The Contemporary International Committee of the Red Cross

The International Committee of the Red Cross (ICRC) was founded in 1863 and is often considered the gold standard in humanitarian action. Despite its many positive achievements over more than 150 years, some former ICRC officials believe that the organization is now in decline because of a series of recent policy choices. Their view is that the organization has undermined its reputation for independent and neutral humanitarian action, while growing too fast and too large, which has weakened its reputation for quick, tightly focused, and effective action in the field.

David P. Forsythe revisits the ICRC policy decisions of recent decades and suggests that the organization is not in fatal decline, but that it does need to reconsider some of its policies at the margins. Though some errors have been made and some corrections are in order, Forsythe argues that its obituary is premature.

David P. Forsythe is Professor Emeritus, University Professor, and Charles J. Mach Distinguished Professor of Political Science at the University of Nebraska–Lincoln. He is a past consultant to the Red Cross Movement and the United Nations High Commissioner for Refugees, as well as author of multiple publications about the ICRC, including the first independent book on it, *Humanitarian Politics: The International Committee of the Red Cross* (Johns Hopkins University Press, 1977).

The Contemporary International Committee of the Red Cross

Challenges, Changes, Controversies

David P. Forsythe

University of Nebraska–Lincoln

Shaftesbury Road, Cambridge CB2 8EA, United Kingdom

One Liberty Plaza, 20th Floor, New York, NY 10006, USA

477 Williamstown Road, Port Melbourne, VIC 3207, Australia

314–321, 3rd Floor, Plot 3, Splendor Forum, Jasola District Centre, New Delhi – 110025, India

103 Penang Road, #05–06/07, Visioncrest Commercial, Singapore 238467

Cambridge University Press is part of Cambridge University Press & Assessment, a department of the University of Cambridge.

We share the University's mission to contribute to society through the pursuit of education, learning and research at the highest international levels of excellence.

www.cambridge.org
Information on this title: www.cambridge.org/9781009386968

DOI: 10.1017/9781009387002

First published 2024

A catalogue record for this publication is available from the British Library

Library of Congress Cataloging-in-Publication Data
Names: Forsythe, David P., 1941– author.
Title: The contemporary International Committee of the Red Cross : challenges, changes, controversies / David P. Forsythe, University of Nebraska–Lincoln.
Description: Cambridge, United Kingdom ; New York, NY : Cambridge University Press, [2024] | Includes bibliographical references and index.
Identifiers: LCCN 2023029889 | ISBN 9781009386968 (hardback) | ISBN 9781009387002 (ebook)
Subjects: LCSH: International Committee of the Red Cross. | Humanitarian assistance. | International relief.
Classification: LCC HV568 .F668 2024 | DDC 361.7/72–dc23/eng/20231010
LC record available at https://lccn.loc.gov/2023029889

ISBN 978-1-009-38696-8 Hardback
ISBN 978-1-009-38701-9 Paperback

For L. M.,
Genuine exceptionalism

Contents

Photographs

Preface: Who and Why

The reader, or maybe a prospective reader, might be interested in knowing how an American academic came to write about the ICRC and why he keeps addressing that subject even after authoring several publications on the topic spanning about fifty years. There are reasons why there are so few books about the ICRC by independent authors, first and foremost being the organization's preference for discretion on sensitive topics. Then there is the related matter that its archives are closed for about five decades after a situation is concluded. So maybe it is best to explain in general how the present author got started on this track and then dealt with the difficulties of research on policymaking at the contemporary ICRC.

Back in the 1970s, relatively fresh from a dissertation on United Nations (UN) mediation and conciliation, I came to Geneva as an independent academic intending to study the ICRC as a neutral humanitarian intermediary. I had little idea about what I was getting into but was acting on the advice of one of my professors in graduate school. He said, in effect, that since I had studied the UN as a diplomatic third party in conflicts, I should take a careful look at the ICRC, which is an intermediary for the Red Cross, and which is also active in many conflicts. (He referred to the organization as ultra-conservative, probably having read something from the era of World War II.) He was certainly right in saying back then that we lacked independent and analytical studies of the ICRC, much of the early literature being predominantly legal if not legalistic, and often in the category of hagiography as it was often written by Swiss ICRC personnel.

As a young novice in every way imaginable, I then met Jean Pictet, Pierre Boissier, and other ICRC leaders. In addition to my own interviewing at ICRC headquarters, I wound up doing some studies for, and having long lunches with, Boissier when he headed a miniscule think tank called the Henry Dunant Institute (defunct since 1998). When the International Red Cross (now officially the International Red Cross and Red Crescent Movement) decided to do a self-study, probably stimulated by decolonization and the creation of numerous weak Red Cross or Red Crescent national societies in fragile new states, Boissier put in a good word for me with the director of the new Red Cross ad hoc international study team, the Canadian Donald Tansley.

So, in the mid-1970s, I became a consultant on Red Cross protection of persons for the "Tansley Big Study" (formally the Reappraisal of the Role of the Red Cross, which made a final report in 1975). At about the same time, the 1974–1977 diplomatic conference was ongoing concerning the reaffirmation and development of international humanitarian law. This led to two Additional Protocols to the 1949 Geneva Conventions. For me personally, since I attended all four sessions, that diplomatic conference enhanced my understanding of the relevant legal issues and extended my contacts with people knowledgeable about international humanitarian law and policy.

My role on the Tansley team, and maybe even my close links to Boissier, got me a foot in the door at the ICRC. (I felt great personal loss when Boissier died prematurely in an accident. He was a wonderful person and my boss at the Henry Dunant Institute – experienced, thoughtful, and unpretentious. He took me for tea one afternoon with one of his older relatives who lived in the Old Town of Geneva so I could experience what he called the "constipated atmosphere" of establishment Geneva. As Pictet reportedly said, one could be in Geneva but not of Geneva. Pierre Boissier was certainly of Geneva, part of the social establishment, as well as in Geneva, but he was the opposite of a stuffy elitist.)

A not-so-charitable view was that some at the ICRC were not very happy with the start of the Tansley Big Study or self-study project, because some of its conclusions might not reflect well on the ICRC as a central leader of the RC Movement. (I often use the abbreviation RC to avoid writing out the longer "Red Cross and Red Crescent" and to avoid prioritizing Red Cross over Red Crescent.) That network has always been fragmented and not uniformly focused.

It was also the case that a few at ICRC headquarters did indeed enjoy playing the role of what was later called "the high priests of humanitarianism,"[1] with Swiss hubristic nationalism leading to some disdain toward non-Swiss like me. I was not the only researcher to encounter at the ICRC what has been termed "ingrained arrogance."[2]

Some others at the ICRC, however, took a more positive view of the Tansley project. After all, it had been established by a Red Cross organ on which the ICRC was represented. Moreover, it not only existed and was going to report, but it could be an opportunity to push for desired changes. In any event, some ICRC officials arranged for me to accompany some ICRC delegations in the field despite the fact that at that time the ICRC was about 99 percent all-Swiss from top to bottom. I may have been the first American to do prison visits as part of an ICRC team.

So I tagged along on some prison visits, searches for missing persons, and other protection activities where the ruling authorities did not object to an American being present (as long as I observed ICRC discretion); in one case they probably did not even know I was there on the ground. In any event, I got to see some conflict situations in the Global South at the grass roots level and how the ICRC operated in the field – in addition to seeing up close the nature of headquarters staff and what went on in a diplomatic conference about the laws of war.

I even survived a small plane crash on the way to visiting a provincial prison, which caused my ICRC colleagues there to help headquarters counter local press speculation that a mysterious American, possibly a Central Intelligence Agency (CIA) agent, had been seen at the crash site. I have never been in the CIA, and they would not have accepted me even if I had applied, which I never did.

Over the subsequent years after the Tansley Big Study I continued to stay in touch with various ICRC personnel, having become deeply interested in both human rights and humanitarian affairs because of the events of the 1960s and 1970s: the Vietnam War, the election of Jimmy Carter as US president, and my own personal experiences in Geneva, Africa, and the Middle East.

In subsequent decades I would show up in Geneva from time to time and get interviews with the top tier of officials at headquarters. I was fortunate to be able to talk one on one with all presidents since Alexandre Hay (Sommaruga, Kellenberger, Maurer), although consistent with my experience of interviewing at the UN, it was at lower levels that one got the best information. I spent two sabbaticals teaching at what used to be called the Graduate Institute, an independent unit of the University of Geneva, which again allowed me to meet informally with lots of ICRC staff, as well as to talk with the top officials that came and went. Thanks to the Internet, I was able to carry on a prolonged back and forth with lots of ICRC types over the years, even when I was not in Geneva.

In general, I would say that the ICRC in the past was not well structured to deal with independent academics like me. Maybe it was a matter of how the bureaucracy was organized. They had no office for outreach to academic researchers. (They do now.) The ICRC archives were officially closed to all outside researchers until 1996. (Some outsiders with special connections to top leaders got exceptional access, but that was just how the old system worked. I never got unusual archival access.) Even now most subjects cannot be examined for fifty years after a dossier is officially closed. Some information is embargoed for a century.

Certainly, ICRC files hold lots of sensitive information, such as on prison visits and quiet diplomacy. The ICRC was never going to leak to me about most of that, and I never asked them to. I respected their need for discretion on those topics and in general they respected my independence as a private academic. I found that most ICRC officials, but certainly not all, were relatively candid where they thought they could be. Moreover, on some topics, such as the details of how policy is made at the top, even 95 percent of staff have no idea what the president said to the director-general, or what the president presented to the governing board (called the Assembly or sometimes just the Committee). There are things I was not told because staff had no information themselves. The ICRC is a very strange and opaque organization in several ways, certainly so regarding the details of policymaking at the top.

Asking questions about internal policymaking at the ICRC is probably like asking a Swiss bank how it decided how to handle certain controversial accounts. A Swiss culture of secrecy and wariness of outsiders seemed to prevail in some offices. (The latter trait still exists. Some ICRC alumni carry on a lively email exchange with each other. It was like pulling teeth to get them to include me; fortunately, I succeeded, with a few exceptions.) The professional staff was internationalized from 1993 and other nationalities sometimes exist in the second tier (Canadian, Belgian, British, Australian, French, etc.). The president, vice president, and other members of the Assembly must statutorily be Swiss, and certain Swiss cultural traditions prevail especially at that top level. All of which is to say that while the organization came to know me, and more than once arranged a program of interviews for me, and even hosted a lunch or two with some important official, certain sensitive subjects were always off-limits.

Still, through a combination of persistence on my part (how many people spend their emeritus years researching ICRC affairs?) and some considerable goodwill on the part of various ICRC officials past and present, I wound up collecting considerable information – more than most outsiders, it is safe to say. And while parts of the ICRC could be difficult to deal with (polite stonewalling some have called it), more than one ICRC official wanted me to understand complex reality and made a genuine effort to answer my questions – within limits of course. For this book there was considerable cooperation at the level of the Directorate (if the director-general is comparable to the prime minister in French politics, then the Directorate is the cabinet). I have even made one or two personal friends out of all the back and forth over the years, even if others took exception to some of my views. But as one ICRC alumnus told me, you should not praise unless you have done a hardheaded analysis, the latter often involving some criticism – hopefully constructive.

So here I am, about fifty years after I met Jean Pictet for my first discussion at the ICRC in 1972. I wanted to try one last time to utilize the information and contacts built up over the decades to reflect on the contemporary ICRC. Each time I went to Geneva I found out that a lot was going on in that organization that one would never know if one stuck to reading the mainstream media, American or otherwise. That was certainly true when I made a trip in 2017 and learned about the controversy that was swirling around the presidency of Peter Maurer, then in his fifth year of leadership – which was long enough for him to make a mark and long enough to stir up considerable debate.

Despite the obscurity of the organization for the general public, there is now a small library on the subject of ICRC history and Red Cross principles, not to mention the laws of war. What I do in the pages that follow is to give some observations about ICRC policy and policymaking in contemporary times. There is intentionally not much on legal details – with the exception of one chapter in particular. I leave most of that to the lawyers and law professors who know the law much better than I do. I cannot stress too much that my project is primarily about policy choice and policy process, with some marginal attention to the specific laws of war.

The ICRC is a fascinating organization, very important for many victims of war and victims of politics. (To be politically correct one now refers not to victims but the beneficiaries of ICRC services.) It manifests a history that is both distinguished and controversial. But we really do need to figure out what is really happening these days in the Geneva headquarters. The organization is either necessarily adapting its role, as it has done constantly since the late 1860s, or it is flirting with major changes that may considerably reduce its internal élan as well as its status in world affairs. It might be doing both at once – necessarily adapting but also undercutting its traditional status.

Still being very much an outsider, I make no claim to being definitive. There is still much I do not know, especially in relation to a number of very smart insiders. But they, having signed nondisclosure agreements, and with the archives closed for recent decades, cannot talk or write about all that they know. So I write what I can. A relative gain is still a gain, even if incomplete.

On almost every topic I discuss, one could write a book on that subject alone: political prisoners, needed adjustments in the laws of war, the link between relief and development, the humanitarian aspects of migration, major debates within the Red Cross Movement, and so on. What I do is introduce the subject in terms of ICRC policy at the time of writing, and thus presumably, in providing a tentative analysis, alert future researchers to leading issues that they will be able to analyze on a firmer documentary basis. I am consciously selective in what I emphasize, and there are many important subjects not covered in any detail. Among the latter is the topic of what used to be called dissemination, or the myriad ways the ICRC tries to spread knowledge about international humanitarian law and the Red Cross Fundamental Principles. That topic alone is (a) extensive and (b) fairly boring, especially if one tries to categorize all the formal and informal meetings, all the introductions and meet-and-greet sessions, that spread the word about ICRC activities, status, and objectives. In the meantime, even with gaps and limits, we should know more about the ICRC and its major policies, pending those later and more definitive studies.

There is a big global humanitarian system out there, and I know I am focused on only one bit of it. One publication, a mapping exercise of many different humanitarian actors with much attention to the Global South, mentioned me as one of those who "merely" focused on organizations based in the West.[3] Others also take a big picture view, with ample criticism of the ICRC, and I touch on some of that literature in the conclusion. But within this big global humanitarian system, one still needs to know how influential actors make their decisions and why. One needs both kinds of studies: the big picture overview and the detailed analysis of influential actors. None of the humanitarian actors has been more influential over the decades than the ICRC. I certainly address the question of whether the ICRC is part of a continuing Western imperialism or colonialism in international humanitarian affairs. In fact, my study of the ICRC sets the organization both within the global RC Movement and the broader global humanitarian system, and indeed within the state system of international relations.

A number of people helped me with this project. Many of them agreed to do so under Chatham House Rule, meaning that I would not name them or quote them but rather use the information they provided as background material to help me form my own views. In some cases, I asked cooperative officials to read certain pages or paragraphs and comment on either facts or sound interpretation. I then made my judgment about how to utilize their commentary.

In one or two cases, ICRC officials agreed to give me certain documents that up until then had been considered internal. In those one or two cases involving several paragraphs of my writing, I agreed to show the organization what I had written as the price I had to pay for obtaining the internal document(s). In some of those cases Geneva asked me to change this or that wording and given the minor nature of changes requested I agreed to do so. In no case was I asked to make a major change regarding a substantive matter or a critical interpretation – with a few exceptions noted below. It was usually a matter of dropping an adjective here or changing a sentence there. In (most) other cases I proceeded with my collection of information and then my interpretations without asking for any opinion from headquarters or staff. That independent process on my part certainly was controlling regarding documents given to me by various sources now outside the organization.

It may be true, as one official said with a touch of exasperation, that in his view the ICRC had provided me with more cooperation than any other independent author – showing some irritation with yet another question from me. And it was true that on numerous occasions for my current book project the ICRC headquarters organized an interview schedule for me when I was in Geneva, or organized a virtual discussion with me via internet video, or responded to requests with emails. In all of those kinds of interactions, the ICRC never sought to unduly restrict my academic freedom as an independent analyst. (Well, there was one exception, which I ignored.)

I will simply skip over the few responders who misrepresented things to me to try to deflect my inquiry, or who refused to cooperate, or who in one case actually threatened me with unspecified negative consequences if I wrote something (in his view) inappropriate. These were the exceptions that proved the more general pattern of considerable cooperation.

There were several ICRC alumni who, being out of office, felt free to greatly assist my quest for understanding policy and the policymaking process either now or in the past. I am very grateful to them. The most important of these was clearly Jacques Moreillon, who had been with the organization for decades, had risen to the position of director-general, had stood for president, and had been co-opted into the Assembly (governing board). At the time of this book, we had known each other since the 1970s.

He was the most cosmopolitan and open of anyone I ever met at the ICRC. He had encouraged numerous writers of whatever nationality in their attempts to understand the ICRC correctly, whether through historical or more contemporary studies. I was not the only one who benefitted from his desire to see that others, particularly academics, properly analyzed the organization. He was devoted to the organization as a matter of personal identity, but he was willing to consider whatever defects or shortcomings someone might assert. He wanted the organization to be true to its own principles and roles and be as effective as possible in responding to the plight of victims of political violence. He might even have used some of us to better his own understanding, which was fine with me.

The book could not have been completed without him: his asking others to cooperate with me, his alerting me to this or that development, his "brainstorming" with me, especially during the last few years. At the same time, he never sought to restrict my freedom and independence. He was very clear about what he could not say. He and I had some different views on some issues, which on balance is a good thing. His being a cosmopolitan humanitarian, and keenly interested in the organization that had seen fit not to elect him president, made this book possible – whatever its worth.

I also want to mention Alain Modoux, former ICRC head of communications, who, despite an episode of serious health issues, was also of great help. He had a special talent for finding obscure documents, especially in Bern, and in explaining much about Swiss diplomatic affairs. He proved an astute and dedicated researcher with a sharp and independent mind.

Also deserving of mention is Yves Sandoz, who held several important ICRC positions and authored several thoughtful articles on Red Cross affairs. He too was co-opted into the Assembly. He was one who often kept his own counsel and then produced a deeply reflective thought piece about the changes underway in Geneva.

Others, too, were of great help but it is best, for various reasons, not to list them here. In a different category were those who helped double check and complete the reference notes: Annette Kovar, Sophia Stockham, and Brianna Martinez. I am grateful to the Political Science Department at the University of Nebraska–Lincoln for providing the support it did. It was again a great pleasure to work with John Haslam at Cambridge University Press. His assistant Carrie Parkinson was a tremendous help. The ICRC was very good about giving me full access to their public photo collection, comprising several thousand items. Most of the photographs included in this book, unless identified otherwise, come from the ICRC public audiovisual archives portal: https://avarchives.icrc.org/. I am grateful for their permissions and for making a few exceptions to their normal restrictions.

What is written in the pages that follow is my responsibility alone. Those who helped me in various ways bear no responsibility whatsoever for any errors of fact or any misguided interpretation that, despite my best efforts, might have crept in.

I made an early effort at understanding recent trends which became a journal article: David P. Forsythe, "A New International Committee of the Red Cross?," *Journal of Human Rights*, 17/5 (fall 2018), pp. 533–549. This book follows on from, and overlaps with, that more limited effort.

The present book also overlaps with my chapter "Humanitarianism: Coping in the Void," in Michael Stohl and Allison Brysk, eds., *A Research Agenda for Human Rights* (Cheltenham: Edward Elgar, 2020), pp. 23–36.

Parts of Chapters 7 and 8 in this book wound up as another stand-alone article: David P. Forsythe, "Human Dignity, the ICRC, and the Swiss Government: The Lessons of History Debated," *Human Rights Quarterly*, 44/2 (May 2022), pp. 313–338.

This book's Epilogue about the ICRC and the Russian invasion of Ukraine was published as a stand-alone article in different form by *Alternatives Humanitaire/Humanitarian Alternatives*, summer 2023: "International Humanitarian Law and the War in Ukraine: The ICRC and Humanitarian Politics" (www.alternatives-humanitaires.org/en/2023/07/21/international-humanitarian-law-and-the-war-in-ukraine-the-international-committee-of-the-red-cross-and-humanitarian-policies/)

Notes

1 Massimo Lorenżi, *Le CICR, le coeur et la raison: entretiens avec Cornelio Sommaruga* (Lausanne: Favre, 1998).
2 D. Rodogno, "Certainty, Compassion, and the Ingrained Arrogance of Humanitarians," in N. Wylie, M. Oppenheimer, and J. Crossland, eds., *The Red Cross Movement: Myths, Practices and Turning Points* (Manchester: Manchester University Press, 2020), pp. 27–44.
3 C. Egger and D. Schopper, "Organizations Involved in Humanitarian Action: A New Data Set," *International Studies Quarterly*, 66/2 (June 2022).

1 The Contemporary ICRC and Its Critics
The Slippery Slope of Decline?

> The ICRC is the oldest of the humanitarian organizations. It is the richest and the best organized, and its mandate is the clearest.
>
> David Rieff[1]

Despite ICRC expanding budgets and staff, one could find a lot of discontent among a range of former ICRC officials during the time frame 2015–2022. This quiet controversy, ignored by elites in places such as Washington and London, not to mention by mainstream members of the media such as the *New York Times,* raised important questions. Apart from issues of personalities and personal style, more than a few among *"les anciens"* – literally "the elders" but in this case the alumni of ICRC employment – thought the ICRC was making grave mistakes that threatened the future of the organization. On the other hand, some defenders of current organizational trends thought, to use the words of one high official of that time, that the whole bruhaha was, as translated from his French, nonsense (*betise*).

Given those clashing views, for those interested in this establishment humanitarian organization and/or global humanitarian affairs, the situation merited a closer look. I published my last big overview of the ICRC back in 2005 and evidently much water has flowed under the bridge in the meantime.[2] In this opening chapter I introduce the views of the critics. In the next chapter I situate the ICRC in the global humanitarian system, which helps to explain at least some of the reasons for the trajectory of ICRC policymaking.

Through a review of selected details, this introduction raises the key question at the center of this book: Is the widely respected ICRC, called by some the gold standard among global humanitarian actors, in the process of losing its unique focus and expertise? Or has its recent policymaking been misunderstood by critics who have a faulty view of developments in a changed and still changing world? Given the ICRC's place – historically and in contemporary times – within global humanitarian affairs, that is an important question to address.

Photograph 1.1 ICRC headquarters, Geneva, main building, as of 2013. Formerly the Carlton Hotel built in 1876, the building with its majestic views was made available to the ICRC by the city of Geneva in 1946. Between 1863 and 1946 the ICRC operated out of different premises in Geneva.

I   Early Details

On August 28, 2015, Thierry Germond, former ICRC official, wrote to Peter Maurer, president of the ICRC, questioning whether the organization under Maurer's leadership since 2012 was acting in violation of Red Cross fundamental principles. Both agreed that the ICRC as a humanitarian actor was supposed to be neutral, independent, and impartial – hence the acronym NIIHA for neutral, independent, impartial humanitarian actor or action. The general issue was whether specific ICRC activities did or did not violate core principles. Had the ICRC adopted so many new and different policies that it had lost its proper focus and in the process was now violating its core principles?[3]

Germond was highly experienced, having had a thirty-five-year career at the ICRC, starting with an assignment in the Biafran–Nigerian war of the late 1960s and including the important post of head of the ICRC delegation in Brussels, which meant liaison with the North Atlantic Treaty Organization (NATO) and the European Union. He had been entrusted by the organization with numerous delicate tasks and had personally negotiated with various high-profile or tough political leaders.

Maurer was also no lightweight, having had a distinguished career in the Swiss foreign service, serving as head of the Swiss delegation to the UN in New York and then as the top professional in the Swiss foreign ministry. He had been supported for the ICRC top spot by the outgoing ICRC president, Jakob Kellenberger, and apparently chosen as president in 2012 without major opposition by the ICRC's governing board (called the Assembly).

I say "apparently" because the board's deliberations are secret for decades, depending on subject matter. All members of the board must be Swiss, including the president and vice president, and the country comes close to manifesting reserve and discretion as national traits. Historically Swiss neutrality has been more conservative or "buttoned down" than, say, Swedish neutrality. For example, Stockholm spoke out much more about the Vietnam War than Bern did. Stockholm also spoke out much more against apartheid in South Africa than Bern did. (In fact, a lot of Swiss corporations were in tight with White minority rule there.) Neutral Sweden joined the UN much earlier than neutral Switzerland. In 2022, Sweden moved to align with Finland in applying to join NATO after the Russian invasion of Ukraine, whereas at the time of writing the Swiss government was still debating how far to go in contesting Russian policies under Vladimir Putin. Joining NATO was out of the question. Relevant was the fact that Swiss banks were famous for discretion, or infamous for dubious secrecy if one prefers.

Germond's five-page letter, in rather small font, seemed to stress three interrelated concerns with no particular hierarchy: (1) the ICRC's endorsing neoliberal capitalism and then selecting a number of members to its governing board that represented that orientation; (2) the ICRC president becoming a member of the board of trustees at the World Economic Forum (WEF), which arguably constituted an informal governing arrangement endorsing neoliberal economics; and (3) the ICRC's close relationship to the Swiss foreign ministry which had, inter alia, concluded in January 2015 that the WEF – headquartered in Geneva – was a "neutral and impartial" international organization, which to Germond distorted the meaning of those words. The retired official believed that the principles of neutrality and independence were being violated by an organization that was no longer fully a neutral humanitarian but was becoming too political and endorsing neoliberal capitalism along the way – which advanced the interests of Swiss corporations. In his view the ICRC, led by Maurer, was departing from its proper status and role, with dire consequences for the organization in the future.

Germond circulated Maurer's reply, which put it in the public domain. In any event, the president's response of October 5 did not contain any diplomatic secrets. Germond was not persuaded by anything in that letter and continued to insist that the fundamental Red Cross principles were being violated. (The two had had a brief verbal exchange at a public meeting in Geneva in September, and Germond had written a second letter that same month.) It was a fact that the ICRC was trying to reduce the dependency on the part of those receiving ICRC assistance, which, while not explained in the letter, was a gateway to the subject of encouraging local micro-capitalism as an alternative to repeated humanitarian assistance. This apparently did not sit well with Germond who apparently believed businesspersons in the ICRC Assembly were unduly benefitting from this orientation. All of this led some at the ICRC to see him as a leftish agitator left over from the 1960s. Be that as it may, Germond clearly did not believe that in fall 2015 the Assembly had properly considered various business and economic links. And he certainly did not believe that the ICRC and its president were being open and transparent about policymaking.

Germond was definitely not satisfied with Maurer's response, to put it mildly. He had already sent copies of his August letter to members of the Assembly, along with a few other persons. Encouraged by some of the bilateral replies if not by others, he continued to advocate for his view that the ICRC under Maurer's leadership was headed down the wrong road and undermining the image and reputation of the ICRC. He thought the acceptance of the organization in conflicts and the security of its staff in the field were, or might be, endangered by arguably departing from earlier versions of independence and neutrality.

Germond dispatched another letter on December 15, 2015 to Maurer but also to others, including the Swiss federal president, who would convene the International Red Cross and Red Crescent Conference later that month in Geneva. (The Conference and other aspects of the international RC network are explained in detail in Chapter 5.) The main focus of this letter seemed to be the WEF and arguably its lack of neutrality, which supposedly then made it inappropriate for the ICRC president to be a WEF trustee. If Germond was hoping the RC Conference, which meets in principle every four years, would take up the subject, he was to be disappointed. The Swiss federal president did not get involved. No doubt high Swiss officials knew of ICRC–WEF links and did not want to rock that boat.

Switzerland is small – about 8.5 million in population. Smaller still (less than 25 percent of the national population) is the French-speaking area in the southwest of the country where the ICRC is based in Geneva. And even smaller is the network of former ICRC officials who stay in touch and care about the organization to which they dedicated much of their careers. After the second half of 2015, Germond's views circulated informally in this latter small network. Various contacts led to the formation of a group of Swiss former ICRC officials who were sympathetic to Germond's views – or at least some of those views. The leaders of this group set a goal of getting twenty-five signatures in support – more or less – of Germond's concerns. Hence it became known to some as the G-25, with voluntary membership and a leadership committee.

Like the G-77 at the UN, made up of states from the Global South that wanted more attention given to underdevelopment, and which grew over time to more than 130 members, the G-25 in Switzerland grew larger – to perhaps double the original size. Being made up of former ICRC high officials as well as routine field staff, it displayed a certain organizational competence and political savoir faire. Among its members was a former director-general, several directors of operations, numerous heads of departments and divisions, multiple heads of field officers, and several regional directors, among other positions – including one former member of the governing board. The group was driven by the fundamental concern that the highly regarded ICRC they had helped build was now being damaged by unwise decisions by the current leadership. They thought the active mandate was no longer clear. Concern for ICRC violation of the principles of humanitarian neutrality and independence was at the top of their list.[4]

Over time three clusters of concerned alumni emerged, focused on ICRC leadership decisions. There was Germond, who remained an independent force, marching to his own drummer, doing prodigious research on this or that aspect of his concerns, and keeping his own counsel about when and how to push his agenda. (It was Germond who in 2015 first circulated the fact that Maurer had become a WEF trustee in 2014. There had been no announcement up until then by the ICRC headquarters.) There was the G-25, with a leadership firmly convinced of the correctness of their cause but keeping a certain distance – at least sometimes – from Germond by mutual agreement. Then there was a third cluster made up of informed former officials who stayed in touch with various persons and developments, both inside and outside the ICRC, but who did not fully identify with the iconoclast Germond or become members of the G-25.

This diffuse and unorganized third group of alumni often felt at least partial unease about the ICRC's evolution and were not content, like some former high officials, to wash their hands of the whole controversy and simply defer to the judgments of Maurer and the other contemporary ICRC leaders. One of these nonaligned alumni thought the old ICRC was dead, replaced by a bureaucratic monster whose tentacles reached almost everywhere. The amorphous and shifting third grouping sought more information and were fairly sure that some mistakes were being made, even if they did not automatically buy into all the views – and style and tactics – of Germond or the G-25.

It is very difficult if not impossible to precisely categorize or summarize the views of all those uncomfortable with the evolution of the ICRC in recent decades. For sure, different individuals saw different gains and losses in that evolution. While the three groupings noted earlier capture some reality, one should not try to categorize too firmly a complicated landscape of debate about challenges, changes, and controversies at the ICRC.

The critics noted earlier might or might not participate in the ICRC Alumni Association, a group of former employees who met regularly and discussed mostly noncontroversial subjects in a collegial and nonconfrontational way.

Into 2016, Germond continued to bombard the ICRC leadership with various letters and other information attacking what he saw as the direction Maurer and "his" Assembly was taking the organization. Most, if not all, of the critiques were apparently ignored by the ICRC leadership during 2015 and most of 2016 in the sense of eliciting no written replies – beyond the first reply to Germond by Maurer. It was also the case apparently that ICRC leaders sought no quiet back channels to Germond to try to assuage his concerns. It may have been the case that the tone and volume of his messages dissuaded them from any such effort. At one point he demanded that the entire Assembly resign for failing to properly oversee the ICRC president and directorate. Over time his name evoked very strong negative reactions from more than one high official in Geneva. In pursuing research for this book, I was told more than once to avoid being seen as carrying water for Germond or even probing some of the issues he had raised.

Subsequent interviews established that at least part of the ICRC leadership did not think the issues raised by Germond, particularly Maurer's membership on the WEF board of trustees, was all that important – at least in 2014 when Maurer took up that outside position. They thought it a minor matter of routine diplomacy and outreach. It is almost certainly the case that at some point Maurer felt himself under unfair personal attack and started refusing to discuss the WEF issue. When this author met with Maurer in Washington, DC in May 2019, I was told ahead of time by ICRC staff not to bring up the subject of the WEF. My later experience through several interactions was that other leaders were willing to discuss the WEF and other subjects flexibly but not the ICRC president.

It remains unclear whether Maurer circa 2015 was convinced he was right on the WEF matter and did not want to discuss things further, or whether he realized he might be out on a limb, at least on the WEF matter, and wanted to avoid further attention on that subject. There are other theories about his thinking. Be that as it may, some insiders thought it important that Maurer basically shut off free, open, and critical discussion about the WEF internally, which to them was more important than failing to respond fully and candidly to outsiders.

In mid-September 2015, after Germond's first letter in late August, there had been one posting on the ICRC web page that, in the context of a discussion about RC principles, showed Maurer briefly mentioning the WEF in passing. Maurer said that it was important to use the WEF platform to talk to important actors that could have an impact on humanitarian affairs.[5] This policy position had some support within the broader international humanitarian community.[6] In January 2016, over a year after Maurer became a WEF trustee, there was a posting on the ICRC website defending in some detail that arrangement.[7] It was not a candid costs–benefits analysis but rather a list of advantages derived from Maurer's double role. (There is much more about this especially in Chapter 10 but also in Chapter 17.)

In December 2016, the G-25 sent a long and complex letter to President Maurer challenging whether his push for close links with the for-profit sector, including his role at the WEF and other actions, were always consistent with the principles of independence and neutrality for a humanitarian organization. A central figure for the G-25 had become

André Pasquier, a former director of operations, among his other important positions. This initiative was supported by forty-four signatures.

Some former officials outside the G-25 wrote to Pasquier indicating encouragement – including former ICRC President Cornelio
Sommaruga. Sommaruga, (president 1987–1999), who was a great
champion of ICRC independence, was later quoted in the press as follows: "*[U]n président du CICR ne peut être que président du CICR.*"[8] (The
president of the ICRC can only be the president of the ICRC.) This
statement, publicly reported in 2016, apparently was made at a meeting
in Geneva in the fall of 2015. (In the video cited in note 4, Sommaruga
speaks from the audience, also in 2015, to emphasize the RC principle of
independence. Candidly, he speaks about his own independence, in the
context of a "weak" Assembly.)

Photograph 1.2 André Pasquier gives a press conference in 1986 when
he was director of operations. The position of director of operations
is normally second in importance only to the director-general for the
daily management of ICRC activities. In retirement, Pasquier became
the leader of the G-25, an organized group eventually of about forty-
five former officials deeply concerned about the expansion of ICRC
programs and staff, and about its interpretation of the principles of
independence and neutrality. In the short term, their concerns fell on
deaf ears. In the longer term, financial troubles and leadership changes
might lead to a different analysis.

By comparison, President Jakob Kellenberger (ICRC president 2000–2011), remained detached from all aspects of this controversy. When he was president, apparently he did not appreciate former President Sommaruga looking over his shoulder and making public comments about ICRC affairs. Kellenberger had mentored Maurer in the Swiss foreign ministry, supported him for ICRC president, and was not going to get involved in second guessing him in his ICRC post. For whatever reason Kellenberger was content to be finished with almost all Red Cross matters. (He did serve on the governing board of the Centre for Humanitarian Dialogue in Geneva, an independent agency cosponsored by the ICRC.)

One can understand the position of either Sommaruga or Kellenberger. The former was quite concerned about the ICRC's independence and did not want to see his track record damaged on that subject. (More on this later, especially in Chapter 8.) On at least some issues he was obviously in favor of a traditional understanding of the ICRC's mandate or mission or role. The latter could well have been tired of Red Cross affairs. The ICRC presidency is not an easy role to fill.

The ICRC president meets with the top leaders of the day, and journalists want to know what he thinks. Some at the ICRC close to the top thought that all three recent ICRC presidents developed an appreciable ego because of access to many of the major figures in world affairs. But the ICRC leader is always being disappointed by fighting parties who fail to take sufficiently seriously the laws of war, or even minimal standards of decency. In the words of one provocative observer, the ICRC president as much as anyone represents "the utopian fantasy of a global village of moral concern."[9] If so, or even if not, that position is bound to lead to frustration.

He (now she) is always confronting the dark side of human nature and seeing up close how global humanitarian tragedies unfold. The president is always trying to raise more money for humane causes. As the external face of the organization, the president has to keep up with changing and complicated subjects such as emerging rules for cyber warfare or how to make use of new technologies and represent the organization's position accurately. And someone is always watching for potential shortcomings. In some circles at the ICRC one can feel a certain siege mentality, a fear that outsiders are trying to play "gotcha journalism" or otherwise unfairly criticize the organization in its complex and difficult role. It has made mistakes, it knows it has made mistakes, and sometimes the defensiveness shows through. David Rieff, the independent writer, actually came around to appreciating the ICRC position in world affairs, but in getting there he wrote: "[K]nowledge of the ICRC's shameful conduct in Nazi-occupied Europe had always made me skeptical of the organization."[10]

Beyond Germond and the G-25, some of the other former ICRC officials who retained deep interest in their former employer and harbored some concern about this or that issue also wrote to Maurer. Some former members of the ICRC governing board wrote to both the ICRC Assembly and the WEF. Much of this correspondence was serious, well-reasoned, detailed, and without polemics. It appears to be the case that there were no replies – at least no formal or written replies.

It may have been the case that some alumni letters had some impact even if no replies were received. At least one alumnus, and then later the G-25, objected to Maurer and the organization talking about win-win situations in which business could make money by operating in conflict areas and fragile societies. According to this critique, the ICRC and the Movement were supposed to be strictly humanitarian and thus disinterested in other subjects beyond serving humanity. In this view, Red Cross promotion of taking profits went over the line.

While the ICRC continued to display much interest in an expanded role on the part of for-profit entities, especially in "early recovery" or micro-development programs, there did seem to be less public talk about the profit motive in ICRC communiqués. One could talk about increased use of business partners in ICRC activities, and the need for donors from the business world, without getting into the more controversial matter of encouraging businesses to make money from involvement with victims of political conflict. Some business roles might be helpful and others exploitative. So perhaps it was best to minimize attention to that complicated subject in ICRC public discourse. (Maybe a researcher with a stable of assistants could do a content analysis of the wording of both ICRC and WEF communiqués to establish the facts of the matter. Did Maurer and others in fact reduce references to "win-win" involving corporate profit?)

At some point Maurer turned the matters raised by Germond and the G-25 over to his vice president, Christine Beerli, a member of the Assembly who formerly had been active in Swiss politics representing a center-right political party. A normal part of the vice president's job is to help with external relations. While the president is meeting with political figures and other leaders of the first rank, the ICRC vice president is interacting with various other outsiders, including those from the Movement, alumni, and even, at the bottom of the totem pole, independent researchers.

There followed an exchange of letters between Pasquier for the G-25 and Vice President Beerli, and then a meeting in February 2017 organized by Beerli with various former and current officials – including some from the Assembly. In subsequent letters there was discussion of possible future meetings, but they never transpired.

Without going into all details about this prolonged and multi-faceted process, one can conclude that nothing much changed on the surface for a time. The leadership of the G-25 believed, along with Germond, that most of their concerns were not being taken seriously. For the ICRC president, he apparently believed that the expressed concerns had been properly examined and found wanting. He presumably believed the leadership had made an adequate response in good faith and the matter reasonably put to rest. After all, on the ICRC website (very briefly) in 2015 as noted earlier, in slightly more detail from 2016 (covered later), internally in 2017 in a couple of different ways (covered in Chapter 10), and in still other ways the ICRC leadership had tried to explain its position on various subjects such as links to private corporations or the reasons for an expanded humanitarian diplomacy and programming in the contemporary world. Chapter 9 shows that in the midst of the Germond controversy, the ICRC came out with a report on the long relationship between the ICRC and the private business sector.

Apparently, in November 2015, after Germond had flagged the issue, the ICRC Assembly had some kind of discussion about links to the WEF and deferred to Maurer being on the board of trustees there. However, when Maurer's first mandate on the WEF board of trustees expired (2014–2017) and he indicated to the ICRC Assembly that he wanted a second term at the WEF, the Assembly could not proceed by the preferred route of consensus. His renewed mandate at the WEF was approved, but by a split vote. All of the back and forth about Maurer and the WEF from 2015 had had some effect on some ICRC Assembly members. At approximately the same time, the Assembly approved a second four-year term for Maurer as president of the ICRC. In 2015–2017, therefore, the Assembly paid more attention to the WEF issue while being satisfied with Maurer's overall leadership and the direction of the organization during his first ICRC term of 2012–2016.

In December 2017, with Maurer having been approved by the Assembly for a second term as WEF trustee, and a possible second meeting with the G-25 therefore canceled for lack of primary purpose, the G-25 leadership drafted a position paper, widely circulated, with broad focus. There was attention to ICRC dubious links with some firms in the private sector, as well as the usual attention to the WEF, expression of concern about various measures pertaining to China (covered later in the book), and attention to the rapid expansion of ICRC activities and staff.

Over time the critics grew more and more frustrated. They, being Swiss and former ICRC officials, had started quietly and without public fanfare. They were concerned not to damage the reputation of the ICRC but to effectuate change within the family.

But then articles appeared in the Swiss press, in each of the three national languages, and Swiss TV reporters began to ask pointed questions. For example, in early April 2016 the *New Zurich Times* (*NZZ*) ran a story on the controversy in German.[11] For whatever reason, the article did not draw broad attention, but it was certainly noted inside the ICRC by both leadership and staff. The article quoted Germond in addressing a variety of subjects: the growth of the ICRC and the decline of staff morale, the competition for funds with especially UN agencies, the apparent loss of ICRC focus as it broadened its economic assistance, the corporate role, the WEF, some presidential travel that might be overdone, leadership and management style, and so on. Maurer was quoted several times in the story in an effort to refute his critics.

It did not help the climate for exchanges between the critics and the ICRC leadership when in early April 2018, the editor of the Swiss *Le Temps*, who was perceived as close to the ICRC leadership, wrote a piece arguing, inter alia, that: (1) humanitarians had no choice but to seek more links to the for-profit sector, and (2) those who questioned this orientation were stuck in a 1968 view of things (referring to the French left-wing street protests of that year).[12] The piece referred to a statement by ICRC Director-General Yves Daccord, dismissive in tone, saying the ICRC was trusted in talking to the Taliban in Afghanistan, but if it talked to banks, the critics feared the worst.[13] Such developments did not endear the ICRC leadership to the critics.

About a month later, in May 2018, the same Swiss newspaper ran a longer story.[14] It was clear that some of the critics, more than Germond, were talking to the press. Several former staff agreed to be quoted by name. The focus of the article was similar to that in the *NZZ*: Maurer was dangerously wearing two hats, one for the WEF and one for the ICRC; there were relations with corporations that had not been properly vetted; there were quotes from a leaked internal survey of staff indicating some criticisms of management; and more.

Toward the end of that year the controversy was picked up by *Le Monde* in Paris, which ran a story on December 2, 2018, based on considerable nonpublic information.[15] The ICRC was said to be in an ethical crisis, and there was much attention paid to President Maurer and the WEF. It was said that, to some, the expanded role of the ICRC was making it into a second UN or "l'ONU-bis." Pasquier thought the

ICRC had become an agent for the WEF. Relatedly, some thought the ICRC was driven by Swiss national interests as defined in Bern. For former official Serge Nessi, the ICRC's treatment of the fundamental Red Cross principles, including independent neutrality, was akin to the Church abandoning the Ten Commandments. Again, there was attention to staff discontents. Rony Brauman of Doctors Without Borders (Médecins Sans Frontières, MSF) thought the critics were right and were trying to save the ICRC from its own mistakes. Germond was pictured as making this controversy the centerpiece of his life. Peter Maurer had refused requests for an interview, according to Rémy Ourdan, the journalist for *Le Monde*.

There were other articles on this subject, not to mention multiple radio and TV programs. For example, there was an article in the Italian region of Switzerland. In Lugano, the award-winning freelance journalist Federico Franchini wrote an article that once more focused on the ICRC's for-profit partners and Maurer at the WEF.[16] While not published in a major media source, it typified the spreading media coverage of the controversy throughout the small Alpine nation.

However, few in the public, either in Switzerland or in the broader readership of *Le Monde*, seemed to care. *Le Monde's* Rémy Ourdan, noting the article by Stéphane Bussard in *Le Temps* from May 2018, wrote that it was met by a "stupefying silence." When Maurer came to Washington, DC in May 2019, he gave a public talk at the Center for Strategic and International Studies and took questions. No one in the audience seemed aware of the controversy. There were no questions about crisis or turmoil or even debate within the ICRC or larger RC network. There have been no articles about the controversy in the American media. The same seems to be true regarding the United Kingdom and other major donor nations, except for the one article in *Le Monde*.

Clearly, however, someone at the ICRC felt it needed to address further the subject of its links to the WEF and the for-profit sector. The result was a longer internet post in 2018 by two staff members, said to be written in their personal capacity.[17] The piece was basically an elaboration of what had been posted on the ICRC website page back in 2016.

In late 2018 the G-25 again wrote to Maurer, with a copy to Assembly members, noting that the WEF was sanctioning certain Russians for supporting Putin's incursion into Crimea and the Donbas which started in 2014, arguing that this showed how political the WEF was – and how Maurer should not be part of its governance. This démarche had no evident impact at the Geneva HQ.

All of this being what it was, in July 2019 Pasquier and the G-25 decided to take their concerns to one of the central organs of the RC network. They submitted a letter to the President of the Standing Commission of the International Red Cross and Red Crescent Movement. (See Chapter 5 for an explanation of where the ICRC and Standing Commission fit in the larger RC global network.)

In that letter they repeated their assertion that the current ICRC leadership was violating its own statutes and the statutes of the RC Movement. The core arguments were the same as before, namely that the ICRC was departing from the requirements that it be a neutral and independent humanitarian actor that avoided political controversies involving political economy and ideology. It was not supposed to be endorsing any of the various versions of capitalism, and it was not supposed to be intertwined with the WEF – particularly since the WEF (like the Swiss government) was supporting economic sanctions on various Russian officials after 2014, when Russia intervened in several places in eastern Ukraine. The WEF was also endorsing the defeat of this or that fighting party such as the Islamic State Group. Maurer, being a WEF trustee, was logically or indirectly implicated in these non-neutral positions at that organization. There was also the argument that the ICRC had departed from neutral humanitarian assistance by getting more involved in development activities and climate change, which were inherently political subjects.

The G-25 was doing what other advocacy groups had done: Having failed to win in one forum (quietly going to the ICRC), and another forum (talking to journalists), it then shifted to another forum (the Standing Commission representing the global Movement). After all, most of the G-25 had been negotiating with states and armed nonstate actors for their careers and knew something about how to try to advance their agenda. They might have been right or wrong about their concerns (or right about some and wrong about others), but they were persistent and determined. Some were clearly true believers in the rightness of their cause.

The Standing Commission of the Red Cross Movement declined to act on the G-25 complaint and did not inscribe the matter on the agenda of the next International Red Cross Conference scheduled for December 2019, where the G-25 hoped to have a debate that would put pressure on the ICRC. It did not help the cause of the G-25 that the ICRC always has two members on the nine-person Standing Commission, making it difficult to pursue a question through that organ that the ICRC leadership finds distasteful. The 2019 International Conference said nothing at all about the controversy. It was all pushed under the rug.

II   Adding Up the Details

Up to that point the various criticisms seem to have been discounted by a leadership that seemed united behind past decisions and unwilling to make major changes. The critics, or at least most of them, remained convinced that their concerns were valid. Germond continued to bombard the ICRC president and Assembly with letters of criticism. He and others also tried to mobilize Swiss public figures, politicians, and political parties to the cause. There were meetings in Bern. In 2018 and 2019, several members of the Swiss Federal Parliament raised questions with the Swiss Federal Council, the collective executive, about ICRC and WEF neutrality. The Federal Council brushed off the inquiries with short and superficial replies, refusing to engage in-depth on substance.

Clearly the ICRC leadership stayed the course chosen regarding such matters as links to the WEF and corporate world, growing the budget and staff, adopting new personnel management practices, taking economic assistance beyond traditional emergency help, working more with migrants, getting more involved in certain urban violence below the level of armed conflict, using internationally recognized human rights more as a reference point, and so on. Above all, the leadership believed it was not violating the Red Cross fundamental principles of independence and neutrality. If it had skated close to the edge of what was permissible, it said that it was evaluating risk and reward and paying close attention. This was a way of saying that Germond and the G-25 – and the other critiques – had been noted and found wanting.

Against the historical background briefly noted here since 2015, this book examines the contemporary ICRC – its policies and principles. The triggers for deciding to do the book lay in the era of President Peter Maurer, or 2012–2022. But once one started in-depth inquiries, it was necessary to go into the roots of some changes. And that produced a work dealing with the ICRC after the Cold War. Rather than seeing just striking and recent changes on this or that subject in the last decade, one sometimes found a build-up of incremental changes over considerable time. One found more adaption than sudden change *de novo*. Or some real change was accompanied mostly by gradual evolution. What some outsiders might see as new circa 2017, to choose one arbitrary date, might sometimes have discernible roots going back to about 1991 and the end of the Cold War.

Having now noted the controversy and mentioned the leading issues, we turn in the following pages to systematic analysis and finally evaluation. Has the ICRC lost its specific focus that helped build the reputation of the organization? Has the recruitment of a more varied and larger staff

Photograph 1.3 Peter Maurer (left) became President of the ICRC in 2012, endorsed by the outgoing President Jakob Kellenberger (right). Maurer dismissed the criticisms of Thierry Germond and André Pasquier, and others. Kellenberger showed no interest in the controversy and, unlike another former president, Cornelio Sommaruga, did not become involved on either side.

killed the goose that laid the golden egg – that egg being a cohesive and dedicated staff in the field? Has the organization's leadership violated the fundamental RC principles that require it to be a neutral, independent, and impartial humanitarian actor?

One can close this opening section in slightly different terms by asking what exactly is at the core of this controversy – this complicated debate among a few humanitarian practitioners that remains quite obscure to most outsiders – as evidenced by the little public attention it has received. At first glance the dispute appears to be centered on two primary subjects: the participation of the president of the ICRC on the board of the WEF, and the links between the ICRC with certain for-profit donors and partners. Some might include relations between the ICRC and Swiss authorities in Bern as a third major issue. Some believed that Bern, through Peter Mauer, had organized a triangle centered on Swiss national interests with the ICRC and WEF as secondary players. But the controversy goes considerably beyond these specific subjects.

It may be that the most important aspect of the controversy covers what traditionalists within the ICRC call its "specificity" or sometimes its "unicity" – namely its primary focus and the limits on its activities. In fact, the scope of some ICRC activities had been considerably enlarged before the Maurer era. In reality, the more important issue might be the very broad interpretation of its original and unchanged self-defined role as a NIIHA. The ICRC used to be an institution that focused on activities where it was pretty much the only one to perform them, clearly centered on war and political prisoners. Now it seems the ICRC is undertaking new tasks with broader scope that it *might* be better positioned to perform than others, at least for a time, or maybe just expanding its tasks because it (temporarily?) has the resources to do so, or maybe just enjoying being a more important actor in the eyes of the World Bank and other major players in international affairs. It is particularly this latter task expansion that this book seeks to analyze. And task expansion entails staff expansion, with greater need for specialization.

The ICRC remains an organization that gave itself the duty to consider, and perhaps act on, any subject linked to violent conflict that it felt required attention from an independent, neutral, and impartial humanitarian agency. Its interpretation of the meaning of this core mandate, a self-adopted mandate not originally given to it by either the Red Cross Movement or international humanitarian law (IHL), but confirmed by both, has always been affected by changing conditions. This everyone acknowledges. Have the expansive changes since about 2000, but in some cases evolving since the end of the Cold War, been well considered as the leadership claims, or poorly thought out as the critics argue? That is the central subject of the pages that follow.

III   Conclusion

Are the critics right but maybe for the wrong reasons? Has the ICRC lost its way not because of links to capitalist actors and the WEF, but because it is spreading itself too broadly without clear limits? Is it dissipating its efforts because it has not established where neutral humanitarianism ends and traditional political activities begin – like promoting development and responding to climate change, or for that matter broadly engaging in a response to pandemics? Has the ICRC become, rather than a unique actor with a specialized focus, another do-gooder organization trying to do almost everything for almost everybody? Has it become like some other nongovernmental organizations – the International Rescue Committee comes to mind – a sprawling do-gooder with activities for anyone affected by crisis, underdevelopment, refugee status, lack of proper education, victims of gender bias and racism, and adversely affected by pandemics and global warming? Does it really have a clear, well-defined interpretation of its mandate anymore? If David Rieff was right as of 2005, that the ICRC had the clearest mandate among international humanitarians, as quoted at the top of this chapter, is that still true?

Notes

1 D. Rieff, *A Bed for the Night: Humanitarianism in Crisis* (New York: Simon and Schuster, 2002), p. 19.

2 D. P. Forsythe, *The Humanitarians: The International Committee of the Red Cross* (Cambridge: Cambridge University Press, 2005).

3 In this chapter and indeed throughout the book, if I refer to unpublished sources, I have the document in my possession. Also, I use the abbreviation RC to avoid writing out each time "Red Cross and Red Crescent." Its use also avoids prioritizing Red Cross over Red Crescent. The abbreviation can also be read as including official aid societies, as in Israel, that use in their international operations the Red Crystal emblem, which was approved by states and then the RC Movement in 2005–2006. There is more on this latter subject in later chapters.

4 The RC fundamental principles are discussed throughout the book. For a start, see ICRC, *The Fundamental Principles of the Red Cross: Commentary* (1979). www.icrc.org/en/doc/resources/documents/misc/fundamental-principles-commentary-010179.htm (accessed August 22, 2022).

5 ICRC, "Stubborn Realities, Shared Humanity: History in the Service of Humanitarian Action," YouTube (2015). www.youtube.com/watch?v=5LyNIXPUl7k (accessed August 22, 2022).

6 A. Slemrod, "Princes and Bankers and Aid! Oh My!" *The New Humanitarian*, May 26, 2017, www.thenewhumanitarian.org/analysis/2017/05/26/princes-and-bankers-and-aid-oh-my (accessed August 22, 2022).

7 ICRC, "Mieux servir les personnes vulnérables grâce à la coopération avec le Forum économique Mondial" (2016). www.icrc.org/fr/document/mieux-servir-les-personnes-vulnerables-grace-la-cooperation-avec-le-forum-economique?amp (accessed August 22, 2022).

8 R. Ourdan, "Suisse-Monde: 'Le CICR est devenu une sorte d'agent opérationnel du WEF et des entreprises partenaires'. Peter Maurer: CICR et WEF sous la même casquette" (2018). https://alencontre.org/suisse/suisse-monde-le-cicr-est-devenu-une-sorte-dagent-operationnel-du-wef-et-des-entreprises-partenaires-peter-maurer-cicr-et-wef-sous-la-meme-casquette.html (accessed August 23, 2022).

9 D. Rieff, *A Bed for the Night: Humanitarianism in Crisis* (New York: Simon and Schuster, 2002), p. 37.

10 Ibid., p. 18.

11 J. P. Kapp and M. Woker, "Die Guten aus Genf" (2016). www.nzz.ch/international/die-guten-aus-genf-ld.12428?reduced=true (accessed August 24, 2022).

12 In French they are called the "*soixante-huitards*," which refers to protestors from 1968 who supported labor rights and were seen by some as utopians, idealists, or modern communards – alluding to the Commune of the French Revolution of 1789 and thereafter.

13 S. Benoit-Godet, "Finance et humanitaire: la nécessaire collaboration" (2018). www.letemps.ch/opinions/finance-humanitaire-necessaire-collaboration (accessed August 24, 2022).

14 S. Bussard, "Les liaisons a risques au CICR," *Le Temps* (2018). www.letemps .ch/monde/liaisons-risques-cicr (accessed December 6, 2022).

15 R. Ourdan, "Crise éthique à la Croix-Rouge internationale" (2018). www .lemonde.fr/international/article/2018/11/30/crise-ethique-a-la-croix-rouge-internationale_5390802_3210.html#xtor=AL-32280270

16 F. Franchini, "I rapporti con partner privati intaccano la credibilità del CICR" (February 2019). www.areaonline.ch/I-rapporti-con-partner-privati-intaccano-la-credibilita-del-CICR-5d581a00 (accessed August 30, 2022).

17 J. Fleurinor and C. P. Cramer, "The ICRC and Partnerships with the Private Sector: Evolution and Ethical Considerations" (n.d.). https://alternatives-humanitaires.org/en/2018/03/15/the-icrc-and-partnerships-with-the-private-sector-evolution-and-ethical-considerations/ (accessed August 30, 2022).

2   The ICRC and the Global Humanitarian System

The Critics in Context

> The international response to humanitarian situations is largely determined by the degree of strategic interests held by the major states.
> Sadako Ogata[1]

It helps understanding to situate the back and forth between the critics and defenders of the contemporary ICRC against the background of the global humanitarian system. As noted many times, no person is an island completely apart from society (save maybe for a few armed survivalists hiding out in rural Oregon!). And no humanitarian organization can be completely unaffected by the international humanitarian enterprise as it has evolved after the Cold War.[2]

The contemporary ICRC is certainly the product of its own leadership and their experiences, but it is also affected by other factors – in no particular order: (1) the practices of other humanitarian organizations; (2) the preferences of the RC Movement; (3) various governmental policies including first of all by the Swiss government but also the other major donors to the ICRC and especially the United States, Britain, Germany, and the EU; (4) thinking within the business community especially about social responsibility; (5) and the changing roles of the United Nations and other intergovernmental organizations. The sum total of all these factors adds up to the global humanitarian system, aka the humanitarian enterprise, aka the humanitarian business. I outline a few preliminary points now, returning to them in more detail in subsequent chapters. The ICRC leadership, or parts thereof, think the critics do not understand the big changes in the global humanitarian picture. Naturally the critics, certainly most of them, reject that characterization.

I   Elusive Boundaries: Some Basics

Nowhere is there a scientific or legal definition of international humanitarianism, humanitarian action, or humanitarian organization. The International Court of Justice (ICJ) or World Court (or top UN court in some popular discourse) had an opportunity to pronounce on some aspects of the subject in 1986 in the case of *Nicaragua* v. *United States of America*.[3]

At one point in its long and fractured judgment, with multiple judges using multiple lines of reasoning, the ICJ addressed the US provision of certain types of aid to the Contras, an armed nonstate group (actually organized by Washington) that was intervening in the hopes of overthrowing – or at least pressuring – the leftist Daniel Ortega government of Nicaragua as punishment for its intervention into neighboring El Salvador. The Court said inter alia that true humanitarian aid, such as practiced by Red Cross agencies under resolutions approved at the International Red Cross Conference, could not be considered impermissible interference in the domestic affairs of states. The Court assumed that RC aid was neutral and impartial and nonpolitical. Political and military assistance was different.

Thus, rather than sharply define humanitarian assistance, the Court basically said that true humanitarian assistance was what the Red Cross practiced, which meant neutral and impartial rather than slanted by strategic politics. Eventually the Court reached the conclusion that US nonmilitary aid to the Contras was part of a policy of illegal intervention in Nicaragua, along with the mining of Nicaragua's harbors and certain other US actions. (The United States, which had contested the Court's exercise of jurisdiction in this matter, basically ignored the substantive judgment.) The Court effectively (and correctly) said that nonmilitary aid to an armed nonstate actor was not really humanitarian assistance.

Insofar as there is informal or unofficial agreement on what makes the core of the humanitarian system, it would be those agencies that try to alleviate human distress in the context of some emergency or crisis – whether from human decisions such as war or natural events such as flood or earthquake. The focus of action is on relieving personal suffering from nonroutine situations. Events such as industrial disasters – as in Bhopal, India in 1984 (often the product of human errors somewhere along the way of design, maintenance, or supervision) – are sometimes lumped in with natural disasters, if only because they do not fit well with the other side of the coin – namely, war and other major political violence.

II   More on Vague Definitions and Elusive Boundaries

As much noted, the distinction between "man-made" political crises and other emergencies is inexact. It is often factually the case that distress from natural causes such as flood or earthquake is affected by multiple human decisions – for example, allowing housing in flood plains and coastal areas, or permitting fragile construction of housing in earthquake prone areas, or failing to provide adequate planning for emergency medical response. These types of human failures often occur within the context of poverty and underdevelopment. (But hurricane Ian in Florida in 2022 in the United States raised almost the same questions.) Even in situations of violence, part of the problem may stem from dissatisfactions with poor governance and underdevelopment.

Many facts lead to difficulties of precise categorization about types of situations. This is true not only regarding "man-made" versus natural disasters, but also regarding humanitarian versus developmental. Are emergency needs all that different from routine or structural deficiencies? The ICRC is traditionally said to be primarily a humanitarian organization even if undertaking some types of development programs (while trying to avoid calling them that). The UN Development Program (UNDP) remains focused mainly on development, even if marginally involved sometimes in a humanitarian response.

It is equally difficult to clearly differentiate humanitarian concern from human rights concern. If one initially assumes that humanitarianism is about relieving distress in emergencies while human rights is about justice for repression and/or deprivation, a close examination shows that those distinctions or comparisons are also not firm or watertight.[4] It will become clear later on that the ICRC, which is almost always called a humanitarian organization, now endorses reference to human rights norms in certain ways and in certain situations. It actually runs workshops on some aspects of human rights, as well as police use of force and police handling of weapons in urban areas.

Returning to the comparison between humanitarian and development actors, one can say that absent the factor of emergency or crisis, it is conventional to speak of development agencies that try to alleviate human distress stemming from poverty and other structural factors such as poor governance, lack of adequate education and health, and failure to adjust to a harsh climate. But we will see in some detail that the dividing line between humanitarian and development actors has sometimes been intentionally blurred. As will be shown, the World Bank, an intergovernmental development organization dominated by Western states and always with an American as president, has moved into the business of funding presumably humanitarian organizations like the ICRC because the Bank decided that various crises interfered with development. In the Bank's view, one needed to address (and fund) response to humanitarian crises as the first step to sustainable development, or to limit backsliding from whatever level of development had already been achieved. The ICRC has always claimed to be a humanitarian organization, but the World Bank, supposedly a development agency, is now among its major donors.

Moreover, some organizations have long claimed a role in acting on both sides of the divide – the humanitarian and the developmental. The private actor Oxfam comes to mind. In fact, Oxfam also advocates for human rights. The evolution of that private agency, dating from 1942, shows a meshing of crisis response to human needs, advancing sustainable human development, and advocacy for human rights and justice. (Oxfam's recent history also shows some scandals, more so than at the ICRC, covered later.) Other NGOs also act broadly on humanitarian response, development, human rights, pandemics, and climate change. Some do not draw a firm distinction between international and domestic problems. The International Rescue Committee has already been mentioned.

We find in the big picture of global humanitarianism that various attempts at neat categorization of actors and action are plagued, if not defeated, by especially the contemporary intentional merging of humanitarian and development activities, while noting the intrusion into both of these two supposedly separate – or at least identifiable – domains by concerns about ecology (climate change) and public health (pandemics) – along with human rights. As will be noted, Peter Maurer of the ICRC, president during 2012–2022, argued that traditional categories of activity have become merged and old ways of thinking have broken down; so it is necessary to think broadly and in new ways, or outside the box, if one is going to be a relevant (and adequately funded) humanitarian actor. Donor governments, the UN system, important other organizations such as the World Bank (officially part of the UN but sometimes acting separately) and the European Union, plus some other private agencies, are all pushing in this same direction of meshing or merging or combining in some way new thinking and policymaking across traditional semantical and ideational boundaries.

Importantly, there has been a desire, broadly shared, to combine the traditional, short-term, emergency, lifesaving humanitarian response with at least some kinds of development. These latter activities go by many names: early recovery, resiliency programs, micro-development, intermediate economic security, basic infrastructure, direct results of conflict, and more. The ICRC was not so much sucked into this vortex of new and badly defined "conflict-development activities" as it was an early practitioner of such activities. Relatively early on it paid for vaccination of cattle so that those pastoralists adversely affected by violence might support themselves economically in the near future and not be so dependent on delivery of food relief. This broader orientation for assistance has now been systematized and expanded at the ICRC, as will be shown. Some critics agree with this orientation but believe it has been taken too far, and without clear limits, to the detriment of other ICRC roles – which will be explained in due course.

III   What about Specificity?

And yet, as especially the critics note, there is still a need for specialized expertise within this swirling mass of new thinking and competing ideas. Not every agency is supposed to do everything. That would be a recipe for over-extension, conflict, and reduced competence. Agencies and programs still need limits, or so the critics emphasize. It was long said at the ICRC, but maybe not so much anymore, that one of its strengths was recognition of its limits. Some note that as Amnesty International (AI) expanded from a focus on arbitrary detention to a defense of all the internationally recognized human rights, its reputation and influence arguably declined.[5] It once had a limited mandate, but now was spread thin with a sprawling focus. Arguably, this resulted in a weaker impact.

Moreover, some emphasize that while most of the global humanitarian system is about material and moral assistance, the ICRC has traditional humanitarian protection as part of its mandate and historically acquired expertise. The critics fear that especially all the attention and money devoted to expanded assistance for civilians in so-called protracted conflicts – or in other terms an overlap with development in violent situations that wax and wane – has diverted the organization from its traditional excellence related to IHL for armed conflicts and protection of political prisoners.

The critics thus claim, especially when other program expansions are added, that the ICRC has lost or is in the process of losing its reputation for excellence in two endeavors: advancing IHL and protecting detainees. As noted in Chapter 1, the leadership dismisses this criticism as nonsense, saying, as one leader told this author, that its traditional activities are grounded in the ICRC's DNA. According to him, forced to choose between protecting prisoners of war (POWs) and responding to low-level violence in Latin American urban centers, the ICRC would always opt for the former. Observers may want to evaluate this statement in the light of events in Ukraine, as discussed in the Epilogue.

IV   Nevertheless, Some Facts and Figures

Despite the difficulty of establishing precise definitions and distinctions, one can still speak of the numbers of humans in need of immediate help from some disrupting event like war, forced displacement from political events, or natural and industrial disaster. Apart from grinding poverty or persistent underdevelopment, there are those persons on the move or in peril from exceptional events leading to forced displacement from routine life, either "man-made" or at least partially natural.

Circa 2022 the UN estimated that more than 300 million people around the world were dislocated from their usual residence. This is approximately the population of the United States. Of this number, some 200 million had not found safety and jobs in a new location but required some type of immediate international assistance. This is just under the population of Brazil. The estimated cost of this need was placed at almost US$50 billion.[6] This is about what one man, Elon Musk, offered in order to buy Twitter. Or, this is about the value of military aid that the United States provided to Ukraine in the first year of the Russian invasion.

Donations and promises of donations in early 2022 fell well short of the projected financial target needed to respond to this humanitarian or relatively short-term need. The number of those in distress and needing assistance was a major increase over previous years. One of the persistent features of the current world order was much disorder. Even back in about 2010, one observer estimated the number of "aid workers" involved in global assistance efforts at 210,000.[7] In the fall of 2022, it was said that aid workers numbered 630,000 on a global scale.[8]

A report in fall 2022 confirmed the big picture: there were more people in need of humanitarian help compared to the past, donations for a needed response fell short, the entire system was dominated financially by a few Western governments and their organizations, the better-funded humanitarian actors were based in the West, there was much talk of localization and collaboration with aid agencies especially in the Global South, but these ideas were difficult to implement in practical ways especially since pandemics and climate change interacted with protracted conflicts to impede progress.[9]

Another report in fall 2022 said that of the 283 million persons who faced food insecurity, 60 percent of them were to be found in countries facing geopolitical conflict – which is of course where the ICRC works.[10] In other words, those with the guns were responsible for most of the hunger and malnutrition that existed, whether one talked about blocking the export of Ukrainian grain or endangering the distribution of grain in east and central Africa, for example.

In late 2022, UN projections for 2023 updated and unfortunately expanded the numbers. More people were displaced, more people were food insecure, there were double standards in that some situations (e.g., Ukraine) got much more attention than others (e.g., South Sudan).[11]

In early 2023 a massive earthquake in Turkey affected broad swathes of the southeast of that country, not to mention northwest Syria, adding great numbers of those killed (about 50,000) and dislocated (maybe 250,000) from "normal" life. The response to the humanitarian crisis not only involved questions about immediate response but also the nature of previous development – namely, why construction of high-rise buildings had been allowed in a quake-prone area, and whether building codes has been ignored through lax governmental supervision. Again, humanitarian and developmental issues were both in play at the same time for the same situations.

To give a few more specific examples with numbers, during the Syrian war of 2011–2022, about half the Syrian population was uprooted, with about seven million becoming IDPs (internally displaced persons), often very hard to reach with help, and another five million becoming refugees and crossing an international border into Turkey or Jordan or wherever. Both groups, forcibly displaced, were not able to provide for themselves, although some places of refuge such as Turkey were more open, for a time, to refugees working than others, for example Jordan or Lebanon. As of summer 2022, at least six million Ukrainian civilians became internally displaced and another six million wound up refugees in Poland and other countries because of the invasion by Russia. This amounted to about one-third of the Ukrainian population under Kyiv's control. In Haiti circa 2020, because of a combination of poverty, earthquake, hurricane, collapse of government, and rise of gang warfare, the number of Haitians in need of immediate help for basic human needs was in the range of five million out of a total population of about eleven million. In Afghanistan, by summer 2022, almost twenty-five million people, or about 60 percent of the population, needed immediate assistance because of political conflict and transition.

A large part of the circa 330 million persons uprooted by late 2022 stemmed from armed conflict or other political violence in a handful of cases: Ukraine, Syria, Yemen, Afghanistan, Myanmar, Somalia, Venezuela, Ethiopia, and South Sudan. In 2023 new and extensive fighting in Sudan added to the problems.

V   Not Just Assistance, but also Protection

The above numbers, driven primarily by a handful of cases, raise the issue of basic human needs and therefore humanitarian assistance. But there is also the matter of humanitarian protection in the narrow sense of the term. The ensuing chapters follow ICRC practice of using the word "protection" with two meanings: There is general humanitarian

Protection, a synonym for humanitarian help, meaning advocacy and diplomacy and services for all the needs of persons harmed by exceptional violent events; and there is protection in the narrow sense of trying to respond to the basic needs of those detained or missing, including restoring contacts with family or loved ones.

To repeat for clarification, everything the ICRC does is intended to respond to the distress of those adversely affected by violent conflict and is thus Protection in the general sense. The ICRC tries to Protect persons from hypothermia, starvation, malnutrition, waterborne diseases, anxiety and depression, and more, by its material and moral assistance. Assistance, formerly called relief and now sometimes called economic security programs, is one type of general Protection. But there is also the matter of ICRC protection in the narrow sense pertaining to those detained or missing, including links to immediate others. One might speak of prisoners of war and interned civilians in international armed conflict, those detained by reason of internal armed conflict (often called civil war), political or security prisoners, and those most sweepingly and blandly called by the ICRC "persons detained by reason of events." The latter phrase reflects an attempt to help detainees while bypassing disputes over labels and categories – and governmental fears of activating law and attention that authorities want to avoid.

Again, to give some specifics, although the numbers are soft rather than definitive, in Syria after the outbreak of demonstrations and repression in 2011 until the present time, several sources estimate the number of detainees tortured to death while in the custody of the Assad regime at perhaps 15,000. Media reports about political prisoners in Egypt put the figure at about 60,000. In Ukraine, during 2022, some fifty Ukrainian POWs were reported killed in some type of event at a prison facility (Olenivka) in Russian-controlled territory. In Yemen in early 2022, a Saudi airstrike on a prison facility in rebel territory killed a reported sixty prisoners.

Especially in armed conflict, the ICRC has a well-recognized special protection role, initially chosen by itself, then endorsed by the rest of the RC network, and then endorsed by states in public international law for certain categories of detainees. But as will be shown, the effectiveness of the ICRC as "guardian" of IHL, and more particularly its role in supervising detention in armed conflict and political violence or instability, hinges on cooperation from controlling authorities. An important, if murky, subject is ICRC wisdom and dynamism, or astuteness, in seeking and even sometimes obtaining this cooperation. I delve into this opaque subject later in more depth, especially in Chapter 14.

VI   Interim Sum: Shared Burdens

To repeat a fundamental point, the ICRC claims a mandate to act in situations of war and "other violence," plus the "direct results" of such situations, mostly leaving to other actors the response to natural and industrial disasters. But Geneva desires to maintain its activities when natural disasters occur in a situation of violent conflict. Northwest Syria was a clear example of this latter type of situation, as the effects of the 2023 earthquake in nearby Turkey collapsed fragile housing in Idlib province. Those adversely affected had been mostly displaced from other parts of Syria during the violence from 2011, the local medical system was meager, and outside assistance was heavily politicized with long-running disputes about access points for humanitarian assistance.

Once upon a time the ICRC might have been one of the few actors focusing on humanitarian services in armed conflict and other violence. These days the ICRC role overlaps with numerous other actors, especially in assistance. In Ukraine in the first half of 2022, the UN reported over 250 organizations active in assistance in that war, with 60 percent of them being local rather than international. Also, in 2014 the UN created the Human Rights Monitoring Mission in Ukraine, which engaged in reporting on, and conducting some field activities about, both protection and assistance.

VII   Partners and Competitors

One can also note the expanded activities of some actors such as the UN Refugee Office (UNHCR).[12] This agency is one of the big three as far as UN humanitarian funding is concerned. The other two are the World Food Program and UNICEF. It was said that these three got about 40 percent of humanitarian funding around the world as of fall 2022.[13]

The UNHCR started with a focus on those fleeing a "well-founded fear of persecution" but evolved to deal also with war refugees and also IDPs sometimes (as internal refugees). It started with a focus on protection, making representations to governments who had the last say on who was entitled to asylum as victims of persecution, but wound up with a major effort in managing assistance (the details of assistance were mostly subcontracted to nongovernmental organizations who ran the refugee or IDP camps).

One of the main criticisms of the UNHCR is that it has been manipulated by Western governments, its major donors, so as to downgrade protection in favor of assistance. (Most of the UNHCR budget is funded through voluntary donations, with only a very small percentage drawn from the regular UN core budget.) Therefore, so the critique goes, Western governments wanted to take in fewer refugees and grant fewer claims to asylum, while also wanting the UNHCR to manage refugees "over there" someplace. As two experts wrote, the UN-centered refugee regime went from a central concern with "rights, asylum, and permanent resettlement in the West, to safety and short term assistance in the region of origin."[14] More generally, questions were raised rather early in the post-Cold War era about how to prevent "the humanitarian enterprise from being hijacked by donor governments."[15]

The ICRC and UNHCR were both active regarding war refugees and IDPs from violent conflict. They were also part of the international response to undocumented migration, along with the IOM (International Organization for Migration) and many others. In general, organizations like UNHCR and IOM had good relations with the ICRC, the latter mostly staying out of legal controversies about who was entitled to non-refoulement and not to be sent back to a situation of danger, which was the métier of the UNHCR. As a head of UNHCR wrote, "The ICRC was always the closest and most reliable partner for UNHCR."[16] Both were funded by Western governments. The head of UNHCR was always from a country friendly to the United States, and there was always an American in a top secondary position.

Photograph 2.1 The ICRC is part of the global humanitarian system, interacting frequently with various UN and other humanitarian agencies. Here, the ICRC runs an office for tracing missing persons in a refugee camp organized by the UNHCR in Jordan in 2016.

Whether the private ICRC was more independent in its policymaking than the public UNHCR is an interesting question. The UNHCR, while officially having a relatively independent head, reported to UN organs and was part of the intergovernmental United Nations. Sometimes the UN secretary-general overruled decisions by the head of UNHCR. For example, in 1993 UNHCR head Sadako Ogata suspended relief operations in the Bosnian war to protest conditions imposed on the agency. She was ordered to resume operations by UN Secretary-General Boutros Boutros-Ghali (whether he had the legal authority to do so is another question). The ICRC had as its highest authority its own governing board. But the United States contributed a third of its budget, and that donation was voluntary – subject to change at any time. The other top five donors to the ICRC were all Western public authorities. One former high ICRC official told this author that the firebreak between donors and ICRC decisions was not always what it should be.

Or take the example of MSF (Médecins Sans Frontières [Doctors Without Borders]). MSF started in 1971 as a spin off from the ICRC and RC Movement, with parts of the French Red Cross unhappy about the restrictions from NIIHA values in the Biafran-Nigerian war of 1967–1970. The original thinking by Bernard Kouchner and others was that MSF would not only provide medical assistance but also speak out, or witness, about human rights and injustice. It would not be so dependent on state consent for its operations. Kouchner and others talked about, somewhat later, a right of interference or in some versions a right of humanitarian intervention. He was driven by the thought that the ICRC had made a mistake by not speaking out against the Holocaust, and he did not want to duplicate that stance in Nigeria-Biafra or any other conflict producing many innocent victims.

MSF evolved out of a political view by some in the French Red Cross that Biafra should be independent, a view closely aligned with French governmental policy. France was one of the very few to recognize Biafra as a state – perhaps because the United States and Britain were seen as tilting toward Lagos! This French recognition of Biafra was later conflated with the propaganda that Nigeria was engaged in genocide against the Ibo people who made up the local population in the breakaway area. There was no genocide in Biafra, and officially MSF, once it existed, never claimed there was – although perhaps over a million civilians died in that conflict.

One can note that much later the Biafra leader C. Odumeguru Ojukwu openly ran for various offices in Nigeria. At his death he was honored by the state. On the part of Lagos, one could not prove an intention to destroy the Ibo people, or even their leaders who had attempted secession.

The ICRC in that conflict, however, was affected by pressures to act from Kouchner and others. It too wound up tilting toward Biafra, notwithstanding its official commitment to neutrality. Reasoning by analogy to the full 1949 Geneva Conventions, one can note that a belligerent state such as Nigeria had the right to control (supervise) humanitarian relief destined for contested areas. Biafra, as we know, refused to cooperate with relief approved by Lagos, since that would imply that Biafra was not an independent state. Biafran leaders used attention to the suffering of the Ibo people to try to override Nigerian sovereignty. Biafra had employed an effective public relations firm, and much of Europe – where of course the ICRC headquarters was located – was pro-Biafra, being not much interested in the details of IHL. The ICRC's main competitor in active relief to Biafra, Joint Church Aid, not much interested in matters of state sovereignty, also pushed Geneva into dangerous decisions with several negative consequences.

For MSF, originally stimulated by the complexities of Nigeria-Biafra, the desired combination of in-country programming and being a public witness about human rights violations has turned out to be a much more

Photograph 2.2 The ICRC often works with not only UN agencies but also private humanitarian groups. Here the ICRC and MSF (Doctors Without Borders) discuss medical aid in Sudan, 2007. MSF was a spinoff from the French Red Cross but evolved to have good relations with the ICRC.

difficult project than originally expected. In fact, MSF has evolved to be very similar – but not identical – to the ICRC, but focusing only on medical services, in that it has had to often recognize the necessity of keeping a low profile rather than denouncing crimes in order to operate in many conflicts. This was true of MSF in Myanmar circa 2023, as we show later in Chapter 6.

Some MSF leaders recognized fairly early on the difficulty of speaking out while operating in-country: "Those who had played Luther to the Red Cross's Rome were, it seemed, more and more ready to heal the schism."[17] For example, it had to join the ICRC mission in Rwanda in 1994, and accept ICRC rules of engagement, in order to keep its personnel in-country during the genocide. Chapter 6 contains a section that compares MSF and the ICRC in the Syrian civil war, and then with references to Myanmar. In general the two organizations, different in mission and administration, have good relations now and cooperate in many places where their mandates overlap.[18] MSF is probably more inclined than the ICRC to try to operate in rebel areas without the consent of the central government, where conditions allow, but the comparison is not absolute.

These brief references to the UNHCR and MSF are used as examples to show that many different types of actors, both public and private, are now involved in situations of war and other violence. One could also speak of the World Food Program, UNICEF, Save the Children, Oxfam, Care, Caritas, World Vision, the International Rescue Committee, and a host of others. At one point there were so many outside actors trying to respond to instability, repression, and poverty in Haiti, which was generating much violence and dangerous flight from the country, that wags said it should be called the NGO Republic. In South Sudan at the time of writing in 2022, the US Agency for International Development (AID) had contracts with at least twenty implementing agencies for humanitarian assistance. We noted already some 250 agencies active in assistance in the Ukraine war. Many agencies, unlike the ICRC (at least in principle), act in situations other than violent conflict, but that is not the point here. The point here is that this situation of multiple humanitarian actors in assistance calls for coordination or at least a rational division of labor to avoid waste, duplication, and competition that impedes relieving the distress of individuals in need of help. There is certainly the matter of competition for funding.

VIII   He Who Pays the Piper, ...

By and large the organized official international response to emergencies and crises, which has been called "organized compassion,"[19] was paid for by Western governments and their partners like the EU and then distributed to UN agencies, RC actors, and some international NGOs. The exact proportion of funding from governments compared to private donations varied among private organizations such as Save the Children, Oxfam, Caritas, International Rescue Committee, MSF, and so on. (For example, only about 2 percent of MSF funding comes from governments whereas for the ICRC it is about 85 percent or higher.) A few non-Western governments, such as Kuwait or the United Arab Emirates (UAE), also contributed to this humanitarian response in reasonably significant ways. Two members of the UN Security Council, China and Russia, along with some of the oil-rich nations such as Saudi Arabia, were not major contributors to the official global humanitarian enterprise. Circa 2022, as noted earlier, there was a sizable deficit between the estimated cost of humanitarian immediate lifesaving help, along with early recovery efforts, and the resources donated. This was true even before 2022 when the war in Ukraine took money and attention away from other crises in Yemen or South Sudan, inter alia. The shortfall was evident even before the 2023 earthquakes in Turkey killed tens of thousands there and in Syria and left many more homeless.

It became fashionable to note, with accuracy, that the extant global humanitarian system originated in Europe on the basis of Christian charity and was intertwined with European colonialism.[20] Chapter 3 will place the early ICRC firmly within this context. It is also accurate to say that the West still dominates the organized global humanitarian response to crises, with Western governments providing most of the resources that are then distributed to mostly Western-based humanitarian agencies – as already noted. A head of UNHCR wrote, "The international response to humanitarian situations is largely determined by the degree of strategic interests held by the major states."[21] Two scholars wrote more simply, "States run the game."[22] The last chapter of the book discusses this situation further, as the ICRC has benefitted from, while being criticized for, this arrangement. Carving out a posture of independent neutrality, and a reputation for superior effectiveness, while maintaining broad support, is no easy task in this context.

It is a fact that in Ukraine at war, and in other crisis situations, local organizations have done much good in response to humanitarian need but get almost none of the international humanitarian funding (globally less than 1 percent). There are some sound reasons for this, such as concern about accountability for handling funds and in particular whether the line is crossed between civilian help and military impact. Here one gets into the debate about a Red Cross or Dunantist approach, which is supposed to be NIIHA (neutral, independent, impartial, humanitarian action), and other approaches that are partial or engaged or committed or biased or preferential or non-NIIHA. Some local aid to civilians in Ukraine trickled down to military personnel.

It is no surprise which side the ICRC takes in this debate, at least in general, as compared to some specific cases where the ICRC was compelled to depart from an independent and neutral and impartial posture (Syria is discussed). It will be shown that there is very broad support, globally speaking, for a Dunantist or NIIHA approach, which was reflected in the ICJ case about the Contras and Nicaragua mentioned earlier. But a number of voices argue now for more consideration of the local – and even nonneutral – approach. There are some very capable local aid organizations here and there in the Global South,[23] and some of them are quite different from the ICRC. At the same time, particularly regarding action in ongoing violent conflicts, there is still very clearly a need for neutral international humanitarians in conflict situations. It may not be politically correct to observe two possible interrelated reasons for the many local aid workers killed during their efforts: they did not have extensive contacts with all armed groups in a conflict zone, and they did not have a clear reputation for NIIHA values.

There is nevertheless a backlash in some circles against the Western-funded and Western-dominated global humanitarian system, including by some analysts in the West. The ICRC is caught up in this debate, since it is one of the Western-based and well-known humanitarians (at least, well known to policymakers) whose top donors are all Western: the United States, the United Kingdom, Germany, Switzerland, the EU. However, being part of the RC Movement, the ICRC sometimes teams up with a National RC Society for action on the ground, which may allow it to escape, or at least minimize, any complaints of outside meddling by a Western neocolonial actor. This linkage, however, may lead to other problems. This, too, is discussed later, especially in Chapter 5.

One should be clear, however, that it is not just Western states that might take a strategic political approach to many aspects of humanitarian affairs. All states seem to view much humanitarianism through the prism of national interests. In 2023, the Assad regime in Syria agreed to two additional crossing points for humanitarian aid to enter the northwest province of Idlib, controlled by opponents, where there was much civilian need after earthquakes. This move by Damascus softened its image in the quest for more reconstruction aid for those parts of Syria under Assad's control. At the same time, other states, for example the UAE and Saudi Arabia, changed policy and increased their relief aid to Assad's government, hoping to lure it into their geopolitical orbit and offset the influence of Russia and Iran. Russia and Iran themselves were providing some relief to their strategic ally Assad, more so than in some other situations of need.[24]

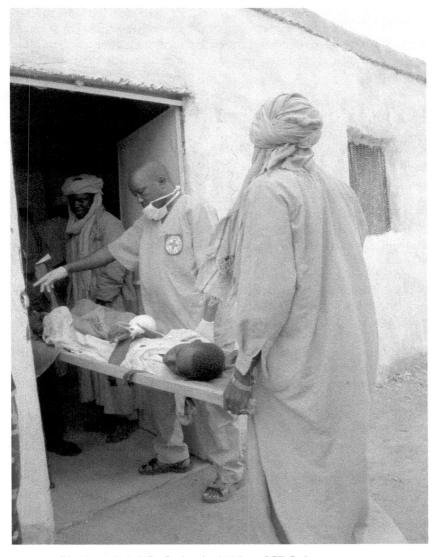

Photograph 2.3 In Sudan in 2005 an ICRC doctor prepares to carry out surgery in a guardhouse at a distribution center run by the UN World Food Program. The ICRC and the WFP often coordinated in their field activities. Sometimes both cooperated in the provision of assistance – sharing warehouses, scheduling, and personnel. The WFP won the Nobel Peace Prize in 2020. The ICRC has won three, in 1917, 1944, and 1963 (shared with the IFRC). Henry Dunant shared the first in 1901.

It is misguided to think that only Western states develop a humanitarian policy with considerable attention to strategic politics. Do Western states show more genuine and purely humanitarian concern than other states regardless of strategic interests? That is a good subject for further research.

IX   The UN Enters the Game

Above all, the global humanitarian system is characterized by a much larger UN role after the Cold War. It seems ancient history to recall that in the Nigerian civil war of 1967–1970 about Biafra, discussed earlier, the UN played almost no role on the ground (or in the air regarding relief flights). This conflict, perhaps the first where humanitarian action played out in the headlines, saw two major relief networks involved: the ICRC and its RC partners, and Joint Church Aid as already mentioned – a coalition of faith-based actors who did not see themselves bound by what the 1949 Geneva Conventions might say about humanitarian relief in armed conflict.[25]

It also seems almost prehistoric to note that in the 1971 events in South Asia involving Pakistan and India, producing Bangladesh out of what was East Pakistan, the UN as well as the RC Movement (then called the International Red Cross) were unprepared to act in response to forced dislocation on a massive scale. An estimated ten million persons fled the conflict from East Pakistan/Bangladesh into India. To try to provide assistance in some way, UN leaders had to cobble together some kind of ad hoc response, borrowing an ICRC official to help lead the effort. The ICRC qua ICRC and its RC partners were blocked from assistance early on, not only by unpreparedness but also by the views of Pakistan.

Also noteworthy, and analyzed later, in 1979 the ICRC and UNICEF put together another ad hoc response when Vietnam ousted the radical and genocidal Khmer Rouges from Cambodia (Kampuchea). This duo of a private and public actor, a unique humanitarian actor with a supposedly UN developmental agency, managed an unprecedented relief and recovery action to avert famine and lay the groundwork for socioeconomic development in that destroyed country. Even into the 1980s, there was no guaranteed, much less well-oiled, UN relief system as such.

The end of the Cold War changed many things including the UN role in emergency humanitarian relief. The details of this are covered later. In short, Western states led in establishing a more coordinated planning and supervisory system, trying to make use of existing UN agencies while creating a few new ones, and trying to bring on board in a more systematic way relevant NGOs. This presented challenges to the ICRC as well as new partnerships. To the extent that the ICRC and its RC partners were presumed to have something of a monopoly on, or at least primacy about, official humanitarian action in wars, that was certainly diluted.

To provide a few summary points, one can note that from 1991 a new UN relief coordinator, heading the UN office for disaster relief, eventually became also the Under Secretary-General for Humanitarian Affairs. He led OCHA, the Office of the Coordinator of Humanitarian Affairs. As the name suggest, this part of the UN bureaucracy was not authorized to act in the field but rather to coordinate the action of others. The UN system eventually adopted the so-called cluster approach to emergency response, with the UNHCR leading those focused on protection in conflicts, the WHO leading on health issues, UNDP leading on early recovery, UNESCO on education, UNICEF on water/habitat, and so on.[26] The ICRC followed developments closely but kept itself apart from the clusters approach, guarding its own roles in protection and assistance, even while it sometimes cooperated with UN and other actors. It did join in when the UN and other agencies adopted the Sphere standards designed to meet minimum targets in the provision of water, food, shelter, and sanitation.[27] UN and RC agencies met with interested NGOs in the Inter-Agency Standing Commission at the UN headquarters in New York to try to coordinate action, agree on divisions of labor, and reduce overlap, waste, and at least some competition.

X The System beyond the UN

Over time a whole range of actors arose to study, plan, evaluate, and share information (and much criticism) about the international response to human need in emergency or crisis situations. For example, there was the Overseas Development Institute (ODI), based in London, which in 1997 created ALNAP (Active Learning Network on Accountability and Performance). So, one had a think tank within a think tank on the subject of development and humanitarian response, with a broad and mixed range of donors. The ICRC Director-General 2010–2020, Yves Daccord, was on the ODI governing board for a time.

There was Devex, a global media platform for development studies but with much attention to humanitarian affairs. It was funded by a wide range of public and private sources. Also, there was the New Humanitarian, formerly IRIN, originally sponsored by OCHA, that became an independent news source focused on humanitarian issues. Unlike Devex, whose in-depth reports going beyond basic information required a paying membership, the New Humanitarian was a nonprofit with free information, funded by a mix of governments (e.g., the

Danish Foreign Ministry), foundations (e.g., the Bill and Melinda Gates Foundation), and individual contributions.

Then there was the organization Humanitarian Outcomes, based in London, comprised mostly of former aid workers, that did research and consulting on humanitarian issues. Also based in London was the Humanitarian Leadership Academy, a spin-off from Save the Children, which provided online learning and other services to help all humanitarian actors, especially in the Global South, act more effectively. Based in Lyon is Humanitarian Alternatives, a web platform and publication centered on analyzing international humanitarian affairs. Bilingual, it was supported mainly by a consortium of French-speaking universities and foundations.

Some of the organizations interested in humanitarian affairs formed the H2H network to provide services to the front line humanitarians. Rather than directly provide relief, this network tried to support those on the front line of action by providing support services such as mapping of events and needs, accounting skills, and expertise in negotiations, inter alia.

Many universities developed various programs analyzing global humanitarianism or aspects of it. There was, for example, the Feinstein Center at Tufts University concentrating on humanitarian crises, especially involving nutrition. Harvard University had a Humanitarian Initiative, run for a time by a Swiss with connections to the ICRC. Not only university programs but also the existence of professional journals showed that international humanitarianism became a defined subject for teaching and research. Space does not permit a full listing of the professional, refereed journals that carry articles touching on the international humanitarian response to crisis. A few examples of those that publish in English suffice to convey the point that global humanitarianism in its different dimensions has attracted increasing attention from serious thinkers: *Disasters, Crisis Response Journal, Forced Migration Review, Journal of Refugee Studies, Journal of Humanitarian Affairs, Journal of Humanitarian Assistance, Resilience Journal*, and so on at great length. Moreover, many journals on human rights, foreign policy, world politics, international law, international organization, or ethics, inter alia, sometimes analyze different aspects of the humanitarian enterprise, whatever its elusive boundaries.

As one who has followed at least some of these practical, professional, and academic developments for about five decades, I would not say that the ICRC is often covered or explained or analyzed in these sources in new or in-depth ways. Its prevalent commitment to discreet diplomacy and its policy of closed archives for mostly fifty years no doubt often leads to the judgment, especially on the part of journalists but also academic researchers, that the ICRC is not a helpful source of information.

I know of a few younger academics who wanted to study the ICRC but gave up, given the difficulty of obtaining useful information there on timely but sensitive topics. Nevertheless, beyond discussions of the ICRC, there is no doubt that the subject of global humanitarianism has attracted much attention especially since the end of the Cold War. It is certainly the case that historians have discovered how interesting the subject of humanitarianism can be, along with the emergence of the field of history of human rights.

If the ICRC found itself alone, or almost alone, as a humanitarian actor in the midst of war and similar violence in the 1950s and 1960s in former Western British Palestine, or violent clashes in Kenya and Algeria, things have become decidedly different now. If there were few humanitarian actors in Afghanistan up until 2001, that is different now – even under the Taliban. (One source said 800 humanitarian actors were active in Afghanistan circa 2022, including most of the well-known ones.) If all humanitarian actors, including the ICRC, had pretty much forgotten about the local scene when China took over Tibet in the early 1950s, a Great Power seizure of territory now would draw much more attention – on humanitarian as on other grounds. The Russian invasion of Ukraine shows that (although Ukraine also shows a bias in the humanitarian response, with much more attention directed there compared to South Sudan or many other conflicts in the Global South). Both humanitarianism and human rights became progressively established as fields of action and study. Whereas lawyers and philosophers had initially studied aspects of both, many more joined in, as global humanitarianism became a fixed dimension of international relations despite continuing discussion of exactly what it was and what it did, should be doing, or needed to change.

XI   Conclusion

The global humanitarian system, warts and all, is now there in all its sprawling and ill-defined dimensions. The ICRC is a part of it and is affected by it. It is a big aspect of the background, or context, for the little-noticed but intensely felt debate among present and former officials of the ICRC (deeply felt on both sides). With many more varied actors in the international humanitarian response to crises situations, the ICRC faces both more competition (especially regarding funding and assistance) and many more potential partners. It also faces more scrutiny and review. When I did my first book on the ICRC published in 1977,[28] some reviews noted that this was the first time the reviewer had read about the ICRC in any framing besides legal. The reviewer knew something about the ICRC and the Geneva Conventions, but that was about it. Now one can discuss and evaluate the ICRC more broadly – at least if one is willing to make the effort. (Lots of inquiries still go ignored in Geneva.) After all, officials there are dealing with multiple weighty matters.

That takes us back to the deeply felt exchange between some former ICRC officials and the current leadership. Is the ICRC making the right decisions in adjusting to a changing world scene, or is it squandering its reputation for excellence by acting too broadly and without clear limits, while not concentrating properly on a few issues where it manifests – or should manifest – a clear expertise or value added?

Notes

1 S. Ogata, *The Turbulent Decade: Confronting the Refugee Crises of the 1990s* (New York: W. W. Norton & Company, 2005), p. 318.

2 L. Miner, *The Humanitarian Enterprise: Dilemmas and Discoveries* (Bloomfield, CT: Kumarian Press, 2002); T. G. Weiss, *Humanitarian Business* (Cambridge: Polity Press, 2013).

3 Military and Paramilitary Activities in and against Nicaragua (*Nicaragua* v. *United States of America*), Merits, Judgment, I.C.J. Reports, 1986, para 242.

4 See especially M. A. Barnett, ed., *Human Rights and Humanitarianism: A World of Differences?* (Cambridge: Cambridge University Press, 2020). The book shows the difficulties of establishing clear and firm distinctions between the two concepts of human rights and humanitarian affairs.

5 For a good review of AI and traditionalists who wanted to keep the focus on political prisoners, and others who wanted to expand AI's mandate, see Stephen Hopgood, *Keepers of the Flame: Understanding Amnesty International* (Ithaca: Cornell University Press, 2006).

6 United Nations Office for the Coordination of Humanitarian Affairs, Global Humanitarian Overview (2022). https://gho.unocha.org/ (accessed September 2, 2022).

7 M. A. Barnett, *Empire of Humanity: A History of Humanitarianism* (Ithaca: Cornell University Press, 2011), p. 3. See also P. Ryman, *Une histoire de l'humanitaire* (Paris: La Decouverte, 2016).

8 *The New Humanitarian*, "State of the Humanitarian System," September 13, 2022, www.thenewhumanitarian.org/news/2022/09/13/State-of-the-humanitarian-system-Key-takeaways (accessed January 12, 2023).

9 ALNAP, *The State of the Humanitarian System*, September 7, 2022.

10 *The Economist*, "How Men with Guns Aggravate World Hunger," November 2, 2022, www.economist.com/international/2022/11/02/how-men-with-guns-aggravate-global-hunger (accessed November 8, 2022).

11 Irwin Loy and Jessica Alexander, "Key Takeaways from the UN's Record-breaking Tally for 2023 Humanitarian Needs," *The New Humanitarian*, December 1, 2022, www.thenewhumanitarian.org/news/2022/12/01/financing-appeals-OCHA-global-humanitarian-overview (accessed December 2, 2022).

12 For background and fundamentals see G. Loescher, *The UNHCR and World Politics: A Perilous Path* (Oxford: Oxford University Press, 2001). An analytical treatment by an insider up through the 1990s is S. Ogata, *The Turbulent*

Decade: Confronting the Refugee Crises of the 1990s (New York: W. W. Norton & Company, 2005).

13 *The New Humanitarian,* "State of the Humanitarian System."

14 A. Aleinifoff and L. Zamore, *The Arc of Protection: Reforming the International Refugee Regime* (Stanford: Stanford University Press, 2019), p. 23.

15 Rieff, *A Bed for the Night,* p. 280. See further especially A. Donini, ed., *The Golden Fleece: Manipulation and Independence in Humanitarian Action* (Boulder, CO: Kumarian Press, 2012).

16 Ogata, *The Turbulent Decade,* p. 196.

17 Rieff, *A Bed for the Night,* p. 331.

18 See R. Brauman, "Médecins Sans Frontières and the ICRC: Matters of Principle," *International Review of the Red Cross,* 94/888 (Winter, 2012) pp. 1523–1535.

19 Barnett, *Empire of Humanity,* p. 50.

20 Barnett, *Empire of Humanity,* provides a good overview as of about 2010.

21 Ogata, *The Turbulent Decade,* p. 318.

22 Aleinikoff and Zamore, *The Arc of Protection,* p. 135.

23 See the reference to the African organization SHOFCO, which did both relief and development and was sometimes intertwined with local governmental authority at: F. Halais, "Weathering the Storm: Building Resilience in the Humanitarian Sector" (2022). https://devex.shorthandstories.com/weathering-the-storm-building-resilience-in-the-humanitarian-sector/index.html (accessed September 9, 2022).

24 See further Declan Walsh, "Syria's Assad Uses Disaster Diplomacy to Inch Back onto World Stage," *New York Times,* February 16, 2023, www.nytimes.com/2023/02/16/world/middleeast/syria-earthquake-assad-diplomacy.html (accessed February 17, 2023).

25 There is good literature on this seminal conflict – seminal for the ICRC, international humanitarianism, and the entire system of international relations. For starters, see T. Hentsch, *Face au Blocus: La Croix-Rouge international dans le Nigeria en guerre (1967–1970)* (Geneva: HEI, 1973). He presents inside information on the ICRC. His book is not so good on relevant state policies. From a vast range of choice see also M. L. Desgrandchamps, *L'humanitaire en guerres civiles: la crise du Biafra (1967–1970)* (Rennes: PUR, 2018), who makes good use of ICRC documents. She sees the conflict having affected ICRC management, personnel policy, and communications policy.

26 UNHCR, Emergency Handbook, "Cluster Approach (IASC)," https://emergency.unhcr.org/entry/61190/cluster-approach-iasc (accessed November 27, 2022).

27 For a short analysis see Dan Price, "Complex Humanitarian Emergencies: Beyond the Sphere Standards," https://medium.com/@mantis.banks/complex-humanitarian-emergencies-beyond-the-sphere-minimum-standards-378559a86f77, February 22, 2017 (accessed November 27, 2022).

28 David P. Forsythe, *Humanitarian Politics: The International Committee of the Red Cross* (Baltimore and London: Johns Hopkins University Press, 1977).

3   History

Part I – The Gentlemen of Geneva and Dunant's Dream

NIIHA.

> The ICRC is a curious animal.
>
> Caroline Morehead[1]

A few literati know, but many in the general public do not, that the ICRC is the founding agency of what is today called the International Red Cross and Red Crescent Movement (or International Red Cross before 1996). The well-informed are aware that early events were inspired by the experiences and writing of Henry Dunant, a Geneva businessman by profession but a religious visionary by nature. Some might even know that the nascent ICRC, led by the Geneva lawyer Gustave Moynier, developed and institutionalized what became known as the Red Cross idea: Neutral, Independent, Impartial, and Humanitarian Action (NIIHA) to victims in need, nongovernmental but operating closely with public authorities. The ICRC has been constant in its desire to advance Dunant's vision of an NIIHA organization – and at the same time engaged in constant change to meet different challenges, incurring various controversies along the way.

I   Origins and Values

Created in 1863 in Geneva (sometimes called the Protestant Rome back then), the ICRC manifested modest beginnings but expanding activities over time. It initially consisted of five public-spirited Protestants who were concerned about the lack of adequate treatment for war wounded. They had no guaranteed budget or staff support, being at first a committee of the Geneva Public Welfare Society – a private charitable organization made up of some 160 prominent citizens. Rather than being a relief organization per se, the Welfare Society undertook studies about social problems and their solutions. The members were not really armchair liberals but rather armchair Christians with a social conscience – albeit part of a larger conservative orientation.

On their own, the five committee members decided to become independent and permanent, even though early and cautious discussions in the larger Welfare Society had focused on the goal of temporarily mobilizing others to the cause of war wounded. From the start, the now-independent committee which eventually became the ICRC promoted the core idea of an international network of permanent, impartial, and neutral aid agencies. Dunant's personalized and *ad hoc* effort at medical relief in the Franco-Austrian war during the 1859 battle at Solferino was to be replaced by something systematic, something more institutionalized.

The idea that the ICRC itself would wind up operating on the ground for the better part of 160 years and in about a hundred nations in the twenty-first century would have been considered a sheer fantasy at the start. But the central idea promoted by Dunant was initially a bit of a fantasy itself, featuring neutral private actors being allowed to help in the midst of war. And it was something of a miracle that events evolved as they did. What was historical happenstance and what was the result of pragmatic planning by individuals who were determined to make a difference has always been difficult to sort out. Context and individual action are often entangled in ways hard to decipher.

It has sometimes been said that states created the ICRC or that its core mandate derived from diplomatic conferences of states. These statements are not true. Hence it bears repeating that the ICRC created itself in 1863, with the five members of a study committee of the Geneva Welfare Society on their own audaciously declaring themselves independent and permanent. It was they who decided to call a meeting of those interested in medical relief to war wounded the same year (a mixture of governmental representatives and private citizens). And it was they who decided to ask the Swiss government to call a diplomatic conference the following year to get states to endorse by treaty what they wanted – namely, neutral private action for war wounded in international war.

Mid-nineteenth-century Europe was a time of rapid change which, along with the slow governmental response, led to inadequate public policies – and thus much private activity to fill the gaps. There were lots of ideas circulating about limits on war, aid to victims of war, improved public health, the moral and material conditions of the working classes, the need to curtail slavery and the slave trade – and the role of "charitable" organizations devoted to all sorts of causes. During 1859–1862 while Dunant was writing his book on the need for private neutral aid to war wounded, based on his observations about the battle at Solferino, similar ideas were already being articulated in France. Some might even accuse Dunant of plagiarism.[2]

Humanitarian norms and war were discussed, for example, during the brief Swiss civil war of 1847 (Sonderbund war). Better known was the role of Florence Nightingale in the Crimean War (1853–1856) and her attention to the health and welfare of British soldiers, then greatly neglected by national leaders. There were parallel developments in the American Civil War (1861–1865) regarding both codifying the laws of war (Lieber Code) and war relief (Clara Barton and various "Sanitary Commissions"). The Union and Rebel armies used flags of truce to suspend the fighting and collect the wounded from the battlefield. The founding fathers of the ICRC did not exist in a hermetic bubble. They both led change and reflected changing ideas already in motion. They both borrowed and innovated. That was also true in the first decades of the twenty-first century, but that gets ahead of our story, even if already alluded to in the previous chapter.

Photograph 3.1 Clara Barton was among those on both sides of the Atlantic concerned about the treatment of war wounded in the mid-nineteenth century. In addition to her efforts for the Union side in the American civil war of 1861–1965, among her other interests, such as response to natural disasters, she was supportive of the emerging ICRC and volunteered with it in the Franco-Prussian war of 1870–1871, aiding both sides. Although the US government did not accept the 1864 Geneva Convention for war wounded in international war until 1882, it recognized the American Red Cross in 1881, with Barton as its first president. She was forced to resign that position in 1904, as a result of controversies within the organization. She died in 1912.

Between the 1859 Franco–Austrian war into which Dunant stumbled and the outbreak of World War I in 1914, there were many humanitarian and social welfare organizations active in the Western world in both war and peace. The Red Cross idea was to find a prominent, unique, and lasting place. It was to be a complex evolution. It is still evolving in complicated ways now. The Red Cross idea has never had a totally fixed form and function.

Of course, there was a more revolutionary or radical reaction to the wrenching changes in industrializing Western nations mid-nineteenth century. Karl Marx and Friedrich Engels produced seminal publications during roughly 1845–1875 attacking capitalism. They, too, saw the harsh effects of industrialization and urbanization under capitalist development – along with inadequate governmental policies to take the sharp edge off capitalism for the many beyond the propertied elites. As is well known, rather than seeking private "charitable" action, religious or otherwise, to mitigate the harshness of capitalism, they sought to overthrow it. They did not believe that elites would agree to ameliorative reform.

With V. I. Lenin expounding on Marxist thought, communism – rather than seek to limit the brutality of war at the edges – advocated the fanciful notion that war was solely the product of capitalist imperialism. In their view, it was capitalism's search for guaranteed foreign resources and markets in order to postpone the internal contradictions of domestic capitalism that generated war. Once the proletariat triumphed in the class struggle, that victory would provide the fundamental solution to war's brutality and other social ills.

Despite a great deal of economic mumbo jumbo about the labor theory of value (only blue-collar work was truly valuable; Jeff Bezos should not be richly rewarded for thinking up and managing the idea of Amazon), and despite comparable nonsense about the purity of industrialized workers (proletarian rule would be bereft of corruption or exploitation as if blue-collar unions were without blemish), parts of early Marxism reflected a humane concern for the fate of many individuals caught up and victimized by the capitalist industrial revolution of the second half of the nineteenth century. In Dunant's Geneva and Marx's London, as elsewhere, it was indeed hard to ignore the evident fact that for many in the 1860s, whether soldier or civilian worker, life was indeed nasty, brutish, and short. Industrialized war and industrialized economies were harsh for the rank and file.

Unlike Marx, early ICRC leaders were firmly attached to property rights and private enterprise, its extension via colonialism, and the superiority of political rule by the (White) upper classes. They were distrustful of democratic movements and labor organizations. They were religious conservatives in economics and politics and were concerned about heading off various "leftist" developments.

As Protestant evangelicals in the Calvinist tradition, both Dunant and Moynier endorsed the notion of Christian charity (well, maybe not so much toward each other!). It was a central factor that drove a life-long and enduring commitment to good works. Hence there was the ICRC motto: *inter arma caritas* ("charity in the midst of war" – "charity" became politically incorrect, smacking as it did of Western superiority, noblesse oblige, or imperial paternalism and the motto was allowed to fade away in active usage); it likewise acknowledges the motto *Per humanitatem ad pacem* ("through humanitarianism to peace"). This Christian charitable orientation was crosscut by at least two other important factors explained in due course: personal ambition and geo-political identity. This complex mixture evolved over more than a century to produce the ICRC of today: a humanitarian organization not at all adverse to economic liberalism featuring property rights, but a persistent if quiet crusader for the human dignity of those victimized – mostly, but today not entirely, the victims of war and other political violence.

By comparison to Marxism, the Red Cross idea originating with Dunant and developed by the ICRC under Moynier's long presidency was always a halfway house – surprisingly capable of mobilizing people but always shying away from a fundamental attack on root causes of victimization. It accepted war and other major ills of the world as persistent problems but mostly sought to limit the negatives rather than root them out. This was because the ICRC and other RC actors officially saw themselves as apart from politics, at least strategic and partisan politics. Their idea of neutral humanitarian action presumably occurred in a zone free of traditional politics. And one cannot solve fundamental problems of victimization outside of political action. As often noted and quoted, there are no purely humanitarian solutions to the root causes of humanitarian problems. (Late in life Dunant became a pacifist, perhaps in a calculated move, but he was not openly so circa 1860. Moynier also flirted, inconsistently, with linking the Red Cross idea to the desire for peace.)

The organization as based in Switzerland and always under Swiss leadership (actually only Genevan leadership until 1923) was from the start closely linked to capitalism – and still is. But in the first half of the twenty-first century most humanitarian actors operated in the context of capitalism, the central debate being what kind of capitalism was chosen.[3] As for governing authorities, the ICRC sought cooperation from those with power of whatever description, autocratic as well as democratic – or some mixture of the two, de jure as well as de facto, to the end of improving the basic dignity of victims of conflict in relative – and mostly incremental – terms.

The Red Cross movement was not officially utopian or really in favor of revolutionary change. This accounted for some of its success as well as limits over time. The National RC Societies, after all, were auxiliary to national authorities. As the establishment aid agency in each nation, they were officially recognized and watched over (if not controlled) by states. The ICRC was mostly funded by the governments of the day – at least during war, and in general, funded by governments (and intergovernmental organizations) in the West. In peace early on, Swiss corporations picked up the financial slack. International humanitarian law (IHL), or the international law of armed conflict, aka much of the laws of war, which was a basis for much that the ICRC attempted, was formally created primarily by states. These are not the building blocks of revolutionary developments.

In sum, the Red Cross idea was institutionalized within the nation-state system of world affairs, even as it adjusted to international organizations and nonstate actors. It sought humanitarian progress in bits and pieces rather than revolution.[4] Its cumulative record reflected the effect of multiple small deeds. There was a lot of adaptation to changing currents of opinion, all the while in its official doctrine avoiding "politics." The Red Cross idea proved to be a globally accepted Band-Aid, but at least the ICRC, if not other RC actors, was flirting with being something more at the time of writing – maybe a larger Band-Aid or one of different shape. That possibility is central to later pages.

Some suspected the ICRC of wanting to be a quiet revolutionary actor – to end war by the back door by pushing for so many limitations that war became impossible to wage.[5] But the truth was otherwise, despite an early comment by Moynier apparently suggesting that if one starts with the 1864 Geneva Convention to neutralize aid to wounded soldiers, then logically, the process must lead to the elimination of war itself.[6] There is not much danger of that happening at the time of this book (circa 2022–2023), written in the midst of the brutal Russian invasion of Ukraine and with plenty of protracted and nasty violent conflicts in Syria, Yemen, South Sudan, Myanmar, Ethiopia, the Democratic Republic of Congo, and so on. Rather than the Red Cross idea and the laws of war undermining armed conflict, the danger is precisely the reverse.

A persistent criticism of the RC idea is that it perpetuates war by making it seem tolerable, acceptable, not so bad. The RC idea has been understood as an effort to humanize warfare. Relevant here is the one pithy quote attributed to the genteel and staid Robert E. Lee, commander of the Confederate Army of Northern Virginia in the 1860s: "It is well this [war] is so terrible [or] we should grow too fond of it."[7] Various peace movements and societies see the RC idea as an impediment to their desire to get rid of war itself. Better, for some of them, is to see war in all its ugliness; if humanized, we might grow to like it too much.

However, evident events led one to wonder, more than once, if the repeated brutalities of contemporary conflict, without accountability, would be the final nail in the coffin of Dunantist humanitarianism.

It is true that Moynier, like Dunant, eventually joined some peace societies, but for Moynier, this seemed a move to blunt the persistent criticism of the Red Cross idea as too accepting of war. He was steadfast in seeing war as not likely to be erased anytime soon. He also abandoned an early belief that it was possible to have a supranational international court with authority to adjudicate state war crimes. (We do now have the International Criminal Court [ICC] with supplemental authority to try individuals, not states, for war crimes inter alia when states are unwilling or unable to do so. It is hanging on by its fingernails and is opposed or barely tolerated by most major military powers, certainly when it comes to allegations against their own personnel.[8] It is one thing to use the ICC selectively against enemies. It is another thing to accept the jurisdiction of the Court without reservation for one's own behavior.)

Lots of grandiose ideas coming out of different locales and eras withered away in the face of belligerent nationalism, crusading anti-imperialism, hatred against the memory of Western colonialism and hegemony, and other widespread policies based on brutal power politics. The Red Cross idea found a way to be permanent, but the price was historically avoiding root causes of victimization (or in today's polished terminology, avoiding the root reasons why there were so many who might benefit from charitable services). One exception, discussed later, was the ICRC's opposition to most forms of nuclear warfare. On that one issue the ICRC was a peace society.

While a few had charged it with opposing war by stealth, the more persistent criticism, as noted above, was that it encouraged war by making it seem (slightly) more humane. A recurring argument, found especially in some military circles, was that the most humane thing to do is to fight a total war and thus get it over with quickly rather than sugarcoat it with superficial "humanitarian" restrictions that draw out the agony. From Helmuth von Moltke, Prussian head of the general staff of the army, to al-Qaeda and the Islamic State group, there have been advocates for total war and for observing few, if any, humane limits. Sometimes this stance is rationalized as a more realistic form of humanitarianism (e.g., get it over with quickly and limit the suffering that way), and sometimes this stance is just oblivious to humanitarian concern (e.g., the evils triggering war are so bad, it does not matter that there is great suffering in attacking those evils). The advocates of total war have proven both temporarily appealing to some – but ultimately disastrous on balance.

It was fundamental to the ICRC that it should not comment on controversies beyond its understanding of humanitarian affairs – such as which side caused war and why. Central was avoiding comment on matters of aggression and self-defense since that was the domain after 1919 (League of Nations Covenant) and 1928 (Kellogg Briand Pact) of *jus ad bellum* (international law regarding the start of war). The United Nations charter continues that legal tradition of *jus ad bellum* norms (in legally allowing only defensive war).[9] The initial domain of the ICRC was *jus in bello* (law for the process of war – including victims and later weapons – the means and methods of violence leading to victims). *Jus in bello* applied to both aggressor and defender in the event such determination could be made.[10] The ICRC was seen by some as the paladin of *jus in bello*. That IHL applied to the defender as well as to the aggressor was not a popular idea in much of Ukraine from February 24, 2022, when Russia invaded. Nor was the neutral ICRC popular there, which is discussed in the Epilogue.

Eventually, the ICRC determined that its humanitarian role pertained not only to international war and then to internal war (civil war) but also to internal troubles and tensions or internal strife (always with vague definition) – now called "other violence" and its aftermath (with no increase in precision). It also decided that its role covered political prisoners (also vaguely defined), who were similar in some ways to detainees in war. After World War I, the ICRC became a major actor in refugee affairs, even if it tried to hand off much of that activity to the League of Nations. Later it tried to hand off caring for some war refugees to others in the RC Movement. From the beginning, there was a constant change at the ICRC regarding what it meant to be an independent and neutral actor focused on an impartial response to victims of political ("man-made") conflict. Sometimes it was pushed by others. For example, the American Red Cross took the lead on Red Cross involvement in internal wars, with the ICRC hesitant circa 1920.

The underlying central fact was that the ICRC defined the scope of most of its changing activities and was not limited by the mandate given to it by others. The ICRC's own governing board was the ultimate "decider" (as George W. Bush might say) as to how the organization determined what constituted a proper understanding of its mandate. The International RC Conference might ask it to do X, or states in a diplomatic conference might indicate that it was allowed to do Y. But the ICRC itself defined its role in the broader picture of world affairs. It

decided whether to accept or reject outside mandates or to stall or rein-
terpret. All of this will be given more attention in subsequent chapters,
especially the tendency by 2022 to interpret its long-standing mandate in
ways that troubled some – as already noted in Chapter 1.

In 1940, ICRC president Max Huber told some journalists:

> This lack of [precisely defined] rights is perhaps the secret of our organisa-
> tion's strength. For the Red Cross sees its work as being wherever people are in
> distress, wherever it can relieve suffering. The Committee is not bound by any
> pre-established [precise] mandate. Suppose it can base itself on any principles
> set out in international law or in treaties between the belligerents – that might be
> of use. Nor does it confine itself to the actual law in force. Rather, it endeavours
> to act in accordance with the idea that originally inspired the Red Cross – to
> take ever more effective action to ease the suffering of people affected by war.[11]

This was a good philosophy and accurate as far as ICRC's official theory
was concerned. But of course, Huber's words did not mean that he and
the organization would actually be dynamic and proactive in responding to human distress generated by violence. A persistent charge about
Huber's time at the ICRC was that in World War II it hid behind international law, saying that the Jews and others persecuted and killed by the
Nazis were not protected by the existing Geneva Conventions and thus
its hands were tied. This is partly true and partly false, as Chapter 7 will
show. The Huber quote above comes from a work that shows the organization was sadly late in dealing with the victims of the Nazi concentration (and death) camps, and when it did so it acted as a by-product of its
concern with prisoners of war. There were other reasons in play besides
legal ones – all analyzed in subsequent pages. The ICRC did have room
to maneuver for victims, then as later. Whether it did so, and effectively,
is grist for the analytical mill in each case. That is as true of Putin's war in
Ukraine as of Nazi Germany's policies in the 1930s and 1940s.

The ICRC evolved to be an organization that remained mostly – or
more accurately partially – quiet in public about many specifics in the
face of all sorts of violations of the laws of war, not to mention violations
of human rights in related situations of instability and unrest, playing
the long game of limited and incremental improvements in the human
dignity of victims over time. Discretion was *not* one of the fundamental
RC principles, synthesized finally by the ICRC and adopted by the rest
of the Movement in 1965,[12] but rather mostly a way to project an image
of neutrality and gain access to victims.

Those seven RC fundamental principles were humanity, independence, neutrality, impartiality, volunteerism, unity, and universality. The
ICRC came to emphasize the first four, with the subject of discretion
being a possible means to those ends but far from an absolute principle

of the first order. All of this camouflages the suspicion that the ICRC might be often secretive by instinct rather than by necessity or through reflective calculation. But exactly how discreet one must be to retain an image of neutrality with fighting parties, and their often emotional supporters, is not an easy calculus. The Epilogue about the Ukraine war will show this.

In effect, discretion might contribute to the perception of neutral access to victims but was far from ironclad – at least in theory. Discretion was an informal tactic for the ICRC as a NIIHA agency. It was also a factor, I suspect but cannot prove, affected by Swiss political culture at the ICRC, which was governed at the top only by Swiss. Just as Swiss political (governmental) neutrality was historically restrained, and Swiss banking culture was devoted to great secrecy until relatively recently, so the Swiss-run ICRC developed much reliance on discreet action and, in particular, avoidance of much but not all specific public criticism of conflicting parties.

It was true that the ICRC would have been very pleased to see the ill-treatment of prisoners of war totally erased, just as it would have been pleased to see the bombing of hospitals in war zones totally eliminated. But when torture occurred and hospitals were intentionally attacked, most of the time the organization declined to huff and puff about specifics in public and continued to try to do the relative good it could do, where it could do it, committed to playing the long game of seeking progress usually through small, incremental steps. It might be direct and candid in its discrete representations but rarely in public. When it did go public, it was usually in a general and matter-of-fact sort of way, discussing how unspecified events differed from the rules of IHL or RC principles.

It was in favor of legal justice for violations of IHL, or for that matter these days for violations of human rights, but carried out in public by others. Attempting to do so itself would probably jeopardize its practical actions on the ground, which, one way or another, required cooperation by those with power rather than their prosecution. Tongue in cheek, one might suggest a new motto for the ICRC: today, practical humanitarian cooperation; tomorrow, maybe prosecution by somebody else.

By 2022, it was doing an enormous amount of good around the world in bits and pieces, but mostly out of sight – namely, mostly without being much noticed by journalists or mentioned by foreign offices. When in 2020 the World Food Program won the Nobel Peace Prize for its efforts to get food into conflict zones, a reasonable argument could be made that the prize should have been shared with the ICRC. My concluding chapter, indeed this entire book, reviews why. Be that as it may, the

ICRC was still having little impact on either recourse to violence or the nature of strategic and partisan politics, at least regarding major states. These objectives were not part of its mandate. Whether it was nevertheless attempting too much and hence endangering what it had already achieved is a major focus of this book.

II   Early Leadership

The above introductory points about history can be fleshed out to advantage by thumbnail sketches of Dunant and Moynier in context.[13] It helps to accompany general organizational trends with some details about human flesh and blood if only to understand better the interplay of success and failure, achievements and mistakes. Challenges, changes, and controversies did not first show up in 1942 or 2022.

A   Henry Dunant

Dunant, a piously Protestant young man from a Genevan middle-class family whose mother suffered from periodic black moods, foreshadowed much of the Red Cross structure by thinking up what is today the YMCA international (Young Men's Christian Association) in the early 1850s.[14] He and a few other young men in Geneva, affected by the Protestant evangelical Awakening Revival of that time, decided to create an international network of social-religious organizations for Christian men. Britain was already the locale of the first YMCA, and similar groups existed here and there in different nations, but they were not linked. Dunant's international network, starting out as prayer groups but evolving into something broader, would have no authoritative center but rather be a string of independent groups, self-governing, in various nations. Dunant became the secretary of his pioneering Geneva group, not the president (he would later have a bitter falling out with Moynier, the result of personality conflicts and concerns about image rather than disagreement on visions and planning). It was a bold, if not audacious, effort by a young man with little money and no status, but the international YMCA found a lasting niche. Dunant showed a talent, if not a genius, for visionary thought and persistent advocacy. But the same traits proved disastrous for his financial plans.

Dunant, the part-time evangelical social activist, was also a social climber who wanted to belong to, and be accepted by, the upper classes. Following somewhat in the footsteps of his businessman father who had investments in France, Henry Dunant (born Jean-Henri but choosing to anglicize his name) worked for a company that invested in

Photograph 3.2 Henry Dunant was thirty-five when he helped create what became the ICRC in 1863. A Christian businessman, Dunant was shocked by the lack of care for war wounded at the battle of Solferino in 1859. His book on the subject was published three years later and helped bring to fruition what today is the International Red Cross and Red Crescent Movement.

French Algeria. The corporate objective was to buy property so as to enable European settlers to move there and live in self-supporting and profit-making agricultural communities. On the basis of his exposure to all this as a salaried employee, Dunant then borrowed money to make personal investments of his own along similar objectives.

He borrowed more and more money as he expanded his dreams and schemes. At one point, he wound up managing a sort of Ponzi scheme: he used some of his new loans to pay apparent dividends to his shareholders as if his Algerian projects were making money, which they weren't. This diversion of borrowed money, of course, reduced his ability to invest productively on the ground in Algeria. To make a long and complicated story short, Dunant failed miserably in his commercial ventures in French North Africa and wound up in 1867 convicted in a Geneva commercial court for deception and fraud in a suit brought by unhappy shareholders.

Among those negatively affected was General Guillaume Henri Dufour (greatly respected in Switzerland for his role in the brief Swiss civil war of 1847), whom Dunant not only enticed into his business ventures but also into the founding of the ICRC. Dufour was the first ICRC president, and he continued to endorse Dunant with French authorities despite losing money in Dunant's commercial projects. Dunant could be charming and persuasive, at least in his early years.

It was, in fact, due to his efforts to find French authorities so he could lobby on behalf of his Algerian ventures that Dunant stumbled upon the bloody detritus of the battle of Solferino in 1859 in what is now northern Italy, a short distance from Geneva. The French, along with their Sardinian allies, were trying to throw out the Austrians. Despite the notoriety of Florence Nightingale and her humanitarian efforts in the Crimean War some five years earlier, the belligerents at Solferino had made scant efforts to care for the wounded and dying after the massive battle. Although some historical points remain debated, it is clear enough that Dunant stepped into the bloody mayhem, his religious social activism supplanting for the moment his business objectives, and he organized medical relief for both sides with the help of local volunteers – mostly female. The total of the dead, wounded, and missing from the Solferino one-day slaughter may have totaled a shocking 40,000, rivaling the butchery of the American civil war that was soon to start. He did what he could for the war victims of both sides – unlike Florence Nightingale, who was concerned only about British soldiers.

It took about two years for Dunant to be persuaded to write about his experiences. But when he did so in the book *A Memory of Solferino*, published in 1862, it met with great popular success in Europe. The key argument, mirroring the YMCA project, was that each nation should have a permanent and official aid society, independent and self-governing, organized in peacetime, ready to act in a neutral way in wartime to come to the aid of wounded soldiers. His spontaneous and amateurish humanitarianism of 1859 was to be replaced by something more permanent and systematic. He was not the only European to talk about such possibilities, but he publicized the idea more prominently and effectively than anyone else.

Part of that success was due to Dunant's cleverness in circulating copies of his book widely, especially to those in elite circles in France, the German-speaking states, and elsewhere. Dunant recognized the importance of selling his ideas to the upper classes that dominated much of Europe in the 1860s. They had the time and connections to support the Red Cross idea. Moreover, he was comfortable dealing with the ruling classes and wanted to be a part of that social stratum. He had cultivated those contacts in Napoleonic Paris, was a loyal Bonapartist, took French citizenship in addition to his Swiss one, and after his financial downfall in Geneva legal proceedings spent much

Christian Zionists in Ottoman Palestine

time in French aristocratic circles (including with one lady in particular) for many years. He did not take a steady job to pay off his debts.[15] He remained more of a thinker and advocate rather than a practical businessman.

The international YMCA and the Red Cross idea were not his only visionary projects, and over the years as a pariah from Geneva, Dunant developed other schemes – for settling Ottoman Palestine with German Christian Zionists, promoting conservative social values like faith and family, opposing war, promoting international arbitration, and so on. Progressively, his mental health declined along with his social status and financial resources. Discovered by the press as he was living quietly in a Swiss village, Dunant was eventually remembered for his efforts on behalf of the Red Cross idea and shared the first Nobel Peace Prize in 1901 with the Frenchman Frederic Passy. His bad business judgments, his many unrealized projects, and his increasingly difficult personality were all but forgotten in a rush to honor the man who had first popularized the idea of permanent aid societies to help victims of war on a neutral basis. He had lobbied tirelessly and cleverly, if inconsistently, on behalf of that vision, often at his own expense, until his circumstances compelled him to retreat and retire.

B   Gustave Moynier

Gustave Moynier was similar to Dunant in some ways but mostly different.[16] From a conservative upper-middle-class family active in Geneva politics, he reacted to the political liberalization of the mid-1840s by decamping to Germany and France to complete his legal studies. Returning to Geneva, he avoided local politics, which he considered too leftist for his tastes, and threw himself into social work mostly designed to deal with the material and moral conditions of the working class under newly industrialized capitalism. He became heavily interested in what we would call today statistical sociology, above all, empirical evidence about those not doing well in European capitalism.

He and his wife both inherited wealth, so Moynier did not need to find a paying occupation. He developed good contacts with elements in Swiss federal politics in Bern, sometimes representing Switzerland at various international conferences about statistics or social welfare. He was both a devoted Calvinist and ambitious. He wanted to prove that his circle of conservative upper-middle-class Genevans had much to offer and had not been completely sidelined by those to the left.[17] By 1863, he was not only President of the Geneva Public Welfare Society but looking for bigger worlds to conquer, maybe something international.

Photograph 3.3 Dunant was a visionary and gifted advocate for his ideas, but the early ICRC and RC Movement were largely the result of the persistent efforts of the Genevan lawyer Gustave Moynier. He and Dunant had a falling out, especially after the latter's financial affairs were exposed as fraudulent. Moynier effectively *was* the ICRC for almost forty years. Both died in the same year, 1910.

A colleague in the Geneva Public Welfare Society, Dr. Louis Appia, was already active on the subject of aid to war victims, especially better surgeries. Like Dunant, he embodied the idea of evangelical good works. There was much attention to that subject in that era, certainly so in Geneva. (Appia, and another Calvinist Genevan Doctor, Theodore Maunoir, rounded out the founding five.) But it was Dunant's *A Memory of Solferino* that piqued Moynier's interest, causing him to invite Dunant to the Welfare Society and discuss matters further. The rest, as they say, is history. In reality, it was not that simple.

With the respected General Dufour as the president of the new stand-alone Geneva committee to aid war wounded and Dunant as secretary, Moynier immediately became the prime mover and shaker – becoming committee acting president and then president in 1864 when the aging Dufour retired (he died in 1874). The distribution of offices was agreeable to Dunant, who had his business affairs to pursue in France and Algeria. As in the YMCA setup, he was content to be the secretary rather than the president. Dunant may have been a social climber, but he was more of a visionary than a pragmatic organizer. His business affairs, unfortunately, showed that. Moynier, by comparison, was the organization man.

Moynier was committed to making Dunant's vision of private, permanent, and neutral aid societies a reality. He first organized in Geneva a meeting of potential aid societies in 1863, the start of the RC network, then moved rapidly to push another Dunant idea: that such aid societies and their neutral work should be recognized in public international law. Moynier and Dufour drafted what became the 1864 Geneva Convention for aid to wounded soldiers. Twelve European states ratified quickly, including major powers France and Prussia. The British were still dubious about private neutral action for both sides, and the Americans thought ratification of this European treaty would violate their splendid isolationism.

A rapid acceptance by some states of Dunant's basic idea was no doubt surprising to many, namely that military powers would agree to a zone of neutrality in the midst of war – a neutral space for wounded soldiers and the private aid societies that tended them. But states had their *raisons d'état* for doing so. They hoped to shore up domestic support for war by better care of soldiers in an era of nascent democracy and more rapid communications. The 1864 Convention was the result of a marriage of humanitarian concern and state self-interest.[18] It would not be the last document of this kind. (Florence Nightingale was not sold on the Red Cross idea, believing that care of wounded soldiers was a state responsibility, not the domain of private groups. British governmental views were similar.)

Dunant greased the wheels in various ways in 1864, including lobbying the French Emperor to have Swiss authorities in Bern agree to call and host the diplomatic conference of 1864. This started the idea that Switzerland had a special role to play regarding IHL. This remains the case, with Bern being the depository state for IHL treaties and the host for IHL legislative conferences, not the United Nations. There is a good bit of muddled thinking about relations between Geneva and Bern, between the ICRC and Swiss authorities. Like some other subjects, that will be probed later in Chapters 7 and 8. The Red Cross idea stressed independent neutrality, but practical action would depend on the cooperation of territorial states and their military establishments. Both Dunant and Moynier understood this from the start. They believed that progress could be made by acting with states and not against them. Unlike Marx, they believed that elites would indeed agree to progressive reforms. And governments sometimes did, but not entirely for humanitarian reasons.

The tandem of Dunant and Moynier briefly looked formidable, the visionary advocate and the pragmatic lawyer operating under the patronage of the respected General Dufour. They shared a Calvinist Evangelism – even if Moynier was a member of the Geneva establishment church while Dunant was more of an independent free thinker – and they shared the belief that the RC project should be a secular venture, despite their genuine religious convictions. However, not only did Dufour move quickly into retirement but the other two were different in temperament and eventually fell out. Dunant's financial disgrace in 1867 was the final straw, with the status-conscious Moynier demanding Dunant's resignation from the Geneva Committee.

As Moynier worked doggedly to build what is today the RC Movement, it was clear his Genevan identity and Swiss nationalism played a role. Some in Paris tried to get the center of things moved there, looking down on small and supposedly provincial Geneva. Moynier would have none of it, maneuvering to protect what became the ICRC as the central communications node in the emerging decentralized network of aid societies, in Geneva of course, with himself as editor of the network magazine from 1869 – which became the *International Review of the Red Cross*. (Dunant was very attached to Geneva early on but he spent much time in Paris, having many contacts there, becoming a French citizen in 1859, and ultimately rejecting a Geneva that was rejecting him – at least until his Nobel Peace Prize. Even then, he feared that his Geneva business investors would come after his Prize money.)

A close reading of what became the flagship journal of the RC Movement, eventually called, as noted, the *International Review of the Red Cross*, would discover articles reflecting Moynier's *amour propre* in being Swiss (and other articles reflecting his dislike of Dunant).[19] Circa 1870, when the Russians floated the idea of replacing the all-Swiss, all-Genevan ICRC with an elected multinational central RC body, Moynier stalled and then used the *Review* to lobby against the idea – successfully. (Earlier, Moynier himself had toyed with the idea of some kind of multinational central authority for the RC network, but he abandoned this thinking in favor of a decentralized network – with important roles for the Swiss ICRC.)

Apparently, most in the RC network preferred the all-Swiss ICRC as the central actor compared to an international group where an adversary might be represented. The other RC units did not care that the founding committee was still all-Genevan; what counted was that the neutral Swiss were presumably not going to be taking sides in future wars. (Of course they did, at least diplomatically, in different wars in different ways, and then more openly in 2014 and again in 2022.) According to some, what preserved the ICRC at the center of the RC Movement was not so much Moynier's maneuvering against the Russian proposal, but the desire of the National RC Societies to remain independent and not be tightly coordinated by anyone.[20]

The ICRC was proud to be Swiss, and Swiss authorities were proud to host the founding agency of the RC network. In 1914, at an exposition in Bern, Swiss authorities presented displays reflecting various positive aspects of the country. Some artwork drawn up by the ICRC was included.[21]

Moynier, like Dunant, was comfortable dealing with the upper classes and European officialdom. When the 1864 Geneva Diplomatic Conference met, the ICRC by-passed city authorities because of their perceived leftist political orientation. Without a doubt, Moynier believed in a supposedly liberal colonialism, one that brought a higher level of civilization to "backward" peoples. While Dunant first worked for a company that was trying to get more White Europeans to settle in French Algeria, and later more passively wanted to help German Calvinists move to Ottoman Palestine, Moynier was serving in Geneva as general counsel for King Leopold of Belgium and his notoriously brutal Congo Free State during 1886–1904.

It is not clear today how active Moynier was in that consular role, which might have been little more than a sinecure, and whether it was bestowed on him or he maneuvered to get it. There seems to be no record of his publicly commenting on the terrible fate of many local inhabitants in the Congo.[22] Without a doubt, his alignment with Leopold's brutal Congo Free State was a blot on his otherwise strong humanitarian record. Moynier was opposed to slavery, helped negotiate an international legal regime for the Congo River, and initially saw his support for the Congo Free State as a way to head off colonial conflict over that region. In this orientation, he may have been affected by the public relations efforts of King Leopold, who tried to cover up his brutal drive for wealth with talk about doing good for the African locals.

But as he aged, bitter about the honors bestowed on Dunant, Moynier was unable to reconcile his determined RC humanitarianism with his support for colonialism as it really was. And so he remained silent in the midst of growing European criticism of King Leopold's brutal record in the heart of Africa.[23] According to one view, Leopold was all about money and African exploitation, but he talked about more noble ventures (e.g., shielding the Congo from great power rivalries under his "protection") to cover his tracks.[24] It is possible Moynier fell for this deception, if that is what it was, until he realized his mistake toward the end of his life.

Dunant might have been intrigued by much of the Arab world and its geography, but it was clear that Moynier had a very low opinion of Africans. At the same time, Moynier developed a respect for efficient non-Europeans like the Japanese. He also welcomed the Ottoman

Empire into the RC network, which was to add the Red Crescent as a network emblem through a fait accompli. Moynier, however, reflecting the dominant views of the time, was openly critical, and not at all neutral or discrete, about Ottoman atrocities in the Balkan wars of the late nineteenth century.[25]

In all these RC matters, both Dunant and Moynier reflected views broadly shared in European ruling classes in the latter half of the nineteenth century. If perhaps the apex of European colonialism, it was certainly a time of assumed Western superiority over non-Whites – at least until Japan defeated Russia in their war of 1904.

Working mostly alone, at best sometimes with a part-time assistant, Moynier had succeeded by the time of his death in 1910 (the same year Dunant died) in establishing both the ICRC and the RC Movement as fixtures on the international scene. Dunant had continued for a time to be a lone wolf in advocating for the Red Cross idea even after he had left the ICRC, sometimes undercutting what Moynier was trying to do. But Moynier was determined and persistent and ultimately successful in building the ICRC and the International Red Cross, now called the RC Movement.

He managed to get the various RC actors through the Franco–Prussian War of 1870–1871, negatively impressed by the narrow and belligerent nationalism of the French and Prussian RC Societies, and therefore convinced that the ICRC in neutral Switzerland would have to play a bigger role in advancing neutral help in war. He also oversaw the first tentative expansion of the Red Cross role, from wounded soldiers to POWs. The ICRC and the RC network were not really prepared for World War I in 1914 (who was?), but they were well enough established by that time to take the next big jump in their activity in world affairs.

III   Conclusion

Some might find it difficult to see the contemporary ICRC, widely respected for its mostly diligent work on behalf of victims of war and other "political" misfortunes, as having emerged out of the world of Dunant and Moynier. The modern ICRC is completely secular, even if many of its officials personally reflect a Christian heritage. But Moynier, despite his deep and genuine evangelical Protestantism, had long ago declared that the ICRC was not a faith-based organization. The pious Dunant had agreed.[26] Dr. Appia was the one who mixed medical service with Christian proselytizing. Moynier, whatever his achievements and faults, did not do that. Nor did subsequent Christian leaders of the ICRC like Max Huber, however much they might describe the ICRC by reference to the biblical story about the good Samaritan.

And so the ICRC wound up operating without regard to sect or theology. For pragmatic reasons, it might try to establish a linkage between IHL principles and the tenets of Islam, but it drew its inspiration from secular IHL and human rights law and a combination of RC principles and Dunantist values. The Christian principle about the value of all human beings in the sight of God probably fed into the enduring RC principle of service to all humanity, but beyond that, religious motivation has long ago withered away for the modern ICRC.

The organization is now known not for good Christian deeds but rather for pragmatic achievements of both a legal and diplomatic nature and, above all, its fieldwork in service to those whose lives have been disrupted by violence. Some say its current objectives may be utopian (more on that later in the last chapter). Still, the ICRC is not at all given to utopian ventures such as promoting world government or one-world citizenship, or even peace on earth.

Despite retaining an all-Swiss governing board, it runs most of its big programs in Africa and the Middle East and, since the 1990s, manifests an international staff with about 130–140 nationalities on the payroll. Being all-Swiss at the top, it is not usually charged with intentionally favoring one belligerent over another. It also knows that in many conflicts, a representative on the ground with a white face, much less an affinity for Christianity, is not necessarily an asset.[27]

Today, it is certainly aware of the charge that the global humanitarian world might reflect some kind of neo-imperialism, if not neocolonialism, with maybe some Western (and Christian) paternalism thrown in. Once again, we will address these issues in more detail later. Mononationality at the top remains a foundation for its claims to neutrality. Whether it has really been neutral (and impartial) in its policy decisions in Geneva and programs in the field is a subject for empirical examination.

The modern ICRC, through all of the changes since 1863, has remained mostly true to Dunant's original vision and Moynier's determined follow-up: the aspiration for independent, neutral, nonpoliticized help to victims of war and other violence, working closely with the public authorities whether de jure or de facto; and seeking to fortify this humanitarian help by having it recognized in public international law as much as possible. Yet it operates in a world often characterized by brutal conflict that sometimes leaves Dunantist values at the point of disappearance. The original Dunantist vision of leaving the practical work to the National RC Societies was altered after the 1870s, and certainly so from World War I. That altered vision, featuring more ICRC action in the field, is being renegotiated now within the Movement – as will be shown in Chapters 5 and 6.

Of course, complexities and controversies have always arisen around the Red Cross idea and within the RC network. They do so now. And that will be duly noted in the rest of this book. Is the ICRC today just making the usual changes that are required to adjust to a changing environment, being flexible as it has always been, with each decade of leaders at the Geneva headquarters having slightly different priorities? Or is the ICRC not just changing but mutating into something fundamentally different, and if so, is that cause for concern?

And in any event, what can the ICRC do if much of world affairs is characterized by amoral power politics? It is not entirely inappropriate to remind the reader of a famous aphorism by the distinguished jurist Hersch Lauterpacht: "If international law is, in some ways, at the vanishing point of law, the law of war is, perhaps even more conspicuously, at the vanishing point of international law."[28] But that was 1952, and more than one analyst (including many at the ICRC) believes that history has moved on in a more positive direction. I am not so sure.

Notes

1 C. Morehead, *Dunant's Dream: War, Switzerland, and the History of the Red Cross* (New York: HarperCollins, 1998), p. 175.
2 Frederic Joli, "Quand George Sand taclait Henry Dunant pour plagiat," *L'Humanitaire dans tous ses Etats*, February 13, 2023, https://blogs.icrc.org/hdtse/2023/02/13/quand-george-sand-taclait-henry-dunant-pour-plagiat/ (accessed February 18, 2023).
3 B. Milanovic, *Capitalism Alone: The Future of the System That Rules the World* (Cambridge, MA: Belknap Press for Harvard University Press, 2019).
4 D. P. Forsythe, "The Red Cross as Transnational Actor: Conserving and Changing the Nation-State System," *International Organization*, 30/4 (Fall, 1976), pp. 607–630.
5 For a misguided view see N. O. Berry, *War and the Red Cross: The Unspoken Mission* (London: MacMillan, 1997). He focuses on modern internal wars.
6 "It is especially when I think of those still far-off consequences that the drafting of a code of laws of war seems to me to have social implications that are as significant as they are beneficial, and that I agree with those who see the adoption of the Geneva Convention as a memorable act, because it has marked the beginning of a new era which will culminate in the liberation of mankind from major ills still prevailing today." Quoted in A. Durand, "Gustave Moynier and the Peace Societies," www.icrc.org/en/doc/resources/documents/article/other/57jnaw.htm (accessed October 29, 2022).
7 A. C. Guelzo, *Robert E. Lee: A Life* (New York: Vintage, 2022), p. 275.
8 The ICC was opposed in varying degrees of determination by the United States, China, Russia, Israel, India, Pakistan, Iran, Iraq, Vietnam, and other significant military powers. It was accepted by all members of NATO, including Britain and France, except for Turkey and the United States. There was

an interlude when the United States cooperated with the ICC in dealing with certain foreign situations. When the Court began to examine the possibility of US war crimes in Afghanistan, that latter state having accepted the ICC, Washington resumed its criticism of the Court. It then developed a more positive view when the subject was Russian war crimes in Ukraine. US policy toward the ICC was entirely transactional, varied over time and by issue, and was anything but supportive of consistent and institutionalized attention to claims of war crimes.

9 Lawyers know that in today's world there are only two types of lawful recourse to military force under the UN Charter: the exercise of genuine self-defense, and use of force approved by the UN Security Council.

10 Essential for understanding the ICRC is F. Bugnion, *The International Committee of the Red Cross and the Protection of War Victims* (Geneva: ICRC, 2003). Bugnion was a staff member, then high official, then member of the governing board. He has much inside knowledge and a photographic memory of recall. He probably knows more ICRC history off the top of his head than any other person on the planet.

11 Quoted in S. Farre, "The ICRC and the Detainees in Nazi Concentration Camps (1942–1945)," *International Review of the Red Cross*, 94/888 (Winter 2012), p. 388. https://international-review.icrc.org/sites/default/files/irrc-888-farre.pdf (accessed October 29, 2022).

12 The ICRC's Jean Pictet extracted the seven principles from preceding RC practice, in the context of friction with the RC Federation, which were then duly adopted by the International RC Conference in 1965. See further, Chapter 5 on ICRC links with the Movement.

13 A very good popular history is by C. Morehead, *Dunant's Dream: War, Switzerland, and the History of the Red Cross* (New York: HarperCollins, 1998).

14 This section relies heavily on C. Chaponnière, *Henry Dunant: la croix d'un homme* (Paris: Perrin, 2010). She is both very well informed and frank in her analyses. An English edition has since been published (*Henry Dunant: The Man of the Red Cross*, London: Bloomsbury, 2022).

15 When Prussia defeated France in 1871, Dunant was living in Paris. As the Empire of Napoleon III collapsed and the Paris Commune briefly held sway in that city, the Red Cross emblem was in use. There seems to be no evidence that Dunant got involved in any way in humanitarian assistance in that unsettled, even chaotic, time. He had left the ICRC four years earlier but was a member of a French committee for aid to wounded soldiers. He operated in aristocratic circles that endorsed his Red Cross idea, but apparently he did not get involved in Paris as he had at Solferino.

16 This section relies heavily on F. Bugnion, *Gustave Moynier, 1826–1910* (Geneva: Slatkine, 2010). The longer book by J. Senarclens, *The Founding of the Red Cross: Gustave Moynier, Its Master Builder* (Geneva: Slatkine, 2005), covers the basics but lacks analytical sharpness.

17 On this and other points treated in this section see I. Herrmann, *L'humanitaire en questions: Reflexions autour de l'histoire de la Croix-Rouge* (Paris: Editions du Cerf, 2018).

18 J. F. Hutchinson, *Champions of Charity: War and the Rise of the Red Cross* (Boulder: Westview, 1996), is very good on the history of this era. It is very

unfortunate that his premature passing prevented a follow-on study that he had planned, taking his analysis into more contemporary times. His was one of the first studies to look hard at the Red Cross idea, moving beyond the Pablum often published by various RC actors.

19 D. P. Forsythe, "The ICRC as Seen in the Pages of the Review: 1869–1913 – Personal Observations," *International Review of the Red Cross*, https://international-review.icrc.org/articles/opinion-note-icrc-seen-through-pages-review-1869-1913-personal-observations (accessed November 29, 2022).

20 Early on Moynier was sympathetic to some sort of Red Cross supreme council, multinational, with the ICRC apparently as implementing bureau. But like some other early Moynier ideas, this one also shifted over time. What he leaned toward circa 1867 was not at all what he maneuvered for some twenty years later.

21 The ICRC office in Paris publishes a blog that is informative in several ways, including on history. https://blogs.icrc.org/hdtse/category/histoire/ (accessed November 29, 2022).

22 See the very engaging book by Adam Hochschild, *King Leopold's Ghost: A Story of Greed, Terror, and Heroism in Colonial Africa* (New York: Mariner Books, 1998).

23 D. Fiscalini, "Des élites au service d'une cause humanitaire: le Comité international de la Croix-Rouge," University of Geneva, Geneva, 1985.

24 H. W. French, "Confronting Belgium's Colonial Legacy," *Foreign Policy* (June 6, 2022), https://foreignpolicy.com/2022/06/06/belgium-congo-colonialism-leopold-ii-commodities/ (accessed November 29, 2022).

25 Forsythe, "The Red Cross as Transnational Actor."

26 Any religious influence on the selection of the Red Cross emblem may be ancient and indirect. The 1863–1864 developments are mute on the reasons for selecting a Red Cross on a white background as both symbol of the RC Movement and neutral signage in war. As the reverse colors of the Swiss national flag, that latter cross can be traced back to medieval times when the use of the cross by various Swiss cantons did have Christian connotations. The modern ICRC plays down its religious origins, and in certain contemporary situations of violence involving Islamic armed actors it removes its emblem from vehicles and personnel. The Dutch were one of the early national aid societies to use the Red Cross emblem, even earlier than the ICRCs formal adoption of "Red Cross" in its title. It seems that while the National RC Society of the Netherlands was the first to use the RC emblem, the Spanish National RC Society was the first to formally adopt the RC emblem. The ICRC then followed suite a few years later.

27 A standard overview is D. P. Forsythe, *The Humanitarians: The International Committee of the Red Cross* (Cambridge: Cambridge University Press, 2005). Compare Shai M. Dromi, *Above the Fray: The Red Cross – the Making of the Humanitarian NGO Sector* (Chicago and London: University of Chicago Press, 2020). The latter work was a dissertation.

28 Hersch Lauterpacht, "The Problem of the Revision of the Law of War," 29 *British Yearbook of International Law* 382 (1952).

4 History

Part II – From the Death of Moynier to the End of the Cold War

> The International Committee of the Red Cross has grown into a formidable non-governmental organization.
>
> Margaret MacMillan[1]

Just as in Chapter 2 where we gave an overview of the global humanitarian system, so we now provide a selective overview of ICRC history. Rather than attempt a full narrative and chronological version, which would necessarily be superficial given the brevity, I want to try to tease out some possible explanations for why the ICRC has endured and become respected across more than 160 years – even while some critics believe it has passed its peak and is on the slippery slope of decline. Such an interpretative exercise will take us from the foundations established by Dunant and Moynier to the end of the Cold War and contemporary times – an era addressed in the rest of the book.

Like similar attempts to explain social developments, one must wrestle with the interplay of individuals and context, leadership and situations, agency and structure. What follows is a thumbnail sketch of a few important junctures in ICRC history, thin to be sure, but sometimes based on new research. Obviously, it leaves out much. It stresses examples of the three main areas of ICRC endeavor in the past: fieldwork, both protection and assistance in various violent situations; development of the RC Movement and IHL; and attempts to help political or security prisoners.

A well-informed review of ICRC history by the top historian working at the ICRC, Daniel Palmieri, emphasizes two factors to explain things over time: the organization's capacity for innovation and its unique specificity.[2] In this carefully considered view, the ICRC has endured and prospered because of its flexible response to changing humanitarian challenges while maintaining a specific role that others did not provide. I will suggest that he is right on the first point, namely the record of flexible response. That basically positive trait is accompanied, however, by several leadership failures and mistakes – but with a successful rebound

65

based on dedication to the cause. It is his second point, unique specificity, that is precisely what is up for debate now.

I   More Field Action and World War I

In an interesting phrase Palmieri says that from the origins of the ICRC to World War I, the main activity of the ICRC was "literary." By that he means that the ICRC was originally intended to advocate and stimulate, with the National RC Societies doing the actual work of tending to the war wounded. True, the organization exercised its right of initiative to dispatch a couple of persons to observe the war in Schleswig-Holstein, and then again pretty much the same thing in one of the many Balkan wars (e.g., Montenegro in 1912). But by and large, for its first fifty years, the ICRC was primarily a communications node in the international RC network. Its primary objective was to build the RC network and get the values of that institution recognized in public international law.

This changed during World War I in 1915, when the organization got into sustained field activities, again based on its own right of initiative, involving supervising the conditions of detention for prisoners of war, mostly on the Western front. Having seen the narrow and chauvinistic nationalisms of the French and Prussian RC agencies in the Franco–Prussian War of 1870–1871, and having overseen the effort of the supposedly distinct POW agency in Basel in that war, it realized the need for neutral action in WWI that it was best placed to provide. Thus, it took an initiative that represented the systematic and direct beginnings of its active expertise in prisoner protection. True, it was the National RC Societies, along with the belligerent governments, that mostly provided the assistance that was distributed in the POW camps. But it was the neutral ICRC that delivered the goods and began to report on conditions. It had no explicit legal permission for its actions but acted anyway – initiating the negotiations with the French and then the Germans to get the process going.

One saw this same type of flexible response on two subjects related to WWI: the organization's work with war refugees and with political prisoners. I have reviewed elsewhere the matter of the ICRC and war refugees in this era.[3] Suffice to say here that its efforts for war refugees in the aftermath of WWI, again based on its own initiatives and without specific authorization in international law, meant that when the ICRC did arrange a handoff to the League of Nations on this topic, the ICRC's status was such that the head of what became the Nansen Office in the League of Nations was first offered to Gustave Ador who had replaced Moynier as president of the ICRC.

White Russian refugees → religious & capitalist.

An interesting question, but by no means the driver of all its actions, was how much it was motivated by the concern for White Russians who had lost the fight for control of Russia and who made up a sizable portion of European refugees as found in Istanbul and other European refugee centers, and how much it was motivated by pure humanitarian concerns regardless of who had been threatened and displaced by the Bolshevik victory by the early 1920s. This question about the deep motivation of ICRC leaders who were religious and capitalist and feared the communist Bolsheviks in Moscow I leave to others.

As for the second topic involving direct results from WWI, one finds the ICRC again exercising its right of initiative in the political turmoil of Hungary and then what became the Soviet Union, on behalf of political prisoners. The parallels with POW affairs are obvious, as both categories of prisoners were seen by the dominant authorities to be enemies. And so, the ICRC sought to use the expertise it had developed in the supervision of POWs to the benefit of politicals.[4] Again, the role of a neutral humanitarian filled a need and, as practiced by the ICRC, was acceptable in principle to various governments. I note later that the ICRC was clever in getting the collective endorsement of this role by the International RC Conference, with states as participants in the voting, even if it has proven impossible thus far to get a treaty adopted on political prisoners. I discuss this subject further at some length in Chapter 14.

Also after World War I the ICRC was part of large, fragmented, and rather chaotic focus by many Western-based humanitarians on conditions in the territory of the collapsed Ottoman Empire.[5] The ICRC was involved in various ways, not only for former POWs and refugees but also civilians more generally. Poorly funded, it nevertheless sought to go beyond immediate relief into support for types of development. Acting independently, it had few contacts with the American Red Cross and other RC agencies active in that area. Like other Western humanitarians, it had big objectives, with a paternalistic attitude of knowing best what the locals needed, and was concerned for image in competition with others, but made little lasting impact. It had tried to do good in a complex arena, with Greece fighting the newly established Turkish state, with the League of Nations mostly absent on the ground, and with Britain and France maneuvering to continue their control through the League Mandates System. In effect, the context defeated well-intentioned humanitarian efforts, and not just by the ICRC.

In a central way, it is the ICRC's early reaction to war that has made it what it became: in 1859, Henry Dunant's ad hoc response to the battle of Solferino between the Austrians and the French, plus working to advance the 1864 Geneva Convention for war wounded; its observations and reactions to the Franco–Prussian War of 1870–1871; and its actions during WWI in 1914–1918 along with its creative responses to the direct result of that war in the interwar years. The conventional wisdom seems right that WWI established the RC network on the world scene as a permanent fixture. This was not simply because of the ICRC's efforts on behalf of POWs (along with other activities such as protesting the use of poison gas) but also because of the roles of the various National RC Societies, chief among which was the sizable presence of the American Red Cross (ARC) in that war.

II   Humanitarian Politics among the Humanitarians

Here is as good a place as any to briefly note the friction from 1919 between the ICRC and the new League of RC Societies, now the International Federation of Red Cross and Red Crescent Societies (IFRC). After victory in WWI, due in no small part to the belated intervention of the United States, the very large and very wealthy ARC sought to reshape the RC network, which involved downgrading the role of the ICRC. After all, WWI was the war to end all wars, the ICRC was pictured as composed of aging legalists fixated on war, and the world presumably needed something like a combination of the later World Health Organization and UNICEF to deal with public health and related social needs. Naturally, some assumed the dynamic Americans should lead the way in this endeavor, especially since all recognized the potential might of the United States in world affairs – witness the central role of President Woodrow Wilson in the much-criticized peace process of 1919.

Several analysts have covered the details of this intra-network conflict, which I will document later, and which pitted the ICRC as the founding agency and central communications node against the parvenu RC League (now Federation). The ICRC's formal objections were clear, namely that the Federation was created in an irregular process reflecting a violation of the basic principle of impartial action for all of humanity. The Federation's founding was due to only five National RC Societies (in the USA, UK, France, Italy, and Japan) and excluded the National Societies of the defeated powers.

I believe that the deeper reasons for the ICRC's determination to continue in its traditional roles are to be found largely in Genevan exceptionalism and Swiss nationalism, along with a belief in the importance of ICRC neutrality as linked to permanent Swiss neutrality. These ICRC substantive – if sometimes latent – views were buttressed by the Swiss government's siding with the ICRC because Bern had long viewed the

ICKC asset for Swiss diplomacy

ICRC as an asset to Swiss foreign policy. And, just as the various National
RC Societies had not wanted to be tightly directed by any international
body as proposed earlier by the Russian RC to replace the ICRC, so the
National Societies of the 1920s did not want to be commanded by the
new Federation – which also was seen particularly in France as under
(irritating if not despised) Anglo-Saxon hegemony.

The outcome was that the ICRC could not block the creation of the
Federation, but it could limit its mandate by protecting the ICRC's traditional activities. This it did by 1928 when new Movement statutes
confirmed the status quo, even while recognizing the Federation as a
new member of the Movement. Palmieri explains things by reference
mostly to developments in Geneva and Bern. But other factors were perhaps equally important: the illness and death of Henry P. Davison, the
champion of the Federation within the ARC; differing views within the
ARC, especially since it was Davison's War Council that had pushed for
the Federation without the full backing of the rest of the ARC leadership; and perhaps most importantly the drift of US foreign policy toward
isolationism or, if one prefers, selective engagement with the rest of the
world – taking the ARC and its resources along that same path toward
domestic retrenchment. (The ARC leadership was tightly intertwined
with the political leadership in Washington, however much RC agencies
were supposed to be independent and nonpolitical. The US president
was also the ARC president; the US Attorney General was also the chief
legal officer for the ARC.) The Federation soon was short of money and
lacked powerful backing.

I am in the camp that tends to emphasize the benefits of the ICRC's
refusal to be pushed aside, while not being prone to either Genevan
exceptionalism or Swiss nationalism and without being especially enamored of the Swiss authorities in Bern. A reputation for neutrality in
humanitarian action has its uses, especially in armed conflict and other
forms of bitter political disputes. It is fair to note that regarding WWII,
the Federation (1) had to flee Paris for Geneva and (2) was prevented
from independent action in Nazi-controlled territories because its multinational leadership was comprised of many enemy nationals. In sum,
the Federation was not seen in Berlin in 1939 as neutral – or even as
particularly effective or efficient.

I do not ignore the views of those who see the ICRC of circa 1919
as defensive and perhaps somewhat paranoid. It may be that I am still
affected by what the Tansley Big Study concluded in the mid-1970s,
namely that the ICRC was one of the more effective members of the RC
network, far superior to the leadership of the Federation at that time.
(My role on the Tansley team was explained in the Preface.) I certainly

acknowledge that the highly independent ICRC has made some big mistakes and can, at times, be difficult to deal with.

But in the last analysis, I think the determination of the ICRC leadership circa 1919 to preserve its unique role, especially in matters of traditional humanitarian protection (which is now more than ever linked to assistance) and legal development, has turned out relatively well. As will be explained later, one of the reasons the ICRC attracted significant support, not to mention funding after the Cold War, was precisely its neutral image amid various conflicts, combined with a reputation for proper administration, which allowed it to operate where others could not or in any event did not. It is fairly clear that the Federation, or the Movement itself, lacked in the past the same image or reputation – for both neutrality and effective administration. The big problem for the Federation is not really its own fault – namely that more than one National RC Society refuses to be coordinated by the Federation according to Dunantist principles.

III   Success and Failure in the Era of World War II

Be that as it may, since war made the ICRC and affected its evolution, it is no surprise that the ICRC was highly active in WWII, especially in POW affairs between the Axis and Allied Powers, but also in civilian relief in places such as Greece, and in a few other subjects as well. It did participate in the Joint Relief Commission with the Federation, which the ICRC seems to have initiated and apparently wanted to continue after 1945, and which I discuss later in Chapter 6. If the ICRC proved to be no factor at all on POW matters between the Nazis and the Soviets, it could be recalled that: (1) neither state was obligated to the other under the 1929 Geneva Convention pertaining to POWs, which was not the fault of the ICRC; and (2) the policy of each of these states was to torment or kill as many opposing POWs as possible, at least the ones not needed for forced labor, which again cannot be laid at the doorstep of Geneva. The Soviet criticism of the ICRC for not doing more to protect Soviet prisoners in German hands was more in the realm of propaganda rather than serious analysis.

Where the ICRC record in WWII can be fairly criticized is on the matter of the Nazi camps beyond POWs – first the concentration camps and later the death camps, where Hitler eventually implemented his policy of genocide against the Jews and other "subhuman" groups by the systematic use of poison gas as compared to earlier genocidal acts via shootings and fatal slave labor. Thus far, we have pictured the ICRC leadership in Geneva as cohesive and dedicated, mostly responding to changing circumstances by expanding the range of well-considered activities in much-needed ways. But when it came to trying to protect the Jews and other persecuted groups from the Axis powers, the all-Swiss governing board overlapped with Swiss governmental personnel in Bern, and probably reflecting the biases of its White, Christian, conservative, upper-middle-class membership, failed to either denounce the genocide, of which it had knowledge certainly by mid-1942, or take dynamic steps in quiet diplomacy to contest German policy. All this and more, including ICRC policy toward Mussolini and Abyssinia, is examined in detail later, in Chapter 7, along with supporting documentation.

Here we note primarily that ICRC leadership can be given high marks for determination and flexibility in advancing the international humanitarian agenda in conflict situations during 1863–1945, but at the same time, manifest a downside stemming from its narrow composition and pattern of co-optation. Its record in WWII, in some ways quite deserving of its second Nobel Peace Prize (third if you count Dunant's shared prize along with the ICRC award from WWI), was accompanied by its greatest failure. And that failure stemmed directly from the cautious, nondynamic, politicized, or biased attitudes of leaders such as Max Huber and C. J. Burckhardt, who, in the last analysis, failed to establish a dynamic policy based on Dunantist values.

Not only was it not dynamic and flexible, but by comparison with examples already noted, it was morally indefensible. It was affected by Swiss foreign policy in two ways. First, it reflected a desire not to rock the boat in Berlin, following the Swiss policy of appeasement of Hitler to forestall any takeover of Switzerland. And second, ICRC leaders reflected prevailing views in Bern in seeing at least some in the German leadership as of future use in resisting the Bolshevik threat and, therefore, to be cultivated rather than criticized. The leadership in Geneva was too similar and too intertwined with the political elites in Bern to be truly independent and impartial. Huber was a legal advisor to the Swiss foreign ministry at the same time that he served as ICRC president. Burckhardt was deeply interested in geostrategic politics as compared to strictly humanitarian roles. This is one of the main reasons Charles de Gaulle wanted him as Swiss ambassador in Paris after the war. It was a main reason the British did not like or trust him during the war.

This record in the Holocaust was not the only reason the ICRC almost went out of business in the late 1940s and early 1950s. It was short of money and personnel. It was mostly boycotted *sur place* by the USSR and most of its allies (even though the USSR participated in negotiating the 1949 Geneva Conventions). It had weak leadership with Huber being ill, Burckhardt still officially president but on leave as the Swiss ambassador in Paris, and no major figure actively minding the store in Geneva. It was for a time heavily criticized by especially the Swedish Red Cross, which sought to internationalize the membership of the ICRC governing board before reconsidering – probably wisely.

IV   Rebounding after the Good War

The ICRC began to rebound and demonstrate renewed flexibility in mostly well-considered ways by several steps. It played its traditional role in being a drafting secretariat in the diplomatic conference leading to the four Geneva Conventions of 1949, these treaties being still the bedrock of modern international humanitarian law. It thus continued to bring to bear its practical and legal expertise in drafting and negotiating IHL, as in 1864, 1909, and 1929. Recent research tells us a great deal about various maneuvers by various actors in the supposedly humanitarian negotiations of 1949, as the ICRC and states made choices about not only how far and how hard to push humanitarian concerns, but also how to protect various self-interests.[6] As ever, humanitarian diplomatic conferences reflected struggles over power and reputation as well as how much humanitarian traffic the political path could accommodate at that juncture.

At the same time the ICRC became active in the conflict over the future of British Western Palestine, proving useful as an intermediary – and acceptable to the new Israeli government despite the history of the Holocaust. And it continued to expand its activities in various ways and directions in Korea, Algeria, Kenya, and elsewhere. If it was often seen as pro-West and somewhat slow to respond to the humanitarian needs of those detained in South Africa or Kenya, for example, it did progressively and more appropriately respond. A good example was its deepening role in the Algerian War for Independence (1954–1962), where it finally obtained some legal and practical concessions on prisoner affairs from the French government. Yet it is fair to note that that war remained a brutal war of terror and torture, with the humanitarian accomplishments slight and marginal at the time.[7]

Perhaps the ultimate example of ICRC flexibility in its history was triggered by the Cuban missile crisis of 1962. Given the very real threat of strategic nuclear war between the Soviet Union and the United States over the placement of attack missiles in Cuba, the ICRC quietly let officials at the UN know that it was prepared to step outside of its normal humanitarian role to assist as needed.

It was quietly agreed that the ICRC would appoint an international panel to supervise the withdrawal of missiles by Moscow, as negotiated by the protagonists. The ICRC knew that a major nuclear war would

Photograph 4.1 In the late 1940s the ICRC was active in the war for the future of British western Palestine. Here its white car, marked with the Red Cross flag, leads a convoy through Jerusalem on the way to delivering relief near the front lines of fighting. The ICRC in that war wanted not only to carry out protection and assistance activities but also to prove to the world that it was still needed and viable after the controversies of World War II. From almost going out of business after that global war, it gradually recovered through various field operations and the negotiation of the 1949 Geneva Conventions.

make IHL irrelevant since such a war would see the obliteration of the distinction between civilian and combatant, as well as the erasure of other legal distinctions designed to limit the process of armed conflict. At the same time, the ICRC wanted to avoid winding up possibly having to pass public judgment on the policies of a superpower. Thus, it was not willing to supervise by itself but willing to appoint others to do so.[8]

As events played out, the crisis was resolved without the projected control panel coming into existence, much less functioning. It is likely that the USSR was just buying time for its decision-making by agreeing to these arrangements. In any event, the ICRC had shown itself ready to take extraordinary steps to help defuse the greatest nuclear crisis of the times.

Geneva had not, however, fully or permanently solved its problems of weak leadership, nor did it always manifest well-trained and dynamic staff in the field. If the Holocaust and then the immediate *après-guerre* of the late 1940s had not finished off the ICRC, the bruhaha over Biafra during 1967–1970 almost did. The ICRC did not fare well in this internationalized internal war, which played out in the headlines, with complicated politics in every way imaginable, and with demands for civilian relief leading to other relief actors who cared little for the rules of IHL or the presumed centrality of the ICRC regarding humanitarian action in armed conflicts. Some details were already mentioned earlier in Chapter 2, and more are given later, with documentation at those other points.

The crux of the matter was that the amateurish ICRC Assembly, its governing board, proved incapable of managing things properly. Under pressure from Bern, which feared the loss of Swiss reputation, ICRC policymaking was contracted out to the well-known Swiss diplomat Auguste Lindt (whom I had the privilege of interviewing in the 1970s) and who was loaned by the Swiss government and initially given full control over ICRC policy in that conflict. A major result of this arrangement was that the dynamic but imperial Lindt became *persona non grata* in Lagos. The ICRC, although decisions taken in its name did much good in the form of civilian relief, wound up sidelined in the conflict after controversial policies led to the shooting down of a Red Cross plane trying to deliver relief inside Biafra without the full and clear approval of the Nigerian government – or at least the Nigerian air force. Parts of the French Red Cross were pro-Biafra and openly revolted against the ICRC and its official NIIHA values – however ambivalently pursued by Geneva – leading over time to the creation of both Doctors Without Borders (MSF) and Doctors of the World (Médecins du Monde).

Once again, the ICRC recovered. It changed its governance and administrative structures in Geneva (explained later in Chapters 15 and 16).[9] It found itself with a permanent presence in the Middle East in the wake of the 1967 War, or the third war between Zionist/Israeli forces and Palestinians supported by neighboring Arab states. Although the ICRC and the victorious Israelis disagreed on both general applicability and particular aspects of the Fourth Geneva Convention (GC) of 1949 containing provisions on occupied territory, the two found a way to avoid a rupture as they interacted on prisoner affairs, civilian assistance, and a wide range of other contested topics. The ICRC became better known and respected in the Arab world for its efforts to protect and aid Palestinians under Israeli control, but it retained stable relations with Israel – in part because the ICRC sometimes played a role in the protection and/or safe return of Israeli POWs.[10]

On the general matter of the applicability of the Fourth GC from 1949 to the territories taken by Israeli forces in 1967, the ICRC decided to agree to disagree with Israel so that it might achieve some humanitarian

Photograph 4.2 On the night of 5–6 May 1969 a cargo plane made available to the ICRC was flying relief for the civilian population (rice, no weapons) into the breakaway region of Biafra, without full agreement from the fighting parties, when it was shot down with loss of life by the Nigerian air force. This led to the end of ICRC operations in that internal conflict, and also had other more long-term effects.

progress on various topics. The ICRC ran the risk of being seen as complicit in some Israeli policies that were in violation of IHL, but from time to time Geneva issued public statements giving an overview of its interpretations and where Israeli policies departed from those. For example, it was an open fact that Israel authorized the use of coercive interrogation of Palestinian detainees. The ICRC could not stop that policy, but it did try to see that the coercion was indeed limited and that the detainee emerged alive from the process – with the ICRC negotiating an agreement giving the organization access to the detainee a few weeks after capture.[11]

So from 1967 in the Middle East, the ICRC engaged in flexible policies in order to do some good, even if IHL was not being implemented as written. The ICRC–Israeli relationship was delicate, not lacking frictions, but managed so as to avoid rupture. On the 150th anniversary of the ICRC, in the *Review*, the article on the Middle East appeared under the name of the president – such were the sensitivities on the subject.[12] This statement, as well as others, made clear that the ICRC took issue with several Israeli policies affecting the territories captured by the Jewish state in 1967. The emphasis of the article was on how the Palestinian civilian population was affected by such policies as the introduction of Israeli settlements into the West Bank and the barrier wall constructed by Israel despite the legal critique by the International Court of Justice. Detention issues were mentioned in passing. It can also be noted that the ICRC had access to detainees held by the Palestinian Authority where there were also reports of serious ill-treatment.[13]

In sum, after the 1967 war in the Middle East, the ICRC sometimes gave a public critique of Israeli policy as occupying power. If state parties to IHL chose not to do anything, or anything effective, about Israeli violations of especially the Fourth GC from 1949, the ICRC collectively shrugged its shoulders at the workings of international politics while doing what it could to aid and protect those adversely affected on both sides, within the limits of its capabilities and practical possibilities. Rather than withdraw in protest or engage in impassioned denunciations of one side or the other, it continued to engage and accomplish what it could.

Photograph 4.3 The ICRC developed a permanent presence in the Middle East from 1967 onward. While it manifested extensive activities concerning Palestinians under Israeli control, here at the border with Lebanon it returns the remains of two Israeli soldiers killed in fighting.

In an understatement, one can say that the ICRC did not lack challenges in the 1960s, not only in Cuba, Africa, and the Middle East but also in Southeast Asia. The Vietnam War, American phase circa 1965–1975, says a great deal about the ICRC of this time, its persistent efforts on behalf of IHL and especially prisoners' affairs, and – through no fault of its own – its often marginal impact on brutal political struggles. Several summary points deserve emphasis from the long and complex conflict.

Given especially the influx of large numbers of US military forces in the mid-1960s, by 1966 the ICRC considered the situation to be an international armed conflict to which the full 1949 Geneva Conventions applied. This view was accepted by US political and military leaders, who issued instructions for compliance.[14] The ICRC legal view fit nicely with the view of Washington that governing authorities in Saigon constituted an independent government representing a legitimate state that was entitled to self-defense against attacks from Hanoi. In the view of Hanoi, however, the ICRC was tilting toward the United States and its allies rather than seeing the conflict as an internal one about who governed within the one state of Vietnam. Neither the Peoples Republic of Vietnam in the north nor the National Liberation Front in the south saw the ICRC as neutral; neither gave it much cooperation.

No doubt more important than legal considerations was Hanoi's determination to take over the south by whatever strategy and tactics were required. Hanoi was never to give much serious or favorable attention to the rules of IHL from 1949, and the ICRC never gained access to US POWs held in the north, including the captured fighter pilot John McCain who later ran for president, and who was clearly very badly treated. The ICRC contacted many communist and other governments in search of better rapport with Hanoi but to no avail.[15] Nevertheless, the US side, at high levels, continued to endorse the 1949 GCs, hoping that a situation of reciprocity would eventually emerge with the north, leading to improved treatment of American POWs.

The ICRC delegation in Saigon, based on the organization's experience in Algeria, got their American counterparts, and later Washington, to agree to expand the definition of who was entitled to humane treatment as a POW. That is, ICRC staff worked out an agreement with US contacts saying that guerrilla fighters captured in combat would be treated as if they had met the provisions of Article 4 in the Third GC of 1949, defining POW status, even though regular North Vietnamese fighters or their allied fighters in the National Liberation Front were not wearing uniforms or otherwise always meeting the terms of IHL. The primary US motivation was not fidelity to IHL per se but securing improved conditions for Americans held in the north.

If captured communist fighters survived capture, field interrogation, and then further questioning and treatment in a US interrogation center – and that survival was not assured – they were placed in five or six POW camps run by Saigon.[16] Here the ICRC had at least some access three or four times each year and supervised a prisoner system that was relatively humane. Where the ICRC did not have access, conditions were worse.

However, first of all, the number of communist prisoners in the POW camps was relatively small, much smaller than estimates of political prisoners. The ICRC and other estimates are in the same range: maybe three or four times as many non-POW detainees as POWs. Most detained communists or suspected communists were declared by Saigon to be civilian defendants or given some other legal label depriving them of POW status. These other detention places, along with interrogation centers administered by Saigon, were often characterized by serious mistreatment, sometimes fatally so. The ICRC had some access to these locales on an irregular basis. US officials in the field sometimes colluded with officials from South Vietnam to delay ICRC prison visits or deny them altogether. These US officials, and their South Vietnamese counterparts, thus undermined what some high US officials were trying to achieve – namely, the image, if not the reality, of humane treatment for detainees and prisoners in the south so as to encourage better treatment for Americans held in the north.

The second thing to be noted about the official POW camps was that often the improvements obtained by the ICRC were then rejected by the prisoners themselves. The POWs, for example, would wreck the improved showers obtained via ICRC recommendations. The fight continued in detention, with Hanoi managing to instruct its fighters, including NLF fighters, to prevent Saigon from projecting an image of humane detention for POWs. Hanoi was able to keep track of events in detention in the south, seeing that its instructions to detainees were carried out. POW detention was not seen by Hanoi as simply a humanitarian quarantine but rather a further field of conflict. Some communist prisoners were killed by their compatriots if they seemed too cooperative with the ICRC or Saigon authorities. This continuation of the strategic political struggle in detention sometimes happened in other wars as well, as in Korea or Iran–Iraq. Sometimes detention did not represent a humanitarian quarantine from brutal power politics, which made the ICRC role delicate and even dangerous.

A third point about the POW camps was that the prisoners could be held for the duration of the war. If persons wound up in other detention centers in the south, and if they survived, they might, in fact, be released sooner than the POWs. In many detention centers, although characterized by poor conditions and mistreatment, there was a certain ebb and flow as persons were arrested but then sometimes released. Detention might be highly arbitrary, with mistreatment, but sometimes it was short.

Especially beyond the low number of POWs in the camps, detention in the South was quite brutal, as was true in the north; the ICRC had limited or no regular and guaranteed access to interrogation centers, civil defendants, political prisoners, and other non-POW prisoners; and overall its impact on prisoner affairs was marginal and frustrating. The ICRC fought the good fight and tried to carve out a humanitarian space, especially for prisoners (RC civilian relief was managed mostly by a few National RC Societies with some supporting role by the ICRC). But as in Algeria, the Vietnam War in the American phase was brutal as fought by both sides, with little charity extended to enemies. One saw this, for example, when the "Tiger Cages" for political prisoners at Con Son prison was discovered and publicized in 1973.[17] Saigon often treated its perceived enemies very harshly, as did the Hanoi regime and its allies.

In sum, US high officials might give official attention to IHL, and the United States had self-interested reasons for doing so, given the desire to have the ICRC gain access to its POWs in the north. (On the other hand, high officials tried to cover up the My Lai massacre of 1968 and other less savory aspects of the war.[18]) But many facts on the ground effectively negated the words and intentions of officials such as Secretary of State Dean Rusk or General William Westmoreland in favor of IHL and especially on behalf of POWs. Pentagon lawyers might be supportive of the ICRC and its objectives, but many facts on the ground were otherwise. The ICRC remained deeply frustrated about its limited humanitarian impact, both in the field and in Geneva. ICRC personnel tried very hard to have a beneficial impact on prisoner affairs in the south, as well as supporting civilian relief, but the results were meager. Detention issues were more complex and disappointing for the ICRC in the American phase of the Vietnam war than in other violent conflicts at more or less the same time in, for example, Malaysia, Thailand, and the Philippines.

However, ICRC diplomacy about guerrilla fighters captured in combat being entitled to treatment as if they were POWs became a new rule of IHL in Additional Protocol I (API) of 1977, Article 43(3). API has now been accepted by 175 states (skipping the subject of reservations or understandings that might qualify acceptance and also skipping the comparison between legal acceptance and proper application).

Here we might pause in reviewing various field activities by the ICRC to pursue the topic of these 1977 Additional Protocols to the 1949 GCs. In fact, legislative action and field activities were related. Just as the

experiences of WWII led to the 1949 GCs, so the process of decolonization – or if one prefers, the push for national self-determination throughout the Global South – frequently violent, led to new IHL. Such events as
the Algerian war and the Vietnam war, not to mention the fighting over
what used to be western British Palestine, among many other events, led
in 1968 to a UN conference in Tehran that was officially about human
rights. Among the topics discussed was human rights in armed conflict.

Whether one used the discourse of human rights law or IHL, the political reality was that the numerous newly independent states of the Global
South wanted increased attention to what they called wars of national
liberation and to enhance the status of those fighting against what the
majority called colonial, racist, or occupying regimes. This was a rhetorical code for enhancing the violent struggles, particularly then occurring
in the late 1960s and early 1970s, against Portuguese authority in Angola
and Mozambique, apartheid in South Africa, and Israel's occupation of
arguably Palestinian land from 1967 (if not 1948).

Whereas after WWII, some sixty states, mostly Western, negotiated the
1949 GCs, with broad agreement that the ICRC should prepare the early
drafts, in 1968, there were eighty-four states, mostly non-Western, at the
UN Tehran Conference. At the start of the 1974 Geneva Diplomatic
Conference on the Reaffirmation and Development of IHL, which was
one outcome of the Tehran conference, UN membership stood at 138
and 125 states attended the 1974 session of the diplomatic conference in
Geneva. Western states by then constituted a distinct minority in international relations. The ICRC retained its position as drafting secretariat
for the 1974–1977 diplomatic conference, having been asked to do so by
the United Nations, but it and the Western states were not as influential
or controlling as in 1949. No doubt, the ICRC saw itself as neutral in its
drafting role, but a number of observers saw it as aligned with most of
the Western states.[19]

A large number of developing or postcolonial states wanted wars of
national liberation to be considered international armed conflicts. They
wanted captured fighters in that cause to be considered prisoners of war.
The tradition in IHL had been not to characterize by name certain wars
as international or internal but rather leave such distinctions to state
practice. In this sense, most of the Western states were traditionalists.
They saw the other side as pushing a "just war" concept into the laws of
war, identifying ahead of time which side of the fighting was just – and
on this subject, which wars were to be definitely seen as international.[20]
Politically speaking, many so-called wars of national liberation were seen
by some Western states as internal conflicts, if not examples of terrorism,
and many fighters on the challenging side in such conflicts were seen by

the West as failing to meet the terms laid out in the 1949 law for POW status. So there were many factual, political, and legal complexities to be sorted out in Geneva during 1974–1977.

This is not the place for a detailed review of those complexities and the twists and turns of negotiations (which I followed *ad nauseum* at the time, attending all four conference sessions as an observer). Suffice it to say that two Additional Protocols, or add-on treaties, were adopted in 1977, the first on international war and the second on internal war. The numerous states of the Global South, supported by what was then the Soviet-led communist alliance, got what they wanted in that the API on international war included reference to wars of national liberation, whether considered anti-colonial, anti-racist, or anti-occupation.

This being so, these postcolonial governments then showed not much interest in a broadly or easily applicable APII on internal wars, which, after all, might restrict *them* since they often represented fragmented nation-states dealing with violent dissent and disaffection. The governments of the Global South helped shape an APII that had a high threshold of violence for application, along with other conditions and restrictions. That an APII was adopted at all, thus reinforcing in principle 1949 Common Article 3 covering internal wars, was due finally to the strong verbal intervention of the Pakistani delegate, whose impassioned speech at the conference in favor of that Protocol may or may not have been approved by his foreign ministry. By 2022 API had been formally accepted by 175 states (as noted already) and APII by 169. Unfortunately, formal consent cannot be equated with a serious application. This is as true in Ukraine as in Ethiopia or Yemen, inter alia.

The United States, as *primus inter pares* among the Western States, entered the 1974 negotiations with an overriding interest in enhancing that part of IHL that would protect its captured military personnel in the future, given its bitter experience on that subject in Vietnam. Other Western states had their own priorities, with Norway, for example, having a distinct agenda at the conference leading it to be labeled behind the scenes by some as "the blue-eyed Arabs." That is, Norway did not object to expanding IHL so as to cover what some called wars of national liberation. It saw that as a plus. Moreover, having been victimized in WWII via Nazi occupation, Norway in the 1970s tended to emphasize the relevance of IHL to other situations of occupation.[21] Norway was the first NATO state to ratify the Protocols and did so without parliamentary debate, whereas the United States has never formally consented to either one.

Whatever the national distinctions and agendas, the conference was as much about geostrategic power and politics – and image and status – as about updating humanitarian concerns. The ICRC might discuss and draft and comment in a low profile sort of way, trying to bring its field experience and other historical knowledge to bear, and there were some humanitarian gains embedded in the Protocols (covered later in Chapter 13). The conference was not totally about power politics. But the large number of newly independent states shaped outcomes greatly; they clearly wanted IHL to reflect their preoccupations – which to them were both geopolitical and ethical at the same time. Given these trends (and votes at the conference), the United States and Israel have never ratified the Protocols. (The subject of whether parts of the Protocols have now passed into customary IHL is discussed later.)

One can close out this brief and selective overview of ICRC activities between the time of Moynier and then the end of the Cold War, which is to say between about 1910 and 1990, with attention to two different kinds of situations: the plight of political prisoners in Chile and Argentina in the 1970s and the Iran–Iraq war in the 1980s. Lots of other subjects merit attention, but the topics chosen gave an accurate flavor of ICRC's broad and complex efforts to limit the human damage from violent conflict.

The Chilean coup of 1973, ousting the elected Salvador Allende, who died in the fighting, came on the heels of a similar right-wing military coup in Greece in 1967. In Athens in 1969, the ICRC had obtained a one-year written agreement to supervise Greek places of detention, the Greek colonels being under considerable international pressure to moderate their policies and restore democracy. There followed a determined effort by the ICRC, and its main man *sur place*, Roland Marti, to check torture and other abuses by the Greek junta. In that era, the ICRC would publish in the *Review* which places of political detention it was allowed access, where it was blocked, where its normal modalities of visit were respected and where not, and where it could see prisoners then under interrogation.[22] After one year, with Marti forced out and with a reduction of some of the international pressure, the colonels did not renew the agreement with Geneva – and the ICRC became sidelined in events.

In Chile, a similar dynamic played out from 1973. General Pinochet and his military associates, as backed by Presidents Nixon and Ford and Secretary of State Kissinger, were determined to eliminate or intimidate much of the left-wing opposition, which had engaged in violent challenges to Chilean dominant trends. Yet the Chilean junta was under much pressure to curtail human rights abuses, particularly after Jimmy Carter was elected president in 1976. (Also, a Chilean dissident was murdered by Pinochet's covert operatives on American soil in that same year, which led to increased pressures against the Pinochet regime.)

The ICRC was able to obtain access to some places of detention, if not others. It was able to moderate some Chilean policies as well as to help free a number of detainees for emigration (which involved the organization in forced emigration as the lesser evil). Many brutal policies toward detainees remained as the crackdown ebbed and flowed over the years. The position and role of the ICRC also ebbed and flowed until Pinochet stepped down from office in 1981.

As in Greece, it was basically partisan and strategic politics that determined events, but the ICRC calculated how best to try to protect detainees, search for the missing, and provide family links within a shifting humanitarian space as negotiated in the midst of brutal power struggles. What sealed the fate of Pinochet was not really a moral revulsion at his policies of political murder and torture. It was more a desire by the Reagan Administration in Washington after its election in 1980 to see that Pinochet did not stay too long, fearing that his continued rule might provoke a swing in favor of renewed leftist politics. By then, Pinochet had crushed the hard left through brutal repression.

Such was the harsh political world within which the ICRC operated, with the Chilean situation unregulated under IHL and thus with the ICRC at the mercy of full state consent. The United States, normally a strong supporter of the ICRC, during 1973–1976 had urged the Chilean military to move against the elected Allende, quickly recognized the Pinochet regime, and continued to support that regime despite its brutal repression – all in the name of US hegemony in the region laced with an anti-leftist fervor.[23]

The 1973 Chilean coup was followed in 1976, by a similar power grab by the Argentine military, resulting in a three-man junta. If anything, the crackdown on perceived leftist opponents was more severe, with the usual political murder and torture, but also people thrown into the ocean from helicopters, children stolen from politically active parents and given to loyal supporters, and other atrocities. Again, in a context of considerable criticism of the junta, the ICRC was able to negotiate some access to detainees but on an inconsistent and unsatisfactory basis. As in Chile, the Argentine junta was determined to eliminate its left-wing opposition; what was allowed to the ICRC was essentially window dressing that did not affect the structure of the brutal political struggle. The junta collapsed because of losing the Falklands/Malvinas war with Britain in 1982.

There is, of course, much more to be said about the history of the ICRC and political prisoners or security detainees, whether one might use the example of another Southern Cone national security state, Uruguay, or perhaps Poland in the early 1980s – the only European communist state to allow ICRC visits to such detainees. Chapter 14 focuses in part on this subject in contemporary times.

We close this history section with a reference to the Iran–Iraq war just before the end of the Cold War. Here we find, as in Vietnam or indeed in a more complicated way Afghanistan during the time of Soviet attempts to control the political picture (1979–1989), a nasty international armed conflict with much violation of IHL. There were indeed some international wars where IHL fared better. A large one of this latter type involved India and Pakistan in 1971, where the ICRC wound up visiting tens of thousands of POWs on both sides. A small one involved Argentina and Britain as they contested control of the Falklands/Malvinas islands in the South Atlantic in 1982. The ICRC is still dealing today with missing persons and exchanges of mortal remains from that brief war of a couple of months – a war fought with much attention to IHL.

One analyst referred to the Iran–Iraq war as an "immoral swamp."[24] An initial Iraqi invasion of Iran was followed over time by Iranian counterattacks regaining lost territory, followed again by Iraqi counterthrusts and eventually a military stalemate after most of a decade. The cost in lives was horrendous, with perhaps more than fifty thousand killed and up to two million injured.

The Saddam Hussein government in Iraq was known for its harsh repression, which limited its open and relatively enthusiastic allies to a few Sunni Arab regimes preoccupied with Iran. As for Tehran, its new Shiite clerical government was brutal at home and expansionist in foreign policy, and was no friend of international law, as witnessed by its 1979 seizure of US diplomats and consular officials as hostages. Most outside powers were content to let two distasteful regimes bleed each other and thus contain each other, regardless of the human cost. Iraq used chemical weapons on a widespread basis, and without serious sanction, to try to offset Iran's numerical advantage in military personnel.[25] Washington, being hostile to Iran, provided Iraq with intelligence information, although Baghdad seems to have obtained its supplies for chemical weapons from other sources.

In this conflict, one to which the four Geneva Conventions applied, the ICRC struggled to achieve humanitarian results. Each side, while permitting some ICRC visits to POWs, hid others and killed and mistreated still others. Shia Iran tried to pressure some Shiite Iraqi POWS into denouncing Saddam's regime, as it was nominally Sunni. An ICRC representative was roughed up as part of these machinations by the clerical regime in Tehran. The POW situation was such that over time the ICRC issued several "White papers" on humanitarian matters, indicating where and when IHL was being violated and its humanitarian diplomacy blocked by the two belligerents.[26] This public accounting of the humanitarian record had slight discernible impact on anyone, as the protagonists mostly continued their illegal policies. Third parties – including those in the supposedly liberal West – mostly continued to pursue their Machiavellian national interests. Few, if any, states displayed serious interest in IHL, which deprived the ICRC of effective allies.

Neither belligerent being able to obtain its desired outcome after almost a decade of fighting, the United Nations was finally able to broker an end to the war in 1989 based basically on the status quo ante. This left many issues unresolved, festering into future eruptions both at home and abroad. The results of the war were negative in almost every respect, especially for the ICRC and IHL. Most governments gave priority to narrow national interests understood in geopolitical terms or were driven by extreme nationalist and/or sectarian ideology. This left little humanitarian space for the objectives of the ICRC against the background of IHL. The ICRC was committed, persistent, and courageous but largely devoid of leverage over important actors.

Notes

1 M. MacMillan, *War: How Conflict Shaped Us* (New York: Penguin Random House, 2021), p. 218.

2 D. Palmieri, "An Institution Standing the Test of Time: A Review of 250 Years of the History of the International Committee of the Red Cross," *International Review of the Red Cross*, 888 (December 2012), https://international-review .icrc.org/articles/institution-standing-test-time-review-150-years-history-international-committee-red-cross (accessed November 29, 2022).

3 D. P. Forsythe, "The International Red Cross: Decentralization and its Effects," *Human Rights Quarterly*, 40/1 (February 2018), https://muse.jhu .edu/article/685697/summary (accessed November 29, 2022). See also Claudena M. Skran, "Gustave Ador, the ICRC, and Leadership on Refugee and Migration Policy," *Cambridge Core Blog*, December 3, 2018, www.cambridge .org/core/blog/2018/12/03/gustave-ador-the-icrc-and-leadership-on-refugee-and-migration-policy/ (accessed November 28, 2022).

4 J. Moreillon, *Le Comité international de la Croix-Rouge et la protection des détenus politiques* (Geneva: HDI; Lausanne: L'Age d'Or, 1973).

5 See Davide Rodogno, *Night on Earth: A History of International Humanitarianism in the New East 1918–1930* (Cambridge: Cambridge University Press, 2021).

6 See especially Boyd Van Dyke, *Preparing for War: The Making of the Geneva Conventions* (Oxford and New York: Oxford University Press, 2022).

7 From a library of sources on the topic, one can start with Paul Aussaresses, *The Battle of the Casbah: Terror and Counter-Terrorism in Algeria 1957–1959* (New York: Enigma Books, 2002).

8 F. Bugnion, "The ICRC and the Cuban Missile Crisis, October-November 1962," *Intercross* (October 26, 2012), https://intercrossarchive.icrc.org/

blog/the-icrc-and-the-cuban-missile-crisis-october-november-1962 (accessed November 29, 2022). A more thorough account can be found in F. Bugnion, "Confronting the Unthinkable: The International Committee of the Red Cross and the Cuban Missile Crisis, October–November 1962," *Swiss Review of History*, 62 (2012), Part 1, pp. 143–155; Part 2, pp. 299–310.

9   Even before the end of the Biafran war in Nigeria, during September 17–21, 1968 the ICRC held a "round table of delegates" in Geneva to review most aspects of ICRC organization and administration. This meeting stimulated important changes in the organization, pushed along by subsequent events in Nigeria. The *procès-verbal* of the roundtable can now be accessed in the ICRC archives.

10 "A Day of Joy in Israel as POWs Start to Return Home," *Jewish Telegraphic Agency*, (November 13, 1973), www.jta.org/archive/a-day-of-joy-in-israel-as-pows-begin-to-return-home (accessed November 28, 2022).

11 ICRC, "Israel, Methods of Interrogation Used against Palestinian Detainees," (n.d.), internet posting, https://casebook.icrc.org/case-study/israel-methods-interrogation-used-against-palestinian-detainees (accessed November 29, 2022). Among a wealth of other material, see "Israel Renews Permission for the Use of Force in Interrogations," *New York Times* (August 17, 1995), www.nytimes.com/1995/08/17/world/israel-renews-permission-for-the-use-of-force-in-interrogations.html (accessed November 29, 2022).

12 P. Maurer, "Challenges to International Humanitarian Law: Israel's Occupation Policy," *International Review of the Red Cross*, 888 (December 2012), https://international-review.icrc.org/articles/challenges-international-humanitarian-law-israels-occupation-policy (accessed November 28, 2022).

13 Amnesty International, "Palestinian Authority Must Investigate Torture Allegations of Hunger-striking Prisoners and Ensure Fair Trial," November 2, 2022, www.amnesty.org/en/latest/news/2022/11/palestinian-authorities-must-investigate-torture-allegations-of-hunger-striking-prisoners-and-ensure-their-fair-trial/ (accessed November 29, 2022).

14 G. S. Prugh, *Law at War: Vietnam 1964–1973* (Washington, DC: Department of the Army, 1975).

15 J. Blondel, *From Saigon to Ho Chi Minh City: The ICRC's Work and Transformation from 1966 to 1975* (Geneva: ICRC, 2016), pp. 38–42.

16 On the ICRC and the fate of communist prisoners in the South, see Marcel Berni, "The ICRC and Communist Captives during Vietnam's American War," in M. Berni and T. Cubito, eds., *Captivity in War during the Twentieth Century: The Forgotten Role of Transnational Actors* (London: Palgrave Macmillan, 2021). This chapter, very solid in substance, was supplemented by the present author's interviews under Chatham House rules. See also the book by Berni, based on his dissertation, *Ausser Gefecht: Lieben, Leiden, und Sterben "communist" Gefangener in Vietnams americanischen Krieg* (Hamburg: Hamburger Edition, 2020). The present author read the relevant parts of this book as translated by a colleague into French. The present author also benefited from a synopsis by another German-speaking colleague.

17 Sylvan Fox, "4 South Vietnamese Describe Torture in Prison 'Tiger Cage'," *New York Times*, March 3, 1973, www.nytimes.com/1973/03/03/archives/4-south-vietnamese-describe-torture-in-prison-tiger-cage-center-of.html (accessed November 29, 2022).

18 J. Goldstein, B. Marshall and J. Schwartz, eds., *The My Lai Massacre and Its Cover-Up: Beyond the Reach of Law? The Peers Commission Report* (New York: The Free Press, 1976).

19 For example, see Henry Lovat, *Negotiating Civil War: The Politics of International Regime Design* (Cambridge: Cambridge University Press, 2020).

20 D. E. Graham, "The 1974 Diplomatic Conference on the Law of War: A Victory for Political Cases and a Return to the Just War Concept of the Eleventh Century," *Washington and Lee Law Review*, 32/1 (Winter, 1975), pp. 25–63, https://scholarlycommons.law.wlu.edu/wlulr/vol32/iss1/4/ (accessed November 29, 2022).

21 B. Egge, "Norway and the 1977 Additional Protocols to the 1949 Geneva Conventions," *International Review of the Red Cross*, 258 (June 1986), pp. 310–312. https://international-review.icrc.org/sites/default/files/S0020860400025638a .pdf (accessed November 29, 2022).

22 ICRC, "External Activities," *International Review of the Red Cross*, 110 (May 1970), p. 279, https://international-review.icrc.org/sites/default/files/ S0020860400064445a.pdf (accessed November 29, 2022).

23 A new biography of Henry Kissinger accurately identifies his key memo to President Nixon urging the US president to move against Allende and picturing the situation in Chile as key to US global containment of communism. The memo was a gross exaggeration of the situation, as the biographer rightly concludes. Thomas A. Schwartz, *Henry Kissinger and American Power: A Political Biography* (New York: Hill and Wang, 2020), p. 111.

24 B. Riedel, "Lessons from America's First War with Iran," Brookings Institute (May 22, 2013), www.brookings.edu/articles/lessons-from-americas-first-war-with-iran/ (accessed November 29, 2022).

25 J. Ali, "Chemical Weapons and the Iran-Iraq War: A Case Study in Non-Compliance," *The Non-Proliferation Review* (Spring, 2001), pp. 43–67. www .nonproliferation.org/wp-content/uploads/npr/81ali.pdf (accessed November 29, 2022).

26 F. Bugnion, *The International Committee of the Red Cross and the Protection of War Victims* (Geneva: ICRC, 2003), pp. 642–644.

5   The Red Cross Movement
Part I – The Swiss and the Rest

> The development of the ICRC ... cannot be separated from that of the Red Cross.
>
> André Durand[1]

From the beginning, the ICRC founding fathers all agreed that their projected international network of aid agencies should be comprised of independent units without an authoritative center. At the first meeting of the prospective groups in 1863, the American participant Charles Bowles raised the question of how effective such a loose network could be, but Henry Dunant and Gustave Moynier and the other Swiss organizers had their minds set on decentralization.

Perhaps they were influenced by the fact that the Swiss confederation itself was decentralized with a relatively weak center in Bern, which left considerable autonomy to the cantons like Geneva. Perhaps they themselves wanted to be highly independent, not tightly regulated by any superior Red Cross body. Perhaps it was because Dunant had already articulated the same scheme for his decentralized international network of YMCAs as we saw in Chapter 3. We could use better records about 1863–1964 but are never going to get them.

Early on, Moynier toyed with the idea of some sort of central union for the national aid societies. However, he later maneuvered against variations of that idea, as did other ICRC leaders still later. For whatever exact reason(s), the Red Cross idea was born basically decentralized and has remained that way. As we have already mentioned in Chapter 4, there was considerable attention to Movement structure after World War I with periodic headaches thereafter.

During World War II, there was a joint ICRC–Federation relief agency (the Federation was then called the League of Red Cross Societies). But it did not last, and it did not erase, but rather was affected by, persistent ICRC–Federation friction.[2] The Joint Relief Commission during World War II reflected an imbalance between the two Geneva HQs, and its termination occurred in the context of renewed tensions between them. The Federation itself had little independent operational capability during that war. It had scrambled to relocate to Geneva from Paris at the start of the war. Given that its leadership was heavily populated by personnel from Allied nations, Berlin did not allow it to operate relief programs for civilians in German-controlled areas.

It seems that most of the activities of the Joint Commission resulted from ICRC-led negotiations and ICRC management. The Federation, however, brought vital links with the National RC Societies to the Joint Commission – helpful in raising funds and providing material goods. The Joint Commission was terminated in 1946 for complicated reasons, despite massive needs by civilians in Europe after the war.

Max Huber, ICRC president, was not involved in critical decisions but later expressed regret at the dissolution of the Joint Commission which had combined the two Geneva headquarters. By 1946 the ICRC and Federation were jousting again, this time over the evolution of the RC Fundamental Principles, covered below, so their relations remained more prickly than collegial. While the Joint Commission manifested some evident achievements during its existence, in Greece for example, it did not provide an accepted blueprint for enhanced cooperation between the ICRC and Federation or how to unite the Movement for civilian relief in the long term.

In recent years there has been renewed discussion about the structure and functioning of the Movement – explained more fully in the next chapter. For the ICRC, there was much thinking about how to maintain ICRC roles and reputation while becoming more of a team player. But how does one mobilize the resources of the entire Movement for more significant impact, while preserving the ICRC niche which was constructed with great effort and considerable success over the past years? We will find there is greater RC coordination here but not there, on this subject but not on that subject. Much global RC action remains fractured. This persistent feature of the network – decentralization or fragmentation – has both advantages and disadvantages for the ICRC.

Decentralization, meaning primarily the autonomy for the national aid agencies, was a good formula for expanding the network. And it fit with the notion of national sovereignty bestowed on territorial states. After all, it would be awkward for the state to be sovereign but for institutions such as the official aid auxiliaries to the national military to be centrally controlled by some international body. At first, Moynier even though each aid society could use whatever name and emblem it wanted. These

Photograph 5.1 The ICRC and the IFRC, along with several National RC Societies, cooperated closely regarding relief to civilians during World War II. This arrangement achieved considerable good in places such as Greece. However, the work could be dangerous, with RC vehicles sometimes the target of attacks. The close cooperation among some RC members during this war did not last but was revisited several times – and yet again in 2022.

views also shifted, and the Geneva committee for the war wounded itself added "Red Cross" to its name in 1875.

Decentralization was never a good formula for ensuring maximum effective action for the network, as Bowles foresaw in 1863, since the national units could pick and choose what they wanted to do or how they wanted to do it. One contemporary ICRC staffer argues that the Movement was never intended to be a unitary and cohesive actor compared to a loose network of multiple actors. Be that as it may, it was relatively easy for national governments to influence or even control "their" aid society because there was no authoritative centralized Red Cross body to firmly contest that national policy.

A fragmented RC Movement has been mostly a constant. Efforts at structural change on this matter have mostly failed. Whether new efforts at "flexible coordination" can make much difference is a subject worth watching.

I   A Decentralized Movement: The ICRC and Three Basic Identities

The essence of the ICRC, already noted as a "curious animal" in the wording of Caroline Morehead,[3] can be viewed in three fundamental ways. Each is correct, yet somewhat different from the other two with some areas of overlap.

A   The Swiss Core

Legally speaking, the ICRC was for a long time described as a private humanitarian organization based in Geneva whose supreme authority is an all-Swiss governing board called the Assembly.[4] It was recognized (and regulated) by the Swiss civil code, Article 60, covering charitable or nonprofit private organizations in that territorial state. In this sense, it was a kind of nongovernmental organization (NGO), civil society organization (CSO), and private volunteer organization (PVO). (These acronyms refer to a nonprofit agency, which is unlike a private organization designed to make money across borders, such as a transnational corporation [TNC].)

But the ICRC is also now widely recognized as a private international organization despite its mono-national governance. Again, because of its functions, international staff, and global activities, it is considered as if it were a private international organization accorded certain rights and immunities. In this sense, one has an international organization nested within an international institution – namely, the RC Movement. The Movement is not an international organization with a centralized authority and bureaucracy, but rather a permanent network of actors who interact in mostly predictable ways – and thus, an institution.

The ICRC also has legal personality in international law due to its functions, now recognized in various treaties and customary public international law – especially the Geneva Conventions of 1949, and 1977 Additional Protocols. It remains a private organization but part of a public international legal regime. This is not entirely unique in public international law – that is, to have a private actor or agency as part of an interstate legal regime.[5]

The ICRC has dual or hybrid legal status, recognized and regulated in both domestic and international law.

One rather doubts that the victims of political violence care very much about all these legal complexities. It does seem to be the case that the various legal considerations serve as foundational building blocks and, in general, help the ICRC carry out its humanitarian activities. However, its ties to public international law can be a constraint, demonstrated by the case study on Syria in the next chapter.

Those so inclined sometimes go into great detail about various ICRC-governmental agreements, written exchanges, and proof of this or that legal status.[6] I am not so inclined, being primarily interested in policymaking and policy outcomes. Therefore, I skip over whether recognition of the ICRC as an international organization alters its status under the Swiss civil code for NGOs. If the ICRC has been transformed into an international NGO (INGO), does that make any legal difference in Swiss law? Apparently not – or perhaps somewhat – but I leave that to the lawyers.

As noted, the ICRC governing board, formally called the Assembly when in session, but often referred to simply as the Committee, charts the basic course for the agency. (The Assembly also sets the rules for the length of service of its Swiss members, their behavior while in that body, and how new members are co-opted from Swiss society. It names the president and vice president, who *must be* Swiss, and other high officials such as the director-general.) Its daily role was reduced after mismanaging the Nigeria–Biafra affair (1967–1970), but it remains the ultimate authority for the organization. No other person, organization, or institution can override the decisions of the Assembly without its consent – subject to some qualifications discussed in the next section. No other nation-state or multinational body can dictate to the all-Swiss governing board, not even the International Red Cross Conference, most of the time.

The ICRC Assembly (meeting about ten times each year), and its Assembly Council, which represents the Assembly when that body is not in session, now plays the expected role, or maybe less. It oversees the budget, approves major budgetary shifts, oversees the fiscal audit, reviews major issues, establishes general policy, approves doctrinal and strategic statements, and perhaps is somewhat similar to most parliaments in most Western-style democracies. Its proceedings are completely closed to outsiders, even to the rest of the staff, for decades. Honorary members, that is, retired Assembly members, will not talk much about it even long after their tenure there. Like certain mafia families, they are sworn to secrecy for life.

During recent years one does not hear about, much less read about, significant initiatives by the governing board itself. Almost all the time, apparently, it knows what the president and the director-general present to it. It seems not to have generated its own information or started major initiatives, and it seems that in recent years it has not asserted itself to challenge the administration (the Directorate under the director-general) in any significant way. In these matters, it differs from some democratic parliaments.

Sometimes the Administration organizes workshops for the Assembly to educate it on this or that subject. This shows the weakness of the Assembly. It may remain a useful review body and sounding board. Some of the elected members of the Assembly Council, who meet more frequently along with the president and vice president, may generate some influence. Some among these Council members may turn out to be perceptive and assertive – probably collegially. There does not seem to be any recent issue where the Assembly or its Council has forced the Administration, or the president for that matter, to change course.

Conventional wisdom has it that recent presidents did not think that highly of the Assembly or take many complicated hot-button issues to it. The president has been a professional diplomat deeply involved in specific problems and interacting with other important leaders on complex matters. On the other hand, Assembly members were and still are businesspersons, medical workers, academics, NGO leaders, and others co-opted from Swiss society. Departing high professionals such as Director-General Yves Daccord were not asked to join, thus breaking with some past practice which had elevated some high ICRC professionals to Assembly membership (François Bugnion, Yves Sandoz, Jacques Moreillon, Jean Pictet, etc.). That practice gave the Assembly some independent knowledge and expertise based on past experience.

It may be that there is some discussion within the organization to clarify when a policy question should be taken to the Assembly for approval. Given the prevailing discretion at headquarters, it is hard to be sure about that.

What one finds at the ICRC today by way of governance is, for sure, the result of the Biafran affair, covered briefly in other chapters, and the desire to get the volunteer and amateurish Assembly out of the day-to-day management of ICRC policy. Moreover, the strategic statements and doctrine (policy guidance statements) adopted by the Assembly are drafted by the Administration, in consultation with the president, and only fine-tuned or polished by the Assembly. (That may change from 2023.) Still further, what one probably has at the ICRC in recent years is a strong-willed president who has great confidence in his course of action.

When, for example, a minority in the Assembly raised some questions about President Maurer's links to the World Economic Forum (WEF) (mentioned in Chapter 1 and analyzed later in this book), the president effectively dismissed their concerns and marshalled majority support from the rest of the Assembly. Later, more than one observer thought the president was careful to place only his supporters in the Assembly (although there is an Assembly recruitment committee). Apparently, some independent-minded Assembly members decided not to stand for reelection, but this is not certain.

Historians will be able to say more about the Assembly in the era of presidents such as Sommaruga, Kellenberger, and Maurer when ICRC archives are open to researchers. What appears to be certain is that at the time of writing there are no strong checks and balances on the ICRC president and Administration (aka the Directorate) from the Assembly. The professional offices are where the power really lies, and the Assembly, if not quite a rubber stamp, does not seem to be a major independent factor. There is, however, the Assembly Council, which is probably where the potential oversight of at least the Directorate resides. I will discuss all this in further detail later. As of fall 2022, a new president (Mirjana Spoljaric) appeared to be interested in restructuring the Assembly in order to make it more of an influential player in general policymaking.

Whatever the proven facts turn out to be about how ICRC governance operates, the organization at the very top remains Swiss and self-governed. It is either a Swiss NGO, a Swiss-based and governed private international organization, or both simultaneously. More important is what it does, with what degree of support, and with what outcomes. If it stays true to NIIHA principles (neutral, independent, impartial, humanitarian action) and meets with some success, the legal or maybe legalistic discussions about its status may turn out to be secondary at best.

To close the circle of analysis for now, it bears stressing that the ICRC governs itself and decides what to do and how to do it – which has been evident from day one. In 1863 it decided to assemble the other interested parties which led to creation of the International Red Cross aka the RC Movement. The following year it decided to ask the Swiss government to call a diplomatic conference to adopt a treaty on the basic idea of neutral aid to international war wounded. Also, in 1864 it decided to dispatch two observers to the war over Schleswig-Holstein, who then dabbled in medical assistance on the ground for both sides – Denmark and Austria-Prussia. In these and certain subsequent activities, it was not states or other units in the RC network that told the ICRC what to do.

This customary right of humanitarian initiative, practiced since 1863, was eventually codified in the various statutes of the organization. The ICRC's right of initiative went unmentioned in its first Statutes of 1915. These written rules of 1915 were developed to allow people to donate to the organization in their estate planning. There was a minor revision in 1922. Then events after World War I caused an important clarification in statutory wording in 1930.

Without going into all the details, one can say that the first Movement Statutes adopted in 1928, after the creation of the RC Federation (League) in 1919, and then the 1929 Geneva Convention on Prisoners of War, caused the Committee to clarify in writing what had been observable all along. Namely, the organization had an open-ended right of initiative, limited only by one's understanding of what was proper for a neutral, independent, and impartial humanitarian actor. Thus, Movement and treaty references to an ICRC right of initiative caused the organization to confirm customary practice on paper in its own 1930 Statutes. This clearly shows one part of the ICRC's hybrid status: its fundamental nature as a Swiss NGO or Swiss-based INGO.[7]

The latest version of this right of initiative reads as follows: "The ICRC may take any humanitarian initiative which comes within its role as a specifically neutral and independent institution and intermediary, and may consider any question requiring examination by such an institution."[8] So, the reach of ICRC interests – and possible action – is unbounded except for whatever limits are understood to be inherent in the words "humanitarian," "independent," and "neutral." The meaning of these words, plus the word impartial, is not self-evident.

The ICRC's legal personality in public international law, now reasonably clear, is often just a confirmation of, and facilitation of, what it had already been doing via its pragmatic right of initiative. That is, the organization likes to say that it has been given a mandate by states in international law, or organs in the RC Movement, to do this or that. This is a clever way to proceed, claiming collective legitimacy for its actions. But this line of presentation often confuses some, who fail to recognize that its right of initiative as a private agency is often key to what it tries to do. For example, it checked on the conditions of prisoners of war (even those not sick or wounded and needing medical assistance) during World War I, only got that activity written into international law in 1929, and only got a right to visit for itself in 1949. Its self-generated right of initiative was key to the evolutionary process.

The ICRC's plenary right of initiative, practiced since 1863 and recorded on paper since 1930, was recognized in public international law in the 1929 Geneva Convention (GC) on Prisoners of Wars (POWs), then again in the four GCs of 1949, and again in the 1977 Additional Protocols. So, there is a broad ICRC right of initiative codified from 1930 in ICRC statutes, and in the context of armed conflict has been recognized in IHL from 1929 on. If one wants to get into other legal waters, one can say that the ICRC plenary right of initiative is now part of customary international law.

B   *The RC Movement*

Secondly, while it is a Swiss independent civil society organization, the ICRC is a constituent member of an international institution, officially private, professing universal principles rather than strictly Swiss values. The RC network, the RC Movement, or more commonly the International Red Cross (IRC), at least in the Western world, manifests an International Conference as its highest deliberative organ. The key word is deliberative. The RC Conference is similar to the UN General Assembly in that most adopted resolutions are nonbinding.[9] The ICRC may value the Conference even more than the National RC Societies and the RC Federation, which have their own international meetings. But the ICRC is not controlled by the RC Conference or its subsidiary statutory bodies (the RC Standing Commission and the RC Council of Delegates). No organ in the RC network is similar to the UN Security Council with the authority to make substantive decisions binding on all members.

What supposedly unites the Movement is not a powerful central authority but a voluntary commitment to principles. The specification of these principles evolved out of changing and expanding practical action. For a long time, the ICRC focused on violent conflict, including direct results such as war refugees and war-induced poverty. The National RC Societies, joined by the League of RC Societies in 1919 (renamed the Federation in 1991, having added Red Crescent to the title in 1983), undertook broader action still. They needed something to do in peacetime, and there were plenty of problems to address – from responding to natural and other disasters to supporting public health programs and more. What could possibly tie all these disparate activities together?

What are now called the Fundamental RC Principles provided one answer. From nothing explicit (the early RC efforts were centered on practical action), there was an abortive attempt to list a few principles, then further efforts along those lines, then a long and confusing list of principles evolving through the RC Federation, and finally what proved to be a culminating effort by the ICRC's Jean Pictet to bring order out of discursive chaos in the 1950s and 1960s. In 1965 the RC Conference endorsed Pictet's seven Fundamental Principles: humanity, neutrality, impartiality, independence, volunteerism, unity, and universality. The first four became essential. Volunteerism was undercut somewhat, but still sometimes valued, by the growing professionalism and paid staff of all component members, although many volunteers continue. Unity was often absent in easily observable facts and often best left undiscussed except as a distant goal. Universalism was redundant with humanity – all humanity or humanity addressed on an impartial basis.[10]

The evolution and final endorsement of the Fundamental Principles showed much about the RC network. If one might venture to summarize a multitude of details, the ICRC early on saw itself as the guardian of RC values, having been responsible for the genesis of things, even if, for a long time, there were no official principles. When the Federation (then the RC League) took the unilateral initiative, without consultation with the ICRC, to define a long list of principles in 1946, the ICRC considered this to be an attack on its central role and *raison d'être*. It responded with a determined effort of its own to control the process and outcome about the principles. In this effort, it was largely successful by 1965.[11]

The four core principles remain important. They define Dunantist protective and relief work. There are politically engaged and, thus, biased relief agencies, which may do some good for selected targets. For example, there were relief organizations in the Spanish civil war that aided only the Republican side. But they were not Dunantist, which is to say not NIIHA. Take away these four basic RC principles, and there would be little to unify RC endeavors around the world. And even with these four, one still faces the reality that how National RC Societies interpret principles of neutrality and impartiality may differ from the ICRC, as shown later. Surprisingly, a former ICRC official, albeit not a long-term professional, wrote in defense of politically engaged rather than NIIHA or Dunantist action, saying there was a role for the former.[12] Be that as it may, it was widely accepted, even for many relief agencies outside the RC Movement, that the Dunantist version of humanitarian action was the preferred way to go.

Multiple relief agencies signed on to a RC Code of Conduct, approved in 1994, even if they were not part of the RC family. The Code started with the big four principles of working to relieve the affronts to humanity on the basis of independence, neutrality, and impartiality. Other ideas were added, such as respect for local customs. By 2022, over 500 private organizations had signed on to the code. The Dunantist core principles and a few other guidelines have attracted broad support.[13] They have been endorsed at the United Nations.[14]

So, the ICRC, which has never shed its Swiss essence in its governance, is part of a decentralized international movement officially held together, to the extent that it is, by a commitment to four cosmopolitan RC principles, supplemented by various other normative guidelines. This condition is both important and often, at the same time, a fiction. The Movement and its Fundamental Principles are both sometimes useful and sometimes made secondary, if not irrelevant, by the stronger-held values of narrow nationalism or seeking geopolitical advantage. In popular jargon, "politics" often dominates any commitment to universal neutral humanitarianism. Still, the ICRC's relationship with the RC Movement is a factor that cannot always be easily discounted, as we will see.

Historians are beginning to study the Movement in more depth, especially the Federation and its member National Societies.[15] They are considering that maybe the ICRC has been given too much attention in the Movement's evolution. Maybe the ICRC was paranoid about the addition of the Federation in 1919, but not so understood partly because of studies by the present author and others, and that we have understated the "ingrained arrogance" (quoted in the Preface) of ICRC leaders. There was certainly a growing demand for more attention to the National RC Societies. (But more attention might show more reason for concern, as will be shown by the subsequent analysis of Syria from 2011.) Here is another subject area, namely ICRC relations with the Movement, where future studies will enrich and challenge what we think we know now.

C   Mandates from IHL

Thirdly, the ICRC is recognized and given rights and duties in public international law and is treated by states – including the Swiss federal government in Bern – as if it were an international organization. The ICRC has a legal personality in public international law. In effect, as noted, the ICRC is treated as if it were an international organization within an international institution – the latter being the Movement.

Perhaps the most cited provision in IHL pertaining to the ICRC is that in international armed conflict, it manifests the right to detention visits for both combatant and civilian detainees. Included is the right to such visits in territory occupied resulting from international armed conflict.

Also important is that IHL recognizes the ICRC right of initiative, namely that the organization has the right to offer its humanitarian services to belligerent parties as decided in Geneva without that offer being considered an unfriendly act.

As already indicated, the present study is not focused on the details of IHL. In this book, the international law of armed conflict is primarily considered in analyzing contemporary ICRC policies and policymaking. But, clearly, the ICRC status in IHL is relevant to many of its operations and its reputation or status across the board. One of the central questions to be addressed later is whether the ICRC, in deciding on a much-expanded interpretation of its mandate, has weakened its position as guardian of IHL and the "go to" private organization for expertise on that subject. This is a central question today for some critics of the organization. Is the ICRC unprepared for its traditional activities in armed conflict because its staff is busy with economic development, migrants, urban gang activity, and all sorts of violence, detention, and social fragility beyond the sometimes ill-defined or contested contours of armed conflict? This is a serious question.

II   The Interplay of the Three Identities

The three ICRC identities play out in different ways and at different times, but always with attention to:

(1) what it decides itself – with wisdom or otherwise – under its own statutes;
(2) what the RC Conference approves according to Movement Statutes and Conference resolutions; and
(3) what IHL authorizes it to do via treaty and customary law.

The latter two roles sometimes depend on the first. That is, the ICRC may suggest to the RC Conference what resolutions it would like to see adopted, and/or tell states in a diplomatic conference what it does and does not want, and therefore often obtains collective endorsement for its preferences. But it always retains its own right of initiative.

I know of no major case where the RC Conference or a state diplomatic conference gave the ICRC marching orders that it did not want or flat-out refused to accept. There are some RC Conference resolutions that the ICRC is not too keen on. In that event, the independent ICRC may make its own interpretation of how it will proceed, drag its feet, or in other ways adopt certain tactics that downgrades the issue or allows the organization to escape what it thinks is an unwise direction.

Three examples are illustrative while leaving a definitive treatment of the subject to others. First, in 1918–1919 the ICRC on its own decided to initiate visits to political prisoners, with political instability in Russia and Hungary eventually leading to the institutionalization of the concern later.[16] In various years the ICRC sought and received from the RC Conference endorsement of this activity. State parties to the then-existing GCs were part of the vote. Hence the ICRC undertook an initiative to expand its activities beyond armed conflict, received endorsement from the RC Conference, and continued those efforts on a firmer diplomatic footing. There was at least RC Conference approval, a form of collective legitimization, for its course of action. Such resolutions are quasi-legal, involving as they do the vote of states.

The ICRC attempts to improve the conditions of detention for political or security prisoners beyond situations of armed conflict still hinged on state consent case by case, and there still is no treaty on the subject specifically buttressing ICRC efforts. There are treaties and other rules prohibiting torture and other ill-treatment of those detained. Still, there is no global treaty specifically on political prisoners and their monitoring – partly due to definition problems and partly to governmental reluctance to codify international supervision when its own policies toward domestic political opponents might wind up being regulated. The humanitarian game as it was played showed both ICRC initiative and use of the RC network to move things along. However, there is no guaranteed humanitarian progress on the ground, as state sovereignty and consent still control ICRC visits. Chapter 14 is devoted in part to further details on this topic.

Second, one has the example of a debate about a substitute for Protecting Powers in the 1970s. At the Geneva Diplomatic Conference on Reaffirmation and Development IHL (1974–1977), there was an effort to improve the application of the law. The declining use of Protecting Powers (a neutral state appointed by a belligerent to advise on IHL issues) was clear, with only five conflicts after 1949 where Protecting Powers had been appointed.[17] In this context, some proposed that the ICRC become an automatic substitute if, in international armed conflict, a Protecting Power was not named. The ICRC firmly opposed that role, and the proposal was not adopted. The ICRC feared that its image of neutrality might be undercut by being a substitute for a Protecting Power on one side only. Here we have an example of the ICRC blocking a legal development, however well-intentioned, that would have resulted in a legal mandate the organization did not want.

Events in the 1970s did not change the fact that in IHL, the ICRC had already accepted a 1949 mandate that it should, more or less automatically, visit detainees in international armed conflict, whether prisoners of war or civilians. This was supposed to occur on both sides of the international war. Treaty wording in 1949 left it to the ICRC to determine the procedure for the visits, which could and did include a certain amount of discretion, as well as the timing of visits as negotiated with the belligerents. In fact, the legal wording reflected much ICRC practice already established. The ICRC let it be known in 1949 and again in the 1970s that it accepted ahead of time the legal wording being considered by states concerning detention visits in international armed conflict. This was, after all, one of the areas of expertise for the ICRC, and had been since the First World War. But all this was seen by Geneva as different from being an automatic substitute for a Protecting Power that might result in public friction with one side only.[18]

Third, during the Cold war, Red Cross societies from the European communist nations pushed a peace agenda and tried to get the RC

Conference meeting in Istanbul in 1969 to endorse more RC action on certain issues related to peace and war. These National RC Societies, part of totalitarian states run by communist elites in the party-state apparatus, sought to take advantage of such subjects as controversy over the Vietnam War and supposedly offensive or destabilizing nuclear weapons as deployed by NATO. The ICRC, seeking to maintain a focus on *jus in bello* – or law for the process of war – and trying to stay away from *jus ad bellum* – or law regarding the start of war – and its inherent strategic political factors, was convinced it was a bad idea for RC actors to get entangled in what it thought were geopolitical controversies. To make a long and complex subject short for present purposes, the RC Conference did indeed adopt several resolutions on promoting peace. The ICRC then tried to steer discussions in RC bodies to relatively safe means of implementing these resolutions, such as talking about how agreement on IHL and promoting human dignity on a universal basis might prove conducive to global peace and peace agreements. One can see this in its report to the World RC Conference on Peace in Belgrade in 1975.[19]

After the Cold War, as we will see in some detail in especially Chapter 11, more precisely between 1991 and 2016, there was much talk in diplomatic circles about "the triple nexus": the linkage between humanitarian relief, development, and peace. The ICRC maintained its dual position on such matters:

(1) it did not do traditional geopolitical mediation and direct peacebuilding because that was incompatible with neutral humanitarianism; and
(2) cooperation on neutral humanitarianism might spill over into a more general political peace.

A concrete example of the latter might be deduced from events in East Africa in the 2020s. In a region characterized by conflict, the ICRC and its Wat-Hab unit (dealing with water and habitation) was active. Eventually, there was a multinational effort to link immediate steps to make access to water secure with longer-term efforts in the same direction – that is, to respond to pressing water needs for refugees and the displaced so as to create lasting improvements, this latter involving development agencies. In so far as this international effort resolved water conflicts among several nations in a particular water catchment basin, the whole affair could be said to be preventing conflict over water and thus contributing to peace. ICRC neutral humanitarianism was not questioned but rather broadly welcomed, and one could say there was a triple nexus at work. Relief bled into development which produced less conflict and hence peace.

The ICRC is still following this approach. At one point in 2020, the ICRC participated in some diplomatic meetings in Berlin, arguing that if the fighting parties in Libya could agree on some IHL matters, it might constitute a confidence-building measure which would lead to a more general peace agreement as negotiated by someone else. This contemporary ICRC approach to peace issues reflects some field activities in the past. In El Salvador in the 1980s, the ICRC agreed that some RC actors should participate in the organization of meetings designed to wind down the fighting between the government and rebel parties. The RC actors would not participate in the substantive negotiations, obviously political by definition, but would limit themselves to helping to set the diplomatic table – for example, by helping to arrange safe passage for rebel negotiators to and from the peace talks. Later we return to the humanitarian–development–peace nexus.

These brief and thin examples, all of which have a richer history, show that the ICRC's policy positions and actions on the ground are affected by all three of the organization's identities: its independence as a private actor with Swiss governance featuring its own decision-making, its membership in the RC Movement, and its status in public international law. Sometimes the ICRC's complicated position relative to other RC actors and states in a diplomatic conference is helpful, leading to humanitarian progress, and sometimes not. For sure, the RC Movement's fragmented structure, with weak central organs, is part of the picture that comes into play.

III   The ICRC and the Movement: Recognition, and Back to the Principles

The ICRC, which from the 1860s has recognized new RC societies according to set criteria, has never sought to withdraw recognition from a National RC Society for improper behavior. This was true even for the German Red Cross under the Nazis, which was, inter alia, participating in the persecution of various groups and even genocide of Jews during that era.[20]

The subject of withdrawal of recognition is a sinkhole with quicksand. More than a few National RC Societies have failed to demonstrate independent, neutral, and impartial humanitarianism in the face of inhumane policies by their government. The normal pattern for most National RC Societies is to tend to the social needs of national military personnel and other cocitizens and not raise the question about the abusive treatment meted out to "enemies" or even to some domestic version of "the other" – for example, unpopular minorities.

Should one have debated the withdrawal of recognition for National RC Societies in Eastern Europe during the Cold War, which were part of a repressive totalitarian state and lacking in almost all dimensions of supposedly NIIHA programs (by a neutral, independent, impartial, humanitarian actor)? What about the South African Red Cross during the apartheid era? (The South African governmental delegation, but not the National RC Society, was barred from the RC Conference in 1986, after which that government blocked ICRC visits to political prisoners there, after which the RC Conference decided to move in different directions in the future, all of which became mute with the collapse of South African apartheid in the 1990s.) Or, for that matter, what about the American Red Cross when it was: (a) racially segregated; and (b) supportive of the US military when engaged in various atrocities (take, for a historical example, the waterboarding of local insurgents during counter-insurgency operations in the Philippines as a follow-on to the Spanish–American war)?

The fact that many, if not most National RC Societies are less than what is fully required under the concept of NIIHA is actually the best argument for a decentralized RC Movement. A decentralized RC Movement reflective of narrow nationalism and other defects, despite its cosmopolitan principles, allows the ICRC, based in (so it is argued) permanently neutral Switzerland and with an all-Swiss governing board, to undertake delicate humanitarian roles beyond the practical possibilities of almost any National RC Society. (This analysis does not suggest that the ICRC has always been free from its own version of narrow nationalism or social bias, a subject taken up particularly in Chapter 7.)

Had the American Red cross (ARC) demonstrated concern for the treatment meted out to foreign terror suspects held and mistreated by the CIA in its secret prisons after September 11, 2001 (9/11), and for a certain percentage of those held at the Guantanamo military prison and also mistreated in that same era, the ARC would have lost financial support, suffered internal dissension and resignations, and incurred the wrath of various governmental officials. (Depending on the year sampled, about 40 percent of the American public supported torturing terror suspects in the years after 9/11).

The ARC's understanding of its NIIHA status was that it would not openly and directly take sides in partisan or strategic politics, would not be armed or directly participate in armed action, and would medically treat enemy wounded as well as its own side. But showing further concern for the human dignity of alleged detained enemies was left to the ICRC or somebody else. This pattern has been widely duplicated within the Movement. National RC Societies manifest a less demanding understanding of NIIHA principles than the ICRC. They endorse the same seven fundamental principles, including the big four, but interpret them differently.

The ICRC offered medical assistance to the Afghan Taliban after 2001, just as it offered the same to the government side in that long-running armed conflict. The ICRC even arranged outside visits by some donors to showcase a medical facility it supported in Taliban-controlled territory, such was its neutral and independent status in the war in Afghanistan. The ARC cannot practically manifest that same kind of independent, neutral, and impartial action, especially as an auxiliary to US military forces. (After the 2021 collapse of the US military effort in Afghanistan, the ICRC had good relations, at least for a time, with the newly restored Taliban authorities, obtained agreement that its female staff could continue in their roles, at least through 2022, and even did prison visits in some Taliban-run prisons, among other developments – not all of them positive.)

The ICRC favors a ban on all anti-personnel land mines. The ARC could not safely duplicate that policy position, given that the US military insisted in the past that it needed certain kinds of anti-personnel land mines in, for example, South Korea. A decentralized RC Movement, rent especially by narrow nationalism, at least allows some RC action by the ICRC. That is, in principle, an upside to the more general problem of a decentralized RC Movement that is often incapable of fully maximizing its humanitarian potential in a unified way.

The ICRC certainly maneuvered to protect its centrality in the Movement in the early years as well as later. From the beginning, it willingly assumed the role of recognizing the one official aid organization per state that met the emerging rules for recognition. However, it never sought a supranational authority to command the other units. And it has remained reluctant to say that the right to recognize implies the right to derecognize. This initial and continuing decentralized RC structure, with minimal elements of any central authority, essentially remains today with some minor tweaks.

These days, if a National RC Society or one of its subunits blatantly violates RC principles, the ICRC and/or Federation may engage in quiet discussion of the matter – a form of quiet pressure.[21] The formal structure of the RC Movement still reflects the strength of noncosmopolitan nationalism and the staying power of the nation-state system of world affairs. This fact of political psychology remains, despite other facts pushing in a different direction – namely that dangerous pandemics and climate change, or even the sheer scale of human suffering worldwide – require a fully international and coordinated response.

Photograph 5.2 Representatives of the ICRC and IFRC discuss the coordination of relief in Haiti, 2010. Each member of the RC network is independent. There is a constant search for the right formula for improved cooperation and coordination. How to deal with National RC Societies that might violate Fundamental RC Principles is a thorny issue.

In 2022, the RC Federation suspended the Peruvian RC. This was not because of a violation of NIIHA values but because of internal chaos and maladministration. The ICRC, skipping the subject of withdrawal of recognition, continued to interact with the Peruvian RC on certain matters while supporting the RC Federation and the Peruvian RC in efforts at reorganization.

IV   Structural Change, Constant Decentralization

In addition to the International RC Conference itself, two minor tweaks created bodies to help give some institutional coherence to the entire Movement. (The RC Federation holds various international meetings, as noted, which is why the ICRC may value the International Conference every four years more than the Federation and its national RC members.)

The Standing Commission represents the Movement in-between Conference sessions. As such, it becomes the highest deliberative body of the movement for issues that might arise during that period. Created in 1928 to mesh primarily the ICRC with the Federation or union of National Societies (created in 1919 against the wishes of the ICRC as we saw), it consists of two officials from each of those two Geneva agencies plus five members elected by the International Conference from among the National Societies. It lacks the authority to command but helps set the agenda for the International Conference and tries to deal with any controversies that might flare up.

We have already noted in Chapter 1 the ICRC's decisions circa 2014, both to further expand its field operations and to allow, after the fact, to be sure, its president, Peter Maurer, to serve on the board of trustees of the World Economic Forum. The propriety of these new policy positions by the ICRC was challenged in a petitioning letter from some former ICRC officials to the Movement's Standing Commission. The complaint, written by former Director of Operations André Pasquier on behalf of the steering committee of the G-25 (explained in Chapter 1) and on behalf of about forty-five former officials, charged the ICRC with departing from ICRC and Movement statutes requiring neutral and independent humanitarian action.

As already briefly noted, the Standing Commission, under a Canadian chairman, declined to act and did not put the matter on the agenda of either the Standing Commission or the International RC Conference. He therefore deferred to the status quo, even if he might have quietly told the ICRC it would be best if the leadership resolved disputed matters within the ICRC family.

Many in the Movement, especially in the subsequent RC Conference, remained completely unaware of this clash of views about properly interpreting the ICRC's long-standing core mandate and whether RC central organs could and should review relevant ICRC decisions. The subject of new ICRC policy positions was swept under the rug as far as the International RC Conference was concerned. This left the ICRC free to continue to make its decisions relatively freely as a Swiss civil society organization. The absence of formal review by central RC organs does not necessarily mean, however, the absence of informal contacts among key actors. Whether or not key donor governments and leading National RC Societies supported the new ICRC policy directions was not irrelevant. Such factors we eventually address.

Then there is the Council of Delegates, meeting every two years in off years from the International RC Conference – as a mini-international conference minus state representatives. It can highlight this or that theme, help supervise what has already been adopted, and generally give attention to international RC efforts. The Council of Delegates called for a Red Cross Code of Conduct, already mentioned, and thus gave its blessing to a project being discussed within the Movement. The Council called for a review of cooperation within the Movement, and that led to a new internal agreement covered in the next chapter. It gives final approval to the agenda for the International Conference.

The Council takes on added importance on those occasions when the Conference is unable to meet. This has occurred in modern times when questions of participation fracture the Movement (or fracture the Movement further), and the path chosen is simply to sidestep the issue by cancelling the Conference. This happened in 1963, regarding how to deal with two Chinas, and again in 1991 regarding whether and how to seat a delegation representing Palestine. The RC Movement is not only decentralized but also often fragmented. The Fundamental RC Principles are sometimes overwhelmed by the dominance of more powerful national concerns and interests. The National RC Societies are usually sucked in. The ICRC maneuvers in these shifting sands.

V   The ICRC and the Movement: Different Notions of Politics

By 2023, those in the know expected to find an ICRC presence – or maybe a request to be present – where there was international war, internal (civil) war, some mixture of the two, political detention by whatever name, or "other violence" in fragile societies. In any given year, one did find an ICRC program of protection or assistance in about 80–100 countries around the world. One might find the ICRC dealing with migrants, gang violence, Ebola, and other epidemics such as COVID-19, water security, and various other situations where, as a neutral intermediary with certain demonstrated skills, it might fill a void in humanitarian help. As noted, it claimed an open-ended right of initiative that went beyond the mandates given to it by states in the Geneva Conventions or approval by the RC Conference – a self-interpreted mandate limited, to be sure, by wording about neutral humanitarianism. As noted earlier, it offered its services even in the 1962 Cuban Missile Crisis and would be marginally involved diplomatically.[22] It was very active in the COVID-19 pandemic circa 2020, especially regarding prisons but elsewhere as well.

Humanitarian help in conflict situations, trying to advance the dignity and welfare of individuals, does not just happen. It is based on a series of decisions or policy choices about where, when, and how to proceed. There are two ways to view this important subject.

The traditional ICRC view is that the organization is nonpolitical and strictly humanitarian. Hence one has the principles of neutrality, independence, and impartiality in humanitarian action. Moreover, it is supposed to avoid controversies about religious, racial, and other public policy issues that might impinge negatively on its humanitarian role. It observes politics but does not participate. To paraphrase Jean Pictet, the legendary ICRC official who first wrote about RC principles, the ICRC swims in the sea of politics but is careful not to choke on the water. Today the ICRC must stick to this mantra, not only as part of its identity but also as a key to the security and other aspects of its operations on the ground. It needs to be seen as neutral and nonpolitical by conflicting parties. Staff safety in conflicts depends on the Dunantist image.

A second view, a deeper or more realistic view, is that this rigid separation of humanitarian affairs and politics is fiction, if one is candid. While the ICRC might very well seek to avoid strategic and partisan politics as practiced by governmental officials and armed nonstate actors, it practices a type of humanitarian politics itself. Its officials struggle with each other within the organization, with officials of other aid societies, and with various other actors regarding the nature, direction, and control of humanitarian programs. In this view, in sum, the struggle to make and implement humanitarian programs is part of a political process. One might even call it the politics of doing good while being seen as nonpolitical.

In this sense, there is a politics of humanitarianism: a contested series of struggles to take this rather than that decision; to try to get involved here rather than there; to do X rather than Y; or to do X in addition to Y; to overcome this or that opposition to what is needed; to gain the support of others for desired policies. If politics is the struggle over who gets what, when, and how, then humanitarian affairs can be understood within this framework. Within the ICRC, and for the ICRC in relation to other actors, this kind of politics – this kind of policy choice among competing alternatives and actors – is always present and has always been present.

For a first example, and as mentioned already, it is perfectly clear that the ICRC maneuvered to protect its position and limit the role of the new (in 1919) League of Red Cross Societies (now the Federation). The American Red Cross, or parts of it, wanted to push the ICRC to the sidelines and create a new powerful RC League that would run international RC programs in a more centralized fashion. American RC leaders such as Henry P. Davison wanted the new League/Federation to be a kind of muscular World Health Organization combined with UNICEF. He and a few others foresaw much RC assistance in peacetime, partly to undercut the appeals of communism in situations of instability and poverty. Davidson, after all, had been an investment banker and had made lots of money on Wall Street. He did not look kindly on leftist agitation.

The ICRC had other ideas about arrangements within the International Red Cross, even as it shared Davison's aversion to communism. While it was not able to block the creation of the League, it was able to limit its authority. It refused to be pushed into the role of narrow prison inspector and defended its historical role as a central node in the RC network. For now, it suffices to note this subject as an example of humanitarian politics within the Movement. It was a struggle about influence, reputation, and which Movement structure would guarantee certain kinds of action. Concern about effective and neutral humanitarian action was mixed with organizational loyalty – with Swiss and American nationalism far from absent.[23]

Or take another historical example. It is also clear in the 1940s that the top of the ICRC debated how to respond to evidence of Nazi genocide. There were differences of opinion within the ICRC headquarters in 1942, debates and proposals, arguments about this or that, involvement by Swiss Federal officials with primary concerns about *raisons d'état*, and finally, an informal compromise (that was not fully implemented). For now, it suffices to observe a type of humanitarian politics within the ICRC, as various persons struggled to establish a precise humanitarian policy: to speak out or not, to be more discretely dynamic or not. As one participant astutely observed, the future reputation of the ICRC was at stake – which indeed it was, to some degree.[24]

Finally, for now, take the Nigerian Civil War of 1967–1970 involving the asserted independence of Biafra, already mentioned. Under various pressures and competitions, the ICRC decided to fly relief into rebel/Biafran territory without the full and complete permission of Lagos, using planes that were also used separately for gun running, and with RC relief flights sometimes mixed in with flights carrying weapons. This policy choice did not work out well in various ways, with a RC plane shot down by the Nigerian air force and the ICRC sidelined for the rest of the conflict. In Geneva, as in the field, there were shifting policy calculations about power, reputation, and proper legal interpretation. There was humanitarian politics in various times and places – all in the name of nonpolitical action. The ICRC was not trying primarily to endorse the claims of either Lagos or Biafra, but in fact, it tilted toward Biafra and collectively became *persona non grata* in Lagos. That was because of a lack of careful policymaking in Geneva and the field. And this the ICRC belatedly acknowledged by changing its policymaking structure in Geneva. Considerable good was done for a time in the Nigerian-Biafran conflict, but at a price.

One sees the clash of views about what is neutral humanitarianism and what is strategic or geopolitics when the ICRC wants to open an office in-country for its work and the authorities resist. The ICRC views the matter as one of effectiveness in neutral humanitarian action. The authorities sometimes resist because of wanting to keep a free hand in their exercise of power and control. They fear an ICRC office in province X will internationalize the subject and lead to de facto or de jure limits on their freedom of action. What the ICRC wants as a NIIHA actor – to be close to victims of political conflict and effectively respond to their needs – is often evaluated by the government in terms of national power and status.

The difference between neutral humanitarianism and politics often is in the eye of the beholder. One sees this in clashing views of the ICRC and the World Economic Forum. The ICRC leadership saw the matter as one of extending humanitarian diplomacy and increasing awareness of humanitarian affairs among various stakeholders such as for-profit corporations. After all, the Swiss government recognized the WEF as a neutral international organization. Critics of the tight link between the ICRC and the WEF saw the matter as the ICRC endorsing an ideology (neoliberal economics) that seeks to informally and nondemocratically govern the world (through informal power). What was neutral humanitarianism to the ICRC leadership was ill-considered political involvement to the ICRC's critics. There will be further attention to all this in later chapters, even though introduced already in the first chapter.

VI   Conclusion

The issue of Movement cohesion, along with leadership issues, was at the center of the clash of views that played out especially in the 1920s after the Federation (nee League of RC Societies) was created. The same subject of Movement cohesion, along with other issues, resurfaced circa 2022 (as explained in Chapter 6).

In the 1920s, the French RC Society, like many others, supported the ICRC and its vision of a decentralized Movement, reflecting the appeal of narrow nationalism closely linked to the State, and seeing in the Federation of that time too much Anglo-Saxon influence (a persistent bête noire in French thinking, not at all limited to the time of Charles de Gaulle).[25] The International Federation of Red Cross and Red Crescent Societies (IFRC), after all, was the brainchild of the Americans who then arranged for a Brit to be the chief executive. The outcome of this post-1919 debate about the Movement confirmed decentralization, as have all other versions of Movement Statutes since that time. Henry P. Davidson for the American Red Cross may have wanted a League of RC Societies, now the Federation, that was authoritative and all-purpose, but that view did not carry the day. It did not even last a decade. The 1928 Movement Statutes confirmed the decentralized status quo – albeit with the League/Federation added as a member of the Movement.

The organization of broader international relations has been much debated over time, from about 1648 and the Peace of Westphalia until today. The benefits and defects of state sovereignty, or originally the right of each prince to determine the religion of his territory, have morphed into debates about the presumably sacrosanct ideas of national domestic jurisdiction and territorial integrity – but supposedly affected by international law. Along the way there has been attention to the clash of ideas about state authority versus: universal human rights and humanitarian norms, international organizations, the state responsibility to protect human dignity, humanitarian intervention, and many other subjects. Debates about the structure of the RC Movement have followed a parallel track, also reflecting tensions between the independence of national member units and the need for greater centralized coordination. The debates in both domains continue, as shown in Chapter 6.

Notes

1 A. Durand, *The International Committee of the Red Cross* (Geneva: ICRC, 1981), p. 15.
2 For basic facts, see Joint Relief Commission of the International Red Cross Committee, League of Red Cross Societies International Committee of the Red Cross, and League of Red Cross Societies, *Report of the Joint Relief Commission of the International Red Cross, 1941–1946* (Geneva: ICRC and League of Red Cross Societies, 1948). See also C. Rey-Schyrr, *De Yalta a Dien Bien Phu: Histoire du Comité international de la Croix-Rouge 1945–1955* (Geneva: CICR, 2007), p. 42 and passim.
3 C. Moorehead, *Dunant's Dream: War Switzerland and the History of the Red Cross* (New York: Carroll & Graf, 1999), p. 175.
4 See further F. Bugnion, *The International Committee of the Red Cross and the Protection of War Victims* (Geneva: ICRC, 2003), pp. 954–972.
5 A. Lindbloom, *Non-Governmental Organizations in International Law* (Cambridge: Cambridge University Press, 2005).
6 E. Debuf, "Tools to Do the Job: The ICRC's Legal Status, Privileges and Immunities," *International Review of the Red Cross*, 897/898, February 2016, https://international-review.icrc.org/sites/default/files/irc_97_1-2-13.pdf (accessed September 20, 2022). See also C. Shucksmith, *The International Committee of the Red Cross and Its Mandate to Protect and Assist: Law and Practice* (Oxford and London: Hart and Bloomsbury, 2017) for many legal points.
7 I have been misunderstood by at least one of the critics as saying in another publication that the Assembly or its president can decide to do whatever is desired at the moment. What I am staying is that the ICRC in utilizing its right of initiative can decide on different courses of action, limited by the meaning of the words neutral, independent, impartial, humanitarian organization. The limits imposed by these words are not always a matter of agreement.

8 ICRC, *Statutes of the International Red Cross and Red Crescent Movement* (Geneva: ICRC, n.d.) www.icrc.org/en/doc/assets/files/other/statutes-en-a5.pdf (accessed September 20, 2022). The wording in ICRC Statutes is repeated verbatim in Movement Statutes.

9 On the binding nature of some RC Conference resolutions, see F. Bugnion, "The International Conference of the Red Cross and Red Crescent: Challenges, Key Issues and Achievements," *International Review of the Red Cross*, 91/876 (December 2009), https://international-review.icrc.org/sites/default/files/irrc-876-bugnion.pdf (accessed September 20, 2022).

10 J. Pictet, *Red Cross Principles* (Geneva: ICRC, 1956). (Translated from the French, *Les principes de la Croix Rouge* [Geneva: ICRC, 1955].)

11 See the blog post by D. Palmieri, "Principes fondamentaux de la Croix-Rouge: une histoire politique" (2015), www.icrc.org/fr/document/les-principes-fondamentaux-de-la-croix-rouge-une-histoire-politique (accessed September 20, 2022). And see J. Glasman, "The Invention of Impartiality: The History of a Humanitarian Principle, from a Legal, Strategic and Algorithmic Perspective" (n.d.), https://alternatives-humanitaires.org/en/2020/11/13/the-invention-of-impartiality-the-history-of-a-humanitarian-principle-from-a-legal-strategic-and-algorithmic-perspective/ (accessed September 26, 2022). This last author adds an emphasis on statistics that is not necessary.

12 See H. Slim, "You Don't Have to Be Neutral to Be a Good Humanitarian" (2020) www.thenewhumanitarian.org/opinion/2020/08/27/humanitarian-principles-neutrality (accessed September 26, 2022).

13 IFRC, "Code of Conduct for the International Red Cross and Red Crescent Movement and Non-Governmental Organizations in Disaster Relief," www.ifrc.org/our-promise/do-good/code-conduct-international-red-cross-and-red-crescent-movement-and-ngos, (accessed March 18, 2023).

14 See further the ICRC posting: Marina Sharpe, "It's All Relative: The Humanitarian Principles in Historical and Legal Perspective," March 16, 2023, https://blogs.icrc.org/law-and-policy/2023/03/16/humanitarian-principles-historical-legal/ (accessed March 18, 2023).

15 For example, N. Wylie, M. Oppenheimer, and J. Crossland, eds., *The Red Cross Movement: Myths, Practices, Turning Points* (Manchester: Manchester University Press, 2020).

16 J. Moreillon, *Le comité international de la Croix-Rouge et la protection des détenus politiques* (Geneva: CICR, 1975). In 1918 in Russia, the ICRC and a few National RC Societies got involved in the Russian civil war, managing to visit some Russian detainees in that process. In 1919 in Hungary, the ICRC alone made a request to the new government to visit political or security detainees, a request that was granted.

17 Melina Fidelis, "War, Law, and Humanity: The Role of the ICRC in International Armed Conflicts," *Humanitarian Law and Policy*, February 16, 2023, https://blogs.icrc.org/law-and-policy/2023/02/16/war-law-humanity-icrc-international-armed-conflicts/_ (accessed February 16, 2023). The five instances were: 1956 Suez Crisis; 1961 Bizerte Incident; 1961 Goa Clash; 1971 India–Pakistan War; 1982 Falklands/Malvinas War.

18 As an observer at the diplomatic conference in the 1970s, I thought then and still think now that the ICRC position was misguided. The ICRC missed

an opportunity to improve the application of IHL, especially so since the practice of appointing Protecting Powers has progressively declined. Note that under the 1949 law, when automatic visits to POWs is supposed to occur, the ICRC may wind up doing visits on one side only. In the Vietnam War, the ICRC was refused visitation rights to American POWs detained by Hanoi despite the Peoples Republic of Vietnam having consented to the Third Geneva Convention of 1949. Had the ICRC become an automatic substitute for a Protecting Power, it could have provided its legal advice in a discreet process, as did neutral states as Protecting Powers during World War II. Nevertheless, it is true that without being a formal substitute, the ICRC can still exercise its right of initiative to try to give advice to a belligerent about various legal questions.

19 Among multiple sources see J. Moreillon, "The Fundamental Principles of the Red Cross, Peace and Human Rights," *International Review of the Red Cross*, 217 (July–August 1980), pp. 171–183. And see another article by an ICRC official, Y. Sandoz, "The Red Cross and Peace: Realities and Limits," *Journal of Peace Research*, 24/3 (1987), https://journals.sagepub.com/doi/abs/10.1177/002234338702400308 (accessed September 26, 2022).

20 The ten rules for recognition can be found at ICRC, "Conditions for Recognition of National Societies" (2005), www.icrc.org/en/doc/resources/documents/misc/6erk5h.htm (accessed September 26, 2022).

21 In 2023, the head of the Belarus Red Cross openly sided with the invasion of Ukraine, while wearing a military uniform, and endorsed the transfer of Ukrainian children to his country. He was publicly called to account by the RC Federation, with the ICRC quietly backing the Federation.

22 F. Bugnion, *The International Committee of the Red Cross and the Protection of War Victims* (Oxford: Macmillan, 2004), p. 1024.

23 ICRC and ARC leaders of the time both shared an antipathy to leftist agitation and attempts at revolutionary change. The ICRC was socially and politically conservative from 1863 until sometime after the end of World War II, from Moynier and Ador through Huber and Burckhardt, to Rugger, as will be shown. Davison was strongly anti-communist and his commitment to the ARC reflected a conviction that social problems and instability facilitated Bolshevik expansion.

24 For detailed exposition see I. V. Cardia, *Neutralité et Engagement: le comité international de la Croix-Rouge et le gouvernement suisse 1938–1945* (Lausanne: Société d'Histoire de la Suisse Romande, 2012).

25 R. Fathi, "Sovereignty, Democracy and Neutrality: French Foreign Policy and the National-Patriotic Humanitarianism of the French Red Cross, 1919–1928" *Contemporary European History* 1/19 (2021), www.cambridge.org/core/journals/contemporary-european-history/article/sovereignty-democracy-and-neutrality-french-foreign-policy-and-the-nationalpatriotic-humanitarianism-of-the-french-red-cross-19191928/6A0D880113 96A1881FDD6DA98E3A0FAB (accessed September 28, 2022).

6   The Red Cross Movement
Part II – Seville and Syria

> Seville 2.0 is a fair weather document.
>
> Confidential comment to the author, 2022

From the beginning in 1863 and especially from 1919 there has been discussion within the RC network about how to coordinate the component members. One can certainly find evidence of this continuing discussion in contemporary times – such as debates and resolutions in the Council of Delegates in 2013. In 2015, a major step occurred when the Council adopted a long resolution on Strengthening Movement Coordination and Cooperation (SMCC).[1] The subject began to acquire more importance for two reasons: a quest for greater impact in emergencies, and because of competition with other humanitarian actors whether these were intergovernmental organizations or in the NGO world. Things limped along in the usual Movement fashion. It takes a long time to find consensus over 190 independent actors – Oman being the only UN member state never to have a national RC society.[2] But the discussions picked up steam in the spring of 2019 when the leadership of the Federation began to push for a revision of the Seville Agreement of 1997 and its Supplemental Measures.

I   Some Facts

In the fall of 2019, so I am told, the ICRC's President Maurer wrote a letter to all the National RC Societies giving the ICRC vision of the future of Movement coordination. The basic idea in the letter, apparently, was not very controversial in the abstract, namely that the Movement should develop better flexible coordination among independent units in shifting coalitions of the willing. He might have taken that initiative when he did to head off other thinking about the Movement that would be more distasteful to the ICRC.

Although Maurer's 2019 letter to the National RC Societies apparently failed to even mention the RC Federation (the Federation was

114

presumably noted in some annexes), the two Geneva headquarters agreed on a common work stream, advised by a group of 15 National RC Societies.[3] The two Geneva HQs established some common ground, even though they were two different kinds of organizations with differing histories. But a more cohesive Movement, functioning with more integration in predictable ways across different cases, was clearly not a simple matter.

Some insiders remarked privately that the ICRC and the Movement were "leaving money on the table." That is, the ICRC and the Movement could increase their funding by more attention to shared action, making a more persuasive case for a greater impact on the global humanitarian crisis. UN humanitarian actors such as the World Food Program, UNICEF, and the UNHCR (refugee office) were getting a large share of global humanitarian funding, perhaps about 40 percent in a given year. RC actors competed with these UN agencies for the humanitarian dollar, not to mention with private actors such as World Vision, MSF, and similar NGOs. As mentioned in the Epilogue, in the early stages of the war in Ukraine starting in February 2022, Red Cross actors got about 10 percent of humanitarian donations directed to that international armed conflict.

A major point to be dealt with was how to treat what is called the Seville Agreement and its follow-on measures. Against the background of long friction between the ICRC and the Federation after 1919, with the established ICRC often feeling – rightly or wrongly – that the parvenu Federation was trying to encroach on its turf, in 1997, at a meeting in Seville, Spain, all RC member units agreed on a set formula for Movement duties. If an international response was required in a "man-made" disaster, the ICRC was to be the lead RC agency. The Federation would be the lead agency for a similar natural or industrial disaster. However, both roles would depend on the relevant National RC Society stating that it could not, itself, handle the problem and would need international help. And the whole arrangement would also depend on various RC actors implementing in good faith what had been agreed to on paper.

That the Seville Agreement did not work all that well can be seen in the fact that various supplemental measures were negotiated over the years, trying to fine-tune the original agreement in order to iron out the coordination problems that arose. The problem of coordinated RC action on the ground remained enough of a problem so that at the time of the 2019 Maurer letter, one had to decide whether to renegotiate Seville in detail, make some summary adjustments once again, or focus on practical coordination across different situations. The ICRC preferred the latter approach. But some views were initially otherwise at the Federation and in the RC Standing Commission – and then the Council of Delegates – reflecting disparate views among the National RC Societies.

One can summarize the leading factors at issue in discussions about the Movement.

(1) The 1997 Seville Agreement, even with supplemental measures, had never worked all that well.

(2) Many National RC Societies were tired of perceived bickering between the two Geneva HQs.

(3) Globally, there was a push for the "localization" of relief actors and a corresponding effort to avoid any taint of colonial or imperial structures in international relief action. This meant more emphasis on the National RC Societies.

(4) At the same time, many National RC Societies lacked NIIHA credibility and capability; many were not truly committed to NIIHA values but rather interested in a narrow and self-interested nationalism, not to mention self-aggrandizement by certain NS leaders. Some National Societies were very weak in terms of capacity for effective action.

(5) The ICRC was still among the most widely respected units of the Movement, with the best and broadest high-level contacts among public authorities – and did not want changes that could threaten its status and traditional activities.

Not surprisingly, in an era when there was much attention to "localization" and avoidance of neocolonialism in international humanitarian affairs, as noted earlier, many National RC Societies asserted their importance within the Movement. To achieve this, some sought to revisit the Statutes of the Movement, which was anathema to the ICRC. In fact, the wording of those Statutes required ICRC approval for major changes. The ICRC seemed sympathetic to closer links with some National RC Societies in at least certain field operations where a reliable partner existed. After all, the ICRC's primary donor, the United States, was making much public noise about the importance of localization.[4] But the ICRC feared any change in legalities that might undermine its own "sovereignty" and freedom about how to interpret its humanitarian right of initiative. The ICRC was open to certain changes and more voluntary coordination, but it had its red lines that were not to be crossed. It was careful not to appear opposed to all change, but clearly was worried about some aspects of the discussion concerning a more coordinated Movement.

The ICRC was only in favor of more attention to coordinated impact for the Movement as long as certain conditions were obtained: (1) there would be no formal change in any Statutes, and certainly no change in the ICRC's core right of initiative; (2) the ICRC would continue to emphasize its traditional protection roles, and even when working more closely with National RC Societies would continue to stress such matters as detention visits, tracing of missing persons, restoring family links, and forensic science – all areas of established ICRC expertise; (3) the ICRC would continue its role as the guardian of IHL, whatever that meant; (4) both the ICRC and the Federation would help develop the National RC Societies.

If one talked to many ICRC officials and staff, it seemed that de facto there was already a more coordinated RC presence in many places. For example, in conflict situations in Ethiopia, the ICRC was already trying to cooperate closely with the National RC Society, especially in relief, economic security, and medical aid matters. At the same time, there might be ICRC contacts and programs with armed nonstate parties, sometimes in cooperation with RC partners. For example, in Zimbabwe, it was already working with the National RC Society to enhance services for tracing of persons, even though there was no large-scale violence in the area. For example, in Central America, it was already working with various organizations, inside and outside the Movement, to provide various services to migrants – some of whom were on the move in search of better jobs or to escape the ravages of natural disasters, not necessarily fleeing violence. There were cases, for example, of cooperation between the ICRC and the Federation, both acting in support of the National RC Society. Even, for example, in Venezuela during the Maduro era, where the various RC actors initially undertook separate roles amidst some competition and suspicion, there was eventually improved RC communication among partners even if not fully integrated cooperation.

It went without saying that in some situations, the National RC Society was an unreliable partner for the ICRC. That had always been the case. But in other cases, the local RC personnel had good contacts with authorities or even rebel parties and thus offered advantages to the ICRC for beneficial impact. In a few cases, the National RC Society even participated in the delicate matter of prison visits to security prisoners. In some situations, there was a written agreement on who was to do what among the ICRC, Federation, and National RC Society (sometimes more than one). But other situations were decidedly otherwise.

II   Seville 2.0

In early summer 2022, the Council of Delegates endorsed a new agreement on RC coordination for international action. It was called Seville 2.0 and replaced the original Seville Agreement and its Supplemental

Measures. More than two years of discussion and negotiation produced a document that:

(1) reflected the times (or was politically correct) in providing much rhetoric about the centrality of the National RC Societies;

(2) did not change ICRC traditional roles under both Movement Statutes and IHL and thus did not cross ICRC red lines; and

(3) left all Movement members still legally free and independent, with the application of the agreement dependent on the goodwill and faithful attention to RC Principles by these members, aided by the historically weak oversight and assistance by Movement organs. (The suspension of Peru from the RC Federation in 2022, mentioned above, might indicate a strengthening of Movement cohesion.)

Seville 2.0 could be seen as significant because it did no fundamental damage to traditional RC activities, including those of the ICRC. It did not authorize any National RC Society to dictate to the ICRC (or Federation) when doing what the Geneva HQs traditionally had done. It also did not disrupt the Movement, maintaining the possibility of cohesion and cooperation. Encouraging improvement in voluntarily coordinated operations might still be an advance in historical terms. It avoided any utopian effort to impose uniformity of action in a top-down command and control process.

The agreement could be seen as insignificant in that most of the old core problems remained, centered on the lack of NIIHA values and effectiveness by several National RC Societies and lack of authority by the two Geneva headquarters – or the International Conference – to correct things. *Le plus ça change, le plus c'est la même chose* – the more things change the more they remain the same. That said, there was a committee at the Federation on integrity with the title of "Compliance and Mediation."[5] This was the body that suspended the RC Society in Peru. It had done the same a bit earlier, essentially for the same reasons of internal malfeasance, regarding the Greek Red Cross. But sanctioning the Greek or Peruvian Red Cross for improper procedures and sloppy finances was decidedly not the same as compelling a National Society to adhere to RC Principles in a conflict situation, as demonstrated by the case of Syria below.

As for key specifics, right from the start in Article 1, Seville 2.0 stipulates that in international RC action, nothing in the Accord affects either the Movement Statutes or the Geneva Conventions and Protocols. This means, inter alia, that ICRC core activity remains as authorized and endorsed as before. To be clear, Article 1.4 says that "the provisions of the Accord will in no case be interpreted as limiting or modifying the particular

Photograph 6.1 A new agreement in 2022 on Movement cooperation tried to promote more coherence among RC agencies without getting into the controversy of changing legal or other fundamental factors. In some countries and programs there was good coordination between the ICRC and a National RC Society, as captured here in Venezuela in 2018 regarding a public health program. At other times and in other places and activities, coherence among members was much lower. The new scheme, Seville 2.0, looked good on paper but, as with past agreements, depended for its effectiveness on voluntary cooperation in good faith.

role and competence of each member [of the Movement] as found in the Geneva Conventions and Protocols and Movement Statutes."

Why then have a new Accord? Article 2 notes the purpose: to provide "guidelines about operational or functional cooperation." In this regard, the Accord intends "to reinforce the central role of the National Societies … since these National Societies form the core of the Movement and are a vital force for it." All of this would arguably position the Movement as a "pillar" of the global humanitarian system.

Lest anyone be confused, Article 3 notes that the basic norms of the Movement remain unchanged, they being the Fundamental RC Principles, the Statutes of the Movement (which faithfully reflect ICRC statutes), and the Geneva Conventions and Protocols.

Whereas Seville 1.0 mentioned lead actors (e.g., the ICRC in conflict situations requiring an international response), Seville 2.0 in Article 4 speaks of facilitators and cofacilitators. Or, the idea of a definite leader is replaced by the notion of a lead facilitator or convenor who coordinates voluntary action among equals. In the case of a conflict situation requiring a Movement response, the ICRC would be a cofacilitator along with the relevant National Society. Hence the position of the two Geneva HQs is rhetorically reduced, without changing the function of what the ICRC was already authorized to do in the Statutes and IHL.

This language reflects, by and large, what was already happening in, say, Ukraine from February 2022, where both the ICRC and the National Society were highly active in an international armed conflict. The rest of the Movement was supposed to support what these two Movement members were doing, and where the ICRC continued with a special role regarding those victims/beneficiaries falling under IHL such as POWs, interned civilians, those in occupied territory, and so on. All Movement members were supposed to coordinate to avoid redundancy and lack of focus.

The first part of a very long Article 5 puts new wine in old bottles. The wording changes, but the division of labor remains the same. The ICRC is seen as a cofacilitator in political conflicts and their direct results. Meanwhile, the Federation is seen as a cofacilitator in other emergencies (such as natural and industrial disasters). They work with the local and other National Societies. Presumably, old competitions are set aside. Notably, the Federation gives up the desire, real or imagined, to take over all assistance/relief, which would have hypothetically left the ICRC with only traditional protection activities narrowly defined. So presumably, this point of friction, however and whenever it existed, is definitively put to rest.

Article 5 also further specifies some details of coordination, noting that the specifics can vary, but articulates the goals of less competition, more coherent communication, and in general, a coordinated Movement presence in an international emergency or crisis situation – whether that might be a war about the status of Ukraine or an earthquake in Afghanistan or Turkey. Of particular interest for present purposes is Article 5.3.b, where the ICRC role is described as a cofacilitator who furnishes guidelines in political conflicts that cause Movement action to conform with RC Principles and IHL. An interesting question is how the ICRC might achieve this vis-à-vis a National Society inclined otherwise. This is discussed further below.

Article 9 endorses coordinated fundraising where circumstances permit.

Article 10 has nine parts trying to specify how to achieve a common communications policy across the members of the Movement, where possible.

Article 12 reiterates the importance of the RC Fundamental Principles, whereas Article 14 speaks of the importance of integrity. These two articles, taken together, can be read as an attempt to pressure the National Societies to live up to NIIHA values.

Article 14.5 indicates that if there is a problem within the Movement regarding the RC's fundamental principles or integrity, the ICRC and the Federation will consult on the subject and discuss matters with the relevant National Society. This wording reflects current practice.

Article 15 indicates that all members of the Movement commit to the application of the Accord. Both the ICRC and the Federation supervise the resolution of any differences that could create an obstacle to good cooperation of the Movement. So, the application of the Accord depends on good faith commitment by the members rather than any formal enforcement provisions. No new authority is given to any central organ to enforce any or all specific provisions, whether that might be the Conference, the Council of Delegates, or the Standing Commission. The Movement remains decentralized with legally independent members who presumably cooperate voluntarily in keeping with the Fundamental RC Principles and other norms such as the 2022 Accord.

The Accord is essentially what Peter Maurer asked for in his letter to National Societies in the fall of 2019: A coalition of the willing who agree to cooperate for enhanced coordination, with the specifics varying from situation to situation and without fundamental change for the ICRC operating under IHL, the Fundamental Principles, and current statutes.

In terms of aspirations, there is not much to quibble with in the 2022 Accord called Seville 2.0. At the end of the day, the wording fits with many emerging practices already visible in Niger, Venezuela, or Ukraine, for example. Apparently, there are some good aspects, such as (perhaps) improved relations between the ICRC and the Federation. But the potential for continuing problems is clear enough, indicated by a review of what happened in Syria. As one well-informed alumnus of the ICRC said privately, Seville 2.0 is a fair weather document. It stipulates what should be. What actually transpires for and within the Movement is often something else.

III   The Case of Syria

In the future enterprising historians who can access various documents should have much of interest to say about the various RC actors and violence in Syria during 2011–2022. The government of Bashar al-Assad required outside humanitarians to provide assistance only through the

Syrian Arab Red Crescent (SARC), a recognized Movement member since the 1940s. This was a unique situation as far as the Movement was concerned.

In the early days of the violence, when the government cracked down hard on street protestors demanding a more effective and less autocratic regime, the SARC, which sought to display some independence and manifested some independent local units, tried to respond to the medical needs of injured protestors. Some of these independent local SARC personnel were fired on or otherwise attacked by government security forces.[6]

Over time the Assad regime tightened its control over at least parts of SARC, replacing some top leaders and forcing out some other personnel. Some of those active in SARC in keeping with NIIHA values were detained, and some were apparently tortured. SARC – or at least parts of SARC – became, in the words of one ICRC staff member, just another government agency. Early on, several foreign Arab regimes, of Sunni identification, refused to support – or reduced their support to – the SARC because it was perceived as controlled by the Alawite/Shia Assad regime.[7]

Anne Sparrow wrote in 2018 in the US widely respected magazine *Foreign Affairs*:

The [Syrian Arab] Red Crescent has long been tied to the Syrian state apparatus, and any hint of its independence was snuffed out after 2011, when the government put Red Crescent elections on indefinite hold, purged independent board members, and dismissed qualified staff. Intelligence agents posing as volunteers also infiltrated the organization, according to ex–Red Crescent volunteers that I spoke with. After these changes, the Red Crescent's new unofficial policy was to deliver aid according to partisan criteria. Staff and volunteers who violated these rules were detained and tortured, even killed.[8]

Some ICRC personnel disagree with this interpretation, considering it too broad and without nuance. They argue that parts of SARC remained relatively independent and committed to NIIHA values. They note that some seventy SARC staffers were killed in trying to assist victims in the Syrian violence. It is not clear which armed actor killed them.

The same author writing in the same publication had already criticized UN agencies such as OCHA and the WHO for prioritizing cooperation with Damascus, and hence being allowed to stay in the country, over a more assertive approach to humanitarian need in the Syrian internal armed conflict. What she wrote about UN agencies might logically pertain to ICRC decisions in the Syrian context:

The defense offered by UN agencies operating in Damascus when challenged for accepting these [government] limitations – that some aid is better than none – is wrong. When the bulk of aid is controlled by the government and is preferentially directed, the main effect is to relieve the government of responsibility for caring for its own citizens, freeing up resources for it to pursue its military strategy of targeting civilians in politically unsympathetic areas, rendering a bad situation there a great deal worse.[9]

Some ICRC personnel also disagree with this evaluation, believing that a great deal of humanitarian good was accomplished, mainly in assistance, in a terribly complicated and brutal situation.

Indeed early on after 2011, RC Movement aid, as was true of UN aid, was sometimes blocked by the security forces, or allowed to proceed only to loyal areas, or distributed in such a way that those Syrians suspected of disloyalty had to report to police stations before receiving aid. It appears to be the case that some of the injured protestors were arrested, even tortured, directly after being taken to hospital by SARC ambulances, in hospitals supported by the ICRC.

There was also the matter of graft and corruption.[10] Circa 2022 in the UN Security Council, the Russians vigorously argued that all humanitarian aid to northwest Syria, where the Assad regime lacked control, should be channeled through Damascus and not brought in cross-border through Turkey. A primary reason for this Russian stance, emphasizing cross-line aid rather than cross-border help, was to allow Damascus to manipulate exchange rates and rake off a portion of the aid. In the past, some foreign humanitarian assistance and funding never reached the victims. (As of the time of writing, the Russians allowed some continuation of cross-border aid from Turkey through one portal but only for six months. As noted, this arrangement was adjusted for a time after the 2023 Turkish earthquakes.)[11]

The ICRC had made the early decision to comply with the governmental edict to channel all humanitarian assistance through the SARC. In this policy stance it was supported by other units of the RC Movement, such as the Red Cross Societies in Britain, Denmark, Norway, and so on, which supplied funds or personnel to the ICRC-SARC effort. By so doing, Geneva could distribute a large amount of emergency assistance in areas controlled by the regime or sometimes in areas still contested. As time went on, it was able to negotiate access for relief efforts in some rebel-held areas. Some water projects served both government and rebel areas and were allowed to continue uninterrupted. Undoubtedly, the ICRC and its Movement partners did some good.

At times, it operated in northeast Syria under the control of the Kurdish Democratic Forces. After the weakening of the Islamic State Group (DAESH or ISIS) in that area, the ICRC and its Movement partners expanded activities with more personnel, including establishing a field hospital, all requiring Damascus' consent, which was not easy to accomplish. Areas controlled by Turkish forces were another matter.

Without a doubt, ICRC operations that achieved some good were also, at times, manipulated by governmental policies requiring cooperation with the SARC. ICRC NIIHA values were compromised to some extent in Syria. The price of delivering assistance was a lack of full independence and, therefore, lack of total neutrality and impartiality – certainly immediately after the start of violence but in more complex ways after that. The ICRC also hired on its staff in Syria the daughter of a regime security official.[12]

In 2017 the ICRC president dealt with these complexities in an in-house interview that was relatively accurate, even if couched in careful diplomatic language.[13] Parts of it are worth quoting at length. He said, apropos of Syria from 2011:

We faced a dilemma: either to do what we could with those belligerents that were engaging with us, or opt not to engage at all. In some critical instances and in the interest of saving lives, we decided to continue to work with one side in the absence of a readiness from the other side. But we never gave up either our efforts or our willingness to engage with all sides and to get a "licence to operate" in all places where people were affected by the conflict.

The Syrian crisis also illustrates the legal landscape of humanitarian action today – the Geneva Conventions and UN Resolution 46/182 on "Strengthening the Coordination of Humanitarian Emergency Assistance of the United Nations," which places humanitarian activities within the context of State sovereignty. Under IHL, there is no unfettered right of access for humanitarian organizations. They must seek and obtain the consent of the State on whose territory they intend to carry out their humanitarian activities.

Sovereignty is the frame within which the international community has decided it wants humanitarian activities to be set...

Although the ICRC has a mandate to fulfil its mission in a neutral, impartial and independent way, and although that mandate is conferred upon it by the four Geneva Conventions of 1949, by which all States are bound, as an organization we must nevertheless have the consent of a State if we are to operate in its territory...

Theoretically, you can always criticize the construct that humanitarian organizations are not automatically granted unrestricted access, but it's what the international community has decided. I'm very much aware that there are organizations which have decided to operate in territory held by non-State armed groups without the consent of the Syrian government, that they have operated from neighbouring countries and with a licence from neighbouring countries. We also recognize that the UN Security Council has made efforts to mitigate the problems in deciding on procedures for cross-border operations applicable to UN agencies and implementing partners only. Ultimately, however, none of these efforts has really changed the nature of the challenges under which we are operating today and which leave some populations outside the scope of the ICRC's humanitarian services.

The last few years have confirmed that the best possible avenue has been to engage with the Syrian government, as, by doing so, we have increasingly been able to do more for all Syrians, including those on the other side of the front lines, gaining access to populations living under the authority and control of armed groups, while maintaining the consent and trust of the Syrian government.

In the last two years, we have considerably increased our operations across front lines – but still not to the extent we would like. In that sense, I do recognize that consensus-building and negotiating across front lines in order to be able to work on both sides is very time-consuming, but it's a concept that very much defines the ICRC, and one which we cannot easily set aside.

The international community has tried to solve this conundrum. In the last fifteen years or so, there has been a lot of discussion around concepts like responsibility to protect and humanitarian intervention, and attempts to define the threshold beyond which States and international organizations would be allowed to respond to important humanitarian crises without the consent of the territorial State. The problem is that these lively discussions have not crystallized into recognized and agreed legal norms, thus illustrating the lack of consensus on this issue within the international community.

The crisis in Syria and the lack of adequate response to the needs of the Syrian people have forced humanitarian actors and political actors to think more about what is fundamentally wrong with the system. While many would agree that the conflict and its impact have taken an unacceptable toll on civilians, there is very little appetite within the international community at the moment to engage openly about other ways of delivering humanitarian assistance in the absence of the consent of the territorial State.

...

A specific aspect of the situation in Syria was the decision by the Syrian government that the SARC was to be not only an auxiliary of the government but also the coordinator of international humanitarian assistance for Syria. That was a political decision.

One can always question whether it was a wise decision or not, but as a political decision it has shaped the humanitarian reality since the beginning of the conflict. This framework gave the SARC the authority to coordinate all the international assistance coming into the country, including via the UN system, the Movement and NGOs. So, it's not only because we are a member of the Movement that we work in this way with the SARC.

We would certainly, as in any other place in the world, prioritize working with a National Society to the extent that we can. And we would ensure the work is divided up so that the National Society is covering certain needs, while the international component of the Movement is covering certain other important activities. That's generally how we operate in most contexts. But I don't know of any other context in which the National Society, as a Movement partner, has been not only an auxiliary of the government but also the chief coordinator of international humanitarian assistance.

This leaves us with a situation in which a lot of our assistance is delivered in cooperation with the SARC, as is a lot of the UN assistance. In practical terms, there has also been a level of trust established between the ICRC and the SARC, which has meant that the ICRC has been able to work alone in certain instances, as has the SARC on certain issues. This is particularly true in places of detention, for instance, where the SARC is not present.

The role of the SARC as the coordinating body for humanitarian assistance in Syria is part of the complexity and also the special nature of the Syrian situation ... [W]e have had to adapt to the particular situation there. In the meantime, the ICRC and the SARC have become mutually dependent: while we cannot operate without the agreement, consent and cooperation of the SARC, the SARC cannot cover the needs of the people without cooperating with the UN system and the Movement.[14]

Unfortunately, there is no evidence that ICRC assistance, as coordinated by SARC, led to any major breakthroughs in traditional protection. Some ICRC prison visits occurred. But those who needed ICRC protection the most in detention did not get it. Despite its desires and démarches, the ICRC was blocked, and large numbers were tortured and killed by Assad's security agencies.[15]

There is no doubt that parts of the SARC failed to live up to a rigorous understanding of NIIHA values in its activities, with early efforts in this direction falling victim to much governmental control over time. Other units within SARC proved more faithful to NIIHA values. ICRC public protests against the Assad regime for its specific violations of IHL in an internal armed conflict and its breaches of Red Cross principles cannot be found in the public record. There were ICRC public protests of a general nature about the conduct of the war but not about specific Assad policies – or those of Russia, which deepened its involvement in 2015. This is why it will be imperative to eventually establish the nature of ICRC quiet diplomacy.

The ICRC head of delegation in Syria told the *Washington Post* in 2013:

It is important to note that we need authorizations both to move personnel and goods. We are able to move both in many parts of the country, but would very much want to reach further. The security situation sometimes makes movements impossible, but frequently, the reason we are unable to reach critical destinations is the lack of authorization. This is particularly true for medical supplies destined for opposition-held areas. In some besieged areas around Damascus and the city centre of Homs, no humanitarian access has been authorized even in situations in which – based on the ICRC's own assessment – it would have been safe to deliver.[16]

There were other press releases or messages on Twitter in which the ICRC said quite clearly that more civilians needed its assistance. Still, the organization did not have permission to move, lacking as it did authorization from the Syrian government. The ICRC staff member quoted above in the *Washington Post* became *persona non grata* to the Assad

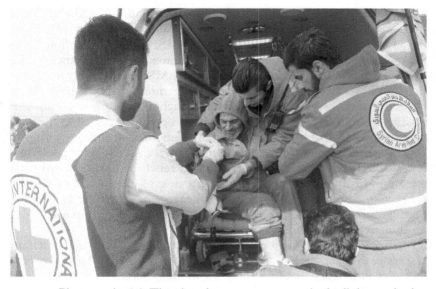

Photograph 6.2 The Assad government required all humanitarian assistance to be channeled through the Syrian Arab Red Crescent Society (SARC). The ICRC worked closely with the SARC – here both agencies are helping civilians near Aleppo in 2016. The SARC was not fully independent but rather subject to political limitations imposed by Damascus. This compromised the position of the ICRC on some matters. By comparison, MSF refused to fully coordinate with SARC but wound up not being able to have much impact on the situation.

regime and was replaced by Geneva with someone who kept a lower profile. Some ICRC personnel believe that over time, the organization achieved considerable good in that long-running and brutal conflict. In contrast, others stress the lack of full ICRC independence – resulting in inroads on neutrality and impartiality.

Any ICRC quiet efforts contesting politicization of humanitarian activities, which included intentional attacks on medical facilities and personnel, and the use of chemical weapons, particularly against civilians, will be important for historians to establish when archives allow. Undoubtedly, the Assad government, supported mainly by Russia and Iran, adopted a brutal approach to fighting opponents.[17] Fully independent and genuinely neutral and impartial humanitarian aid on a broad scale was essentially impossible in that context. The ICRC was periodically or partially restricted in the face of Assad's insistence that SARC control humanitarian assistance.

Relevant to the ICRC experience of working with the SARC in Syria from 2011–2022 is the record of Doctors Without Borders (MSF) in the same conflict in the same time frame. MSF refused to comply with the governmental demand to link all its humanitarian assistance to the SARC. From outside Syria, mainly Turkey, MSF tried to rely on unauthorized cross-border operations to deliver most of its medical aid in northeast and northwest Syria. This approach did not prove feasible on a large scale over time. MSF found itself operating almost entirely in areas not controlled by the government. Sometimes it did so by remote contact – that is, phone or video – with partners inside rebel areas. Thus, it consulted with doctors long distance in rebel medical clinics, which were eventually moved underground because of intentional attacks by the government and its allies. Even so, because of attacks by the Islamic State group and other extremists, it was forced to curtail many, if not most, activities it desired.[18]

MSF was able, at the end of the day, to provide much less humanitarian assistance in Syria than the ICRC working with the SARC. However, critics believe the ICRC became complicit in many severe violations of IHL and RC principles by continuing to link to the SARC within parameters set by Assad officials. MSF escaped these charges of complicity and bias by maintaining more independence from the government and SARC. But MSF did less humanitarian good compared to ICRC-SARC operations. (Mercy Corps, based in the United States, was also barred from Syrian government areas for refusing to coordinate relief aid with the SARC.)

Seville 2.0 contains nothing to prevent future cases like that of Syria 2011–2022. The wording of the Accord puts rhetorical pressure on members of the Movement to respect IHL and RC Fundamental Principles. But where a National RC Society, such as SARC, acts otherwise, at least in part at the bidding of its government, with dire consequences for NIIHA behavior, the Movement cannot offer an adequate response. Indeed, in Syria, the ICRC itself engaged in a controversial trade-off, violating the fundamental principles to some degree in exchange for being allowed to deliver considerable if partial assistance, and a very minimum of protection that did not stop significant amounts of cruelty, torture, and political killing. But emulating MSF and opting for purity of principle at the cost of being marginalized in humanitarian matters was not a perfect alternative.

Later, in Myanmar, MSF seems to have adopted the approach of the ICRC in Syria. An MSF report states that MSF "has had to compromise heavily on the principles of independence and impartiality in order to operate in Rakhine. For example, project locations for both regular and emergency interventions were often chosen by authorities, and not always based on medical needs. MSF was also not allowed to conduct independent needs assessments."[19] This is what happened to the ICRC for much of the time in Syria.

MSF was prepared to openly state, with regret, how it was being compelled to violate NIIHA values in Myanmar to be able to do some good. While MSF was eventually candid about the general disregard for IHL in that conflict,[20] the ICRC in Syria clung to the myth that it had acted mostly in accord with NIIHA principles. What it did, in actuality, was do the good it was allowed to do, while, as an establishment humanitarian organization linked to public international law, it deferred to the controlling principle of state sovereignty and state consent.

Syria was not Biafra. The ICRC was not going to try to deliver assistance without the explicit consent of the Assad government, which mostly used the SARC as an instrument of partisan and strategic political calculation.

IV   Conclusion

From 1863, until today, the ICRC has never been able to work out a completely satisfactory formula for relations with all the other members of the RC Movement that both preserved its NIIHA goals and accomplishments and maximized the impact of the Movement as a whole. Maybe it just couldn't be done. ICRC's full independence to interpret its humanitarian right of initiative as it wished, crucial both to a widely respected neutral humanitarian protection (even if tainted by mistakes now and then) and a reputation for effectiveness in assistance, meant a decentralized Movement that struggled to be taken seriously as Movement. On the other hand, a Movement with more formalized central authority meant less freedom for the ICRC to project itself as a reliable and respected NIIHA actor.

In the view of the ICRC about 2020, the way forward was more coordinated fundraising and communication and more operational cooperation when possible *sur place*, but no significant change in decentralized authority within the Movement. Above all for the ICRC, the pursuit of more Movement coherence had to occur without a change in fundamental norms as found in IHL, the RC principles, and current statutes. That proved to be an arduous effort that resulted in the 2022 Accord known as Seville 2.0. There certainly was more lip service to the centrality of the National RC Societies in Movement affairs, which fits with the anti-colonial, anti-imperial times. The ICRC is as "woke" as any other agency in being sensitive to past discrimination, especially in the era of European colonialism. But the rhetorical adjustment to changing contexts did not alter some realities. Chief among these was the possibility of the National RC Society that violated the NIIHA norms to varying degrees, at the bidding of an illiberal or brutal government uninterested in broad human dignity.

This could cause the ICRC to make a Faustian bargain, violating NIIHA values itself, at least sometimes, to achieve minimal but manipulated attention to humanitarian concerns. What the ICRC wound up doing in Syria after 2011, ran parallel to its record in Abyssinia in the 1930s. As discussed in the next chapter, the ICRC remained silent in public about many specific violations of IHL and RC Principles while doing some good on the ground. However, the calculations in Geneva were not the same in the two cases.

Seville 2.0 is undoubtedly an improvement over past attempts at coordinating Movement activities, even if real problems remain.

Notes

1 Council of Delegates of the International Red Cross and Red Crescent Movement, "Strengthening Movement Coordination and Cooperation (SMCC): Optimizing the Movement's Humanitarian Response," Progress Report, December 7, 2015, https://rcrcconference.org/app//uploads/2015/03/CoD15_SMCC_report-FINAL-EN.pdf (accessed September 27, 2022).
2 In 2023 the government in Nicaragua closed down the National RC Society there. Its substitute agency was not automatically accepted into the RC Movement because of lack of independent neutrality. Thus there are currently 191 National RC Societies.
3 Members of the advisory group were from Palestine, Kuwait, Lebanon, the Philippines, India, Australia, Ukraine, France, Sweden, the USA, Panama, Costa Rica, South Sudan, Kenya, and The Gambia. The RC Standing Commission had observer status. From summer 2021, the ICRC and the Federation dealt directly with all the National RC Societies in the negotiations, this advisory group having served its primary purpose of initial input.
4 M. Igoe, "Devex Newswire: Samantha Power Goes Local" (2021), www.devex.com/news/devex-newswire-samantha-power-goes-local-102027 (accessed September 28, 2022). The ICRC was certainly aware of her views, as she interacted directly with the ICRC president on occasion. In the global humanitarian system, there was discussion about whether a local affiliate of an international institution was really "local" for purposes of broader sharing of funding.
5 The case of the Belarus RC has been referred to this Compliance and Mediation Committee in 2023 for actions that appeared to violate the RC principles of independence and neutrality. The head of that RC Society was openly supporting controversial and indeed illegal policies by both Belarus and Russia. So there was a new effort to enforce RC principles and correct improper action by National RC Societies.

6 Syria Justice and Accountability Centre, "Inside the Syrian Arab Red Crescent" (2019), https://syriaaccountability.org/inside-the-syrian-arab-red-crescent/ (accessed September 28, 2022) and A. Sparrow, "Syria's Assault on Doctors" (2013), www.nybooks.com/daily/2013/11/03/syria-assault-doctors/ (accessed September 28, 2022).

7 *The New Humanitarian*, "Syrian Red Crescent Fighting Perceptions of Partiality" (2012), www.thenewhumanitarian.org/report/95204/analysis-syrian-red-crescent-fighting-perceptions-partiality (accessed September 28, 2022).

8 A. Sparrow, "How the UN humanitarian Aid Has Propped Up Assad: Syria Shows the Need for Reform" (2018), www.foreignaffairs.com/articles/syria/2018-09-20/how-un-humanitarian-aid-has-propped-assad (accessed September 28, 2022).

9 A. Sparrow, "Aiding Disaster: How the United Nations' OCHA Helped Assad and Hurt Syrians in Need" (2016), www.foreignaffairs.com/articles/syria/2016-02-01/aiding-disaster (accessed September 28, 2022).

10 For a general analysis of how the Assad regime manipulates foreign humanitarian assistance for its own interests, see N. Hall, "How the Assad Regime Systematically Diverts Tens of Millions in Aid" (2021), www.csis.org/analysis/how-assad-regime-systematically-diverts-tens-millions-aid (accessed September 28, 2022).

11 See further Natasha Hall and Harden Lang, "The Weaponization of Humanitarian Aid: How to Stop China and Russia from Manipulating Relief Money," *Foreign Affairs*, January 9, 2023, www.foreignaffairs.com/world/weaponization-humanitarian-aid (accessed January 10, 2023).

12 Raya Jalabi, "Spy Chief's Daughter Highlights UN's Tangled Relations with Syrian Regime," *Financial Times*, March 7, 2023, www.ft.com/content/00c4e905-2245-4594-9dee-7ca8e94c8aaf (accessed March 11, 2023). The woman in question was hired first by the ICRC and then by a UN agency. The ICRC said that she did not handle sensitive protection matters.

13 V. Bernard and E. Policinski, "Interview with Peter Maurer: President of the ICRC" (Geneva, 2018), https://international-review.icrc.org/sites/default/files/906_2.pdf (accessed September 28, 2022).

14 Interview with Peter Maurer: President of the ICRC, *International Review of the Red Cross*, 99/906 (2017), pp. 875–884. doi:10.1017/S1816383118000620 © Cambridge University Press, reproduced with permission.

15 Anne Barnard, "Inside Syria's Secret Torture Prisons: How Bashar al-Assad Crushed Dissent," *New York Times*, May 11, 2019, www.nytimes.com/2019/05/11/world/middleeast/syria-torture-prisons.html.

16 E. Londoño, "What Syria Looks Like to Red Cross Workers on the Ground" (2013), www.washingtonpost.com/news/worldviews/wp/2013/09/16/what-syria-looks-like-to-red-cross-workers-on-the-ground/ (accessed September 28, 2022).

17 See, for example, L. Rubenstein, *Perilous Medicine: The Struggle to Protect Health Care from the Violence of War* (New York: Columbia University Press, 2021).

18 Z. A. Tahhan, "MSF: Attacks on Aid Groups Part of Syrian Regime Plan" (2016), www.aljazeera.com/news/2016/10/10/msf-attacks-on-aid-groups-part-of-syrian-regime-plan (accessed September 28, 2022).

19 S. Healy, U. Aneja, M. DuBois, and P. Harvey, "Lone Ranger No Longer: MSF's Engagement with Ministries of Health" (2020), www .humanitarianoutcomes.org/publications/msf_lone_ranger_2020 (accessed September 28, 2022).

20 V. Bernard, "Conflict in Syria: Finding Hope amid the Ruins" (2017), https://international-review.icrc.org/sites/default/files/906_1.pdf (accessed September 28, 2022). ICRC official Vincent Bernard wrote that he deplored Syria for "the significance of this conflict as a new paradigm of war and the utter contempt that has been shown for international humanitarian law (IHL)…" (p. 866).

7 ICRC Relations with Bern
Part I – Losing the Moral Compass

> Nor does the ICRC's insistence upon its entire separateness from the Swiss Federal Government convince sophisticated observers...
>
> Geoffrey Best[1]

It is clearly not surprising that the ICRC now endorses Dunantist values as a neutral, independent, impartial, humanitarian actor (NIIHA). The organization is the oldest of this type of actor, one that has the confidence of many contemporary governments, international organizations, and even some armed nonstate groups. Some of its Swiss traits, and hence organizational culture, may make it less than beloved and less easy to deal with, but its status and reputation have remained generally high for recent decades. Until the COVID-19 pandemic of 2020 forced some temporary financial retrenchment, the ICRC found donors to fund its annual budget which is now pushing almost US$3 billion. Then in 2023, in the context of galloping inflation, tightening monetary policy, and increased military spending, there was a severe shortfall in contributions for ICRC planned activities. This is discussed later.

Historically, however, the ICRC manifested muddled thinking about NIIHA values in its own decision making. The theory was better than the practice. With the benefit of historical research, we can now see that this was the case continuing into the 1930s even before matters came to a head in the 1940s. Even in modern times, some ICRC leaders have been more careful about these Dunantist norms, or optics about these norms, than others. There was a comparable muddle involving the independence of Amnesty International and British governments, with lessons that could benefit all RC actors. Naturally enough, the Swiss leaders of the ICRC are not the only ones who let nationalism and social biases corrupt their commitment to cosmopolitan standards like Dunantist principles in humanitarian affairs.

I   Early ICRC Practice of NIIHA Principles

We have already seen that Dunant, Moynier, and the other founding fathers of the ICRC always saw their humanitarian project as private and nongovernmental, even if working with national authorities. This independence from governments was then immediately violated by Moynier, who joined with General Dufour in serving on the Swiss governmental delegation at the 1864 diplomatic conference that produced the first Geneva Convention for victims of war. It was one thing to draft the prospective treaty. That could be done by a fully independent Geneva Committee. It was another thing to put oneself under instructions from Swiss national authorities in Bern by joining the governmental delegation.

This muddled thinking about independence from, but cooperation with, national governing authorities was then repeated by the ICRC for a long time. Many ICRC leaders served simultaneously in Swiss public positions at federal, cantonal, and city levels. A number of Committee members agreed to be Swiss ambassadors or other foreign policy officials. When the ICRC set up a relief agency to deal with the Balkan war of 1913, a Swiss consular official headed that RC agency. Max Huber served as legal advisor to the Swiss foreign ministry much of the time that he was ICRC president (1928–1944). He accepted to be the Swiss governmental representative to the 1932 Disarmament Conference while heading the ICRC. Giuseppe Motta, Swiss foreign minister in 1920–1940, was a member of the ICRC governing board during most of that time. After World War II when C.J. Burckhardt and Paul Ruegger were Swiss Ambassadors, in France and the United Kingdom respectively, they mixed Swiss and ICRC business, discussing the ICRC's future in terms of Swiss national interests.[2] ICRC examples of lack of appropriate independence from Bern are legion.

When ICRC President Gustave Ador joined the Swiss Federal Council in 1917 in order to resolve a crisis there, eventually becoming Swiss president in 1919, he took an official leave of absence from the lCRC. But he continued to make decisions on behalf of the ICRC, even presiding over some ICRC meetings. Clearly, he mixed the roles of ICRC humanitarian neutrality with Swiss political neutrality.[3] When C. J. Burckhardt became Swiss ambassador in Paris in 1945, Max Huber returned as interim ICRC president. As per the source above, however, Burckhardt remained involved in ICRC affairs. An official leave of absence was a pro-forma status that did not necessarily mean distance from participation in key ICRC decisions. What was a Swiss political concern and what was an ICRC humanitarian concern were not always separated.

This was true on many levels during the interwar years of 1919–1939 either because Geneva sought the assistance of Bern, or perhaps more often Bern sought to co-opt or advance the role of Geneva.[4] But here we concentrate attention on the 1930s and 1940s, and then on the post-1945 era.

It should be noted that the same intertwining of humanitarian and government roles, or worse, was found throughout the RC Movement. At one point the head of the Belgian Red Cross was the Belgian defense minister. At one point the head of the American Red Cross (ARA) was the president of the United States. The top legal counsel for the ARC used to be the US Attorney General. It was only in 1986 that the International Red Cross Movement forbade a state that had accepted the relevant Geneva Convention and the respective National RC Society from being represented by one combined delegation to the International RC Conference.[5] There seems no record, or personal recall now, of how many times before then a nation manifested one combined delegation to the RC Conference. But there had to be some evident reason, now maybe lost to history, for adopting the 1986 wording.

Many, if not most, National RC Societies had become de facto state agencies, with minimal independence. Some might be private and independent in the economic sense of operating from citizen donations, but otherwise they remained quasi-state in nature. Throughout the RC world, the principle of independence from governments was observed mostly by its breach, even as the idea of independence was written into the RC Fundamental Principles.

(There were apparently some occasions on which a National RC Society voted differently from its governmental delegation at the RC Conference, although no one seems to have records on this point. This apparently happened in 1996 on the question of expelling the South African governmental delegation from the Conference because of its apartheid policies.)

One might guess that a kind of unexamined nationalism impeded careful thought much of the time. No one seemed to want to carefully sort out the difference between national citizenship and the NIIHA realm-meaning cosmopolitan RC principles. Maybe it couldn't be done to the satisfaction of all, or maybe the subject required choices that were too difficult – and the preservation of the RC Movement required leaving everything unexamined.

There were plenty of egregious examples of National RC Societies violating NIIHA norms, not at all limited to the German Red Cross in the Nazi era. Other totalitarian states presented the same picture: the National RC Society was incorporated into the structure of a state that was not known for its humanitarian accomplishments. Totalitarians aside, the basic problem remained widespread. In the Serb region of Bosnia circa 2002, the head of the Bosnian Serb Red Cross (The Red Cross of the Republic of Serbia), an autonomous subunit of the Bosnian Red Cross, was Ljiljana Zelen-Karadzic, wife of the now-convicted war criminal Radovan Karadzic. She was openly supportive of his discriminatory political campaigns, even as he evaded capture until 2008 to stand trial for war crimes, so much so that the ICRC apparently asked for her resignation.

In the previous chapter we discussed the ICRC refusal to exercise withdrawal of recognition from a recognized National RC Society. The Bosnian Serb case comes very close to such a withdrawal, complicated by the complex arrangements in Bosnia and Herzegovina, which apparently the ICRC had facilitated. The ICRC, which never had formally recognized that particular subunit, asked for her to step down on the grounds of driving away supporters – at least if one can believe what was reported by multiple media sources.[6] (The ICRC declined to clarify that history, it being part of the closed archives at the time of writing.)

As for the ICRC over time, from 1863 through the Second World War, from Moynier to Huber, they and their colleagues in Geneva seemed to often assume that ICRC neutrality and Swiss neutrality, if not the same, were almost the same. This error was compounded by a failure to confront their social biases that undermined the notion of impartiality. In short, lack of proper independence and lack of rigorous self-examination about biases sometimes compromised ICRC claims to neutrality and impartiality. The narrow sociopolitical background of most ICRC officials did not help matters. The record on such conflicting values was, if anything, worse in much of the rest of the RC Movement.

II   The 1930s and Mussolini

As noted, the ICRC was started by French-speaking Genevans of Protestant persuasion mostly from the upper classes. These male Christian conservatives with a social conscience, accompanied by skepticism about things on the political left, kept the enterprise going in pretty much the same format from 1863 until the First World War. (The first female was co-opted in 1918.) Family links were strong, with a few prominent families being well represented.[7] Uncles were replaced by nephews; relatives by marriage were often co-opted as well. The first German speaker was asked to join only in 1923, the first Catholic in the same year. So it was only from the 1920s that the governing board became national rather than strictly Genevan. What did not change, for the most part, was an unexamined Swiss nationalism and demonstrable conservatism. This led to inroads on the practice of humanitarian independence, neutrality, and impartiality.

We will skip the Spanish civil war where we still do not have much independent research on the ICRC.[8] Instead we focus on the Italian invasion of Ethiopia (Abyssinia) in 1935–1936 where we have an extremely well-researched source.[9]

Switzerland was an important trading partner with Mussolini's Italy. In particular, the Swiss-Italian region in the southeast of the country was intertwined with Italy not only economically but also culturally. And just as Bern might fear an invasion from the Nazis from the north, so it might fear Italian irredentist claims in the south. The Swiss foreign minister between 1920 and 1940 was Giuseppe Motta, from Ticino. He was well known for his view of Mussolini as a counter to both the Nazis and the Bolsheviks.[10] He was also on the ICRC governing board. His man in Rome, Georges Wagniere, held similar views; he was co-opted onto the Committee in 1936.

President Huber at the helm of the ICRC was close to Motta personally and helped Motta draft the legal approach that allowed Switzerland to soften League of Nations economic sanctions on Italy after it invaded Ethiopia in 1935. Also, Huber had economic connections to firms heavily invested in Italy, firms which greatly profited from military spending in both Italy and Germany.[11] Bern, since Switzerland was a member of the League, felt obliged to do something given the vote for sanctions in the League, but did not want to hurt Italy, or itself, too much. ICRC President Huber, legal advisor to the foreign ministry, showed Motta how to do what the latter wanted to do as part of Swiss national interests.

Switzerland had never recognized the Soviet Union from 1917, even after its consolidation of power by about 1922, and still had no diplomatic relations with Moscow in the 1930s. It was only in 1940 that ambassadors were exchanged. Since 1933 Bern had been worried about trends in Germany – in addition to the Soviet Union. It followed that good relations with Mussolini's Italy loomed large in Bern's calculations of national interest.

Given the above, in retrospect it is not completely surprising that the ICRC followed the lines of Swiss foreign policy toward Italy, tilting toward Rome. Geneva was less than neutral and impartial in responding to humanitarian needs in the Italian–Ethiopian war of 1935–1936. There was indeed a broad RC presence in the conflict, with the ICRC working with a number of European RC Societies to provide medical and other assistance. Many RC staff in the field upheld NIIHA principles and even pressured their headquarters to do more, especially in calling out Italian airstrikes on medical facilities, not to mention use of poison gas. The

Photograph 7.1 The ICRC clearly tilted in favor of Mussolini's regime in its brutal invasion of Ethiopia in 1935–1936. It did not protest when Italy attacked facilities marked with the Red Cross, or when Rome resorted to mustard gas to subdue continued Ethiopian resistance. The exact year of this photo is not recorded but is either 1935 or 1936. The ICRC leadership lost its moral compass in the 1930s and 1940s.

ICRC had publicly protested the use of poison gas in World War I; it did not do so regarding Italy in Ethiopia.

In various other ways the ICRC favored Italy, as Baudendistel conclusively shows. At headquarters in Geneva two views in particular prevailed, both reasonably well documented. First there was racism, with Huber and others, both in Geneva and Bern, believing that Haile Selassie's Ethiopia should not have been recognized and admitted to membership in the League of Nations. There was thus the view that a bit of Italian colonialism might not be a bad thing, assisting the Ethiopians to make a more orderly future. Then there was the view, already mentioned, that the Italian Black Shirts were a useful counterweight to the Nazis and the Soviets. Mussolini played to this view after coming to power in 1922 until he aligned with Hitler in the later 1930s. For Bern and the overlapping ICRC leadership, black was better than brown or red. Mussolini's Black Shirts were preferable to the brown clad Nazi storm troopers and to the red flag of the Bolsheviks.

When the history is closely read, it is undeniable that the ICRC under Huber fell far short of a reasonably sound application of NIIHA norms regarding Mussolini and his brutal policies in Ethiopia. Part of the problem was lack of independence from Bern, not because the ICRC was pressured to conform to Swiss policy, but because the ICRC leadership was too close to Swiss authorities and voluntarily followed the line of Swiss foreign policy. Huber and his colleagues were not inclined to establish a rigorously independent humanitarian policy. They were not inclined toward a firm humanitarian stand in the face of Mussolini's policies.

Part of the problem also stemmed from the social conservatism of the ICRC and its racist demeaning of Africans, maybe as much under Huber as under Moynier earlier. And part of the problem stemmed from how both of these factors coalesced into ICRC support for the reigning version of Swiss national interests – namely, that one should go slow about contesting Italian atrocities in Ethiopia in order to prioritize Swiss larger political interests. Huber failed to distinguish a proper NIIHA stance from his Swiss identity. What was good for Switzerland was assumed to be the right policy for the ICRC as well. Huber might have been a well-recognized jurist, but he was lacking as a clear-minded humanitarian policy maker. And he carried the rest of the ICRC governing board with him.

III   Hitler and the Holocaust

By early fall 1942 the ICRC in Geneva was in possession of reliable information from various sources about the Nazi genocide. Nazi genocidal actions had become more systematic after the Wannsee Conference of Nazi leaders in early 1942, and then undeniable on a systematic and large scale by that summer. A mail poll of Committee members indicated support for a draft public statement about this and other humanitarian issues roiling events.

The Swiss government had put Edward de Haller in charge of supervising humanitarian organizations, and the ICRC had made him an honorary member of the Assembly. De Haller was related to others in the Swiss foreign ministry and politically close to still others. When de Haller saw the responses to the mail survey and realized the possibility of an ICRC public statement about humanitarian affairs in the Second World War, including treatment of detainees, he alerted key figures in Bern. One of these was the Swiss president, Philippe Etter, also a member of the ICRC governing board. Although Etter was usually not one to take part in specific ICRC decisions and activities, he and some others called for an in-person meeting of the governing board to discuss the pending draft public statement, attended the meeting, and spoke against a public statement.[12] Clearly he became involved in ICRC meetings to head off any public statement that might offend Berlin.

During the years of Nazi rule Swiss authorities, finding themselves surrounded by fascist states and well aware of the power of their brutal neighbor to the north, had engaged in policies that tilted toward the Nazis – as did Sweden, which was another leading neutral.[13] The Swiss version of partial appeasement involved cooperation with the Nazis primarily in matters of banking (helping convert gold, much of it stolen, to convertible currency, inter alia) and refugees (helping to identify German Jewish refugees and turning them back to a dark fate). Much of the country more broadly speaking, including the Swiss Red Cross, had been reasonably generous in wanting to receive many Jewish refugees, especially children, from neighboring states.[14] But clearly Swiss official policy represented a kind of appeasement so as not to provoke Berlin unduly. Other small liberal European states such as Belgium and the Netherlands had not fared well under the Nazi boot. Was Hitler likely to invade the small Alpine state that had made preparations for armed neutrality? Why take any chances that Hitler might actually implement invasion plans?

It was true that the Swiss government per se did not officially pressure the ICRC to remain silent about the Holocaust and other humanitarian subjects. The Swiss Federal Council, which was the collective executive, and the Swiss Parliament never adopted any stance regarding the ICRC meeting of October 1942. Moreover, a larger perspective showed that during the war the ICRC was not always simply in the pocket of Bern, because there were numerous differences of opinion between Geneva and Bern on this and that subject. While the ICRC had its own activities going, and Switzerland was the Protecting Power for several belligerents, the two Swiss entities sometimes cooperated and sometimes had stiff arguments about who was to do what and who was to pay for what. The ICRC manifested some independence during the war, and Swiss officials officially respected that independence. But only up to a point.[15]

In October 1942, the Swiss officials in Bern who were also members of the ICRC governing board all argued against a public statement by the ICRC regarding a shortlist of humanitarian issues including the fate of political detainees. The hidden agenda of appeasement remained officially hidden, as Bern officials argued for more quiet diplomacy, or suggested that a public statement would make no difference and have no impact. In the last analysis the double membership on the ICRC board allowed the governmental members to join with other conservatives in adopting a position that led to much controversy. The draft public statement was not adopted, but that was not the entire story.

Part of the denouement in 1942 was that in lieu of a public statement, the ICRC was supposed to carry out a more vigorous discrete diplomacy toward Berlin in favor of IHL and victims. But this never transpired. J. C. Burckhardt and other ICRC conservatives never followed up on that agreement. Huber was ill, did not participate in the 1942 meeting, and effectively turned ICRC leadership over to Burckhardt. The latter was not trusted by the British for being too close to certain German leaders in this era.[16] Burckhardt is seen by more than one historian as favoring the German conservatives, but not necessarily the Nazis, as a barrier to an expanding communism. And Swiss nationalism was certainly not absent in his thinking. (All this would fit with how Huber, and Motta, viewed Mussolini as covered above.)

After 1942 the good that was done for Jewish victims of the Nazis by the ICRC was done by local ICRC representatives in peripheral areas, such as Friedrich Born in Budapest. It was not the ICRC in Geneva that authorized the dynamic action in saving many Jews, and the proactive ICRC staff members were not recognized and rewarded by the Geneva headquarters after the war.[17]

Photograph 7.2 While the Geneva HQ neither publicly condemned Berlin for its atrocities in the 1930s and 1940s, about which the ICRC had reliable information by 1942, nor developed a dynamic quiet diplomacy in defense of Nazi victims, some individual staff members, such as Friedrich Born in Hungary, successfully helped many Jews escape the Holocaust. This photo is not dated but was taken in either 1944 or 1945.

IV   Contested Lessons of History about the 1940s

The reigning version of "lessons learned" about the ICRC and the Holocaust stresses the failure to take a public stand in the face of great evil: rather than independently standing for humanitarian principle in publicly opposing the Nazi genocide and other violations of human dignity, and thereby protecting its reputation for the future, the ICRC remained silent under personal pressure from high Swiss officials, which resonated with the ICRC conservatives of that time.[18] In the 1942 debate several members of the Assembly urged, unsuccessfully at the end of the day, a public statement lest the future status of the ICRC be negatively affected.

In April 2015, at a meeting on the Shoah cosponsored by the World Jewish Congress, ICRC President Peter Maurer gave a talk in which the theme of speaking out rather than remaining silent figured prominently. He said, in part:

> Over the past seven decades, we have heard innumerable versions of the perverse justifications for the horrors of the Shoah.... Tragically, the leaders of the International Committee of the Red Cross were part of the by-standers who – when confronted with questions about the silence of the institution – defended standard responses to extraordinary circumstances.... In institutional terms, the ICRC also learned some hard lessons. It had failed to protect civilians and most notably the Jews persecuted and murdered by the Nazi regime; it had failed to understand the uniqueness of the inhumanity by responding to the outrageous with standard procedures; it had looked on helplessly and silently, not really trying – certainly not hard enough – to live up to the principle of humanity.... It failed as a humanitarian organization because it had lost its moral compass. This failure has become an intrinsic part of our institutional history.[19]

Maurer continued:

> Since then, we have chosen to confront our past and to embrace transparency. Our public archives are proof of our acknowledgment of the past and our continued effort to confront uncomfortable truths. The ICRC has also adopted a new policy on confidentiality, explicitly acknowledging that there is a path to condemnation of acts of inhumanity. We have chosen not to let ourselves be cornered by the binary logic of silence vs. denunciation, which inevitably leads to paralysis.

This speech in its entirety is consistent with contemporary ICRC doctrine both about communications[20] and about steps to take when confronted with violations of IHL or human dignity.[21] Maurer, while appearing to take a stand in favor of more public diplomacy, actually was rejecting a simple dichotomy between silence or denunciation and indicating the various steps the ICRC might take short of specific denunciation of a particular authority. His speech, when analyzed carefully, was actually an endorsement for a varied discreet diplomacy that saw public denunciation as a rare last resort. Later in this book we show that Maurer was almost always in favor of quiet diplomacy rather than public criticism, and he explicitly acknowledged this trait in an interview. Nevertheless, his carefully chosen words could be understood, and probably were, as furthering the notion that the ICRC was once again rejecting the silence of the Assembly in 1942 in the face of Nazi atrocities.

Almost entirely unnoticed, in 2006 the Assembly adopted a statement about the Nazi holocaust.[22] This appeared to "come out of the blue," in the sense that nothing in the ICRC's external environment compelled more attention to the history of the 1940s. That doctrinal statement of 2006 was consistent with ICRC contemporary policy on communication and response to violations of human dignity, but it projected a different emphasis. One should read the 2006 Assembly statement as saying that the primary problem in 1942 was not remaining silent but not having a sufficiently dynamic quiet diplomacy, and not pursuing that effort even if it had no practical impact. In other words, the ICRC did indeed lose its moral compass in the 1940s (and for that matter in the 1930s regarding both Mussolini and the early Hitler), but primarily because it did not take a firm and courageous stand by way of high-level if discrete overtures to top officials – even if not grounded in IHL, and even if the overtures would have no practical impact.

The 2006 statement acknowledging ICRC failure, even if with reference to the failure in all of Western civilization in the face of the Holocaust, reads in part:

This failure is aggravated by the fact that the ICRC did not do everything in its power to put an end to the persecutions and help the victims. The organization remained a prisoner of its traditional procedures and of the overly narrow legal framework in which it operated. Having abandoned the idea of public condemnation – convinced as it was that this would not change the course of events, fearing that it would jeopardize the activities it was carrying out for other victims, especially prisoners of war, and not wishing to exacerbate Switzerland's relations with the belligerent States – the ICRC essentially relied on its delegates to make confidential representations to the authorities of the Reich or its satellites. However, these delegates had no access to the corridors of power. Only towards the end of the war did the ICRC's leaders make high-level representations to certain leaders of the Reich and its satellites.[23]

The Assembly statement continues:

Having confined itself to two options – that of the very limited aid operation it was carrying out for the victims of Nazi persecution, with derisory results in regard to the situation of the victims and no impact on the genocide, and that of public condemnation, an ultimate weapon that the ICRC felt it could not use, the organization was unable – until the last months of the war – to make determined, sustained, high-level diplomatic representations to the leaders of the Reich.... Such approaches should have been attempted, even if it could be doubted that the desired results would be achieved....

Within the Assembly the view was articulated that the various ICRC comments and publications about the Holocaust since the late 1980s did not add up to a consistent ICRC position and had not been widely understood correctly. In this view, the ICRC during World War II was correct for worrying about the effect of a public statement in 1942 on POW matters. The Germans were, more or less, adhering to the 1929 GC on POWs with the Allies (but not with the Soviets who had never ratified that GC), the ICRC was being allowed to act as a neutral intermediary on that subject, there were tensions between the Allies and the Nazis regarding POW affairs, and it was possible that the Nazis might pull out of reciprocal POW arrangements and block various ICRC activities.

Photograph 7.3 ICRC representatives talk to POWs (mainly French) at a German POW camp at Rawa-Ruska, on the border between Poland and Ukraine, 1942. Fear of collapse of these kinds of prison visits was one reason some at the ICRC did not want to press the Nazis very hard about treatment of Jews and other detainees who were not POWs and not legally protected under the 1929 Geneva Convention. It was in 1942 that the Nazis escalated plans for the Final Solution.

In 2006 the Assembly was endorsing the view that the ICRC's big failure in the 1940s was failing to send someone like Burckhardt, with good access to high levels of German officialdom, to press the case about unacceptable violations of human dignity – even if such matters were not then fully covered by IHL. In this view the Nazi policies were so grave that the ICRC should have made that high-level effort even if Geneva believed the démarche would do no good. The effort itself would show that the organization had tried every reasonable option and thus had protected its reputation in the future, as well as protecting ongoing POW arrangements. The Assembly seemed to imply in 2006: If dynamic quiet diplomacy failed, and if there were ongoing humanitarian programs, the ICRC would be correct not to publicly denounce specific atrocities. The Assembly statement did recognize the role of Swiss nationalism in ICRC thinking in 1942 by including the polite phrase "not wishing to exacerbate Switzerland's relations with the belligerent States...."

In any event the Assembly, with apparently little debate, approved what had been drafted by a staff member and what President Kellenberger supported. But then apparently it was Kellenberger who decided not to publish the statement in the *Review* or otherwise give it great publicity. It was posted on the ICRC website but not featured prominently. Probably the ICRC did not want to stir up any new controversies by calling attention to its past mistakes. This official statement about the ICRC and the Holocaust, and for now the last document on the subject, has languished in the shadows ever since. Some staff persons did not know it was in the public domain.[24]

Maurer in 2015 was not really disagreeing with the 2006 statement but rather was presenting ICRC doctrine on public denunciation of atrocity in a way that was tailored to his audience – talking about publicity and transparency but closing with an emphasis on other steps besides full silence or explicit denunciation. ICRC doctrine as well as practice continues to emphasize confidential dialogue, with specific public denunciation of war crimes or gross violations of human rights as an exceptional last resort. Even then, specific public denunciation has to be seen as in the interest of victims, which in practice it almost never is at the Geneva headquarters.

V   Lessons Applied in Rwanda

Rwanda in spring 1994 is illustrative about what the ICRC really learned from 1942, and what ICRC doctrine on communication and response to atrocities really means in contemporary times. In the face of atrocities by militant Hutus primarily against Tutsi but a few others (and with some

Tutsi massacres of a smaller number of Hutus), resulting in the estimated deaths of around 800,000 Tutsis, the ICRC stayed in the country
to do what good it could while making calculated public statements. It
operated on the edge of danger to its personnel there.

According to Philippe Gaillard, who was head of the ICRC delegation
in Rwanda at the time of the genocide:

The Rwandan genocide was so well covered by the media, especially by the western media, that everyone could follow it on TV, radio or in newspapers every
day. One could say that it was transmitted live, at least live enough to inform the
governments and public about what was really happening there.... The ICRC
contributed to this media coverage and reporting like it maybe never had done
in its almost 130 years of existence at that time. On 28 April 1994, some three
weeks after the beginning of the genocide, the ICRC called on the governments
concerned including all members of the Security Council to take all possible
measures to put an end to the massacres. The words used – *"systematic carnage,"*
"the extermination of a significant portion of the civilian population" – left no room
for doubt about what was going on.[25]

So the ICRC was not silent about the Rwanda genocide, but it crafted
its language so that (just barely) it could stay in the country in order to
run a hospital that continued to function on the basis of impartiality –
and was seen as neutral. It made representations to the authorities that
resulted in children being spared in some orphanages, or Tutsi adults
saved in this or that jurisdiction. It did what it could in terms of some
humanitarian good, even as the genocide continued until the victory of
the invading and Tutsi-dominated Rwandan Patriotic Front.

Of course, the Rwandan genocide was different from 1942. In 1994
ICRC officials did not have to pay much attention to complicating
Swiss national interests and whether some high officials in Bern might
object to an ICRC pending decision. Rwanda had no plans to invade the
Helvetian Republic.

VI   The Same Lesson Regarding Russia in Syria

ICRC relations with Russia in recent years demonstrated how the ICRC
deals with atrocities, in keeping with what happened in Rwanda, and
with what the Assembly said in its doctrinal statement of 2006. It is all
of one piece, with the 1940s in the background. Here we are not talking
about genocide but about major war crimes. But ICRC thinking and
process remain the same on both matters.

In Syria 2011 to 2021, from the government side, with Russia fighting on the side of the Assad regime from about 2015, there were many
attacks on medical facilities and use of chlorine bombs, as well as the

failure to consistently exercise due diligence in distinguishing between civilian and military targets. Human Rights Watch eventually released a highly critical report about Russian–Syrian bombing policies.[26] The ICRC, active on the ground mainly in government-controlled areas, protested against inhumane violence in general, but did not call out Moscow by name for its role, directly or indirectly, in war crimes as it supported the Assad government. In government-controlled areas the organization was allowed to deliver some humanitarian relief working with the Syrian Arab Red Crescent. It manifested a few cross-border operations to rebel held areas. It carried out some routine prison visits but not to detainees under interrogation held by the security services. (Recall the analysis of the ICRC and the Syrian civil war at the end of the last chapter.)

The ICRC had a general strategy underway of engagement with various Russian officials for long-term confidence building. Moreover, it, was engaged with Russia and its allies with some limited humanitarian achievements in Eastern Ukraine from 2014, Libya, Nagorno-Karabagh, and probably elsewhere. Geneva had discussions with Foreign Minister Lavrov and other high foreign policy officials which the Geneva headquarters saw in positive terms. In 2021 the Russian Foreign Ministry awarded the F.F. Martens Medal to Peter Maurer representing the ICRC for its humanitarian record, whatever that signified. (Winning the prize could be seen as success for the ICRC strategy of building confidence and good relations, or as a Russian effort to reward the ICRC for keeping silent about, and thus being complicit with, Moscow's controversial policies.)

In any event ICRC policy was to avoid explicitly denouncing Russia for war crimes in Syria especially from Russian air force bombing. The big picture about ICRC programs not only in Syria but also about dealing with Russia across different situations was controlling, and a good example of how the ICRC normally operated, consistent with various doctrinal statements, and consistent with arguably the main lesson learned from the Holocaust. The main focus was said to be on dynamic quiet diplomacy and not explicit public protest, especially if some humanitarian progress was being made somewhere with a particular actor. Public denouncement of specific violations of IHL and/or human dignity, and active prosecution for war crimes, was almost entirely the domain of others. That posture facilitated some pragmatic help for victims – at least sometimes. Doctrine allowed for public specific protest as a last resort, but it was almost never a favored course of action. This was the ICRC general policy followed in the Ukraine war in 2022, discussed in the Epilogue.

There seems no evidence that the evolution of ICRC doctrine and particular decisions about public protest, or the lack thereof, involved Swiss officials in Bern. Rather, ICRC doctrine and policy practice about public protest stemmed from ICRC experience and thinking at the top in Geneva. Such was not the case, of course, in 1942.

VII   Further Reflections

After World War II, Huber and Burckhardt wrote a letter to President Truman seeking clemency for the German convicted war criminal Ernst von Weizsacker, who had been secretary of state, or the top civil servant, in the German Foreign Ministry – and later German ambassador to the Vatican. This letter, ill-advised for a humanitarian organization, confirmed the view that ICRC key leaders saw conservative Germans (and Italians), even those complicit in war crimes, as being useful in blocking the advance of communism, which they saw as threatening Switzerland and the rest of the West. For Burckhardt, the letter to Truman culminated a sizable effort on behalf of several Nazi war criminals who had been friendly to Switzerland or who had helped Burckhardt in his extracurricular efforts to mediate a peace with Britain during the war. Huber, never decisive, went along with what was no doubt a Burckhardt initiative.[27]

In the fall of 1943, the Nazis had taken over Rome from the collapsed Mussolini regime. The Vatican arranged a meeting with Ambassador Weizsacker. The relatively new Pope, Pius XII (Pachelli), had decided to pursue a belated concern of his predecessor, Pius XI (Ratti), and contest the Italian anti-Semitic laws. (The latter had drafted a long statement opposed to Nazi policy toward the Jews which was never published.) The Pope's emissary, Cardinal Maglione, asked Weizsacker to intervene to protect slightly more than 1,000 Jews detained in a nearby building. Weizsacker refused, declining to undermine Hitler's instructions. A couple of days later the Jews were deported to Auschwitz. Only sixteen survived.[28]

That Huber and Burckhardt would petition Truman on behalf of Weizsaker indicated the nature of the views at the top of the ICRC during the Nazi years. Such views represented a moral low point in the history of the ICRC. Deference to Swiss national interests and calculations about the dangers of communism loomed large.

VIII   Universal Humanitarianism and Universal Religion

National RC Societies were not usually paragons of virtue when it came to NIIHA values, and the historian John Hutchinson has written about how the RC Movement had become nationalized and militarized even before the Second World War.[29] But the ICRC, too, has had its own controversial eras as well. Just as it is difficult to keep religion from being nationalized, so is it difficult to avoid the same fate for a cosmopolitan humanitarianism. This was quite evident at ICRC headquarters.

The German Lutheran pastor Dietrich Bonhoeffer famously argued that Christianity was supposed to be a universal religion whose tenets were not supposed to be nationalized or made secondary to national or other secular interests. Christianity, being a universal faith, required tough choices for its believers in resisting popular trends.[30] He was killed by the Nazis for his beliefs. Many, if not most, Christian churches – indeed many, if not most, religions – conform to prevailing national sentiment about the priority of national interest and national security.

One way to understand ICRC history is to see it as an evolution toward a rigorous and professional commitment to NIIHA universal norms, trying to improve on its amateurish start complete with fuzzy thinking about things such as Swiss nationalism and deference to the Swiss government. The 1930s and 1940s show the details of why that evolution had not proceeded very far back then.

Just as Moynier never seemed to have engaged in self-evaluation about his support for colonialism and King Leopold's brutal Congo Free State, so Huber and Burckhardt never seemed to have engaged in self-evaluation about their humanitarian failures in the 1930s and 1940s – witness the letter to Truman after the war. If there was private agonizing, Huber seems to have done more of it than Burckhardt.[31] The Assembly statement in 2006 about the Holocaust wanted to make sure there *was* reflection about 1942 and adjacent years, and that the reflection hit on arguably the right points. Even so, the 2006 ICRC Assembly statement contained only diplomatic language and soft reference to the role of persons in the Swiss government in the defective decisions of the ICRC in 1942.

IX   Comparison with Amnesty International, London

Here one might usefully bring in a rough analogy from the history of Amnesty International (AI). The founder of AI, Peter Benenson, was a bit like Henry Dunant: he was a visionary rather than a systematic manager, was very good at promoting a cause with much energy, was outraged by a certain injustice, was a committed religious believer, and became the author of various schemes and visions beyond the one for which he is mainly remembered. But that is not the main point here.[32]

Benenson, a British citizen who was based in London and pushing for more attention to political prisoners from 1961, assumed that the British government, especially when Labour was in power, shared his commitment to human rights and was equally concerned about the fate of political prisoners. And so there developed between Benenson representing AI and British governments various joint maneuvers in, for example, South Africa, Haiti, Southern Rhodesia, and Aden. Some of this cooperation was both under the table and of dubious ethics.[33]

It turned out that, whereas Benenson and AI were interested in detained individuals per se, the British government was interested in burnishing its image and other aspects of its national interests as it defined them. The joint convergence on political prisoners was for different reasons, with different objectives. When the bubble of secret dealings eventually burst, Benenson had to resign from AI. The organization decided on rejecting any donations from governments in the future, a policy position which remains today.

This historical comparison between Amnesty in London and the ICRC is not exact, and today the ICRC continues to have close relations with the Swiss government both diplomatically and financially. The last four ICRC presidents, and now the current one, Mme. Mirjana Spoljaric, first had careers as Swiss federal officials (but not all entirely with the Foreign Ministry). But the comparison holds on an important point: At times both the leaders of the early Amnesty in London and of the early ICRC in Geneva assumed that *their* government was different, more ethical, more genuinely committed to human rights or human dignity than other governments, and in the Swiss case more genuinely neutral – and worthy of some deference. And so both AI and the ICRC sometimes fell into the trap of not guarding their independence enough and not keeping a necessary distance from their national political leaders. A shared nationalism, complete with shoddy thinking, was pervasive early on.

X   Conclusion

There is much more to be said about ICRC relations with Swiss authorities, and the subject is continued in the next chapter.

Notes

1 G. Best, *War and Law Since 1945* (Oxford: Oxford University Press, 1994), p. 376.
2 Gerald Steinacher, *Humanitarians at War: The Red Cross in the Shadow of the Holocaust* (Oxford: Oxford University Press, 2017), pp. 104–105. Burckhardt at that time had been ICRC president and Ruegger would be in the future.
3 Cédric Cotter, *(S')Aider pour survivre. Action humanitaire et neutralité suisse pendant la Première Guerre mondiale* (Chêne-Bourg: Georg Editeur, 2017), esp. pp. 243–248.

4 For an English summary of his book in German, see Thomas Bruckner, "The ICRC and Switzerland 1919–1939: A 'Special Relationship' Examined," *Imperial and Global Forum*, May 28, 2018, https://imperialglobalexeter .com/2018/05/28/the-icrc-and-switzerland-1919-1939-a-special-relationship-examined/ (accessed November 16, 2022).

5 *Handbook of the International Red Cross and Red Crescent Movement* (Geneva: ICRC-Federation, 1986), 14th ed., p. 527.

6 BBC News, "Karadzic's Wife Quits Red Cross Post," December 13, 2002, http://news.bbc.co.uk/2/hi/europe/2571579.stm (accessed November 17, 2022); Reuters, "World Briefing/Europe: Bosnia: Karadzic's Wife Quits Red Cross Post," December 13, 2002, www.nytimes.com/2002/12/13/ world/world-briefing-europe-bosnia-karadzic-s-wife-quits-red-cross-post .html (accessed November 17, 2022); Radio Free Europe and Radio Liberty, "Balkan Report," May 31, 2002, www.rferl.org/a/1341067.html (accessed November 17, 2022); Reuters, "Timeline: Events Leading to Trial of Radovan Karadzic," www.reuters.com/article/us-warcrimes-karadzic-trial/timeline-events-leading-to-trial-of-radovan-karadzic-idUSTRE 59M3I720091023 (accessed November 17, 2022).

7 Diego Fiscalini, "Des elites au service d'une cause humanitaire: le Comité International de la Croix-Rouge," Mémoire de license, University of Geneva, Faculty of Letters, Department of History, 1985. Some say this student account is not entirely accurate, but no one has produced a better study so far.

8 The standard account on Spain, promoted by the organization, was by Marcel Junod, *Le Troisième Combattant* (Geneva: ICRC, 1947). Baudendistel, cited later, suggests that Junod was not a completely reliable source concerning both Ethiopia and Spain. The ICRC research historian has produced a short account on Spain: Daniel Palmieri, "Une neutralité, sous influence?: le CICR, Franco, et les victimes," *Revue Suisse d'Histoire*, 59/3 (2009), pp. 279–297.

9 The definitive source is Rainer Baudendistel, *Between Bombs and Good Intentions: The Red Cross and the Italo-Ethiopian War, 1935–1936* (New York and Oxford: Berghahn Books, 2006).

10 See also "Guiseppe Motta," *The Anthology of Swiss Legal Culture*, www .legalanthology.ch/motta_guiseppe_1871/ (accessed November 17, 2022).

11 Yves Sandoz presents a rather positive view of Huber in "Max Huber and the Red Cross," *European Journal of International Law*, 18/1 (2007), pp. 171–197 while noting his controversial corporate connections. See also "Le Comité International de la Croix-Rouge," in *L'Observatoire de l'Action Humanitaire*, no date, www.observatoire-humanitaire.org/en/index.php?page=fiche-ong.php& part=commentaires&chapitre=311&id=84 (accessed November 17, 2022) where one reads the following: "Max Huber was first attacked by the Swiss communist press in July 1936, because his firm's subsidiary in Venetia, the SAVA (Società Alluminio Veneto Anonima), was producing aluminum and trading with the defense industry in Italy as the fascists invaded Ethiopia. From 1929 onwards, Max Huber also directed his father's metallurgical company, Alusuisse & Oerlikon, which manufactured weapons for Nazi Germany during World War Two. When conflict broke out in 1939, Max Huber decided to donate his salary to the ICRC, but did not resign from his

position. Meanwhile, his company's factory in Singen, Germany, violated the Geneva Conventions by using OST (Ostarbeiter) labor provided by deported persons and Soviet prisoners of war captured after 1941."

12 Isabelle Voneche Cardia, *Neutralité et engagement. Les relations entre le Comité international de la Croix-Rouge et le gouvernement suisse pendant la Seconde Guerre mondiale* (Lausanne: History Society of Swiss Romand, 2012).

13 A short and journalistic, but accurate, comparison can be found at: Roger Cohen, "The (not so) Neutrals of WWII," *New York Times*, January 26, 1997, www.nytimes.com/1997/01/26/weekinreview/the-not-so-neutrals-of-world-war-ii.html (accessed November 17, 2022).

14 One independent historian summarized the Swiss overall record toward Jewish refugees as "commendable, but not impressive." Yehuda Bauer, *The Holocaust in Historical Perspective* (Canberra: Australian National University Press, 1978), p. 91, https://openresearch-repository.anu.edu.au/bitstream/1885/114693/2/b12168439.pdf (accessed November 17, 2022). See further the extensive, official, and more critical Bergier report on Swiss–German relations during the Nazi era, published in 2002, "Independent Commission of Experts: Switzerland-Second World War (ICE)," www.uek.ch/en/index.htm (accessed November 17, 2022).

15 David P. Forsythe, *The Humanitarians: The International Committee of the Red Cross* (Cambridge: Cambridge University Press, 2005).

16 James Crossland, *Britain and the International Committee of the Red Cross, 1939–1945* (Basingstoke: Palgrave Macmillan, 2014).

17 It should be stressed that this is not the place for a detailed review of the ICRC record in World War II, including the Holocaust. That record has been recorded not only by the organization but also by independent scholars such as Jean-Claude Favez, *The Red Cross and the Holocaust* (Cambridge: Cambridge University Press, 1999; the earlier French edition was *Une Mission Impossible?*, Lausanne: Editions Payot, 1988) and Arieh Ben-Tov, *Facing the Holocaust in Budapest: The International Committee of the Red Cross and the Jews in Hungary, 1943–1945* (Boston: Martinus Nijhoff, 1988).

18 Favez, *The Red Cross and the Holocaust*, p. 282, concludes that the ICRC should have spoken out about the Nazi genocide.

19 ICRC, "Remembering the Shoah: The ICRC and the International Community's Efforts in Responding to Genocide," April 2015, www.icrc.org/en/document/remembering-shoah-icrc-and-international-communitys-efforts-responding-genocide-and (accessed November 17, 2022).

20 ICRC, "The ICRC's External Communication Doctrine," May 2, 2016, www.icrc.org/en/document/icrc-external-communication-doctrine (accessed November 17, 2022).

21 ICRC, "Action by the ICRC in the Event of Violations of International Humanitarian Law or of Other Fundamental Rules Protecting Persons in Situations of Violence," no date, https://library.icrc.org/library/search/notice?noticeNr=20414 (accessed November 17, 2022); and ICRC, "The ICRC's Confidential Approach: Specific Means Employed by the ICRC to Ensure Respect for the Law by State and Non-State Authorities," no date, https://library.icrc.org/library/search/notice?noticeNr=37714 (accessed November 17, 2022).

22 ICRC, "The Nazi Genocide and Other Persecutions," October 25, 2007, www.icrc.org/en/document/wwii-nazi-genocide-and-other-persecutions (accessed November 17, 2022).

23 Ibid.

24 This doctrinal statement No. 64, posted in 2007, was a slightly different version of a 2002 statement by François Bugnion posted in 2002: "Dialogue with the Past: the ICRC and the Nazi Death Camps," ICRC, November 5, 2002, www.icrc.org/en/doc/resources/documents/misc/6ayg86.htm (accessed November 18, 2022). In his post on the ICRC website, Bugnion, who played a large role in the fashioning of Doctrine 64, writes: "Even more than the absence of public condemnation, it is, in my opinion, the timidity of the confidential representations that weighs most heavily against the ICRC." For a recent exposition of the same theme about dynamic quiet diplomacy, against the same historical background, see Daniel Palmieri, "Savoir et se taire: le Comité International de la Croix-Rouge et la Shoah," *Revue d'Histoire de la Shoah*, 2019/1 (No. 210), pp. 117–129. Palmieri is the senior historian at the ICRC.

25 Philippe Gaillard, "Rwanda 1994: '… kill as many people as you want, you cannot kill their memory'." ICRC, March 29, 2004, www.icrc.org/en/doc/resources/documents/misc/5xfncq.htm (accessed November 18, 2022).

26 Human Rights Watch, "Syria/Russia: Strategy Targeted Civilian Infrastructure," October 15, 2020, www.hrw.org/news/2020/10/15/syria/russia-strategy-targeted-civilian-infrastructure# (accessed November 18, 2022).

27 Steinacher, *Humanitarians at War*, pp. 126–136.

28 David I. Kertzer, *The Pope and Mussolini: The Secret History of Pius XI and the Rise of Fascism in Europe* (New York: Random House, 2014), pp. 193–195.

29 *Champions of Charity: War and the Rise of the Red Cross* (Boulder: Westview Press, 1996).

30 From a multitude of sources on the subject, one can start with Bonhoeffer, *The Costs of Discipleship* (New York: Simon and Schuster, 1959), translated from the original 1937 publication.

31 In Favez, *The Red Cross and the Holocaust*, the author closes with a thumbnail sketch of some leading personalities including Huber and Burckhardt. Neither comes off especially well. He shows that neither were careful about the difference between humanitarian neutrality and Swiss political neutrality. Even ICRC President Sommaruga, who as we will see was very keen on ICRC independence, took exception to what Favez said about Huber, as recorded in the final pages of the Favez book. On this matter Favez was right and Sommaruga was overly touchy and defensive about ICRC history.

32 Tom Buchanan, *Amnesty International and Human Rights Activism in Postwar Britain, 1945–1977* (Cambridge: Cambridge University Press, 2020).

33 See also Kirsten Sellars, "Human Rights and the Colonies: Deceit, Deception, and Discovery," *The Commonwealth Journal of International Affairs*, 93/377, 2004, www.tandfonline.com/doi/full/10.1080/0035853042000300197?scroll=top&needAccess=true (accessed November 18, 2022).

> The federal authorities should avoid mixing up Switzerland's policy
> with the activities of the ICRC and the neutrality of the State with
> the Committee's humanitarian neutrality. They should not attempt
> to influence the decisions of the ICRC and should respect its
> independence.
>
> Swiss Federal Report (1992)

For a long time, as already noted, the Swiss Confederation has been
proud to be the host state for the ICRC and at the origins of the RC
Movement. The relationship feeds into the Swiss governmental narrative
that it is a force for good in the world and a leading humanitarian actor.

Of course the Swiss arms industry, as regulated by the state, sells
weapons abroad, which sometimes wind up being used in dubious ways,
but that is another matter.[1] Of course Swiss banks, as regulated by the
state, attract a lot of money from those trying to hide wealth and avoid
taxes, but that too is another matter.[2] And these banks, again under state
regulation, were slow to return unclaimed property to the heirs of Jewish
depositors who perished in the Holocaust, and did so only under considerable
outside pressure, but that is another matter.[3]

It remained true that Switzerland did manifest a special role in humanitarian
affairs. The Confederation covered about 9 percent of cash contributions
to the ICRC's total budget in 2019, or roughly the same as the
European Union made up of twenty-seven states. (Those states might
make separate donations as well.) The US government was the top contributor,
covering about 27 percent of the total budget. But Switzerland
ranked high among donors, especially given its small size. Bern usually
covered the ICRC's expenses at headquarters, then made additional
donations for field activities in response to special appeals for funding.

By tradition, as already demonstrated, the Confederation hosts diplomatic
conferences on IHL, consulting closely with the ICRC on
whether or when to call for such a conference. That was the case in
2005, the last Geneva Diplomatic Conference regarding victims of war.

The Confederation issued the invitations for the conference limited to the subject of neutral emblems, although in some views the conference turned out to be mostly about the legitimacy of the state of Israel. (The opposition to a new emblem was coordinated by the Organization for Islamic Cooperation.) The ICRC helped negotiate the deal among states that led to recognition of the Red Crystal as a new neutral emblem in armed conflict. This allowed the Israeli official aid society, Magen David Adom, which agreed to use the Red Crystal or Red Diamond in its international operations, to be recognized by the ICRC and enter the RC Federation. All of this reflected well on the state of Israel.

Photograph 8.1 The exclusion of the Israeli official aid society, Magen David Adom (MDA), from the RC Movement had long been a troublesome issue. The technical problem was that the Israelis refused to use either of the two neutral emblems approved by states, the Red Cross or the Red Crescent. This prevented recognition by the ICRC as a first step to membership in the IFRC. Under pressure from the American Red Cross, the ICRC finally helped broker a deal in 2005–2006 in which a third emblem was adopted by states, the Red Crystal, which MDA agreed to use in international activities. This solved the recognition and admissibility issues and was accompanied by recognition and admission for the Palestinian Red Crescent Society. Here ICRC President Jakob Kellenberger meets with MDA President Noam Yifrach in Haifa in 2006.

(As a by-product, this diplomatic development also led to acceptance into the Movement of the Palestinian Red Crescent, even though the state of Palestine was not universally recognized and had no agreed borders. There are rules, and then there are package deals that grease the wheels. The ICRC pays attention to both. As noted, it has a lot of lawyers on staff, but its emphasis is on pragmatic accomplishments – presumably within the bound of NIIHA values.)

The Swiss Confederation and the ICRC will sometimes undertake joint programmatic initiatives, such as the long-running (and disappointing) effort to inquire of states about how to improve compliance with IHL. There was also a joint effort (more successful on paper) to get a diplomatic agreement on rules for private security contractors (aka mercenaries) and their operations in situations of violence. If one cannot get hard law, better to get soft law than no law. A diplomatic nonbinding agreement that actually shapes policies can be said to become soft law.[4]

A few examples show some different dimensions and continuing debates about ICRC relations with the Swiss government.

I   The Bonnard Affair, 1950s

Aside from IHL and diplomatic conferences, if we go back to the 1950s the little known Bonnard affair showed several relevant things. One was that Bern was very protective of the ICRC's neutral image, which was no doubt seen as buttressing the state's claim to neutrality as well. The government sought to use the ICRC for its own purposes and probably overreached.

André Bonnard was a Swiss left-wing academic, an expert on Greek culture and language, and active on Greek political affairs. He lobbied the ICRC on Greek matters and was known to the organization.

In the early 1950s the ICRC was engaged not only in Greece but also, among other places, in Korea where an armed conflict was underway during 1950–1953. For reasons which have been recounted elsewhere,[5] the ICRC was seen in some circles as tilting toward the West and biased against communist North Korea and China. In this context the head of the World Peace Council, a Soviet-front organization in which Bonnard was active, asked him to document the links between ICRC Assembly members and Swiss defense corporations. The intent was to discredit the ICRC by proving it was pro-West, supportive of Western military efforts, and thus not neutral.

Bonnard compiled such a report using open sources. Being under surveillance by Swiss authorities, he was arrested on his way to a Council meeting in Berlin, his papers seized, and eventually he was prosecuted for espionage. While the court convicted him, it gave him a meagre penalty of fifteen days in jail, suspended, which could be seen as an indication that the court thought the government had been overzealous in prosecuting him. It was not the ICRC but a public prosecutor who had brought the legal complaint. The ICRC leadership probably did not care for his politics but did not seem overly exercised about the matter. Swiss judicial authorities did share confidential information with the ICRC, showing the close relations among governmental and private elites.

It was a fact that several Assembly members did have economic links to various Swiss defense corporations, just as ICRC President Max Huber had had links to various defense contractors in Italy and Germany that benefitted from various fascist policies in the 1930s and 1940s. Just as the ICRC had not been attentive to its Assembly members having real or perceived conflicts of interest back then, so the status quo on that subject continued to prevail in the 1950s – and beyond for a time.

The larger picture, which is perhaps why Bern went after Professor Bonnard, was that while the Swiss state was legally and militarily neutral, it was pro-West politically and ideologically. It did not join NATO, or even the United Nations until 2002, but it bought its weapons for its armed neutrality only from the West, and secretly it shared its defense planning with the United Kingdom.[6] Clearly it was part of the democratic-capitalist world. Bern was sensitive to any challenge to its neutrality, being keen to make sure that the Soviet Union and its communist allies regarded it as neutral. As part of this sensitivity, it wanted to protect ICRC claims to neutrality as well.

The Bonnard affair is not much recalled by anyone these days, not in Switzerland, not at the ICRC, and certainly not in the broader world – a very few historians excepted.[7] But in the 1950s with the Cold War in full bloom, Swiss leaders were both strongly anti-communist and desirous of being accepted as neutral by Moscow. This was certainly true of Foreign Minister Max Petitpierre, who later became an Assembly member at the ICRC. This paradoxical combination of anti-communism and neutrality led to considerable efforts to stress the neutrality dimension, even if the neutral claims at issue in the Bonnard affair pertained to the ICRC. One could say that at the time of Bonnard's arrest and prosecution, Switzerland was having its own version of McCarthyism which involved suppression of peaceful views supportive of communism, but at the same time wanted to preserve a version of neutrality in foreign affairs.

For present purposes it is secondary that the Swiss paradoxical position worked. Moscow accepted Switzerland as neutral, despite the latter's political and ideological preferences for the West, which was also true for Austria and Sweden and Finland. The key for Moscow was that these states should exercise military neutrality and stay out of NATO.

As for the ICRC, one could say, even without a detailed study on the subject, that Moscow over time softened its views about the organization by comparison with some earlier years, even cooperated in the drafting of the 1949 Geneva Conventions (for strategic rather than humanitarian reasons), but never cooperated with the ICRC regarding field operations involving communist countries – not in Korea in the 1950s, or Vietnam in the 1960s, or Hungary in 1956, or Czechoslovakia in 1968. (Toward the end of the Cold War the ICRC carried out detention visits in Poland; that was after Moscow has lost full control of the Warsaw communist regime.) But all that goes far beyond the Bonnard affair. We return to the subject of conflicts of interests by Assembly members later.

II   Nigeria–Biafra, 1967–1970

Similar to the Bonnard affair, the Swiss government in Bern showed much interest in the image and reputation of the ICRC regarding the Nigerian civil war, in this case not so much about its neutrality but about its competence. As an amateurish, fragmented, and under-resourced ICRC stumbled and fumbled and bumbled its way through the early stages of this conflict, some Swiss diplomats expressed concern that ICRC difficulties were reflecting badly on Switzerland as a whole. It followed that when the ICRC turned to Bern for help in dealing with its predicament, at that time increasingly under the spotlight of media coverage and world attention, Bern responded not only with a loan of a high-profile diplomat, August Lindt (among other staff and resources), but with instructions that ICRC officials were not to interfere with his role.[8]

This is not the place for an extended discussion of the ICRC and Nigeria–Biafra, which was extremely important not only for the future of the ICRC but for the evolution of large-scale humanitarian relief in general. The conflict and some French critics of ICRC policies led to the creation of Doctors Without Borders and other developments that continue today. The conflict also comes up in many discussions of the Red Cross/ICRC approach to topics such as remaining discreet or speaking out, or acting only within the principles of IHL as compared to a more radical humanitarian intervention. There is a vast literature on Nigeria–Biafra concerning these and other topics.

For present purposes, what is to be emphasized from this conflict is the extremely close relations between Geneva and Bern as of the late

1960s, the orientation of Bern (and its legations abroad) in seeing the ICRC as a means to a larger Swiss national reputation, and eventually considerable friction between Lindt and some Committee members as the latter sought to recover some of their separate identity and autonomy that had been given away under duress to Bern and Lindt.

As in the Bonnard Affair so in Nigeria–Biafra, and so one would guess in a number of other cases, Bern never viewed a particular case strictly in terms of NIIHA values, or Red Cross principles, or IHL principles, but rather with some aspects of the above combined with Swiss national political interests. This observation fits with southern Africa in the 1970s as per below.

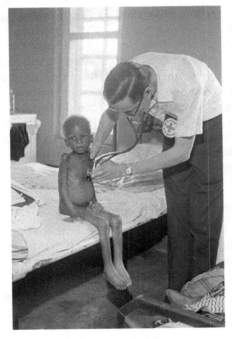

Photograph 8.2 An American doctor examines a malnourished child in 1968 in the Biafran–Nigerian war. The ICRC, short of staff, incorporated several persons from other organizations into its field mission. The issue of the fate of civilians, especially children, in Biafra became politicized. Biafran authorities and their public relations firm based in Europe utilized images of malnourished children to build support for the secessionist movement. The ICRC, also under pressure from competing relief actors, took controversial decisions as a result.

III   Southern Africa, 1970s

Continuing close relations between Bern and Geneva were again demonstrated by a minor matter in the 1970s.[9] The Swiss foreign ministry, hoping to improve its image with newly independent Black authorities in southern Africa, loaned some personnel to the ICRC so it could better carry out its humanitarian assistance operations in places such as Angola and Mozambique. Bern had not been in the forefront of efforts to terminate Portuguese colonialism by comparison to other European neutrals, for example Sweden. And so it wanted to be seen in the newly independent southern Africa states, even belatedly, as interested and supportive.

There is no known evidence that Bern's loan of personnel was anything but supportive of what the ICRC decided itself in Geneva. But it would not be out of the question if, on return to the Foreign Ministry, these couple of staff persons working for the ICRC might turn out to have commented on political as well as humanitarian matters. But no humanitarian values seem to have been compromised by this seconding of Swiss governmental staff personnel to the ICRC. It seems the ICRC had purely humanitarian objectives in its activity in southern Africa, whereas, as usual, the Swiss government had mixed motives: support humanitarian programs by the ICRC as a means to improving Swiss diplomatic relations. This example was, however, similar to British Labor governments financially supporting Amnesty International for reasons of more narrow national interests.

IV   ICRC–Swiss Agreements, 1993–2020

More important than the Bonnard Affair and the southern Africa case, but less important than Nigeria–Biafra, were certain ICRC-Swiss agreements in contemporary times.

Cornelio Sommaruga, the ICRC president in 1993, despite having been himself a high Swiss official in Bern but not always part of the foreign ministry, was determined to reinforce ICRC independence and its humanitarian neutrality. His stance was triggered by continuing discussion of the ICRC record during World War II, as well as by the persistent view in some circles that the organization was little more than the humanitarian arm of the Swiss foreign ministry. He therefore negotiated a binding Headquarters Agreement with the Confederation trying to make clear that such a view was mistaken.

On the government side, a consensus developed in Bern that the best way to support the ICRC was to fully respect its independence and the way it fashioned its humanitarian neutrality as per a new document. To quote from a governmental report in 1992 mentioned at the start of this chapter:

The federal authorities should avoid mixing up Switzerland's policy with the activities of the ICRC and the neutrality of the State with the Committee's humanitarian neutrality. They should not attempt to influence the decisions of the ICRC and should respect its independence. This position would become clearer if Switzerland were to conclude a headquarters agreement with the Committee, granting it the international immunities and privileges usually accorded to international organizations in Geneva.[10]

This 1992 view in Bern can be compared with a 1965 governmental view, recorded in a memorandum that was published later.

That the ICRC wants to present itself as free of any influence and allegiance to any government, even that of Switzerland, is derived from the need to be able to invoke at all times this necessary freedom from the threat of foreign interference. But the ICRC has never had any secrets from the Swiss government, which has always had a way into the Committee.[11]

Sommaruga, wanting to put to rest the 1965 view that reflected the traditional interlocking of Bern and Geneva, and wanting to take advantage of the 1992 consensus in Bern, was happy to conclude the new 1993 headquarters agreement which was legally binding.[12] The Swiss government agreed to treat the ICRC as if it were an international intergovernmental organization (IGO), with the rights and immunities that that status entailed. Most other states then took the same view. Thus, the ICRC was officially treated the same way as, say, a UN agency. It had already been afforded permanent observer status at the United Nations in 1990. The 1993 HQA stated that ICRC premises, including the archives, were inviolable by Swiss authorities, similar to a foreign diplomatic mission. ICRC communications were also said to be off-limits to Swiss authorities. There were provisions on tax matters and other administrative details that need not concern us here. The document was a cut-and-dried legal instrument, speaking to the details of ICRC independent status, spelling out in concrete and boring terms the limits of Swiss legal authority for the organization. The document was reprinted in full in the RC *Review*.

The ICRC during the presidency of Peter Maurer felt the need to add protocols to this document three times by 2021. There had been no such additions or clarifications of understandings during the twelve-year presidency of Jakob Kellenberger. In fact, as will be shown later, Kellenberger kept his distance from Bern. The Maurer additional protocols occurred in 2013, 2017, and 2020. None has ever been published

Photograph 8.3 ICRC President Cornelio Sommaruga (left) hosts Swiss President Flavio Cotti in 1998. Five years earlier, Sommaruga had negotiated a headquarters agreement with Bern formalizing ICRC independence. Years later ICRC President Peter Maurer negotiated protocols to the HQ agreement stressing the closeness of ICRC–Bern relations. Sommaruga kept good relations with Bern while emphasizing ICRC independence. Maurer did not change any legal arrangements with Bern but, more than Sommaruga, promoted the image of tight ICRC coordination with the Swiss foreign ministry.

but only announced in press releases by Bern.[13] They have not been mentioned at all either on the ICRC website or in the *Review*.

The last or 2020 protocol, approved by the Swiss Federal Council, appears to be legally binding and a technical addition to the 1993 HQ agreement covering a variety of specific mundane subjects including the inviolability of computerized data held by the ICRC. It can be found as an official Swiss Federal document.[14]

The protocols of October 17, 2013 and May 1, 2017, which appear to be nonbinding "gentlemen's agreements," never approved by the Swiss Federal Council, have leaked. (It is not clear if they were approved by the ICRC Assembly as compared to just being negotiated by the Office of the President.) They are different in many ways from what Sommaruga negotiated in 1993. Importantly, the general thrust of the two protocols that we can read is to show the closeness of ICRC relations with

Bern, whereas the 1993 Memorandum of Understanding (MOU) was all about separateness.

Analyzing the 2013 protocol, we certainly find many references to the independence of the ICRC and its NIIHA values. It is clear that the 2013 document is additional in an informal way to the 1993 HQA. But much of the 2013 addition is about the virtues of Bern and its close role in ICRC activities. A reader might easily draw the conclusion that one central point of the document was to provide a positive view of Swiss foreign policy.

In my English translation from the French, the document says that Bern is quite attached to IHL and is constantly involved in its application. The document reminds of the Swiss financial support to the ICRC. The reader is reminded of "high quality" exchanges between Bern and Geneva, and the long humanitarian tradition of the former. The details and different levels of cooperation are then spelled out at some length, giving the impression that the Swiss Foreign Ministry spends much time, effort, and money on the ICRC and humanitarian affairs. The document indicates Bern intends to support ICRC operations, but then adds the words "if possible" or "to the extent possible." So one finds bold humanitarian commitment by Bern but with diplomatic double speak. The two actors pledge to exchange information and coordinate, but then add "if such be the case," meaning if it transpires.

Article 3 of the document pledges the two parties to hold an annual high level meeting organized by the ICRC president and the Swiss foreign minister with the participation of other top officials from both sides. Other bilateral meetings are mandated for lower levels of the two organizations. Then there are more details about Swiss financial support.

One might be forgiven for thinking that the general point of this 2013 addition was to provide an ode to the Swiss Foreign Ministry, the Swiss government more generally, and the Swiss people who pay the taxes to undergird governmental support to the ICRC. There are no real alterations to the 1993 HQA terms of the nitty-gritty details of ICRC independence. That is to say, there is no evident substantial or factual-legal reason to have the 2013 additional agreement regarding ICRC independence from Bern. But in terms of semantical emphases and therefore optics, the new document is not primarily about independence and separation, or the difference between state neutrality and humanitarian neutrality, but essentially about cooperation and coordination between Geneva and Bern.

The 2017 additional protocol, again nonbinding, is not about refining the details of the original 1993 HQA but about reiterating cooperation and adding certain subjects on which Bern and Geneva will cooperate. There is mention of "Geneva International," which is a government-sponsored public relations program to emphasize the city and canton of Geneva and all the international organizations that have an office there. There is mention of "protracted conflicts," which is a theme stressed by the ICRC and, as we discuss elsewhere, said to justify certain policies such as more attention to economic resiliency and not just emergency, short-term relief.

As for Article 3 in the 2017 protocol on an annual high-level meeting, the changed wording reads (my translation): "a high-level bilateral meeting is organized one time each year between the head of the DFAE [Federal Department of Foreign Affairs] and the ICRC President." The required presence of other officials has been dropped, leaving the two leaders possibly meeting alone. The reason for this change is entirely opaque. It is a change that Sommaruga, and probably Kellenberger, would not have approved. Having the ICRC president and the Swiss foreign minister meeting alone to discuss unspecified subjects is contrary to the image that Sommaruga was trying to create with the original 1993 HQA emphasizing ICRC independence and separateness. It seems contrary to the 1992 Confederation report saying the government should not get involved in ICRC policy making. It is contrary to the behavior of Kellenberger who, during his ten years at the ICRC, apparently had few private meetings with Bern officials.

The 2017 document, even more than the one in 2013, creates an impression that does nothing to dispel the notion that the relations between Bern and Geneva might be suspect, otherwise why should the two leaders have the right to meet alone. It leads to speculation about whether the Swiss Foreign Ministry has too much influence on ICRC affairs, especially if a one-on-one meeting of the leaders of the two organizations should discuss personnel matters such as who should be in ICRC leadership positions or, possibly, how to manage the triangular relationship between Bern, the ICRC and the WEF – the latter being then quite important to the first two.

Such a concern is not without basis. In 2020, Swiss Foreign Minister Cassis said the following in an interview (my translation):

From a legal point of view, the [ICRC] independence is total. We have no right of decision within the organization. But that would hide the truth that affirms that there is a moral and political interdependence [between the two organizations]. It is not by accident if the ICRC is directed by a former Swiss diplomat [Peter Maurer], if we allocate 150 million francs in Swiss donations to finance the ICRC, and if myself and the ICRC director general call each other regularly. We are proud to have the ICRC headquarters on Swiss territory.[15]

Indeed, reading the 2013 and 2017 protocols together in comparison with the 1993 HQA, one gets the impression that Maurer thought Bern was being held at too great a distance, given its diplomatic and financial support. Or, he was agreeable to a request from Bern that it be given more recognition in ICRC affairs. Under either interpretation, the origin of the push for revisions being unknown to outsiders, then Maurer apparently agreed to create a semantical platform mostly extolling the virtues of Bern, but with some continued attention to ICRC independence and humanitarian neutrality. The fact remains that the core details negotiated by Sommaruga all remained unchanged pertaining to inviolability, taxes, and other concrete matters. All the changes in 2013 and 2017 had to do with optics, chief among which was recognition of the special role of Swiss foreign policy, and concrete collaboration between Bern and the ICRC.[16]

The 2013 and 2017 protocols, especially the latter, may be somewhat explained by a Swiss document that became public. The Swiss Agency for Development Cooperation (SDC), a division within the Foreign Ministry (e.g. the Agency for International Development within the US Department of State) made an evaluation of the ICRC in 2017 – apparently the first ever by Bern. Written for the Swiss SDC by outside (American) contractors supervised by Bern, it essentially asked: since the Swiss state donates considerable money to fund ICRC headquarters, what are we getting for our money?[17]

The answer was mostly structured in terms of Swiss narrow, even parochial, national interest: We expect the ICRC to be supportive of our "international Geneva" project (already identified above as a marketing and public relations effort), to create a well-structured process for dialogue with Bern, and to stay in Geneva rather than moving out! There was one brief, if positive, mention of the relations between ICRC HQ and field delegations. The report said the ICRC had a favorable competitive position on the global humanitarian scene. There was a comment that the ICRC was good at self-evaluation. But the analysis was not much concerned with ICRC humanitarian protection and assistance in the world compared to returns on the Swiss franc in terms of narrow-minded Swiss self-interest. This was partially because the consultants were told to focus on the Swiss donation to ICRC headquarters expenses and not to ICRC field operations, the latter funded by special appeals for particular operations and programs. That such a report failed to emphasize whether the ICRC was good at humanitarian programs can partially be understood as indicative of the narrow nationalistic and nonhumanitarian (and nonhistorical) approach of Bern to the ICRC.

In the light of this document and possibly others like it, it seems the ICRC decided to placate Bern by creating a precisely defined process of consultation, by mentioning "international Geneva" in the second protocol to the HQ agreement, and in general by ensuring the continued flow of Swiss funding in a time of ICRC expansion and budget needs by scratching Bern's itchy back. It used to be that the Swiss donation to the ICRC HQ was by special and separate legislative act. Now that donation comes out of the regular budget for the Foreign Ministry and its subsidiary SDC. That change contributed to Bern's evaluating the ICRC in terms similar to other budget lines: how is the ICRC serving our Swiss interests, not how well is the ICRC advancing humanitarian values and programs globally.

Sommaruga openly, and his successor at the ICRC Jacob Kellenberger more quietly, had clearly distanced themselves from the Swiss foreign ministry. This was striking in the case of the latter, who had been the top civil servant in that ministry. But when he became ICRC president, Kellenberger seems to have severed almost all connections with his former employer. He was rather like the well-respected American diplomat Ralph Bunche who, when seconded to the UN Secretariat, was almost never seen in the presence of US officials so as to cultivate not only the image but also project the reality of being strictly a UN official.[18]

Peter Maurer was different from his immediate predecessors. (And Foreign Minister Cassis expressed a different view from the 1992 Swiss report in favor of the government not getting involved in internal ICRC policymaking.) Maurer was often seen in the presence of Swiss officials, spent considerable time in Bern (he kept a bicycle there!), and negotiated the two diplomatic protocols that seemed to draw him and the Swiss foreign minister closer together in private meetings.

Maurer's style on the matter of relations with Bern, very different from Sommaruga and Kellenberger, gave rise to all sorts of theories about what was going on. But given the lack of transparency about such subjects in Swiss elite circles, no outsider was sure of the relevant facts. There are those who see Maurer as more driven by Swiss national interests than humanitarian principles. (Apparently when he gave notice in late November 2021 that he was leaving the presidency in the fall of 2022, he did not give advance notice to Bern and he did not consult Bern about his successor, as best outsiders can tell.) But for sure, at least in terms of optics, Maurer had shrunk the distance between Bern and Geneva that Sommaruga had created.

The situation from 2013 and especially 2017 did nothing to dispel lingering criticisms from the 1930s and 1940s. In those protocols, Maurer seemed to have a blind spot as to why Sommaruga did what he did. Or, he kept the essence of the Sommaruga HQA, but placated Bern. Either way, the optics about ICRC independence, and about the difference between state neutrality as practiced by Bern and humanitarian

Photograph 8.4 In the field in conflict situations the ICRC depended on an image of independent neutrality in order to be able to operate. Nevertheless, sometimes its personnel or facilities were attacked. Here one can see its office in Peshawar, Pakistan, closed after a British staff member was killed. In this case the organization was forced to suspend its activities for a time until guaranties of security could be reestablished.

neutrality as practiced by the ICRC, were altered for many close observers. This had possible relevance to the Ukraine war, as discussed in the Epilogue.

V   The Crypto A.G. Affair, 2020 and Beyond

Logically interesting was the disclosure of a Swiss connection to an American–German spying operation during the Cold War. The Crypto A.G. affair once again demonstrated that Swiss political neutrality was different from ICRC humanitarian neutrality, and that the humanitarian organization should be diligent about maintaining its independence from the pro-Western state. The affair erupted at the time when some close observers were critical of the 2013 and 2017 MOUs and thought President Maurer ought to emulate Presidents Sommaruga and Kellenberger and display more independence from Bern.

During the Cold War, the United States and Germany were the secret owners of a Swiss electronics company that was part of a spying program.[19] The company's software, used for coding messages, was sold to governments. It contained a component that allowed Washington and Bonn to read supposedly encrypted communications involving governments in Argentina and Chile, among others. The role of the Swiss government in all this remained unclear for a time.

Two parliamentary reports, one public and one never released, seemed to conclude that the Swiss intelligence agencies knowledgeable about Crypto held the information closely, not informing the government or foreign ministry.[20] So the Swiss government and foreign ministry were in a position to claim plausible ignorance about this controversial cooperation with the West in the Cold War. If true, which can be debated, almost certainly none of the information gained through electronic spying was shared with the ICRC.

It was perfectly clear, and had been for some time, as discussed previously, that Swiss neutrality was a pro-Western neutrality that in various ways took sides in strategic or geopolitics in spite of claiming to be neutral. Or, Bern said Swiss neutrality was strictly military, whereas diplomatically the Swiss state was partial toward widespread Western practices of politics and economics, democracy, and capitalism. This latter understanding was articulated explicitly (a) after Switzerland joined the United Nations (and was elected to its Security Council), and (b) after Russia fully invaded Ukraine. As already noted, during the Cold War Bern shared Swiss defense plans with the United Kingdom and bought weapons systems only from the West.

It is possible that Swiss intelligence agencies had knowledge of general arrangements regarding Crypto A.G. but not necessarily the detailed results of that spying as obtained by American and German intelligence agencies. It remains unclear who in Bern exactly knew the contents of intercepted foreign governmental communications. If the Swiss intelligence agencies had inside knowledge about atrocities in Argentina and Chile in the 1970s, for example, most probably it did not share such information with the ICRC – which was trying to mitigate the gross violations of human rights in those countries, which included arbitrary detention, torture, murder, and so on. On the other hand, if elements of the Swiss state were privy to inside information but did not pass that along to the ICRC, what should be said about Bern's asserted devotion to protecting human dignity?

Did President Maurer and the rest of the ICRC leadership draw the right conclusions from following this Crypto A.G. affair? Was there a discussion in Geneva about the ICRC being sucked into geostrategic controversies that could damage its NIIHA image? After the Crypto affair, did Geneva have a high-level discussion reaffirming the difference between ICRC humanitarian neutrality and Swiss state neutrality – the latter allowing for taking sides nonmilitarily in political conflicts? There is no public evidence about any ICRC meeting and conclusion.

Other links between Bern and Geneva could be discussed, but space imposes limits.[21]

VI   Conclusion

Overall, ICRC–Swiss relations remained close and complex – and sometimes troubling – whether one focuses on 1942 or 2022. We mention this linkage in other chapters and the Epilogue.

Notes

1 MENAFN, "How Do Swiss Arms End Up in Conflict Zones?" April 2, 2020, https://menafn.com/1099652307/How-do-Swiss-arms-end-up-in-conflict-zones (accessed November 18, 2022). In 2020 a Swiss referendum rejected a ban on weapons sales.

2 Lisa Jucca, "Special Report: How the U.S. Cracked Open Secret Vaults at UBS," *Reuters*, April 8, 2010, www.reuters.com/article/us-banks-ubs/special-report-how-the-u-s-cracked-open-secret-vaults-at-ubs-idUSTRE6380UA20100409 (accessed November 18, 2022). This is one reliable source, among many, dealing with use of Swiss banks for avoiding taxes.

3 Stuart E. Eisenstadt, *Imperfect Justice: Looted Assets, Slave Labor, and the Unfinished Business of World War II* (New York: Public Affairs, 2003).

4 On both subjects see David P. Forsythe, "The Geneva Conventions after 70 Years: The Fate of Charity in Turbulent Times," *Global Governance*, 25/3 (2019), pp. 359–369.

5 Catherine Rey-Schyrr, *History of the International Committee of the Red Cross: From Yalta to Dien Bien Phu, 1945–1955* (Geneva: ICRC, 2017). The published edition benefitted greatly from the revisions made by François Bugnion. See also Forsythe, *The Humanitarians*, cited in previous chapters.

6 Marco Wyss, *Arms Transfers, Neutrality and Britain's Role in the Cold War: Anglo-Swiss Relations 1945–1958* (Leiden and Boston: Brill, 2013).

7 Hadrien Buclin, "Swiss Intellectuals and the Cold War: Anti-communist Politics in a Neutral Country," *Journal of Cold War Studies* 19/4 (2017), pp. 137–167.

8 An early source based on ICRC archives (before the archives were open to all) is Thierry Hentsch, *Face au Blocus: La Croix-Rouge international dans le Nigeria en guerre (1967–1970)* (Geneva: HEI, 1973); but better for present purposes is Marie-Luce Desgrandchamps, "'Organizing the Unpredictable:' The Nigeria-Biafra War and Its Impact on the ICRC," *International Review of the Red Cross*, 94/888 (Winter, 2012), pp. 1409–1432. https://library.icrc.org/library/docs/DOC/irrc-888-desgrandchamps.pdf (accessed November 18, 2022).

9 Sabina Widmer, "Neutrality Challenged in a Cold War Conflict: Switzerland, the International Committee of the Red Cross, and the Angola War," *Cold War History*, 18/2 (2018), pp. 203–220.

10 *Swiss Neutrality Put to the Test – Swiss Foreign Policy between Continuity and Change, Report by a Study Group on Questions of Swiss Neutrality*, Berne, Federal Chancellery, March 1992, p. 25.

11 Quoted in Frederic Burnand, "The ICRC as a Swiss Political Tool," *Swiss Info*, September 4, 2017, www.swissinfo.ch/eng/politics/dangerous-liaisons-_the-icrc-as-a-swiss-political-tool/43487480 (accessed February 6, 2023).

12 "Agreement between the International Committee of the Red Cross and the Swiss Federal Council," *International Review of the Red Cross*, 293 (1993), pp. 152–160; footnotes omitted.

13 Swiss Federal Council, "Enhanced Cooperation with the ICRC," October 17, 2003, www.admin.ch/gov/en/start/documentation/media-releases.msg-id-50634.html (accessed November 18, 2022); Swiss Federal Department of Foreign Affairs, "Innovative Measures to Help People in Need: Switzerland and the ICRC to Expand Cooperation," May 1, 2017, www.eda.admin.ch/eda/en/fdfa/fdfa/aktuell/news.html/content/eda/en/meta/news/2017/5/1/66539 (accessed November 18, 2022); Swiss Federal Council, "Switzerland and ICRC Sign Protocol Amending Headquarters Agreement," November 27, 2020, www.admin.ch/gov/en/start/documentation/media-releases.msg-id-81392.html (accessed November 18, 2022).

14 Swiss Federal Council, "Accord du 19 mars 1993 entre le Conseil fédéral Suisse et le Comite international de la Croix-Rouge en vue de déterminer le statut juridique du Comité en Suisse," November 27, 2020, www.fedlex.admin.ch/eli/oc/2020/969/fr (accessed November 18, 2022).

15 Stéphane Bussard, "Ignazio Cassis: La Suisse doit montrer au monde qu'elle croit encore fermement au droit international humanitaire," *Le Temps*, August 12, 2020, modified August 13, 2020, www.letemps.ch/suisse/ignazio-cassis-suisse-montrer-monde-croit-fermement-droit-international-humanitaire (accessed November 18, 2020).

16 The 2020 MOU apparently had something to do with the inviolability of ICRC computerized data. www.admin.ch/gov/en/start/documentation/media-releases.msg-id-81392.html (accessed November 19, 2022).

17 SDC, "Swiss Contribution to the ICRC Headquarters," July 2017, www.newsd.admin.ch/newsd/NSBExterneStudien/820/attachment/en/3465.pdf (accessed November 18, 2022).

18 See further Brian Urquhart, *Ralph Bunche: An American Odyssey* (New York: W. W. Norton & Company, 1993).

19 For a mainstream journalistic account, see Greg Miller, "The Intelligence Coup of the Century," *The Washington Post*, February 11, 2020, www.washingtonpost.com/graphics/2020/world/national-security/cia-crypto-encryption-machines-espionage/ (accessed November 18, 2022).

20 Reuters, "Swiss Cabinet Blames Intelligence Community for Crypto AG Affair," May 28, 2021, www.reuters.com/technology/swiss-cabinet-blames-intelligence-community-crypto-ag-affair-2021-05-28/ (accessed December 14, 2022).

21 In spring 2020 a draft paper was circulated in the state bureaucracy in Bern suggesting one should view the ICRC as important to Swiss national interests. The wording suggested the ICRC was mostly working for Swiss interests. While ICRC headquarters was publicly silent, without apparent protest,

some ICRC alumni saw the problem and made contacts in Bern. The wording was changed. The alumni involved knew the organization's history from the 1940s and were sensitive on the matter of ICRC independence from Bern. We do not know what contacts, if any, the ICRC HQ might have made in Bern on this matter. But they were not public. It is likely that the early wording stemmed from some government fonctionnaire who was oblivious to ICRC history. That would be common, even in Switzerland where the ICRC is still not terribly well known in non-French-speaking areas.

The 2017 evaluation of the ICRC by Bern, cited above at note 17, is all about internal management in Geneva and whether Bern is getting a good return on its money; there is no reference to a historical reason why Sommaruga would want to establish some formal distance from Bern, and why Bern would have been in favor of some distance back at that time in the early 1990s.

9 Humanitarians and Business
Part I – For Humanity?

If every corporation felt a need to give away 5% for general humanitarian purposes we'd be in better shape.

Andrew Young, US civil rights leader and Ambassador to the UN[1]

The ICRC has a long history of close relations with the business community. Early leaders were strong believers in private enterprise, and some were actively engaged in private business while serving the ICRC. This is understandable since early on all Committee members served in a voluntary capacity. (Gustave Moynier – who as we know built the ICRC up until about 1905 – and his wife came from wealthy families. While trained in law, he never took a salaried position because financially he did not need to.)

Early ICRC leaders, particularly Moynier, who basically *was* the ICRC from 1867 to about 1905 (he died in 1910), were obviously skeptical about political parties that were critical of, or would highly restrict, the private for-profit sector. As noted earlier, in pushing for the first Geneva Convention of 1864 the ICRC bypassed Geneva city officials who were seen as too far on the political left. The organization was sustained for a time by donations from the business sector, first in Geneva and then in Switzerland as a whole. To put it mildly, the rise of Marxist ideology and then the consolidation of the Soviet Union greatly troubled the ICRC's leadership. The Bolsheviks challenged both private property rights and religion, two central pillars of the world view held by early ICRC leaders.

The ICRC leadership early on was dominated by conservative, pro-business circles of opinion. Early Committee members included not only businesspersons from the upper classes including more than a few bankers, but also those from other usually conservative professions such as lawyers, doctors, and Swiss military and diplomatic personnel. Labor leaders are notable mostly by their absence in the leadership over time. Few have been the members of the governing board, and only one president, who would clearly self-identify as politically left-center.

Rather typical among recent officials was the ICRC vice president during 2008–2018, Christine Beerli, who had been active in the Swiss Free Democratic Party, which was center-right in Swiss politics.

An earlier chapter demonstrated some evident conservative slants in ICRC policymaking during past eras – for example, tilting toward Mussolini in the 1930s regarding Abyssinia, failing to adopt a dynamic discreet diplomacy toward Nazi Germany and its genocide in the 1940s. However, it is quite possible that in other eras the members of the ICRC Assembly, whatever their professions, were diligent in exercising their NIIHA mandate. That would be a good subject for historians in the future, looking at eras as recorded in the open parts of the archives.

Against the background of its social and political history, as already mentioned in several chapters, it is not very surprising that the contemporary ICRC would endorse the idea of a beneficial role for business and continue to reach out to the private sector for both donations and partnerships.

The ICRC was certainly not alone in this orientation. The idea that private enterprise should only make money for its owners and shareholders (as per, for example, the arguments of Milton Friedman and the Chicago Schools of Economics), while certainly not dead, was increasingly challenged by the view that business had a responsibility to benefit various stakeholders – not just shareholders. With some form of capitalism dominating the global scene after the collapse of European communism in 1991, even in nominally communist countries such as China and Vietnam, the question was raised with renewed vigor about what kind of capitalism should be preferred.

In 2000 the United Nations launched the UN Global Compact, an effort to get the private capitalist sector to voluntarily accept the notion of business social responsibility and play a positive role regarding human rights, humanitarianism, and ecological affairs. Across the globe in the first quarter of the twenty-first century, one saw a broad push demanding that business adopt "responsible" positions whether the topic was climate change, women's equality, police brutality, complicity in atrocities, voter suppression, domestic abuse, various forms of racism and neocolonialism, Russian aggression in Ukraine, or some other topic. Numerous business schools introduced courses on business social responsibility, not only to deal with substance but to relate to students increasingly interested in that topic.

To be sure, some major foreign companies did not pull out of Russia after its invasion of Ukraine (e.g., Burger King, Marriott), and there was a pushback against ESG investing (with attention to environmental, social, and governance issues) in some circles of opinion.

One can easily see that the push for business social responsibility was fraught with difficult decisions, and ICRC contemporary relations with the business community were certainly not free from controversy. There were some new and complex dimensions to the old subject. Were there some donors that the organization should avoid? Were there some partnerships that were ill-advised? Was the Assembly careful about the appearance of conflicts of interests between member's economic links and the ICRC's image as a NIIHA actor? Did ICRC connections to the private sector actually have very little impact on its financial situation? But did those links actually increase questions about the ICRC's commitment to dynamic pursuit of responding to humanitarian need?

I   Budgets, and Both Public and Private Donors

The ICRC has almost never had a surplus of funds and so it was logical that the early ICRC leadership would look to the business community for help. It can be recalled that the original Geneva committee on aid to the military wounded, which evolved into the ICRC, declared itself into permanent existence without any promise of financial help from its former parent, the Geneva Public Welfare Society. Immediately thereafter it operated on a financial shoestring, with good intentions far outstripping resources. For years Moynier ran the Committee, such as it was, out of his Geneva residence, sometimes with one assistant to help with correspondence. While the Committee officially had between five and ten members depending on the year up until 1914, most of that time it was largely a one-man operation with a few Swiss banks donating the meager funds needed.[2] During the Franco–Prussian war of 1870–1871, special voluntary donations flowed in from governments and private sources, but all that was short-lived.

In a way it is curious, but in a way understandable, that the rest of the RC Movement has never covered much of the ICRC's expenses. The National RC Societies have their own budgets to worry about, being officially independent from the ICRC and having their own varying programs. The RC Federation, certainly first as the League of RC Societies from 1919, was in tension if not outright conflict with the ICRC for a time over Movement leadership. After the early death of John P. Hutchinson who had championed the RC League as *the* leader of the International Red Cross, and as the American Red Cross retrenched after World War I taking its funding with it, the League itself was hurting for money. During that Great War, which solidified the ICRC and at least some National RC Societies as permanent actors on the world stage, the ICRC operated mostly on donations from the governments using its services plus private donations – mostly from Swiss banking and industry. If the National RC Societies paid little into the Geneva headquarters, they did pay for most of the relief parcels that the ICRC distributed in the POW camps.

The general pattern continued in the interwar years of 1919–1939, with the ICRC short of funds. The National RC Societies made donations that covered about a third of ICRC expenses. In fact, budgetary pressures explain why the ICRC had adopted its first statutes in 1915. Moving from pragmatic practice to a more formalized statement of purpose and structure, it wanted to be able to accept estate gifts under Swiss law. Once it started the POW agency in August 1914 with salaried employees, it needed a steady flow of income rather than depend heavily on state donations during wars. Then after the RC League had been created in 1919, by 1928 one also needed broad Movement statutes to go along with revised ICRC and National RC Society statutes. But the original ICRC statutes were devised out of financial need. Once again in the interwar years the ICRC relied heavily on donations from the Swiss private sector, especially in the absence of governmental contributions during nonwar years.

Even in World War II, governmental and RC donations only covered about 60 percent of the ICRC's expenses, with most of the rest being eventually met by the Swiss public and certain corporations. The IBM corporation, for example, based in the United States, donated staff and machines to the ICRC in Geneva for its tracking efforts concerning prisoners of war. (IBM also contracted with Nazi Germany for less enlightened projects.[3] IBM worked both sides of the street.) Some shipping firms donated their services for transport of humanitarian relief under the ICRC aegis.

For perhaps two decades after World War II the ICRC was faced with the possibility of going out of business. There was the controversy about its stance when confronting the Holocaust, covered primarily in Chapter 7. There was the decline in governmental funding after 1945 when the world war ended. There was only lukewarm, or worse, acceptance of the ICRC in the communist world. There was the cost of sizable and ongoing diplomatic protection efforts in places such as former British Palestine, as the ICRC tried to prove to the world it was still needed and relevant.[4] In 1967 the ICRC manifested a global staff of about 160 persons.

There were no large-scale relief efforts, which helps explain the organization's unprepared status at the start of the Nigerian–Biafran war, also already mentioned in preceding chapters. (When in 1971 there was a mass movement of persons into India because of violent developments

Photograph 9.1 During World War II, IBM donated early computers to the ICRC Central Tracing Agency that utilized punch cards to
track missing persons and prisoners, as seen here. During the same
era, IBM sold its services and products to Nazi Germany for a variety
of purposes, including tracking the changing capacity of concentration
camps and also the movement of trains that sometimes carried political
prisoners as well as POWs. IBM worked both sides of the street.

in what had been east Pakistan and what was to become Bangladesh,
neither the United Nations nor the Red Cross system was prepared to
cope with relief on that scale.) Government and Movement donations
only covered perhaps 40 percent of the ICRC's costs for the first couple
of decades after 1945. The rest again came from Swiss corporations and
a Swiss public collection, as the ICRC in 1999 finally got into fundraising campaigns more systematically.[5]

If we summarize the contemporary situation running from about 1990
until 2020, we find that governments and their intergovernmental organizations cover about 85 percent, more or less, of the ICRC's expenses
via voluntary donations. The National RC Societies (NRCS) cover
about 10 percent of the remaining costs through their voluntary donations. (There are required NRCS dues to the Federation but not to the
ICRC.) This leaves about 5 percent of costs covered by the private sector. Somewhat more precisely for these years, business donations might

average 3.5 percent of total ICRC income, or close to it, with some slight variation, with private foundations and individuals contributing approximately the last 1.5 percent.

To fully understand the matter of ICRC business relations, it helps to have a good understanding of some details of the *public* financing of the ICRC. One aspect of this situation is the Donor Support Group (DSG), created by the ICRC in 1997–1998 to reward major governmental donors and entice others to join.[6] In recent years private donations have stagnated at a low level, with the ICRC being overwhelming dependent on public contributions. State donors, when they contribute 10 million Swiss francs annually, are recognized by DSG membership which entitles them to special briefings and sometimes a trip to observe certain field activities. Since 1998 the number of qualifying states has ranged from ten to twenty-four, with a steady increase over time.

ICRC briefings to the DSG cover such matters as management, human resources, operations, funding, and so on. These meetings were both a reward for significant donations and an opportunity to raise questions about the directions of ICRC policy.[7] Between 1998 and 2020, the donors that were always members of the DSG were (in alphabetical order): Canada, Denmark, the EU Commission, Japan, the Netherlands, Norway, Sweden, Switzerland, the United Kingdom, and the United States. Other donors sometimes represented were: Australia, Austria, Belgium, Finland, France, Germany (missed only one year), Ireland, Italy, Kuwait, Luxembourg, New Zealand, Spain, the United Arab Emirates, and (only recently) the World Bank.[8]

There is no evidence that any of these key donors reduced their financial support of the ICRC because of strong disagreements with the direction of ICRC policy including an expanded understanding of its basic mandate. That is, they supported in general how the ICRC interpreted the meaning of its NIIHA role.[9] Indeed, the Europeans were strong proponents of a linkage between humanitarian relief and development, as explained further below. In 2020, the only DSG members not usually thought of as part of the core political West were Kuwait and the United Arab Emirates (UAE). Kuwait was aligned with the political West on several issues, having been saved from an Iraqi takeover in 1991 by the United States and its allies. The UAE in recent years has sought to enhance its global influence by a variety of initiatives.

A reputation for violation of various IHL and human rights norms, designed to protect human dignity, does not disqualify a state from DSG membership. One can recall US torture of detainees in its "war on terrorism" after September 11, 2001, not to mention atrocious treatment of detainees at the Abu Ghraib prison in Iraq after the 2003 invasion.

There was also European states' harsh treatment of undocumented migrants in recent years; this included paying for migrants to be intercepted on the way to Europe who were then sent for abusive detention in Libya. For contributors such as Kuwait and the Emirates, there were allegations about arbitrary detention and torture. In 2022, the UAE again qualified for DSG membership, credible reports continued about mistreatment of detainees there, and it was announced that the ICRC mission to the UAE had been upgraded to a delegation.

The DSG seems to have been successful in attracting more donations over time. Some critics believe, however, that the DSG should not exist, because many donors are too poor to ever achieve membership and the status that goes with it. Some critics see it as a mechanism that gives preferential treatment to the wealthy, contributing to a Western-centered and biased – rather than impartial and fair – humanitarian system.

In sum to this point, business donations, mainly Swiss, were very important in the early years of the ICRC. They are much less important now, as governments and intergovernmental organizations (such as the EU) regularly dominate the organization's funding. The RC Movement still provides only a small percentage of the funds required. The ICRC would like to increase the corporate contributions, but so far the general financial picture has not changed much over the past thirty years regarding sources of funds, at least until the 2020 pandemic imposed its effects of reduced governmental donations. President Maurer's being on the WEF Board of Trustees during 2014–2022 did not significantly increase corporate funding to the ICRC. By early 2023 the expanding ICRC was facing its worst shortfall of funding in its long history.

After a period of great expansion in activities, staff, and budgets during particularly 2010–2020, the ICRC was forced to retrench. In 2020, when the COVID-19 pandemic was both creating new challenges and siphoning off governmental contributions, the ICRC faced a budget deficit of about $140 million. It had run a deficit for the previous three years. It therefore began a program of budget cuts each year of about 5 percent spread over various programs and situations. It closed an expensive hospital in Lebanon that specialized in surgery for war wounds that served as a trauma center for various conflicts, having to think about a public health approach that reached large numbers of victims compared to expensive specialized surgery that impacted much smaller numbers. The organization also let go some personnel at the Geneva headquarters.[10] Such were the painful choices driven by budgetary factors. All the talk about more reliance on the for-profit sector, and the closer links between the ICRC and the WEF, had not changed the budgetary picture in any significant way.

There was a temporary financial recovery in 2021–2022, but by 2023 the ICRC was in deep financial trouble – as was the entire global humanitarian system (which was noted in Chapter 2). Protracted conflicts continued; new major conflicts erupted as in Ukraine; inflation rose both in major donor countries and otherwise; financial demands continued for such matters as climate change, future pandemics, and security fears; movements pushed for reparations for past injustices; and more. In both domestic and foreign affairs, there was never enough money, while many fretted over past borrowing and a growing national debt.

The ICRC was correct in seeing much humanitarian need but perhaps not so prescient in anticipating evident trends about reduced funding. By early 2023 the ICRC was without doubt going to have to do some financial trimming to meet a short fall of – over 400 million Swiss francs. Its projected activities were underfunded by around 15 percent. Before, during the last financial pinch of 2020, it had cut a little here and there across the board. Now it was faced with more significant cuts. New President Mirjana Spoljaric was faced not only with the major war in Ukraine, which actually had been *over* funded as far the ICRC was concerned in its first year, but with the need for a major rethink in programming and staff for all other situations.

There are of course many budgetary issues to address, such as the Western nature of almost all sizable donations, and the failure of most oil-rich non-Western countries to contribute much to the ICRC despite several large relief operations in the Middle East and North Africa, and so on. The ICRC continued to court the favors of wealthy Saudi Arabia at humanitarian meetings. For now we note the relatively small role that the business community plays in contemporary ICRC financial affairs. (A major donor such as the United States, and its Agency for Development (AID), was also hoping for more contributions from the private sector. That hope too had been disappointed by early 2023.)

II   Business Donors

In 2005 the ICRC created the Corporate Support Group (CSG). The original members were: ABB Ltd., Lombard Odier Darier Hentsch & Cie, Roche, Swiss Re, Vontobel Group, Foundation Hans Wilsdorf, and Zurich Financial Services. Its membership has varied over time but has run at between ten and twelve members. They have mostly been based in Switzerland but some have other links or focus. The biggest of the non-Swiss members has been Philips based in the Netherlands. In a recent year the ICRC CSG consisted of: ABB, Avina Stiftung, Credit Suisse, Fondation Hans Wilsdorf, Fondation Lombard Odier,

Novartis, Philips Foundation, Roche, Swiss Re Foundation, Vontobel, and Zurich Insurance.

One does not find on the CSG the biggest of the global corporations in terms of sales, income, profits, or any other indicator – such as Amazon, Walmart, General Motors, Volkswagen, or Coca-Cola, and so on. Nor does one find the big financial management firms that invest billions of assets – such as Bridgewater, BlackRock, and so on. Some of these big global corporations may or may not donate to the National RC Society where their headquarters is located. The membership of the CSG suggests that the ICRC remains mostly a Swiss organization, which accurately reflects its governance but not its international staff and global scope of operations, or its influential position in the global RC Movement. If the ICRC tried to recruit Volkswagen into its CSG, would that offend the German Red Cross and/or the German government? Probably. Same question and answer for Coca-Cola and the American Red Cross. And on down the list of possibilities.

In return for a defined donation – at the time of writing in 2023 it was 500,000 Swiss francs each year for at least six years – the private corporation (or foundation) not only received in return a good image for public relations purposes, but also other perks as well – such as access to some internal information, a couple of field trips each year to observe humanitarian programs in progress (except during the COVID-19 pandemic), special dinners and briefings with high officials, and so forth. The CSG thus operated similar to the DSG as per above.

To join or remain in the CSG, one had to be reviewed in a very detailed and complicated process organized at the Geneva headquarters. The *Ethical Principles Guiding ICRC's Partnerships with the Private Sector* and the *Movement Policy for Corporate Sector Partnerships* were approved by the Assembly on June 1, 2017. In general, as with all business links, the ICRC insists that major donors and partners must not be involved in violations of IHL or conduct operations that violate the RC Fundamental Principles. Businesses are supposed to respect internationally recognized human rights and also the labor standards adopted by the International Labor Organization, as well as health standards established by the World Health Organization (the latter rules out involvement with tobacco). Certain business activity is automatically disqualifying, such as weapons production and sales, or involvement with gambling or pornography. Links to fossil fuels are not automatically prohibited but fall into a "cautionary" category. So the standards for the CSG are actually higher than for states in the DSG, at least on paper.

Business donors outside the CSG, including Foundations and also individuals, are subjected to a similar review process, which is in principle updated every four years with a report from the lead office going to the Directorate. Businesses that invest in conflict zones and otherwise fragile societies are not subjected to the same standards as ICRC donors and partners.

This ICRC review process, almost mind-numbing in the number of rules and internal offices involved, is much more demanding on paper than the process at the UN for reviewing corporate promises to respect the principles of the UN Global Compact. The World Economic Forum, with its efforts to enlist the private sector for "improving the state of the world," has no established and systematic review process at all for the corporations who choose to join and pay various levels of membership fees. National RC Societies may have rules concerning which corporations can donate and benefit from that status in their public relations, but it seems that none are as complex as at the ICRC. In any event there appears to be no comprehensive and comparative study on this issue about the units of the RC Movement and for-profit donors.

If a member of the ICRC CSG runs afoul of media coverage or some national legal process, that almost always triggers a review in Geneva. For example, charges of bribery or corruption may lead to telephone calls to, or meeting with, corporate leaders and a close monitoring of the situation. Charges that a member might have donated goods or money that then got transferred to violent or corrupt actors also triggers a review and monitoring. Hence the matter of indirect support of terrorism can be a red flag. It could be that a corporation does not make or sell weapons itself, but it might invest in other businesses that produce weapons or engage in controversial behavior in war zones. This, too, is likely to trigger investigations and monitoring and possible future action.

There has been one recent striking case in this matter. Holcim, a Swiss cement company, was a member of the ICRC CSG. It merged with a French company to become Holcim-Lafarge. Before the merger, Lafarge as based in France was charged in effect with aiding and abetting Daesh (aka ISIS, aka the Islamic State Group) through the policies of its subsidiary in Syria after 2011. Specifically, the charge was that Lafarge had paid money to Daesh in order to operate in parts of Syria controlled by Daesh, despite the latter's well-known atrocities in the Middle East. A company internal investigation confirmed the reports, French legal procedures moved forward, and the ICRC removed Holcim-Farage from its CSG. The corporation was not just a donor but also a business partner, working with the ICRC in Nigeria to build affordable housing. That link too was terminated.

However, one could not say that the ICRC review process for all donors was free from all debate, despite the overall thoroughness of the review process on paper. As this book was being wrapped up in 2023, a whistle-blower leaked information showing that Credit Suisse, a longtime member of the ICRC's CSG, had opened secret bank accounts for all sorts of controversial figures, including leaders of poor countries who turned out to be quite wealthy, those suspected of criminal activities, those linked to human rights violations, and more.[11] The disclosed accounts were mostly from the past. Credit Suisse was a member of the CSG between 2008 and 2023. The bank claimed that its policies of the past were then legal, that changes had been made over time, and that the still-existing accounts that were mentioned had been reviewed and found proper.

Photograph 9.2 From the beginning the ICRC developed close relations with the business community, especially in Switzerland. From 2005 it created the Corporate Support Group (CSG) to encourage and reward significant donations from major corporations and/or their foundations. A steady member of the CSG was Credit Suisse, part of the socioeconomic Swiss establishment but one that nevertheless compiled a record on the edge of legal propriety. The ICRC could never bring itself to fully split from the controversial investment bank, and here ICRC President Peter Maurer seeks business support at an investment conference sponsored by Credit Suisse in Hong Kong in 2016. In 2023 the long train of controversial management decisions by the bank led to its takeover by UBS bank with guarantees provided by the Swiss government. The relationship between Credit Suisse and the ICRC turned out badly for both sides, at least in terms of optics.

It was clear that the bank had been involved in multiple scandals and paid multiple fines under court judgments in a variety of cases.[12] In June 2022, a Swiss court found Credit Suisse guilty of allowing money laundering back in 2007–2008 from a Latin American drug cartel as arranged by an employee of the bank, holding the bank responsible for lax rules and procedures.[13] Various media publications referred to a lengthy scandalous reputation for Credit Suisse. Its overall financial situation was so shaky, but its position in the global banking industry so central, that in early 2023 the Swiss government indicated it would come to the rescue of the bank if necessary. All of that became moot when the Swiss banking giant UBS took over Credit Suisse slightly later in 2023.

It is still worthwhile to examine how the ICRC dealt with Credit Suisse in the past. According to the ICRC after repeated inquiries from this author, the organization said it had reviewed matters with Credit Suisse in a "confidential bilateral dialogue" and would "continue to closely monitor related developments and take action as needed based on the results of our due diligence assessment." Some facts were indeed different when comparing Holcim-Lafarge to Credit Suisse. The former had been paying money directly to one of the fighting parties in the Middle East, the latter had not. It was also the case that the former was partly French, whereas the latter was very much part of the Swiss establishment. At the end of the day, any objective reading of the situation would conclude that Credit Suisse had manifested a quite unsavory reputation in many financial matters. But it was not clear that its documented misdeeds directly impacted ICRC activities in the field.

Was Credit Suisse using the ICRC to burnish its controversial reputation? Probably. Was a complex ICRC review process leading to vague outcomes regarding several corporations? Probably. Was the ICRC going to publicly and clearly distance itself from a major Swiss banking corporation? Probably not.

It is possible that at the ICRC there were too many rules and offices regarding corporate donors. The man that has multiple masters maybe has none. Given all the rules, it might be the case that ICRC leaders found some rule somewhere to justify an interpretation retaining good relations with a deep-pocket Swiss corporation. Credit Suisse probably fit into that possibility.

Then there was the underlying strategy. About Credit Suisse the ICRC told this author: "The aim of this dialogue has been to raise our concerns, seek assurances from the bank and continue to provide a humanitarian perspective on the issues it faces. We remain convinced that our confidential bilateral dialogue is the best way" to move forward. This is like the US State Department's prevalent approach to advancing human rights, especially among aid recipients. The game is played by asking questions about the situation, and the questioning itself generates pressure. If one pulls the trigger and publicly condemns, then often one may well be out of the game of trying to influence and improve.

There is also an ICRC Foundation, existing since 1931, which tries to raise money from mostly the private sector for various projects. As of 2022 it had announced a new fundraising project to try to raise money for four topics: the evolution of IHL, the application of science and technology to humanitarian affairs, new models of fundraising, and contributions to a sustainable environment. It said it would share resources with the rest of the RC Movement. It noted a contribution from the Swiss government, but the new project would be headed by the private sector. It hoped to show creativity and a breakthrough on these four topics.[14] But it was hard to see progress on these topics when the ICRC in its annual operations was short – over 400 million Swiss francs.

III   Business Partners

For-profit partners of the ICRC were subjected to the same review process as the members of the CSG, according to the same standards. (Here we might mention in passing that the ICRC as of the early 2020s had enlisted a vast array of nonprofit partners from the fields of education, development, negotiation, peace and security, and more. Whereas the ICRC had been criticized by the 1975 Tansley Report for being excessively unilateralist and reclusive,[15] in current times the ICRC seemed willing to reach out to anybody and everybody who might advance its global humanitarian agenda in all its expanding complexity. Universities, think tanks, study groups, development institutes, experts on negotiation, and more, all might have a formalized link with the ICRC. One doubts that any ICRC official or office could completely track and evaluate all of this activity with these nonprofit partners. The emphasis here remains on the for-profit sector.)

The ICRC manifested a number of business partners at headquarters or in the field who might also be major donors. Holcim, later Holcim-Lafarge, has already been mentioned as both a big donor and a partner in the field. The same was true for Philips, which was a big donor and a field partner helping with, for example, the lighting in camps for those forcibly displaced.

As for business partners beyond the CSG, they comprised a long list ranging from those providing security for warehouses to those designing secure computer programs for data storage at headquarters. In general, the ICRC tried to review them all according to the usual standards regarding no violation of RC Principles, or of IHL rules, or of international standards on human rights, labor rights, refugee rights, and so on. The ICRC declined to provide this author with a list of current business partners at the time of writing, and it might be the case that a comprehensive list did not exist, given that the ICRC was active in about 90–100 nations around the world, with numerous suboffices. Some ICRC partners were chosen by local field delegations, perhaps in consultation with the local RC society, making the construction of a master list of business partners a big, if not impossible, challenge.

The case of Swiss-based Nestlé is interesting. Nestlé, the iconic food manufacturer, was a sizable donor to various RC projects, sometimes including the RC Federation also based in Geneva. It was not a member of the CSG at the time of writing in 2023 (but was a member of the WEF as well as the UN Global Compact). Nestlé sometimes partnered with the ICRC on various projects.[16] It had a long history of support for RC programs and other charitable activity. It had also been involved in past controversies such as the marketing of infant formula as a substitute for breast feeding in underdeveloped areas that allegedly endangered the health of infants.[17] A related controversy involved the marketing of Nestlé milk products at a later stage of childhood.[18] A report in the *Financial Times* in 2021 argued that over half of Nestlé's food products were unhealthy.[19]

Also, it was a codefendant in a US legal case about the use of slave labor, including child labor, in the production of cocoa, which goes into chocolate, in West Africa. One substantive issue was whether Swiss-based Nestlé, or for that matter its codefendant Cargill, which was US-based, could be expected to control all aspects of its supply chain, including where and when informal recruiters for small farms might enlist child workers in exploitative conditions in the harvesting of cocoa beans. Nestlé had pledged to eliminate child labor in known cocoa suppliers, but the matter of the informal market or gig labor complicated matters.[20]

In 2021 the US Supreme Court held that the case presented insufficient connection to the United States for the Court to rule on substance.[21] The Court, as had been true in recent years, was reluctant to hold corporations acting abroad to rigorous human rights standards. It was also reluctant to have US courts adjudicate all sorts of human rights disputes from around the world. The Court disposed of the case on procedural grounds, namely the scope and application of the US Alien Tort Statute from 1789. Nestlé policy and profits benefitting from child labor were never addressed. A US Supreme Court judgment against Nestlé would have complicated life for the ICRC and other RC agencies who benefitted from occasional Nestlé largesse.

Photograph 9.3 Some private corporations have a long history of supporting the ICRC and other RC agencies. Here a RC worker unloads boxes of Nestlé condensed milk in Indonesia. The photo is not dated but perhaps was taken in the early 1960s. Nestlé was never a member of the ICRC's Corporate Support Group but nevertheless regularly supported a variety of Red Cross members and programs. It, to a lesser extent than Credit Suisse, was involved in various controversies.

A perhaps less complicated case of an ICRC business partner was the Danish pharmaceutical Novo Nordisk. It agreed to establish a program in conflict areas, including urban areas, to treat chronic, noncommunicable diseases such as diabetes and hypertension. One can certainly understand that war zones and situations of other violence would be correlated with high blood pressure. It was also the case that many amputations, including in violent areas, resulted from diabetes. And so the Danish corporation teamed with the ICRC and the rest of the RC Movement, principally the Danish Red Cross, to announce in 2018 a program of about US$4 million to provide drugs and other services in conflict areas in order to treat hypertension and diabetes. Other partners were also involved in the research and monitoring of this project.[22]

There was the related matter of the ICRC role when the UN and others encouraged for-profit corporations to invest and operate in conflict situations and fragile and vulnerable societies in order to help provide economic security. The ICRC conducted workshops and in other ways tried to sensitize businesses to the various international standards that might intersect their activities. For example, the ICRC conducted a workshop in China for businesses involved in the Chinese Belt and Road Initiative. As China pushed this big infrastructure project at many places around the world as part of its effort to enhance its global influence, the ICRC tried to spread the word about business social responsibility in all its many forms, including attention to IHL norms in armed conflicts. Another example involved ICRC programs in areas of Mozambique prone to violence, where again the ICRC tried to inform the relevant business community of ethical and legal standards that were relevant to business activity in conflict and otherwise fragile areas.

Beyond attempts to sensitize business circles concerning human rights and humanitarian norms or values, there was the matter of actively crossing the line between helping individuals as a humanitarian concern and contributing to a politicized development that might be good or bad for individuals, depending on particulars. This perplexing subject is covered both here and in other chapters.

In 2016 President Maurer wrote a foreword to a WEF report about corporate investing in fragile and violent situations that read in part:

The World Economic Forum is in a unique position to connect corporate leaders with a variety of other stakeholders to share knowledge of the challenges posed by fragile situations and to co-create solutions, particularly at the local level. It can be a prominent platform to advance dialogue on how such environments can affect a company's bottom line, the opportunity costs of nonengagement and the methods to ensure that they invest in a way that does no harm.... Regardless of whether we are primarily driven by profit or humanitarian objectives, fragility affects us all. There is immense potential to combine the complementary attributes of the private sector, civil society, governments and local communities to build resilience in the face of instability and violence.[23]

In this view, the difference between a neutral humanitarian and a profit-oriented business operating under various political regimes seems to disappear – or at least become insignificant.

On its face, President Maurer's statement is an appeal for investment and profit-making that does no harm. But it might not turn out to be a fully neutral position. One can call neutral humanitarian assistance a resiliency or early recovery program, but it can also be political development without clear limits or boundaries as to projects enfolded in its embrace. The issue is not so much that it freely mixes neutral humanitarianism with business in search of profit. The stated position indicates no clear conception of neutral early recovery programs or neutral infrastructure compared to "regular" or "normal" political development, which might not be good for individuals, or some individuals, as governed by a particular political regime.

Helping in early reconstruction in Syria under Assad is allowed, even asked for by Maurer. After a trip to Syria in 2021, the ICRC quoted him and then added further information.

"This is not about having a political divide on reconstruction, this is about finding practical solutions in water, sanitation, education, health, basic electricity, basic income for people," he [Maurer] said.... On a visit to the Damascus suburb of Darayya, he met Syrians who had returned after years of displacement and started small businesses, with the support of the ICRC and the Syrian Arab Red Crescent.... Last year, the ICRC in cooperation with the SARC gave support to around 9,000 Syrians including returnees, displaced families, households headed by women and people with disabilities to set up small businesses in eight governorates.[24]

We will return to this important subject in Chapter 11 on the ICRC and interpreting its mandate today – namely, where is the dividing line between neutral humanitarian resiliency or early recovery programs, often involving business partners, and political development benefiting a brutal government with lots of blood (and torture) on its hands? What exactly is the difference between neutral humanitarian resiliency programs and making a profit under an autocratic government that has done great damage to lots of people? There is conceptual fuzziness in all the talk about "resiliency." The notion of neutral humanitarian assistance can be politically corrupted. One needs to discuss the ethics of impact and not stop with the ethics of intentions.

In fact, the ICRC and its local business partners in Syria faced the same conundrum confronting all providers of aid there – well captured by the *Economist* magazine: "In working out how to help the people living amid the devastation of Syria while not rehabilitating a blood-soaked regime, there are no easy answers."[25]

IV   Social Impact Investing

In many places around the world and seeking to address a variety of issues, there arose the practice of social impact investing. Some investors wanted not just a decent return on their invested money, but to do good in the process. In this broad context, in 2017 the ICRC devised its first Humanitarian Impact Bond (HIB) to run for five years as a test case.[26] On the basis of commitments by a group of states and a foundation, the ICRC offered an investment opportunity centered on some of its prosthetic centers. If three new centers, built in conflict areas, and dealing mostly with those wounded in violent conflicts, met certain targets over a five-year period, investors would receive a predetermined return on their money. The experiment was small, capped at US$30 million, with a maximum return set at 7 percent.

On the one hand this scheme offered the possibility of building on the commitment by the original sponsors by attracting other funds. The US$30 million was raised in the private sector, and the new prosthetic centers were built and other expenses covered. These activities did not come out of the existing ICRC budgets. Sponsors committed to possibly paying the maximum of 7 percent of US$30 million, thereby putting themselves on the hook for up to US$2.1 million.

On the other hand, this ICRC-sponsored HIB, which was not really a bond sale in the technical sense, did not provide a great expansion of humanitarian funding over time. The initial focus on prosthetic goods and services was not extended to other activities. Moreover, no other humanitarian agency adopted a similar scheme, although the RC Federation, UNESCO, and some other agencies were discussing options. MSF, for example, did not buy into this kind of approach to fundraising.

The HIB did raise new monies from private investment markets. The important factor of raising new monies aside, the initial sponsors could have achieved the same result, namely donating US$30 million in humanitarian funding, by increasing their donations by that amount directly to the ICRC – along with asking the ICRC to meet efficiency targets. US$30 million was not an insurmountable sum, given the budgets of the sponsors of the HIB scheme.

However, the ICRC as well as the contributing sponsors wanted to test a new way of raising money. For the ICRC, it wanted to demonstrate to states and foundations that it was engaged in creative thinking and dynamism. In quest of this last objective, it probably succeeded. It also wanted to stimulate efficiency within the organization.

At the end of the project in August 2022, investors broke even.[27] There were no financial gains for investors, but no losses either. It was a win-no win situation. The ICRC won via raising new monies; the investors did not lose anything, except they tied up their money but did not reap any positive returns. In that, despite the ICRC putting a positive spin on things when it announced final results, it was a de facto loss for investors. They could have invested elsewhere and arguably received positive returns. There was no discussion of what they might have earned from putting their money to other uses.

When all the factors were considered, some called the various social impact investing schemes, including the one developed by the ICRC, smoke and mirrors.[28] This is probably too harsh. True, social impact investing in general has not been highly valued by some independent analysts.[29] This too should probably be discounted at least somewhat. Social impact investing was proving popular in general, especially with younger investors.[30] But there was a pushback against ESG investing in a number of conservative political circles that objected to mixing investing with social justice issues.

Certainly the ICRC version had not proven a game changer in terms of humanitarian funding. However, the ICRC was likely to experiment in this domain further. As this book was being completed in 2023, the ICRC had part of its bureaucracy in Geneva devoted to devising new investments schemes for the private sector. Several projects were in the pipeline.

The ICRC plays an important role in the world through its prosthetic centers and services. It is the largest provider of such goods and services in the world. Many injured persons depend on ICRC mobility devices and related expertise. But despite the initial hype, its 2017 well-intentioned effort to increase funding for this worthwhile endeavor did not meet the very high initial expectations for fund raising. In May of 2022 the WEF issued a report on social impact investing that did not mention the ICRC experience at all.[31] The ICRC initiative was probably worth trying and had the expertise behind it of some very experienced financiers. But in the last analysis the scheme did not seem cost-effective in a major way.

The above being what it was, when the ICRC in early 2022 created a new fund for Climate and Environmental Transition, private investing was only projected to be a future and small part of it. In order to reduce its own carbon footprint and to promote environmentally sound assistance toward beneficiaries, it sought grants from public and private sources. Private sector investment in this fund was a medium-term possibility, not seen as a major component.[32] Once again the ICRC was creative, trying new policies including new sources of funding. But social impact investing in this particular new fund was anticipated to be small.

Then there were other policies such as the Goma West Water Resilient Project. In West Goma, a densely populated area in a region long characterized by armed conflict and other violent clashes, the ICRC led in the creation of a public–private partnership to ensure better water supply over the long term. Early studies and preliminary steps were undertaken by the ICRC and its partners, paid for via the usual ICRC funding sources that included governments and private foundations along with a few RC partners. A public entity, part of the local government within the Democratic Republic of the Congo, was eventually to take over the project and issue shares to be purchased by private investors. It was

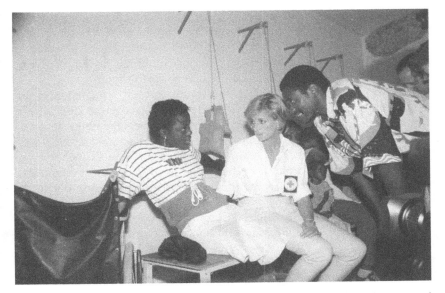

Photograph 9.4 The ICRC sought a total ban on all anti-personnel land mines because of their danger to civilians, who were often killed or seriously injured long after the fighting had ended. To dramatize its concerns, the organization enlisted the help of the well-known Diana, Princess of Wales (of the UK). Here in an ICRC prosthetic center she talks to someone in Angola in 1997 grievously injured by a landmine.

anticipated that by 2026 over 300,000 people would benefit from an improved and secure water system. This project not only reflected a public–private partnership but also an example of blending humanitarian assistance with development activities (hence an example of the double nexus discussed in an earlier chapter). In so far as conflict over water was reduced or eliminated, the project could also be seen as making a contribution to peace (hence the triple nexus). Private investment was a feature of the second phase of the project.[33]

V   Conclusion: Elusive Boundaries

Global events show broad recognition of the benefits of some kind of capitalism. It is often dynamic and can produce economic growth and the benefits that come with it. But it always needs proper regulation (the exact nature of which is always subject to debate), and increasingly its dangers are manifest – whether one speaks of global warming from markets in fossil fuels or lack of purchasing power to buy adequate medical care in a pandemic. There are also the usual or widespread problems of corruption and gross inequality. Winston Churchill has often been quoted on the subject: "The inherent vice of capitalism is the unequal sharing of blessings. The inherent virtue of Socialism is the equal sharing of miseries." The United States and Cuba come to mind.

In a mostly capitalist world, it is certainly natural – indeed advantageous – for the ICRC and other RC agencies to have some kind of relationship with the for-profit sector. Even so, all the hype about business social responsibility, not to mention those cheerleading for the World Economic Forum, has not changed the fact that the ICRC remains hugely dependent on voluntary donations from Western governments. The business sector remains marginal not just to fundraising but to the ICRC's field activities. There might be a bright spot or good example here and there, but corporations exist to make money, not primarily to be a Good Samaritan. It still remains difficult to do both at the same time.

Business likes stability and set rules. It does not like conflict, violence, and uncertain contexts. There is no business model for making lots of money in Yemen or South Sudan or northern Ethiopia and eastern Ukraine or most of Myanmar. Business has to turn a profit to continue to exist, and it is difficult to do that until the guns go silent (except for the arms industry and security contractors, of course).

Humanitarian crises may be too important to be left only to humanitarians, but the profit motive is not the answer. The answer to ending humanitarian crises is to be found in the right kind of politics – for example, appropriate mediation, compromise, and in general political peacemaking. Business might help at the margins but cannot be central. The ICRC is counting on business and investors to play a role in protracted conflicts and early recovery efforts, while waiting for the Godot of peacemaking to arrive and succeed. Again, one can find a positive case here and there in the midst of violence, such as the ICRC partnering with Novo Nordisk on hypertension and diabetes in conflict areas.

There is nothing wrong with the ICRC seeking out business donors and partners, but it does have to protect its genuinely neutral humanitarian role from those who would instrumentalize it for profit, power, or status. I have no trouble concluding that ICRC leaders have strictly humanitarian intent (along with a concern for their own reputation) 99 percent of the time, but others may seek to utilize the organization for other purposes. I believe Credit Suisse and the WEF, not to mention the Swiss government, have all sought to utilize the ICRC for profit or power, or both. Whether the ICRC has then extracted appropriately meaningful benefits for its humanitarian purposes is a very good question for analysis.

The strong push for corporate social responsibility will remain with us for the foreseeable future. Milton Friedman's model of shareholder capitalism where the only thing that matters is the bottom line of profit accounting, along with the Reagan–Thatcher endorsement of freeing business actors from most shackles of regulation, is rightfully under attack. But the corporation that forgets about adequate profits will not be in business for long.

It merits recall that while some corporations pulled out of Russia given the Putin regime's invasion of Ukraine and follow-on war crimes, others did not. Similarly, while some corporations in the United States took a stand to pay for female staff abortions after the Supreme Court revoked the constitutional right to that procedure, others did not.

This divide in the business world, with some corporations prioritizing ESG policies and others not, mirrored the split among governments. Regarding Ukraine we note that governments such as India or South Africa, inter alia, did not fully oppose the Russian invasion and did not compel their business corporations to interrupt business as usual. Indeed India, a great champion of anti-imperialism and state sovereignty during the Cold War, in that era a leader in the Non-Aligned Movement, propped up the aggressive and repressive Putin regime by buying Russian oil at discounted prices. Amoral economic self-interest still looms large, for governments and businesses, much of the time.

Still, in general, what was in play in Ukraine and other conflicts was not just the policies of governments but the policies of the for-profit sector as well. The old idea that the realm of business was business, and not taking a stand on ESG issues, was largely or at least sometimes (but not entirely) cast aside. The economic muscle of Microsoft, Apple, Google, British Petroleum, Shell, Exxon, and so on, all took a stand on the question of aggression versus self-defense, and then war crimes. Other business did not. No doubt the facts would be otherwise in other situations. Ukraine was not Myanmar or Ethiopia or Yemen. Still, the public–private response to violations of international law in Europe, mainly concerning aggression but also war crimes, was a noteworthy possibility.

The ICRC says it is a strictly humanitarian organization that seeks to carve out a humanitarian zone of endeavor in the midst of war and other violence. But corporate profit and power either intrude or are actually invited in. Sorting out the resulting mix, and figuring acceptable trade-offs, is challenging. How does one correctly evaluate, even if now for historical purposes, the donation from Credit Suisse to the ICRC compared to its unsavory record?

Chapter 10 continues the focus on business by a deep dive into the WEF. The result is more complexity and controversy.

Notes

1 A. Young, "An Interview," *Non-Profit Forum*, 1/1 (2010), p. 8.
2 This early section relies heavily on Daniel Palmieri, *The ICRC and the Private Sector* (Geneva: ICRC, 2016). Palmieri is the resident historian at the ICRC.
3 Edwin Black, *IBM and the Holocaust: The Strategic Alliance between Nazi Germany and America's Most Powerful Corporation* (Washington, DC: Dialog Press, expanded ed., 2012).
4 Dominique D. Junod, *The Imperiled Red Cross and the Palestine-Eretz-Israel Conflict, 1945–1952: The Influence of Institutional Concerns on a Humanitarian Operation* (London and New York: Keegan Paul, 1996).
5 Palmieri, *The ICRC and the Private Sector.*
6 "The ICRC Donor Support Group," *ICRC*, April 1, 2018, www.icrc.org/en/document/icrc-donor-support-group.
7 Ibid.
8 Ibid., Annex 1.
9 If space permitted one could trace the role of the EU with regard to humanitarian assistance and its links to development and peace. The EU was a major player in this issue-area and a major donor to the ICRC. One could start with certain basic documents: "European Consensus on Humanitarian Aid," *European Commission: European Civil Protection and Humanitarian Aid Operations,* https://ec.europa.eu/echo/who/humanitarian-aid-and-civil-protection/european-consensus_en; "Humanitarian Principles," *European Commission: European Civil Protection and Humanitarian Aid Operations,* https://ec.europa.eu/echo/who/humanitarian-aid-and-civil-protection/humanitarian-principles_en; "Resilience & Humanitarian-Development-Peace Nexus," *European Commission: European Civil Protection and Humanitarian Aid Operations,* https://ec.europa.eu/echo/what/humanitarian-aid/resilience_en.
10 "ICRC to Pull Out of War Hospital in Lebanon in Wide-ranging Cuts," *The New Humanitarian*, November 30, 2020, www.thenewhumanitarian.org/investigation/2020/11/30/ICRC-Lebanon-hospital-closure-budget-cuts (accessed March 3, 2023).
11 Christiaan Hetzner, "Credit Suisse Whistleblower Claims of Deals with Drug Dealers and Dictators Adds to List of Missteps That Has Made It Europe's Most Scandal-ridden Bank," *Fortune*, February 21, 2022, https://fortune.com/2022/02/21/credit-suisse-whistleblower-claims-deals-drug-dealers-dictators-europe-most-scandal-ridden-bank-archegos-greensill/ (accessed March 3, 2023).
12 "Factbox: Spies, Lies and Losses: Credit Suisse's Scandals," *Reuters*, November 4, 2021, www.reuters.com/business/finance/spies-lies-losses-credit-suisses-scandals-2021-11-04/, (accessed March 3, 2023).
13 Jack Ewing, "Credit Suisse Is Fined for Helping a Bulgarian Drug Ring Launder Money, a Court Said," *The New York Times*, June 27, 2022, www.nytimes.com/2022/06/27/business/credit-suisse-fine-bulgarian-drug-ring.html (accessed March 3, 2023).
14 ICRC, "The Foundation for the ICRC Launches Its Objectives through 2031," September 16, 2022, https://blogs.icrc.org/hdtse/2022/09/16/la-fondation-pour-le-cicr-lance-ses-objectifs-2031-pour-accelerer-l-innovation-humanitaire-de-rupture/ (accessed March 3, 2023).

15 The reader is reminded that the present author was part of the Tansley team that was mandated by the Movement to do a "Re-appraisal of the Role of the Red Cross" and which produced the 1975 document, "Final Report: An Agenda for Red Cross." My specific charge was to analyze RC protection, which linked me primarily to the ICRC. I had a hand in drafting the final report.

16 For example, Nestlé and the ICRC cosponsor a coaching or mentoring program of relevance to what might be generally called personnel management; see "ICRC and Nestlé Recognized for Outstanding Organizational Coaching," *LeNews*, June 5, 2014, https://developingtalent.ch/wp-content/uploads/2019/04/ICRC-and-Nestl%C3%A9-recognized-for-outstanding-organizational-coaching.pdf (accessed March 3, 2023).

17 Stephen Solomon, "The Controversy over Infant Formula," *The New York Times Magazine*, Section 6, p. 92 (December 6, 1981), www.nytimes.com/1981/12/06/magazine/the-controversy-over-infant-formula.html (accessed March 3, 2023).

18 For a surprisingly good review of the issues, given its Swiss source, see Jessica Davis Pluss, "Nestlé Struggles to Win over Baby Formular Critics," *SWI: Swissinfo.ch*, January 10, 2020, www.swissinfo.ch/eng/milk-for-older-babies_nestl%C3%A9-struggles-to-win-over-infant-formula-critics/45473338 (accessed March 3, 2023).

19 "Nestlé Document Says Majority of Its Food Products Unhealthy," *Financial Times*, May 30, 2021, www.ft.com/content/4c98d410-38b1-4be8-95b2-d029e054f492 (accessed March 3, 2023).

20 In 2020, a Swiss referendum rejected a proposal, despite sufficient support in the popular vote, to hold Swiss companies responsible for human rights violations in all aspects of their supply chains. The measure failed to secure enough support from the required number of cantons. Jessica Davis Pluss, "Responsible Business Initiative Rejected at the Ballot Box," *SEI: Swissinfo.ch*, November 29, 2020, www.swissinfo.ch/eng/swiss-to-vote-on-holding-companies-accountable-for-supply-chain-abuses/46184500l (accessed March 3, 2023).

21 *Nestlé USA, Inc.* v. *Doe et al.*, 593 U.S. ___, 141 S. Ct. 1931, 210 L. Ed. 2d 207, (2021), www.supremecourt.gov/opinions/20pdf/19-416_i4dj.pdf (accessed March 3, 2023).

22 "Novo Nordisk, Red Cross Team Up to Tackle Chronic Diseases in Conflict Zones," *Reuters*, April 18, 2018, www.reuters.com/article/us-novo-nordisk-aid/novo-nordisk-red-cross-team-up-to-tackle-chronic-diseases-in-conflict-zones-idUSKBN1HP0UR; www.icrc.org/en/document/red-cross-and-novo-nordisk-announce-ground-breaking-partnership-tackle-chronic-care (accessed March 3, 2023).

23 WEF, "Responsible Investment in Fragile Contexts," 2016, https://igarape.org.br/wp-content/uploads/2016/05/GAC16_Responsible_Investment_Fragile_Context.pdf (accessed March 3, 2023).

24 "Syria: ICRC President Urges 'New Approach' by International Community after Decade of Brutal Crisis," *ICRC*, March 29, 2021, www.icrc.org/en/document/syria-icrc-president-urges-new-approach-international-community-after-decade-brutal-crisis (accessed March 3, 2023).

25 *The Economist*, February 18–24, 2023, p. 44.

26 "The World's First 'Humanitarian Impact Bond' Launched to Transform Financing of Aid in Conflict-hit Countries," *ICRC*, September 6, 2017,

www.icrc.org/en/document/worlds-first-humanitarian-impact-bond-launched-transform-financing-aid-conflict-hit (accessed March 3, 2023).

27 ICRC, "First Humanitarian Impact Bond Brings Physical Rehabilitation Services Successfully to Conflict Affected Communities," July 28, 2022, www.icrc.org/en/document/humanitarian-impact-bond-brings-physical-rehabilitation-services (accessed March 3, 2023).

28 Ben Parker, "Saving Lives and Making Money: Can Humanitarian Impact Bonds Marry the Two?," *The New Humanitarian*, August 15, 2019, www.thenewhumanitarian.org/analysis/2019/08/15/humanitarian-impact-bonds (accessed March 21, 2023).

29 "Report: Measuring the Success of Impact Bonds," *Brookings*, September 2, 2020, www.brookings.edu/multi-chapter-report/measuring-the-success-of-impact-bonds/.

30 Andrew Mayeda, "As Impact Investing Grows, So Do Expectations," *International Finance Corporation*, April 2021, www.ifc.org/wps/wcm/connect/news_ext_content/ifc_external_corporate_site/news+and+events/news/insights/impact-investing-for-growth (accessed March 21, 2023).

31 "Cultivating Investment Opportunities in Fragile Contexts: Catalyzing Market-Driven Solutions to Strengthen Community and Economy Resilience," Discussion Paper, World Economic Forum, 2022, www.weforum.org/reports/cultivating-investment-opportunities-in-fragile-contexts-catalysing-market-driven-solutions-to-strengthen-community-and-economy-resilience (accessed March 21, 2023).

32 ICRC, "ICRC Launches a New Fund to Support Long-term Climate and Environment Initiatives," January 17, 2022, www.icrc.org/en/document/icrc-fund-climate-environment-initiatives (accessed March 21, 2023).

33 ICRC, "Partnerships and Innovative Financing Solutions Boost Access to Safe Water for Hundreds of Thousands of People in DR Congo," May 21, 2022, www.icrc.org/en/document/partnerships-financing-solutions-boost-water-access-dr-congo (accessed March 21, 2023).

10 Humanitarians and Business
Part II – The World Economic Forum

We need Davos now more than ever.

William Burke-White
(The Brookings Institution, 2020)

I think Davos is totally irrelevant.

Rana Foroohar, *The Financial Times* columnist
(as quoted on CNN, 2023)

Since 2014 one must address the issue of the ICRC being closely intertwined with the World Economic Forum (WEF). The latter is now officially said to be a neutral international organization based in Geneva – and enfolded in the warm embrace of the Swiss government and its hyping of "Geneva International." Was the fact of the ICRC president wearing two hats and helping to manage the WEF, officially in his role on the WEF board of trustees during 2014–2022, an extraneous controversy that should have been avoided? Or was the ICRC president's joining the WEF board of trustees a proper part of humanitarian outreach and broadened diplomacy, subject to the usual costs-benefits analysis? Even if seen as an error and a violation of ICRC rules, did the close links to the WEF cost the organization in any important and practical way? Even if a controversial step, might the ICRC president's being at the center of the WEF actually turn out to have had humanitarian benefits?

The first chapter has already indicated that a number of ICRC alumni took exception to the organization's close links to the WEF from 2014. That the situation evolved as it did reflects a blend of international and Swiss factors in a complex mix not easy to fully untangle. The details of the subject, however, remain important for what might be said about the nature of contemporary ICRC leadership and programs. ICRC links with the WEF overlap with the topic of ICRC relations with Bern, discussed in previous chapters.

I   International Economic Trends

I have given a short overview of the ICRC and the WEF in another publication.[1] The relevant international trends that contextualize the subject can be briefly summarized.

By the 1980s economic globalization was a fact of international relations in much of the world, with much endorsement of "free trade," which meant in effect giving much free reign to transnational corporations (TNCs), which were lightly regulated. This situation of economic liberalism – or neoliberal economics, market fundamentalism, or shareholder capitalism – was strongly endorsed, especially by the influential Reagan and Thatcher governments in Washington and London. To paraphrase Reagan, a rising tide (supposedly) raised all boats. Pursuing the profit motive in relatively unfettered fashion would supposedly benefit all.

There followed a strong pushback against this view, including street demonstrations and protests at various meetings of the World Trade Organization, the World Bank, the International Monetary Fund, the World Economic Forum, meetings of the G-7 group of some major economic states, and other venues. The disruptive protests were very strong in 1999 and continued for another decade. To summarize a great mix of critics, one can say that the protestors saw economic globalization and its emphasis on freedom of action for TNCs as detrimental rather than beneficial. In the critics' view, private for-profit corporations comprised an unelected governing structure that had contributed to global warming, gross inequality, much violence, gender discrimination, and a variety of other ills in the world.[2]

As a result of this clash of views, a longstanding effort directed at corporate self-regulation intensified, with various efforts to get TNCs to exercise greater social responsibility through greater attention to ecological protection, human rights, gender equity, humanitarianism, and a variety of other issues. Given that most governments had clearly indicated they would not support a treaty directed at tight regulation of TNCs on socioeconomic issues, there seemed no alternative but to pursue once again nonbinding codes of conduct but accompanied by various forms of social pressure and in some cases institutionalized review and supervision under agreed-to norms. A main effort in this regard was the UN Global Compact, already mentioned, created in 2000 under the aegis of UN Secretary-General Kofi Annan. It specified certain principles of corporate social responsibility, including a set of rules on human rights, and entailed a supervisory or evaluative mechanism – although the code was nonbinding and corporate membership voluntary.

Whether one saw TNCs as broadly beneficial or a great threat to human dignity, there was no doubting their economic and hence political power. "In 2019, the market value of Apple, Microsoft, and Amazon was *each* higher than the annual GDP of every country – except for the United States and China. In that same year: the annual revenue of Walmart was roughly equivalent to the annual GDP of Belgium; Shell's income was slightly greater than the GDP of Israel; Aramco was about that of the Philippines; Apple was almost equal to Finland."[3]

II   Swiss Policy

Here we need to shift gears and focus on Swiss foreign policy, in the context of economic globalization and efforts to reform it. There are two dimensions that are relevant: the acceptance of stakeholder capitalism entailing the idea of the social responsibility of corporations, and the desire to obtain benefits for the small alpine nation including benefits from "international Geneva."

As for accepting business social responsibility in world affairs, for the Swiss this was a continuation of domestic policy. The Swiss, characterized by three major language groups and two major religions, have developed a national consensus in favor of compromise and pragmatic adjustment to changing trends with a view to a broad range of beneficiaries. This aspect of Swiss political culture is sometimes summarized as multi-stakeholder democratic capitalism. Through a combination of federalism combined with occasional referenda, the latter involving both a popular vote and requirements for cantonal acceptance, there is a complicated but continual process of trying to navigate the ship of state through competing demands for the benefit of a broad swath of citizens. To take but one resulting example, both Geneva and Zurich are listed in the top ten of most livable cities around the world, according to the Intelligence Unit of the *Economist* magazine. Rankings reflected such factors as stability based on compromise and ecological protection. In 2020 the Swiss public voted to hold corporations broadly responsible for respecting human rights and environmental standards, but the referendum measure failed to pass because of an insufficient number of approving cantons.

This Swiss trait of multi-stakeholder concern contributed to Bern's trying to find a compromise between the competing views about economic globalization. Swiss leaders, endorsing capitalism and proud to be the home of some major TNCs such as Nestlé and Novartis, nevertheless took into account those protesting the negative aspects of international economic interdependence as led by corporate managers. One aspect of this Swiss response has not been much noticed but is relevant to the ICRC and WEF during Peter Maurer's tenure as ICRC president – the creation of the Global Humanitarian Forum.

In this context and against this background, Bern along with the Kofi Annan Foundation and the city of Geneva launched the Global Humanitarian Forum (GHF) – not to be confused with the later World Humanitarian Forum.[4] This GHF project was realized briefly during 2007–2010. In reality it was a platform for an exchange of views mainly on (under)development and the environment (climate change). It sought to promote progressive views about meshing international capitalism with environmental protection, but also used the language of humanitarianism. Kofi Annan, the former UN secretary-general and said by some to be the most Swiss of the UN secretaries-general (he retired to Geneva) was head of the governing board. Among the lengthy list of board members was Jacques Forster, then the primary vice president of the ICRC. Attending some of the GHF meetings in Geneva was the president of the ICRC, Jakob Kellenberger.

The GHF had the strong support of Walter Fust, head of the Swiss Development Cooperation Agency (DCA). When he retired in 2008, or when he "was retired" by others in Bern, he became director of the GHF. When the GHF wound up on shaky financial footing, Micheline Calmy-Rey, the Swiss foreign minister and president arranged for its funeral. Her right-hand man on humanitarian affairs was Peter Maurer, but apparently it was Tony Frisch from the Swiss DCA who handled the details of the GHF demise. He arranged a handoff of humanitarian affairs from the GHF to the WEF.

The GHF was formally suspended in 2010 for lack of financial resources. Fust proved better at spending than fundraising, and Annan was apparently used to a generous lifestyle. Whatever the details, Bern and the Kofi Annan Foundation had proven unable to raise the matching funds necessary to make the project sustainable over time. Bern, insofar as there was a coherent foreign policy on these matters, which is in doubt, showed a desire through the GHF to at least tolerate a new initiative on public–private partnerships and an ill-defined humanitarianism. For sure, some in Bern had also seen the GHF as useful in trying to keep Switzerland at the center of developments. Importantly in the light of subsequent events, when the Swiss Foreign Ministry announced the end of the GHF in 2010, it said: "The objectives of the GHF will continue to be pursued by integrating a part of its topics into the World Economic Forum (WEF) within the scope of its annual meeting in Davos."[5]

In sum to this point, Bern believed in stakeholder capitalism and tried to promote it in its foreign policy via the GHF, but with ample attention to Swiss interests and image. The latter point merits further elaboration.

After the end of the Cold War the UN was able to become more active on humanitarian affairs. As noted earlier, in 1991 the General Assembly created the Office for the Coordination of Humanitarian Affairs (OCHA). Shortly thereafter it also created an Inter-Agency Standing Committee (IASC) for coordination of humanitarian fund raising and subsequent programming. The Security Council also became more active in this domain, authorizing field missions for the protection of civilians, and declaring that its decision-making authority had broad scope, including responding to complex humanitarian emergencies and gross human rights violations. From the viewpoint of some in Bern, New York might challenge Geneva, the home of the Red Cross, as *the* diplomatic center for humanitarian affairs. True, the ICRC was still often alone or almost alone in the field in active conflicts, compared to UN agencies, but reputational concerns remained in Bern about a challenge to the ICRC as based in Geneva on humanitarian affairs. For sure, Bern liked to emphasize its links to global humanitarianism and a progressive international diplomacy.

Bern had been pushing the slogan of "international Geneva" from 1996 and was proud of the hundreds of international organizations based there, and proud of the diplomatic conference and summits held there. Then there was the matter that protests against the WEF might drive that organization out of Davos, where its most prominent meetings were held, and out of greater Geneva where its headquarters were found. Promoting Geneva was not without its financial aspects, which Bern did not want to endanger. Local hotels, restaurants, shops, and real estate all benefit from Geneva being home base to hundreds of international organizations, as well as the major European center for the United Nations and some of its various agencies. The same financial and reputation gains were true for WEF meetings in Davos (even if Bern paid for most security arrangements).

The GHF would have been a double accomplishment for Bern had it endured: it would have contributed to a more responsible global capitalism (mostly regarding ecology) and given prominence to Geneva. Its official handoff to the WEF, whatever the merits on substance, kept that particular project in Switzerland and in Geneva (and Davos). The origins of the GHF and the WEF were distinct, and some Swiss leaders, perhaps Calmy-Rey, and by implication maybe her main assistant Peter Maurer, were never heavily invested in the GHF. But once the handoff occurred, someone had to make it work.

Photograph 10.1 The World Economic Forum (WEF) is based in the greater Geneva area, and its annual meeting in Davos is attended by business, political, and social elites. The nation-state of Switzerland derives many benefits from the WEF being associated with the small country, and so Bern agreed to provide security for the Davos meeting and its many high-profile participants – as here in 2018. For a time, ICRC officials did not become deeply embedded in WEF activities, protecting their independence and neutral image – aware that the WEF was controversial. From about 2014 the ICRC deepened its involvement with the WEF, which led to questions about ICRC motivations, priorities, and prudence.

III   The WEF

Given this background, we turn directly to the ICRC and the WEF. What is now the World Economic Forum was started in 1971 by the German-born business professor Klaus Schwab (educated partially in Switzerland, he taught at the University of Geneva). The early focus was decidedly mundane: spreading the word about best management practices for business corporations, primarily so that European corporations could compete better with their American counterparts. This international network and its meetings then went through several iterations, one stage involving political mediation. The claim is now made that Schwab was always interested in stakeholder capitalism on a global scale, but his early focus was on business management and the organization was first called the European Management Forum. It became the WEF in 1987.

From 2006 to 2007, in the midst of the global debate about economic globalization and corporate social responsibility, it adopted new statutes designed to promote social responsibility in and for the corporate world, as part of a public–private partnership for the grand, if vague, objective of improving world affairs. (The WEF statutes were revised in 2015 but without major change on the points of interest here.) True, WEF statutes do not mention social responsibility. (One wag said that if they did, 50 percent of the WEF membership would have to leave.) But the WEF now makes recommendations on topics that add up to a focus on business social responsibility such as: reduction of executive pay or tying that pay to achievement of social goals, more attention to climate change, more attention to the UN's Sustainable Development Goals, more required reporting on economic, social, and governance factors, and so on.[6] The very phrase "stakeholder capitalism," which the WEF endorses, can be understood as a synonym for business social responsibility. It is linked to ESG investing.

Its annual meeting in Davos evolved to become a major media and social event, with leaders from business, politics, governance, and civic society combining to, officially, "make the world a better place."[7] Schwab may have been initially uncertain about the changing purposes of the WEF, but he was very good at advocacy and marketing of his malleable or Protean ideas. In some ways he was a modern Henry Dunant.[8]

The WEF meeting at Davos brought money and attention to small Switzerland and a chance for its leaders, often marginalized in world affairs, to rub shoulders with the leading global personalities of the day. Whether various Swiss leaders directly worked with and advised Schwab about what to become, and how to achieve it – and how to be fully well received in Switzerland – is not entirely clear. Given what we know about the goals of the GHF, the public handoff of its role to the WEF, and concerns in Bern that the WEF might be forced out of Switzerland in response to protests, it would be reasonable to assume a close relationship between some officials in Bern and Schwab regarding the revised statutes and continued location of the WEF. Not all developments are written down in public documents.

One might also assume that various protests against economic globalization as managed by unelected elites triggered a decision at the WEF to broaden its participants. On the one hand, we noted above the various protests and disruptions at certain international meetings, including those of the WEF. On the other hand, one could see the WEF increasingly including personalities and organizations from international civic

Photograph 10.2 The WEF annual meeting in Davos evolved to be a major media event attended by elites from around the world. It allowed WEF President Klaus Schwab and officials from small Switzerland to rub shoulders with prominent persons. Here in 2008, Schwab (left) talks with Swiss President Pascal Couchepin and US Secretary of State Condoleezza Rice. Mrs. Schwab is also seen (center background).

society, as well as a few educators, in addition to business managers and governmental leaders. From 2003 it had held a meeting for international civil society called Open Forum Davos, parallel to its main annual meeting for corporate and governmental leaders. The first parallel Open Forum was attended by the Swiss Red Cross but not by the ICRC. This broadened participation in the WEF was formalized in its 2006 statutes, first applied in 2007. In 2008, during the short life of the GHF, the WEF officially added humanitarian affairs to its concerns.

Eventually in 2015 the Swiss authorities recognized the WEF, surprisingly to some, as a neutral international organization.[9] That solidified its status as part of "international Geneva," a public relations and marketing designation, with the WEF headquarters located in a suburb of Geneva. One reasonable way to look at the current WEF after 2006 is that it developed a stream of activities that became a continuation of the GHF, but with the former having much greater resources and visibility than the latter. Corporate Strategic Partners in the WEF pay circa US$650,000 for an annual membership, depending on the year discussed. For Bern, supporting the WEF was a better deal than trying to fund the GHF, with more visibility – even if with more controversy. As noted above, Bern agreed to pay for most security arrangements in Davos but got many benefits in return, some tangible and some otherwise.

IV   President Maurer at the WEF – a First Take

Peter Maurer was certainly in positions to be informed about all the events and trends described here. During 1996–2000 he was the Deputy Head of the Swiss Observer Mission to the UN (before state membership in 2002). He thus had a front row seat about UN increased activities regarding humanitarian affairs, including preparations for the launch of the UN Global Compact to encourage business social responsibility. The primary mover and shaker at the UN for the Global Compact, the late John Ruggie, an American political scientist, told the author before his passing that Maurer was supportive of, but played no special role in, that project. In 2000–2004, Maurer was the first head of the Human Security division within the Swiss Foreign Ministry with responsibility for planning and execution in that domain. He was charged with adapting Swiss foreign policy to changing factors involving peace, development, human rights, and humanitarian affairs. In the period 2004–2009 he was posted back to New York as Swiss ambassador to the United Nations. During 2010–2011 he was Swiss Secretary of State, or the top administrative official, at the Foreign Ministry in Bern. In his various positions for the Swiss foreign ministry Maurer often endorsed a public–private partnership for global problem solving.

Maurer was chosen ICRC president in 2012 with the support of outgoing ICRC President Kellenberger, who had also been secretary of state in the Swiss Foreign Ministry and who had mentored Maurer in that department. According to some insiders, Kellenberger supported Maurer for his talents and record, not because of any desire to advance strictly Swiss interests. In 2014 Maurer agreed to join the board of trustees of the WEF. We do not know the exact details of this development – for example, who initiated the idea and whether Maurer responded to an invitation by others or whether he sought out and helped construct arrangements.

Before the GHF handed off its humanitarian agenda to the WEF in 2010, the WEF had created a council or discussion group on that subject in 2008. The leadership of that council changed regularly on a short-term basis, and a lot of its discussions focused on response to natural disasters and development plans. The ICRC director-general then, Angelo Gnaedinger, attended a WEF "councils summit" in 2008 in Dubai, but he was not active in the specific discussions of the humanitarian assistance council (despite the fact that his name was listed on certain WEF humanitarian reports). Maurer, by joining the WEF board, could become the primary mover and shaker on WEF humanitarian topics within that organization, give persistent leadership on that subject, move things in directions that interested the ICRC – and perhaps keep WEF humanitarian developments tightly associated with Switzerland.

His becoming a WEF trustee was a clear departure from some ICRC previous practice. Like other leaders from civil society, ICRC Presidents Sommaruga and Kellenberger had gone to the Davos meeting to make contacts and try to advance humanitarian values and programs through that channel. They met lots of leaders from governmental and business sectors, sometimes sponsoring working dinners at Davos. They used the WEF for more than "meet and greet" brief encounters. The ICRC Directorate of that time supported these kinds of links to the WEF, as long as the ICRC retained an independent voice and as long as it was free to also attend various meetings of anti-globalization activists.

Photograph 10.3 ICRC President Peter Maurer joined the WEF Board and Trustees in 2014. There was no announcement of this at the ICRC HQ in Geneva. Top ICRC officials described this and related developments as normal humanitarian outreach and diplomacy, seeking to influence and learn from a range of important persons. Critics saw a departure from Dunantist principles and possible endangerment of ICRC staff in the field. ICRC President Mirjana Spoljaric did not replace Maurer on the WEF Board of Trustees in 2022. Here Maurer participates on a panel at the WEF in 2016 with Queen Rania of Jordan and WEF Managing Director Philipp Roesler.

Sommaruga and Kellenberger never accepted a position on the inside of the WEF and never became officially responsible for its various activities and reputation. Some WEF activities have nothing to do with humanitarian values traditionally understood but rather involve spreading the WEF brand and promoting various profit-making ventures such as tourism. It publishes a report on economic competitiveness, among its many activities. Sommaruga and Kellenberger did not put themselves in a position where outsiders could question their priorities or motivations. They stayed independent from the WEF while periodically using that platform and network for ICRC objectives.

Given ICRC rules about its Assembly and the secrecy there, we do not know the facts for sure, but the following sequence seems likely. In November 2015 the Assembly debated the matter of its president joining the WEF board of trustees. Apparently at this stage some Assembly members voiced concerns, but no votes were taken. There was deference to what the president wanted, although it seems there was agreement to revisit the subject half-way through his WEF three-year mandate.

His director-general at the time, Yves Daccord, was supportive of the move. Daccord himself was on the board of the Overseas Development Institute while he was ICRC director-general. ICRC Vice President Jacques Forster had been on the governing board of the GHF. As noted above, ICRC Director-General Gnaedinger had attended one WEF meeting in Dubai and was listed as a member of the WEF Council on Humanitarian Assistance, even if not active in producing its reports.

Perhaps because of continuing intense criticism from some ICRC alumni (covered in Chapter 1), of which Assembly members were made aware, Maurer's renewal of the WEF trustee role in 2017 was subjected to a renewed and intensified debate in the ICRC Assembly. This time there was a divided vote (the Assembly tries to proceed by consensus), but ultimately his continuation inside the WEF, with the comfortable but incomplete support of the ICRC Assembly.[10] Then in 2020 his position on the WEF Board was renewed yet again. There was no formal announcement from the ICRC about any of these Assembly details involving the WEF during 2014–2021. There had been no references to the WEF on the ICRC website or in the *Review* during and immediately after 2014. It was Thierry Germond, the ICRC alum, in 2015 who found an announcement of Maurer as WEF trustee dating from 2014 on the WEF website. This led to the first Assembly discussion of the matter in late 2015.

In early 2016 there was a posting on the ICRC website indicating that President Maurer had joined the WEF board, more than a year after the event. It listed six general advantages to that move, ranging from enhanced cooperation with others to benefitting from the expertise within that organization.[11] There was a further posting about the WEF one year later.[12] Then there was mostly "radio silence" about the two organizations as far as ICRC postings were concerned. There was nothing in the *Review* about Maurer being a WEF trustee. On the WEF website there were many postings by Maurer, or Maurer and other authors, about humanitarian subjects. The ICRC Office of the President considers all these statements over Maurer's "signature" to be official ICRC statements, even if posted via the WEF. To the ICRC, there is no such thing as Maurer speaking personally or only for the WEF and not for the ICRC.

In 2017, the same year that the Assembly had an in-depth discussion about Maurer being renewed as a WEF trustee, Maurer gave an interview on his role at the WEF that circulated only internally at the ICRC. He stressed his opportunity at the WEF to meet and work with important persons from other organizations, as well as his ability to add humanitarian programs to the WEF agenda. He noted the increased number of events related to humanitarianism at the annual WEF meeting in Davos. So while the ICRC president declined in-depth or unstructured interviews on the topic of the WEF with journalists and others outside the ICRC, he did do a controlled interview on the subject that was made available to ICRC personnel.

Some have suggested that President Maurer was active at the WEF in his personal capacity. But the 2016 ICRC web posting indicated otherwise: his presence on the WEF board was a matter of an organization-to-organization linkage. And there were formal agreements between the two, noted below. Other ICRC officials also participated in WEF events and held WEF positions. This might be seen as strange, in that WEF rules prohibit WEF trustees from acting there for personal or professional interests. To use WEF wording: "In their work on the Board, members do not represent any personal or professional interests."[13] But if President Maurer was not there to advance the professional interests of the ICRC and other humanitarian actors, why join the board?

In 2015 and 2020 the ICRC signed agreements of cooperation with the WEF. The ICRC has never released these and would not do so in response to a specific request. So we know about the details of 1993, 2013, and 2017 agreements between the ICRC and Swiss government, and the outlines of another agreement in 2020, as noted in Chapter 8. And we know about understandings between Bern and the WEF. But we have incomplete details about links between the ICRC and WEF.

No doubt Maurer, with his knowledge of both the Swiss-sponsored GHF and the UN Global Compact – and knowing that ICRC officials had been involved with the GHF – saw a positive opportunity in joining the WEF board of trustees in 2014. Membership on the WEF board would give him greater influence in the adoption of WEF programs touching on humanitarian affairs, as noted above in the 2016 posting on the ICRC website, even if Maurer never became a managing trustee and thus one of those actually running the entire WEF on a daily basis. In the last analysis the WEF has been mostly a talk shop, and its "councils" on different subjects, along with its other meetings, debate and discuss. Similar to the UN much of the time, the WEF is often a platform for the spread of ideas and the promotion of action by others.

How much Maurer was motivated also by Swiss national interests in keeping the WEF in Switzerland, and according to one close observer being the eyes and ears of Bern inside the WEF, we do not know – and no doubt will never be told explicitly one way or the other. It is possible, but not very probable, that Maurer at the WEF, similar to Vice President Forster at the GHF, was there partially to block any infringement on ICRC independence in humanitarian affairs – at least when the WEF began to consider becoming a humanitarian actor in the field and not just a talk-shop.

V   The Debate Continued

One initially had a choice about how to interpret Maurer's double role: (1) an advantage in advancing the ICRC's humanitarian concerns; (2) sowing doubts about the priority of those humanitarian interests compared with maintaining good relations with WEF participants; and (3) advancing the reputation and resources of Switzerland.

Not only some ICRC Alumni but also some staff members questioned the wisdom of Maurer wearing two hats at the same time, that of ICRC president and WEF trustee. It was not just that ICRC internal rules prohibited Assembly members from taking part in controversies of a political, religious, racial, or ideological nature. After all, taking part in humanitarian controversies was not prohibited. The line between a political and humanitarian controversy existed in the eye of the beholder, rather than objectively in the material world. Was the WEF intrinsically part of a humanitarian or a political controversy? Which was it? Was the WEF a big part of the informal governing of the world based on neo-liberal ideology, by and for economic elites? Was it a neutral platform for the exchange of views? Was it an organization that, in part at least, promoted values and programs consistent with the Red Cross idea? Like blind men feeling different parts of the proverbial elephant, descriptions of the WEF varied.

The argument that Maurer's "double chapeaux" or "double casquettes" compromised the ICRC's sole focus on its humanitarian concerns is important to pursue. Was he primarily interested in advancing the WEF brand in China, which he was obligated to do as a WEF trustee, or working so that the ICRC gained accesses eventually to detained Uighurs in the context of charges of genocide? Was he primarily interested in seeing that WEF meetings went according to plan in the UAE, or maneuvering so that the ICRC gained access to political prisoners there in the context of reports of torture? When he had meetings with this or that top national official, did he sometimes discuss only WEF affairs and ignore humanitarian topics such as access to political prisoners?

Some well-respected insiders believed that Maurer's wearing of two hats indeed compromised the status of the ICRC – potentially at least. If the Russians had wanted an excuse not to deal with the ICRC in Eastern Ukraine during 2014–2021, Maurer's membership on the WEF board and the WEF initial support for sanctions on certain Russians after Moscow's invasion of Crimea in 2014 would have given Moscow an easy way out. Officials in Moscow could easily claim, given the WEF brief sanctions on certain Russian oligarchs after 2014, that he was biased against them and not neutral. They did not do that (and the ICRC had a strategic campaign going of engaging with Russia in various ways). But some thought the ICRC was not pushing hard for access to various detention centers in places such as Belarus, an ally of President Putin in Russia. Maurer's role as a WEF trustee contributed to doubts in some circles about his commitment to a tough stand in matters of ICRC humanitarian action. These doubts may have been misplaced, but they existed because of his WEF role as trustee. It seems Maurer was not careful about the image he might project as WEF trustee.

Furthermore, many Russian oligarchs and their companies, with a record of dubious economic dealings, were deeply embedded in the WEF. They might even have been essential for funding the WEF.[14] Did this controversial Russian presence in the WEF, private but with close links to Russian President Putin, affect President Maurer who as trustee had a legal obligation to look after the best interests of the WEF? One might very well doubt that Maurer was affected by the Russian role at the WEF, especially given Maurer's tireless global diplomacy for humanitarian causes, but the complexities of WEF arrangements lent credence to the view that the ICRC should not be so deeply linked to that organization. If the WEF was a sham, as many thoughtful individuals believed, why would the ICRC align itself with that kind of organization?

The WEF certainly remained highly controversial in some – maybe most – circles of informed opinion, containing corporate members that sold weapons and armaments (as did of course Swiss corporations with the approval of the Swiss government), had members who were big investors in fossil fuels and thus made major contributions to global warming and climate change, involved businesses engaged in perpetual controversies of various sorts (such as Swiss-based Nestlé), and in general was centrally made up of paying corporate members who had contributed mightily to the global inequality, conflicts, and polluted planet that was so evident. Corporations attending Davos might pay their top executives perhaps 300 times what their typical worker earned.[15] Corporate leaders in attendance often paid no income taxes whatsoever.[16] Such facts hardly suggested that most WEF paying members were making the world a better place.

Of course, a problem for organizations such as the ICRC was that most of the world was characterized by some form of capitalism. The question came down to a choice between a harsh version compared to a socially responsible version. The ICRC during the Maurer era apparently saw the WEF as promoting socially responsible capitalism, which was arguably compatible with Dunantist humanitarianism. The critics saw the WEF as a sham, pretending to support broad stakeholder capitalism whereas, to the critics, dangerous neoliberal capitalism continued to contribute to the problems that the ICRC was left to deal with.

Moreover, at times the WEF took clearly political positions, as in enforcing (for a time) economic sanctions on some Russian oligarchs, criticizing Houthi leaders in Yemen, or calling for the defeat of the Islamic State group. (How the Swiss government could see it as a neutral international organization is an interesting question, especially in the light of the above examples and also when some political leaders who came to Davos made all sorts of clearly political speeches.)

After Russia fully invaded Ukraine in 2022, the WEF purged itself of a number of Russian participants. Whereas Schwab had previously stressed WEF neutrality and keeping lines open to especially Putin, after the invasion things were decidedly different. Russian names simply disappeared from the WEF board of trustees or other bodies, with no explanation. At Davos in 2022, the meeting was openly favorable to Ukraine and openly critical of Putin's Russia and its supporters. How could this WEF programming be considered neutral in taking the side of the Ukrainians against Putin's Russia? Of course the "neutral" Swiss government also joined its European trading partners in sanctioning Putin and his oligarchs.

Maurer and most of the ICRC leadership were certainly not defenseless in the controversy over the WEF, even if the Geneva headquarters rarely addressed his dual role. An ICRC web post in 2016, mentioned already, while skipping controversies about the WEF, argued that being on the inside of the WEF offered an opportunity to deepen relations with important actors, advance humanitarian programs, and present the ICRC as on the cutting edge of developments.[17] This was consistent with what Maurer said in his 2017 internal interview. But this was a one-sided account, not a real cost-benefits analysis. The ICRC declined my request to provide a real costs-benefits analysis of its close relationship to the WEF. It might not exist, at least not on paper. Reportedly, an outside consultant was retained circa 2015–2016 in order to write an analysis of the ICRC–WEF linkage. If so, that report has not been made public.

A balanced or fair accounting of Maurer at the WEF would note that he indeed helped establish certain WEF programs: the 2014 WEF Global Agenda Council on Fragility, Violence, and Conflict (terminated in 2016); the 2017 WEF Global Agenda Council on Global Humanitarian Response (terminated in 2018); and the 2019 WEF Humanitarian and Resilience Investing Initiative. This latter project linked the ICRC to other major public and private actors to try to continue to stimulate creative investing in conflict-prone areas greatly affected by violence, underdevelopment, climate change, and poor governance. It was an impressive and broad set of major actors from business, the UN system, and international civic society.[18] It fit exactly with the rhetoric coming from the ICRC leadership in Geneva about especially protracted conflicts and the need to move beyond traditional "truck and chuck" emergency aid. But it had only existed for a few years at the time of writing, too short a time for firm evaluation. The WEF had discussed humanitarian assistance before 2014 – witness the WEF Council on Humanitarian Assistance from 2008 – but it did more in the humanitarian domain after Maurer became a trustee.

A second line of defense about Maurer's double role stated that the ICRC was prepared to take some risks, such as helping to manage the WEF, in order to promote humanitarian values and activities, then watch for any serious negatives especially concerning field operations and any dangers to staff.[19] And in this the ICRC leadership might be correct – at least as far as known operations were concerned. There seems to be no case where Maurer's being on the WEF board impeded ICRC practical operations. President Maduro in socialist Venezuela did not say: I will not deal with you ICRC types because you are tied to global capitalism via the WEF. Rather, he actually developed closer relations with the ICRC as of circa 2021 regarding both protection and assistance. The ICRC got the consent of the Maduro government for detention visits there, worked to expand the scope of those visits, and provided different types of humanitarian assistance in various parts of the country.

Maurer was dismissive of the argument that his presence on the WEF board endangered field staff. He said in a brief interview with Swiss media in 2019, having mostly kept a public silence on the issue until then, that such criticism was just a lot of hot air, and that the ICRC knew how to protect its field staff – which was by talking to the relevant political actors. He said he took note of the criticism but paid it no serious attention.[20] It was a curt and dismissive response, not entirely diplomatic, showing he had little patience for the complaint. He was probably right on substance, at least as far as we know based on public reporting, even if somewhat short tempered. That is, there seems to be no evidence of Maurer as WEF trustee interfering with or endangering an ICRC field operation. There was still the matter of potential problems from his wearing two hats, as well as matters of image and reputation.

It seems to be the case that most non-Western or even anti-Western armed groups were too busy fighting local battles in places such as Yemen or various parts of Africa to have the luxury of worrying about what was happening in Davos. As one ICRC staff member commented from the field, certain Islamic armed groups would be opposed to Maurer being on the WEF board if they knew about it, and thus his being so intertwined with mostly Western power circles, but they didn't know about it. "Communist" states such as China and Vietnam were actually at Davos and had developed their own versions of capitalism.

A third line of defense about Maurer's being a WEF trustee made a comparison to states. So the argument went, the ICRC dealt with all kinds of governments that did not have clean hands when it came to humanitarian affairs, so why not reach out to corporations even though they too, as a collective group, were less than perfect? The United States, its largest donor, after 2001 engaged in the ill-treatment of prisoners held in secret prisons run by the Central Intelligence Agency, and also some ill-treatment in prisons run by the Pentagon. Yet the ICRC continued to accept US funding and dealt with Washington on a variety of issues – with mixed results. In places such as Syria and Yemen, not to mention Ethiopia and Myanmar, the ICRC dealt with a lot of political operatives who had much blood on their hands. Why should relations with the for-profit sector be treated differently?

It is hard to say if WEF programs to date have had a major impact on violent situations or "fragile contexts." The 2014 WEF Futures Council on Violence produced reports indicating some best-case practices of for-profit firms in fragile and conflict prone areas.[21] Were other companies duly sensitized? Hard to say. There seems slight impact from the 2017 WEF Futures Council on Humanitarian Response.

The 2019 WEF Humanitarian Investment Initiative looks impressive on paper but had yet to prove itself "a game changer" in terms of attention to, and funding for, humanitarian concerns. The MasterCard Foundation made a gift of US$1.3 billion in 2021 for COVID vaccination programs in Africa. Was there any link between MasterCard officials being active in the WEF, and cochair (with Maurer) of the Futures Council on Violence, and the 2021 donation? Hard to say. When the US Biden administration renewed attention to the root causes of extra-legal migration from Central America to the United States, it enlisted several major corporations who promised to invest in a handful of fragile and violence prone states – mainly Guatemala, Honduras, El Salvador, and Nicaragua. Was any of this affected by ideas and programs circulating via the WEF? Hard to say. And was such promised corporate investment in Central America part of neutral humanitarianism, or part of a US governmental desire to stem unwanted migration into the United States? Did the distinction matter?

VI   NIIHA Values Debated

The WEF remains very controversial, and not just in the world of leftist, anti-capitalist, and anti-globalist intellectuals. The *Economist* magazine, pro-business and widely respected, has persistently probed the bona fides of the WEF and been consistently critical of "Davos man."[22] This is not the kind of controversial entity that the ICRC normally associates itself with, much less agrees to help direct and manage. The ICRC as an organization is now associated with the WEF in various practical ways – witness various (unpublished) cooperation agreements between the two organizations. There are staff exchanges between the ICRC and the WEF, with a given person working for first one, then the other organization. An ICRC Assembly member has also been a member of one of the WEF humanitarian councils.

Since Maurer refuses to discuss with outsiders in detail the subject of his being a trustee at the WEF, much less to fully explain his thinking over time, we remain much in the dark about the how and why of his landing on the WEF governing board. Some observers remain convinced that some strictly Swiss interests were helping to drive decisions – such as the desire to advance the reputation of Geneva and Switzerland. These critics believe that Maurer, unlike especially Sommaruga but also Kellenberger, had not walled off these strictly Swiss interests. As we have noted, for Sommaruga, his distancing the ICRC from the Swiss Foreign Ministry, at least in terms of some legal arrangements, was a strategic decision. For Kellenberger, maintaining few personal contacts with officials of the Swiss Foreign Ministry, confirmed by multiple sources, may have been a conscious strategy or a reflection of his personal style. But both kept a certain distance from the WEF, even while making contacts there.

In a previous chapter we showed that Maurer was very different in relative terms from particularly Sommaruga about emphasizing the ICRC as very distinct from Bern. But even so, that would not explain why the ICRC Assembly majority and the Directorate went along with the president's deep involvement in leading the WEF. There are naturalized Swiss and non-Swiss in the ICRC Directorate. In going along with Maurer's being on the WEF board, it is unlikely they were driven by concern for Swiss interests.

Then Director-General Yves Daccord made an interesting comment in 2018, saying one should not personalize ICRC policy directions.[23] This perhaps reminded that the ICRC president's being a WEF trustee had the backing of the Geneva headquarters – meaning the Administration, meaning the Directorate. There was also endorsement by the Assembly, even if not unanimous. All this suggests that the Directorate did some kind of costs-benefits analysis, even if only inside the director-general's head, and decided that being inside the WEF was the right course. Again, the organization refused to candidly clarify its analysis in terms of costs and benefits. It has refused to release a consultant's study of the issue, if it existed. Maybe the Directorate just caved in to the strong desires of a strong willed president. After all, if you want to keep your position in the Directorate, maybe it is wise not to address the WEF matter, since it was clear the president had little patience with further discussions on that subject.

According to a scholar associated with the Brookings Institution, a respected think tank in Washington, DC, there was plenty to criticize about the WEF, but in his view one might as well try to use it in order to advance corporate social responsibility and a relatively more effective public–private partnership. After all, governments themselves had done a poor job in managing international relations and its central problems such as climate change, so why not see if TNCs, or some new public–private partnership, might not do a bit better.[24]

One could, in fact, find examples where a corporation had been socially responsible and had used its role, along with financial muscle, to advance a good cause. In India, the NGO named Breakthrough had teamed with Vodaphone to implement a successful campaign to keep girls in school and thus reduce the incidence of child brides – at least in urban if not rural areas. A creative and practical approach had been pursued without sacrificing human rights principles.[25]

In this sense, if one had to choose between relying on narrowly nationalistic and nativist and illiberal governments in various states, or relying on new ventures via the WEF, the latter might not look so bad – or at least be worth a try. After all, one big reason for protracted conflicts and underdevelopment was the inability of the outside states with wealth and military muscle to agree on meaningful solutions. Official bodies such as the UN Security Council were often in gridlock because of political differences among key member states. Perhaps the WEF, as a coordinator and stimulator of nonstate actors, might do better on some matters in relative terms.

One way to view matters under discussion here was to say that politics as usual had for a long time produced a bad crop of national leaders who then had failed to conduct responsible and progressive foreign policies. The result was protracted conflicts and many fragile, failing, or failed states. Given this void of responsible and progressive political leadership by national leaders, especially the great powers, humanitarian actors such as the ICRC then sought to do the best they could – in part by looking for new partners (maybe with deep pockets for donations and investments and/or relevant expertise on the ground).[26] It might be recalled that MSF refused to attend the 2016 UN Humanitarian Summit in Istanbul because the agenda (as set by the UN) refused to address precisely the matter of the nature of state foreign policies and their responsibility for the very large humanitarian crisis facing the world.

But that state of affairs still left the ICRC president wearing two hats, which meant that there could logically be some question about priorities and basic motivations and potential dangers. For the top of the ICRC, what exactly was the interplay of humanitarian concerns, WEF links, and Swiss interests?

How does one evaluate the results of the WEF humanitarian councils compared to the view that the WEF is a sham and a money-making machine for Klaus Schwab and his family – not to mention use of the WEF to clean up the reputation of the Russian oligarchs, at least in the past? We return to this question in the final chapters.

Notes

1 David P. Forsythe, "A New International Committee of the Red Cross?," *Journal of Human Rights*, 17/5 (fall, 2018), pp. 533–549.
2 To understand the critics of economic globalization, lightly regulated international economic interdependence, and TNCs, one can start with Susan George, *Shadow Sovereigns* (Oxford: Polity Press, 2015). For a later critique, see Peter S. Goodman, *Davos Man: How the Billionaires Devoured the World* (New York: HarperCollins, 2022).
3 David P. Forsythe, *The Politics of International Human Rights* (Cheltenham and Northampton: Edward Elgar Publishing, 2021), p. 59.

4 The World Humanitarian Forum, not to be confused with the Global Humanitarian Forum in Geneva, was started in 2019 as a follow-up to the 2016 UN Humanitarian Summit in Istanbul. It is an annual meeting in London for the exchange of views about humanitarian affairs, led by a variety of persons including former government officials such as the UK's Jack Straw and NGO leaders. The annual event is run by the same firm that managed the 2016 Istanbul meeting.

5 "FDFA Supports the Dissolution of the Global Humanitarian Forum with Socially Compatible Measures," Swiss Federal Department of Foreign Affairs, March 31, 2010, www.admin.ch/gov/en/start/documentation/media-releases.msg-id-32496.html (accessed December 14, 2022).

6 Michael Posner, "What's Driving the New Push to Measure Companies on Social Performance," *Forbes*, February 20, 2020, www.forbes.com/sites/michaelposner/2020/02/20/whats-driving-the-new-push-to-measure-companies-on-social-performance/?sh=51fa5bd05199 (accessed December 14, 2022).

7 One might recall the line from the Harvard historian and journalist Jill Lepore: "Research surveys suggest a rule of thumb: the more ethically dubious the business, the more grandiose and sanctimonious its mission statement." "Mission Impossible," *The New Yorker*, August 2, 2021, p. 74.

8 Unlike Dunant, Schwab and some relatives became wealthy. His annual salary was reported to be about US$400,000. It was said that various for-profit activities were created as spin-offs from the WEF, and he was reportedly appointed to various advisory positions at handsome renumeration. Some said that the WEF was a cash-cow for Schwab and his family. Peter S. Goodman, "'He Has an Incredible Knack to Smell the Next Fad': How Klaus Schwab Built a Billionaire Circus at Davos," *Vanity Fair*, January 18, 2022, www.vanityfair.com/news/2022/01/how-klaus-schwab-built-a-billionaire-circus-at-davos (accessed December 14, 2022).

9 The French version indicates the accord was concluded on January 23, 2015. In a strange paragraph, the Swiss government states that the WEF is "guided by the principles of neutrality, impartiality, and integrity...." Why the government brings up the subject of WEF integrity suggests that, in the classic phrase, "he doth protest too much." Why vouchsafe for WEF integrity unless there is question about it?

10 Yves Daccord, ICRC director-general at the time, said in an interview with the Swiss newspaper *Le Temps* on July 25, 2018 (my translation): "The Assembly of the ICRC has approved the mandate of the [ICRC] president at the WEF despite several votes in opposition." The full citation is: Stéphane Benoit-Godet and Stéphane Bussard, "Yves Daccord: 'Les attentes envers le CICR ont changé'," *Le Temps*, July 24, 2018 modified online by the newspaper, July 25, 2018, www.letemps.ch/monde/yves-daccord-attentes-envers-cicr-ont-change (accessed December 14, 2022).

11 ICRC, "Mieux servir les personnes vulnérables grâce à la coopération avec le Forum économique mondial," January 19, 2016, www.icrc.org/fr/document/mieux-servir-les-personnes-vulnerables-grace-la-cooperation-avec-le-forum-economique (accessed October 27, 2023).

12 ICRC, "Better Serving People in Need through Cooperation with the World Economic Forum," January 20, 2017, www.icrc.org/en/document/

icrc-cooperation-with-world-economic-forum (accessed December 14, 2022). This is identical to the reference in note 11, but indicates a different date, suggesting perhaps a typo on the Internet.

13 WEF, Regulations, Article 2(3), www3.weforum.org/docs/WEF_Reglement_2015.pdf, which is a subcategory of WEF, "Leadership and Governance," www.weforum.org\\about\\leadership-and-governance (accessed December 14, 2022).

14 Ryan Heath, "Davos Freezes Out Putin and Russian Oligarchs," *Politico*, March 8, 2022, www.politico.com/news/2022/03/08/davos-putin-russian-oligarchs-00015344 (accessed December 14, 2022).

15 Lawrence Mishel and Jori Kandra, "CEO Compensation Surged 14% in 2019 to $21.3 Million," *Economic Policy Institute*, August 18, 2020, www.epi.org/publication/ceo-compensation-surged-14-in-2019-to-21-3-million-ceos-now-earn-320-times-as-much-as-a-typical-worker/ (accessed December 14, 2022).

16 Alan Rappeport, "Wealthiest Executives Paid Little to Nothing in Federal Income Taxes, Report Says," *New York Times*, June 8, 2021, www.nytimes.com/2021/06/08/us/politics/income-taxes-bezos-musk-buffett.html (accessed December 14, 2022).

17 ICRC, "Mieux server les personnes vulnerables."

18 WEF, "Humanitarian Resilience Investing Initiative," no date given, www.weforum.org/projects/humanitarian-investing-initiative (accessed December 14, 2022). See also Boston Consulting Group, "Humanitarian Investing Initiative Update," no date given, https://irphsg.ch/wp-content/uploads/2020/01/WS3_Galligo_ICRC.pdf (accessed December 14, 2022).

19 Yves Daccord told *Le Temps* in July 2018 (my translation): "It is above all the formal membership of Peter Maurer at the WEF which is criticized because of the perceived risks that could cause for our delegates in the field. We have followed the situation with a lot of attention without ever finding those risks proven." www.letemps.ch/monde/yves-daccord-attentes-envers-cicr-ont-change (accessed December 14, 2022).

20 Celine Tzaud and Mouna Hussain, "Le president du CICR répond à la polemique sur sa double casquette," *Monde*, January 23, 2019, www.rts.ch/info/monde/10161640-le-president-du-cicr-repond-a-la-polemique-sur-sa-double-casquette.html (accessed December 14, 2022). My summary of the French.

21 World Economic Forum, "Responsible Private Sector Action to Address Fragility, Conflict and Violence," (February 2016), www3.weforum.org/docs/WEF_Responsible_Private_Sector.pdf (accessed December 14, 2022).

22 See, for example, Bagehot, "The Party of Davos," *The Economist*, November 16, 2019, p. 54. See also Anand Girdharadas, *Winners Take All: The Elite Charade of Changing the World* (New York: Knopf, 2019).

23 "Yves Daccord: 'Les attentes envers le CICR ont change'," *Le Temps*, July 25, 2018.

24 William Burke-White, "The Word Economic Forum Deserves Criticism, but We Need It Now more than Ever," blog post, Brookings Institution, January 18, 2020, www.brookings.edu/blog/order-from-chaos/2020/01/28/the-world-economic-forum-deserves-criticism-but-we-need-it-now-more-than-ever/ (accessed December 14, 2022).

25 Rajshri Sen, "Being Flexible while Staying True: The Balance of Engaging Corporations in Human Rights," *Open Global Rights*, May 3, 2018, www .openglobalrights.org/Being-flexible-while-staying-true-the-balance-of-engaging-corporations-in-human-rights/?lang=English (accessed December 14, 2022).

26 David P. Forsythe, "Humanitarianism: Coping in the Void," in Michael Stohl and Alison Brysk, eds., *A Human Rights Research Agenda* (Cheltenham, UK: Edward Elgar Publishing, 2020), chap. 3.

11 Interpreting the Mandate
Part I – From Relief to Resilience

> The ICRC is a flexible institution and therefore adapts to change.
> The International Committee of the Red Cross[1]

More important than ICRC–WEF relations in the long run was the issue of the changing interpretation of the ICRC's mandate. There is no doubt but that the ICRC has enlarged its understanding of what is required of a neutral, independent, impartial, humanitarian actor (NIIHA) in contemporary times. The written mandate as found in the ICRC statutes and as endorsed by the RC Movement remains the same in wording. But the meaning of the verbiage has indeed been enlarged over time – frequently in piecemeal steps that were then systematized and consolidated later.

As conflicts became protracted, as urban violence short of armed conflict affected more and more people, and as extra-legal migration became a pressing problem, the ICRC added to its tasks without officially abandoning its past concerns. These changes in ICRC operations did not start with Maurer's tenure as president from 2012 but years before then. When the roles did expand, it was not simply because the organization had a new president from 2012, but rather because a broad review that was centered mainly on the Directorate supported change – or, more accurately, supported systematizing and consolidating the bits and pieces of change that had been evolving already. All this was approved periodically by the Assembly.

It contributed to trends that destructive international wars of a traditional nature were episodic rather than regular features of international relations. Between the Iran–Iraq war of the 1980s and the Russian invasion of Ukraine in 2022, the were few international wars between military powers with even intermediate capability for destruction. True, the first Gulf War of 1991 involved the United States forcing Iraq to end its invasion of Kuwait, but that combat lasted only about six weeks and was largely fought in unpopulated areas. More destructive and longer was the US invasion of Iraq in 2003 to topple Saddam Hussein, which lasted in some accounts until 2011 (when most US combat troops were withdrawn) and involved much destruction to civilians and civilian infra-structure. (I make no attempt to list the wars that were essentially over intranational issues, such as who governs in Rwanda or Syria or Yemen, but manifested international dimensions.)[2]

Insofar as the Directorate thought it had to persuade Maurer in 2012 when he assumed the presidency to continue the changes already in pro-cess during the Kellenberger era, that would be pushing on an open door. Mauer was not a traditionalist. In terms of personal philosophy, he was sympathetic to new initiatives, maybe even risky ones. As he said in a 2016 interview, he thought it important to: "Se poser les questions à l'envers du courant normal. C'est ce qui est important. Quand les trends politiques vous disent qu'il faut penser dans cette direction, c'est tou-jours important de penser l'inverse. Ne pas suivre les *trends* politiques."[3] ("Ask oneself the questions that run against the current. That is what is important. When the policy trends tell you it's necessary to think a cer-tain way, it's always important to think the opposite. Don't just follow the political trends.")

The ICRC of circa 2022 is mostly new because of its evolving field operations. This is more important in the long run than the passing issue of Peter Maurer's being on the governing board of the WEF – especially since that ended in 2022 and President Mirjana Spoljaric did not auto-matically assume that trustee position. The ICRC's necessarily special links with the Swiss government, also not set in stone, will also be endur-ing in one form or another.

If there is a new ICRC as of the first quarter of the twenty-first cen-tury, which there is in some important respects, its understanding of how it interprets its mandate is crucial. The complicated and not always publicized role of the ICRC as demonstrated by its global operations suggests something indeed new – at least in terms of scale of systematic action. This has led to other important changes such as nature and size of staff. What is beneficial and sound, and what is problematic, remains to be sorted out – both by outsiders and more importantly by the orga-nization itself.

We try to decipher the new complexity of ICRC field operations with attention to: (1) protracted violence and socioeconomic resiliency; (2) urban violence short of armed conflict; and (3) attention to extralegal or irregular migrants. These three topics give us a representative sample, or a short-form summary, of the expanding nature of ICRC activities on the ground in many nations around the globe.

There were also changes in themes or emphases within these three broad categories. There was shifting and overlapping attention to women and girls, mental health concerns, race relations, sexual violence, technological issues, recruitment of specialist personnel, utilization of for-profit partners, and more. But one has to address core policy changes somewhere, dealing with other subjects along the way.

I   Expanded Assistance, the Context

Two contextual factors set the stage and help explain an ICRC expanded notion of humanitarian help after the guns fall silent – or at least temporarily fall silent.[4] First there is the fact of protracted conflicts with much complicated violence that ebbs and flows. Sometimes Geneva says it is involved in an armed conflict but often not – describing the situation as one of "situations of other violence." Second there is the demand for a broader and different notion of humanitarian assistance coming from multiple circles of opinion. The result at the ICRC, as elsewhere, has been change – or more precisely expanded change – in order to adjust to these two contextual factors. Other factors are likely at work as well, such as the need for the ICRC to compete with other organizations in raising money in a crowded international humanitarian system, which involves maintaining or even expanding the support of key donors.

The ICRC, based first of all on its own experience, has been very clear about recognizing the fact of protracted conflicts in places such as Democratic Republic of Congo, or South Sudan, or Yemen, or Syria, or Iraq, or Afghanistan, or many other places.[5] One sees violence that persists and fluctuates over the years, with governmental and armed nongovernmental fighters of various allegiances and motivations, often with outside backing. Most often there is an inability of anyone to quickly make a permanent peace. As of 2019, "The average time that the ICRC has been present in its 10 largest operations is 42 years. The duration of humanitarian operations in protracted conflict settings has caused organizations like the ICRC to re-think their way of working."[6]

From a humanitarian concern and for present emphases, there are prolonged civilian needs. From the UN view, there is an inability to move further toward achieving sustainable development goals such as increased longevity or declining infant mortality. There may be a regression on issues like gender equality and youth literacy. There is broad recognition that the efforts to improve societies and meet internationally approved development goals are negatively affected by armed conflict, or other systematic violence, or a perpetual state of fragility and vulnerability featuring instability from intermittent violence. This fragility often results from the combined effects of violence, underdevelopment, climate change, and poor governance.[7] The early phase of the COVID-19 pandemic circa 2020–2021 added another layer of difficulties – and setbacks.

Hence one finds President Maurer writing in the introduction to the 2019 ICRC Annual Report: "The realities on the ground are moving further away from some of the classical administrative distinctions created to deal with issues of concern: human rights, peacebuilding, development, humanitarian action. Partnerships between all of us with a role to play in developing lasting solutions to humanitarian challenges will be key to ensuring our collective impact is powerful and sustainable."[8]

Persistent civilian distress is also hampered by the unpopularity of foreign assistance in richer countries, and their other pressing needs ranging from public health (e.g., locally fighting a pandemic as per vaccine nationalism) to national security (e.g., continuing foreign and domestic counterterrorism operations plus attempted deterrence of strategic competitors). Peace and progress in foreign lands, especially in poorer or nonstrategic countries, is rarely the priority of the Great and Intermediate Powers. States such as France and the United States may manifest extensive and self-interested counterterrorism policies in Africa and the Middle East in order to deny safe haven to enemies, but durable peacemaking and well-funded development programs remain elusive.

Henry Kissinger, highly influential in US foreign policy during the Nixon and Ford Administrations, was well known for his focus on China and the Soviet Union and willingness to sacrifice the welfare of smaller countries, such as Cambodia, Chile, and Bangladesh, to great power relations. Then there is the matter of the lack of a serious approach to climate change – at least thus far. One can note in passing that the United Kingdom drastically cut its budget for development assistance in 2021. The United States cut its international development budget in 2022.

The importance of protracted conflicts and their broadly deleterious results have been recognized by a variety of actors – donor agencies, the United Nations, the European Union, and various agencies within the RC Movement. Crucially, the World Bank is now part of this coalition of the aware, with programs and funds targeted to "fragile, conflict, and vulnerable" countries (FCV).[9] The UN's Global Humanitarian Summit, meeting in Istanbul in 2016, crystallized this awareness. Some of its nonbinding resolutions addressed the relevant factors by calling for more action along the humanitarian–development nexus, or the humanitarian–development–peace nexus. In fact, the UN was calling for a double nexus, a tighter link between humanitarian aid and development assistance, much earlier.[10] In sum, in addition to the ICRC's own grassroots experience, there was a broad push, in the context of protracted conflicts, to link emergency humanitarian assistance, development aid, and efforts at peacemaking.[11] We noted this in an introductory way in Chapter 2.

Here we might note that the situation of fragile societies with protracted conflicts that ebb and flow caused, among other things, the ICRC to want to stay on the ground and be in touch with various political actors. It had an incentive to keep delegations going regardless of whether there was major violence at a given point in time. It feared losing relevance by losing its dialogue with different political actors. As one staff member said, the ICRC used to work in the matchbox of war and other big violence plus political prisoners; now the ICRC faces this undefined spread – some of it well intentioned. If one wanted to do something in conflict-torn Somalia, at times it was important to talk to the leaders of Ethiopia, even if Ethiopia was not undergoing major violence right then. If one wanted to act in Chad, it might be important to be engaged in Sudan, even if Darfur had gone quiet. Global conditions and the realities of diplomacy made it difficult to gear up only for war and major violence and then leave. Moreover, the problem of political prisoners was pervasive.

One should reiterate that prolonged human insecurity was never high priority in the foreign policies of the leaders of wealthy and stable nations. No leader from a permanent member of the UN Security Council attended the Istanbul Humanitarian Summit. Only one leader from the G-7 countries did so, Prime Minister Angela Merkel of Germany. In this political void at the highest levels of national governments, humanitarian organizations struggled to do what they could, working with the interested parts of governments and intergovernmental organizations, and with the nonprofit and for-profit sectors.[12]

On the one hand, one sees much rhetoric and some diplomatic agreement on terms such as civilian distress, complex humanitarian emergency, human security, and the responsibility to protect. On the other hand, in a particular crisis with clear evidence of atrocities and gross violations of human rights, national leaders find reasons not to engage in a deep or profound (and costly) way. These leaders are often supported by national public opinion. This pattern has been all too evident regarding Syria, Yemen, South Sudan, Myanmar, Ethiopia, and many other places. Jacques Forster, vice president of the ICRC 1999–2007, noted that in 1994 the concept of human security increasingly informed UN debates while in the same year major states refused to get involved to stop the genocide in Rwanda.[13]

Either an effort at effective peacemaking was seen as too costly, or the national leaders sought particular advantage from the conflict rather than pursue a more balanced and durable peace – for example, Russia in Syria. This leaves those genuinely concerned about what is happening to individuals who find themselves in harm's way operating in the void created by lack of concerned national leaders who have the power and resources to make a difference. Perversely, these self-interested states may support humanitarians to salve their conscience and show that they are at least doing something (and may support international criminal justice after the fact of atrocities for the same reason).

In sum of these contextual factors, one can say (as have others) that the end of the Cold War by 1991 actually intensified humanitarian problems. According to one source, in 2020 the number of deaths from political violence was ten times higher than in 2005.[14] The fear of Superpower confrontation and dangers of escalation no longer imposed limits on many conflicts in the Global South. Longstanding ethnic and other intranational tensions could erupt without danger of sucking in Moscow and Washington – with threats of escalation to nuclear war, at least outside of Europe. The power centers in the Global North downgraded the importance of many conflicts in the Global South since they were no longer perceived as affecting the bipolar balance of power and its ideological competitions.

In fairness to those in Washington and other capitals who *were* concerned about the fate of those victimized by protracted conflict abroad, some disappointing trends might have been inevitable. After all, there were many situations of nasty conflict particularly in Africa and the Near and Middle East, and not forgetting the Asian case of Myanmar. Moreover, Somalia in 1991–1992 showed just how difficult it could be to make a difference for the better.

Toward the end of the George H. W. Bush Administration, in Somalia there was a deployment of US military force in the context of protracted conflict with massive starvation and attacks on a Red Cross assistance program. But the follow-on Bill Clinton Administration took decisions that led to a deepening conflict with fatalities, and eventually the scaling down and eventual withdrawal of this multifaceted attempt at "humanitarian intervention" cum coercive pacification efforts. Such events, and others, indicated how difficult it was for well-intentioned outsiders to prevail in the face of determined local fighters.

Somalia also showed that the American public, and therefore Congress, was loath to pay costs in blood if not treasure for situations apparently devoid of immediate self-interest. There was no reason to think the American public was unique in this regard. Domestic support was difficult to sustain if a mostly altruistic effort to save strangers turned costly. The broad facts about Somalia in the early 1990s help explain the paucity of outside constructive involvement in the Rwandan genocide of 1994. US difficulties in Iraq from 2003, and then in Afghanistan especially by 2021, solidified the idea that deep foreign involvement in conflicts could be a costly sinkhole. "Forever wars" were not popular. Ukraine in 2022 was an exception, at least for some months. There the victims were White Europeans, set upon by the West's archenemy during the Cold War, Moscow. The future of NATO was said to be at stake, and maybe even Taiwan, not just difficulties for Ukrainians.

As for the ICRC, faced with sprawling and ill-defined internationalized domestic violence in many places, with numerous private armed actors who might manifest various transnational connections, and both suffering and observing attacks on humanitarian persons and facilities, it tried to reiterate its role and the importance of its NIIHA values. The Director of Operations addressed much of this back in 2004.[15] The rest of this section examines the basics of this evolution of ICRC activities in the post-Cold War world, complicated by the increased saliency of terrorism and counterterror concerns, and then affected still further by climate change and pandemics.

II   ICRC Early Expansion of Assistance

The ICRC had already started moving toward a systematically expanded role in protracted conflicts at least a dozen years or more before the Istanbul humanitarian summit of 2016. This change was consolidated and systematized during the time of President Kellenberger, with a big push coming from the then Director of Operations Pierre Krähenbühl, who had the confidence of both the president and Directors-General Paul Grossrieder and then Angelo Gnaedinger.

This orientation that was chosen in Geneva some 20 years ago could not have endured had the United States as the largest donor strongly objected, or the EU, or other key governments, or other partner RC Societies. But they evidently did not. Here one should mention the Donor Support Group (DSG), a designation for the largest donors to the ICRC among public authorities. (This body should not be confused with the Corporate Support Group (CSG) for businesses and foundations.) The details of the DSG and CSG were covered in Chapter 9 where funding of the ICRC is discussed. For now, the point to be noted is that an expanded understanding of the ICRC mandate has been supported by its major donors.

As usual there had been constant discussion in Geneva of how best to understand and apply its humanitarian right of initiative, or core humanitarian role. As early as the mid-1990s one could document that the ICRC was evaluating how it supplemented emergency assistance, usually called relief, with efforts at resiliency or socioeconomic recovery – with concrete examples from about half a dozen countries.[16] There followed agreement at headquarters to systematically broaden this push for rehabilitation or socioeconomic security. Trends were consolidated and expanded when Krähenbühl took over as director of operations (2002). Headquarters and field staff were generally, but not entirely, in agreement about what needed to be done.

There was thus broad and deep concern about the limits to traditional emergency relief. True, life-saving emergency relief was needed. But it would be better if one were not condemned to repetition over and over because no structural improvements occurred. There was frustration with the lack of resolution of the root causes of violence and human insecurity.[17] In that context, the ICRC leadership was agreed on the need to do more for victims, at least up to some undefined point. Even back then, not all at the ICRC agreed with the broader conception of ICRC assistance, but the collective leadership, while hearing the dissidents, continued with their expanded vision. The president, the Directorate, and the Assembly were all in general agreement. So were many staff, best as one can judge. The expanded policy direction was solidified in meetings between the Director of Operations and staff in the different geographical regions.

The organization first confirmed that it wanted to take a broader approach to what was involved in emergency relief. (This included, for example, more attention to mental health issues. As early as the Bosnian war of 1992–1995 the ICRC director-general fought internal battles to get more counseling for grieving Bosnian widows. By 2020, the ICRC was sponsoring sporting events for people with disabilities, helping those injured in war or natural disasters to have confidence in themselves and reintegrate into society.) Then it confirmed that it wanted to supplement or integrate traditional short-term lifesaving assistance with a more systematic expansion of intermediate assistance directed to what was sometimes called resiliency programs – when security conditions allowed. Over time this desire to implement a broader socioeconomic dimension to humanitarian assistance went by various names: development holds, micro-development, early recovery, resiliency programs, socioeconomic security.

As noted above, here and there the ICRC already had been providing not just emergency relief in the form of short-term food, clothing, shelter, and health care, but also seeds for the next round of planting, farming equipment, fishing equipment, improvements in water and sanitation systems, or vaccination of cattle. Sometimes a truce was negotiated so as to allow the vaccination of children against disease. These sporadic programs, mostly agricultural, with central attention to water and habitat, were a recognition of the limits to narrow emergency relief

Photograph 11.1 In Somalia in the early 1990s, the ICRC not only ran an important program of traditional food assistance in the context of famine, a program that required military protection to stop banditry attacks, but also helped pastoralists protect their livestock in the interest of longer-term economic security and reduced dependency on outside aid. ICRC resiliency programs, in addition to short-term aid, are not a new phenomenon, except in terms of extent of the practice and budgetary costs.

and the dangers of creating victim dependency in situations where development actors were not present.

In the early 2000s, therefore, the ICRC started expanding broad socioeconomic assistance on a more systematic basis, while not abandoning traditional short-term emergency relief where needed. Expansion was controlled and monitored. Budget increases were modest. Eventually Economic Security became one of the six specialized units at HQ that provided expert support to the field delegations (the others were Protection, Health, Weapon Contamination (e.g., demining), Water/Habitat, and Psychology (e.g., mental health). See further the ICRC organizational chart in the Annex.

ICRC policy about expanded humanitarian assistance was part of a global trend by a variety of humanitarian actors toward supplementing emergency relief with more socio-economic development activities. No man is an island, and the ICRC was not isolated from global developments.[18]

In historical fact, the ICRC was operating where conditions allowed along the lines of what later came to be called the triple nexus – and long before that verbiage became popular. Traditional emergency humanitarian relief sometimes overlapped with a kind of limited local development (which often supported a kind of local capitalism or buying and selling in local markets). It was rare but did happen that the ICRC, while avoiding political mediation as such, did help arrange local agreements that suspended the violence for a time or even arranged safe passage for negotiators who then engaged in the partisan or strategic political bargaining that the ICRC itself avoided.

III ICRC Expanded Assistance and UN Affairs

Some have speculated that it was greater UN involvement in humanitarian affairs after the Cold War that propelled the ICRC into enlarging its conception of humanitarian assistance. This seems both true and false: False, in that the direct trigger early on for expanded ICRC views of its assistance in conflicts seemed to be its own experience, as noted above; True, in the sense that over time the ICRC aligned its view with where the UN and its member states wanted to go. This continued evolution aided ICRC fund raising and diplomatic support. Some of the points discussed below were mentioned in Chapters 2 and 9 but merit further attention here.

We briefly set the stage in this discussion by looking back to the Cold War. At the start of the UN era, that body focused greatly on security and socioeconomic development and left most humanitarian assistance matters to what was then called the International Red Cross, with the ICRC being the supposed lead actor for programs in conflicts that the local National RC Society could not fully handle. However, after the ICRC failed to distinguish itself in the Biafran–Nigerian conflict of 1967–1970, and then early on offended Pakistan in the conflict over Bangladesh starting in 1971, the UN progressively did more on matters of humanitarian assistance.[19] Up to that era, the UN refugee office (UNHCR) mostly focused on protection not assistance, UNICEF focused on development involving women and girls, and there was no UN lead agency for humanitarian assistance. The resulting fragmented UN situation continued for some twenty years, roughly from 1971 to 1991.

After 1991 both the General Assembly and the Security Council begin to deepen their attention to humanitarian issues. The Assembly stressed the need for a greater UN response to pressing humanitarian needs in 1991 and decided at the same time to create what evolved to be OCHA

(Office for the Coordination of Humanitarian Affairs) with a reorganization in 1998.[20] Also in the early 1990s the president of the Council issued a Presidential Statement, with the agreement of Council members, indicating that threats to international peace and security, which allowed the Council to reach a binding decision, could arise from various conditions including humanitarian emergencies.[21] There followed in fact more UN action related to humanitarian concerns as one moved beyond the constrictions of the Cold War. Both the Assembly and the Security Council took various actions to try to assist and protect those caught up in internationalized civil wars and other forms of organized violence from the early 1990s onward.

At this time at the UN, pushed by European states as led by the Netherlands, there was talk not only about better UN coordination but also about linking humanitarian assistance to rehabilitation and development. In the same 1991 General Assembly resolution that directed more attention to humanitarian assistance and created an early version of OCHA, one finds the following wording: "There is a clear relationship between emergency, rehabilitation and development. In order to ensure a smooth transition from relief to rehabilitation and development, emergency assistance should be provided in ways that will be supportive of recovery and long-term development. Thus, emergency measures should be seen as a step towards long-term development."[22]

This linkage between humanitarian relief and development in the 1990s eventually came to be called the double nexus. Moreover, again led by the European states and the European Commission Humanitarian Office (ECHO), one found discussion of the triple nexus, with peacemaking added to relief and development.[23] So the discourse about a double or triple nexus was broadly shared by the time of the UN Humanitarian Summit in Istanbul in 2016.

However, according to those directly involved on behalf of the ICRC, it was not competition with an increased UN presence in humanitarian crises, or pressure from UN organs and agencies, that affected ICRC policymaking so much circa 2000 but rather its own experiences – a policy direction supported by major donors. True, the ICRC had observer status at the UN from 1990 and followed UN proceedings closely. But despite the view of some outsiders that the UN was trying to take over Red Cross humanitarian roles and that the ICRC was primarily motivated to protect its traditional zone of action, ICRC officials maintain that their expanding role was not driven by competition with the UN. However, later, by the time Yves Daccord became director-general (2010–2020), the need to raise money in competition with UN humanitarian agencies was no doubt a consideration in play.

According to officials in the Kellenberg–Krähenbühl era, often UN agencies were absent when it came to humanitarian assistance in ongoing violence. OCHA was not operational on the ground but rather a coordinating agency in New York. The same limits on field work were true for many humanitarian NGOs, with the exception sometimes of Doctors Without Borders (MSF) and occasionally a few others. The violent situation was too dangerous for most other actors to operate in, lacking as they did an established image of neutrality. UN security forces authorized by the Security Council to protect civilians often did not have a humanitarian mandate concerning relief and were often weak and slow to deploy. To the extent that UN field operations were based on a coercive mandate, the Blue Helmets were not seen as neutral. The same view pertained to other UN field operations if in New York the Security Council or General Assembly had criticized one of the fighting parties.

It seems that the ICRC, being involved on the ground around the world as it was, often alone or almost alone, knew firsthand about protracted conflicts. It followed UN developments in New York and elsewhere but maintained its usual independence and ran its own programs according to decisions in Geneva. Over time it might not object to UN language about New Ways of Working and coordinated outcomes,[24] but it was careful about its image of independent neutrality. In a widely used phrase in Geneva, the ICRC was willing to sometimes *coordinate with* the UN but not be *coordinated by* the UN.

It did not, for example, endorse the UN's Agenda for Peace under Secretary-General Boutros-Ghali because that document mixed military, political, and neutral activities. It was therefore wary of the concept of the triple nexus except for limited exceptions noted above. It refused to explicitly sign on to the UN "clusters approach" that created different UN lead actors for different sectors of humanitarian action. UNHCR might be given the lead for protection, and UNDP for assistance, and so on. The ICRC observed all this, might cooperate occasionally in the field with one or more agencies as the situation required, but did not blend itself totally with UN approaches. It might cooperate regarding fundraising appeals, in order to control for duplication, but not so much regarding field operations.

The ICRC had indeed joined with UNICEF in running an aid program on the Thai–Cambodian border from 1979. Pushed by ICRC Director of Operations Jean-Pierre Hocke, and led on the ground by the ICRC's François Bugnion, this combined operation eventually developed a budget that was three times the size of the ICRC's existing annual budget. The program was multifaceted with much attention to what is now called resilience or early recovery. It showed the flexibility of the

ICRC. Faced with exceptional distress after the fall of the fanatical and genocidal Khmer Rouge at the hands of the invading Vietnamese, it implemented a broad program of relief and basic development in cooperation with a leading UN agency.

This was a limited exception to the general rule back then of ICRC operational independence from the UN. At various times and places the ICRC might join with MSF in supporting a medical hospital in this or that conflict zone. But mostly it was careful about the RC principles of independence and neutrality. It was those principles, plus impartiality, that allowed it to operate in conflict situations characterized by a variety of armed actors. As always, one had to be careful about how one was viewed by those with the guns. Many other actors including UN agencies in the 1990s found the situation on the ground too dangerous, or never got authorization to act from a fragile government skeptical about UN politics.

IV   Effect of US Global War on Terrorism on ICRC Views

The ICRC posture of independent neutrality, which some at the UN found annoying, was reinforced by events after September 2001 pertaining to Afghanistan. The United States, most prominently its Secretary of State Colin Powell, argued that humanitarian NGOs should join the team of the Western good guys and become "force multipliers" for Washington and its allies in that conflict against the Afghan Taliban and al-Qaeda which started after the attacks on the United States on September 11, 2001. The ICRC, alarmed, responded by publicly reiterating its commitment to NIIHA standards.[25] This was crucial for the security of its field staff.

And so ICRC headquarters relied on its own traditions and perspectives to resist being incorporated into either UN programs or Western foreign policies. It did not see the UN as an actor that threatened its traditional role, primarily because particularly UN development agencies were mostly absent in the heart of the violence. And it did not see the United States and its allies as having monopolized international humanitarian action, whatever their quest for political hegemony after the al-Qaeda attacks on New York and Washington, because their approach was obviously not neutral. Ironically the United States, having called on humanitarian NGOs to be force multipliers in the US "war on terror," continued to be the largest donor to the ICRC as an NIIHA actor. In Afghanistan, the United States tolerated the fact that the neutral ICRC had contacts and programs with the Afghan Taliban. After all, under prevailing norms of neutrality and impartiality, wounded Taliban fighters were entitled to medical assistance and other humanitarian considerations. Some at the ICRC held their noses in dealing with the Taliban, given who they were and what they did, but nevertheless stuck to NIIHA values.

V   Continuation of (Often Broad) Emergency Relief

It is clear that the ICRC has not abandoned the role of providing emergency relief in conflict, whatever some official might say in a slip of the tongue. But this emergency relief may sometimes be very broad. If we arbitrarily fast forward to the Central African Republic in early 2021, we find a situation that ICRC President Maurer tried to publicize by a personal visit. In that situation of prolonged conflict, the immediate and short-term relief needs were enormous. According to the International Crisis Group and many other reliable sources, a personal power struggle for control of the central government going back to 2013 lay at the heart of the violence. National elections in late 2020 only deepened the crisis.

In much of the country the state had ceased to function. Armed political and criminal groups ran rampant. There were hundreds of thousands of displaced persons. The ICRC came across entire villages where the residents were traumatized in their residences and where the local economy had ceased to function. More generally, much commerce across the country had collapsed due to the violence. Where markets existed, they had priced their scarce commodities out of the reach of many citizens. Sexual assaults were common, and the ICRC had transported more than a thousand females to places where they could receive medical and psychological help. In addition to food assistance, the ICRC had tried to keep medical facilities functioning, but about 20 percent of these had been destroyed. It had trucked in water to several communities. Assistance was extremely hazardous, given the number of armed groups and the difficulty facing the ICRC in maintaining contacts so as to explain its role. Attacks on neutral personnel were up 40 percent over the preceding year.

Foreign involvement by the UN, EU, African regional organizations, and various states such as France, had been unable to fully stabilize the situation. Even before getting to the subject of intermediate-range resilience, just the matter of immediate humanitarian assistance often required enormous resources and much diplomacy. Traditional humanitarian emergency relief and protection were not by any means passé. But even ICRC emergency action could be very broad. This is a reason why the ICRC cannot or will not estimate how much of its assistance goes to traditional relief and how much to resiliency programs. In the Central African Republic, the ICRC's emergency response was often inseparable from economic recovery efforts. Geneva decided not only to deliver food and water and other immediate help, but also to try to get persons on their feet again as autonomous and independent citizens engaged in normal socioeconomic activities.

At the end of an official statement regarding the Central African Republic in 2021, the ICRC said: "Without hope of individual or economic development, without hope of security, the unremitting trauma ravaging the citizens of the Central African Republic will destroy the future of an entire nation."[26] This was a statement linking humanitarian assistance to much larger perspectives. And this broader perspective was exactly what many donors, policymakers, and victims (aka beneficiaries) wanted.

VI   Further on Humanitarian Assistance

When and if immediate civilian needs could be met concerning lifesaving food, water, clothing, shelter, and medical care including more attention to the psychological issues of especially vulnerable groups, for decades the ICRC was prepared to consider further assistance of a socioeconomic nature. The organization sought the right terminology for this expansion. Was it rehabilitation, or early recovery, or reintegration, or reconstruction, or economic security, or resilience, or micro-development?

In 2016 President Maurer gave a talk in which he called this expansion of humanitarian assistance a matter of providing "development holds," by which he apparently meant limited economic development focused on individuals and their basic socioeconomic needs. The driving contextual factor was protracted conflict in a situation where most development actors were absent, causing civilians to remain in deep distress. There was often arguably no other actor in place, or very few, to address basic or intermediate socioeconomic needs. Interestingly, ICRC staff did not much use the language of "development holds," but President Maurer certainly did. Staff also did not much use the term micro-development.

According to Maurer: "These developments [prevalence of protracted conflict with multiple armed actors] change our business fundamentally: the short-term emergency relief in well circumscribed conflict zones in favour of individual victims has largely disappeared as standard operating model. Humanitarianism 2.0 is about medium to long-term presence to stabilize the most fragile contexts and build development holds to prevent further contagion and disintegration."[27]

One could and should quibble with his apparent downplaying of short-term emergency relief, because in fact the organization in practice still prioritizes that role. But his term "development holds," while not always

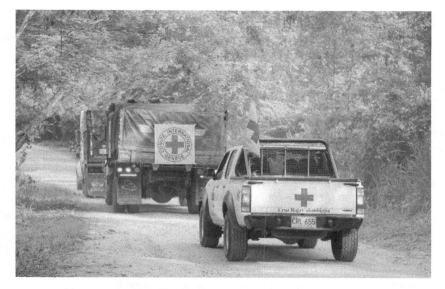

Photograph 11.2 Despite more importance directed to resiliency or early recovery programs as a form of micro-development, traditional emergency relief was still widely needed. Here in 2018 the ICRC and Colombian Red Cross deliver food assistance to civilians whose movements were restricted by fighting in the area. But especially in protracted conflicts the ICRC, like others, remained concerned about creating dependency through repeated emergency relief. It tried to support local economic self-reliance where security conditions allowed.

used by staff, fairly accurately captures the expansion of socioeconomic assistance that has been occurring for decades. It is a limited form of socioeconomic development that falls short of aspiring to change entire societies as per some formally approved national development model. At the UN it came to be called early recovery.

In a press interview in 2018, ICRC Director-General Yves Daccord was quoted this way:

L'assistance reste l'une de nos missions prioritaires, mais elle n'a rien à voir avec ce que font les acteurs du développement. Ces derniers poursuivent un agenda de changement social. Le CICR n'a pas l'ambition de changer la société. Il veut humblement faire en sorte que les systèmes vitaux en place ne s'effondrent pas. Nos 15 opérations les plus importantes durent depuis trente ans en moyenne. Pour avoir de l'impact, nous devons changer notre mode opérationnel. D'où la nécessité de mener des interventions de longue haleine pour réparer des infrastructures vitales.[28]

(My colloquial translation: Assistance remains one of our priority missions, but it has nothing to do with what development actors do. These later follow an agenda of social change. The ICRC does not have the desire to change society. It just wants to see that the vital [infrastructure] systems in place do not collapse. Our most important fifteen operations have gone on for thirty years on average. To have impact, we must change our mode of operations. That explains the necessity to manage interventions of long duration in order to repair vital infrastructures.)

In the same year President Maurer was quoted this way:

Dès qu'une région en crise atteint un seuil minimal de stabilité, c'est-à-dire dès que nos actions humanitaires ont garanti la survie de la population, nous devons tenter de mettre fin à la dépendance de cette région afin d'y attirer les investissements. L'humanitaire vise à devenir obsolète. Cela n'est possible qu'en relançant un minimum les cycles économiques. Il s'agit donc toujours de favoriser la transition des dépenses humanitaires vers les investissements dans un avenir plus durable. C'est en cela que le savoir-faire du secteur privé nous intéresse. Quels instruments faut-il employer, dans quel contexte et à quel moment? C'est ce qu'il nous faut définir et tester ensemble.[29]

(From the time that a region in crisis achieves a bare minimum of stability, which is to say that from the time that our humanitarian actions have guaranteed the survival of the population, we should try to terminate the dependency of that region by attracting [business] investments. The [traditional] humanitarianism is tending to become obsolete. All that is possible only in launching again a minimal economic cycle. Thus it is a matter of always favoring the transition from humanitarian expenditures to investments in a more lasting future. It is in that context that the know-how of the private sector interests us. Which instruments should be employed, in which context and at which moment? That is what we should define and test together.) In sum, to move from delivery of emergency humanitarian assistance to create development holds that meet basic human needs, one needs to involve the business community in order to reestablish a locally functioning economic system.

In the ICRC budget for 2021, about 70 percent went for humanitarian assistance. About a third of this sum went for economic security, both short and longer term. (Other types of assistance were health, water/habitant, demining plus other "weapons contamination" programs.) It remains unclear how much of this "economic security" was comprised of traditional relief and how much of resiliency projects aka development holds. The ICRC tracks spending for items – such as trucked-in water or cost of fishing nets, purchase of food or startup costs for a local poultry operation. Perhaps strangely, the organization does not track different costs for emergency relief versus development holds. The reference above to the Central African Republic shows the intermingling of traditional emergency relief and development holds, making easy separation a challenge.

VII   The Triple Nexus Reconsidered

In an important but not widely noted publication in 2017, an ICRC official addressed the relief–development nexus and suggested that in a number of situations there was too much insecurity for the organization to implement resiliency programs.[30] This suggested that the major limitation on implementing development holds was continued violence. Without stability, one could not attempt micro-development. He apparently was trying to temper all the trendy talk about the relief–development nexus by a reminder of the frequent facts on the ground. One might desire a sustainable humanitarian impact, by seeing RC assistance within the context of the UN Sustainable Development Goals. One might desire to make a first step in that direction. But it could not always be attempted because of the security situation.

He also indicated, quite accurately, that in all the talk about a relief–development–peace nexus, humanitarian protection (in the narrow sense) had been slighted. ICRC humanitarian operations involved not only socioeconomic assistance, but also various forms of protection narrowly defined (covered in different chapters, especially Chapter 14). He then, quite accurately, as far as Geneva was concerned, threw some cold water on the triple nexus idea by pointing out that the ICRC was not going to overtly do traditional peacemaking or peacebuilding, because it could not do that and guard its status as a neutral humanitarian actor. Whether this clear view of frequent realities was understood and shared by the entire leadership is an interesting question, particularly since other ICRC officials continued to use the discourse of the double and triple nexus. And the person who wrote the 2017 statement did not stay with the ICRC all that long.

Two authors at the respected Stockholm International Peace Research Institute also indicated similar concerns about the double or triple nexus. In a 2019 report, these SIPRI authors suggested that the double nexus was not working well, and particularly the triple nexus endangered the neutral status of the humanitarians such as the ICRC.[31]

VIII   Types of Development Holds

In some cases these "development holds" are directly related to violence and a clear extension of the emergency aid already occurring. Having created and staffed prosthetic centers for those who lost limbs to violence, often because of land mines, the ICRC then started making cash payments to those it had helped so they could get training and earn a living and operate independently in society. Likewise, having provided food relief, the ICRC then provided financial assistance so that some locals could start (or resume) and maintain a bakery to feed locals – allowing a reduction in, or termination of, food relief. For a third example, the ICRC was active in eastern Ukraine from 2015 trying to provide access to education as part of its efforts to help the civilian population in a war zone. Rather than trying to affect what was taught in schools near the contact line of fighting between government and separatist forces, the ICRC focused on safe access to education in material and moral/psychological ways. There was much consultation with local communities, and much interaction with the Ukrainian Red Cross.[32]

In some other cases the "development holds" or resiliency programs seemed more distant from traditional response to violence and maybe not so closely linked to traditional ICRC relief.

Sometimes the ICRC made payments to isolated senior citizens long after an armed conflict had ended when various tensions and blockages remained. Those benefiting from what might be termed ad hoc social security payments were at some distance timewise from the violence of years earlier. To be sure, social good was being done, but was such action really within the mandate of the ICRC? How should one understand the idea that the ICRC should concern itself with the "direct results" of violence? Social security payments to isolated seniors ten years after the end of armed conflict? Was that really the role of the ICRC as compared to a National RC Society? But suppose the National RC Society was impoverished or disorganized?

In another country, the ICRC was active supporting an agricultural college and its training of students in the feeding of cattle from local materials. This looked like a development activity, providing training and thus potential jobs for the young people. It also seemed not neutral, as it was justified sometimes as keeping young people from being recruited by local armed groups. This ICRC activity seemed quite distant from armed conflict, or other major violence, and its direct effects. It might be an example of how the ICRC fit into the paradigm of the triple nexus. It might also be an example of too much sprawl and lack of concentrated focus in ICRC activities.

In yet another situation, the ICRC was engaged with regional authorities to repair and expand a water system in a limited area. As in the example above of supporting an agricultural college, there was a history of violence in the area, and some continuing sporadic violence from time to time, but there was no longer major combat in that region. Some 80 percent of the locals were "regular" or "normal" residents, with only 20 percent being IDPs (internally displaced persons from past conflict). What the ICRC was supporting was basically longer-term development of infrastructure, in cooperation with public authorities, in a region that was stabilized at least at that time. It was mostly water infrastructure development per se, with some limited or distant link to political conflict.

Enterprising ICRC officials, aware of the policy direction of things at HQ, and wanting to show initiative and accomplishment, might be prone to stretch the link to political conflict and other violence. Of course good was being done for individuals, so what did it really matter if the local feeding of livestock or an improved water and sanitation system looked more like development than humanitarian assistance in war and major violence. This was the direction of policy, desired by locals as well as important outsiders.

IX   Back to the Future: NIIHA Values

One of the key factors in play for various kinds of resiliency programs was once again the matter of NIIHA values. An official of the World Bank explained clearly why the Bank was financially supporting the ICRC and its humanitarian orientations – both old but especially new. The ICRC was able to operate in conflict situations, with unique or almost unique access to those in need, because it was seen as neutral. If the ICRC were not seen as neutral on the ground, it would throw away the key factor, along with efficiency, that made it such a useful partner for the Bank and others with money as they pursued development holds or minimal development activities. In South Sudan, for example, the ICRC cooperated with the World Bank in improving all-purpose health-care clinics despite the nasty protracted conflict there. The program was more than short term, it led to medical treatment far beyond just the war wounded, and it depended on being perceived as neutral and impartial and hence off-limits to attack. It might provide a foundation for more general socioeconomic development if national political stability could be achieved.

Long-term or society-wide development is inherently a political process involving governmental choice about who directs development according to what model of political economy and which sectors of society benefit. Hence an important question arises: where do "humanitarian development holds" stop, and where does traditional development begin? In other words, macro-development is highly political, so the boundary of action that the ICRC should not cross becomes a crucial factor (in addition to the need to raise sizable resources). A clear view of the limits to ICRC "development holds" may be difficult to establish in general because crucial factors vary case to case. Some donors have raised questions about the outer limits of ICRC economic security programs, but headquarters has not been able to give a clear answer about programmatic boundaries that obtain across varied cases.

There is thus ample room for debate about the difference between neutral "development holds" or humanitarian resiliency programs and political development. It used to be the case that the ICRC leadership would ask: what is it that the organization is best placed to do, or the only organization that can do it? An internal ICRC study, transformed into an article in the RC Review, phrased it slightly differently: what is it that the ICRC can do that adds "something extra,"[33] which is maybe the same thing as a unique "value added." This key question might be answered by looking for examples of where the ICRC stopped its socioeconomic work, or backtracked on a program, because its neutral "development hold," which only it could provide, was becoming development per se and therefore perceived as political – which endangered its neutrality. Or, in some situations there might be development actors available for a handoff.

Independent research suggests that circa 2008 in northern Uganda the ICRC pulled back from its operations as its work with internally displaced persons morphed into something close to routine development.[34] Also, it appears to be the case that in one country, the ICRC field delegation decided not to respond positively to a request for repair of electric pylons that had been intentionally damaged by an armed group. To do so might be perceived as opposing the actions of that armed group, which remained active in that area. Repair might be seen as a nonneutral step by one of the fighting parties.

One ICRC publication suggested that the organization tended to avoid development projects that had been approved by a government, but also said that the ICRC would indeed sometimes cooperate with governmental plans and agencies.[35] Geneva certainly did manifest cooperation with governmental plans and offices when developing water/sanitation systems for all, sometimes in cooperation with the World Bank and UNICEF, two actors often called development agencies.

This left matters unclear. It seems that the difference between humanitarian micro-development and politically approved larger development remains undefined and unspecified. If true, this gray area of public policy is exactly where the ICRC operates in some of its actions today.

At the end of the day, on the subject of expanded version of neutral humanitarian assistance, we have three categories: (1) a direct and logical and clear extension of traditional assistance (e.g., cash payments and training to those benefitting from ICRC prosthetic services, being mostly war wounded, so they can get a job and function in society); (2) a mixture of logical extension combined with new expansion (e.g., supplementing food relief with support for the resumption of local food markets that operate on a profit-making basis, or building and supporting medical clinics that will treat more than the war wounded); and (3) borderline examples of "development holds" mixed with macro-development (e.g., cooperation with governmental agencies for a backup system guaranteeing the general water supply well into the future).

It may be that the degree of acceptance of ICRC resiliency programs depends on subjective views about what is an NIIHA program. If subjective views are in agreement on supporting an ICRC broad assistance program, firm and clear definitions and distinctions may not matter – at least for a time. In academic jargon, what counts is not clear and objective definitions but intersubjective agreement.

X   Humanitarian Resilience versus Political Reconstruction

Not all expanded ICRC assistance may be viewed as neutral: while neutral and impartial in intent, it might make a political impact. This is not a new problem.

In Syria, the ICRC established several "economic security" projects in areas controlled by the Assad regime. While benefitting persons, this action had the effect of reinforcing the Assad desire to make its control look sustainable and beneficial. This is precisely why the Western democracies were slow to commit to the reconstruction of Assad's Syria, because such economic reconstruction would contribute to the stability and consolidation of his brutal rule – as propped up by Iran and Russia. And this is precisely why the new Republican chair of the House Foreign Affairs Committee, in early 2023, wrote a letter to the State Department challenging US policy decisions regarding Syria.[36] He argued that US foreign assistance, including support for private organizations activating such projects as "bakery resilience," were propping up the detested Assad regime. "Bakery resilience" was a major ICRC objective in Syria at the time.

Circa 2023 most Western states were not keenly interested in correcting the economic chaos and dysfunction characterizing Assad's Syria, despite citizen hardship, because of calculations of power and interests. It seems that some officials in the EU told the ICRC leadership about this red line: yes to support for some micro-development, but no to large-scale reconstruction and development. So this distinction, difficult to define, remained politically important. Similar issues arose in Afghanistan after the Taliban returned to power in 2021: how to assist persons in need without supporting the legitimacy and continuation of a government that violated many human rights and might endanger the security of other states.

Photograph 11.3 In the Central African Republic in 2022, the ICRC supports a local business person with money and training so as to provide economic security and lessen the need for emergency assistance, which might create dependency. This "double nexus" of linking relief to local development became extensive by the ICRC if security conditions allowed, until major budget problems arose. The "double nexus" was popular with both donors and recipients and was endorsed by relevant international institutions.

It is relevant to note a UN Security Council resolution in 2021 regarding Syria that contained the following language: "Welcomes all efforts and initiatives to broaden the humanitarian activities in Syria, including water, sanitation, health, education, and shelter early recovery projects, undertaken by the International Committee of the Red Cross (ICRC) and other organizations, and calls upon other international humanitarian agencies and relevant parties to support them...."[37]

Here we find high-level endorsement of ICRC early recovery programs, but still no clarity about where they end and political development or reconstruction begins. As noted, some on the political right in the US Congress, which is where the donation to the ICRC originates, might manifest a quite narrow view of what is a neutral humanitarian assistance program and what, by comparison, is political involvement ill-advisedly propping up a strategic enemy.

Now if the ICRC were also able to implement similar economic security measures in opposition-held areas – for example, by restoring the water system of Idlib in the northeast of Syria, for some time not under the control of Damascus – then it could be argued that the ICRC impact was indeed neutral and impartial because various humanitarian projects were effectuated on all sides of the conflict. While the ICRC was promoting some kinds of economic recovery in the government-held areas of Syria, it was also operating in the northeastern areas still held by Kurdish Democratic Forces. It, along with partners such as the Norwegian Red Cross, was active in providing medical and other services in the al-Hol detention camp. The residents of al-Hol were mostly women and children linked to fighters of the Islamic State group. The overall ICRC effort within the traditional borders of Syria might be said to be neutral and impartial because of the sum total of assistance and protection activity on all sides. Still, a relatively large proportion of ICRC spending in Syria during 2011–2022, mostly for assistance, occurred on the government side. (The ICRC was unable or unwilling to provide a specific estimate in this regard.) The subject was dealt with in Chapter 5 regarding ICRC relations with the rest of the Movement.

In other situations, the same questions about ICRC neutrality and impartiality could be raised. In Libya or the Central Africa Republic, for example, the ICRC might undertake to rebuild the functionality of a village by providing and paying for agricultural, sanitary, and medical measures, plus stimulating the restart of the local economy by economic grants to individuals. One saw economic recovery measures on a very limited scale, not part of an official governmental development program. This ICRC resilience activity would work to the political advantage of the ruling authorities in whose territory the village existed. There might be no comparable rehabilitation program in areas controlled by other armed groups – who might in fact lack persistent control of set territory. One supposes that the ICRC decided that the good done for individuals outweighed any projected political impact, especially if no armed actor disrupted ICRC programs.

This conundrum seemed to be just an inherent complexity of humanitarian assistance in many violent situations, whether pertaining to emergency relief or expanded "development holds." The ICRC mostly avoided charges of politicized *intent*, or willfully taking sides in the conflict. How one evaluated its indirect political *impact* might be a different matter. Some Republicans in the House of Representatives certainly thought so in early 2023, noted above. They were concerned about humanitarian programs that would have the effect of solidifying Assad's power.

The problem was more serious in internal armed conflicts and domestic violence. The ICRC often worked in conjunction with the local National RC Society, which was an auxiliary to the government. So not only in Syria but also Ethiopia, for example, it wound up providing assistance, short or intermediate term, mostly in government-controlled areas. While ICRC motivations reflected NIIHA values, the consequences might be seen by some as nonneutral or unbalanced.[38] I already noted the complex case of Syria in Chapter 6 on the RC Movement in contemporary times, stressing that the ICRC was blocked from being fully independent, impartial, and neutral by the dictates of the Assad government effectuated through SARC (the Syrian Arab Red Crescent Society).

The ICRC does decline to pursue some versions of expanded humanitarian assistance. In some cases there is too much insecurity, or the proposed project exceeds the organization's expertise and capability, or the ICRC is not sufficiently well connected to make the project work well, or the proposal has too much of a political impact. Apparently in Yemen the ICRC turned down a proposal by the World Bank because of lack of capability, with the Bank program finally undertaken by UNICEF and others. But situations vary and it is very difficult to establish clear lines everywhere about what the organization will and will not do by way of socioeconomic human security programs. If there is a universal rule on this subject, it is that the ICRC will engage in a resiliency program if it can produce a value-added for individuals affected by conflict, and it is the best placed to do it.

Hence in Afghanistan as of 2022, the organization not only provided medical relief to a couple of dozen hospitals, but also paid impoverished medical staff. Still further, it helped support a medical college that trained medical personnel for the future. ICRC staff, including females at least for a time, helped train future Afghan medical staff, including females.

But the Taliban's highest religious authorities intended to operate medical facilities that were segregated by gender. One can argue that the ICRC was supporting discrimination in violation of the principle of impartiality, in that Afghan women would not be allowed to receive treatment at certain medical facilities supported by the ICRC. Or one could argue that the ICRC was ensuring that when females were treated at female-only clinics, they received expert medical care of an equal nature – or as equal as the situation allowed.

At the time of writing, in Afghanistan the ICRC had publicly protested discrimination against women (documented in the Epilogue), but then kept a low profile while some other humanitarians suspended their operations because of restrictions on female staff. (Still other humanitarian actors continued operations with only male staff.) But the ICRC tried to keep its existing programs going where it could, including with female staff, relying on good local relations with some parts of the fragmented Taliban leadership, and encouraging local citizens to approach Taliban authorities asking for ICRC activities to continue.[39] It could not help all those it wanted to, but it continued to keep some of its programs going as previously constructed. One could see a flexible and pragmatic organization doing the good it could, with attention to NIIHA principles as best it could. This orientation was part of a longstanding historical pattern. It pursued pragmatic, incremental progress in an imperfect world with many trade-offs.

If the ICRC does cooperate with governmental agencies whether regarding water rehabilitation or medical assistance, for example, it does try to follow NIIHA values at least in relative terms. We discussed Afghanistan above. Or to use another example, an ICRC water rehabilitation project in Africa benefited not only some IDPs but "regular" local citizens persons as well. In this way officially sanctioned infrastructure programs, whether medical or water, were as neutralized and impartial as possible.

Likewise, one can find examples where the ICRC, having run or helped run a program of expanded assistance, will eventually hand off to another actor of coalition of actors. It is trying to do so in Goma, Democratic Congo regarding a long-term water rehabilitation project. It did so in Bolivar state, Venezuela, regarding a health program to combat malaria in a region wracked by conflict. So there are at least some examples showing it shies away from becoming a long-term development actor. Again, situations vary; negotiations vary; the availability of other competent actors varies.

Lots of other humanitarian actors were also engaged in the same notion of expanded humanitarian assistance aka development holds or resiliency programs. This is where the entire humanitarian system was headed. In Haiti, a private humanitarian actor was trying to stimulate local agriculture rather than deliver food assistance from outside.[40] But for this particular scheme to work, the armed gangs that dominated so much of Haiti would have to leave the local farmers alone to raise and then sell their crops. The gangs would have to resist the temptation to "tax" or "shakedown" or exact "protection money" from the process. Again, the "double nexus" only works if the security situation allows.

By and large, major donors to the ICRC faced the same dilemmas and uncertain boundaries between types of assistance. The United States objected to paying for reconstruction or development projects in Afghanistan under the Taliban from 2021. The Taliban in 2022 was restricting education for women and had killed some supporters of the former pro-Western government, among other contested policies. However, Washington continued to have good relations with, and made the usual donations to, the ICRC – which was not only providing medical relief there but also (as mentioned above) supporting a medical school that was training medical personnel for the future. The ICRC was helping maintain and build medical infrastructure for Afghanistan under the Taliban, and that was acceptable to major donors. Or, those were facts at the time of writing in 2023.

The world is messy and ICRC assistance roles in protracted conflicts are varying and fluid.

XI   Conclusion

We defer a conclusion here and do a cumulative conclusion about contemporary interpretation of the ICRC's mandate until the end of Chapter 12.

Notes

1 The International Committee of the Red Cross, "The International Committee of the Red Cross's (ICRC's) role in situations of violence below the threshold of armed conflict," *International Review of the Red Cross*, 96(893) (2014), p. 277. doi: 10.1017/S1816383114000113.

2 The Bosnian War of 1992–1995 is difficult to characterize. It was essentially over borders and power following the breakup of the former Yugoslavia. Serbia, for example, did not officially invade Bosnia and Herzegovina, but rather lent support unofficially to the Bosnian Serbs in their struggles with Bosnian "Turks" or Muslims. Croatia was of course also involved in complex ways. The central point in this section remains: much violence in world affairs took the form of complex internal wars or locally inspired violence not always characterized as war or international war.

3 Radio Suisse Romande, "Tous en soi dit," Septembre 29, 2016, Rediffusion, Octobre 8, 2016, 16h03.

4 For an excellent overview of the subject, see Marion Harroff-Tavel, "Do Wars Ever End? The Work of the International Committee of the Red Cross When the Guns Fall Silent," *International Review of the Red Cross*, 85/851 (2003), www .icrc.org/en/doc/assets/files/other/irrc_851_haroff-tavel.pdf (accessed November 7, 2022). Note the relatively early date. This article resulted from a larger internal study.

5 A visit to the ICRC website pulls up almost 11,000 references to the term during the past five years.

6 Ellen Policinski and Jovana Kuzmanovic, "Protracted Conflicts: The Enduring Legacy of Endless War," *International Review of the Red Cross*, 101/912 (November 2019), pp. 965–976, https://international-review.icrc.org/reviews/ irrc-no-912-protracted-conflict (accessed November 16, 2022).

7 For an accurate journalistic version of this view about multiple causes of violence and civilian distress, see Thomas Friedman, "Trump, Niger, and Connecting the Dots," *New York Times*, October 31, 2017, www.nytimes .com/2017/10/31/opinion/trump-niger-africa-desertification.html (accessed November 7, 2022).

8 ICRC Annual Report 2019, p. 7, https://library.icrc.org/library/docs/DOC/ icrc-annual-report-2019-1.pdf (accessed November 16, 2022).

9 The World Bank, "Fragility, Conflict & Violence," September 30, 2022, www.worldbank.org/en/topic/fragilityconflictviolence/overview (accessed November 16, 2022). The present section of this book is about expanded ICRC assistance in order to make victims of violence more independent and less dependent on aid, with some of it funded by the World Bank. Exactly the same goals and trends are noted by the International Rescue Committee, again with reference to the World Bank. The arguments of the ICRC and the IRC are virtually identical. See David Miliband, "A Battle Plan for the World Bank: Why Refugees Are at the Center of the Fight Against Poverty," *Foreign Affairs*, February 19, 2019, www.foreignaffairs.com/articles/2019-02-19/ battle-plan-world-bank (accessed November 16, 2022).

10 Barbara Rijks, "Transition and Recovery: The Missing Middle," April 2018, Perry World House, Penn University, https://global.upenn.edu/sites/default/ files/Rijks.pdf (accessed November 16, 2022).

11 For a useful summary see Rescue Global, "The World Humanitarian Summit: A Summary of the Major Outputs (Part 1)," August 3, 2016, www .rescueglobal.org/news/view/the-world-humanitarian-summit-a-summary-of- the-major-outputs-part-1 (accessed November 16, 2022). For one overview of the follow up to Istanbul at the UN, showing among other things an emphasis on the link between humanitarian relief and development, see United Nations, "ECOSOC Events on Transition from Relief to Development," no date, www.un.org/ecosoc/en/node/14973644 (accessed November 16, 2022). This ECOSOC document is useful for showing the long and broad concern with protracted conflicts and their socioeconomic ramifications. A companion document traces ECOSOC concern back at least to 2005, which is when, more or less, the ICRC also began to emphasize the same problems. United Nations, "'Transition from Relief to Development' Special Relief Assistance Focus, As ECOSOC Opens Humanitarian Affairs Segment," July 13, 2005, www.un.org/press/en/2005/ecosoc6165.doc.htm (accessed November 16, 2022). ICRC Vice President Jacques Forester participated in some of the ECOSOC discussions at his time. So both the ICRC and the UN were interacting regarding the socioeconomic dimensions of protracted conflicts.

12 David P. Forsythe, "Humanitarianism: Coping in the Void," in Alison Brysk and Michael Stohl, eds., *A Research Agenda for Human Rights* (Cheltenham, UK: Edgar Elgar, 2020), chap. 3.

13 Jacques Forster, *Coopération Nord-Sud: la solidarité a l'épreuve* (Neuchâtel: Editions Livreo-Alphil, 2021), Vol. II, p. 67.

14 United Nations, "ECOSOC Events on Transition."

15 Pierre Krahenbuhl, "The ICRC's Approach to Contemporary Security Challenges: A Future for Independent and Neutral Humanitarian Action," *International Review of the Red Cross*, 86/855 (September 2004), pp. 505–514,

www.icrc.org/en/doc/assets/files/other/irrc_855_krahenbuhl.pdf   (accessed November 16, 2022).

16 ICRC, François Grunewald, "From Prevention to Rehabilitation: Action Before, During and After the Crisis: The Experience of the ICRC in Retrospect," *International Review of the Red Cross*, 306, June 30, 1995, www.icrc.org/en/doc/resources/documents/article/other/57jmh5.htm (accessed November 16, 2022). The EU and its ECHO used the same concepts and language as the ICRC.

17 One can trace this same frustration in the community focused on refugees, with UNHCR leadership calling for more state attention to root causes of flight, but at the end of the day finding itself left holding the bag regarding caring for refugees who were not resettled and could not return to their habitual homes. See, for example, Ogata, *The Turbulent Decade.*

18 Michael J. Barnett, "Humanitarianism Transformed," *Perspectives on Politics*, 3, 4 (December 2005), pp. 723–740. Some of the global trends within the international humanitarian community the ICRC resisted, as noted later.

19 Florian Hannig, "The Power of the Refugees: The 1971 East Pakistan Crisis and the Origins of the UN's Engagement with Humanitarian Aid," in Simon Jackson and Alanna O'Malley, eds., *The Institution of International Order: From the League of Nations to the United Nations* (London and New York: Routledge, 2018), pp. 111–135.

20 A/RES/46/182.

21 UNSC presidential statement, UN Doc. S/23500, January 31, 1992: "The non-military sources of instability in the economic, social, humanitarian, and ecological fields have become threats to international peace and security...."

22 A/RES/46/182, Annex, Guiding Principles, para. 9.

23 International Council of Voluntary Agencies (ICVA), "Learning Stream: What Is the Triple Nexus," no date, www.icvanetwork.org/uploads/2021/08/Topic-One-Briefing-Paper-The-nexus-explained.pdf (accessed November 17, 2022).

24 OCHA, "Humanitarian Development Nexus, The New Way of Working," no date, www.unocha.org/fr/themes/humanitarian-development-nexus (accessed November 17, 2022).

25 Krähenbühl, "The ICRC's Approach to Contemporary Security Challenges."

26 ICRC, "It Is Time to End the Violence in the Central African Republic," February 12, 2021, www.icrc.org/en/document/it-time-to-end-violence-in-central-african-republic (accessed November 16, 2022).

27 Peter Mauer, "What Are the Triggers for Global Conflicts, and What Can We Do about Them?" *ICRC*, April 8, 2016, www.icrc.org/en/document/what-are-triggers-global-conflicts-and-what-can-we-do-about-them (accessed November 16, 2022).

28 Stéphane Benoit-Godet and Stéphane Bussard, "Yves Daccord, Les attentes envers le CICR ont change," *Le Temps*, July 24, 2018 modified July 25, 2018, www.letemps.ch/monde/yves-daccord-attentes-envers-cicr-ont-change (accessed November 16, 2022).

29 Manuel Rybach, "L'humanitaire vise à devenir obsolete," *Credit Suisse*, December 12, 2018, www.credit-suisse.com/about-us-news/fr/articles/news-and-expertise/the-goal-of-humanitarian-work-201812.html (accessed November 16, 2022).

30 Hugo Slim, "Nexus Thinking in Humanitarian Policy: How Does Everything Fit Together on the Ground," *ICRC*, October 25, 2017, www.icrc.org/en/document/nexus-thinking-humanitarian-policy-how-does-everything-fit-together-ground (accessed November 16, 2022).

31 Marina Caparini and Anders Reagan, "Connecting the Dots on the Triple Nexus," *SIPRI*, November 29, 2019, www.sipri.org/commentary/topical-backgrounder/2019/connecting-dots-triple-nexus (accessed November 16, 2022).

32 Geoff Loane and Ricardo Fal-Dutra Santos, "Strengthening Resilience: The ICRC's Community-based Approach to Ensuring the Protection of Education," *International Review of the Red Cross*, 99/2 (2017), pp. 797–820, https://international-review.icrc.org/sites/default/files/irrc_99_905_17.pdf (accessed November 16, 2022).

33 Harroff-Tavel, "Do Wars Ever End?"

34 Jon Harald Sande Lie, "From Humanitarian Action to Development Aid in Northern Uganda," *Development in Practice*, 27/2 (March 28, 2017), www.tandfonline.com/doi/abs/10.1080/09614524.2017.1275528 (accessed November 18, 2022).

35 "Q&A: The ICRC and the 'Humanitarian-Development-Peace Nexus' Discussion, in Conversation with Filipa Schmitz Guinote," *International Review of the Red Cross*, 101/912 (2019), pp. 1051–1066, https://international-review.icrc.org/sites/default/files/pdf/1602948923/IRC101_3b/S1816383120000284a.pdf (accessed November 17, 2022). This was a substantive and sophisticated discussion of particularly the relief–development nexus, but it covered so many factors at such a level of generality that key distinctions remained unclear.

36 Adva Saldinger, "Exclusive: Top Republican Urges State Department to Rethink Syrian Aid," *Devex*, January 25, 2023, www.devex.com/news/exclusive-top-republican-urges-state-department-to-rethink-syria-aid-104840 (accessed January 26, 2023).

37 UN Security Council, "Resolution 2585, The Situation in the Middle East," July 9, 2021, http://unscr.com/en/resolutions/2585 (accessed November 17, 2022).

38 See further Rajeesh Kumar, *The International Committee of the Red Cross in Internal Armed Conflicts: Is Neutrality Possible?* (Singapore: Palgrave Macmillan, 2019).

39 A careful observer could discern ICRC policy from sources such as Ali M. Latifi, "After the Taliban Ban on Women NGO Work, Local and Foreign Aid Groups Take Different Approaches," *The New Humanitarian*, March 2, 2023), www.thenewhumanitarian.org/news-feature/2023/03/02/afghanistan-ingos-find-workarounds-taliban-ban-on-women-ngo-work (accessed March 18, 2023).

40 Frank Guistra, "The International Aid System Is in Need of Reform," *Toronto Star*, June 1, 2022, www.thestar.com/business/2022/06/01/the-international-aid-system-is-in-need-of-reform.html (accessed November 17, 2022).

> ICRC programs in Rio de Janeiro were a great success and are never to be repeated again.
>
> Anonymous joke that circulated inside the ICRC, 2021

It is all well and good, in principle, for the ICRC to have been flexible over time and respond to new threats to human dignity with an expansion of practical action. Flexibility was, after all, one of the traits of the organization cited by the historian Daniel Palmieri and referred to earlier in order to explain the enduring status of the ICRC since 1863. But the second factor cited by him explaining ICRC success was specificity or concentrated focus. How could the organization be flexible in responding to human need but still retain a precise focus – in reality and not just rhetorically? Given the various forms and broad extent of violence in the world after the Cold War, what were the limits to ICRC activity and programs? Was there still a real core focus? After all, the ICRC was not the only humanitarian actor active in the world.

If one noted not only development holds or early recovery programs in conflict situations where the violence had ebbed, as we did in the previous chapter, what about affronts to human dignity in situations of low-level urban violence and also irregular migration? On these topics one found expanded ICRC action as well. Was this well considered or a bridge too far? Were there perhaps some aspects of this expanded activity in these domains that were merited but other aspects not so much? Was there a way to do all this but keep costs to manageable proportions, perhaps by getting the right partners and eventually handing off programs to them? Was the major budget crisis of 2023 going to compel some hard decisions?

I   Low-Level Urban Violence

At approximately the same time that the ICRC systematically moved into broader programs of economic security beyond emergency relief, it also started new programs designed to address the humanitarian consequences of urban problems in situations of "other violence." It of course had much experience in observing urban distress in international armed conflicts, from Berlin and London in World War II to Baghdad and Mosul more recently – not to mention Mariupol or Kherson in Ukraine. It continued to be concerned about the effect of war on cities, including such subjects as the use of cluster bombs in crowded areas.

But in the first decade of the twenty-first century the ICRC began to also focus on what was happening to many people in urban areas experiencing violence quite clearly short of war. There were armed gangs that controlled parts of cities, neighborhoods where the police feared to tread, use of weapons similar to war situations, armed private actors with enough persistent if sporadic power to interfere with the basic human needs or socioeconomic security of residents. Human dignity could be under major attack from urban low-level violence, as life in Port au Prince in Haiti clearly demonstrated.

Just as the ICRC often used "protracted conflicts" as a frame for its policies of economic resilience, so the organization talked about trends in population growth and urban migration for its programmatic expansion into urban distress and dysfunction with violent dimensions. Citing figures about how many persons lived in cities (projected to be 70 percent globally by 2050), and how many were moving from rural to urban areas (e.g., African cities were expected to triple in size by 2050), and how many lived in slums or shanty towns or bidonvilles (about one billion or one-seventh of global population), the ICRC asserted a need to be more active regarding urban distress. The result, as seen in Geneva, was a decision to confront considerable humanitarian distress for innocent civilians trapped in dysfunctional urban areas. Certainly some type of violence was often evident.[1]

More than once the ICRC referred to its right of initiative, already explained, as the basis for its action. Clearly the situations discussed here did not rise to the level of an armed conflict, and so the organization could not base its action on IHL – although it might draw on analogies with, and experience in, that domain. In a fifty-two-page booklet on the subject, the ICRC noted that it drew on its experience in war to note three fundamental targets for its action in urban areas: the need of civilians for a livelihood; their access to vital services such as medical care and education; and their mobility to enable the first two.[2] Consequently, it wound up relying on its war experiences but additionally drawing on RC principles and also human rights standards. (We explain the ICRC's increased reference to human rights in some depth in Chapters 13 and 14.)

While one could find ICRC passing reference to urban problems earlier, and while the ICRC might be found working with local police forces in the late 1990s, the start of an expanded and systematic concern with urban violence is to be found in decisions circa 2005. From that time there was a period of thinking and planning regarding how a NIIHA agency such as the ICRC might deal with Rio de Janeiro in Brazil and its favelas (slums). The decision was taken in Geneva to try ICRC involvement as a limited case study, then evaluate. The Rio program was launched in 2008–2009, with periodic evaluations. There followed in fairly short order similar programs in places such as Cape Town, South Africa; Belfast, Northern Ireland; Ciudad Juarez, Mexico; Karachi, Pakistan, and elsewhere.

Photograph 12.1 The ICRC became progressively concerned about extensive violence in urban areas below the level of armed conflict, which created much civilian distress. Starting with Rio de Janeiro, Brazil, the organization made a number of interventions. While much good was done, some thought this type of varied activity was a bridge too far beyond traditional concerns for the ICRC, especially as budget cuts kicked in. Photo: Rio, 2010.

It proved quite difficult to say what this ICRC expansion of programming into urban areas entailed as a general rule because situations varied. Some areas, for example Belfast, were more developed in socioeconomic terms than a shanty town outside Cape Town. In Belfast the ICRC was already reasonably well known by community leaders, who might welcome some humanitarian mediation about the human dimension of partisan/sectarian conflict. The situation was mostly otherwise in the shanty towns outside Cape Town, where basic utilities and other government services were clearly deficient. Another variable was ICRC success, or not, in carving out a zone of agreement where it could operate and be perceived as a NIIHA agency. In some cases such as Karachi, whose urban dysfunction was great enough to attract the attention of *The Economist* magazine, the ICRC might do little more than help negotiate an agreement with those possessing weapons not to interfere with ambulances on their way to hospitals. In other cases the ICRC role was multifaceted, involved commitment of resources across time (which necessitated multi-year funding), and might include detention visits.

One can see the differences in cases by looking at some thumbnail sketches of ICRC involvement in low-level urban violence as presented by the organization.[3]

A   Rio de Janeiro, Brazil

There was a five-year project (2009–2013) implemented in partnership with the local health and education authorities in favelas affected by armed violence, aimed at improving people's access to health care and education and enhancing their general safety. In the area of primary health care, for instance, the project addressed issues such as limited access to health services, mental health problems, and specific vulnerabilities aggravated by armed violence. The programs were designed to better measure the effects of violence on people's health, increase the availability and quality of health services, and make health professionals less exposed to the risks of armed violence, thereby facilitating their access to affected communities. Particularly vulnerable groups, such as adolescent mothers and their children, were provided with health and psychosocial support tailored to their specific needs. Many of the activities developed through the project were subsequently turned into public policies by the Rio health authorities and implemented in areas of the city where a need was identified. They have also served as a model for other cities in Brazil facing similar issues.

B   *Belfast, Northern Ireland, UK*

Since 2013, the ICRC's activities have aimed to mitigate the impact of violence perpetrated on armed groups against communities despite the 1998 agreement meant to end decades of conflict. In addition to its direct dialogue with weapon bearers on these issues, the ICRC supports a number of community organizations that mediate on behalf of those under threat of violence, and engages directly with some of the armed groups in a dialogue around humanitarian concerns, including the consequences of armed violence and sexual violence, as well as problems faced by ex-combatants and ex-detainees.

The ICRC works to influence decision-makers to protect and assist victims or their families, and to improve conditions of detention and treatment of detainees, including access to proper health care.

It also commissioned a report on psychological trauma among ex-combatants and a mapping of the violence in Northern Ireland.

C   *Karachi, Pakistan*

An ongoing project that began in 2014, the ICRC activity was designed on the basis of in-depth studies and large-scale consultations with the health-care community, authorities, and other partners, to address the problem of violence against health care workers or health care institutions in a complex context of urban violence. This context is characterized by armed attacks on health-care facilities and a broad range of violent incidents of lower intensity, many of them perpetrated by health providers and members of the public. In response, wide-ranging activities include protection-focused training and developing manuals and other materials for health-care workers and medical colleges; influencing decision-makers to improve legal and administrative mechanisms for the protection of health care; a high-visibility media campaign to increase respect for ambulance services; engaging with law enforcement agencies; and assessing the physical safety of health-care facilities and sharing recommendations with relevant stakeholders. The impact of all the aspects of the project is continuously and rigorously monitored. The ambulance campaign, for example, resulted in a marked increase in the number of drivers giving right of way to ambulances.

D   *Khayelitsha, Cape Town, South Africa*

Here one finds a three-year project (2011–2014) using sports to mitigate the effects of violence in Khayelitsha township. With a clear correlation between poor school attendance and violence, the program targeted at-risk youth – particularly young men aged 14–17 – and provided them with a safe space and alternatives to joining gangs or engaging in antisocial behavior. Football coaching was complemented by academic tutoring, life-skills coaching and a leadership program, all designed to promote behavioral change and positive empowerment. Former gang members were also involved in workshops as facilitators. In collaboration with its local civil society partner, the ICRC developed an evidence-based approach to tackling urban violence. According to a follow-up study, the project resulted in a decrease in violence in and around the project area.

E   Ciudad Juarez, Mexico

The Creating Humanitarian Spaces program was launched in Ciudad Juarez in 2012, in partnership with the Chihuahua State education authorities and the Mexican Red Cross, with the aim of helping communities affected both directly and indirectly by armed violence. Their access to essential public services – such as health, employment, and education – had been reduced. The program seeks to strengthen the resilience, dignity, and respect of people living in these situations, working primarily with students and teachers. Areas of focus include peer-to-peer education, first-aid training, psychological and psychosocial support, community development, and formal education. In the five years since its introduction, the program has reduced school dropout rates; improved relationships between students and teachers and among students themselves; and has had a positive influence on students' behavior towards their families and communities and improved their prospects for the future. The program has also created safe communal spaces, such as a school medical facility and a sports ground, which helps strengthen social ties.

Mostly the fundamental or structural problems in blighted urban areas stemmed from lack of governmental services resulting in a lack of socio-economic development including lack of provision of responsible public order. In some cases the ICRC, working with various local partners both inside and outside the RC Movement, might find itself advocating for, or arranging, medical clinics which then addressed vaccinations, sexually transmitted diseases, tuberculosis, or dengue fever, inter alia. This role went far beyond treating gunshot wounds. Beyond this type of continuing medical assistance, there were issues of employment, education, transportation, various forms of training, and more. As in war, so in these types of urban areas, the ICRC came to be known for its expertise in constructing water-sanitation systems, many of which were eventually turned over to public authorities, as was the case in Port-au-Prince, Haiti in a certain era. There were other obvious connections to war as well. Projects for micro-urban agriculture in places such as Gaza City were not that different from economic resilience efforts in rural areas elsewhere that had been necessary because of violence. There was indeed some overlap with economic resiliency concerns.

This ICRC expanded involvement in urban problems below the level of armed conflict was rationalized as being consistent with RC Conference resolutions calling attention to urban problems and calling on all members of the Movement to support each other. Equally important was the fact that major donors such as the United States and the EU were supportive. In 2012 the ICRC and the EU Institute for Security Studies sponsored a joint workshop on the topic of humanitarian action in low-level urban violence.

Much like "development holds" or economic resilience in protracted conflicts, the ICRC role in urban violence frequently involved micro-development projects, for example training carpenters and plumbers or arranging for traditional schools to function in safety and with adequate resources. In a way the ICRC and its local partners, some in the RC Movement and some not, provided basic health, education, and economic services in the absence of governmental effectiveness in these areas. This was really a type of urban development over time, just as much ICRC programming in protracted conflicts was really long-term infrastructure development or creation and support for local market activity. True, one often had to negotiate a path through the violence, but call it what you will, this was urban socioeconomic development in various ways and means.

Sometimes nongovernmental armed actors did not object if they were left alone to pursue their own interests, which more likely than not involved some kind of criminality. This was the price the ICRC paid for being seen as a NIIHA agency and allowed to operate without being attacked. The ICRC might be found arranging détente between police and gangs, which was different from trying to eliminate the gangs. On the other hand, trying to keep kids in school so as to deter them from joining gangs was not, in fact, neutral in impact. Encouraging kids to play sports which again might keep them away from gang activity was a desirable goal, but it was not a purely neutral activity in that it undercut the appeal of one or more of the armed actors in conflict with public authorities. It undercut the position of the gangs – one of the violent parties.[4]

One might say that just as the ICRC was not neutral when it came to promoting and applying IHL and human rights, so the organization was often not neutral when it came to endorsing and working for a humane life in urban settings. Sometimes this meant pursuing programs which undercut the appeal of certain armed groups, and sometimes this meant turning a blind eye to some of the activities of those groups in order to achieve other humanitarian objectives. If one was going to get more safety for ambulances on their way to hospital, maybe one had to skip over what some armed groups were doing in their other activities. If the groups involved in criminal activity agreed not to shoot up medical resources, maybe that was all that could be achieved in that situation. ICRC NIIHA principles were practiced in different ways in different contexts.

As with socioeconomic recovery in protracted conflicts, so with micro-development in urban violence short of war, questions arise about the ICRC role. Does the ICRC have the expertise to do what it is trying to do, especially when its programming involves advocacy for human rights standards rather than IHL? What is the division of labor within the RC Movement? The Seville Agreement 2.0, negotiated by 2022, and already analyzed in Chapter 6, presumably highlights the role of the National RC Societies and their Federation in situations outside armed conflict, especially when what is needed is some kind of assistance rather than protection as per detention visits. Are the critics right that the ICRC risks losing it specificity and reputation for effectiveness in war zones by this broad and varying role in urban distress? Where are the clear limits to ICRC action in urban areas? Where are the consistent guidelines for ICRC and NIIHA programming in urban human insecurity?

It is worth recalling that the 1975 Tansley Report, which as noted was a broad reappraisal of the global role of the Red Cross idea, faulted the Movement for its sprawling activities without central focus. For Tansley and his research team, too many RC actors were undertaking too many disparate activities, hence his recommendation for a renewed focus on emergency response to exceptional human need. One can wonder if that report, despite its date, is now relevant to ICRC varied actions in situations of urban distress short of armed conflict.

If back in the day the National Societies and its Federation were criticized for having too many disparate programs resulting in programmatic sprawl (as per teaching swimming, being concerned with road safety, teaching how to do proper childcare, etc.), was the ICRC getting sucked into the same expansion now? Yes, there was much violence in many cities. But as with early recovery in protracted conflicts, where were the limits? Where were the situations, or proposed activities, that were turned down or rejected because the ICRC mandate was exceeded? This question might be even more relevant in low-level urban violence than in resiliency programs in protracted conflicts, given the clearly multifaceted nature of the former.

There is another point worth discussing. After the international armed conflict between Armenia and Azerbaijan over Nagorno-Karabakh in 2020 where the ICRC was active on the ground, there was in 2022–2023 continuing ICRC activity to help those displaced or injured by the fighting. Should the ICRC be expending resources on urban violence short of war when human needs from armed conflict, the traditional focus of the ICRC, were going unmet? Should not the ICRC devote more of its human and financial resources to places like Nagorno-Karabakh, which was indeed an international armed conflict with continuing problems not to mention periodic flare ups of violence, rather than to Juarez, Mexico? And of course there were the massive humanitarian needs from the international war in Ukraine from 2022.

And finally, did some of the results justify all the time and resources devoted to ICRC activities in low-level urban violence? Achieving more traffic deference to ambulances in Karachi? Achieving stronger social ties connected to schools in Juarez? These are improvements for sure, but are these the best accomplishments that can be cited? Are these urban improvements really in line with the core mandate of the ICRC?

Similar questions can be raised about ICRC expansion into a still further area: migration.

II   Migration

About the same time that the ICRC was interpreting its role to include widespread programs for economic recovery as a result of violence, and to include low-level urban violence, it began to pay more systematic attention to migrants. By the first decade of the twenty-first century there was growing attention to international migration both at the United Nations and beyond.[5] During 1970–2017, international migration increased from 82 million to 244 million, the latter figure amounting to 3 percent of the global population. This pattern was affected by such factors as the end of the Cold War, technological change in communication and transportation, continuing poor quality of life in many countries, alongside awareness of relatively better conditions in other countries, much repression and violence leading to forced displacement, and eventually more disruption because of climate change and pandemics accompanied by deficient local policies.

In this context, in 2007 both the RC Council of Delegates and the RC Conference endorsed greater attention to migrants for all members of the RC Movement.[6] Officially for the Movement, migrants are defined broadly: "persons who leave or flee their habitual residence ... to seek opportunities or safer and better prospects. Migration can be voluntary or involuntary, but most of the time a combination of choices and constraints are involved." The ICRC accepts this definition, saying it is advantageous to recognize mixed motives on behalf of those on the move. Especially in irregular international migration – namely, outside the pathways of legal movement across borders, and for vulnerable migrants – namely, those in need of protection and assistance, the ICRC asserted a need for more programming on its part, often in conjunction with Movement partners. Migration was mentioned in the ICRC Strategic Statement for 2015–2018 for the first time.

There was no doubt but that irregular migration could be fraught with dangers. The ICRC was aware of factors mentioned above: harsh policies adopted by various receiving states to deter unwanted entrants, the possibility of attacks and other dangers along the migratory path, the problem of disease in an era of pandemics, the loss of contact with loved ones, even death during migration. In one month alone in 2022 (November), over 200,000 migrants were intercepted by US border agents along the border with Mexico.[7] That tracks out to 2.4 million per year. No country wants to encounter those numbers or is prepared to accommodate that number of new people crossing its borders without advance notice. The cost to social services is high. Those who manage to stay in the new country change the country in many ways, causing much debate and even disruption or instability.

Those kinds of numbers do indeed result in mass detention, expulsion with resulting homelessness and hunger, exposure to the elements and criminal behavior, and all manner of other humanitarian difficulties. Almost all developed democracies faced increased migratory pressures as seen in, particularly, Europe, North America, and Australia. And all of the countries, despite being called liberal democracies, adopted harsh or restrictive policies as a result.

It can certainly be argued on the basis of numerous facts that all of the developed democracies had aging populations and needed immigrants to bolster the work force (and pay taxes!). And there were elements in the business community and pro-business political parties who recognized the validity of that view. But that was a long term economic and financial consideration that did not always shape the policies of the receiving states.

Moreover, many of the would-be immigrants lacked marketable skills; they were more likely to be short-term wards of the state, needing social assistance, than productive members of the economic system. This is one reason why Denmark, a genuinely progressive liberal democracy with an excellent human rights record at home and a relatively generous foreign assistance program, has adopted a hard line on migrants and refugees. Denmark has a very generous social assistance program as part of its large and expensive welfare state. Danish citizens have been paying very high taxes to support its welfare state. Would-be refugees and other immigrants have not. They would benefit from extensive services they have not paid for.

Regardless of various arguments for and against a generous and humane policy toward migrants, all developed democracies that were under migratory pressure had adopted various restrictive measures. In the United States the Democratic Biden Administration came around to a tougher border policy by 2023, adopting various measures that penalized migrants for trying to cross the border without permission – for example, requiring them to first seek asylum in countries they had passed through, such as Mexico or other neighbors. The United Kingdom, by comparison, initially wanted to deport illegal migrants to Rwanda, with the cooperation of the Kagame government in Kigali, the latter having the expectation, no doubt, of increased British foreign assistance. All of this got entangled in British court judgments.

Photograph 12.2 Here an ICRC staff member interviews an irregular migrant detained in Greece in 2010. Detention visits concerning migrants were also sometimes carried out by National RC Societies, as was the case in Australia. The ICRC organized training sessions concerning protection activities, conveying its procedures and experiences to National RC Societies manifesting the requisite Dunantist principles, such as independence and avoidance of partisan and strategic politics.

As was the case concerning new forms of urban violence, in addressing the problems facing migrants the ICRC could bring a skill set from its traditional activities focused on armed conflict: the tracing of missing persons, the restoring of family links, detention visits, the handling of mortal remains with dignity. A central issue was detention, and the ICRC developed a list of concerns and norms that it pursued.[8]

In some regions the ICRC would help create a communications system for migrants so they could stay in touch with relatives. This seemed to have little to do with armed conflict or systematic or large-scale "other violence." In some cases it was a stretch to claim this was a protection measure, because in these cases there was not much danger facing the economic migrants on the move. If there were sporadic attacks on migrants, those attacks did not seem political, or part of any sizable group violence. Such communications networks might have been locally well received as a timely social service, but should the ICRC be doing this? Perhaps the ICRC could be seen as helping start a social service that would be taken over in the future by the local RC society. But if we take the case of Zimbabweans going to South Africa to seek work, there was no armed conflict or organized systematic "other violence" involved. On the other hand, RC Conference resolutions could be cited to justify the ICRC training and then supporting a National RC Society in its tracing efforts. That tracing capability might be useful in future armed conflicts, if that transpired.

Likewise in a number of cases, the ICRC provided water, digital connections, and medical assistance along migratory routes, sometimes supporting civil society organizations outside the RC network. In some of these cases, as per the example above, violence was either absent or very infrequent. There was certainly a humanitarian need, but was the ICRC the proper agency for action? Where was the RC Federation? In such cases, what was occurring seemed like a social service normally provided by the local National RC Society, with little connection to systematic or sizable violence, and not really a "development hold" or matter of economic resiliency. Again, however, there were Movement resolutions aimed at increasing the impact of the Movement as based on increased cooperation among its independent members. The Movement had endorsed more attention to migrants.

Noteworthy is that fact that for many irregular and vulnerable migrants, the ICRC cannot use the norms of IHL in dealing with authorities. These migrants are sometimes not seen as fleeing armed conflict. Consequently one finds the ICRC, as in new forms of urban violence, relying on appeals to international human rights law. It used to be the case that some at ICRC headquarters demeaned human rights standards as both political and idealistic, seeing IHL as neither. Now one finds the ICRC making extensive appeals for migrants based on human rights standards. There is also international refugee law as interpreted principally by the UNHCR (the UN refugee office). When it is a matter of advocacy about a well-founded fear of persecution in the genesis of migration, the ICRC normally defers to and coordinates closely with that UN actor. It should be noted that at headquarters, the ICRC has no administrative unit on human rights or on refugee law (see the Annex). It has plenty of lawyers, but most are specialized in IHL and not human rights or refugee law.

In addition to the UNHCR regarding refugees, there is also the International Office for Migration (IOM), now part of the United Nations since 2016. It manifests a very broad mandate including protection and assistance for migrants. Its actual role is not easy to summarize, and its history is not free of controversies. It is widely seen as deferential to the interests of the governments of the wealthy democracies. One analyst sums up the situation this way:

> IOM speaks to three political agendas: (1) security concerns and states' control over their borders, (2) labour market preoccupations with economic migration, and (3) the imperative to protect migrants through humanitarian interventions and development. This enables IOM to interact with a wide range of actors, including not only governments but also the private sector, the UN system, NGOs, media, or researchers ... IOM is a kind of 'hub' for discussions and policy debates on migration....[9]

Then too, there are private organizations, or INGOs (international nongovernmental organizations) such as the International Rescue Committee (IRC) concerned with migration. The IRC was started by Albert Einstein because of the needs of Jews trying to flee Hitler's persecutions, but it has been continued and now deals with a broad range of human rights issues. The point here is that various public and private agencies exist dealing with various types of migrants. They are active on the ground as well as in public policy debates in Washington, New York, Geneva, and elsewhere.

Since various other organizations exist with great focus on migration or aspects of migration, the question arises as to the exact value added that the ICRC brings to this subject, along with the other members of the Movement. When migration occurs in relation to armed conflict and other similar violence (large-scale, organized, systematic), the presence of the ICRC is a given. This is the case, for example, in Libya circa 2021. A main migration path from central Africa to Europe passes through Libya. Libya itself being torn by an internationalized internal armed conflict, many migrants find themselves detained, exploited, used as forced labor, and more. There is no question but that there is an expected and broadly supported role for the ICRC in that and similar situations.

Photograph 12.3 Immigration outside approved legal channels increasingly became a broadly recognized problem, particularly in Europe and North America. Here one sees ICRC and Tunisian Red Crescent staff members try to help a migrant survivor of a shipwreck in 2015 who had tried to reach Europe. In some cases ICRC traditional expertise was relevant, as in prison visits to, and restoring family links for, detained migrants. In other cases one saw a more controversial expansion of ICRC activities for migrants.

However, when dealing with other migration situations that manifest no large-scale violence or dangerous detention, it is not always clear what are the limits to ICRC concern. That is to say, that it is not always clear what is the "value added" that the ICRC brings. It is not sufficient to say simply that a flexible approach is the value added, if only because the IOM and the IRC also have a broad and elastic approach to the multidimensional notion of migration. Outside of situations of armed conflict and their *direct* effects, thus far it is the other members of the Movement that are supposed to be the primary RC actors. And indeed that has been the case in Australia, for example, when the National RC Society, not the ICRC, has been deeply involved in matters of irregular migration – including carrying out visits to places of detained migrants.[10]

According to one scholar, ICRC primary objectives regarding migrants can be summarized as: providing practical protection and assistance across different legal categories of persons informally on the move; doing this in keeping with its traditional emphasis on persuasion and public nonconfrontation; and emphasizing its traditional areas of expertise such as detention visits, tracing of missing persons, and restoring family links.[11]

In sum, regarding the ICRC and migration, the central issue is not so much whether the organization can play a needed role in some situations, but whether it has clearly established where it should focus its attention in this domain (especially so, given periodic budgetary problems). Some of its activity in this domain seems remote from armed conflict and similar large-scale or systematic violence. And some of its activity might be handed off to other actors. Here again, as per its critics, the issue of specificity and focus rears its head.

III   Conclusion

Summing up our two chapters on interpretation of today's mandate regarding (1) resiliency programs, (2) urban violence short of armed conflict, and (3) extra-legal migration, we conclude that it is difficult for an outsider to understand clearly what the ICRC will *not* do or mostly avoid. While one might understand why the ICRC started doing what it did by way of expanded action, there is still the question about outer limits and guardrails against overextension. That is an important matter in a time of funding shortfalls but also new demands for humanitarian action because of pandemics and climate change. One can understand why some critics believe the ICRC has lost its traditional identity and concentrated focus. Their views about loss of specificity and unicity reflect a serious concern.

The ICRC, it seems, really does *not* seek to become a development actor or be all things to all people. But its guidelines for deciding how to interpret its mission are complicated and subject to different judgments in different situations. Its roles are decided: case by case, with attention to NIIHA values, with some concern for what the ICRC can bring as value-added, and with due regard for security considerations. Especially the boundaries between NIIHA programs and support for political authorities remain open to discussion. Also needing discussion is whether trying to be a good and cooperative team player within the RC Movement might actually suck the ICRC into ventures it actually should avoid or decline. These subjects are revisited in the concluding chapters.

Notes

1 See, for example, ICRC, "Urban Violence and the ICRC's Humanitarian Response," October 2016, with associated analysis that can be downloaded from www.icrc.org/en/document/urban-violence-and-icrc-humanitarian-response (accessed December 13, 2022).

2 ICRC, *Present and Engaged: How the ICRC Responds to Armed Conflict and Violence in the Cities*, no date indicated. www.icrc.org/en/document/present-and-engaged-how-icrc-responds-armed-conflict-and-violence-cities (accessed March 10, 2023).

3 ICRC, "Urban Violence and the ICRC's Humanitarian Response."

4 Regarding the non-neutral impact of the ICRC in low-level urban violence, see Miriam Bradley, "From Armed Conflict to Urban Violence: Transformation of the International Committee of the Red Cross, International Humanitarianism, and the Laws of War," *European Journal of International Relations*, 26/4 (2020), https://journals.sagepub.com/doi/10.1177/1354066120908637 (accessed October 16, 2023).

5 Alexander Betts and Lena Kainz, "The History of Global Migration Governance," Working Paper Series No. 122, Refugee Studies Center, Oxford University, July 2017. www.rsc.ox.ac.uk/publications/the-history-of-global-migration-governance (accessed November 18, 2022).

6 This paragraph is based on Stéphanie le Bihan, "Addressing the Protection and Assistance Needs of Migrants: The ICRC Approach to Migration," *International Review of the Red Cross*, 99/1 (2017), pp. 99–119. https://international-review.icrc.org/articles/addressing-protection-and-assistance-needs-migrants-icrc-approach-migration (accessed November 18, 2022).

7 John Gramlich, "Monthly Encounters with Migrants at U.S.-Mexico Border Remain at Record Highs," Pew Research, January 13, 2023, www.pewresearch.org/fact-tank/2023/01/13/monthly-encounters-with-migrants-at-u-s--mexico-border-remain-near-record-highs/ (accessed January 14, 2023).

8 "ICRC Policy Paper on Immigration Detention," *International Review of the Red Cross*, 99/1 (2017), pp. 359–363, https://international-review.icrc.org/sites/default/files/irrc_99_19.pdf (accessed November 17, 2022).

9 Antoine Pecoud, "What Do We Know about the International Organization for Migration?," *Journal of Ethnic and Migration Studies*, 44/10 (2018), pp. 1621–1638. www.tandfonline.com/doi/full/10.1080/1369183X.2017.1354028 (accessed November 17, 2022).

10 As far back as 2014 the Australian Red Cross was reporting on its services for migrants, including visiting places of detention. See Australian Red Cross, "Supporting Migrants," 2013–2014, www.redcross.org.au/sites/annual-reports/2014/year-in-review/supporting-migrants/ (accessed February 24, 2023).

11 Miriam Bradley, "A Humanitarian Agency in Global Migration Governance: The International Committee of the Red Cross's Migration Policy and Practice," in Antoine Pécoud and Hélène Thiollet, eds., *Research Handbook on the Institutions of Global Migration Governance* (Cheltenham: Edward Elgar, 2023).

13 Has the Traditional Focus Been Lost?
Part I – Laws of War

> Humanitarian practitioners do not live by law alone.
>
> Geoffrey Best[1]

Some critics believe that with all the changes at the ICRC, especially regarding an expanded interpretation of its basic mandate, the organization either has already lost or will lose its status as the "go to" private agency on international humanitarian law (IHL). These critics also fear that the ICRC has downplayed its protection role especially concerning political prisoners, having arguably become mostly about assistance – which is where the big money is. They also think the ICRC's links with the World Economic Forum, while violating NIIHA values, has put a premium on good relations with governments and their corporations, rather than rocking the boat about prison visits and other delicate protection matters.

This chapter asks: are the critics correct? In dealing with this central question, I try to avoid a deep dive into many specifics of IHL. Not being a law professor, I am inclined to focus mostly, if not entirely, on policy and the policymaking process rather than the details of most legal specifics in the Geneva Conventions and Protocols.

While some authors have it backwards, asserting that IHL created and defined the ICRC, it is certainly true that right from the start in 1863 the private and independent ICRC always saw a close relationship between itself and the public international law for armed conflict. To realize its vision of NIIHA help to victims of war, as a private agency it would need the cooperation of states. To create an enduring system featuring that help, it wanted its idea of private and neutral humanitarianism embedded in public international law as approved by states. In historical fact, as we showed, it was the ICRC's right of initiative as a private agency that led to both the RC Movement and the 1864 Geneva Convention, but that central point does not lessen the historical place of IHL in the organization's activities. Later IHL then recognized the organization's right of initiative, first for POWs and then more generally.

Gustave Moynier – the central figure in the building of the ICRC – was a lawyer, the only one of the founding five to have that training. While he never practiced law as a professional career, he had a legal mind. He helped create and was then active in the Institute for International Law first organized in Ghent in 1873. As we will see shortly, that Institute – with Moynier in the leadership – tried to reinforce ICRC efforts in advancing the laws of war. In his commitment to turning Henry Dunant's dreams into practical action, law always loomed large.

I   IHL as a Negative?

We also noted in the early chapters that state foreign policy is rarely made up of only altruistic intentions, accepting that in 1864 states had their self-interested reasons for adopting the first treaty in modern IHL: the 1864 Geneva Convention neutralizing wounded soldiers in international war along with those who tended them. In so doing, as we observed, the participating governments in 1864 responded to domestic concerns about the wounded in an era of growing democracy with a more independent press, volunteer or conscript armies, and more rapid means of communication. For the original twelve European ratifying states, the 1864 treaty was a win-win development in terms of self-interest: establish a reputation for humanitarian concerns and respond to criticism at home about the fate of the troops. There had been plenty of that kind of criticism – well founded in fact – in the Crimean War of 1853–1856 and then again in the Franco–Austrian war of 1859 about which Dunant wrote. The 1864 Convention did indeed help states keep war as a viable option, in their view.

A persistent view, noted already, is that the most humane way to fight a war is to engage in total war, or almost total war, and get it over with quickly. (As if the total war approach was always guaranteed to lead to a quick victory rather than a prolonged and hellish quagmire.)

Helmuth von Moltke the Elder, writing in 1880 while still chief of staff for the Prussian army, endorsed an almost-but-not-quite-total war approach to military affairs. In replying to correspondence about a new law of war manual being drafted at the new Institute of International Law, where Moynier was active, he wrote:

The greatest good deed in war is the speedy ending of the war, and every means to that end, so long as it is not *reprehensible*, must remain open. In no way can I declare myself in agreement with the Declaration of St. Petersburg that the sole justifiable measure in war is 'the weakening of the enemy's military power.' No, all the sources of support for the hostile government must be considered, its finances, railroads, foodstuffs, even its prestige.[2]

Von Moltke did reject, but did not define, reprehensible actions in war. Moreover, he accepted the medical neutrality found in the 1864 Geneva Convention, while reflecting a certain hauteur of the ruling classes:

In war, where everything tends to be comprehended individually, only those paragraphs directed essentially at the leaders will, I believe, be effective. Among these are what the [draft law of war] manual wants to establish with regard to the wounded, the sick, doctors, and medical supplies. Universal recognition of even these principles, as well as those concerning treatment of prisoners, would already represent substantial progress toward the goal which the Institute for International Law strives toward with such praiseworthy steadfastness.[3]

Then there is the persistent view that war is hell and there is no point in sugarcoating it with other pretenses. At more or less the same time as the start of the ICRC, and while Francis Lieber was articulating his code setting a few, if elastic, limits on use of force for the US Union Army in the American civil war, General Sherman of that same Union army said about his destructive march through Atlanta and Georgia: "My orders are not designed to meet the humanities of the case.... You cannot qualify war in harsher terms than I will. War is cruelty, and you cannot refine it.... You might as well appeal against the thunderstorm as against these terrible hardships of war."[4] And indeed Lieber accepted the sacking of Atlanta by General Sherman because it presumably hastened the end of the war, a war that would also rid the United States of chattel slavery.[5]

Perhaps Sherman had read Karl von Clausewitz, often quoted to the effect that to introduce moderation in war would be an absurdity. In the words of the British Admiral Jackie Fisher, this axiom became known as: "restraint in warfare is imbecility."[6]

Such minimalist or skeptical views about IHL have proven persistent and indeed resurfaced in contemporary times. In 2021 a book resurrected arguments about a presumed downside to IHL.[7] So the argument went, too much attention was being paid by the United States to IHL issues to limit wars, and not enough to whether armed conflict should be undertaken in the first place. The laws of war plus modern technology might make war seem antiseptic to some, and – so the argument went – major states such as the United States had paid insufficient attention to peace efforts to avoid war.[8]

II   The Ugliness of Total War

One rather doubts that the critics of IHL, at least those who see it as a distraction from the greater good of preventing war, would be happy with the absence of IHL, or at a minimum the absence of its humanitarian principles, in the here and now. Violence without limits is not a pretty picture. Consider this description of areas of the Sahel by the ICRC regional official for Africa in 2021, in my translation:[9]

On 13 August [2021], 37 persons, of which 13 were children, have been killed by armed men in the region of Tillaberi, in Niger, near the border with Mali.... This situation tends to make worse the resumption of conflicts and criminal activities, the inter-communal tensions, and the breakdown of public services. These last months, the situation is particularly dramatic in the area of Liptako Gourma which sits astride the borders of Burkina Faso, Mali, and Niger. The level of violence has been turned up a notch, increasing the suffering of the civilian population which is already very vulnerable. In these three countries, hundreds of deaths and wounded, including men, women, and children, are to be deplored since the beginning of the year. On the regional roadways, more and more civilian vehicles and ambulances are victimized by improvised explosive devices attached to engines. In 2020, speaking only of Mali, our [ICRC] teams have recorded more than 39 incidents which have affected 224 civilians of which 61 died and 163 were wounded. Medical institutions are also not spared from the violence. They are no longer sanctuaries: the attacks against medical personnel, the theft of ambulances and medicine, deprives thousands of persons of vital care.

Photograph 13.1 ICRC Vice President Gilles Carbonnier arrives from Geneva for an assessment of a camp for internally displaced persons, Niger, 2022. The Sahel region of Africa was wracked by much violence, many civilians were at risk, and armed groups often displayed little respect for the laws of war or basic principles of human rights. The dividing line between internal war and "other violence" was often unclear, with protracted conflicts displaying an ebb and flow to the violence.

The absence of limits on political violence is indeed not a pretty picture. For many of us, such a situation offends our moral intuition. Michael Ignatieff is right in arguing that the laws of war are part of the effort to construct firewalls against barbarism.[10] IHL, along with human rights and other measures, is part of the attempt to contest atrocious behavior and for many has much independent merit apart from the subject of recourse to violence in the first place.

But it is evident that at times some armed actors believe the status quo is so objectionable, that history has been so oppressive, or that a compromise agreement with opponents so unacceptable, that violence without limits – or almost without limits – is the right choice. As noted already, the French–Algerian war (1954–1962) was not the only war accurately described as one of terror and torture, as each side sought to prevail through almost any tactic. But that kind of totalistic thinking, sometimes on both sides, has never convinced the ICRC to give up its quest for at least some mutual humanity during political violence. One might believe either that a focus on IHL will eventually spill over and lead to peace, or that such a focus on IHL simply accepts the persistent fact of war in human history and tries to reduce its horrors.

Either way, in the abstract the ICRC has the formal if perhaps superficial support of what is loosely called the international community, witness the universal acceptance by governments of the 1949 Geneva Conventions. But much hypocrisy is evident. From Russia to the United States, one sees states officially accepting IHL, then adopting unrestricted bombing polices as in Syria after 2011 or adopting policies of torture in the "war on terror" after September 11, 2001. Stephen Krasner has written about endorsement of state sovereignty as organized hypocrisy.[11] The same might be said about much lip service to the supposedly hallowed 1949 Geneva Conventions.

One can argue, nevertheless, and it might even be true, that the ICRC has made its most important humanitarian contribution by pushing for IHL in countless ways since 1863–1864. Its role in diplomatic conferences that legislate (the most recent in 2005 on the matter of the emblem) is supplemented day in and day out in countless ways that are so vast and varied that they cannot be categorized or summarized here. This relative judgment about the legal side of things involves a comparative evaluation of the ICRC's role in helping to develop IHL, compared to helping develop the RC Movement, compared to the nature of its field operations – many, if not most, of which now occur in a context of legal ambiguity. (More so than in the past, the ICRC now makes a judgment about the legal nature of a situation among international armed conflict, internal armed conflict, and other violence. It may or may not publish that determination. Its view may or may not have impact on fighting parties.) In this book's conclusion I stress this last contribution of pragmatic field work, but without denigrating the first two.

At the end of the day we still have the general fact that all states and their military establishments officially accept that there should be legal limits on war. In both international and internal armed conflict, war is not supposed to be a license for wanton destruction. Even in some national special forces, often given to clandestine action out of uniform, one can be prosecuted or otherwise sanctioned for engaging in wanton violence unrelated to, or in excess of, the official (and presumably legal) mission. It can be documented that any number of US military officers were incensed about the treatment dished out to certain foreign detainees after September 11, 2001 and who were tortured by their American colleagues in the US "war on terrorism." Military lawyers sometimes are among the champions of military honor and commitment to the laws of war. Obviously we are not talking about most legal advisors in the Russian military (did they exist?) during the 2022 invasion of, and then much destruction in, Ukraine.[12]

Playing a central role in constructing a universal legal regime on behalf of limits on armed conflict is no small achievement. In the long struggle to put legal limits on the process of war (*jus in bello*), the ICRC refused to yield to the views of General Sherman and others like him. The organization always advocated for more and more "development and reaffirmation" of IHL if that is what it was, but only with the right timing. The ICRC wanted more attention to the up-close reality of what happens to individuals in armed conflict, but it was careful about any diplomatic conference that might undo the legal restraints that had already been adopted. It hoped for further legal advances but was wary about a forced retreat.

III   ICRC Field Activities and Legal Codification

A dominant pattern in the history of the ICRC was to take creative action on the ground and later try to have that humanitarian action endorsed in law. This may have meant that one saw the updating of IHL one war too late, in that ad hoc humanitarian advances during conflict were only legally formalized later. The ICRC got into the business of visiting POWs in World War I. Legal codification of much ICRC experience occurred via the 1929 Geneva Convention on that subject. Its experiences with POWs in World War II were further refined in the Third GC of 1949.

A good contemporary example of this process was the subject of IHL and guerilla fighters. (The subject was introduced in Chapter 4 when discussing the ICRC in Vietnam.) To obtain prisoner of war status in international armed conflicts, the 1949 third GC, Article 4, requires detained fighters to have been a member of the regular armed forces of the enemy (or associated groups), to have been organized under superior orders, to have worn a distinctive insignia (e.g. a uniform) recognizable at a distance, to have carried arms openly, and to have followed the laws of war. These fighters when captured became POWs – resulting from their status as lawful combatants.[13]

In the French–Algerian war, which to the Algerian side was an international armed conflict, the ICRC finally got the French to accept that for opposition irregular fighters openly displaying weapons in combat or just prior to combat, that fact entitled them to humane treatment upon capture as if they were POWs (even while not being so labeled). They were, after all, a type of enemy combatant in fact. And that agreement in turn led to US military agreement with the ICRC to the same basic provision in Vietnam – namely that guerilla fighters who carried arms openly were entitled to humane treatment upon capture, even if wearing "black pajamas" rather than military uniforms. Varying views about the legal label for the conflict ("other violence" v. internal war v. international armed conflict) did not prevent some flexible agreement and practical humanitarian accord.

None of these provisions covered those who posed as civilians to throw bombs or carry out assassinations while concealing their combat status. In nonlegal terminology, there were irregular fighters who were still entitled to humane treatment in detention under IHL principles, and then there were terrorists (but who were also entitled to humane treatment when detained, under non-IHL legal norms – viz., human rights law). The argument was often about status: should IHL recognize irregular fighters? Should one recognize in humanitarian agreements the farmers by day but fighters at night?

Against this brief recounting of agreements in the Algerian and Vietnam wars, one can now read Article 44 in Additional Protocol I from 1977. This is a long and complex legal norm consisting of eight paragraphs. The crux of the legal requirement is similar to the ad hoc field agreements in the Algerian and Vietnam wars, namely, in terms of the 1977 article: that the fighter who "carries his arms openly ... during each military engagement, and during such time as he is visible to the adversary while he is engaged in a military deployment preceding..." shall be treated as if that person were a POW.[14] This was one of the provisions in API that caused the United States not to ratify that legal instrument, even though the United States had informally agreed with the ICRC on the same essential rules in Vietnam. (API has separate provisions on spies, mercenaries, and other categories of persons.)

The matter of treatment of detained fighters of various types is complicated by: (1) the GCs, Common Article 3, which mandates humane treatment for all persons affected by all armed conflicts (if one follows the ruling of the US Supreme Court in the 2006 Hamdan judgment, covered later); and (2) those human rights standards that continue to be valid in armed conflicts (and which cannot be suspended for reasons of national emergency), such as, inter alia, prohibitions on torture and cruel treatment. So even if one rejects API, Article 44, one is still legally bound by other applicable provisions of international law. There is also the point that parts of API, Article 44, may have become part of customary IHL.[15] Furthermore, if the United States continues to reject API, Article 44, but its NATO allies accept that rule, which most do, as a practical matter the United States will be pushed into implementing the rule to maintain cohesion within NATO in joint operations. For now the point to be stressed here is clear: ICRC field experience can feed into new IHL norms and debates about norms. There are many examples of that process. This is one reason, and a central one, that the ICRC with its extensive field experience in violent situations has an important status in debates about the construction of IHL.

Stephen C. Neff has captured some historical trends nicely, noting that before 1864 the laws of war as found mostly in custom were about the rights of belligerent states. After 1864, as pushed by the ICRC and RC Movement, the law of war progressively emphasized legal limits on states and the corresponding protection of individuals.[16] One might add that this historical trend is a major reason the international law of armed conflict is often called IHL. As Neff notes, this humanization of the laws of war became especially so when the RC or Geneva tradition of law, which focused on individuals, also incorporated The Hague tradition dealing often with state choice about means and methods of violence. Legally limiting the impact of means and methods of warfare, especially concerning civilians and their essential needs, became more important over time. It was thus broadly important that the ICRC's early focus on wounded fighters evolved to other concerns, including detained fighters, irregular fighters, and also civilians.[17] Right from 1859 and then 1864, one sees Dunant and then the ICRC taking practical action, and then at least some of this field experience becoming part of IHL.

There are still plenty of people who accept the old axiom that in war law is silent, but these people cannot explain the sizable numbers of lawyers in the Pentagon and other military establishments and how much they affect military operations – at least sometimes.[18] This situation today, at least in some states, can be usefully compared to the 1860s and 1870s when the laws of war, mostly in the form of custom about the rights of states, were so vague and confusing that particularly in the Balkan wars of that time, belligerent governments issued no clear instructions to their troops on legal matters.[19]

If one takes the long view, there has been some progress. This is not the same as saying IHL works well and is usually broadly applied in good faith. The history of the ICRC, and noting how its field activities sometimes leads to new laws of war, indicates caution and modest expectations but not hopelessness.

IV   Contemporary Realities and IHL

There are those with a more legal orientation than the present author who compile tombs on the details of IHL, including provisions in national law and national military manuals, which are largely drawn from the principles found in the relevant treaties.[20] Then there are the court cases, military and civilian, national and international, about judicial enforcement which likewise fill in the details about IHL in specific situations.[21] I make no attempt to evaluate recent international criminal courts such as the International Criminal Tribunal for the Former Yugoslavia (ICTY) and the International Criminal Tribunal for Rwanda (ICTR), or the International Criminal Court (ICC), and how much they used, and perhaps refined, IHL. This is a good topic for others.

One could fill a retirement, or maybe a lifetime, reading all the material that the ICRC has put in the public domain about IHL. That law is both a reality, and full of weaknesses and gaps and limitations. The existence of law should not be confused with its effectiveness. In the midst of an asserted Western dominance of international relations centered on the US unipolar moment as the only Superpower after the Cold War, an astute observer asked, "Why is so much of today's IHL so badly observed?"[22]

V   Enforcement

Just when one despairs about using law to limit war, and just when one is ready to laugh when someone says that the main goal of the early ICRC was to humanize war, something happens to remind us of what has been achieved in legal terms since 1864. In 2006 the US Supreme Court declared in its Hamdan ruling that Common Article 3 from the four GCs of 1949 was applicable in all armed conflicts, including George W. Bush's proclaimed "war on terrorism" after September 11, 2001.[23]

Common Article 3 (CA3), originally designed for essentially internal wars such as the Spanish civil war of 1936–1939, as compared to international wars, and once upon a time criticized as consisting of "affectionate generalities,"[24] actually prohibits a sizable list of illegal policies including "cruel treatment and torture." The US Supreme Court asserted in the Hamdan case that CA3 was now a baseline minimal standard in all armed conflicts. While this Supreme Court judgment did not end all maneuvers by the United States to mistreat various prisoners in various contexts after 9/11,[25] it did strike a major legal blow in favor of humane policies even amid a violent and sprawling conflict manifesting all sorts of atrocities by more than one fighting party.

What can be said for sure about Hamdan, and for myriad other actions in support of IHL, is that the struggle continues in modern times to limit the destruction of war – with a few juridical battles won here and there. There is a direct line of developments from the first GC in 1864 to the much-cited four GCs in 1949, including CA3.[26] And then there are the two Additional Protocols concluded in 1977. Less broadly accepted than the 1949 GCs (about 70 percent of states have accepted the Protocols, compared to 100 percent for the 1949 law), they nevertheless have made their contribution to protecting individuals in war. Especially noteworthy in the two Additional Protocols were efforts to regulate the conduct of hostilities.[27]

It is only a slight overstatement to say that Charles Taylor and Radovan Karadzic, among others, are in jail today because of the ICRC and the persistent push for IHL dating back to 1863–1864. That is, one can note modern "warriors without honor" who engage in total war without limits,[28] but some of whom have been convicted and incarcerated for violating IHL and certain other legal norms. If one takes the long view, all is not lost in the effort to limit war's damage to individuals.

Taylor, from his position as strongman of Liberia, organized atrocities in neighboring Sierra Leone. Convicted by a transnational criminal court, he is now serving a fifty-year sentence in a British jail. Karadzic, political leader of the Serbian autonomous republic as part of Bosnia, authorized various atrocities against non-Serbs. Convicted by a UN criminal court, he is now serving a life sentence in a British jail.

The idea of individual responsibility for war crimes – or maybe grave breaches or other major violations of IHL – is now well established, even if its application across time and place remains dependent on shifting political factors. And of course others were involved in the long legal struggle in favor of IHL combined with international criminal law, certainly including state officials who consented to the key legal instruments. Other authors have written about various important private actors, for example Ralph Lemkin and his advocacy for the concept of genocide, and Hersh Lauterpacht and his push for the concept of crimes against humanity.[29] These concepts can overlap with the idea of war crimes; all three concepts entail now individual responsibility aka legal accountability. It was not as if Henry Dunant had said all that needed to be said, or that Moynier and his colleagues had done all that needed to be done. (Then there were those who focused on crimes against peace aka aggression, part of *jus ad bellum* or war for the start of war.[30]) The ICRC remained a key player across time in these legal matters, concentrating as it did much of the time on developing the laws of war and pushing in general for their proper application.[31]

These days it seems that there are many warriors without honor, for example those in the various versions of the Islamic State group or al-Qaeda and its affiliates, which means they believe in something close to total war. The same could be said for the Junta in Myanmar, or for Eritrea intervening in Tigray in Ethiopia, and so on. Civilians and medical clinics are attacked, prisoners tortured and killed, aid workers gunned down, females (and sometimes men and boys) raped. Particularly the Russian military strategy and tactics in Ukraine from February 2022 raised the question of whether there will be serious and practical attention to flagrant violations of IHL in current times, discussed further in the Epilogue.

In general, aspects of IHL continue to have some role. The safest thing to say about legal basics is that if a leader is responsible for establishing policies that violate IHL, criminal prosecution for that fact cannot be ruled out. A skeptic (or maybe one who is just well informed) might add: especially if that leader has a weak political position and is without a major protector. Charles Taylor was not Vladimir Putin, ultimately responsible for many war crimes in Ukraine, or his ally Bashar al-Assad in Syria in the brutal fighting of 2011–2021. Radovan Karadzic was not George W. Bush or his allies who authorized secret prisons where torture occurred after September 11, 2001. What has been said about the UN Charter could be said about IHL: There is no article in the legal corpus saying that power was no longer relevant in the application of the law.

It remains true, and especially so for a time after the end of the Cold War, that some specific violations of the Geneva Conventions have been successfully prosecuted in various courts. One can see this in the proceedings of the ICTY and the ICTR. These violations may also entail universal jurisdiction, which means that when the political will is there, any state can prosecute for certain war crimes such as torture regardless of the nationality of the accused or the place of the alleged crime.[32] Germany, for example, has utilized the legal concept of universal jurisdiction to conduct trials for events arising out of both Bosnia and Syria. The modern IHL is there to be activated, and sometimes it is – despite political double standards and all the other factors that allow war crimes to go unpunished.

VI ICRC Constancy about Enforcement

The ICRC has developed a workable posture about IHL, helping to develop IHL and disseminate its terms, but almost always leaving its formal and public enforcement to others. This has been noted already at several points. Avoiding most public pronouncements about who specifically has violated IHL where and when, the ICRC leaves itself with the opportunity to try to achieve the consent of fighting parties for practical humanitarian work on the ground, or in the field, or *sur place* for the French speakers. This is a well-considered position. It has been recognized as a good trade-off, with the ICRC now exempt from a duty to testify in international criminal courts such as the old ICTY or the current ICC. If you want the ICRC to do practical things – for example, get into places of detention to help prevent or correct bad conditions or mistreatment – you do not want the ICRC having to testify in court about what it has seen. Such testimony would make future access to detainees more difficult, given the self-protective proclivities of authorities.

Photograph 13.2 Here the ICRC and Ukrainian Red Cross aid civilians in Mariupol in 2014. The ICRC was one of the few humanitarian organizations active in eastern Ukraine when violence occurred, starting in 2014. The full Russian invasion of 2022 led to both more humanitarian need and many more agencies active in relief and recovery – whether local or international.

That does not mean that the ICRC never states publicly a legal position. It does, as on the applicability of the Fourth GC from 1949 to territories taken by Israel in 1967 and 1973. And the ICRC avoidance of testimony in court about facts on the ground does not mean that it never states its legal opinion in discrete representations to authorities. It does, at least sometimes, either in writing or by an in-person visit by a high ICRC official, or both at the same time. The ICRC is not always reticent or noncommittal when it comes to articulating its view about the relevance of IHL. But it does shy away from specific and public condemnation for violations of IHL. This is the price paid for attempts at practical cooperation on a variety of humanitarian matters. Again, the Epilogue delves into this complicated matter a bit more with regard to Ukraine after the Russian invasion of 2022.

VII   Knowledge and Training

Equally important, if not more so, there is the matter of the training of those bearing arms. Most states teach IHL (somewhat) in (some) military training. If we assume that some serious teaching and learning occurs, that is at least as important a means of implementation as prosecution after illegal action. Proper training can help reduce violations before the fact. After all, one of the major problems in violent Somalia in the early 1990s was that, so it was said, no local fighter with a weapon had ever heard of the Geneva Conventions. One can also see the problem in Ukraine in 2022, with Russian conscripts (and others) rushed into combat with only a couple of weeks of minimal military training.

Training in the law is important for military discipline and professionalism, as well as to advance humane values. After the terrorist attacks of September 11, 2001, the George W. Bush administration declared that those apprehended in Afghanistan and other places in the "war on terrorism" were not protected under the Geneva Conventions. They were arguably unlawful combatants, neither regular military nor fully civilian. But US leaders did not clearly and consistently make clear what rules *did* apply to detainees in place of the provisions of IHL. Confusion on this matter at the main military detention center at Guantanamo, Cuba then "migrated" to Iraq after the US invasion of that state in 2003. Even though Washington acknowledged that its invasion of Iraq constituted first an international armed conflict and then an occupation, one saw the horrors of US military behavior at the Abu Ghraib prison there, eventually captured in photos which were widely distributed. US military personnel ran amok, sadistically engaging in torture, cruelty, and other levels of prisoner abuse. This caused the United States great embarrassment and loss of soft power. Without the guidelines of IHL pertaining to detainees, US military detention became amateurish, unprofessional, and out of control.[33]

(The ICRC had been present in Abu Ghraib, had submitted critical reports to the authorities, had quietly suspended its visits to demonstrate its concerns, but did not go public with the facts – although some officials wanted to. Whether the ICRC demonstrated too much discretion and patience in this matter is an interesting question. After all, prisoners were being badly abused while the ICRC waited for Washington to correct matters in response to its candid reports. Whether Washington's status as the biggest donor to the organization had any bearing on developments is also an interesting question. It is quite possible, as one former official told this author, that a firewall between donations and operations was not as effective as in the past. After events, the US government changed procedures about the handling of ICRC detention reports so as to provide wider distribution in the Executive Branch, which made lack of proper response more unlikely.)

The ICRC certainly knows well this factor of ignorance of the law, which is why across the globe it is engaged in what used to be called dissemination efforts.[34] From China to Mozambique, from Colombia to Mali, it tries to spread the word about IHL, its rules, principles, and objectives. Out of the glare of media coverage and in a thousand ways, it conveys the fundamentals of IHL to political and military and penal authorities, armed nonstate actors, influential religious leaders, and even business managers who find or may find themselves in violent situations.

VIII   Human Rights Law as Supplement

There is a small library of materials on the relationship between IHL and international human rights law (IHRL). I am not qualified to analyze all those links, nor is it necessary for current purposes. On the one hand, one can find those who emphasize differences, and on the other hand, there are those who point out similarities, overlap, and mutual influences. I have interviewed high ICRC officials who said candidly, if off the record, that they preferred to keep IHRL at a distance, and I have read ICRC officials who accept IHRL as useful but quite clearly prioritize IHL. It used to be said that human rights was only thrust upon the ICRC in the 1970s, to the detriment of wise thinking. But recent research has indicated that as far back as the 1949 Geneva Conventions, one year after the UN adopted the Universal Declaration of Human Rights, ICRC officials were thinking seriously about how human rights ideas should or should not be incorporated into emerging IHL.[35]

For some, IHRL was idealistic and overreaching, seeking to produce universal good governance. It was supposedly highly politicized, obviously the result of state bargaining and ideological confrontation at the United Nations. IHL, by comparison, was presumably more realistic in that it sought minimal notions of human dignity only in war, which precluded optimism and overreach.

Then there was the argument, sometimes made sincerely and with a straight face, that IHL was produced outside the UN in special diplomatic conferences hosted by the Swiss state and thus with minimal politicking apart from humanitarian concerns. The latter argument is misguided, but there is no reason in these pages to beat a dead horse – especially after the highly politicized diplomatic conference of the 1970s. As Giovanni Mantilla has persuasively indicated, "However one appraises the impact of changes to IHL [in that conference] my analysis clearly demonstrates that the process of lawmaking is a political battleground...."[36] Or, as Geoffrey Best noted some two decades earlier, "What in any case remains indisputable is that humanitarian multilateral treaties, however else they may be regarded, are political products."[37]

In IHRL, specifically in the International Covenant on Civil and Political Rights, adopted at the UN in 1966 and entered in legal force in 1975, there is a list of nonderogable rights which apply in war as in peace. While other listed rights might lead to suspension because of reasons of state in national emergencies, including war, this handful of rights always are in legal force (for example, right to life, freedom from cruel treatment and torture, freedom from medical experimentation, right to legal personhood in law, etc.). At the same time, from 1949 the four GCs of that year contained Common Article 3 for internal wars. So while IHRL regulated some aspects of war as well as peace, IHL came to regulate some situations that were geographically internal to a state. If one uses CA3 to direct concern to large numbers of civilians affected by internal war, one is reaching into formerly state domestic jurisdiction in a major way. The evolution of IHL and IHRL clearly reflected some convergence or overlap.[38] The nonderogable provisions of the UN Civil-Political Covenant are similar to parts of CA3 found in the 1949 GCs.

In keeping with my proclivities and because others are more qualified to do it, I am not going to trace in further detail the textual evidence of this convergence or overlap. One can note some important nontechnical matters: that at the UN in the late 1960s there was increasing talk not so much about developing IHL as about emphasizing human rights in armed conflict. Then some of this changed discourse affected some

Photograph 13.3 In Colombia in 2014, an ICRC staff member talks with a member of the ELN armed group about protecting civilians. At certain times and places in that country, the ICRC considered that an internal armed conflict existed to which parts of IHL applied as found in GC Common Article 3 from 1949 and/or GC Protocol II from 1977. At other times and places, the ICRC believed the situation was one of "other violence," to which international human rights law applied along with domestic law.

of the wording in various parts of the two Additional Protocols adopted in 1977. For the diplomatic conference that started in 1974, in the run-up meetings the ICRC still played the role of drafting secretariat and low-key facilitator. But in particular, the postcolonial, newly independent states sent the same personnel to Geneva who had participated in UN debates and used the same discourse about human rights in armed conflict – not to mention the new discourse on wars of national liberation.

International politics was continuing to blur the line between IHL and IHRL as a practical matter. And in any event both bodies of law reflected a central concern with human dignity or human security, even if that concern was pursued in the state system of international affairs with its central principle of state sovereignty. Unfortunately, however, it was a frequent fact that governments representing states argued that evident violence remained below the level of any kind of armed conflict.

In its fieldwork, the ICRC often sought to justify its activities according to some type of agreed-upon international norm. Ergo IHRL. Rather than say simply that ICRC headquarters was pushing X, it was more diplomatic and legally well grounded (and presumably more efficacious) to say that the international community had agreed on X (such as humane treatment for all prisoners), and the ICRC was prepared to offer its services to help authorities implement that norm.

Today the ICRC, for example being concerned about urban violence short of armed conflict, might not only invoke human rights norms instead of IHL but might find itself leading workshops for police officials on human rights, police brutality, and techniques of crowd control. It might find useful some reference to RC Fundamental Principles, or general principles drawn from IHL – or, and this is the point here, from human rights law whether in treaty form or diplomatic form such as the UN Standard Minimum Rules for the Treatment of Detainees. In various ICRC transactions one can sometimes find references to the Mandela Rules (or the UN Standard Minimum Rules for Treatment of Prisoners) and the Bangkok Rules (UN adopted rules for female prisoners). These documents are part of human rights soft law, or diplomatic agreements providing guidelines about personal rights, produced at the UN. These UN human rights norms are utilized in the 2020 version of the ICRC's Commentary on the 1949 Geneva Conventions.

The ICRC Assembly now has adopted a doctrinal statement, or a statement of policy guidance, concerning human rights: Doctrine No. 63, never published. This guideline supplements, among several doctrinal statements, Doctrine No. 52 on "Other Violence" short of armed conflict. Doctrinal statement No. 63, so it is reported, is a long and complex essay showing the flexibility of the ICRC even as it shows lack of precise guidance. It apparently states that the ICRC has long been involved in conflicts other than war, and that in these other conflicts the organization may (or may not) refer to human rights law.

More specifically Doctrine No. 63 on human rights, still unpublished, was supplemented by an internal memo intended for guidance to staff. The memo indicates, so it has been said, among other points, that: the ICRC has been quietly referring to IHRL "for years;" the organization will be selective in referring to IHRL on the basis of whether such reference helps or hurts what the ICRC is trying to achieve; the ICRC will give priority to IHL but even in armed conflict may refer to IHRL if it fills a void; the ICRC does not invoke IHRL on matters such as freedom of speech or voting rights which lie beyond its traditional focus; the organization remains the guardian of IHL; the

ICRC still prefers a discrete approach and does not seek to emulate the denunciation of violations practiced by some well-known human rights NGOs.

In sum, when – as is often the case – the ICRC finds itself operating in a situation whose legal status is other than war or is contested, it may reference international human rights law as well as whatever norms can be extracted from IHL and/or RC Principles. After all, the main point of all these sets of norms, as well as the main objective of the ICRC, is to help secure human dignity, which can be a synonym for human security. Whether one tries to help, or protect, individuals in some situations by reference to IHL or IHRL has become a pragmatic judgment. The primary objective is to advance human dignity on the ground, not run a conceptually coherent legal seminar. The ICRC these days has a greatly changed view of the utility of human rights law in addition to IHL compared to some time ago. (Not only immediately after World War II and planning the 1949 Geneva Conventions, but also the 1997 "Avenir" project by the ICRC, an exercise in taking stock of contextual trends and planning for the future, one finds the ICRC thinking about IHRL as well as IHL.) It may be that IHL is in the ICRC's organizational DNA as the preferred reference point, but there has been a mutation toward more use of human rights standards.

IX   Importance of Customary IHL

In 1949 it took a few months for some fifty states, mostly from the global north, to negotiate the four Geneva Conventions of that year. (Some governments who agreed to attend did not consistently do so, and thus one reads about different numbers of states involved.) In the 1970s it took four years of off-and-on negotiations to produce the two 1977 Additional Protocols. The clash between the postcolonial states and the major democratic states mostly from the global northwest was impossible to ignore, as were the blatant political calculations at work. We have mentioned some details already.

It has now been over forty years since that fractured diplomatic conference produced a once controversial Protocol 1 (API) for international wars, and a barely surviving Protocol 2 (APII) for internal wars. API presents the merit of emphasizing civilian protections in the midst of combat, more so than in the 1949 law. APII presents the merit of reaffirming the general idea of international legal regulation of internal war. However, it is only in a handful of situations that anyone at the ICRC speaks of APII being recognized as applicable by a government – and even these few cases leave some room for debate.

A brief diplomatic conference on the sole subject of emblems was held in late 2005. As mentioned earlier, it resulted in a divided vote on the matter of adding a third neutral emblem to the Red Cross and Red Crescent symbols. Given the facts in the run-up to that conference, with the American Red Cross withholding its dues to the RC Federation to protest the exclusion of the Israeli official aid society, Magen David Adom (MDA), from the RC Movement, it was clear that the continuing controversy about Israel was at the center of calculations. On the ground, there was sometimes de facto cooperation among the ICRC, the MDA, and the Palestinian Red Crescent (also unrecognized in the past). So some humanitarian issues were being managed. Despite that, the broader political controversy remained. One can note that the opposition to accepting the third emblem of a Red Crystal was organized by the OIC (Organization of Islamic Countries), and that among those voting in the negative were a number of states that had either failed to recognize the Jewish state or were highly critical of its policies.

Admitting MDA to the RC Movement was seen by more than one conference participant as a matter of adding to the legitimacy of Israel. So much for the separation of humanitarian affairs from international politics. In that regard, 2005 was not very different from 1974 to 1977. In the diplomatic conferences, those who hoped to completely wall off a NIIHA space from geostrategic or power politics were bound to be disappointed. For that matter, was the ICRC motivated to find a solution to the MDA controversy in order to protect its reputation and smooth relations with Israel or to address concrete humanitarian problems as broadly as possible? Well, the two are related.

The prospects for a new diplomatic conference of a wide-ranging nature that would actually improve IHL were so dim as of about 2022 that the Swiss government and the ICRC have been agreed for some time on the wisdom of letting sleeping dogs lie as far as the treaty law is concerned. The notion that over 190 contemporary states could reach substantial agreement on improving IHL, and that most states would set aside their immediate self-interested geopolitical concerns for the sake of the "dictates of humanity," was slim to none.

The idea that the various highly nationalistic state leaders, more than one of them with a deep suspicion of international or multinational arrangements, would actually take progressive steps on behalf of IHL obviously strains credulity. This skeptical view is reinforced by the fact that the ICRC and the Swiss government carried out a long diplomatic effort for about ten years to get states to agree to discuss ways of improving the application of existing IHL, with disappointing results.[39]

If there is a bright spot in this state of affairs concerned with the legislation and application of IHL in general, it is that the ICRC has been leading a project to clarify customary IHL. As Giovani Mantilla has suggested, given the political divisions in the world affecting the last two rounds of IHL diplomatic conferences, focusing on customary IHL might be a productive route for reaffirmation and development.[40] But trying to emphasize customary IHL and ensure that it is au courant is not without its problems.

In 1993 a meeting of government experts dealt with various aspects of IHL, including customary law. In a follow-on meeting in 1995, these governmental experts explicitly recommended a new study on the customary dimension. Then the International RC Conference in that same year approved a proposal for a study updating customary IHL.[41] It seems it was awareness of gaps and fuzziness in IHL that led to the customary study, not an explicit judgment that a diplomatic conference would be either useless or dangerous. The ICRC, securing the collective endorsement from the RC Conference, then did a major study starting in 1996 led originally by Louise Doswald Beck and Jean-Marie Henckaerts.

All of this resulted in the publication in 2005 of a two volume study consisting of (1) proposed clarification of customary IHL rules and (2) the practice underlying them. There is now an online database on these twin subjects, with the volume on practice updated repeatedly to take into account new developments.[42] The volume on draft rules has yet to be revised at the time of writing in 2022.

A number of states, particularly the United States, while endorsing the process in general, challenged some of the methodology used and some of the conclusions reached.[43] For example, how much should one take into account the views expressed by smaller or weaker states who rarely were engaged in armed conflicts, as compared to the views of those states with sizable military establishments who actually were involved in armed conflicts with some regularity? But these smaller or more pacific states are not excited about being dominated by or dictated to by the major military powers. Some of the small states are strongly supportive of the ICRC's approach.

Early on some private experts who made the effort to wade through the approximately 500 pages of documentation, while praising the ICRC for its efforts, found some reason to question this or that assertion by the ICRC authors about the contents of customary IHL.[44] The ICRC then engaged in a conversation with these and other commentators with a view to defending its study and arriving at agreement on customary IHL.

In brief sum, with an eye on the IHL legislative process in political context, and trying to avoid getting into the deep weeds of legal technicalities, this focus on clarifying customary IHL seems wise. Not only did one at least partially bypass a dangerous diplomatic conference that might undermine past agreement but also, as it turns out, at least some humanitarian advances were made, noted later.

On the other hand, on any number of particular rules, it did not prove easy to achieve agreement on the specifics of the actual contents of modern IHL in customary form. Some states sought to preserve considerable autonomy in military decision-making, particularly when opponents might be following a policy of total war. The principle of reciprocity, an important incentive for fighting parties to devise and implement IHL, had been weakened in many recent conflicts.[45] So some states were reluctant to clarify further legal limits when responding to brutal enemies. Some states seemed to suggest that the ICRC was pushing too far ahead of what states had actually accepted and considered now to be legally binding. Some thought the ICRC was trying to get most of API accepted as customary IHL, whereas about one-third of states, including many important military powers, still had not ratified or acceded to that legal instrument.

In general the ICRC leadership belied that first of all its approach in the customary IHL study was sound, with lots of positive feedback.[46] They argued they did not engage in advocacy or wishful thinking but rather followed an inductive approach looking at documented practice and resulting clear rules. For example, there were parts of API that they did not think were widely enough accepted so as to constitute a rule of customary IHL. Other parts of API, some experts noted, had been accepted even by Israel and the United States, who had never consented to that entire legal instrument. Secondly, they believed that the IHL rules particularly for internal war has been much clarified, and this is pursued later. And thirdly, they thought that the study had made an important contribution to furthering awareness of IHL, as the suggested customary rules had been translated into approximately fifty languages.

One of the primary substantive achievements of the customary study was to clarify and indeed expand the IHL regulation of internal war – a major form of armed conflict in contemporary times. The gap between the extensive regulation of international war compared to internal war has now been narrowed, with apparently many new norms arising out of practice identified, and broadly supported, concerning NIACs (noninternational armed conflicts). Ironically, if one asked states to explicitly legislate in a diplomatic conference further restrictions on internal war, expectations would be low. But if one asked, as this study did, what the international community was already practicing on this subject, the answer might indicate much fleshing out of IHL beyond Common Article 3 from 1949 and APII from 1977.[47]

Whatever the long-term outcome of this process about customary IHL, which was ongoing at the time of writing in 2023 and would continue to be so, it could hardly be said that the ICRC had forgotten about IHL or was downplaying it in relation to its multifaceted other activities. Whatever the substantive merits of the proposed rules put forward, and whether or not the ICRC research team had identified and properly interpreted the relevant practices, the ICRC had devoted much time and effort to the subject and given states an opportunity to articulate their positions.

Its study of customary IHL had received several awards, notwithstanding some evident state desire to protect the realm of military necessity. Indeed, by the logic of the situation, if a state disagreed with a proposed rule or how practice was interpreted, it was compelled to address the subject – lest it might wind up being legally bound in a way it did not want.

The ICRC teamed with the British Red Cross and with a five-person study team at the Lauterpacht Centre of the University of Cambridge to keep the subject alive and the discussion ongoing about the dynamic evolution of customary IHL.[48] It could not be said that the subject was high priority for many states, more than one of which was busily engaged in violent conflicts that IHL was supposed to limit, and had not reacted to the 2005 study – or its subsequent updating. Nevertheless, the ICRC was doing what it could to identify customary IHL in an era when other legislative avenues looked unpromising if not decidedly dangerous.

X   Cyber Space

While the project on customary IHL might be said to be looking back, to find binding IHL rules that had emerged from past practice, the ICRC was also trying to look forward. That is, it was trying to anticipate how technological developments were going to change – or were already changing – the nature of armed conflicts and how they were fought. The subject of cyber space was central. On this legal issue, as on many others, the ICRC devoted much time and effort.[49] As on the subject of human rights, a focus on how technology might change future wars and their regulation was an immense subject. There is no pretense here to cover most aspects of changes in IHL needed in the future. Subjects such as war in outer space, and with automated weapons, are important topics but left to others. Attention to cyber space as a battlefield remains a useful example of ICRC attention to ongoing IHL matters.

The ICRC was not alone in focusing on wars in the computer age. Among the private institutions making studies about trends in digitalized warfare were the Rand Corporation, the Brookings Institution, Chatham House, the Carnegie Endowment for International Peace, the Atlantic Council, the Council on Foreign Relations, and many more. Did the ICRC retain an elevated position among those concerned with cyber warfare? This is difficult if not impossible to say.

The reputation, moral authority, and standing of the ICRC in legal affairs constitute a matter of perception, to a considerable degree. Legal reputation is not a material object that can dissected under a microscope. With regard to the last general diplomatic conference in the 1970s, at least one serious study questioned the ICRC's ability to properly anticipate developments and relate well to the postcolonial states.[50] Others might or might not share that view about the ICRC. What can be said about cyber affairs is that the ICRC retained its focus on IHL norms and principles to limit war's effect on persons, whereas an organization such as the Rand Corporation did not consistently keep a central focus on humanitarian legal rules to limit the process of war.

On the subject of armed conflict and cyber space, ICRC legal and technical experts tracked meetings at the UN and other international forums – and the broader negotiations among states – about cyber communications, cyber attacks, and armed conflict in cyber space. It was clear enough that states and nonstate parties were already using computer interactions as part of political or economic strategies to do harm.

The ICRC was invited to observe the study of law and cyber space carried out by leading specialists mostly associated with NATO countries that produced the Tallinn Manuals on that subject. Bruno Demeyere participated in that study representing a Belgian university; he then joined the ICRC and became Editor of the *Review*. Similar to the ICRC's study on customary IHL, the Tallinn group put forward its view on the rules for cyber warfare and cyber conflicts. But these so called "black letter rules" were nonbinding.[51] They did not always emphasize IHL as compared to other parts of international law.

Just as there had been longstanding difficulties in definitively establishing when a traditional armed conflict of a kinetic nature commenced, so it was challenging to distinguish the exact moment of a cyber attack, who executed the attack, and when a cyber attack might cross the threshold to cyber war. States agree in general that international law regulates cyber affairs, and that IHL regulates armed conflict involving cyber space. One can have cyber operations in situations already recognized as an armed conflict, and also such operations that might trigger the label of armed conflict for the first time. But most details remain unsettled. Indeed, if international law regulated recourse to kinetic force and the process of fighting, as in *jus ad bellum* and *jus in bello*, it was new and different to think about cyber "force." When does a data stream become "force" in the sense used in international law? That is not clear.

It *is* clear that since many military operations involve computers, there would be – and already have been – attempts by an enemy to disrupt those networks. It is also clear that much civilian damage could be done by cyber manipulations, as electrical grids, water/sanitary systems, the control of dams, and the functioning of hospitals inter alia could be disrupted. Hospital computers have been blocked sometimes by various forms of ransom malware. Banks and other important institutions have had their computers intentionally frozen up. According to media reports, an Israeli cyber attack disrupted the workings of gas stations in Iran for over a week, causing civilian inconvenience and loss of income. According to the same reports, Iran hacked into various computer accounts in Israel causing civilian disruption and embarrassment. The ICRC was exploring the subject of digital emblems of neutrality that could be used on a widespread basis to make particularly hospitals and other institutions, which are vital to the civilian population, off-limits to cyber attack.[52] Medical installations are also vital for treating wounded combatants; these persons too are protected by existing IHL.

There were ample debates, mostly unresolved, about applying traditional core IHL principles to cyber armed conflict – principles such as distinction between civilian and military targets, proportionality of any collateral damage (with military gains compared to civilian losses, a very complex comparison), and how to evaluate "attacks" on dual use targets (having both military and civilian functions). Equally perplexing was how to evaluate the significance of computerized data streams in determining the existence of armed conflict in the first place: does one look at killing of people, extent of injuries to people, permanent destruction of property; temporary blocking of vital machines, freezing of data vital to civilian society, and so forth.

Some of the complexities can be seen in a further example involving Iran. If, as widely reported but never confirmed, the United States and Israel used malware to disable certain computers alleged to be involved in actual or potential weaponized nuclear energy production in Iran, circa 2009, with some destruction of physical matter, this seems to have been treated by most parties as something short of international armed conflict. If, on the other hand, the United States or Israel were to carry out kinetic bombing of those same nuclear reactors and their computers, that would certainly be seen by much of the world in a different way.

Something similar might be said about Estonia circa 2007 when many computers important to the government and the economy were temporarily disabled, allegedly by actors having some connection to the Russian government. The matter was not treated as an international armed conflict giving rise to the right of self-defense, perhaps involving similar measures directed against Russia. But if a kinetic bombing attack had produced the same results, disabling vital communications networks, the legal evaluation no doubt would have been different.

On these matters involving cyber operations in an armed conflict, and whether cyber operations themselves might trigger the judgment that an armed conflict existed, the ICRC was persistently and broadly engaged. On some subjects it stated its view, while recognizing that states would determine the status of IHL pertaining to cyber affairs. It often tried to take certain norms of API from 1977, designed to protect civilians in traditional international armed conflicts, and apply that logic and those principles to cyber space.[53] It argued in general that failure to do so would leave especially the civilian population, and objects vital to it, at great risk in future cyber operations. It therefore continued with its legal preoccupations, from the 1930s onwards, about protecting civilians in war, and tried to extend legal protections in future armed conflicts involving computerized connectivity. The process was ongoing, and the ICRC was deeply involved in it.

Trying to extend humanitarian concerns to cyber space might bring one back to the subject of customary IHL. If one looks at space law or maritime law by comparison, one sees much early attention to customary principles and then customary rules as states, and private corporations, slowly extended their operations in – and knowledge about – those areas. Only later did one explicitly legislate on those subjects by negotiating comprehensive conventions. Logically, the same process was likely regarding cyber space. With so many uncertainties it would be logical to move slowly, with multilateral treaties negotiated later rather than sooner.

XI   Conclusion

By now the reader of this book (if still awake) should be convinced of two things for sure: first, that the world is a complex and messy and uncertain place; and second that the ICRC is in the process of making lots of changes to adjust to its environment. This chapter has tried to show that despite all sorts of changes in process, the ICRC still devotes considerable time and energy to traditional concerns about promoting IHL and trying to help implement it.

I think this is clear enough. Whether one looks back via customary IHL or forward regarding IHL and cyber space, the ICRC is deeply involved in both, making major investments in time and personnel resources. The ICRC is absolutely central to discussions about customary IHL, and perhaps central enough about such trending subjects as cyber space and war.

I am not suggesting that all is in order regarding the ICRC and IHL, and the book's Epilogue in particular will raise some contemporary concerns.

Notes

1 G. Best, *War and Law since 1945* (Oxford: Oxford University Press, 1994), p. 228.
2 Count Helmuth von Moltke letter, in Harry Pross (ed.), *Die Zerstörung der deutschen Politik: Dokumente 1871–1933* (Frankfurt, 1959), pp. 29–31, available at: www.gwpda.org/1914m/moltke.html (accessed November 15, 2022).
3 Ibid.
4 Quoted in H. W. Brands, *The Man Who Saved the Union: Ulysses Grant in War and Peace* (New York: Anchor Books for Random House, 2012), p. 339.
5 See further Leonard Rubenstein, *Perilous Medicine: The Struggle to Protect Health Care from the Violence of War* (New York: Columbia University Press, 2022), who frames the book in terms of a comparison between Henry Dunant and Francis Lieber.
6 Vice Admiral Mark Hammond, AM, Royal Australian Navy, "Chief of Navy Speech to Naval Warfare Officers Association," *Royal Australian Navy* (October 30, 2015), www.navy.gov.au/sites/default/files/documents/20151030_NWOA_Lunch_Address.pdf (accessed November 15, 2022).
7 Samuel Moyn, *Humane: How the U.S. Abandoned Peace and Reinvented War* (New York: Farrar, Straus & Giroux, 2021). The book is less scholarly history than popular history, designed to provoke. It repeatedly uses snide and snarky phrases in reference to efforts to limit war rather than regulate its start.
8 See the critical review of the Moyn book in Stephen Pomper, "Has War Become Too Humane? What Really Allows the War on Terror to Persist," *Foreign Affairs* (September 21, 2021), www.foreignaffairs.com/articles/united-states/2021-09-21/has-war-become-too-humane? (accessed November 15, 2022). The central argument of this review, written by a former US government lawyer, is that attention to IHL by the United States in its global "war on terror" after September 11, 2001, as in rules for drone strikes, did not necessarily reduce or change attention to *jus ad bellum* issues.
9 Patrick Youssef, "Au Sahel, la guerre confisque tout espoir à la population," *Tribune libre* (September 6, 2021), cited at *CICR L'Humanitaire Dans Tous Ses Etats*, https://blogs.icrc.org/hdtse/2021/09/06/au-sahel-la-guerre-confisque-tout-espoir-a-la-population/ (accessed November 15, 2022).
10 Michael Ignatieff, *Human Rights as Politics and Idolatry* (Princeton: Princeton University Press, 2001), p. 5.

292 The Contemporary ICRC

11 Stephen Krasner, *Sovereignty: Organized Hypocrisy* (Princeton: Princeton University Press, 1999).

12 For an analysis of probable war crimes by Russia early in its armed conflict with Ukraine from February 2022, see the independent UN report "Situation of Human Rights in Ukraine in the Context of the Armed Attack by the Russian Federation," UN Office of the High Commissioner of Human Rights (June 29, 2022), cited at *reliefweb*, https://reliefweb.int/report/ukraine/situation-human-rights-ukraine-context-armed-attack-russian-federation-24-february-15-may-2022-enuk (accessed November 15, 2022).

13 ICRC, "Geneva Conventions, Commentary, 2020, Article 4 of Third Geneva Convention of 1949 relative to the Treatment of Prisoners of War," *ICRC*, https://ihl-databases.icrc.org/ihl/full/GCIII-commentary (accessed November 15, 2022).

14 "The Protocols," *International Review of the Red Cross*, 197–198 (August-September 1977), pp. 30–32.

15 See ICRC, Database for Customary IHL, rules, number 106.

16 Stephen C. Neff, *War and the Law of Nations: A General History* (Cambridge: Cambridge University Press, 2005.)

17 The Hague diplomatic conferences of 1899 and 1907 certainly dealt with the subject of prisoners of war. But lacking a permanent sponsor, advocate, or guardian, over time the ICRC took over this subject in a leading way, which one can see in the 1929 Geneva Convention on prisoners of war drafted in cooperation with the ICRC. Also by the 1970s, one could see that the subject of addressing the means and methods of war had been incorporated into the two Additional Protocols of 1977, even more so than had been the case in the diplomatic conference of 1949. Hence it is said that The Hague legal tradition about numerous belligerent subjects was meshed with the Geneva legal tradition that started with a focus on individuals.

18 Moyn, *Humane*, argues that for the influential United States, greatly affected by the Vietnam War, from the 1991 war to liberate Kuwait onward military lawyers began to approve military targeting and otherwise greatly affect various military operations.

19 André Durand, "The Role of Gustave Moynier in the Founding of the Institute of International Law (1875)," *International Review of the Red Cross*, 303 (December 1994), pp. 542–563, https://international-review.icrc.org/articles/role-gustave-moynier-founding-institute-international-law-1873-war-balkans-1857-1878 (accessed November 15, 2022). See also James Crossland, *War, Law and Humanity: The Campaign to Control Warfare, 1853–1914* (London: Bloomsbury Academic, 2018). This is a fine comparison between those seeking to prevent war and those seeking to limit it once initiated. It is more scholarly than the Moyn popular and provocative and personalized history.

20 To take but one example, see Adam Roberts and Richard Guelff, *Documents on the Laws of War* (Oxford: Oxford University Press, 2004). See further Françoise Bouchet-Saulnier, *The Practical Guide to Humanitarian Law* (New York: Rowman & Littlefield, 2014), 3rd English ed.

21 See, for example, Gary D. Solis, *The Law of Armed Conflict: International Humanitarian Law in War* (Cambridge: Cambridge University Press, 2010).

22 Geoffrey Best, *War and Law since 1945* (Oxford: Oxford University Press, 1994, 1996), p. 403.

23 126 S. Ct. 2749 (2006).

24 Thomas J. Farer, "The Laws of War 25 Years after Nuremberg," *International Conciliation*, 538 (1971), p. 31.

25 An overview of much open source information can be found in my *The Politics of Prisoners Abuse: The United States and Enemy Prisoners after 9/11* (Cambridge: Cambridge University Press, 2011). See also the fine summary of events in Lisa Hajjar, *The War in Court: Inside the Long Fight Against Torture* (Oakland: University of California Press, 2022). Both books show that a group of lawyers tried to contest torture by the United States after 9/11, not very successfully. The role of the ICRC is mentioned along the way.

26 Best, *War and Law since 1945*.

27 Nils Melzer, *International Humanitarian Law: A Comprehensive Introduction* (Geneva: ICRC, 2016), chap. 3, "The Conduct of Hostilities," www.jep .gov.co/Sala-de-Prensa/Documents/4231_002-IHL_WEB_13.pdf (accessed November 15, 2022).

28 Michael Ignatieff, *The Warrior's Honor: Ethnic War and the Modern Conscience* (New York: Vintage, for Random House, 1999).

29 Philippe Sands, *East West Street: On the Origins of "Genocide" and "Crimes against Humanity"* (New York: Knopf, 2016).

30 Crossland, *War, Law, and Humanity*, p. 407.

31 I want to remain focused on general trends and not get bogged down into legal hairsplitting. Why exactly was the Serbian leader Slobodan Milosevic charged with war crimes, crimes again humanity, and genocide in the ICTY? I prefer to note that he was charged with authorizing various atrocities in the Balkan War of 1992–1995 and died of natural causes while made to stand trial in the international criminal proceedings of the ICTY. Hence I find useful the concept of atrocity law, part of which is made up of IHL. See further Karen Alter, *The New Terrain of International Law: Courts, Politics, Rights* (Princeton: Princeton University Press, 2014).

32 During 2020–2022, there were trials in Germany of Syrians accused of torture and other crimes in the Syrian civil war from 2011, under the principle of universal jurisdiction.

33 Reed Brody, "The Road to Abu Ghraib: A Policy to Evade International Law," *Human Rights Watch* (June 8, 2004), www.hrw.org/report/2004/06/08/ road-abu-ghraib. (accessed November 15, 2022).

34 The ICRC has published and posted a mountain of information on this subject. For one example, see the *International Review of the Red Cross*, 96/895–896 (December 2014) on the theme of "Generating Respect for the Law."

35 Boyd van Dijk, *Preparing for War: The Making of the Geneva Conventions* (Oxford and New York: Oxford University Press, 2022).

36 Giovanni Mantilla, *Lawmaking under Pressure: International Humanitarian Law and Internal Armed Conflict* (Ithaca and London: Cornell University Press, 2020), p. 167.

37 Best, *War and Law since 1945*, p. 407.

38 For an introduction to the relationship see ICRC, "What Is the Difference between international Humanitarian Law and human Rights Law?," January 22, 2015, www.icrc.org/en/document/what-difference-between-ihl-and-human-rights-law (accessed November 18, 2022); and A. H. Robertson, "Humanitarian Law and Human Rights," in Christophe Swinarski, ed., *Studies and Essays on International Humanitarian Law and Red Cross Principles* (The Hague: Martinus Nijhoff, 1984; copublished by the ICRC in Geneva), pp. 793–802. For a current concise overview see Katharine Fortin, "The Relationship between International Human Rights Law and International Humanitarian Law: Taking Stock at the End of 2022," *Netherlands Quarterly of Human Rights*, November 10, 2022, https://journals.sagepub.com/doi/full/10.1177/09240519221134723 (accessed November 18, 2022). For those who want to explore in depth the complexities about the two bodies of law, see Marko Milanovic, "The Lost Origins of Lex Specialis: Rethinking the Relationship between Human Rights and International Humanitarian Law," in J. D. Ohlin, ed., *Theoretical Boundaries of Armed Conflict and Human Rights* (Cambridge: Cambridge University Press, 2016); and Andrew Clapham, "The Complex Relationship between the Geneva Conventions and International Human Rights Law," in A. Clapham, P. Gaeta, and M. Sassòli, eds., *The 1949 Geneva Conventions: A Commentary* (Oxford: Oxford University Press, 2015), pp. 701–735. An issue of the RC *Review* (No. 871, 2008) was devoted to human rights. In my reading, the more one talks about the two bodies of law as black letter law argued in courts, the more one finds conflicts, complexities, ambiguities, and uncertainties. How much all this legal debate is necessary for understanding ICRC policy and field operations is another matter.

39 For a summary see David P. Forsythe, "The 1949 Geneva Conventions after 70 years: The Fate of Charity in Turbulent Times," *Global Governance* (published online September, 25 2019), 25/3, pp 359–369. https://brill.com/view/journals/gg/25/3/article-p359_2.xml (accessed November 18, 2022).

40 Mantilla, *Lawmaking under Pressure*, p. 172.

41 Jean-Marie Henckaerts, "Study on Customary International Humanitarian Law: A Contribution to the Understanding and Respect for the Rule of Law in Armed Conflict," *International Review of the Red Cross*, 87/857 (March 2005), pp. 175–212, www.icrc.org/en/doc/assets/files/other/icrc_002_0860 .pdf (accessed November 15, 2022).

42 "Customary IHL Database," *ICRC*, originally published by Cambridge University Press in 2005, https://ihl-databases.icrc.org/customary-ihl/eng/docs/home (accessed November 15, 2022).

43 John B. Bellinger, III and William J. Haynes II, "A US Government Response to the International Committee of the Red Cross Study Customary International Humanitarian Law," *International Review of the Red Cross*, 89/866 (June 2007), pp. 443–471, https://international-review.icrc.org/sites/default/files/irrc_866_11.pdf (accessed November 15, 2022).

44 Elizabeth Wilmshurst and Susan Breau, eds., *Perspectives on the ICRC Study on Customary International Humanitarian Law* (Cambridge: Cambridge University Press, 2007.)

45 Mark Osiel, *The End of Reciprocity* (Cambridge: Cambridge University Press 2009).

46 Marko Milanovich, "Assessing the Authority of the ICRC Customary IHL Study," *EJIL: Talk, a blog of the European Journal of International Law*, July 21, 2022, www.ejiltalk.org/assessing-the-authority-of-the-icrc-customary-ihl-study/ (accessed November 15, 2022).

47 Jean-Marie Henckaerts, "Civil War, Custom and Cassese," *Journal of International Criminal Justice*, 10/5 (December 2012), pp. 1095–1111, https://academic.oup.com/jicj/article-abstract/10/5/1095/817233 (accessed November 15, 2022).

48 "Customary IHL Project Updates ICRC Database," *Lauterpacht Centre for International Law* (December 18, 2020), www.lcil.cam.ac.uk/press/news/2020/12/customary-ihl-project-updates-icrc-database (accessed November 15, 2022).

49 For an overview see Laurent Gisel, Tilman Rodenhauser, and Knut Dormann, "Twenty Years On: International Humanitarian Law and the Protection of Civilians against the Effects of Cyber Operations during Armed Conflicts," *International Review of the Red Cross*, 913 (March 2021), pp. 287–334, https://international-review.icrc.org/articles/twenty-years-ihl-effects-of-cyber-operations-during-armed-conflicts-913 (accessed November 15, 2022).

50 Henry Lovat, *Negotiating Civil War: The Politics of International Regime Design* (Cambridge: Cambridge University Press, 2020).

51 For one overview and evaluation see Eric Talbot Jensen, "The Tallinn Manual 2.0: Highlights and Insights," *Georgetown Journal of International Law*, 48 (2017), pp. 735–778, www.law.georgetown.edu/international-law-journal/wp-content/uploads/sites/21/2018/05/48-3-The-Tallinn-Manual-2.0.pdf (accessed November 15, 2022).

52 Tilman Rodenhauser, Laurent Gisel, Larry Maybee, Hollie Johnston, and Fabrice Lauper, "Signaling Legal Protection in a Digitalizing World: A New Era for the Distinctive Emblems?," *Humanitarian Law & Policy* (September 16, 2021), https://blogs.icrc.org/law-and-policy/2021/09/16/legal-protection-digital-emblem/ (accessed November 15, 2022).

53 ICRC, *Avoiding Civilian Harm from Military Cyber Operations in Armed Conflicts* (Geneva: ICRC, 2020), report of an expert meeting.

14 Has the Traditional Focus Been Lost?
Part II – Political Prisoners

> [T]he law is less important than the opportunities and motivations available for the [M]ovement....
>
> Peter McAlister-Smith[1]

Some critics claim, as observed already, not only that the ICRC has squandered its traditional position as the guardian of IHL, both in developing and supervising the application of that law, but assert that the organization has largely forgotten about humanitarian protection regarding political prisoners. This is at least plausible – given all the big money chasing humanitarian assistance and micro-development, and given all the talk about broad activities in low-level urban violence and helping migrants. Humanitarian protection of political prisoners is perhaps the most difficult subject for an outside analyst to address, given the amount of secrecy about particulars surrounding the subject in contemporary times. Nevertheless, the very fact of the accusation requires an attempt to answer.

I   Conceptual Distinction

On the ICRC website, one can find the following wording:

For the ICRC, protection is all activities aimed at: (1) ensuring that authorities and armed actors comply with their obligations under International Humanitarian Law and other bodies of law and (2) at reducing the vulnerability of individuals and communities affected by armed conflict and violence. Protection activities include: improving the life and dignity of detainees, reducing human suffering during the conduct of hostilities or law enforcement operations, restoring family links and searching for missing persons (including forensics expertise).[2]

As mentioned already, it would have been clearer if the ICRC had said, there is Protection and protection – or Protection as general and broad ranging advocacy, and protection in the narrow or traditional sense. Protection with a capital "P" refers to diplomacy for, or advocacy

296

for, the rights of persons affected by violent conflict and other situations, as enshrined in IHL and some other parts of international law. This Protection, with a capital "P," includes advocating for various forms of relief and micro-development. By comparison, protection with a lower-case "p" refers to detention visits and related actions, tracing of missing persons, and restoring family links. The latter notion of protection also includes efforts based on forensic science, both for identification of mortal remains per se in order to bring closure for next of kin, and, if timely, for discreet representations to fighting parties. It does not release that information to other parties for prosecutions. In the 2020s it was still engaged in forensic science from the Falklands War (1982) and the Bosnian War (1992–1995), among other past conflicts.

In the first sense, Protection for the ICRC means almost all humanitarian diplomacy, or diplomacy on behalf of almost everything the ICRC tries to do. It is similar to Protection by the UNHCR on behalf of refugees.[3] It is diplomacy to urge other actors, mainly governments speaking for states, to implement the international legal rules or other norms they have agreed to concerning the human dignity of persons caught up in war and other violence.

Advocating for assistance or socioeconomic security is part of Protection. That is not a conflict in logic but an oxymoron. In reality, providing assistance Protects against death and socioeconomic suffering. This meaning the wording on the website suggests but does not make clear. Actually providing the assistance directed to socioeconomic human security is assistance. It can be intertwined with protection in two ways: checking on treatment and conditions of detainees can lead to provision of assistance; and provision of assistance can enhance how authorities view ICRC protection. At the Geneva headquarters there is a protection division. That is the administrative unit that dispatches specialized personnel to work with ICRC field delegations concerning detention visits and related actions, tracing, restoring family links, and forensic science.

II   Political Prisoners

That said, the rest of this chapter focuses on the one subject of protection of political prisoners.[4] It is mostly this protection topic that the critics claim has been increasingly downgraded. I give short shrift to other aspects of protection for lack of space. On the ICRC website and in the RC *Review* one can find much basic information about tracing of missing persons, restoring family links, and forensic activities. I do return to the subject of ICRC protection activities in the international armed conflict in Ukraine in the Epilogue.

In the last decade or so there have been few prisoners of war and civilian detainees in international armed conflicts, to which the ICRC is legally guaranteed access by IHL – specifically GCs 3 and 4 from 1949. Great powers find such conflicts too dangerous to fight. Or, they say they are not doing what they are doing, as when Russia detached Crimea from Ukraine in 2014 using its soldiers in (thin) disguise. This major trend was altered by the Russian invasion of Ukraine in 2022, but that sort of big traditional international war happily remained the exception that proved the general rule that major military powers avoided direct violent confrontation most of the time. (In the Ukraine war, both Russia and NATO members tried to avoid direct combat against each other as of early 2023.)

As for other states, there might be an international armed conflict now and then, as between Armenia and Azerbaijan over Nagorno-Karabagh. There were some prisoners of war there, some of whom were repatriated after some early fighting by Russian peacekeepers rather than by the ICRC. In that war the ICRC was the only outside organization active on the ground during and after the fighting. UN and EU agencies were not *sur place*, hamstrung by the controversy about who rightfully governed the contested territory. But all that did not mean that the ICRC had a monopoly on POW affairs. After all, the main point was the proper treatment of POWs and their timely release, not who supervised the process.

In various manifestations of noninternational armed conflicts, Common Article 3 from 1949 and APII from 1977 give the ICRC no special right of access to detainees. The ICRC may offer its services, which it normally does in internal armed conflicts, but the process is subject to consent by the fighting parties.

Short of armed conflict, whether international or internal, the ICRC may or may not offer its services to help protect the dignity of detainees by eliminating mistreatment and/or poor conditions. It is this subject we pursue here.

However, one can overdo this tripartite legal framework. It is true that in international armed conflict one finds IHL specifying extensive obligations for detaining authorities. In internal armed conflicts, IHL lays out some core principles relevant to detainees, with customary IHL clarifying more rules, as we analyzed in the previous chapter. But across all three categories or levels of conflict, what the ICRC specifically does regarding actual detention visits is mostly the same. Law affects, or is supposed to affect, the subject of ICRC access to detainees. But what the ICRC does by way of actual visit, and maybe supporting activities related to a visit, is the same in principle across different legal situations. The ICRC has adopted a general detention strategy for 2020–2025 the basics of which mostly transcend legal categories of situations and persons.

Governments, usually attentive to matters of image and reputation, resist the notion that they detain political prisoners. They are also not keen on verbiage about security prisoners. And sometimes there is genuine debate about what legal label properly applies to conflict detainees. So in a classic example of cautious diplomacy in search of practical achievements, Geneva refers at times to "persons detained by reason of events." You cannot get blander than that. And in any event, the authorities know very well who comprise the real targets of ICRC interest, whatever the wording used.[5]

III   General Strategy

At first glance it would be hard to accept that the ICRC has ignored attempted protection of political prisoners in recent years when there have been general reviews at headquarters of protection matters in 2011, 2015, and 2020. Protection strategies have been adopted. It is possible (but not entirely clear to an outsider) that each national field office may be evaluated by headquarters regarding what it has done on protection matters over a five-year period, with perhaps ten major offices reviewed in any given year. If all that is accurate, it would be difficult for either HQ or field staff to ignore either Protection or protection, including the subject of political prisoners.

On paper and in-house, the ICRC asserts that its traditional concern with humanitarian protection remains unchanged. It states internally that its reputation, indeed its identity, is bound up with proper attention to this role. It articulates a desire to use its status on protection to influence others. It professes general satisfaction with its record on the subject and foresees no radical changes in strategy or tactics. In dealing with detained migrants, it is willing to train other units in the RC Movement in its procedures, which it believes have been proven over time to be valuable.

For decades for sure, if not longer, the ICRC paid systematic attention to protection of political prisoners. It at least talked about doing a costs–benefits analysis about a potential request to visit, trying to weigh the prospects for success against the possibility of an offer of services doing harm to these detainees – a subjective calculation. It also discussed whether it had the personnel and other resources to be systematic in its protection efforts so as to be neutral and impartial across different situations.

In its annual report the ICRC presents numbers of detainees visited, perhaps wisely not organizing the numbers into POWs, civilian detainees, those detained in internal wars, political prisoners, and others. Such a classification would get the organization bogged down into legal

Photograph 14.1 From World War I the ICRC developed a concern with conflict prisoners as a primary focus. After that war the organization added political prisoners to its active agenda. In contemporary times the ICRC sometimes takes an all-prisoner approach in its detention visits, either as a way to eventually get to interview the conflict and political prisoners, or because the common criminals are in dire straits. The Covid-19 pandemic further pushed the ICRC in this latter direction. Here, an ICRC employee discusses with an officer of the detention authorities to plan the detention visit and the planned distribution of relief items for the prisoners at Monrovia Central Prison, Liberia.

hairsplitting and political controversies. Such numbers do not tell us how many detainees should have been visited but were not. That number is unknown and maybe unknowable.

It would be very helpful to know how many times, and where, the ICRC "offer of services" regarding detainees was declined. But this accounting would also lead to some controversy, and Geneva has sought to avoid that.

Let us assume for sake of discussion that the ICRC offered its services to supervise detention on the US southwestern border during the Trump Administration where there was much controversy and allegations of poor conditions and inhumane policies. The issue was migrants and not political prisoners, at least as usually conceived, but the same analysis applies to politicals. Public knowledge of that hypothetical offer and any response would have added to controversy on the subject, as critics would have seized on the offer as demonstration of serious problems. Would such controversy have improved the conditions or treatment of detainees? After all, the primary goal is protection, not avoiding controversy. We are not privy to such discussions within the ICRC on contemporary issues and how the organization evaluates productive public controversy. Historically it has tended to opt for discretion on such particulars, with the organization itself admitting to what one interlocutor called a "customary reserve," although in the past from time to time it did publish the fact that a démarche for detainees had been rejected. There are other actors that try to stir up what they see as productive controversy, including the media and human rights organizations.

Its contemporary discretion about offers of service and resulting findings, on a consistent basis, is one reason governments favor the ICRC and donate to it. When there was a leak to the American media about ICRC reports documenting abuse of certain detainees in Iraq after the US invasion in 2003,[6] ICRC President Kellenberger condemned the leak (which almost certainly came from somewhere on the US side) as endangering ICRC access to other prisoners. The leaked material showed a candid and knowledgeable ICRC, but Geneva still condemned the publication of its findings. It wants detaining authorities to have confidence in its procedures. Another leak about ICRC reports at the Guantanamo prison played out the same way: demonstration of ICRC diligence in discretely reporting serious problems, but Geneva's condemnation of the leak.

It would be very useful to know how many times, and where, the ICRC was not just visiting prisoners in the routinized penal system but rather visiting prisoners under interrogation, especially as held by security services in special places of detention. And to know how many times, and where, did the ICRC start with routinized detention visits in regular prisons but was able to expand those visits to persons under interrogation, held by the military and by other security services or clandestine special forces. It is one thing to say the ICRC is doing prison visits at location X, which involves improving the water/sanitation system in a regular prison because the conditions are bad. It is another thing for the ICRC to have early access to "high value" detainees presumed to have "actionable intelligence" about current conflicts – and thus more likely to be ill-treated.

There are prison visits and prison visits. After all, when Dres Balmer published a book against the wishes of the ICRC about his experiences as a staff member in El Salvador (it was set as a novel, but everyone knew it was about the ICRC there), he wrote: "When a political [prisoner] arrives in a prison, he is no longer in danger of death. We did not have a lot to do in the prisons."[7] After all, whereas the ICRC did prison visits at the US military detention center at Gitmo, on Cuba, where maybe "only" 20 percent of the prisoners were intentionally ill-treated early on, it never did gain access to separate CIA detention centers where during about 2002–2006 probably most of the detainees were seriously ill-treated.[8] After all, when a Palestinian detainee who was seen as a security threat of some kind eventually landed in a regular Israeli prison, which was supposed to happen within fifteen days according to a negotiated agreement with the ICRC, the Balmer rule kicked in: there wasn't always a lot for the ICRC staff person to do – except to record what had happened for presentation after the fact to Israeli authorities.

However, such a role for the ICRC was not always useless. If we assume for sake of discussion that the Israeli policy for a time was to use "moderate physical pressure" to extract information from detainees during a two-week period, after which the ICRC got a private conversation with the detainee, and if the ICRC could present to the authorities a list of persons who had been tortured, and if the authorities wanted to avoid torture as compared to lesser forms of coercion, then ICRC documentation *ex post facto* in regular prison confinement might moderate interrogation policy.[9]

These types of analytical distinctions and patterns are known at ICRC headquarters, but they are not public for contemporary times and are not going to be divulged to researchers. However, historians in the future should find a rich trove of information when examining ICRC and other archives concerning the details of contemporary protection efforts. And ICRC officials of the future will have to answer for the policies of the past, just as we can now evaluate the mixed ICRC protection efforts in the 1950s and 1960s in, for example, Algeria, Kenya, South Africa, and the Middle East, not to mention during World War II. Anticipation of future review may cause contemporary officials to be extra diligent in protection policies today, even when particulars are closely guarded in real time, if they are concerned to protect the reputation of the organization on down the road.

My guess is that most ICRC staff take ICRC protection seriously, including regarding political prisoners, but future review of the historical record is an added incentive for diligence. However, one cannot rule out *ipso facto* the possibility of excessive caution and misjudgment. Maybe the "customary reserve" of the ICRC pertains not only to procedures but to the subject of dynamism in seeking access. As far as I know, when China took over Tibet in 1951 after some forty years of Tibetan independence, the ICRC did not assert itself in any way and certainly not about follow-on detention. It is also quite possible that a high ICRC official here or there or once in a while did not see protection of political prisoners as within the really important priorities of the ICRC, as compared to action in armed conflicts and protracted conflicts.

IV   Some Particulars

At times in the past the ICRC would use an "all prisoner" as well as a structural approach. These approaches are not entirely new. But this broader approach has become more common. This broad approach was certainly in evidence during the pandemic year of 2020 when the ICRC would often distribute face masks and sanitizer to crowded, poor prisons in the Global South. It was one of the few humanitarian agencies active on the ground focused on the health of prisoners. How could one ethically focus only on conflict detainees or political prisoners and ignore others when all prisoners were endangered by the pandemic virus?

Similarly, even if primarily concerned with a narrowly focused interest in conflict and political detainees, often now the ICRC situates its concerns – and the actual process of checking conditions and treatment – within a much broader structural approach. It may occasionally pay for and/or help construct a prison in an impoverished area where the alternative is to guarantee that all detainees – regardless of legal status – are held in miserable conditions. It did so in Rwanda, for example, after the genocide of 1994. It may construct or reconstruct the water-sanitation system, which benefits all prisoners. It may organize seminars or workshops for prison managers (and do the same for those in the judiciary) using human rights as well as IHL guidelines regarding proper treatment and processing of detainees. Again, all prisoners benefit. But that includes conflict and political prisoners.

According to interviews, when the ICRC attended a professional meeting on prison administration, it made sure to include in its conference delegation some experts on particular situations where the organization faced challenges in accessing politicals or getting its usual modalities of action accepted. The all-prisoner approach was combined with a targeted effort on behalf of certain conflict or security prisoners.

The local situation determines the ICRC approach, broad or narrow. The existing physical infrastructure, the prison budget, the alimentary and health conditions, the training and expertise of the authorities all feed into what the ICRC may do on the ground. The needs and defects of the detaining authorities are so great in many places that the ICRC might be seen as approaching the role of a global detention agency, despite its professing to concentrate on conflict and political prisoners. Yet in some situations it would be difficult to help political prisoners

Photograph 14.2 One would like to know a lot more about ICRC visits to political prisoners, an activity pursued by the organization since just after World War I. It remains difficult to say whether it has been appropriately dynamic on the subject, or whether it is easily diverted by authorities into activities such as improving sanitation in regular prisons while the organization is blocked from seeing detainees likely to be mistreated elsewhere. Often the modalities of a prison visit are the same for conflict, political, and common prisoners. Here, an ICRC staff member interviews detainees in Panama City's notorious La Joya prison during 2017.

only, as a kind of preferred class of detainees, and ignore common criminals who were equally threatened by disease, malnutrition, and lack of clean water. The broad approach usually contributes to a positive appreciation of the ICRC by local and national authorities, leading sometimes to a breakthrough regarding visits specifically to politicals. But outsiders do not know the details of such developments – when, where, and how often.

This broad approach, all-prisoner or structural, often the result of truly appalling detention conditions in poor countries, demands a broad range of expertise among protection staff. Finding qualified protection specialists, and retaining them on staff, is a major concern in Geneva – especially when adjusting for linguistic and cultural needs. And if one recruits broadly from former police and prison personnel with experience, one must control for humanitarian values and *esprit de corps* when they represent the ICRC.

There is also a breadth to ICRC protection efforts because of more follow-up with certain detainees. When dealing with detention of child fighters, which sometimes happens in situations not recognized as an armed conflict. and then they are released, the ICRC is inclined to follow up to see if they are well integrated into civilian society. Often they have witnessed terrible things, or have been forced to commit terrible acts, and their relocation and reintegration becomes problematic.

There may also be follow-up when prisoners are released on condition that they go to a third country and be supervised. For example, the ICRC has followed up regarding certain prisoners released from the Guantanamo military base on Cuba, as accepted by some third-party state in negotiated arrangements. Such ex-prisoners may face language and other cultural adjustments as they try to avoid being returned to their home country where they might face renewed detention or worse. There is often the problem of obtaining income and self-sufficiency in the new environment.

One also sees the problem of foreign fighters, and/or their wives and children, who are detained in a foreign locale and not wanted in their home country. The detention facility at al-Hol camp in Syria can be cited as an example of this problem. There one finds both residents (numbering maybe 70,000 at the time of writing in 2022) and detainees presumably linked to the Islamic State group, with the Kurdish Democratic Forces being in charge, and the detainees originally from dozens of nations. The home governments not wanting them back, not knowing how to prosecute them for unproven actions or for just being sucked into the vortex of violence, they wind up in legal and political limbo. The ICRC and its partners do what they can in the al-Hol camp, including the detention facilities, but also serve as intermediary in attempts to relocate those confined there. If relocated to Iraq, for example, the ICRC checks on their situation there. Sometimes the ICRC finds it needs to do humanitarian outreach to the local community, explaining who the newcomers are, why they are there, and why they should be accepted rather than rejected. The exact legal status of such detainees and those relocated may not be clear. So ICRC protection may evolve very broadly and become diplomatically complex.

Increasingly the actual modalities of the prison visit are the tip of the iceberg, important but only part of the picture. Having obtained consent for the visit, the ICRC meets with authorities, then speaks privately with prisoners or their representatives, makes a confidential report to the authorities, and then returns at varying times for a follow-on visit to see what has changed. Detaining authorities, including democratic ones in presumably rule-of-law countries, still play the game of hiding detainees from the ICRC and thus trying to cover up the facts of abusive treatment. The game is an old one and the ICRC has much experience in that regard.

Given all the different situations the ICRC encounters, Geneva strives for consistency in its protective activities so that it will be seen as truly neutral and impartial and therefore respected and accepted. But situations vary so much, and the ICRC has often resorted to the "all-prisoner" or structural approach so much, that consistency is an elusive goal. (Ironically, the ICRC has dealt with protracted conflicts so much in changing and hazy legal frameworks that it may not be as consistent with the past in international armed conflicts. I visit this subject in the Epilogue regarding the Ukraine war.)

If one speaks to enough people at different levels of the ICRC, and reads the published material, one gets the impression that the ICRC is indeed highly active on protection matters – including "those detained by reason of events." But one also gets the impression that much of the process is more art than science, full of complexity and ethical trade-offs. The organization's commitment to protection of politicals is now part of the bureaucracy. Bureaucracies tend to do what they have always done. It is possible, however, that systematic emphasis on politicals might vary at the highest levels, as some top leaders might prefer to focus on IHL or assistance cum resiliency programs. That would be another good topic for historians.

When is the time right for an offer of services? After all, as one UN secretary-general said to this author about not taking an issue to the UN Security Council, there is no point in diving into an empty swimming pool. A poorly timed offer may lead to a negative reply, and that negative reply can affect matters for a long time. Should the ICRC undertake visits with a government official present to demonstrate the process? If so, for how long or how often repeated? There might be the same calculation for a visit that excludes certain persons of interest: how long and how often should one engage in that kind of explanatory visit? Should one involve the local National RC Society? Are they a NIIHA actor that can be trusted? Do the benefits of involving them outweigh the dangers? Can one generalize about that? After all, there is no study of the NIIHA status of the National RC Societies (now officially numbering over 190), and it would change along with political events.

If prisoner abuses are documented but the detaining authority is committed to abusive treatment, should the ICRC continue its presence, perhaps curtailing the very worst, even if some bad continues? Presumably

Photograph 14.3 In 1990 after his release from the Robben Island prison off Cape Town in South Africa and twenty-seven years of detention, Nelson Mandela visited Geneva to express his appreciation for the organization's moral and social support. He was greeted by ICRC President Cornelio Sommaruga, and Jacques Moreillon, who had visited him in prison on numerous occasions. Mandela had previously advised the ICRC not to suspend the visits to protest conditions, a policy option then being debated in Geneva.

Nelson Mandela told ICRC staff visiting him on Robben Island, at a time when the organization was considering a suspension of visits as protest: you should continue; it is not so much the good you can do now as the bad you will prevent in the future. But what about ICRC complicity in abuse of prisoners through its continued presence and discreet reporting? Should the ICRC protect its integrity and withdraw, even if detainees are left without any visits? It did this for a time at Abu Ghraib prison in Iraq.

V Necessarily Imprecise Conclusion about Protection

There are some general reasons the critics exist about the ICRC and political prisoners. The first of these reasons is that everything transpires in the diplomatic shadows and no outsider, even a former high official, knows the current facts for sure. And then there is a second reason: there have been no high-profile success stories that have gotten into the public domain. What is the nature of ICRC thinking and action concerning the Uighurs in China, dissidents and protestors arrested in Belarus, reports of torture in the United Arab Emirates, the situation in Myanmar? Whatever the state of play regarding ICRC protection efforts in those and other situations, one cannot read about the details in *Le Monde* or the *New York Times*. One certainly does not read about many major successes for the ICRC in protection matters involving arbitrary detention. So room for suspicion exists.

Another contributing reason that critics exist about the ICRC and contemporary protection is President Peter Maurer's becoming a trustee at the World Economic Forum. That subject has been covered in detail already in Chapter 10. His position there did give rise to logical concern. Once he had an obligation as trustee to promote the fortunes of the WEF, what were his priorities in China, for example: to advance the WEF brand or make progress protecting persons who were widely seen as political prisoners? Or what about Rwanda, where some well-informed persons believe that Maurer met with President Kagame in Kigali and perhaps discussed only WEF matters, never addressing the subject of security detainees? Or maybe the subject of politicals was mentioned but in a pro forma way without evident conviction or concern. The ICRC leadership never really addressed the ICRC president's double role directly and specifically with regard to a possible conflict of priorities, or problems with image and optics.

No outsider knows the nature or extent of contemporary ICRC policy debates about humanitarian protection in, for example, China. In general, one can logically and ethically argue either of two basic approaches. The two approaches certainly show the complexity of the subject.

One approach is to play the long game, which the ICRC often chooses. Given the clearly repressive views of the highly nationalistic Chinese political leadership during the era of President Xi, was there any realistic option for the ICRC but to build bridges over time, seeking areas of cooperation, perhaps taking no initiative about the Uighurs or other repressed groups, and hoping for a better opportunity in the future when an offer would lead to positive results? Would that approach not be consistent with the apparent situation in Russia, where politicals like Alexei Navalny were apparently not visited but where extensive ICRC contacts were ongoing with various parts of the state and nation?

(However, there is a well-considered long game of building bridges, and there is a long game that goes off the track. In the final chapter I address some situations where the ICRC's public diplomacy has appeared quite laudatory of some repressive regimes, raising questions about the ICRC's commitment to protection efforts in those cases. Yes, the ICRC likes to present itself to authorities in a positive way, but there remains the question of whether there really has been a strong commitment to trying to protect political prisoners in certain parts of the organization.)

The second general approach concerning arbitrary detention in China would be consistent with the 2006 ICRC doctrinal statement about the Holocaust, covered already. When faced with truly dire events, the ICRC needs to have an active private diplomacy for victims even if it does no practical good in the short term and even if not based on clear international law. Only that kind of action protects the reputation and integrity of the ICRC as a NIIHA agency. Some actors see the situation of the Uighurs as at least cultural, if not physical, genocide. Even if falling short of genocide, the situation might still properly be seen as one of massive detention, forced labor, and curtailment of reproductive rights, not to mention serious restrictions on religion. If the ICRC does not make an offer of services in China by 2023, saying in effect that the subject of the Uighurs is just factually a "no go" or "no win" situation, will it face the same reckoning one day as it did about the Holocaust as already discussed? But as a matter of conjecture, suppose the organization raised the question about detention of Tibetans and got a negative. Would that show conclusively that, as a practical matter, one should not take an initiative about the Uighurs?

In the last analysis one cannot definitively evaluate ICRC policymaking regarding arbitrary detention around the world in contemporary times when the specifics are so closely held. One has to read the tea leaves, and there is plenty of room for differing views to exist. At the time of writing in 2022, some interlocutors believe with regard to protecting politicals that some ICRC decisions have lent themselves to the appearance of a looming train wreck rather than an independent and dynamic policy based on NIIHA values.

Many at the ICRC involved in protection efforts acknowledge the difficulty of achieving consistency on the matter of protecting political prisoners, as well as the ethical complexity of the calculations and trade-offs involved. But the subject in general has clearly not been ignored or forgotten, even if it turns out to be the case that in certain situations involving political prisoners the ICRC decides not to make an offer of services – at least not today. Or maybe it did.

As for the delicate subject of protection of politicals, I have at least presented some views for future historians to refine. On that subject I am in no position to pretend to be definitive. I have tried to clarify general policy, while indicating the complexity of some particulars. Outsiders cannot do more, or at least not much more on contemporary – and discreet – protection. Not until either the ICRC changes its views on what it can say publicly, or time passes and historians can study the archives.

Notes

1 P. McAlister-Smith, *International Humanitarian Assistance* (Dordrecht: Springer, 1985), p. 92.

2 For a longer but sometimes not always conceptually sharp overview of ICRC protection, see "ICRC Protection Policy: Institutional Policy," *International Review of the Red Cross*, 90/871 (September 2008), pp. 751–775, https://international-review.icrc.org/sites/default/files/irrc-871-icrc-protection-policy.pdf (accessed November 15, 2022).

3 David P. Forsythe, "Humanitarian Protection: The International Committee of the Red Cross and the United Nations High Commissioner for Refugees," *International Review of the Red Cross*, 83/843 (September 2001), pp. 675–697, www.icrc.org/en/doc/assets/files/other/675_698_forsythe.pdf (accessed November 15, 2022).

4 The early history is covered by Jacques Moreillon, *The International Committee of the Red Cross and the Protection of Detainees* (Lausanne: L'age d'homme, 1973). More recently see Alain Aeschlimann, "Protection of Detainees: ICRC behind Bars," *International Review of the Red Cross*, 87/857 (March 2005), pp. 83–122, https://international-review.icrc.org/sites/default/files/irrc_857_5.pdf (accessed November 15, 2022).

5 For a very good discussion of political prisoners in modern times, see Padraic Kenney, *Dance in Chains* (Oxford and New York: Oxford University Press, 2017).

6 The *Wall Street Journal* ran several stories about ICRC confidential reports on detainees in Iraq, the first on May 7, 2004.

7 My translation of Dres Balmer, *L'Heure de Cuivre* (Lausanne: Editions en bas, 1984), p. 67. The original was in German a year earlier.

8 Forsythe, *The Politics of Prisoner Abuse.*

9 A great deal of information about Israeli detention policies and problems can be found in open sources. See, for example, "Torture and Abuse in Interrogation," *The Israeli Information Center for Human Rights in the Occupied Territories* (November 11, 2017), www.btselem.org/torture (accessed November 15, 2022). Since Israeli harsh detention policies are an open secret, and since the ICRC has long done prison visits to Palestinians detained there, the subject of ICRC possible complicity is a perennial and complex subject, too big for full treatment here. One can also find open sources about mistreatment of Jewish detainees under various Arab authorities, and open sources about Palestinian detainees being mistreated by the Palestinian Authority security forces.

15   ICRC Governance and Management
Part I – The Top Level

En réalité, le CICR est en réorganisation permanent...

(In reality, the ICRC is in constant reorganization...)

Jacques Freymond[1]

The study of how the ICRC organizes itself for humanitarian action might not initially seem to be one of the sexier subjects for either author or reader. Yet there is much of interest to be found in that topic. Certainly in recent decades the organization has become widely respected for two things: advocacy of Dunantist or NIIHA values through both law and diplomacy, and effectiveness in humanitarian action. Both depend on adept organizational decisions. The ICRC has been able to attract and maintain significant diplomatic and financial support – primarily in order to respond to the growing needs of victims of conflict – not only because of its image as an independent neutral in conflict situations, but also because it has a mostly proven track record in providing assistance and executing protection policies. This does not happen by accident.

This chapter's focus on such topics as decision-making structure, nature of governance at the highest levels, and record of the three most recent presidents starts the process. The following chapter continues the analysis from other perspectives. Without successful choices regarding governance and management, reputation and access to victims decline – with budget problems sure to follow.

I   Decision-Making Structure

The Biafra crisis eventually showed the power of negative learning, and that has affected the ICRC ever since. The Assembly, having mismanaged its involvement in the 1967–1970 internationalized civil war, indeed having made a muddle of things and then turned over policy-making to the diplomat Auguste Lindt, who was on loan from the Swiss government, knew it had to make radical structural changes for the organization to survive. Historians may be able to determine if it was Roger Gallopin, the executive director (equivalent to today's director-general) who played a key role in this historic transition, building on a four-day meeting in 1968 called the "Round Table of Delegates," which was mentioned earlier.

Whatever the precise fact of particulars and personalities, the result of Biafra internally was a reduction in the role of the volunteer Assembly (unpaid except for the president and senior vice president) and an increase in the role – aka power or influence – of the director-general (D-G) and the Directorate. The director of operations within the Directorate was normally second in importance only to the D-G. The president remained the face of the ICRC to outsiders but was usually also deeply involved in much internal policymaking – certainly so during the time of Sommaruga and also Maurer.

The ICRC thus wound up with a structure of policymaking similar to French politics. There is a double executive, president and D-G, with the latter being essentially a prime minister who interacts with their cabinet. Just as in Paris there often is some question as to what is in the domain of presidential powers compared to the prime minister, so in Geneva there is some shifting practice as to the scope of presidential action compared to the D-G and Directorate. Just as in Paris foreigners may recognize the president but sometimes not even know the name of the prime minister, so in Geneva the president is much better known than the D-G. This can be misleading, since at the ICRC – at least in the past – it was rare for an important policy decision to be made by the president alone without consultation with other high officials, especially the D-G.

In the era of the construction of the double executive, Jacques Freymond, a member of the Assembly, for a time acting president, and a major intellectual force within the organization, feared that the Assembly would be sidelined too much by the new scheme. He thought that the Assembly, without direct responsibility for daily affairs, could not possibly exercise much influence on the specific policies of "la maison." He was right, but that gets ahead of our story. His idea of a smaller Assembly with control over operations, aided by associate members with specialized expertise, did not prevail.[2]

Officially the president is primarily responsible for representing the ICRC to external actors, or in other words for leading on humanitarian diplomacy – with the help of the vice president. The president handles outside actors of the first rank, with the vice president dealing with much of the rest, although the D-G or others in the Directorate may engage with important outsiders as well – normally in relation to field operations or important IHL issues. The president presides in the Assembly and in its Council (more on that later). This leaves the D-G with the main responsibility for the conduct of daily affairs, including internal management.

The key relationship for constructing ICRC policy now lies in the interactions of the Office of the President and the Directorate or parts thereof, who are required by ICRC internal regulations to engage in regular consultations.[3] The president is charged with presenting an institutional strategy for the approval of the Assembly, and this requires presidential consultation with the D-G and the rest of the professional staff. Moreover, at least one recent D-G, and probably others, operated on the principle that the president should never be taken by surprise by ICRC specific actions. He thus kept the president informed of important operational issues as they evolved. That process gave the president ample opportunity to raise questions or even concerns about quotidian affairs. More on this later.

All of this internal interaction between the president and the professionals reporting through the D-G and Directorate, often several times a day, makes locating the precise scope and degree of influence by the various offices and officials a formidable challenge. The informal discussions among president and D-G, and with others, are not in the public domain. Indeed, some of this interaction probably is never recorded in documents. And ICRC high officials simply do not publish memoirs, candid or otherwise, which of course happens in other organizations.

Even the Vatican, well known for a history of secrecy in policymaking, is sometimes faced with the publication of a revealing memoir by an important official.[4] To this author's knowledge, this has never happened at the ICRC. At one point a junior staff member published a novel that was obviously based on his time in El Salvador, but in fact the book revealed very little that was sensitive about his time there.[5] Headquarters started legal steps to confiscate copies, fearing problems with the host government, but gave up when public opinion in the German-speaking parts of Switzerland started to align with the Swiss German staff member and against top ICRC officials in French-speaking Geneva. The book revealed nothing important about policymaking in Geneva, and the brief episode faded into oblivion.

The Assembly, comprised of fifteen to twenty-five Swiss citizens, rather than being in the thick of managerial decisions as at the start of the Nigerian civil war, is now a review board and general supervisor of budgets and major policies. What happens in ICRC field activities does not normally and directly and immediately involve the Assembly or its Council. The Assembly discusses and formally approves the organization's annual budget, strategic policy, and appointment of high officials, although most of the specifics of what is approved has been drawn up by others – meaning the president perhaps in consultation with the D-G, or vice versa. The Assembly only meets bimonthly in principle, but with the possibility of special sessions. There is also a Council of the Assembly for governance issues when the Assembly is not in session, as already noted. More about the Assembly level of governance later. The central introductory point is that the role of a volunteer Assembly has been reduced, and the role of professional side of the house has been increased. This is the primary legacy of Biafra and its policy confusions for ICRC policymaking back then. Whether there is some reconsideration of all this under the presidency of Mirjana Spoljaric (Egger) merits watching.

II   Governance: The Assembly and Its Council

It is very difficult to say much that is entirely certain about the ICRC governing board in recent times since its proceedings are secret for decades. Even though the ICRC is treated as if it were a public international organization with diplomatic rights and immunities, and even though it overwhelmingly relies on tax-based financial donations from Western democracies and their organizations such as the EU, we know little for sure about contemporary specifics in the Assembly. Western taxpayers largely fund the ICRC governed by the Assembly but know almost nothing about the latter's policymaking details. Rather than hold open sessions but go into *in camera* proceedings on sensitive subjects pertaining to protection or personnel matters, the Assembly now prevents even former members (honorary members) from having access to the records of its deliberations. Perhaps major donors are told more about at least some Assembly proceedings but that is not clear.

A   Some Basics

At the end of 2021 the Assembly had 19 members including the president and vice president. (There are term limits for Assembly members: three four-year terms, and a mandatory retirement age of seventy-two.) Of the remaining seventeen members, ten were males and seven were females. There were no persons of color, excepting one woman of Sri Lankan heritage. Given that some Assembly members had varied careers, it is difficult to definitively list their primary fields of endeavors. That is, some combined business with education, some education with media roles, some finance with politics, and so on. With that complexity understood, an observer found (more or less) the following breakdown: six had primary involvement in business and finance, five in education, four in medicine, and two in nonprofit management. To paraphrase a joke, in the Assembly there was much diversity, because there were many different shades of white.

(Toward the end of 2021, of thirty-two living honorary members of the Assembly, 22 percent were female. There were no persons of color, or from organized labor. One was Jewish. Other members of an ethno-religious minority were not evident. There were of course native speakers of French and German and Italian, as well as Protestants and Catholics.)

In the Assembly of late 2021, there were no professional diplomats (aside from President Maurer) although there had been many in the past. This fact might be seen as an effort to separate ICRC humanitarianism from Swiss foreign policy, but then the selection of the ICRC president from the ranks of officials in Bern created the opposite impression of close linkage.

There were no professional soldiers, although some had been members in the past. One might recall the brief stint of General Guillaume-Henri Dufour in the early ICRC, indeed as the first president, which gave the ICRC a certain status and credibility with states and their militaries. Then there was Samuel Gonard, a former Swiss army commander, who was ICRC president in the 1960s. The modern lack of military expertise might seem striking given the extent to which the ICRC focused on the laws of war and situations of armed conflict. One supposes it is hard to make a name for oneself in the Swiss military, leading to co-optation by the Assembly. That profession has not been prominent on a broad scale since at least 1945, although the official Swiss security policy is armed neutrality and a willingness to use force in self-defense. Swiss personnel occasionally participate in a UN security field mission, but not in any role likely to involve fighting.

There are no Assembly members associated with organized labor, which fit with the historical pattern that the Assembly was well stocked with business leaders but not labor leaders. There had been only one major labor leader in the Assembly some decades ago, Waldemar Jucker in the 1960s and 1970s. Some members had law degrees but there were no contemporary practicing attorneys aside from one or two who were really in business/finance positions. There had been numerous lawyers and law professors in the past. One contemporary member had extensive service with Doctors Without Borders (MSF), and a few others helped manage other charitable nonprofit organizations, at least two of these with a heavy focus on feminist concerns. There were no former high ICRC officials, although at least two Assembly members had served the organization in the field for a limited time.

Photograph 15.1 Modern ICRC presidents are usually drawn from, or close to, Swiss governing elites. Here, ICRC President Max Huber, who was also an adviser to the Swiss Foreign Ministry, bids goodbye in Geneva in 1941 to Swiss General Henri Guisan, key defense strategist during World War II. The ICRC has always focused on the laws of war, but only two ICRC presidents have been drawn from the Swiss military, and no military personnel have been on its governing board recently. Huber, a well-recognized jurist, turned out to be a controversial ICRC president. During his presidency the ICRC lost its moral compass. The same was true for his alter ego and successor, C. J. Burckhardt.

The last point is potentially significant. In the past some high officials had been elected to the Assembly upon completion of their professional roles. This practice produced an Assembly with increased expertise in relevant matters. From time to time some of these officials felt comfortable in challenging this or that development emanating from the professional side of the organization. (On the other hand, some of these ex-professionals were not known for activism or challenges within the Assembly.) Absence of ICRC former professional humanitarians in the Assembly weakened it, at least in theory. For whatever reason, Yves

Daccord was not elected to the governing board when he retired as D-G in 2020. (Some other former D-Gs had also not been co-opted.) By comparison, Jean Pictet, Jacques Moreillon, Yves Sandoz, François Bugnion, and Jean de Courten had all been co-opted into the Assembly, bringing their extensive ICRC professional experience along with them.

B   Selection of Leaders and Checks and Balances

There are two Assembly standing commissions of potential importance. One is on recruitment and remuneration. How much this commission operates independently from the president, particularly regarding selection of high officials including the next president, is a good question. One pattern is that presumably the recruitment committee checks with the president about a possible candidate for membership, to see if there is strong opposition. Sometimes a special committee is created for the presidential search. Even regarding election of regular Assembly members, it is not so clear whether the standing recruitment commission exercises full independence from the president who may want more personal supporters on the board. So one has the actual or potential politics of selecting board members, as in the business world. Some think that President Maurer exercised a strong influence on selection of new members but that remains unproven. Some believe there are too many businesspersons on the board, but that remains a subjective matter.

In principle the Assembly is always presented with a choice about the presidency. There was real choice within the Assembly when in 1987 there were two candidates and the Assembly selected the outsider from Bern, Cornelio Sommaruga, over the experienced insider, Jacques Moreillon. In 1998 when Jacob Kellenberger was selected, there were other candidates. In 2009, the Assembly formally wound up with a choice between the then-outsider Mauer and the experienced insider, Pierre Krähenbühl.

Conventional wisdom holds that outgoing President Kellenberger strongly supported Maurer, even though he had given Krähenbühl a key post at an early age, and a majority of the Assembly confirmed that preference. It seems that professional insiders such as Moreillon and Krähenbühl were seen by some Assembly members as being in the wrong "class." They did not bring an outsider's address book with them, and they might have known "la maison" too well for Assembly control over them. They were neither from the upper classes nor did they have status as Swiss federal officials. No doubt other factors came into play. Moreillon with his deep experience and systematic mind might have been perceived as threatening to some Assembly members. Krähenbühl was relatively young when he sought to move from director of operations to the presidency. (He became head of UNRWA dealing with Palestinian issues and later reentered the ICRC and was first posted to a sensitive role in Beijing, then to another sensitive position at HQ.)

When in the fall of 2021 the Assembly named Mirjana Spoljaric-Egger as the first female president to succeed Maurer, we do not know the internal dynamics of that choice. One supposes that the international context played a role. There was much attention to the transnational "me too" movement and its focus on women's equality. There was also considerable attention to the "Black lives matter" movement with its focus on racial equality. (It was surprising to some how much developments first within the United States affected international trends.) Within the Assembly, which was not unaware of these trends, there was almost certainly some self-generated pressure to choose a female – especially since the governing board was not remotely likely to select someone of color for the top post. It was easier for the all-Swiss governing board to find a qualified woman than a qualified person of color, given the social – including racial – composition of elites in Switzerland.

President Spoljaric had considerable international experience both at the Swiss Foreign Ministry and the United Nations. She had developed particular expertise in socioeconomic development, which related to the humanitarian–development nexus that was much discussed at ICRC headquarters as elsewhere. If the Assembly had been concerned to establish more distance from Bern it might have moved in a different direction, but for the fifth consecutive time it selected as president someone with connections to the Swiss state – even if Spoljaric had not spent her entire career at the Foreign Ministry, as had been true of Kellenberger and Maurer. In fact, Egger had had a complicated relationship with the Foreign Ministry and may not have been particularly enamored with how she had been treated there. One view is that her name was first floated within the Assembly Recruitment Committee and not by Maurer. But she had been on his staff in New York and was eventually supported by him.

The second standing commission of some importance in the Assembly is the audit commission, which has broader potential than the name might suggest. In addition to outside financial audits done by professional CPA firms, the Assembly audit committee is supposed to ensure that Assembly decisions have been carried out, whether financial or on other matters of operational policy such as the official strategic plan. This gives it a broad authority to examine and then refer almost any matter to the Assembly as a whole. How assertive this committee, and indeed the Assembly itself, has been since 2012, or even before, is not clear.

Photograph 15.2 In this 2023 photo, ICRC President Mirjana Spoljaric makes a point with Frank-Walter Steinmeier, president of Germany, who was in Geneva to give the ICRC an award for its commendable services. The ICRC had good high-level contacts in governmental circles, at the working level and not just for ceremonies. For example, the ICRC president met with the US president in principle every few years for a discussion of substantive issues. Spoljaric assumed office in October 2022, had to learn the details of ICRC principles and programs in the midst of the war in Ukraine, and was then faced with major budget cuts. Germany remained one of the top financial and diplomatic supporters of the organization.

We do not know for sure if there is an effective system of checks and balances that actually functions, and thus if the president and D-G face meaningful review via the Assembly or its Council. For recent years one hears about some "lively" debates and also about one contentious debate, and vote, regarding the ICRC and WEF in 2017, which represented an open discussion of the president's preferences. There have been other votes in other years, but we do not know how often or on what subjects. Other matters remain shrouded in secrecy.

The Assembly has the option of creating various ad hoc committees, not to mention the existence of a standing commission on data protection that has two non-ICRC members in addition to several Assembly members.

Then there is the Assembly Council, a body of up to seven members consisting of the president, vice president, and additional members chosen by the governing board. It represents the highest level of ICRC governance when the Assembly is not in session and has not pronounced on a matter. While its role varies depending on presidents and Council members, it is the locus of potential supervision of the Directorate. It has the authority to approve special budget extensions to cover events not foreseen in the regular budget.

Once the organization had reduced the role of the governing board in daily affairs (as noted it now meets bimonthly in principle), it had experimented with various administrative arrangements to provide governance oversight to the operational side of the house. At one point, for example, there was an Executive Committee of mixed membership, some from the Assembly and some from the Directorate. This Executive Committee for a time was the real locus of power within the ICRC, containing as it did some highly active Assembly Members along with some experienced professionals.

Now all members of the Assembly Council are from that body. In theory, the Assembly elects to this body its more committed and analytical members. In the past, sometimes the members of the Assembly Council might challenge or even rarely override a policy favored by the president. Such action required confident Council members. One doubts such actions occurred in the Maurer era. But questions could be raised and requests for further information posed. Some recent D-Gs have indicated satisfaction with the role of the Assembly and its Council, but perhaps that is because the members were not especially assertive or intrusive. No outsider really knows. Conventional wisdom holds that both the Assembly and its Council have been weak during the tenures of both Kellenberger and Maurer. Historians should examine this view.

Additionally there is an independent audit commission made up of professionals. It has broad jurisdiction to examine any matter affecting whether the ICRC is "in charge of its own activities." The ICRC does not lack for self-scrutiny and self-evaluation, from multiple sources. Still, the nature of the president, his interests and operating style, greatly affects the organization. At the top of the ICRC, there is at the end of the day a culture of consensus and compromise. Major and disruptive disputes have been rare. Persons resigning on principle, in opposition to some policy dispute, have been rarer still.

C   Mono-Nationality

In earlier chapters we noted that the all-Swiss nature of the ICRC governing board was a historical accident, or, if one prefers, the product of historical happenstance. That characteristic has been maintained, sometimes despite various national challenges from within the RC Movement rather than from states. So the highest authority in the ICRC has remained strictly Swiss, but this is not really because of a belief in Swiss inherent wisdom or other unique national virtue. No doubt there are those who believe in Swiss exceptionalism, in the sense of the Swiss version of a shining city on a hill. (Originally and during its early decades there was probably some Genevan exceptionalism at work.)

The all-Swiss Assembly has endured mainly because it avoids a major problem as at the United Nations where national rivalries can distort response to humanitarian problems or block action. In dealing with political conflict, all know that the ICRC will not be in gridlock because of national competition. And fighting parties know that an adversary or its allies will not be represented in the ICRC Assembly. The ICRC might have evolved more or less in similar fashion to the existing historical record had its top board been all-Swedish, or all-Irish, or all-Costa Rican, or some other leadership group in a historically neutral state.

The advantages of an all-Swiss Assembly have been broadly recognized, especially in avoiding inter-national conflict, and there have been no major challenges on that point since the 1940s. Disadvantages do arise from time to time but have been mostly managed since 1945. Chapters 7 and 8 reviewed some details in the Geneva–Bern relationship – that is, in the links between the all-Swiss ICRC leadership and the Swiss Federal Authorities.

From 1984 for a time there was a council of external advisers made up of prominent figures and experts in international relations from various nations. The creation of this body was perhaps a response, at least in part, to the charge that the ICRC before then was too insular, despite being part of the global RC Movement. That criticism had been articulated by the 1975 Tansley Report. Or perhaps the external advisors were created to offset any lingering criticism about the Assembly being all-Swiss.

In any event this council of external advisors, meeting in informal consultation twice a year, was allowed to lapse in 2011–2012. The conventional wisdom is that Sommaruga thought more highly of it than Kellenberger (even if Sommaruga might not have used it well, perhaps talking too much and not listening enough), and that Maurer followed in the footsteps of Kellenberger in allowing it to lapse. The Assembly could have kept it going but did not. Everything else known about the council of advisors is based on speculation or anecdotal bits and pieces at this point. There has been no public statement about its demise. One problem was that there was no institutionalized means of follow up, even in the Sommaruga era. The informal consultations occurred under

Chatham House rules, and that was the end of the matter. Or maybe the outside advisors were only presented with the details that ICRC officials were willing to share, which might had made meaningful advice difficult to generate.

D   Conflicts of Interest?

The Assembly is supposed to control for any conflict of interests among its members. These latter are supposed to declare any actual or potential arrangements that might conflict with the ICRC role. Lurking in the background is the history of the Assembly in the 1930s and 1940s when its President Max Huber had direct connections to defense industry firms in both Germany and Italy, already noted. At a minimum this was bad public relations. The way the current system is supposed to work can be seen in a recent example. A member of the Assembly, a retired Swiss diplomat, was asked to serve on an outside body that was charged with mediating the situation in eastern Ukraine. She took a leave of absence from the Assembly, since her involvement in political mediation could be seen as incompatible with the humanitarian neutrality of the ICRC. She then retired from the Assembly.

Some outside critics in contemporary times have argued that the Assembly is not properly policing its members and especially their economic connections. This criticism fails to persuade, at least based on what is known thus far, if one links Assembly membership to ongoing ICRC policies.

It has been said that one or more Assembly members have economic investments in Belarus, where political repression exists. But these investments are not likely to affect ICRC policy. If the ICRC is or is not active on political detentions there, or, as is likely, is closely following the situation to see if further initiatives would be beneficial, the Assembly has nothing to do with this type of grassroots calculation by the ICRC team in the field and its supervisors at the regional level or at headquarters. The Assembly is not normally involved in specific operational decisions in Belarus or elsewhere. One might question on individual ethical grounds whether an Assembly member should be investing in a firm doing business in such a brutal dictatorship, but as for a concrete conflict of interest with ICRC policy calculations, that did not seem to exist. The support of Belarus for the Russian invasion of Ukraine in 2022 did not change any factors on the present topic. Assembly members were not involved in any ICRC initiatives toward Belarus, or any that were discussed and discarded on the operational side of the organization – as far as any outsider can judge.

Also, there was criticism of an Assembly member whose investment firm was trying to raise capital for investment in conflict areas or fragile societies. But that course of action was precisely what the ICRC and the United Nations and other responsible parties were calling for, given that official humanitarian and development aid was inadequate to meet existing and projected humanitarian needs around the world. Lots of actors were urging more business involvement for "early recovery" from conflict and sustainable development, as already noted. No evidence was presented showing that the Assembly member got any special treatment or was deriving any untoward benefits by being a member of the Assembly while his firm was promoting business investment in fragile societies and conflict situations. Should one promote business investment in Syria under the brutal Assad regime? That is similar not just to Belarus but also to Afghanistan, and the subject of "early recovery" efforts with some inherent political impact has been discussed in earlier chapters, in particular Chapter 11.

Still further, there was criticism that an Assembly member had been involved in controversies when a manager in a foreign investment bank. Whatever those issues involving risk management and controversial loans to perhaps borrowers of dubious financial standing, and borrowers from the arms industry, there was no evidence that any of that had a connection to ICRC policy decisions. Maybe it would have been better for such a person not to have been elected to the Assembly in the first place, although his record showed positive attributes such as major charitable gifts – as well as, later, some controversy. Again, there was no evidence that his business or banking record directly impacted ICRC policies, as compared to a general evaluation of what kind of person had been co-opted into the Assembly.

In addition to the matter of any links between Assembly members and ongoing ICRC policies, there is certainly the matter of election to the Assembly in the first place. The history of the organization clearly shows a heavy reliance on businesspersons on the governing board, and one can debate the wisdom of this. It is also the case, as mentioned in passing above, that some members were elected (or remained on the board) despite the fact, and it was a fact, that their companies had been linked to misconduct such as price fixing in the drug industry, or pollution of the local environment where firms were located, or manipulation of the Libor rate setting the terms for borrowing among major financial institutions.

There were indeed business leaders on the ICRC Assembly that had held high positions in firms that had paid multiple fines for legal violations in multiple countries. Some violations were important, and some fines were significant. The subject of the nature of Assembly members over time is important but requires a detailed and in-depth inquiry that exceeds what the present overview can offer. There was some further attention to all this in the chapter on ICRC relations with the business community.

Every two years the Assembly is supposed to evaluate itself. There is no other body with authority over the Assembly.

E   Doctrine – Policy Guardrails?

In addition to approving the annual budget, the Assembly approves the general policies of the organization. Some of these make up "doctrine." Statements of "doctrine," or general policy guidelines, used to be a prominent feature of the organization. Such guidelines were considered the keel or the compass of the ICRC ship. Adopted by the Assembly, they usually were drafted by the professional side of the organization and proposed by the Directorate. They were intended to clarify and consolidate the preferred policy orientations of the ICRC and thus to insure the coherence and credibility of ICRC actions and attitudes. They were directed internally to guide staff and often externally to inform outsiders. In 2022 there were more than twenty statements considered to be doctrine, the exact number being difficult to determine since some had never been published.

Officially there were fifteen statements said to be part of doctrine and listed online. These constituted a rather mixed collection consisting of: (1) statements regarding basic mission and core functions such as protection, assistance, and prevention; (2) statements regarding particular strategies and tactics such as external communications, response to hostage taking, response to torture and ill-treatment, approach to violence below the level of armed conflict; (3) a variety of other topics including an article in a legal journal by Professor Sassòli of the University of Geneva (not a member of the Assembly) on the death penalty that apparently reflected the view of the Assembly. Some of these doctrinal statements were published in the *Review* and some were not.

As for general policy statements by the Assembly considered to be doctrine but regarded as internal, this too was a somewhat mixed collection, if one can believe various interlocutors. Why the official ICRC view toward human rights law should be kept internal, when the subject was openly addressed in the *Review*, as already noted, is not at all clear. It is not a secret that the ICRC today refers to human rights norms as well as IHL, and that subject has been covered already. The same comment can be made about general policy on the immunity of ICRC personnel from testimony in criminal judicial proceedings, since that policy has been openly recognized in some international legal documents such as the Rome Statute creating the International Criminal Court. It is not new or surprising for the ICRC to say, as it has in public, that if its personnel must testify in court about what has been seen, public authorities may – and probably will – block the organization from entering prisons or undertaking other sensitive action.

It is well known that the ICRC has opposed nuclear weapons, openly supporting treaties to that effect,[6] yet the doctrinal statement remains internal. Perhaps some internal subjects are considered to be either sensitive or technical, such as security in field operations, or guidance about headquarters agreements, or when to include National RC Society representatives in ICRC diplomacy. I do not discuss those, although it is well known that the ICRC will work with or bypass the local National RC Society depending on particulars. The subject of the interface between humanitarian action and economic sanctions imposed by public authorities is much discussed in open sources; it would be interesting to learn the basic ICRC views on that subject and why they are kept internal. In 2022 the ICRC issued a press release about Afghanistan, praising the UN Security Council for creating an exception for humanitarian work in the face of economic sanctions against the Taliban government there.

The present author is not the only one who thinks the subject of ICRC doctrine could use some housekeeping and updating. This view might even be shared by key players within the organization but who lack the time and staff to, in a quaint phrase, tidy things up a bit. A new Directorate from July 2022 and a new president from October of the same year may, or may not, change the declining status of ICRC doctrine.

Statements of new doctrine have declined in frequency and importance over time. Of the fifteen doctrinal statements listed online, only two were adopted after 2012. Back in the day there was a high official in charge of doctrine who paid much attention to the subject. But over time official doctrinal statements were seen as a bit old fashioned. Circa 2021 the matter of doctrine was lodged with the office whose priority was humanitarian diplomacy. Official statements of doctrine had become partially supplanted by the institutional strategy statements about policy objectives that were adopted by the Assembly in principle every four years (and discussed below).

In broad discussions about new policies with their focus on impact on victims/beneficiaries, there was certainly some attention to basic identity, roles, mandate, parameters, and general principles. But official new doctrine had become partially passé. It seems the controlling view in Geneva up to 2022 was that the world was complex, difficult to organize into definite and well- defined categories and policies. The Assembly had a brief discussion of doctrine circa 2015 but not much came of this, at least in terms of public developments. This is another subject that may be under review after the tenure of President Maurer and perhaps with the blessing of President Spoljaric.

Some humanitarian diplomats preferred a flexible approach to matters and did not seem overly concerned about clear definitions and conceptual or legal boxes. Peter Maurer was quoted in a radio interview in 2016 as saying: "Je ne suis pas quelqu'un qui est à l'aise dans les casiers, les tiroirs, les hiérarchies, le haut et le bas. Pas à l'aise dans la clarté. Je préfère les tensions, les discussions animées, les ambivalences."[7] (I am not someone who is comfortable with pigeonholes, slots, hierarchies, and high and low categories. I am not comfortable with certainties. I prefer tensions, animated discussions, ambivalences.)

Shortly after his presidential term ended, Maurer coauthored an op-ed with an academic in the Swiss *Le Temps*, in which he spoke about the changing nature of world affairs and how traditional state diplomacy was now joined by diplomacy by nonstate actors, with much attention to public–private partnership involving the for-profit sector.[8] The emphasis was not on classical diplomacy in the state system as practiced by the likes of Henry Kissinger but rather an arguably new diplomacy by new actors utilizing new arrangements. The view articulated might be less than clear, but clearly the emphasis was on change, complexity, and not classical categories of thought:

If the State remains the privileged place for articulating the interests of the nation, the inclusion of different components of society remains, itself, a challenge in view of the fragmentation of political action.... The more the separation of the economic, security, political, and social and cultural domains creates an unstable understanding of the hybrid reality, the more diplomacy should "lead from the middle"... and be positioned as facilitator of dialogue. (My translation.)

Whatever that means, it was not a traditional view based on established ideas and approaches.

One understanding of this view was that the focus was on action and results. Clear definitions and categories could be sorted out later. There might be dangers in this approach, as it seemed mostly transactional and not guided by set principles or policy guardrails, not to mention by precedents drawn from patterns of practice (and not yet codified in doctrine), but in any event official ICRC doctrine either had already been set or new doctrine was seen as premature.

To summarize this topic, there are three underlying reasons for this decline in new statements of doctrine. First, with over twenty statements of doctrine, many of the basic orientations have been established regarding such matters as core mission, or discretion compared to publicity, or conceptions of assistance and protection.

Second, and relatedly, particularly during the era of President Kellenberger, there was a push to make the ICRC and its policies systematic and predictable in order to enhance acceptability by other actors. Most of the fifteen public doctrinal statements were adopted or amended during the Kellenberger era.

Third, in recent years there has been much change and complexity in humanitarian affairs, as already discussed in preceding chapters. This is arguably not conducive to new doctrines on humanitarian issues that are clear and firm. The ICRC operates in a world of fluid forms of violence and with many armed nonstate actors of various shapes and sizes. An ICRC publication in 2022 reported that by comparison to 193 UN member states, in 2021 there were 600 armed nonstate actors of some importance globally, the ICRC was in touch with about 450 of them, with about 100 of these capable of producing significant humanitarian effect.[9]

Even in the past, it was difficult to produce concise and clear guidance on particular subjects. The doctrinal statement adopted in 2004 on ICRC assistance, when published, ran to sixteen pages, single-spaced in a small font. One could extract some clear guidance from parts of these statements, but most were complex essays that did not usually limit the ICRC in precise ways. They might indicate general preferences, but always with exceptions.

A classic example of traditional doctrine is the statement about public denunciation of violations of IHL or other controlling norms. A key section reads:

The ICRC reserves the right to issue a public condemnation of specific violations of international humanitarian law providing the following conditions are met:

(1) the violations are major and repeated or likely to be repeated;
(2) delegates have witnessed the violations with their own eyes, or the existence and extent of those violations have been established on the basis of reliable and verifiable sources;
(3) bilateral confidential representations and, when attempted, humanitarian mobilization efforts have failed to put an end to the violations;
(4) such publicity is in the interest of the persons or populations affected or threatened.

This part of the statement is clear and short, but the last point provides a "loophole" or escape clause that hinges on a subjective evaluation. In practice, the ICRC almost never believes that a public denunciation of specific norm violations will benefit victims/beneficiaries. It is difficult, if not impossible, to find a recent example of a clear and unambiguous example of such a denunciation of specific acts, especially involving a major or intermediate power. We mention this further in the Epilogue when discussing the war in Ukraine.

We discussed earlier what the ICRC said publicly about events in Rwanda in 1994 – namely, that the ICRC came close to calling the mass killings genocide but not quite. It called attention to the atrocities but without using the most provocative language available, and without saying exactly who was doing what. This doctrine concerning denunciation of violations of IHL fits well with the doctrine preferring confidential dialogue over public denunciation as a regular course of action. It also fits with the idea of staying close to victims (and thus not getting kicked out of the country).

To repeat for emphasis, most of the doctrinal statements in fact are lengthy and complex, with clear sections, but with much complicated language that does not much place the organization in a tight corner with no exit. The doctrine on use of human rights law is anything but clear and concise, if one can judge from related commentary. In essence, the ICRC might or might not refer to internationally recognized human rights. It prefers recourse to IHL, but it will sometimes use human rights standards depending on context and activity undertaken. We already noted the length of the doctrinal statement on assistance, and yet a reader is still not informed about the limits of that activity and what kind of early recovery programs are avoided because they overlap too much with political development.

One takeaway from all this is that the ICRC is essentially a pragmatic and flexible organization that is wary about boxing itself in with firm doctrinal statements that do not allow a shifting adjustment to changing contexts. Another takeaway is that despite the problems inherent in establishing clear doctrine as general policy guidelines, the organization in the past did become known for reasonably clear policies: focus primarily on armed conflict and similar organized violence, emphasis on discretion rather than public denunciation, active on traditional or specific protection as well as assistance and indeed a linking of the two, and so on.

III   The President – Selection, Leadership Style, Legacy

By comparison to Gustave Moynier who was active as president for about forty years and then his successor (and nephew) Gustave Ador who served for almost thirty, including a formal leave of absence, recent ICRC presidents have served about ten to twelve years. The current rule is that a president is elected by the Assembly for four years, renewable. Our primary focus remains on changes during the last thirty years, or approximately since the end of the Cold War.

A   Selection

The Assembly chose Cornelio Sommaruga as president in 1986, effective the following year, passing over the insider Jacques Moreillon who had held multiple positions within the organization. Sommaruga started his professional life in private banking and then held many positions in the Swiss Foreign Ministry. He held several positions in international organizations and wound up as a senior official in the Swiss Office of Foreign Economic Affairs.

He was a practicing Catholic with deep spiritual values. After his stint at the ICRC, among many other positions he joined the Caux Foundation, which earlier had promoted the conservative and anti-communist movement for social or personal moral rearmament. At the turn of the century and with Sommaruga in the lead, the once controversial Caux Foundation reinvented itself as Initiatives for Change, an effort to promote an ethics-based improvement in international understanding and cooperation. It continued to attract persons of faith with a conservative philosophy, including not only ex-President Sommaruga but also Christine Beerli, ICRC vice president during 2008–2018, who had been active in a center-right Swiss political party.

Also after his ICRC presidency, Sommaruga agreed to serve on a UN panel authorized to look into an alleged misbehavior by Israeli forces in the town of Jenin on the West Bank. This willingness to serve troubled some at ICRC headquarters who feared that his passing public judgment on controversial matters in that long-running conflict, which often inspired deep emotions, would cause problems for the ICRC and its quest for a neutral image. Perhaps fortunately for the ICRC, the role he accepted to play never materialized – for reasons that need not be covered here. Some believed the affair reflected badly on the man, supposedly showing that he did not always properly calculate the proper limits to his ambitions. Others saw nothing wrong with his willingness, having left the ICRC, to help investigate possible wrongdoing in the Middle East.

In retirement Sommaruga served on a very large number of civic society organizations and foundations. He displayed a strong and broad willingness to be active on ethical or social justice issues.

Kellenberger was selected to replace Sommaruga, no doubt on his record of recognized diplomacy as the highest professional staffer (secretary of state) in the Swiss Foreign Ministry and having successfully handled the complicated negotiations about Swiss relations with the European Union. He was seen as a man of high moral standing, dignified, interested in classical music, without hint of scandal or controversy.

What he might lack in charisma, public persona, or speaking ability he presumably made up for in careful thought, diligent preparation, and persistence.

While he accepted the ICRC position and served three terms, when he retired from that office he lost interest in RC affairs. Unlike Sommaruga, he was not active in numerous civil society or other organizations (but was active in a few). It seemed he liked his privacy and retreated into a relatively private life.

Maurer's selection to replace Kellenberger, again over an internal alternative (Krähenbühl), highlighted the importance of Swiss diplomacy once more. Maurer, too, had been secretary of state at the Foreign Ministry among other highly important diplomatic posts, which I review below. Unusually for the ICRC, he identified with the Swiss Social Democratic Party and had been especially close in Bern to several Social Democratic officials. No doubt it was noted in Geneva that he had overseen the office in the Foreign Ministry responsible for human security in Swiss foreign policy.

Given his retirement in the fall of 2022, it was impossible to say definitively what his record after leaving the ICRC might say about his values and interest in various issues. When he announced in the fall of 2021 his impending retirement the following year, he first indicated he intended to contribute to the activities of two small and relatively unknown Swiss foundations.

He was slated to become president and head of the board of trustees at the Basel Institute on Governance, an NGO linked to the University of Basel. Funded mostly by state development agencies with a primary goal of fighting corruption, it had a modest budget of slightly over CHF 10 million. He was also set to join an advisory board of the elea Foundation for Ethics in Globalization. This was a private Swiss group, led by a husband and wife team, promoting social impact investing consistent with sustainable development. His name by far was the most well-known on the advisory board.

It was also announced later that he would join the governing board of the Zurich Insurance Group, a high-powered corporation that was a member of the ICRC Corporate Support Group. The Zurich Group had a reputation for charitable works, and Maurer could have been chosen in a serious effort to obtain advice about business social responsibility. What critics saw was a crude trade-off: An official from the Zurich Group had been co-opted into the ICRC Assembly in 2018, and in 2022 the retiring Maurer was offered a handsome position at that same corporation, which no doubt enhanced the status of that firm.

Sommaruga did not accept any positions in the business world after his ICRC presidency. Kellenber accepted an advisory position with Swiss Re, a reinsurance company.

Maurer's announced plans certainly fit with his role at the WEF, as he continued to show interest in linking private investment to ethical socioeconomic development on an international scale. An op-ed in *Le Temps* cited earlier, mentioned public–private partnerships. And his Swiss origins continued to be important. He also agreed to be a Senior Distinguished Fellow with the Graduate Institute for International and Development Studies, a part of the University of Geneva.

B   *Leadership Style*

Sommaruga was quite different from the previous president, Alexander Hay, both in personal style and in seeking to directly impact a broader range of specific policies. Whereas Hay kept a low profile while broadly delegating and supervising (D-G Moreillon and Director of Operations Jean-Pierre Hocké ran the organization day to day), Sommaruga was more directly activist on numerous issues. As a contemporary of his stated later, he wanted everything to be in his hands. Sommaruga's first D-G, Guy Deluz, resigned. This indicated a clash of personalities, or frustration with the lack of clear demarcation between roles, or both. Since then, at least to surface appearances, the double executive system has functioned reasonably smoothly, with presidents and D-Gs finding a way to work together without major eruptions or disruptions. There is a tradition of seeking consensus and cooperation both within Swiss culture and within the ICRC, witness the Assembly rule of preferring to proceed without voting if possible.

While Sommaruga had a strong personality and came across to some as overbearing, he succeeded in raising the profile of the organization through numerous speeches and other public appearances. He carried the torch for NIIHA values. He could be feisty about independence from Bern. After the fact, he indicated that only once did he make a major decision for the organization himself. At one point he found himself under time constraints and had to decide the ICRC's policy on a land-mine issue.[10] On all other major issues his policy preferences were enmeshed in a web of consultations with the Directorate and the Assembly. Like Hay, but unlike Kellenberger, at least in his first term Sommaruga paid much attention to the Assembly, which during this time was attentive and relatively independent.

Photograph 15.3 Cornelio Sommaruga (right) handed the ICRC presidency to Jakob Kellenberger in 1999. The two had different styles in many ways. The former was extroverted and wanted most ICRC decisions in his hands. The latter was introverted and was selective with his time and focus. Both were former Swiss officials in Bern but both reinforced ICRC independence.

From 1999, Kellenberger represented a return to the low-profile style of Hay and clear contrast to Sommaruga in many ways. Kellenberger, who could exude relaxed warmth in personal meetings, was a shy and retiring personality who did not like, and did not see the point of, cocktail diplomacy and personal networking. He did not court the limelight as Sommaruga had but was known for tenacity in quiet negotiations on issues that interested him.

Whereas Sommaruga displayed broad – some would say undisciplined – interests and activities, Kellenberger was content to leave some policy areas mostly to the D-G. On other subjects Kellenberger played a major role, often after deep and careful reflection on the matter. He did share with Sommaruga a record of emphasizing ICRC independence from Bern. As already indicated, for Sommaruga this was a strategic calculation perhaps to try to lay to rest criticisms centered on the era of the Holocaust, but also probably because of a deeper personal belief in ICRC independence. For Kellenberger, his lack of persistent and systematic personal dealing or private meetings with Swiss officials may have reflected personal style. Both presidents continued as usual to deal extensively with Bern on official matters such as budget contributions and promotion of IHL.

In both cases, presidential power was exercised mostly in nonpublicized consultations with the D-G and Directorate. According to more than one insider, Kellenberger had a lower opinion of the Assembly than Sommaruga and consulted it less in a serious way.

Unlike Sommaruga, Kellenberger did not publicly reflect on his time as ICRC president and did not cooperate with any publications about his tenure there. Once he stepped down in 2012, he mostly left Red Cross affairs behind. He did serve on the board of the Centre for Humanitarian Dialogue, an NGO in Geneva cosponsored by the ICRC. He was also president of Swisspeace, another Geneva-based NGO. For a time he was on the faculty of a couple of universities. Contrary to Sommaruga, until declining health kicked in, Kellenberger did not exchange views with other ICRC alumni who continued to be engaged – and sometimes intensely so – about various ICRC issues. Kellenberger did not attend events at HQ headquarters after 2012, although invited to do so. He seems to have done nothing to burnish his legacy at the ICRC – perhaps being quietly content with his role there. And whereas some ICRC alumni who, when they moved on continued to manifest an intense interest in the ICRC to which they had devoted their primary careers, when Kellenberger moved on, he moved on. Perhaps he considered his accomplishments while in the Swiss Foreign Ministry to be his primary legacy.

Maurer, who became president in 2012 as strongly supported by Kellenberger, was a successful diplomat by any definition: secretary of state in the Swiss Foreign Ministry, head of the Swiss diplomatic mission to the United Nations with the rank of ambassador, elected head of the UN fifth standing committee on administrative and budget affairs, head of the unit on human security within the Swiss Foreign Ministry, and right-hand man for a time of Swiss Foreign Minister Micheline Calmy-Rey. He was polished in multiple languages with an informal and relaxed demeanor in public. More sociable than Kellenberger (who wasn't?), he avoided the bombast of Sommaruga.

When he surprisingly announced his resignation in the middle of his third term in fall 2021, effective fall 2022, a Swiss reporter, doing an overview of his presidency, noted that he was controversial and with more than one critic.[11] There was his role as a trustee at the World Economic Forum and in the final chapter we review some other controversies about his diplomacy. He had presided over the continuing expansion of ICRC activities, staff, and budgets, which had begun before

2012, but which some critics feared had gone too far or too fast and was changing the essential nature of the widely respected organization. Some critics thought he had cut the organization off from its past by: stopping publication of official ICRC history books, preventing former Assembly members from receiving details of recent Assembly discussions, and privately expressing little interest in or conviction about the matter of political prisoners. He seemed not to be aware of some institutional patterns, such as speaking out more about abuses in international armed conflicts compared to other situations of violence.

Such critics saw him as genuinely committed to his active and personalized diplomacy but not so much interested in continuity with the past. If true, this orientation would weaken a priority of Kellenberger, which was to make the ICRC fully consistent across time and space. More than one critic thought that his diplomacy was too compliant with the preferences of especially major states, rather than standing tough for humanitarian norms and principles. These critics contrasted him unfavorably in this regard with particularly Sommaruga.

But he had his outspoken supporters too, who believed he had led the ICRC through necessary changes in a complex and dangerous time. Some insiders believe his highly active diplomacy led to the organization being taken more seriously by many key players in international relations. Many seemed to like his pragmatic and well-informed approach to many international issues, seeing and valuing his advice. He certainly cut a respected figure in many elite or attentive circles. Throughout all the back and forth between critics and supporters, Mauer refused several opportunities to reflect on his record and explain his thinking more fully – at least until he gave several exit interviews in early fall 2022.

For reasons already outlined, it was difficult to say how much the policies at the ICRC during 2012 to 2022 were primarily or importantly because of the president and how much because of collective agreement on policy directions. It is well to recall a quote from then Director-General Daccord in an interview, already cited, that one should not personalize policy developments at the ICRC. This of course implies that primary strategies and major policies were the result of collective consultations and decisions, which was certainly the normal situation through the time of Kellenberger and including the era of the high-profile and broadly active Sommaruga. The D-G during 2010–2020, Yves Daccord, seemed in agreement with his president on almost all major issues, if one can judge from the latter's multiple interviews with reporters. It may be a fool's errand to try to specify what idea came from the president and what from the D-G.

It is relevant to note, although not dispositive of the issue of presidential influence, that the size of staff serving the president, vice president, and Assembly increased in size at a much faster rate than for HQ staff in general. In 2012 there were six support staff in the Office of the President. By 2018 that number was eighteen. In 2012 HQ staff overall numbered 814. By 2018 that number was 918. Maurer's immediate staff tripled during this period while all HQ staff increased by less than 13 percent.

However, in the president's office were staff with a variety of duties, some assigned on a temporary basis. How many substantive policy advisers were found there at a given time is not clear. By comparison there were staff who kept track of schedules and drafted speeches. Staff in this office served both the president and the vice president. For a time this office also was the home of the president's personal representative in Beijing, but this position was later moved to another office. The growth in staff in the Office of the President, modest when tracked out to 2022, was certainly indicative of more high-level diplomacy and outreach compared to the Kellenberger era. Whether it proved a more influential president in internal policymaking is less certain.

We do not know for sure the details of the recent decision-making process in Geneva unless and until Maurer and other key players decide to become more candid. There is the view, which future historians can research, that Maurer was more broadly influential than other recent presidents, but with a companion view that beneath his smiling and polished demeanor in public was an arrogant or autocratic streak that, like Kellenberger but more exaggerated, led to his not tolerating fools (or dissidents) gladly. As an experienced and touted diplomat, one who was in touch repeatedly with the highest national and international officials, it would be logical for him to manifest considerable confidence in himself, particularly in comparison to most Assembly members.

When, in 2017, some Assembly members challenged his being a trustee at the World Economic Forum, he did not take that as a warning or yellow light and back off but rather continued full steam ahead with his WEF activities. He did garner majority Assembly support on that divisive issue. It was said, but of course without definitive proof given the nonpublic proceedings at issue, that from that time he made sure that the Assembly contained an ample number of personal supporters and treated some dissident members in an abrupt fashion. But that is not yet a proven fact. It is doubtful that the archives are going to cover such issues.

According to some circles of opinion, all three recent ICRC presidents developed a sizable ego the longer they were in office – probably to varying degrees. Not only did all three have access to powerful leaders, but we know that in Maurer's case some of these leaders took the initiative to contact him and ask his advice about certain situations and policy questions. Additionally, all presidents have access to confidential information that is closely held even within the organization. All of this can lead to a superiority complex, although Alexander Hay, president before Sommaruga, seems to have resisted this danger.

The clearest example of an imperious or dominating streak in Maurer pertains to the WEF issue. While there might have been some early agreement with his D-G that this was a routine matter of humanitarian diplomacy, when attacks grew on the subject, Maurer largely shut down, certainly after 2017, and refused to discuss the subject further for most of his tenure. Within the organization staff members learned to avoid that topic. There is every indication that he was convinced that he was right and was going to continue to be a trustee, with various activities involving the WEF, and no concern expressed in the Assembly or elsewhere was going to alter his course. It did not help matters that some of the critics from outside could be perceived as shrill, demanding his resignation *and* the resignation of the Assembly en masse, for this alleged breach of RC Fundamental Principles and NIIHA values such as neutral and impartial commitment to humanity. A softer critique, raising questions but without such firm certitude, might have produced a different kind of response at least in terms of more willingness to explain. Then again, maybe not.

In any event, Maurer, after responding via one letter to his chief outside critic, refused to give any further response. Maurer also refused to discuss the matter quietly with other alumni or reporters, some of whom were not hostile or self-assured. It is alleged that Maurer instructed Assembly members not to be in contact with the primary critic of his role at the WEF. All of this apparently intimidated some sitting ICRC officials and maybe blocked a candid costs-benefits analysis within the organization about close links with the controversial WEF.

Later analysts of the Maurer era will have the advantage of more documents and the seasoned perspective that comes with time. In Washington, DC, for example, there are always those in the know who leak to journalists about who said what to whom, and who was an insider with influence and who was not. This is mostly not the case with the ICRC in Geneva, as noted already. There is a collective loyalty to the organization by most officials and former officials most of the time, not to mention binding nondisclosure agreements. Alumni may reflect candidly among themselves, but it is rare for those who hold or have held high office to comment candidly to an outsider about anything sensitive, much less to use leaks to the press to advance a policy preference. (The comments to the press about the WEF issue came from former, not sitting, ICRC officials about 99 percent of the time.)

Away from the public spotlight in internal policy discussions, was Maurer equally smooth and pleasant in his demeanor? That will be for historians, or maybe investigative journalists, to dig out. Rémy Ourdan, the journalist who wrote about the ICRC for *Le Monde* in Paris, wrote a piece in 2018 for a different source quoting various staff members who were highly critical of Maurer's internal demeanor and management style.[12] It seems pretty clear that as of about 2019, there was still considerable internal dissension about how he and his D-G were managing internal affairs. One summary view was that internally he inspired a mixture of awe, respect, and fear, while externally some saw him as manifesting impressive skills in highly active diplomacy but sometimes getting out of his NIIHA lane via his comments. That he was broadly active for the ICRC is not in doubt. I address later the view that he was not always sufficiently attentive to the image and impression created by his actions.

In sum of the leadership style of ICRC presidents, a review since about 1990 – drawing on numerous interviews and discussions – shows first of all that styles vary. Some presidents (Hay, Kellenberger) are more low profile than others. Some (Sommaruga) are more public – and ebullient – than others. But regardless of personal style, normally ICRC major policies emerge from a collective process of consultation among principally the president and the Directorate, with the Assembly as review body of last resort. Still, within this collective process, a president like Maurer was surely likely to be seen as first among equals.

Some presidents engage broadly (Sommaruga), some are more selective – picking and choosing where to focus their time and effort (Kellenberger). In terms of breadth of interest and involvement, and especially extensive diplomacy, Maurer was more like Sommaruga and less like his mentor Kellenberger. But Maurer was different from Sommargua in the latter's commitment to certain values such as organizational independence and a type of public criticism of fighting parties who violated IHL. Maurer was seen by some as being too compliant with state policies; one almost never heard that critique about Sommaruga. Was President Spoljaric going to be a feminine Kellenberger – substantive but low key and without public charisma?

C   Legacies

Attempts to define legacies are especially subjective. Sommaruga probably raised the profile of the organization and RC principles within the Red Cross world and maybe the attentive public – at least in some nations.

Certainly by comparison to Maurer, he was determined to emphasize the independence of the ICRC and lay to rest the argument that the ICRC was too much in the pocket of Bern. This may have been a conscious strategy, but it also reflected his sizable ego. He did not want Bern intruding on his turf, even as he appreciated Bern's support for various humanitarian concerns. It was widely believed, probably correctly, that he did not carefully choose his battles and did not concentrate his energies on major issues. He had great personal integrity and was committed to advances in social justice broadly defined. He was definitely fond of the limelight.[13]

It might turn out to be the case that Kellenberger made a lasting imprint on ICRC fortunes in three major ways. First, despite the terrorist attacks on the United States in September 2001 leading to various frictions between Geneva and Washington primarily over treatment of detainees, Kellenberger and the rest of the ICRC conducted themselves in a professional way that won the respect of US officials despite various policy disagreements. (It might also be the case that the United States was pleased with ICRC confidentiality, satisfied that the ICRC did not complain, at least not much, in public about abuse of detainees and efforts to avoid broad application of IHL.) The start of the final chapter revisits this subject.

Despite events and tense meetings, over time the United States remained a strong supporter of the ICRC diplomatically and financially. This was also in significant part because in the second George W. Bush Administration, Secretary of State Condoleezza Rice and State Department Legal Adviser John Bellinger maintained a generally favorable view of the ICRC as acting in the long-term interest of the United States, compared to powerful officials in Bush's first term such as Vice President Dick Cheney and Secretary of Defense Donald Rumsfeld. Kellenberger led the way in quietly challenging some US policies but without alienating its most important donor. This was an important highwire balancing act.[14] Did he tilt too far in avoiding public criticism of Washington? That is hard to say as an objective matter.

Secondly, Kellenberger may be remembered by insiders mostly for striving for consistency and professionalism, trying to treat all interlocutors the same – even as some believed that objective was not fully realized. Many doctrinal statements were adopted during his presidency with the object of making the ICRC known and predictable in mission, roles, strategies, and tactics.

Third, Kellenberger arranged for Peter Maurer to be his successor. Kellenberger early on appreciated Maurer's talents and had mentored him in the Swiss Foreign Ministry, but there is no evidence Kelllenberger looked over Maurer's shoulder or advised him on any issues after 2012. Kellenberger probably did not enjoy it when Sommaruga continued to comment on ICRC affairs, and he acted quite differently in his post-presidency.

If Kellenberger contributed to the image of the ICRC as a careful, thoughtful, and dependable humanitarian actor, his personal retiring style cost the ICRC something in terms of lack of prominence and expansive influence.

Maurer, by comparison, clearly raised the profile of the ICRC with other policy elites, projecting the organization into many policy debates – with considerable success but also some controversy. An expansive humanitarian diplomacy was probably his greatest contribution. But this had some possible downsides as discussed above and also in the concluding chapters.

Whereas Kellenberger presided over a modest expansion of ICRC budgets and staff, Maurer supported a much greater growth in ICRC action. This probably also had mixed results, discussed more fully later.

Maurer was generally seen in positive terms, witness the Geneva Foundation presenting him their highest award in 2022 – an award given to Kofi Annan, Sadako Ogata, and other international luminaries (including Klaus Schwab of the WEF). Neither Sommaruga nor Kellenberger was so recognized. We note other awards to Maurer by governments in Germany, Russia, and Kazakhstan. But for Maurer there were also intense critics.

All ICRC presidents in the last thirty years were smart and capable in different ways, and all tried very diligently to see that IHL and other limits on violent conflict survived in a harsh political context. There were no documented personal or institutional scandals during their tenures, which could not be said of several other international agencies and their leaders. As is evident by now, there were critics of Maurer who questioned his basic motivations and values, seeing him as fundamentally working to advance narrow Swiss and corporate interests and other non-humanitarian values. On these matters there were more theories than documented evidence. Some missteps, however, are recorded in the closing chapters.

IV   Conclusion

The topic of organizing the organization turns out to be not so boring after all, and indeed one can learn much about the ICRC by closely inquiring into its overall administration. The subject is continued in Chapter 16.

Notes

1 Jacques Freymond, *Guerres, Révolutions, Croix-Rouge: Réflexions sur le rôle du Comité international de la Croix-Rouge* (Geneva: HEI, 1976), p. 15.

2 Ibid., pp. 23–35.

3 ICRC, "Internal Regulations of the International Committee of the Red Cross," January 1, 2018, www.icrc.org/en/document/internal-regulations-international-committee-red-cross (accessed November 1, 2022).

4 Associated Press, "Pope Meets with Benedict's Aide amid Revelations in a New Book," January 9, 2023, https://news.yahoo.com/pope-meets-benedicts-aide-amid-123752795.html.

5 Dres Balmer, *L'Heure de Cuivre* (Lausanne: Editions d'en Bas, 1984), original published in German.

6 ICRC, "Nuclear Weapons," October 10, 2018, www.icrc.org/en/document/nuclear-weapons (accessed November 1, 2022).

7 "Entre Nous Soi Dit," Radio Suisse Romande, September 29, 2016, Rediffusion, October 8, 2016, 16h03.

8 Mohammad-Mahmoud Ould Mohamadou and Peter Maurer, "Pour une diplomatie réinvente," *Le Temps*, October 27, 2022, www.letemps.ch/opinions/une-diplomatie-reinventee (accessed November 1, 2022).

9 ICRC, "Twelve Issues for 2022: What States Can Do to Improve Respect for International Humanitarian Law," no date, www.icrc.org/en/publication/4610-twelve-issues-2022-what-states-can-do-improve-respect-international-humanitarian.

10 Cornelio Sommaruga and Massimo Lorenzi, *Entretiens avec Cornelio Sommaruga, président du CICR* (Lausanne: Favre, 1998).

11 Stéphane Bussard, "Départ de Peter Maurer du CICR: Quel Bilan?," *Le Temps*, November 26, 2021, www.letemps.ch/monde/depart-peter-maurer-cicr-bilan (accessed December 14, 2022).

12 Rémy Ourdan, "Suisse Monde: Le CICR est devenu une sorte d'agent opérationnel du WEF," December 3, 2018, https://alencontre.org/suisse/suisse-monde-le-cicr-est-devenu-une-sorte-dagent-operationnel-du-wef-et-des-entreprises-partenaires-peter-maurer-cicr-et-wef-sous-la-meme-casquette.html (accessed November 1, 2022).

13 For an accurate depiction of Sommaruga's ego and desire for control, see Caroline Morehead, *Dunant's Dream: War, Switzerland, and the History of the Red Cross* (New York: HarperCollins, 1999), p. 679.

14 See further John Bellinger III, "Observations of the 150th Anniversary of the ICRC," *International Review of the Red Cross*, 94/888 (Winter, 2012), https://international-review.icrc.org/sites/default/files/irrc-888-bellinger.pdf (accessed November 1, 2022).

16 ICRC Governance and Management
Part II – On Down the Line

> ... the ICRC's reputation as a leading actor in humanitarian action has been facing some challenges. Overcoming such challenges will require a more ambitious footprint....
>
> ICRC, Institutional Strategy Statement, 2015–2018
> (adopted in 2014), p. 11

Beyond the subject matter of the ICRC Assembly, its Council, and the Office of the President, there is much to analyze of importance. Indeed, the recent directors-general and their decisions about staff and technology – to be sure, taken in agreement with others – comprise topics of supreme importance for the organization.

I   The Directorate

It is instructive for understanding the ICRC and especially the nature of changes in recent decades to note major steps in management of operations during the terms of the last four directors-general: Paul Grossrieder (1996–2002), Angelo Gnaedinger (2002–2010), Yves Daccord (2010–2020), and Robert Mardini (2020–2023). The emphasis here is not so much on personalities as on the major management policies they helped develop. Also, my emphasis is not primarily on the management of particular conflicts (e.g., Bosnia or Iraq) or substantive issues (e.g., land mines or mercenaries) but on changing general aspirations and how the ICRC organized or reorganized itself to pursue those goals. Such an approach also shows which general trends in world affairs were seen as having a major impact for ICRC humanitarian efforts. I first note some general developments of importance during the time of each of the four D-Gs, then go into more detail on selected matters such as personnel policy and values, and digital transformation.

Breaking things down into set periods, at least initially, has its uses. But it is well to note what one D-G and another staff member wrote in 2004: "Within the ICRC, some variables have been 'in play' for three decades.

They are as relevant today as in the past.... What was an issue yesterday, remains ever present today, and while expressed differently, will likely be repeated tomorrow."[1] So we should not expect to find always fully distinct eras in management so much as recurring challenges and slightly varying efforts to respond. How best to respond to the changing needs of victims (or how best to offer services to beneficiaries), how best to relate to the rest of the Movement, and how best to adjust to new developments in global context are examples of issues that are not going to be definitively solved by one set of leaders.

The various institutional strategies adopted by the Assembly, as drafted by the Directorate in consultation with the president, are of some utility and are also linked to set periods (2007–2010; 2011–2014; 2015–2018; 2019–2022 and extended to 2024). They tended to get larger over time and become little booklets of multiple pages. They came to summarize a great variety of trends in world affairs rather than a few main developments. They built a wish list of desirable specific administrative targets. The strategy statement adopted in 2006 was three pages, noting four major challenges, with four major goals. The one adopted in 2018 was nineteen pages, surveying multiple trends in international relations, listing multiple general bromides ("navigate ... between principled action and pragmatism"), and indicating five strategic goals followed by over sixty (!) specific policy objectives.

From time to time their wording does shed some light on important developments, but these nuggets of wheat have to be extracted from considerable chaff. One has to know what to look for, or how to make use of the expanded wording.

A good reason for starting with the 1996–2002 era is that that was when the Executive Council, with mixed membership between the Assembly and Directorate, gave way to the Assembly Council, thus more clearly separating the Assembly from the Directorate. Governance was thus more clearly separated from management, at least on the organizational chart. Some in the Directorate during this era were determined to carve out a zone of professional policymaking.

However, to expand a point mentioned earlier, the president normally has a big footprint in both governance and management. For a first example, at the same time that the president was consulted about daily affairs and had some impact on the drafting of the institutional strategy statements, he managed the review of the draft strategy statements in the Assembly. He presided over the Assembly review of what he had helped construct. For a second example, before the Assembly adopted the doctrinal statement on the Holocaust in 2006, the person driving the process consulted several times with the president before the matter was formally advanced; the president then presided over the Assembly session in which it approved what the president had helped shape, even if most of the document had been written by a member of the Directorate. For a third example, in the Maurer era several messages to staff informing them of internal policy or administrative developments were signed by both the president and the D-G. Still, the modern ICRC management structure dates from that change from Executive Council to Assembly Council in 1999.

Directors-general shuffled the membership of the Directorate at various times. "Communications" might be a separate department or an office within another department. The reverse might be true for Information Technology; once an office, it was elevated to a department. New departments might be created or renamed. Human Resources might become Culture and People. Different offices or subunits might be put in different departments. The D-Gs had their reasons for this shuffle and had to justify things to the Assembly or Assembly Council. Whether any of this

Photograph 16.1 Director-General Yves Daccord, second from right, presides over a meeting of the Directorate in 2011. To his left and speaking is Pierre Krähenbühl. The latter was director of operations at an early age, was later given a sensitive post in Beijing, and under a third ICRC president was named to another important position linked to the Assembly. Daccord had a career of several decades at the ICRC, served two terms as director-general, was an influential figure, and then left the organization for journalism.

administrative realignment made a major difference in policy outcomes was difficult to say. At least temporarily it did create some added burdens, if not stress, on HQ staff particularly, as reporting channels and personal networks changed. In the Annex the reader will find the ICRC organizational structure published in the Annual Review of 2022.

These sorts of administrative changes were reviewed by the Assembly or at least its Council. What type of decision or policy statement or change in administrative structure had to be reviewed by governance was not always clear. Apparently Mardini drafted a statement to help resolve this ambiguity about what issue had to go to the governance level and what could be handled entirely by the Directorate. But despite repeated requests, that subject remained unclarified. What was a subject of sufficient gravity to require at least approval by the Council, and what was a matter moved along by the Directorate itself, remained unspecified. There was some invisible threshold of importance in play, but ICRC internal rules about governance and management left outsiders in the dark on specifics.[2] The ICRC could be very transparent, until it wasn't.

A   Grossrieder Period, 1996–2002

From 1996 one of the more significant developments, beyond changing the Executive Committee into the Assembly Council, was the creation of the second "Avenir" process. The first by that name had been in 1982–1984. It had been a joint Directorate–Assembly deep study, held outside ICRC premises, that took stock of internal changes since Biafra and tried to project ICRC policies into the future. The second Avenir was likewise a broad planning exercise, led by Grossrieder and involving almost all levels of the organization, in trying to anticipate and adjust to international trends after the Cold War.

Its concerns and themes had lasting impact beyond its early years: how to improve security in the field after fatal attacks on staff in Chechnya and Burundi and other places; how to better respond to particularly the economic needs of victims beyond core emergency relief; how to improve relations with, and the division of labor within, the RC Movement; how to expand services but not lose traditional ICRC identity; how exactly to utilize international human rights law in addition to IHL; how to mesh the views of field staff with systematic direction from HQ; even how to get more diversity within the Assembly. It was clear the Directorate, indeed the organization as a whole, was alert to and grappling with, important and persistent trends after the Cold War that challenged its humanitarian work. One sees in the Avenir process attention to a number of issues that would remain central in debates about global humanitarianism for years to come.[3]

Parallel to the Avenir project was the development of a more systematic and demanding budgeting process called Planning for Results or results-based budgetary calculations. Rather than base the budget planning on desired activities in general, there was an attempt to calculate the impact more precisely of existing programs so as to enable more precise planning for the future. The new approach required an effort to statistically measure impact on people (victims became beneficiaries over time) rather than proceed on general objectives and macro-statistical reporting. It had lasting impact in subsequent years, pleasing donors and eventually being accepted by staff despite more exacting demands for a different kind of reporting. Much later by about 2020, a critical view developed arguing that all the attention to statistical reporting was changing the nature of ICRC field activities and links to victims/beneficiaries, and not for the better in terms of staff's real understanding of humanitarian needs and policies.[4]

There was also more coordination with the UN in humanitarian endeavors, especially regarding budget projections. There was much independence in terms of field operations, but much joint planning between the ICRC and the UN's OCHA (Office for the Coordination of Human Affairs) and the IASC (Inter-Agency Standing Commission).

One aspect of the Avenir discussion received much attention by the top levels of management, namely how to expand activities so as to better meet the needs of those harmed by violence while remaining a humanitarian organization and not an all-purpose human rights or development agency. Internally, when dealing with an assertive president, there was a quiet determination to follow policy lines that were carefully calculated and based on professional experience.

B   Gnaedinger Period

During 2002–2010, while the Avenir process was evaluated and the first steps of implementation made, the Directorate had to deal with the aftermath of September 11, 2001. It was not unreasonable to think that the very existence of the ICRC and IHL were at risk, given the total war thinking of al-Qaeda and similar armed nonstate actors, *and* the extensive and brutal response of Western states who adopted controversial "counterterrorism" policies. How to devise the right humanitarian policies in this new dialectical situation preoccupied the leadership. It was in this context that the director of operations published a commentary, cited earlier, stressing the importance of NIIHA values – and thus reaffirming the ICRC's determination not to be co-opted into a political cause, even that of the Western democracies that were the main donors to the organization. Hence there was a determination to clearly reaffirm the idea of independent and neutral humanitarianism in its multiple forms. This positioning, or reaffirmation of its traditional position, was communicated to all relevant actors at multiple levels of contact.

In responding to this major challenge, the Directorate compiled a list of its major assets, which was not short. It then noted risks and challenges, which also were not brief. The resulting core ambition was for the ICRC to remain "the benchmark organization for independent humanitarian action."[5] This was followed by four more specific goals: to stay close to victims, to make an accurate understanding of situations so that operations could go forward, to use dialogue to clarify the ICRC NIIHA identity, which was of practical significance, and to combine consistency with innovation. These four goals were then followed by ten more specific plans having to do with field activities, global positioning, and resource management.

In general, the Directorate reaffirmed the traditional norms and orientations of the ICRC while trying to fine-tune policymaking in quest of improved performance. The usual pursuits were noted: better teamwork, better relations with the Movement, better promotion of IHL, better communications policy, and so on. Internally, on many issues the Directorate had considerable room to advance its preferences since the president was selective in his involvement and the Assembly was not given to ambitions of micro-management.

The intention to stay close to victims meant, among other steps, that there was a delegation of security evaluations to delegations and subdelegations in the field. Some ICRC personnel were attacked, being viewed as part of a Western organization, and so it became crucial to operations to have a clear understanding of threats to field work. Staying close to victims also meant zero tolerance for any behavior that offended local culture, such as staff contracting with local sex workers.

The ICRC wound up with more fieldwork during this era, but organizational growth was not a strategic objective. Rather than being a driving concern, growth was the result of evaluating changing needs.

C   Daccord Period

In a focus on 2010–2020, one sees new prominence for issues such as decolonizing Western based humanitarian help, along with the parallel issue of "localizing" international humanitarianism, which melded into older issues – for example, how to improve relations with National RC Societies and their Federation.

It was certainly accurate to state that the ICRC "has evolved significantly in the last ten years" as indicated in the 2011–2014 strategy statement. Planned budgets had gone from CHF 441 million in 1990, to CHF 1.052 billion in 2000, to CHF 1.175 billion in 2010, to CHF 2.16 billion in 2020. The projected budget for 2023 was CHF 2.7 billion. Staff had increased from an average of about 6,500 in 1990, to around 12,000 in 2000, to 12,150 in 2010, to 18,800 in 2020. (Numbers of staff in 2020 represented a slight reduction from 2019, due to budget deficits and budget cuts.) In 2018 there were 140 different nationalities on staff.

There was no doubt but that the organization was committed to becoming larger. As stated in the 2015–2018 strategy, the ICRC wanted "a more ambitious footprint," given the more numerous actors involved in armed conflict and other violence. It wanted to do something about the fact that its relative share of humanitarian action had declined on a global basis, with UN agencies and INGOs controlling something like 80–90 percent of the international response to conflicts.

It was not content to remain small, with what I have called a "canary in the mineshaft" model that was satisfied with warning others based on knowledge, flexibility, reputation, and key access to policymakers. It wanted to be a major player with major resources, presumably to do more good for victims. It is possible it decided to grow in size to convince donors such as the EU or the World Bank that it was worthy of significant funding. This both enhanced the status of the organization and led to more programming for those in need, especially regarding assistance. More assistance might mean it was sometimes taken more seriously regarding protection narrowly understood.

Given the great expansion of ICRC staff, based on expanded budgets and expanded interpretation of its mandate as already explained, during this era there was much attention to personnel management or human resources. A proper working environment was listed as one of the organization's strategic objectives for the first time in 2018. The Directorate adopted a "one staff" policy, breaking down the rigid distinctions between expatriate and local staff. Locally hired staff could now aspire to longer contracts and higher assignments, with a common pay scale and benefits. The term "delegate" was discouraged, since it implied special status for expatriates, and simply "staff member" was preferred. In the new terminology, there were mobile and resident staff members.

It was also the case that more outsiders were brought into middle-level positions, or even higher, at the Geneva HQ without having experienced grass roots activities in the field. Some of those with considerable public visibility or even a position in the Directorate as head of a department actually knew little about ICRC history or field activities. They had never been in a prison or had to negotiate with a drunken soldier at a checkpoint to get assistance to victims. Presumably the trade-off was more fresh thinking and expertise of a certain sort at HQ. If one wanted a more adept communication or IT policy, it might make sense to have officials with experience in that domain coming from other organizations rather than working their way up internally in the ICRC. More on personnel policy later.

There was also increased attention to digitalization, both in terms of trying to make computerized records and transactions secure, and also in properly managing electronic cash transfers in place of delivering assistance such as food. For the first time, digital transformation was listed as one of the five strategic objectives in 2018. It became a department in 2022 and thus had a seat in the Directorate.

D   Mardini Period

The COVID-19 pandemic altered the ICRC's operations across the board from early 2020, regardless of what was written in the relevant strategy statement. In the poorer countries of the Global South the organization broadened its structural or all-prisoner approach regarding on-site protection matters, distributing relevant materials (sanitizer, face coverings, personal protective equipment) regardless of the status of prisoners (conflict prisoner, political prisoner, common prisoner). Overcrowded and underfunded detention sites were a breeding ground for COVID-19, and the pandemic threatened the lives of prisoners regardless of their official sentence. Detention was not supposed to be a death sentence. Sometimes the organization did virtual or video prison "visits." It broadly cooperated with National RC Societies in public health matters without great attention to whether an area was characterized by large-scale or organized violence.

The existing emphasis on developing the right personnel policy for a larger and multi-cultural staff was continued and expanded. There were several surveys of, and systematic exchanges with, staff. These revealed some discontents and tensions. The D-G stated openly, albeit internally, that leaders were surprised by some of the alarming findings in the survey and were determined to make improvements. The Directorate responded by emphasizing not only the seven fundamental RC principles, but also extracted four core values that presumably staff endorsed as unifying norms: focus on impact, compassion, respect, and collaboration. These were to add up to a "values compass" that was to unify and motivate ICRC personnel at all levels. Special emphasis was placed on diversity and inclusion.

Photograph 16.2 Robert Mardini, here on the right, became ICRC director-general in 2020. Before that he was Regional Director for the Near and Middle East, where he helped manage the ICRC response in the Syrian violence of 2011–2022. Walking with him in Homs, Syria is Marianne Gasser, head of the ICRC delegation in Syria at different times. Some analysts inside and outside the ICRC thought the organization compromised too much in the Syrian conflict and implemented a policy reflective of too much compliance with the Assad regime. Others disagree. As director-general, Mardini had to deal with the Russian invasion of Ukraine and major budget shortfalls, among other pressing issues.

An experienced staff member, Jacques de Maio, circulated a "farewell letter" when he retired from full-time service. It contained a wonderful vignette of the old ICRC in the field when it was staffed only with Swiss, explaining the attractions of working for the ICRC and trying to do good for victims of political conflict in an era when there was little micro-management from the Geneva headquarters. But it also contained ample criticism of recent management trends. He sent the author a condensed email summarizing parts of his longer letter. No diplomatic secrets were revealed. The ICRC blocked my using it in this book. Yet the ICRC continued to employ him on special assignments to evaluate this or that program.

The old question of relations with the RC Federation and its member National RC Societies took on increased salience, as once again there was an attempt to improve cooperation and Movement coherence. If this effort was officially led by the president, parts of the Directorate, especially Operations, were deeply involved. They were the ones familiar with what did and did not work well in the field, or in other terms what had worked well and was perhaps to be replicated. At the same time, the Directorate was part of the effort to protect the traditional and specialized activities of the ICRC, which had allowed it over the years to build the reputation it had achieved as guardian of IHL and respected neutral intermediary. This required a certain independence within the Movement. This was analyzed in Chapter 6.

By 2023 there was also the matter of instituting budget cuts in an era of the COVID-19 pandemic, economic slump, and donor fatigue, but maintaining staff morale. Staff naturally harbored some insecurities about their future in a time of major budget deficits. Manifesting a funding shortfall of perhaps CHF 430 million in a 2023 budget projected to be almost CHF 3 billion was indeed a big problem.

II   Persistent Themes in Contemporary Communications

Looking back across the different D-Gs and their Directorates, this author was impressed by the constant, organized, systematic attention to changing factors in international politics and attempts to accommodate the ICRC to those perceived factors. If we look at major themes in ICRC public communications recently, an analyst might be able to make an interpretation about how the leadership saw the world in terms of changes and challenges today. Combing through the voluminous ICRC communiques during 2012–2022, I would say there are seven major themes that have preoccupied the ICRC leadership up to the start of the Russian–Ukraine war. Some of them have roots in the organization's activities that go back further. By listing them I give a snapshot of what the ICRC saw as the major challenges confronting the organization in contemporary times. These challenges have, as a result, structured the ICRC's policies as it tries to stay relevant to mainly armed conflict and other large-scale or systematic violence. I note just a few of the policy consequences.

A. *Multiplication of armed actors and prolonged duration of violence.* These factors, for example, have made the security of humanitarian operations more difficult to achieve. The ICRC must explain its role to a multitude of armed actors. At one point it was estimated that over half of ICRC activities occurred in territory controlled by armed nonstate actors. These factors have also led to more emphasis on expanded humanitarian assistance via types of socioeconomic development. Traditional truck-and-chuck relief has been accompanied by more attention to longer-term socioeconomic security.

B. *The importance of major contextual factors such as climate change and the COVID-19 pandemic as they affect the twenty major conflicts that have generated the greatest threats to civilians especially through displacement.* Efforts at intermediate economic security, for example, must plan for trends in climate change and also public health. The ICRC's programs on water and protection of habitat are now even more important than before. The ICRC has had to adapt to the global pandemic both through strategy (for example, a broad approach to detention matters) and tactics (for example, more use of video discussions and even video inspections).

C. *A tri-corned great power competition among the United States, China, and Russia now intersects with the preceding emphasis on terrorism and counterterror policies.* While there remain multiple armed nonstate actors capable of creating much humanitarian distress as noted in point A, there is now a much more evident great power struggle in play. US-led Western dominance of global affairs during the 1990s is under challenge. Great power maneuvers are big factors in conflicts in Syria, Ukraine, and elsewhere. ICRC policies have to adjust to these changed macro-factors especially by systematic engagement with the key players.

D. *The continuing computer revolution, or the increased digital connectivity in all domains, has affected warfare and indeed everything else of concern to the ICRC.* From cyber warfare to the electronic transfer of assistance payments, from collecting and securely storing computerized humanitarian data to limits on automated weapons, the digital revolution has a pervasive effect.

E. *Increased demands for a double or triple nexus, which is to say a demand or expectation that humanitarian activity be linked to development and/ or peace.* This makes maintaining NIIHA norms more difficult – but still necessary. One is asked to pursue a type of socioeconomic recovery after conflict but without getting sucked into political development. One has to respond to demands for attention to peace but without losing the status of neutral humanitarian. This can be done in principle, but it is difficult to do it to the satisfaction of all since concepts and categories of activity are much debated as of now.

F. *The economic side of humanitarianism has been affected by much state spending on security, plus public health.* The concern with global terrorism from September 11, 2001, then the disruption from internationalized internal wars in places such as Syria and Libya, and then the return of great power competition as in Ukraine has led to much security spending and hence more strains on humanitarian budgets, all exacerbated by needed spending on pandemics and climate change.

G. *ICRC funding remains primarily dependent on Western states.* One can search for more funding from and greater involvement by the business community, but so far the main financial parameters of ICRC have not changed. One option is more connectivity to other units in the Movement.

III   More on Personnel Policy

At some point in time the ICRC record for dynamic and accomplished field activities was to a significant degree the product of its delegates (as they were then called). They were almost always but not entirely Swiss (until 1993, but Swiss are now only about 20 percent of total staff, in some years less). Staff were always male (until 1963, when Jeanne Egger broke that glass ceiling).[6] Field staff were sent off with little more than a handshake and wish for good luck (more systematic training started in the early 1970s) and told to do humanitarian protection and assistance as loosely instructed and (barely) supervised by a more experienced superior. They were urged to be active and creative but also told on occasion to be prepared to be disavowed if they crossed some invisible line and got into difficulties. The technology back in the day did not permit tight and timely control from HQ.

The organization itself hyped the relatively independent role in the field of Marcel Junod in Abyssinia and Spain in the 1930s, for example.[7] Iconic delegates such as André Rochat in Yemen did whatever they did in the 1960s, and HQ found out about it later.[8] Many of these staff members considered themselves to be the real ICRC and took their role extremely seriously. Laurent Marti was typical of this kind of staff member during the Cold War.[9]

The amateur system of staffing – choosing Swiss males of good social standing but with no training – could occasionally produce controversial consequences, even if overall the system, actually an ad hoc non-system, worked reasonably well. One of the amateurs, Maurice Rossel, was apparently taken in by Nazi propaganda in 1944 when he made a brief and superficial visit to the village aka concentration camp at Theresienstadt (Terezin). He submitted a favorable report to Geneva, despite not speaking privately with many inmates and despite not inspecting many sectors of the camp, apparently not realizing how the Nazis had gone into elaborate and lengthy detail to construct a Potemkin village of happy and well-treated inmates. (He was accompanied by two officials from Denmark who did not report otherwise themselves.) In fact, conditions were quite grim, and many had been sent on to the death camp of Auschwitz to reduce overcrowding before his arrival. Some debate remains about what Rossel understood at the time and then reported, and it seems the Geneva HQ treated his report with considerable caution.[10]

With internationalization and then considerable expansion of staff, by 2018 – as noted earlier – devising a proper human resources policy became one of the five top strategic objectives of the ICRC. However, considerable concern about management of human resources or personnel policy dates back at least to the early 2000s, if not 1993 with staff internationalization, if not the early 1970s after Biafra with better training. There was a meeting as early as 1968, reacting to early problems in Nigeria, focusing on staffing needs among other issues (already mentioned several times).

Top ICRC leaders increasingly over time aspired to manage the larger and more diverse staff according to standard business management practices, albeit still paying lip service to the idea of considerable delegation of responsibility "to the man in the field" –including now female staff who by 2020 made up 48 percent of headquarters staff, 37 percent of heads of delegations in the field, and about 40 percent of field staff overall. Paying attention to distribution of posts by gender had been the subject of special studies and follow-on decisions. (Marguerite Cramer had become the first female member of the Assembly back in 1918, as already observed.)

But with internationalization and expansion, and with more supervision if not control by HQ, did the elan of staff change? How did the organization both devise a modern human resources policy for circa 20,000 staff but not kill the goose that laid the golden egg? That is, how can one provide an appropriate personnel policy for a relatively large and multinational staff but not stifle the creativity and dynamism and commitment to NIIHA values in the field? It was precisely that combination that had greatly helped make the smaller ICRC what it became, especially after Biafra. More bureaucracy in a larger organization, more reporting requirements, and hiring staff from other organizations on set contracts for specified purposes, was certainly a challenge for those trying to maintain an impressive *esprit de corps*.[11] If at HQ one hired from Microsoft or the Gates Foundation or Nestlé or the WEF, and so on, did this create problems? At one point the ICRC hired someone at high level in human resources who had helped develop the market share for Chiquita, the fruit trading firm, then worked as WEF staff. And if in the field one hired various experts on short-term contracts for water engineering or prison

Photograph 16.3 Delivery of assistance in South Sudan, 2019. Before budget problems forced cutbacks, ICRC staff totaled about 20,000, with some 130–140 different nationalities, and many local or resident hires as compared to mobile staff, who used to be called expatriate delegates. Proper personnel management across the organization became a strategic priority. There was much debate and rumblings of discontent.

management, would this not change the "soul" – or cohesion and *esprit de corps* – of the ICRC staff as it had evolved over the past decades?

A prevalent previous pattern was that one started as a lowly delegate in the field and then became a head of delegation, then a regional official, then an official at headquarters with important general responsibilities, with a handful of these eventually selected for the governing board. This was the pattern, with some variation, shown by Jean Pictet, Pierre Boissier, François Bugnion, Jacques Moreillon, Yves Sandoz, Jean de Courten, and others. The pattern was still personified by the D-G in 2020, Robert Mardini, who started as a water engineer and then worked his way to higher responsibilities. (He also started as a Lebanese and later became a naturalized Swiss.) For these types of staff members, the ICRC was not so much a job as a devoted career and matter of personal identity.

One can then understand the surprise of many alumni when in 2020 the ICRC advertised in Swiss newspapers, and in English, for applications for seven heads of department, apparently willing to bring in complete outsiders for positions of general and important responsibility at HQ.[12] However, in the new Directorate taking office mid-2022, as expected, the key slots went to experienced ICRC staff as per director of operations, director of protection, and director of humanitarian diplomacy (to use shortened titles).

It should be noted that the organization for a long time has used short-term contracts, to a great extent because funding was short term and it was difficult to guarantee long-term employment. If some ICRC staff in the field, mostly managed by the Department of Operations, advanced through the ranks and came to personally identify with the ICRC, others did otherwise. It was not unusual for a Swiss male to graduate from university, work for the ICRC for a few years, and then take a position in the business world – having his bona fides certified by employment with the respected ICRC. By 2021 the ICRC was asking donors to provide a commitment to about 40 percent of the budget for multiyear funding and not tied to specific projects, but the matter of short-term and project-specific hires remained. Donors liked to earmark their contributions for pet projects, whereas the ICRC needed the flexibility stemming from unrestricted and multiyear donations.

As for contemporary hiring, it helped that the ICRC could be selective. In 2020 it had approximately 35,000 applications and wound up hiring less than 700. Thirteen National RC Societies loaned another 139 staff members for specific projects, presumably drawing on experienced and proven national talent. The organization started a "values" program, mentioned above, or campaign to try to ensure that staff possessed the traditional commitment to NIIHA values.

The ICRC manifested an office, ERCO (Ethics, Risk, and Compliance Office), with a relatively large staff. The organization wanted to be attentive and even proactive, as well as responsive in a timely manner, regarding any ethical lapses or misconduct by staff. As of early 2021 the ICRC had avoided big problems of staff misconduct, certainly by comparison to the World Health Organization,[13] or various UN peacekeeping units,[14] or others including the UNHCR, Save the Children, and Oxfam.[15] In 2018 it revealed it had dismissed or allowed to resign 21 staff members over a three-year period, out of about 17,000 annual employees, for violating organizational rules.[16] Those dismissed represented much less than 1 percent of staff.[17] The ICRC code of conduct prohibits, for example, paying for sex, inter alia, even when on leave or in private time, and even where paying for sex workers is legal.

In 2020 the number for those terminated in that year alone because of violation of the ICRC code of conduct was slightly higher compared to what was quoted above for 2015–2018. More attention to staff ethics from HQ might have meant more complaints and reporting and cases.

Some might be surprised that alleged cases of corruption or fraud were reflected in the numbers, but the ICRC was, after all, managing a budget of over US$2 billion with many contracts signed at different levels of the organization with various partners. The dollar amounts lost to corruption or fraud in 2020 were relatively small compared as a percentage either to the total budget or other organizations. The subject of traditional sexual exploitation, which had plagued other international organizations, was miniscule. There were other types of harassment, and other sanctions short of termination, but those details are not necessary here. In general, the organization showed a broad and multifaceted effort to control for risks to ICRC operations and reputation. Major donors were informed of the facts so they would have confidence that the organization was controlling risks and problems.

An outside study back in 2008 indicated some tensions between the generalist staff member, often a mobile staff member (the old expatriate delegate), and the experts hired from outside for specialized duties. The authority of the former and his/her ability for general management might be challenged by the expert who, as in other organizations, might not think the generalist knew best what to do or how to proceed.[18] On the other hand, the generalist might be better at developing a politically sensitive "big picture" of the situation and its requirements. The 2008 study showed top-level concern with personnel policy a decade before it was listed as a top strategic objective.

Then there was the occasional situation when a former mobile staff member with much field experience was brought back into the organization to deal with some pressing problem only to find himself taking instructions from some new and allegedly ill-informed head of delegation or regional official who had been appointed to that position in part to satisfy gender, cultural, or linguistic objectives. One supposes this type of problem was not widespread, but broad evidence is lacking.

Reading the tea leaves, one might also suppose there was the problem that local hires, or nonmobile residential staff as now labeled, reflecting the local culture, might sometimes exhibit discriminatory views toward females or ethnic/clan minorities. After all, many non-Western cultures were not known for strong records on gender and other forms of equality (which is not to say that Westerners were unblemished in that regard). The global push for localization of aid and avoidance of neocolonialism in aid policies might produce its own problems. It was difficult to say how often the ICRC dealt with the "big man syndrome," whereby some local male was hired and promoted up the ladder but who then proved more haughty than sensitive toward those perceived to be of lower status. Or maybe mobile staff looked down on resident staff.

In 2017 a group of Swiss academics interviewed twenty-two ICRC employees then serving at HQ, being interested in the interplay of Swiss and global values among respondents.[19] Not only was the study sample small, but the duties of those interviews ranged from one Assembly member (who therefore was not staff) to various other positions. Other characteristics also varied, such as Swiss nationality, times served in the field, and so on. The significance of the study was limited not only by the small "n" but also the nature of responses: traditionalists bemoaned the loss of the strictly Swiss nature of the ICRC, internationalists did not, while pragmatists believed the organization had no choice but to become more international and less Swiss. The latter two groups did not regret that the lingua franca of the organization was more and more English and less and less French. Regardless of these differences, there seemed considerable agreement on – and commitment to – NIIHA values and RC fundamental principles, regardless of whether these values were seen as having Swiss origins or were simply the right global values.

In 2019 another group of Swiss academics did a sophisticated study of ICRC management policies, including personnel policy, based on seventeen interviews in Geneva and with the support of the D-G, Yves Daccord.[20] Noting relevant trends about increasing size and budgets and scope of mandate, along with internationalization of staff, the study looked at the ICRC through the lens of the standard principles of corporate management – with much attention to stakeholder theory. For the ICRC, this meant it should be responsive to the changing needs and demands of victims/beneficiaries, along with donors, partners, and conflict actors.

Among the numerous points made were the following that seemed important:

- field delegations will lose some autonomy, as it is HQ and its specialized service units that have broad vision as well as expertise;
- the maintenance of traditional norms and values is crucial to the continued existence of the organization;
- there are "high tensions" within the ICRC, as staff feel overwhelmed with reporting requirements and other changes, including a high rate of burnout at HQ;
- the addition of longer-term economic security programs beyond emergency action requires a different kind of planning, recruiting, and budgeting;
- contextual uncertainty, urgency, and insecurity make humanitarian policymaking different from most business models;

- about 80 percent of what the ICRC does is not confidential, and the organization needs a better communications policy;
- the organization should make use of social media analytics, which means deep analysis of social media sites in planning and policymaking.

One major takeaway from this study – and consistent with the present author's own observations – is that, as already mentioned, a current leader was right when he said openly, if internally, that he was surprised by various internal (and external) surveys showing the extent of concerns by staff. That being his view, he was determined to address the problems. The organization had already hired a London-based consulting firm, Pecan, that specialized in personnel management, and which touted itself as promoting diversity, feelings of inclusiveness, and creative productivity in the work force.[21] The fact that most of its clients were for-profit corporations, and that its sales pitch often referred to satisfied customers rather than victims or persons in need might not lessen its relevance to the ICRC. This personnel management firm promised expertise in handling rapid change in the face of cultural challenges.

The ICRC also, in cooperation with outside partners, created its own internal management school. In 2014 the ICRC entered into a partnership with Hult Ashridge Executive Education to create the HLMS, a Humanitarian Leadership and Management School. The goal was to create at the ICRC "a transformative and inclusive leadership culture" there.[22] ICRC personnel at various levels of authority can participate in various courses or modules, some online and some in-person, to develop various skills relevant to human resources – or maybe just to people skills or interpersonal relations. One can achieve a certificate or diploma rather analogous to a master's degree in administration. For those wanting a career at higher levels in the organization, participation in the HLMS might become a prerequisite (although to repeat, the ICRC was now hiring outsiders at relatively high levels).

At the end of the day, a larger ICRC, with more rules emanating from HQ and more input from regional officials, with more centralized review and supervision, with more statistical reporting requirements, and hiring from outside for specialized roles, is bound to be a different organization – namely, having a different organizational culture – than the old ICRC of, say, 1980 or 1990. The combination of internationalization of staff, expansion of the interpretation of the mandate, need for specialized experts, and communications technology allowing a greater role for HQ, must inevitably make some difference. Compensation levels were also reduced, so that ICRC staff wound up being paid less than UN personnel and more along the lines of MSF. This was a change from the past.

(For the record, the compensation package for the ICRC president in 2023 was about US$500,000. For the director-general, about US$300,000. For one comparison, the compensation for the head of the International Rescue Committee was reported to be about US$1 million. This latter figure is a scandal for a humanitarian agency but it allowed the organization to hire and retain a former British foreign secretary, David Miliband, as leader.)

The ICRC might still compile a better record than other international agencies in terms of staff morale and ethical behavior. However, for increasing numbers at HQ and in the field, working for the ICRC was a temporary job and not an expression of personal identity. Many employees came and went, both at HQ and in the field. They did not make a commitment for a lifetime. And all the rapid changes had indeed produced tensions and pressures. A perpetual and perhaps unanswerable question was to identify the right combination of guidance from HQ and regional officials and deference to grassroots knowledge in the field. Views varied on this subject.

It used to be the case that the ICRC was known for rapidity of well-considered action based on experienced and knowledgeable mobile staff in the field. This record is no longer so clear. In the war in Ukraine, addressed in more detail in the Epilogue, which also affected neighboring areas, the ICRC did not always demonstrate rapid, flexible, and well-considered operations. Sometimes it had the wrong staff in the field. Sometimes it was slow to sign up temporary personnel, and slow to provide financial and other support. Some believed that in Ukraine and neighboring areas, as in other areas such as Yemen in the past, the ICRC had appointed staff that had applied for the position but were in over their heads, rather than appointing staff that had proven their mettle in other major operations. Some believed that stints at headquarters, and the personal networking that went on there, had become more important than field experience in building ICRC careers. Set bureaucratic rules and regulations in Geneva might be hindering what was needed at local level, at least in nonroutine situations such as the outbreak of war or sudden increase in insecurity. Some messages that circulated on these subjects elicited no definitive reply from top officials and no identifiable changes.

Despite all the evident changes, commitment to NIIHA values seemed reasonably strong, even if proven experience in translating principle into policy was not as evident. A larger ICRC was certainly providing more assistance to those facing socioeconomic insecurity from conflicts. Whether anything much had changed regarding protection in the narrow sense is more difficult to say. Better protection does not necessarily hinge on more funding or bigger programs, or even general management skills as compared to knowledge of local officials and their policies – and the details in that domain are more closely guarded.

IV   Digital Transformation

Like almost all organizations in the world, the ICRC was adjusting to the digital transformation that characterized the modern age. If true that the Internet was progressively invented and computer usage became pervasive between 1969 and 1983, by 2018 digital transformation was listed as a top strategic priority by the ICRC. The subject of a digital humanitarianism was vast, and many of the relevant issues were addressed by multiple authors in a special issue of the *International Review of the Red Cross* in March 2021.[23] Chapter 13 included a section on cyber warfare, and there were other digital issues now in play regarding violent conflict.

In passing we note one episode involving the ICRC that showed the dangers of technology and then Internet-based social media. According to various reports, the ICRC's usual practice of meeting with various armed actors in and around Burkina Faso so as to explain its neutral humanitarian roles was weaponized against the organization. Apparently ICRC conversations in the field with a nongovernmental armed actor were recorded, then false stories planted in social media to discredit the Geneva organization. It seems some element(s) on the Burkina Faso side paid a tech company in Israel to plant false stories in a right-wing French online publication. Other sources picked up the fake story. Perhaps one or more elements in the state administration were unhappy with ICRC efforts at humanitarian protection. In any event, whoever started and paid for these developments, events endangered ICRC staff and activities. A private company seemed only too willing to spread false reports on the Internet for profit.[24] This sort of "fake news" was endemic to the Internet, whether for pecuniary or political reasons.

Certainly one major priority for the ICRC was protecting the data collected and stored in digital form by it and its humanitarian partners, in order to maintain the trust of victims/beneficiaries who relied on the organization for help in their often delicate and vulnerable situations. In this regard one of the ICRC's major nightmares became all too real in January 2022 when a technology partner storing data in Switzerland for the Central Tracing Agency was hacked, jeopardizing the security of some 515,000 accounts collected by the ICRC and sixty RC partners involving searches for missing persons. Some of the information about missing persons related to conflict situations and also detention.[25]

According to Geneva, this was a sophisticated electronic attack by unknown sources. The purpose of the penetration and seizure of records was not clear, as relevant digital systems were not frozen and blocked for payment. The ICRC found itself in the position of appealing to those who had done wrong to now do the right thing and not release to the public the stolen information. At the time of writing the information about families and the particulars of the missing person had not been put in the public domain. Naturally there was a rapid and intense review of the situation and search for improved data security. The digitalized portion of the program concerning "Restoring Family Links" had to be shut down for a time.[26] There was speculation that due to the nature of the hack, it was done by a state or other political actor with advanced technical capabilities. Very disturbing was the finding that the hackers had penetrated the ICRC data for seventy days before the hack was discovered.

Broad evidence from around the world raised the question of whether any digital storage system could be truly said to be protected against unauthorized penetration. Even government security and military agencies had been sometimes hacked, not to mention banks and other important financial institutions. All had tried to institute state of the art protection and security systems. The ICRC was left with the fundamental question of whether computerized storage systems were worth the risks to reputation and trust.

It is also worth noting, out of many relevant issues, the costs and benefits of some digital technology as applied to humanitarian assistance. Cash and voucher assistance (CVAs) through digital transfer became a growing form of help across the humanitarian scene, with the ICRC increase in the use of this measure rising 600 percent during 2012–2020.[27] CVAs were fast and empowering, allowing victims/beneficiaries to make their own choices about sustenance and recovery, among other benefits. Of course in some places traditional relief and recovery through provision of physical goods, not to mention cash payments, continued.

As with data storage, so with digital CVAs, there were risks. Data including personal identification and financial arrangements could be monitored or intercepted and then used for nonhumanitarian purposes – commercial or political. These risks can be mitigated but not completely eliminated. But doing nothing or acting slowly also creates problems for victims/beneficiaries. The ICRC on this issue seemed to be prudently adjusting, studying the benefits and risks, compiling information on its experiences, and certainly monitoring its service provider partners – that is, the private firms under contract who handled the CVA transfers.

V   Conclusion

This chapter and the previous one have looked into the black box of ICRC policymaking. Hopefully the reader has not become glassy eyed or laid low with a migraine headache. The author firmly believes the subject matter covered in these chapters will determine the future of the ICRC. That is, it is not so much what is written in IHL or human rights law that will control the organization and its future, although legal norms remain highly relevant. But if the ICRC is to survive, prosper, and be influential in world affairs, it will have to have the right policymaking structure, be led by the right individuals, who make the right decisions about topics such as size, funding, resources, relations with other actors, personnel policy, digital transformation, and other specifics of governance and management. Law does not implement itself, and neither do humanitarian good intentions.

Notes

1 Angelo Gnaedinger and Wayne MacDonald, "The ICRC in a Changing World: Ambitions, Assessments, and Priorities," in Liesbeth Lijnzaad, ed., *Making the Voice of Humanity Heard: Essays on Humanitarian Assistance and International Humanitarian Law* (Boston and Leiden: Nijhoff, 2004), p. 141. The authors write in their personal capacity while indicating that some of their views also reflect ICRC policy.

2 Readers can try to figure it out for themselves at ICRC, "Internal Regulations," www.icrc.org/en/document/internal-regulations-international-committee-red-cross

3 For an early overview see ICRC, "The ICRC Looks to the Future," *International Review of the Red Cross*, December 12, 1997, https://international-review .icrc.org/sites/default/files/S002086040009081la.pdf (accessed November 1, 2022). For a more complete treatment see ICRC, "The ICRC's 'Avenir Project:' Challenges, Mission, and Strategy," December 12, 1997, www.icrc .org/en/doc/resources/documents/misc/57jnwk.htm (accessed November 1, 2022).

4 Julie Billaud, "Master of Disorder," *Social Anthropology*, 28/1 (2020), pp. 96–111. Billaud was ICRC staff during 2016–2018, charged with studying ICRC communications. This article is highly academic, with the use of much terminology and many concepts that can be debated.

5 Gnaedinger and MacDonald, "The ICRC in a Changing World," p. 152.

6 However, a few female members of the Assembly were made delegates for particular missions, and as early as 1921 there might have been a de facto female delegate although she might be listed as wife, volunteer, assistant delegate, or some such label. See Brigitte Troyon and Daniel Palmieri, "The ICRC Delegate: An Exceptional Humanitarian Player," *International Review of the Red Cross*, 89/865 (March 2007), pp. 97–111, https://international-review .icrc.org/sites/default/files/irrc-865-5.pdf (accessed November 1, 2022).

7 Earlier I noted that Junod and his memoire, *Le Troisième Combatant*, may not have been as honest and reliable as pictured by Geneva, according to a critique by Blaudendistel.

8 André Rochat, *L'Homme à La Croix: Une Anticroisade* (Vevey: Editions de l'Aire, 2005).

9 Laurent Marti, *Bonsoir Mes Victimes* (Geneva: Labor and Fides, 1996). See also, for a more recent staff memoir, Serge Nessi, *Autrefois … L'Humanité* (Geneva: Slatkin, 2019).

10 The Rossel visit has been much discussed, especially by close observers of the ICRC and the Holocaust. For starters, one can consult Jean-Claude Favez, *The Red Cross and the Holocaust* (Cambridge: Cambridge University Press, 1999), pp. 43–44, 73–74. For one recent account, see Christophe Lamfalussy, "A Theresienstadt, une mise en scene des nazis qui prefigures le 'Fake News,'" *La Libre*, January 28, 2023. www.lalibre.be/international/europe/2023/01/28/a-theresienstadt-une-mise-en-scene-des-nazis-qui-prefigure-les-fake-news- (accessed October 18, 2023).

11 See Billaud, "Master of Disorder."

12 The departments listed were: Operations; Protection and Essential Services; International Law, Policy, and Diplomacy; Mobilization, Movement, and Partnerships; People and Culture; Support and Digital Transformation. See also the chart in the Annex.

13 Emma Farge and Hereward Holland, "WHO Employees Took Part in Congo Sex Abuse during Ebola Crisis, Report Says," *Reuters*, September 28, 2021, www.reuters.com/world/africa/who-heartbroken-by-congo-sex-abuse-probe-findings-2021-09-28/ (accessed November 1, 2022).

14 Skye Wheeler, "UN Peacekeeping Has a Sexual Abuse Problem," *Human Rights Watch*, January 22, 2020, www.hrw.org/news/2020/01/11/un-peacekeeping-has-sexual-abuse-problem# (accessed November 1, 2022).

15 Emmanuel Noyer and Françoise Duroch, "Sexual Abuse Perpetrated by Humanitarian Works: From Moral Relativism to Competitive Victimhood," *Humanitarian Alternatives*, 16, no date, https://alternatives-humanitaires.org/en/2021/03/24/sexual-abuse-perpetrated-by-humanitarian-workers-from-moral-relativism-to-competitive-victimhood/ (accessed November 1, 2022).

16 Susan McFarland, "International Red Cross Says 21 Staff Members Paid for Sexual Services," *UPI*, February 24, 2018, www.upi.com/Top_News/World-News/2018/02/24/International-Red-Cross-says-21-staff-members-paid-for-sexual-services/4951519520459/ (accessed November 1, 2022).

17 ICRC staff misbehavior is sometimes misrepresented, with the ICRC lumped in with other international actors displaying serious staff problems. See Scarlett McArdle and Christy Shucksmith-Wesley, "International Non-State Humanitarian Actors Outside of the International Legal System," *Journal of Conflict and Security Law*, 26/3 (2021), pp. 525–550.

18 Sowon Kim and Susan Schneider, "The International Committee of the Red Cross: Managing across Cultures," *Graduate Studies in Commerce*, University of Geneva, 2008.

19 C. F. Brühwiler, P. Egli, and Y. Sánchez, "The ICRC at a Crossroads: Swiss Roots – International Outlook," *International Journal of Humanitarian Action*

4/13 (July 9, 2019), https://doi.org/10.1186/s41018-019-0060-0 (accessed November 1, 2022).

20 G. Muller-Stewens, T. Dinh, B. Hartmann, M. J. Eppler, and F. Bünzli, *The Professionalization of Humanitarian Organizations: The Art of Balancing Multiple Stakeholder Interests at the ICRC* (Cham: Springer Nature Switzerland, 2019).

21 Pecan online, https://pecanpartnership.co.uk/clients/ (accessed November 1, 2022).

22 EFMD Global, "Creating a Transformative Leadership Culture," *Global Focus: The EFMD Magazine*, www.globalfocusmagazine.com/creating-a-transformative-leadership-culture/ (accessed November 1, 2022).

23 Saman Rejali and Yannick Heiniger, "The Role of Digital Technologies in Humanitarian Law, Policy and Action: Charting a path Forward," *International Review of the Red Cross*, 913 (March 2021), https://international-review.icrc.org/articles/digital-technologies-humanitarian-law-policy-action-913 (accessed November 1, 2022).

24 Cécile Andrzejewski, "The 'Masters of Perception,' Burkina Faso and the International Committee of the Red Cross: Anatomy of a Manipulation Campaign," *Forbidden Stories*, February 16, 2023, https://forbiddenstories.org/story-killers/percepto-icrc-burkina/ (accessed February 17, 2023).

25 ICRC, "Sophisticated Cyber-attack Targets Red Cross Red Crescent Data on 500,000 People," January 29, 2022, www.icrc.org/en/document/sophisticated-cyber-attack-targets-red-cross-red-crescent-data-500000-people (accessed November 1, 2022).

26 At the time of the attack, the US State Department issued a statement praising the ICRC and highlighting the dangers presented by the events. Ned Price, Department Spokesperson, "U.S. Statement on the Hack of the ICRC," US Department of State, www.state.gov/u-s-statement-on-the-hack-of-the-icrc/ (accessed November 1, 2022). This of course came from the state that had blocked the ICRC from visiting prisoners in secret CIA detention sites after September 11, 2001, where torture and cruelty occurred, and that had tried to hide prisoners from ICRC personnel at the Guantanamo Island prison, where a segment of prisoners had suffered various levels of ill-treatment.

27 Jo Burton, "Doing No Harm in the Digital Age," *International Review of the Red Cross*, 913 (March 2021), https://international-review.icrc.org/articles/doing-no-harm-digitalization-of-cash-humanitarian-action-913 (accessed November 1, 2022).

17 Conclusion
Part I – Summing Up

The ICRC was a small non-governmental organization with no muscle behind it and a library of conventions that had gone unheeded in the past.

Samantha Power[1]

Not your father's Red Cross.

David B. Rivkin, Jr. et al.[2]

It is easy to downplay the ICRC, as Samantha Power did in her award-winning book about the lack of proper response to genocides. The Geneva agency is rarely front and center about policy discussions in public. The organization does indeed often prefer quiet dialogue over public denunciation, and it often operates in the shadows based on discrete diplomacy rather than "sounding the alarm" as Power had wanted it to do – or do with louder voice – about atrocities in Bosnia in the early 1990s.

It is certainly true that the organization normally has "no muscle behind it," although in Somalia in the early 1990s it accepted some US military protection for its assistance operations, and in Bosnia at roughly the same time it accepted armed UN protection for some civilians being evacuated in a dangerous context. ICRC President Sommaruga lobbied for adequate military action to advance humanitarian causes in both Bosnia and Somalia in the early 1990s.[3] When faced with daunting challenges beyond its capabilities, the ICRC sometimes calls for the military muscle that it obviously lacks itself. And the ICRC does indeed push for continuing attention to international humanitarian law, no matter how much that law has been violated by both states and armed nonstate actors.

By 2022, however, when Power was head of the US Agency for International Development (AID), she sought out the ICRC president for consultations and advice. As another of her books indicated, it was one thing to crusade as a private academic and journalist, letting one's personal morality have full reign. That has its uses. But it was another thing to face the responsibilities of governing and try to officially advance humane policies in a harsh world. She became more educated in a practical sense, with a much higher regard for the ICRC.[4]

Certainly among major donor governments, if one judges not just by continuing financial donations but by the frequency of diplomatic communications, the ICRC remains greatly respected in these policy-making circles. True, most of the major donors are Western, but the ICRC is known by elites the world over. One did not have to introduce the ICRC to President Putin and Foreign Minister Lavrov and similar top Russian officials in 2022 at the time of the full invasion of Ukraine. They knew the ICRC and its leadership. Whether this made any difference in Russian policymaking in the Ukraine war I discuss in the Epilogue.

The preceding pages have tried to make their own evaluation of the ICRC despite the organization's discretion and preference for the shadows. I have tried to explain why Henry Dunant and Gustave Moynier would hardly recognize the contemporary ICRC, given all the changes that have occurred – including, especially, since the end of the Cold War. Neither Dunant nor Moynier advocated for the vaccination of cattle, as former ICRC official Yves Sandoz noted in a pithy observation. Vaccination of cattle and similar resiliency programs are broadly supported within the organization today as a means to independent and sustainable human security in protracted conflicts. On the other hand, providing cell phone recharging stations to migrants, some of whom may not be fleeing armed conflict or major violence, indicates a broader change that is more debatable.

Despite ICRC archives being closed for events of the last fifty years on most subjects, I have nevertheless done what I could to give a *tour d'horizon* showing a broad view of what are the major challenges facing humanitarian action in conflict, what changes have occurred in Geneva and the field, and what controversies have arisen for the ICRC. What is gained in breadth and timeliness in this book has not been matched by definitive depth, but then that is what historians are for (joke). Even with a certain breadth of coverage based mainly on interviews and open sources, some subjects have been given little or no attention, such as ICRC lobbying for the relatively new treaty banning nuclear weapons or the organization's demining efforts. This book has presented a snapshot of some major challenges, changes, and controversies as of the early 2020s without pretending to be comprehensive, encyclopedic, or definitive about these developments.

In a way it is accurate to say that the contemporary ICRC has changed so much that it is very different from "your father's Red Cross." But it is different not in the way asserted by some American ultranationalists who regarded any ICRC statement about US harsh policies after September 11, 2001 as biased carping from just another left-wing European bleeding-heart organization.[5]

When ICRC officials confirmed in public what had leaked to the *Wall Street Journal*, probably from the US side, namely that some US policies at the Guantanamo prison facility holding detainees in the US "war on terrorism" were "tantamount to torture," which was factually true, this confirmation provoked outrage among some on the American political right. But as President Obama eventually said, "We tortured some folks."[6]

Photograph 17.1 Two ICRC staff members discuss matters at the entrance to Camps 5 and 6 in 2014 at the US military prison at Guantanamo Bay, Cuba. The ICRC was present at this facility from early 2002 and came to have a permanent office there. By comparison, it knew about, but never received permission to conduct visits at, CIA prisons at other locations after 9/11/2021. From 2006, CIA prisoners taken in the "war on terrorism" were transferred to "Gitmo," where they were interviewed by the ICRC. Also in 2006, the US Supreme Court held that prisoners in the US "war on terrorism" were legally covered by Common Article 3 of the 1949 Geneva Conventions.

Nevertheless, some American uber patriots charged the ICRC with political bias in a departure from neutrality – and moreover with supporting terrorism. In a perverse sort of way this contretemps, which misrepresented the ICRC and the history of Additional Protocol I of 1977, showed precisely why the ICRC prefers discretion and the shadows. Speaking out on particulars often gets you charged with departing from neutrality and thus abandoning "your father's Red Cross" – a phrase that suggests that back in the day the organization was always rigorously neutral. Such charges about departure from Dunantist principles threatens what you can do by way of practical help to victims/beneficiaries.

At the same time, if the ICRC remains totally silent, it will probably be seen as complicit in violations of IHL and/or human rights as well as lacking courage, as per the early months of the war in Ukraine and issues about POWs. It may well lose control of a humanitarian discourse based on facts, leaving the field to "fake news" and distortions. Also, other actors, some well-intentioned, may move into ICRC traditional areas of expertise when there is much silence from Geneva. This, too, can be seen in Ukraine. UN agencies filled the void in the wake of ICRC considerable (but not total) silence about POW details. UN agencies published their own reports both about POWs and civilian distress in that international war.

Those inflamed by a self-righteous indignation do not extend much charity to neutrals, much less to those speaking truth to power – in public anyway. One of the many difficulties facing an effective IHL is that the law is supposed to be applied by the defender as well as the aggressor – for example by Ukraine as well as Russia. In the American case of September 11, 2001, most Americans were rightly shocked that much death and destruction among civilians was produced by the surprise attack in New York city (and also at the Pentagon). So some on the American political right saw the ICRC as very misguided when it (reluctantly) criticized in public the "shining city on a hill" and its counterterrorism policies. The ICRC faced demands for a cutoff of vital US funding, partially based on a distortion of the ICRC's historical record.[7]

With legal technicalities set aside for the moment, this affair in the United States shows that when the ICRC pushed for treatment of detainees that avoided torture and cruelty, and let that be known, however reluctantly in public, the organization was accused by some American ultranationalists of being another European advocacy organization, just another Amnesty International, rather than a unique neutral one. A self-congratulatory nationalism, often uninformed or misguided, is a persistently powerful force in the modern world – and not just when Russia invaded Ukraine. That inflamed nationalism is a big part of the context in which the ICRC normally operates.[8]

And so the ICRC usually flies under the radar in the sense of adopting mostly a discreet NIIHA stance on sensitive matters, remaining mostly unknown to the attentive public (excepting Switzerland, or maybe only French-speaking Switzerland) and in the sense of attracting little consistent media attention. True, some policy elites and specialists know the organization even if they do not always cooperate with it or endorse its policy choices.

It may also be true that ICRC discretion waxes and wanes with the times. Some believe it was less devoted to complete discretion in the 1980s and 1990s, particularly in the Sommaruga era, compared to the Maurer era. I think that is probably true, and I cite some examples in the Epilogue covering the Ukraine war.

Relatedly, some believe that in recent years the ICRC has been less assertive, certainly in public, in contesting governmental policies, becoming too compliant with governmental demands and expectations. Some critics talk about a policy of compliance. I think this interpretation plausible, but necessarily I leave a full examination to others who will have access to various archives. When the ICRC was operating in northeast Syria in areas beyond the control of the Assad government, and when that government objected to what the ICRC intended to do, was it true that the organization quietly deferred to Damascus perhaps because of fear that some of its other programs would be shut down – even though it was the Kurdish Democratic Forces that were in control of northeast Syria? There is a lot to discuss about the ICRC and Syria from 2011, which I already showed in Chapter 6.

It does bear stressing that discretion per se has never been one of the fundamental RC principles, and the practice of discretion at the ICRC has never been endorsed as absolute – witness Doctrine No. 15 and its mention of public criticism as permitted in certain cases. This reminder is timely, given that new President Mirjana Spoljaric several times erroneously mentioned discretion as a basic principle for the organization. Rather, it is a varying tactic in quest of an image of impartial neutrality.

That brings us to a review of exactly what has remained constant at the mostly discrete ICRC after the Cold War, what has changed that is important, and what issues merit further attention. What one finds overall is some change *de novo* but also a great deal of adaptation. ICRC flexibility lives on, maybe too much so, on some issues.

I   **The Big Changes: Systematically Expanded Action and Size**

There are two major changes at the ICRC as of the first quarter of the twenty-first century that are related: a broader interpretation of its mandate and larger size. The first is not completely new but rather reflects in part a good deal of incremental adaptation across time. The second is quite new if the comparison point is about 1991 and the end of the Cold War, which came with the collapse of the Soviet Union (capping declining East–West friction quite evident by 1989 and the fall of the Berlin War or maybe even the mid-1980s when Gorbachev rose to power).

To go beyond traditional emergency relief and do early recovery or intermediate socioeconomic development and do it systematically where security conditions permit; to get more deeply involved in urban violence short of armed conflict on a broad scale; to be more active on irregular migration issues again in a broad way; to take an "all prisoner" approach to humanitarian protection and advise on how to design and manage prisons, one needs more staff, more specialized experts, and a larger budget. The ICRC is indeed raising more money and hiring more staff, including specialized staff. For better or worse, or for better and worse, it has indeed met its strategic objective of having "a larger footprint" in global humanitarian affairs. At least until the unprecedented budget problems of 2023.

At the end of the Cold War, say in February 1992, the ICRC employed 5,940 persons. These were active in fifty countries. Relatedly in 1991, its total budget ran to CHF 236,100 (core budget of CHF 65,179 plus special funding of CHF 170,922 to cover field activities).[9]

In 2021 it sought CHF 2.3 billion for its activities in about 100 countries. It projected costs of CHF 2.7 billion for 2023. In 2021 it employed just over 20,000 staff members.

This expansion of activities and staff is well intentioned but not without risks. It probably now requires some stocktaking and trimming. This is especially so when funding fell short of appeals by about CHF 430 million in early 2023.

A   Early Recovery Assistance

Expansion of humanitarian assistance, which as noted makes up about 70 percent of the ICRC budget, to include pursuit of socioeconomic development – or a broad conception of human security – first of all speaks to one of the major criticisms of traditional humanitarian action: namely that it solves nothing in a fundamental or structural sense but is only a temporary Band Aid that has to be reapplied again and again. If one can promote longer-lasting socioeconomic human security in a reasonably sustainable way, then one has achieved something good in both material and moral terms. This double nexus, meaning better linkage (or overlap) between relief and development, is desired by both victims/beneficiaries and major donors. It has been endorsed by both the UN and the RC Movement. Specifics were covered in previous chapters.

On this point what we need are some candid evaluation reports indicating the results over time of ICRC resiliency or early recovery programs – also called development holds. Where have such programs worked or not worked, and why – say, five years after the start? Have they become self-sustaining so that the ICRC can move to only monitor from the sidelines? How often have they provoked a backlash, in that, say, internally displaced persons get ICRC help for early recovery but other persons in the conflict area do not – although also negatively affected by events? How many resiliency programs failed because of renewed violence in the area, and what was their duration while they were operative? How often were they undertaken by an ICRC that wanted to stay in touch with authorities and be "relevant" in future events, even if the project did not make much socioeconomic sense or have much immediate importance? Thus there was the matter of ICRC diplomatic positioning for the future regardless of the intermediate needs of beneficiaries – which might be better provided by some other agency. After all, if the ICRC retires to the sidelines and hands off a resiliency project to Oxfam, Geneva might not be perfectly positioned to react to a future crisis with close and favorable connections to ruling authorities.

On this first matter of expanded humanitarian assistance, there are some yellow flags. Is the organization attempting too much, missing opportunities to hand off to development agencies, public or private? Is the ICRC engaging in duplication, undertaking what others are supposed to do and presumably already trained to do? Is the organization getting sucked into political development schemes, working too closely with governmental planning that jeopardizes the ICRC's NIIHA values? In other words, does the ICRC calculate the political impact of its good intentions, or does it fail to analyze where its activities contribute substantially to the legitimacy and staying power of governing authorities who are actually hostile to human dignity in the way they govern?

Saying that humanitarian assistance in the form of early recovery programs is not political reconstruction or political development does not automatically make it so. If you help people establish a livelihood under a brutal dictatorship, that assistance contributes to the acceptance and stability of the dictatorship. Saying otherwise, calling it something else, does not change the facts. And this is precisely why the democratic West (or in some cases the semidemocratic West) has not rushed to provide generous assistance to people in Syria under Assad. The same is true regarding Afghanistan under the Taliban. Saving lives with emergency and maybe intermediate assistance is one thing. Indirectly contributing to the longevity of a repressive (and maybe anti-Western) government is another. Where is the conceptually sound position paper sorting all this out? In how many cases did ICRC economic recovery programs contribute substantially to the legitimacy and consolidation of power of political authorities, and how does one calculate that?

Conversely, does ICRC involvement in such matters as improving water infrastructure in an area for the foreseeable future, or supporting nursing schools and medical colleges, help neutralize the project and actually draw a government into better services for all, without concern for partisan, ethnic, or strategic politics? In how many cases can the ICRC show that its resilience programs have not only helped all relevant individuals into the intermediate future, but also laid a strong foundation for a dignified longer future with less discrimination and persecution?

In Afghanistan in 2022 the ICRC continued to help develop the medical infrastructure of the country, paying the salaries of maybe 10,000 medical staff and helping support medical teaching schools. There are benefits to many persons, but at the same time indirect help to the image of the illiberal Taliban authorities. If the Taliban are going to discriminate against women, should the ICRC see to it that at least they get competent medical care? Is that the controlling criterion for a humanitarian organization? If the Taliban are going to create a medical system based on gender segregation, and if that system is separate but not equal, should the ICRC continue to support it? If the medical system is separate but not equal but still meets the basic needs of women, does that merit ICRC support? And if the authorities do not allow female staff to work for NGOs, what then? (At the time of writing in 2023, ICRC female staff continued to quietly operate under Taliban rule in Afghanistan, with the knowledge of relatively pragmatic Talib governmental personnel in Kabul, but with uncertain status and future given the opaque decision-making of top Talib religious authorities located in the area of Kandahar. This was discussed at the end of Chapter 11.)

In parts of Africa the ICRC is helping develop water and sanitation infrastructure with a time frame of twenty-five years; this helps numerous persons on an equal basis but lends a positive image to local authorities. How does one sort out the costs and benefits involved in helping persons but bucking up ruling authorities who may be less than praiseworthy?

We need more clear and objective studies on all this. Maybe they exist internally at ICRC headquarters. If so, they need to be made public. It seems sometimes the ICRC commissions outside experts to do independent studies. If the organization has good studies on the problem of humanitarian intent for resiliency programs that lead to a large political impact in partisan or strategic politics, these should be made public.

A major step forward would be an ICRC publication that shows clearly what the ICRC rejected doing in terms of expanded assistance aka early recovery programs, and why, in discussion of concrete cases. How many times did the ICRC reject a proposed project for lack of capability, or for lack of neutrality – aka too much political impact? That would show something about the elusive and complex boundary between presumably neutral humanitarian resiliency efforts and more conventional political development programs designed in part to advance governmental interests. I asked repeatedly for such studies but was never able to obtain them. I had the impression that some (many?) ICRC officials were interested in doing good and not terribly concerned about limits in accord with NIIHA values. I had the impression that some key ICRC officials in this domain were very well intentioned but not terribly conceptual. After all, every humanitarian action had some political dimension, did it not? At the end of the day, what has happened to the old ICRC maxim that ICRC long-term success is based on knowing its limits?

After repeated inquiries on this subject I was told the following: "Finally, in response to your more comprehensive research question regarding the limits to the ICRC's activities in various areas, this clearly is not an exact science but requires complex assessments in light not only of our humanitarian mandate, but also of operational, budgetary, security and other institutional and contextual factors, as well as the constantly evolving humanitarian landscape as a whole." This tells me that the ICRC has no clear conception of the double nexus or maybe that this particular person has no clear vision or definition. I do not know if the response was personal or the result of internal consultation. I have been told by some who would know that ICRC resiliency programming is all practice and no theory. If those in the field get no clear guidance concerning what works and what doesn't, what should be prioritized and what is marginal?

Later some higher-ups conveyed a couple of basic points. As said years ago by D-G Yves Daccord, the ICRC is driven by what beneficiaries need for a life with some dignity, not to try to transform society according to some development plan adopted by authorities. (Some high officials dislike the term development, double nexus, or even development holds used by President Maurer.) The organization does reject some resiliency programs because of security problems or because of lack of its own capacity to implement the proposed plan. It seems it turned down participation in a World Bank funded program in Yemen directed to improving education. At more or less the same time it joined the Bank and UNICEF on a program to enhance water security there, reflecting a "layered" combination of humanitarian and development concerns.[10] It does insist that the program be impartial and neutral, not giving preferential treatment to some faction favored by local authorities. Beyond these core points, there remains much variation regarding ICRC early recovery programs. It may be that much still depends on whether the head of delegation someplace is assertive, seeking to develop early recovery programs with the support of experts from the HQ economic security unit, or whether he or she is more passive. The economic security unit seems to be not always well integrated with the Operations Department.

B   Lower-Level Urban Violence and Migration

Development holds are not always separate from situations of low-level urban violence or migration, but sometimes they are. As for ICRC expanded activity in such urban violence below the level of armed conflict, one can understand the organization's desire to get involved. As argued by Geneva, there is much urban violence affecting many in a serious way. But each case tends to be different, making general conclusions difficult.

Take Haiti, for example. In Port-au-Prince, Haiti, the ICRC in the 2000s was doing mainly its traditional prison visits. After several years it concluded that (a) its reporting and recommendations were having slight effect due to lack of proper governmental support and response in a chaotic context, and (b) the UN might manifest better prospects for making beneficial change. After withdrawing from Haiti, later the ICRC was asked by the Haitian Red Cross and others to return. So the ICRC resumed its protection efforts given the terrible situation in prisons there.

It then expanded its operations somewhat in conditions of real anarchy with armed gangs running rampant. Effective government had collapsed in much of the nation. The ICRC was trying to employ its traditional skills, making contact with armed groups, sometimes via yet another third party, in order to, for example, make the delivery of traditional emergency relief secure to blighted and lawless areas. It had done something similar in Rio de Janeiro, Brazil and other cities. Such action did benefit a large number of urban civilians. In the view of some ICRC staff, Haiti by 2021 was really a situation of armed conflict, with violence among armed gangs affecting millions. In Port-au-Prince, the area of Cité Soleil alone contained more than 1.5 million endangered persons.

Again there were yellow flags of caution. Beyond Haiti, why was the ICRC leading so many meetings with the urban police about human rights law when there were other organizations well known for their expertise on human rights, or perhaps even prison affairs? Was it truly the case that it was only the ICRC that had the right reputation and acceptance with both authorities and armed groups? Had the ICRC strayed too far from its focus on armed conflict and similar large-scale violence? After all, NGO status and influence stem from real expertise. Did the ICRC really have that expertise concerning police use of force in urban settings?

Had the organization stretched itself too thin for effective action? After all, the population of Karachi, Pakistan, where the ICRC was active, was about 15 million, that of Lagos, Nigeria 17 million. Was the ICRC role a mere drop in a very large bucket, meaning that its resources ought to be focused elsewhere? After all, more resources could have been directed to civilian need in Nagorno-Karabakh or Ukraine and other situations affected by international armed conflicts. What was lacking in areas of urban dysfunction and violence was provision of proper municipal services. The ICRC was never going to be able to fill that need. And there were already literally hundreds of NGOs trying to provide humanitarian assistance in places such as Port-au-Prince. On the other hand, as with development holds, the ICRC had proceeded slowly, over many years, with test cases, and making evaluations along the way as it developed a general program or focus.

Where were the truly objective evaluations of urban humanitarian roles? We could use more studies, or maybe more publication of existing ICRC internal studies. Was the inside joke true: the work in Rio was a great success and never to be repeated. It was too costly and not sustainable on a large scale. Were these operations in the Western Hemisphere – Haiti and a few other places excepted – undertaken because of the lack of big armed conflicts and thus the need to do something to justify one's existence? Did one wind up paying for some funerals among the urban poor caught in the crossfire but having little impact on the overall situation? If the point of ICRC action was to serve as an intermediary between governmental authorities and various gangs and/or drug cartels, what happens to ICRC neutrality in that kind of conflict? If the ICRC was acting to protect education and keep kids in school, and thus undercut the appeal of gangs and their violence, that was really not a neutral stance among the conflicting parties. Should the ICRC aspire to neutrality when dealing with gang warfare interlaced with illegal drug trafficking? What happens to ICRC neutrality when dealing with armed criminal elements violating domestic/national law?

Photograph 17.2 In Karachi, Pakistan, as captured in this photo from 2016, the ICRC tried to improve the movement of all ambulances, whose transport of patients to hospitals was often impeded by armed groups and indeed by lack of respect from the local population. Whether the ICRC should be trying to solve this kind of problem in large urban areas was a matter of debate.

The subject of more ICRC activity regarding migration presents a similar picture. Global irregular or unofficial migration was both a political and humanitarian problem of major proportions. Many people on the move outside of legal migration procedures found themselves in dire straits. One of the telling snapshots of the situation was to be found in Libya, a major waystation between sub-Saharan Africa and Europe. The North African country was itself in disarray without a strong central government – or sometimes any functioning central government. Migrants trying to reach Europe often found themselves intercepted, detained, used for forced labor, extorted, mistreated, and sometimes killed. Detention centers were sometimes run by brutal figures linked to criminal elements. The ICRC was surely right to try to use its experience in detention matters to do the good it could, especially since Libya itself was plagued by periodic large-scale violence during and after 2011. The ICRC did manage to negotiate access to certain places of detention and did carry out a broad humanitarian diplomacy on the subject with Libyan, European, and other officials.

Other aspects of ICRC involvement on the topic of irregular migration raised familiar questions. When active along migratory routes in Central America, for example, was it really the ICRC proper role to provide various services along the way pertaining to cell phone links and other socioeconomic services? There was no large-scale violent conflict in the area. Were not these socioeconomic services the primary responsibility of various national RC societies along with their Federation based in Geneva? Was the ICRC drawn into this activity because of a desire to be a good team player within the RC Movement? If so, what were the limits to ICRC activity? What was the division of labor within the Movement?

This type of ICRC activity regarding migration seems less justified than working on detention in violence-prone Libya, and it may be undergoing a downsizing. In other places beyond Central America, as also in East Africa, the ICRC found itself working on migration issues having nothing to do with large-scale violence or detention, but rather helping families locate relatives who had left home searching for a better job. No doubt some unit in the RC network could be helpful, but what were the limits to ICRC activity? Was it indeed losing its focus and core identity by spreading itself so broadly? We need objective studies on that, but for now I suspect the organization could use more focus and reduce mission creep. Being more of a team player within the Movement, and supporting sprawling National Society activity, tends to erase traditional limits in ICRC activity. The critics are right about this.

On ICRC roles concerning low-level urban violence and also irregular migration, not to mention so-called crisis development, given the rapid growth in 2012–2022, maybe it was time for serious reevaluation and trimming. Maybe there had been so much innovation and growth, in only a decade, that it was time for the classic "agonizing reappraisal." Maybe the budget crisis of 2023 would force this debate to the forefront.

C   Prisoners

If one talks to enough persons in Geneva, one might get the impression that the ICRC has become a global prison inspector, manager, and advisor. In numerous places around the world the ICRC was highly active on detention matters, taking an all-prisoners approach. This trend was pushed along by the Covid-19 pandemic. Rather than just focusing on conflict and political prisoners, the ICRC sometimes was trying to help prison authorities and all prisoners in general. In addition to referring to the hard and soft law on human rights (diplomatic agreements plus binding treaties and other obligatory documents), the ICRC was conducting meetings with judicial authorities about due process.

Photograph 17.3 An ICRC staff member speaks with detainees in El Salvador, 2014. The ICRC often adopted an "all-prisoner" approach to its protection activities, trying to improve the overall situation regardless of legal distinctions among common prisoners, conflict prisoners, and political prisoners. It often consulted extensively with those who designed and built prisons, as well as with the juridical authorities that supervised application of the law to prisons and prisoners.

It was clearly the case that the ICRC, even with the expansion of socioeconomic assistance, had not forgotten about humanitarian protection in the narrow sense of detention conditions, restoring family links for prisoners, and similar actions such as following up on released prisoners and their integration into civil society. The organization utilized modern technology such as video links when relevant.

An all-prisoners approach had a long history in ICRC practice; it was not really a new phenomenon. In Rwanda after the 1994 genocide the ICRC helped build prisons to alleviate severe overcrowding in that collapsed state. Even before then, the decision had been taken at various levels of the organization to move beyond a strict focus on conflict and political prisoners either (1) as a way to get to see the conflict or political prisoners eventually, or (2) because the conflict or political detainees were actually better treated than the common prisoners – and the plight of the latter was dire. In any event what was going on now was not totally new, except in frequency and scale. Once again there was adaption and broad application of something that dated way back in bits and pieces.

On this subject one is not sure about the existence of yellow flags because the subject is indeed shadowy for outsiders. One factor that can be noted is not so shadowy – namely, that the more the ICRC can present itself in a positive way, and provide material and ideational help to authorities, the more its comments regarding treatment of conflict and political prisoners might be seriously considered. No one likes a perpetual nag who has nothing positive to offer. Moreover, those in the comfort of the Western middle class (or higher) have no idea about the conditions often found in the detention places of the poorer countries, not to mention detention places run by armed nonstate actors. The ICRC was often providing basic relief such as clean water, soap, and food and medicine to counter disease and malnutrition. This was so even before the Covid-19 pandemic and widespread need for face coverings, sanitizers, personal protective equipment, and vaccines among general prison population and staff.

As usual, questions remain. Did the all-prisoner approach in practice mean a downgrading of the effort to stop abuse of political and conflict prisoners? Did the organization get a false satisfaction from doing something about prisons, even if one was diverted from traditional concerns? In short, was the ICRC pushing hard enough about mistreatment of conflict and political prisoners? Was it correctly evaluating the situation and properly seizing opportunities as they arose? Or was it too cautious, trapped by its ideology of seeking mostly a positive relationship with authorities? Was any of this affected during 2014–2022 by a closer link to the World Economic Forum – and ICRC officials interacting closely with governments and corporations within that forum, whatever their treatment of dissidents?

This will be a very good line of inquiry when ICRC archives are open, permitting serious research in the documents. Just as we now know something about the ICRC record regarding detainees in, for example, Kenya and Algeria in the 1950s and 1960s (and those situations were not always praiseworthy for the ICRC), eventually researchers will be able to say more about ICRC detention policies circa 1990–2020. This fact logically pushes the ICRC to be properly assertive about detention policies, knowing that the record will eventually be examined. But we all know that reason does not always prevail or control. The ICRC was slow in asserting itself on detention matters in colonial Kenya and Algeria. It will be interesting to find out what the archives show about Belarus and the UAE in our time, not to forget about Egypt, Venezuela, and literally dozens of other complex cases. If we accept that the ICRC correctly concluded that it was pointless to offer its services to China regarding visits to detained Uighurs in Xingjian province, what about other cases?

There is a reasonably widespread view that cuts in programming might be in order across these three policy areas of (1) development holds, (2) low-level urban violence, and (3) irregular or undocumented migration. By trying to position itself to be relevant to this expanded operational mandate, while at the same time trying to demonstrate its traditional expertise regarding armed conflicts and political prisoners, was it opening too many offices here and there and trying to be every-thing to everybody? Was it not true that the ICRC was highly active in a number of places that did not manifest large-scale violence? Was it not true that in talking about "fragile societies" rather than armed conflict, internal tensions, and political prisoners, the ICRC had slid into a very expansive series of activities having no clear and firm limits? If one had the strategy of "being there" in case of future major violence, did that not imply a very broad and unclear orientation that did indeed indicate a lack of concentrated focus? We will see later that one ex-ICRC official said that the current orientation of the "big humanitarians" was "uto-pian." On the other hand, was not the ICRC better positioned now, say compared with the Cold War era, to act when major political violence erupted or resumed? Was an old guideline now passé in Geneva, namely that a strength of the organization was to know its limits?

But what if this broad approach without clear limits was precisely what was wanted by the Movement, UN members and officials, and donor governments? What was the cost to the ICRC in resisting these stake-holder desires, not to mention the wishes of many victims/beneficiaries? Could the ICRC really fall back to a narrower focus and a more precise anchoring, given contemporary trends and demands?

D   A Bigger Organization, with Implications for Staff

The ICRC after the tenures of President Maurer (2012–2022) and Director-General Daccord (2010–2020) is a much bigger, more bureau-cratic organization. A slow growth in size circa 2000–2010 became a huge bump in 2010–2020. Growth was intentionally pursued as a stra-tegic objective, primarily to increase resources, impact, and reputation in competition with other humanitarians, but with the ultimate goal of doing more good for persons. Swiss governance at the top of the ICRC aside, it is now really a more typical international organization pursuing standard business practices of administration including hiring of outside management consultants.

During the Maurer–Daccord era there was more top-down management, rather widely but not entirely perceived as imperial in style. Generational differences might account for some views, with the older and more experienced staff articulating more discontents than the younger personnel – but not always. Some older staff aspired only to be head of delegation, making decisions in the field that really counted. Now they see lots of maneuvering to obtain this or that position at headquarters, with, in their view, the field delegation downgraded in importance.

The nature of the organization has changed as a result of growth in budgets and staff, driven by an expanding interpretation of its mandate. Along with the demise of the canary-in-the-mineshaft model, featuring quick action by a small actor providing warnings to others about impending dangers, and normally manifesting quite flexible, if limited, field action itself, one sees the relative demise of the staff member who devotes his/her life to the cause. Both in the field and at headquarters, one sees more staff moving in and out of important positions, shuffling between the ICRC and the World Bank, universities, the WEF, private corporations, the Swiss government, and so on. This, combined with the expanded operational mandate, and an imperial management style for a time, has led to staff tensions and frustrations. I have already mentioned the well-informed even if critical "farewell letter" of the veteran staff member Jacques de Maio that circulated rather widely, albeit privately, comparing the old and new ICRC. Some promotions were sometimes perceived as based on personal connections and loyalty to the top. Staff discontents seemed pronounced in 2018–2019. They were documented in internal surveys, which top managers were wise to have authorized.

By 2022 staff tensions and frustrations had been kept within tolerable bounds. Yet if one did extensive interviews, it became clear that there remained many discontents about what was called inclusion and diversity. Gender and race remained contentious issues. International staff were not always happy that the key spots in the Directorate were still going to European males. One might even imagine that this type of discontent would eventually spill over to more criticism of the all-Swiss governing board, especially since Swiss political neutrality was not absolute in an era of Swiss sanctions against Russia and other examples of taking sides short of military involvement. This more flexible Swiss political neutrality, clearly affected by Swiss membership for a term in the UN Security Council,[11] logically weakened the key idea that the ICRC Assembly had to be all-Swiss as tied to the permanent neutrality of the Swiss state. However, as noted, Swiss state neutrality had always been a pro-West, pro-democratic, pro-capitalist neutrality. Swiss neutrality as practiced in Bern was never absolute. It still remained true that the mono-nationality of the Assembly avoided the problem of international disagreement and gridlock that plagued organs of the UN.

From a concern with strictly personnel management style, the shift from Daccord to Mardini in the office of director-general was probably beneficial. Daccord clearly had a fertile mind but could sometimes convey an imperial image. To some, he did not always appreciate that multiple changes should be spread out across time to be digestible.

However, Mardini was a protégé of Daccord and climbed the ranks under the latter's aegis. Personal low-key style aside, he was widely seen as mostly continuing the policies he inherited. When a new Directorate was announced to take over from July 1, 2022, with Mardini continuing as D-G, there were grumblings within the ranks that key positions such as director-general, director of operations, and director of law and policy were held by European males. (Mardini was a naturalized Swiss, from Lebanon.) Indeed, the only nationalities represented in the new Directorate were Swiss and French. True, there were two women in the Directorate not to mention the incoming female president. But in the Directorate, there was no one from the Global South. This did not go unchallenged within the ranks.

Director-General Mardini, rightly or wrongly, took a lot of heat for not anticipating better the failure of donations to keep up with needs. A letter from experienced staff circulated internally in early 2023; it criticized Mardini sharply regarding the anticipated budget cuts; it picked up widespread support quickly. I have already noted the de Maio circular letter and private email message to this author; it too criticized top ICRC leaders for several contemporary trends. That was a farewell letter from a staff member who was leaving the organization – at least concerning regular duties as compared to spot evaluations. The 2023 critical circular was from someone who intended to stay, and those who signed on also intended to stay. Such open protest and sharp debate would not have happened in the old ICRC of circa 1985.

Working at the ICRC had become similar to working at the UN – more like a job and less like a matter of personal identity and lifelong commitment for sizable numbers of staff. This is a factor that bears watching. The surprising numbers of staff committing fraud as they implement ICRC activities may be the tip of the iceberg of possibly less devoted staff members. Whether those numbers are much higher than circa 1990, relatively speaking and all factors considered, would be good to know. In the recent past I have done interviews in an ICRC office where the more junior staff were visibly scared of their superiors. A broad approach to matters suggests staff morale and cohesion had not necessarily improved. But it remains difficult to generalize about a staff of some 20,000 persons of various nationalities and backgrounds, and skills and roles, with both mobile and residential status (formerly, delegates and the locally hired), and with both generalists and specialists.

In the past the ICRC was often thought of as synonymous with the personages of leading humanitarian figures such as Max Huber, Jean Pictet, Pierre Boissier, François Bugnion, Jacques Moreillon, Laurent Marti, André Rochat, and a few others – including of course Gustave Moynier in the early years. (Gustave Ador had a long tenure at the ICRC but he was also active in journalism and politics.) One does not often see the same type of identity and commitment today in many ICRC officials. They come and they go. Some have primary careers in other organizations, arriving at the ICRC in semiretirement.

A few are semi-free spirits, saying or writing things that do not fit so easily with ICRC guidelines. Of course with more centrally mandated rules and regulations, free spirits do not last long in today's ICRC.

In the last analysis, a larger and well-funded ICRC (up until 2020–2023) is doing more good via its expanded scope of activities, but this has been achieved at the price of loss of concentrated focus and with a weakened sense of organizational identity. In a way, the organization has effectively redefined itself along UN lines in progressive steps since it internationalized its staff in 1992. Now staff cohesion is less, there are more tensions over gender and diversity, and there is almost certainly more variation in quality of staff in the field. There is more open staff criticism of governance and management. The outer limits of its activities are not clear concerning socioeconomic assistance, activities in lower-level urban violence, and various roles regarding undocumented migrants. It has more visibility especially among relevant Western policymakers, and it has not been stressed by lack of resources until recently. But it is less the agile and expert organization than it was before the end of the Cold War.

II   NIIHA Diplomacy

It should be clear by now that the ICRC has not officially changed its general mission or fundamental values. On paper it remains a neutral and impartial humanitarian intermediary, taking up whatever humanitarian question that, in its view as an independent private agency (now seen as an international organization), requires attention.

The chapter on organizing the organization has already given an analysis of ICRC governance since about 1990. Here I review and update the role of the president and his humanitarian diplomacy. One of the hardest analytical nuts to crack is whether ICRC diplomacy or other action was the result of the president alone or of some broader collective policy process. I leave further attention to that distinction for those with future access to the archives. (The archives, however, are sometimes silent on matters of policy process. On that general subject, I have found it easier to get commentary via interviews about the relatively distant past as compared to contemporary affairs.) For now I simply talk about ICRC humanitarian diplomacy and whether it was appropriately NIIHA – and properly assertive.

A   The WEF Again

President Maurer's decision to become a trustee on the governing board of the World Economic Forum, ratified *ex post facto* by the ICRC Assembly ultimately in a divided vote, has been discussed in considerable detail and will not be replayed here. Two critiques stand out: first, that he formally aligned himself with a controversial way of informally managing world problems that was not really neutral (however the Swiss government might label the WEF); second, that he put himself in a position where his priorities could be questioned (rightly or wrongly) among three competing goals – recognizing Swiss national interests in keeping and promoting the WEF, participating in a Western-dominated system of global policymaking rife with negatives, and advancing ICRC traditional NIIHA values.

I would not be surprised if in the post-Maurer era, under President Spoljaric-Egger (who prefers to use the name Mirjana Spoljaric) sometime after fall 2022, the organization undertook a real cost-benefits analysis of the linkage between the ICRC and WEF. I also would not be surprised if that anticipated candid analysis showed both positives (such as expanded attention to humanitarian affairs from some key actors at the WEF) and negatives (such as increased suspicions that the ICRC was going soft on protection matters in places such as China and the UAE and other states important to the WEF). Finally, I would not be surprised if President Spoljaric reverted to the policies of Sommaruga and Kellenberger, avoiding membership on the WEF board of trustees but continuing various interactions as mutually agreed. Such a change, actually a reversion, would enhance the ICRC reputation for unquestioned NIIHA values. As a former director-general commented, the ICRC should be free to utilize the WEF for its NIIHA goals, but also free to attend anti-WEF meetings for the same objectives. One cannot do the latter with the ICRC president as a WEF trustee.

It might be icing on the cake that the WEF expelled certain Russians from Davos meetings and from the board of trustees after the Russian full invasion of Ukraine in February 2022. That was not a neutral act, and the neutral ICRC – and its president – should not be tightly linked to any of that.

If one is going to keep a certain distance from UN organs and agencies and programs, one should do the same regarding the WEF – but cooperating from time to time by mutual agreement on specified matters. The Swiss government's referring to the WEF as a neutral organization, since that label is erroneous on several dimensions, should not be controlling.

The pattern at the WEF in the future might be similar to proper relations with the Swiss authorities – keeping a proper distance under the principle of independence and neutrality but cooperating on specific matters by mutual agreement.

On balance it was a mistake for Maurer to become a WEF trustee, but not a major one, as some NIIHA gains were achieved. The negatives were mostly in the realm of optics, image, and suspicions rather than in proven defects empirically verified. We have no evidence, for example, that Moscow saw the WEF as an obstacle or complicating factor in dealing with the ICRC regarding Ukraine. But anything that brings into question the organization's reputation is to be avoided.

Did Maurer understand or care about how he might be perceived when wearing both his ICRC and WEF hats? Almost certainly not, and he was no doubt irritated to have his motives questioned. In a radio interview in 2016 he said: "Jamais socialement à l'aise avec le milieu diplomatique. Milieu fortement imprégné par la bonne bourgeoisie. Pas un endroit où je me sentais particulièrement à l'aise. Clivage social. N'était pas intéressé par l'image mais par les relations internationales."[12] (I was never socially comfortable with the diplomatic milieu. It is a milieu strongly infused with attention to proper middle-class values. It was not a place where I felt particularly comfortable. Too many social distinctions. I was not interested in the image but in the substance of international relations.)

On another occasion when Maurer was asked by a journalist about photos showing him in friendly mode with Russian Foreign Minister Sergei Lavrov, he was quoted as saying: "The public perception is not so important. Our goal is to change the lives of those affected – be they soldiers or civilians. As long as we have the recognition and understanding of these people and the respective warring parties view us as legitimate, then that is enough."[13]

On the WEF and some other diplomatic matters, he was not always careful about the image he might project. He emphasized active diplomacy and did not worry all that much about RC history or what he saw as theoretical debates or set models of action.

He remarked on a couple of occasions about how the ICRC reflected a tension between its legacy and contemporary needs, between the organization's traditions and new challenges. He said one could debate the "dosage" or extent of each, but one could understand the ICRC according to that dialectic.[14] Maurer seemed to think that attention to the ICRC past hampered what needed to be done in the present.

Historians might want to address the hypothesis that President Maurer emphasized active diplomacy in an era of change while de facto downgrading ICRC traditions and legacy. He may have made his mark via extensive and active diplomacy in ongoing conflicts, which is mostly commendable, but without giving much reflection to what the organization had done in this or that conflict or situation by way of precedent and continuity. Not only did he join the WEF board and was criticized for it by Sommaruga, but he stopped publication of a series of books on ICRC history and he cut off the Honorary Assembly members' access to Assembly verbatim records. In general he, unlike at least some other high officials, did not seem to have much use for the former officials and their experience. He, and some others, eventually tired of former officials in general and not just Thierry Germond, who were raising questions about consistency with past practice. He went through the formalities of hosting lunches or dinners for the Honorary Assembly members now and then, but he was not much interested in whether the needs of today, as he saw them, led to ICRC action that was fully consistent with the Sommaruga or Kellenberger eras.

His primary concern seemed to relate to contemporary humanitarian needs, which he saw as linked to protracted and irregular conflicts – at least until the Russian full invasion of Ukraine. Hopefully communication specialists will eventually study his verbiage about "fragile societies" compared to situations of armed conflict, or the changing needs of "beneficiaries" as compared to victims of war.

Despite being trained in history and law, Maurer did not care all that much about images or history when they bumped up against contemporary events. This will be made clear in the Epilogue about the war in Ukraine. That could be a problem for the ICRC in the future, especially when one recalls that Kellenberger had wanted to make the ICRC consistent and predictable across cases. True, Maurer wanted the ICRC to be seen as a NIIHA organization, and that was a partial key to attracting World Bank and other donations. But he was not always careful about how his diplomacy related to that core image, much less whether he could be abrupt with or disdainful of various persons in his personal diplomacy.

One can agree with Maurer, as he said at a public ceremony in 2022 when receiving an award from the Geneva Foundation,[15] that modern humanitarianism needs to relate to private business and finance. One can do that but still keep a certain distance from the controversial WEF (as well as some controversial firms). He made a strong argument at that 2022 ceremony in saying that humanitarianism is too important to be left to strictly humanitarian agencies alone. One can follow that axiom and still skip the WEF board of trustees.

Former official Thierry Germond was logically correct when in a letter to ICRC officials on February 22, 2017 he noted that the WEF had strongly condemned the Islamic State group (or ISIS, aka Daesh). Other critics, such as the G-25 in December 2017, were right to note this same subject. If ISIS personnel had been paying attention to Maurer being a WEF trustee, its fighters could have abducted or attacked ICRC staff in the Middle East in retribution. The person who wrote the anti-Daesh essay for the WEF soon reverted to her position at the ICRC. Fortunately for the ICRC, ISIS was not paying attention to such connections. What was a logical possibility did not become a reality. But all that guaranteed nothing about the future and other brutal armed groups in other conflicts.

Maurer was quoted in the Swiss press as saying in 2022: "Bien sûr, je suis très content qu'aucune des prédictions négatives qu'on m'avait répétées en devenant membre du board du WEF ne se soit réalisée, mais je ne pouvais pas l'exclure."[16] (Indeed, I was very happy that none of the negative predictions that one had repeated to me in becoming a member of the WEF board were realized, but I could not exclude that possibility.) So Germond's logic about the WEF was correct, even if happily events in fact turned out better than logic feared.

B   ICRC Diplomacy Writ Large

In a larger view one finds an ICRC humanitarian diplomacy that was broadly active over especially the last ten years, mostly appropriate, with a few hiccups here and there. President Maurer traveled incessantly and said mostly the right things during his ten years at the helm of the ICRC. His energy, demeanor, and knowledge caused the ICRC to be better known and accepted in policymaking circles. He kept track of various complicated issues and explained the ICRC position well to his interlocutors. He helped double the ICRC budget in 2012–2022. Major gaffes are few (one is discussed later, another in the Epilogue). Extensive humanitarian diplomacy is a main part of his legacy, as endorsed by the ICRC Assembly and supported by the Directorate. He was more broadly active and visible than the restrained Kellenberger, and he was more measured in his public demeanor than the Napoleonic Sommaruga.

(This is not to forget that both his predecessors made their own positive contributions in their own way.)

Maurer's public persona, projecting modesty and commitment, traveled well. He was honored not only by the Geneva Foundation but also by the German government, with many other honors sure to come. Russia and Kazakhstan had also honored him, discussed later, whatever their game was. Whether the same positive evaluation could be made for his up-close dealings with those who differed with him, or whom he thought might criticize him, is a good subject for future analysts.

Maurer did cross the line into unnecessary or unwise political commentary on several occasions, but these seem marginal or unimportant as things have played out. In May 2017 he praised the Chinese policy known as the Belt and Road Initiative (BRI). China presents the BRI as a public service to the world. However, this policy is, in the view of several analysts, a program to extend China's political influence around the world through primarily soft loans to help countries develop their infrastructure. Loans at concessionary rates might make countries dependent on China. When they cannot pay their debt, these countries may wind up doing China's bidding.[17] In Sri Lanka, China took over control of a port for 99 years in lieu of debt repayment.[18] Balanced analysis suggests that overall, for all of its serious economic problems, Sri Lanka is not simply in a debt trap to China – its problems are more general than that. However, the BRI presents many problems and merits close analysis.[19] The safest description is that the BRI is controversial with clear political dimensions.[20]

Praising the Chinese BRI would be like praising the US Marshall Plan after World War II, which was designed to expand US leadership as Europe recovered, according to a capitalist, noncommunist model – and part of the US effort to contain Soviet-led communism. A neutral humanitarian ICRC has no business commenting on such foreign policies central to states' strategic maneuvers.

One can appreciate what Maurer was trying to do vis-à-vis Beijing in 2017 but he still got out of his NIIHA lane. The mistake was in saying: "At ICRC we've been following the development of the Belt and Road Initiative with great interest. We commend this ambitious project, and like many others recognise its great potential ... I can see the huge potential of the Belt and Road Initiative in terms of development, trade and connectivity...."[21] He then went on to make his main point, which was that the Chinese should add a humanitarian dimension to its Belt and Road Initiative.[22] But he did not need to say, and should not have said, the first part in order to get to the second.

There were other similar statements that were either ill-advised or close to crossing the line into unnecessary political endorsement. True, historically the ICRC tried to take a positive approach to governments in public, hoping for more cooperation on humanitarian affairs. But one can still question whether it was really part of appropriate NIIHA diplomacy for the president to praise Saudi Arabia for its humanitarian programs when that government was widely known for torture and political murder.[23] Likewise, was it correct to praise the UAE for its humanitarian efforts when multiple respected institutions were charging that government with torture of political dissidents?[24] Such statements were borderline appropriate at best. They might suggest to some that the ICRC had downgraded its humanitarian protection concerns. But again, this was a matter of image, and Maurer was not terribly interested in images.

There is one alleged breach of NIIHA values that was pushed under the rug: in September 2015 the ICRC, having opened an office for East Asia in Beijing in 2005, apparently signed an agreement with Xinhua, the official voice of the People's Republic of China, to cooperate in matters of communication of interest to both sides.[25] Xinhua is involved in both propaganda and attempts at censorship on behalf of China's autocratic and repressive ruling elite. This would be tantamount to the ICRC signing an agreement of cooperation with Pravda, the official mouthpiece of the communist party of the USSR, during the Cold War. Pravda was the last place one would go to for objective information on any subject.

The 2015 document was strange, as reported to me, as was the ICRC decision to sign it. Xinhua apparently described itself in the agreement as reporting in an objective, way. This was often not true, and the ICRC should not have signed off on it. One provision of the memorandum supposedly indicates that the signatories will cooperate to advance the global influence of each of them. Why the ICRC would pledge to strengthen China's global influence is not at all clear. Still another part of the MOU apparently says the two sides will keep the agreement secret, although facts leaked to the press. It was as if the ICRC had doubts about the propriety of the MOU even as it was affixing its signature.

The MOU was said to be of one year's duration, to be extended automatically unless one of the signatories gave notification of a desire to terminate. Contrary to what I expected, this agreement was apparently still in force at the time of writing in 2022, although perhaps it had led to few cooperative ventures between the two organizations. It was similar to Maurer's being on the WEF trustees: a mistake but without major consequences. Maybe the situation was too embarrassing for the ICRC to give notice of termination since that would offend the Chinese side.

Privately after the fact, certain ICRC officials agreed that the arrangement with Xinhua was a mistake. They were certainly willing to discuss it with me. Similar to the statement by Peter Maurer noted earlier concerning praise for Beijing's BRI, the MOU with the Xinhua Press Agency reflected an overly enthusiastic push by the ICRC to build bridges with the rising major power in Asia. Similar was the ICRC decision to attend a military parade in Beijing celebrating the victory over the Japanese in 1945. This could not have been viewed in Japan as a neutral stance. (When I was traveling with an ICRC delegate in an African country in the 1970s, he was invited to appear on the platform at a rally of one of the armed militias fighting for control of the country. He declined.)

The episode about the Xinhua News Agency shows that an ICRC penchant for signing agreements was not always accompanied by careful attention to NIIHA values. At least the ICRC–Xinhua agreement on communication matters was never posted on the ICRC website and has gone unmentioned in recent broad overviews of relations between Geneva and Beijing. Several analysts who write on Chinese humanitarian policy do not cite the ICRC–Xinhua agreement because they do not know it ever existed.[26] ICRC alumni who were critical of some contemporary developments knew about it and complained about it. The agreement was not a secret in informed circles of opinion. And it has been covered in the Swiss press.

More complicated was the president accepting an award from the Russian Foreign Ministry for ICRC humanitarian efforts in 2021, given brutal Russian bombing policies in Syria from 2014, or given the fact that in Russian-ruled Crimea from 2014 the authorities sometimes engaged in forced disappearance of dissidents. There were places, for example in Nagorno-Karabakh, where there was indeed some humanitarian cooperation and responsible policies from Moscow – at least in relative terms. It certainly would have bruised feelings, with no humanitarian gain, to have turned down the award. At least the ICRC did not publicize the Russian award either externally or internally.

Something similar happened regarding Kazakhstan. After violence and a deadly crackdown on protestors in early 2022, the autocratic Kazakh president presented Mauer with an award for ICRC policies at the Kazakh consulate in Geneva. Again, the ICRC did not publicize the award, which would have been difficult to reject on the spot without triggering an unhelpful diplomatic kerfuffle.

When some attentive alumni complained about ICRC officials accepting awards from controversial political leaders, the ICRC leadership – apparently caught off guard –and themselves noting that the Ortega regime in Nicaragua had recently given an award to an ICRC official (at approximately the same time that the regime kicked the head of delegation out of country), promised to review policies.

The ICRC has a rule against Assembly members accepting individual honors from any government. This leaves open the option for an ICRC official, when surprised by an award without advance notice, of accepting on behalf of the organization to avoid a diplomatic spat and then quietly hiding the award away in some basement closet, with no public comment. There is also the option of extending the rule barring accepting honors from governments for Assembly members to all staff.

Notes

1 Samantha Power, *A Problem from Hell: America and the Age of Genocide* (New York: Perennial, 2003), p. 411.

2 David B. Rivkin, Jr., Lee A. Casey, and Mark Wendell Delaquil, "Not Your Father's Red Cross," *National Review*, December 20, 2004, www.nationalreview.com/2004/12/not-your-fathers-red-cross-david-b-rivkin-jrlee-casey-mark-wendell-delaquil/ (accessed October 31, 2022).

3 International Commission on Intervention and State Sovereignty, *The Responsibility to Protect: Research, Bibliography, Background* (Ottawa: International Development Research Center), 2001, pp. 92, 213.

4 Samantha Power, *The Education of an Idealist: A Memoir* (New York: HarperCollins, 2019). She does not mention the ICRC in her memoir. Her higher regard is shown by her consultations with Geneva and support for the ICRC via US AID. (The main conduit for US donations to the ICRC is the State Department Bureau of Population, Refugees, and Migration. The money is authorized by Congress.)

5 The affair started with an essay in the *Wall Street Journal* which provoked a back and forth within the political class and included a further piece in *The National Review*. See David B. Rivkin Jr. and Lee A. Casey, "Friend or Foe? The International Committee of the Red Cross Should Stop Championing Terrorists or Lose U.S. Funding," *Wall Street Journal*, April 17, 2005, www.wsj.com/articles/SB122702174282237329 (accessed October 31, 2022) and David B. Rivkin, Lee A. Casey, and Mark Wendell Delaquil, "Not Your Father's Red Cross," *National Review*, December 20, 2004, www.nationalreview.com/2004/12/not-your-fathers-red-cross-david-b-rivkin-jr-lee-casey-mark-wendell-delaquil/ (accessed October 31, 2022).

6 Among numerous reliable sources, see Reuters on August 1, 2014, www.reuters.com/article/us-usa-cia-obama/obama-says-that-after-9-11-we-tortured-some-folks-idUSKBN0G14YY20140801 (accessed February 15, 2023). Obama was speaking about the CIA, but it should be recalled that the CIA was in charge of one of the cell blocks in the Gitmo prison.

7 In the *Wall Street Journal* and *The National Review*, the authors attacking the ICRC for API from 1997 and its provisions on detained fighters in wars of national liberation, anti-racism, and anti-occupation, attributed key developments to the organization. In fact, the origins of the legal wording lay with postcolonial states in an effort that troubled the ICRC, which was generally seen as aligned with the West and not with "Third World" states. At the end

of the conference, the head of the US delegation, George Aldrich, decided to make the best of a bad situation and recommended US acceptance of API, perhaps with a statement of understanding or reservation about some of the wording. President Reagan chose rejection of API altogether, which has never been reversed. The authors also accused the ICRC of leaking information about Guantanamo. Probably the leak came from the American side. No evidence was ever presented showing that the leak came from the ICRC. The ICRC stated that it was opposed to the leak since it undermined the ICRC's preference for discreet diplomacy that built trust in the organization.

8 At the same time, some conflicts can be fueled by too little nationalism. The former Yugoslavia in the early 1990s was characterized by too little Yugoslav nationalism and too much ethnic fervor in subunits such as Serbia. The same dynamic has been at work in Ethiopia: too little Ethiopian nationalism and too much ethnic identity with its subregions.

9 ICRC, *Annual Report*, 1992. ICRC, *Annual Report*, 1991. The ICRC annual reports are completely transparent about income and expenditure, as well as staff numbers.

10 Jennifer J. Sara, Ted Chaiban, and Dominik Stillhart, "Joining Forces to Secure Water and Sanitation in Protracted Crises: A New Report," ICRC, March 5, 2021, www.icrc.org/en/document/joining-forces-secure-water-and-sanitation-protracted-crises (accessed November 11, 2022).

11 In early February 2023, the Swiss representative in the UN Security Council explained that the Swiss government was not neutral when it came to violations of IHL and the UN Charter, although Swiss policy on these matters would stop short of military action. www.eda.admin.ch/eda/en/fdfa/foreign-policy/international-organizations/un/swiss-speeches-statements .html/content/missions/mission-new-york/en/meta/speeches/2023/august/24/un-security-council-briefing-on-the-maintenance-of-peace-and-sec (accessed February 15, 2023).

12 "Entre nous soi dit," *Radio Suisse Romande*, September 29, 2016, Rediffusion, October 8, 2016, 16h03.

13 Barbara Luthi, "ICRC President: 'I Had an Impact; That's What Counts,'" *Swiss Info*, September 13, 2022, www.swissinfo.ch/eng/business/icrc-chief---i-had-an-impact---that-s-what-counts-/47884890 (accessed November 11, 2022).

14 Aline Jaccottet, "Peter Maurer: Pour obtenir du soutien, le CICR droit se le mériter," *Le Temps*, September 22, 2022, www.letemps.ch/monde/peter-maurer-obtenir-soutien-cicr-meriter (accessed November 13, 2022).

15 www.youtube.com/watch?v=hk96XS9wki4

16 Jaccottet, "Peter Maurer: Pour obtenir du soutien."

17 Andrew Chatsky and James McBride, "China's Massive Belt and Road Initiative," *Council on Foreign Relations*, January 28, 2020, www.cfr.org/backgrounder/chinas-massive-belt-and-road-initiative (accessed November 11, 2022).

18 *The Economic Times*, "Sri Lanka Seeks Chinese Debt Reschedule for Crashing Economy," January 9, 2022, https://economictimes .indiatimes.com/news/international/world-news/sri-lanka-seeks-chinese-debt-reschedule-for-crashing-economy/articleshow/88792770 .cms?from=mdr (accessed November 11, 2022).

19 Chatham House, "Chinese Investment and the BRI in Sri Lanka," March 24, 2020, www.chathamhouse.org/2020/03/chinese-investment-and-bri-sri-lanka (accessed November 11, 2022).

20 Wade Shepard, "How China's Belt and Road Became a 'Global Trail of Trouble'," *Forbes*, January 29, 2020, www.forbes.com/sites/wadeshepard/2020/01/29/how-chinas-belt-and-road-became-a-global-trail-of-trouble/?sh=2898b411443d (accessed November 11, 2022). And Peter Coy, "China Is Playing Hardball with Troubled Debtors. That's Dangerous for All of Us," *New York Times*, July 22, 2022, www.nytimes.com/2022/07/22/opinion/china-debt-belt-road.html (accessed November 11, 2022).

21 ICRC, "Why There Should Be a Humanitarian Dimension to China's Belt and Road Project," May 15, 2017, www.icrc.org/en/document/humanitarian-dimension-belt-and-road-initiative (accessed November 11, 2022).

22 Ibid.

23 Arab News, "King Salman Receives International Committee of the Red Cross President," October 16, 2017, www.arabnews.com/node/1569536/saudi-arabia (accessed November 11, 2022).

24 News Agency-WAM, "President of ICRC Lauds UAE's Humanitarian, Development Initiatives," February 4, 2021, https://wam.ae/en/details/1395302907239 (accessed November 11, 2022).

25 China issued a press release on September 1, 2015. http://french.china.org.cn/foreign/txt/2015-09/01/content_36474394.htm The ICRC did not. The Swiss newspaper *Le Temps* covered the story belatedly on May 10, 2018, revised on May 11, by reporter Stéphane Bussard, "L'accord controverse entre Chine Nouvelle et le CICR," www.letemps.ch/monde/laccord-controverse-entre-chine-nouvelle-cicr. The ICRC director-general, acknowledging criticism, tried to defend the agreement whereas the vice president did not.

26 Lina Gong, "Humanitarian Diplomacy as an Instrument for China's Image-building," *Asian Journal of Comparative Politics*, 6/3 (September 2021), pp. 238–252, https://journals.sagepub.com/doi/full/10.1177/20578911211019257 (accessed November 11, 2022); and Jacob Kurtzer and Grace Gonzales, "China's Humanitarian Aid: Cooperation amidst Competition," Center for Strategic and International Studies, November 17, 2020, www.csis.org/analysis/chinas-humanitarian-aid-cooperation-amidst-competition (accessed November 11, 2022).

18   Conclusion
Part II – The Future

> [T]oday's humanitarians have recognized a proliferation of new needs
> that would have been unimaginable to Dunant at Solferino, and which
> make humanitarian aid increasingly ambitious, complicated, expensive
> and utopian.
>
> Hugo Slim[1]

Hugo Slim, who was ICRC head of policy and diplomacy during
2015–2020, has written a book on the future of global humanitarianism.[2] He had already startled some in Geneva by writing that one did
not have to be neutral to be a good humanitarian,[3] which may be true
in some ways and in some cases but was nevertheless surprising coming from one who was an ICRC official for a time. (He was a scholar in
the UK both before and after his ICRC stint.) But as one high official
at the ICRC said to this author, Slim had a complicated relationship with
the organization. This is a diplomatic way of saying he was widely seen
as a fresh thinker but was not regarded as a heavyweight on important
policy decisions. Similarly, another staffer said Slim was not disliked but
was not seen as a central policymaker. Still another offered the opinion
that the president was not unhappy to see him go.

Before going further into his arguments, this is a useful point to recall
the fate of Fred Cuny. He was an independent freelance humanitarian from Texas who did much humanitarian good in the Bosnian War
and other places but who disappeared – never to reappear – in the first
Chechen War. There were always rumors that he had close links to the
US government and its security and diplomatic agencies. In all probability he was killed by one side or the other in Chechnya, probably by
some Chechen faction, because he lacked a neutral image. At the time
that he failed to return from an ill-advised trip in 1995 in a sensitive area
of Chechnya, he might have been looking into weapons issues of interest
to the US government.[4]

The key point here is that almost certainly someone among the fighting parties regarded him as partial, seeing him as someone likely to report

to US officials, and killed him. (Two doctors who sometimes worked for the Russian Red Cross also disappeared in the same incident, in the context of Chechen suspicions that the Russian Red Cross was not neutral and had been penetrated by Russian security agents.)

Per Slim, it may be true that one can find examples of politically partial humanitarian efforts of some merit. But if you want to operate in the midst of violent situations, it can be fatally dangerous not to be seen as neutral. This is one of the main reasons some of the critics of the ICRC objected so strongly to the ICRC president being also a WEF trustee, since the WEF was not always seen as a neutral platform or organization. To repeat a point made earlier, there are two interrelated reasons why local humanitarians manifest more casualties than the larger international actors such as the ICRC: (1) they do not have the same reputation for NIIHA values, and (2) they do not have the same extensive contacts with armed groups, useful to actors like the ICRC in explaining who they are and what they do – sometimes on a regional or transnational basis.

Neutrality in humanitarian affairs is not to be taken lightly.

I   More about the Future

Beyond the notion of neutrality, some of Slim's themes in his book overlap with my list of seven major concerns in ICRC communications noted in a previous chapter. This is not surprising since he was an ICRC official for some five years and observed and indeed participated in ICRC policy debates. No doubt he drew on his ICRC experience in informal or indirect ways in writing his 2022 book.

For present purposes I emphasize Slim's arguments that (1) there will never be just one international humanitarian system, dominated by the West, whether through the United Nations or the RC Movement, because China, Russia, and the Islamic world will never fully buy into existing global systems; and (2) prioritizing large bureaucratic "super-agencies," with it being understood that the ICRC is one of those, is not the best way to proceed. Rather, so the argument runs, one should emphasize local agencies that are more authentic and closer to the action.

This latter point is also articulated by other analysts. The scholar of humanitarian affairs, Michael N. Barnett, sees international humanitarian actors as forming a club.[5] He does not quote Robert Michels about the iron law of oligarchy, but he could have.[6] In Barnett's view, international humanitarians manifest a network with an elite within it. In Michels' view, all institutions manifest an elite, aka an oligarchy, as some rise to the top through more creativity or hard work or whatever. Barnett, and many others, consider the ICRC as part of the global humanitarian elite. It is among those who get more money than others. To make his longer analysis shorter, one can paraphrase him to say that the ICRC is among those who benefit from the current global humanitarian system, whereas many organizations from the Global South do not. There is a hierarchy within the network of global humanitarians and the ICRC part of the crème de la crème.

The fact that the ICRC has over the years built a reputation for NIIHA values and effectiveness is noted by Barnett, but rather than simply being virtues to be admired and rewarded, they are seen as part of the reason for a neocolonial or neo-imperial global humanitarian system. The fact that the ICRC arose out of white European Christian charity in an age of European colonialism contributes to this kind of analysis. The analysis is not wrong about historical origins, or that Western donors and Western-based agencies do in fact dominate much of the reported humanitarian action.

But this kind of critical argument does seem to downplay the importance of neutral and effective humanitarian action while emphasizing geographical distribution of resources and the right of conflict victims in the Global South to be masters of their own fate – even if sometimes they lack the capability to do so. There also seems to be an expectation in the academic circles populated by Slim and Barnett that Western sources of humanitarian funding, such as citizens and legislatures, should not put so much emphasis on reporting and accountability, as if interest in how tax money was spent was not very important. These latter concerns about accountability are seen as just another unreasonable or unfair or unethical aspect of humanitarian neocolonialism and elitism.[7] (The US Agency for International Development [AID] was trying to make it simpler for organizations to apply for its grants.)

It is true that UN humanitarian agencies and the ICRC are both paid for mostly by Western states, directly but also via the EU and World Bank. It is also true that the BRICS (Brazil, Russia, India, China, and South Africa), among others, often chafe under Western preeminence in international relations. It is not by accident that all the other BRICS declined to fully support the Western response to the Russian full invasion of Ukraine. It is also true that Saudi Arabia and most other leading Islamic states have their own preferred charities and have never been among the top donors to the ICRC – even though they sometimes benefit from ICRC services. (Kuwait and the UAE *are* important contributors to the ICRC.) After the Turkish earthquakes of 2023 which also created a humanitarian crisis in northwest Syria, Saudi Arabia provided its own humanitarian relief to Syria and was not content to just contribute to UN relief programs. (Saudi Arabia manifested mixed motives, both strategic and humanitarian, and thus preferred bilateral over multilateral assistance.)

Photograph 18.1 A female staff member, arranging a family visit to detainees, Thailand, 2010. Not just detention visits but restoring family links remained core activities for the ICRC. Especially during the COVID-19 pandemic but at other times as well it utilized video links to allow prisoners to talk to their loved ones. Sometimes when prisoners were released, the ICRC did follow-up tracking concerning their integration into civilian society.

That said, first of all, the universal RC Movement – even as decentralized and fragmented – is not about to collapse or fade away. That global network is there and likely to endure. For the ICRC, the global Movement presents a ready-made framework that allows it to combine its own activities, essentially paid for by the West, with local National Society action through the local affiliate. Warts and all, that arrangement presents unique opportunities that one saw in Ethiopia, among other cases. In sometimes getting special access to conflict areas in Tigray, the ICRC emphasized its links to the Ethiopian RC Society. ICRC experience and capabilities were brought to bear in a process that featured cooperation with National RC Societies – and that reduced charges of European (white, Western) imperialism while increasing the capabilities of the local National Society over time. (Perhaps it was by chance, but some staffers for MSF were killed in northern Ethiopia whereas ICRC staffers managed to escape that fate.) In Chapter 2 I mentioned in passing that the global humanitarian system is not quite sure how to view the local affiliates of international institutions such as the RC Movement: are they to be seen as truly local or not when allocating funding from Western capitals?

In some cases like Ethiopia (but not in all cases), the Movement framework gave the ICRC good access to key policymakers and reduced (but did not eliminate entirely) the probability of charges of outside, aka neocolonial, meddling. This Movement framework is not easily duplicated by other humanitarian actors or systems. It has its limits and defects, to be sure, one of which is often a tilt to the government side in internal armed conflicts, as we saw in Syria, but some advantages too. The Movement proved useful again in Ukraine in 2022. In that armed conflict, the ICRC had contacts with the Russian Red Cross, asking it for help on certain subjects, as well as with the Ukrainian Red Cross – and about fifty other National RC Societies.

As for Slim's other main argument emphasized here, seconded by the likes of Barnett, namely that one should fund and otherwise support local humanitarian actors rather than the "superagencies" such as the ICRC, that is often problematic in reality. One can note that in one of his exit interviews in 2022, Peter Maurer declined to support an easy emphasis on "localization" as it was usually understood. If one reads the transcript of that long interview, also a podcast, it is not entirely clear what kind of new model of humanitarian assistance he preferred. It might be that he thought a set or firm arrangement for humanitarian assistance was premature in contemporary international relations. He seemed to believe in diplomacy and action on a case-by-case basis. But he did agree that he was not a big fan of localization as usually discussed, even while he remained vague about concrete alternatives.[8]

And here we can return to some of the major defects of the Movement, evident for a long time. What I say about National RC Societies can be said of some other grassroots humanitarian organizations. If one looks at some of the big humanitarian crises of modern times as in Yemen, South Sudan, eastern Democratic Republic of Congo (DRC), and similar cases, turning primarily to national or local humanitarian actors is mostly a nonstarter. They often lack funding and capabilities. In some cases they barely exist. Often they are fragmented by ethnicity, clan, or political orientation. If every state had a Red Cross or other humanitarian agency as the Scandinavians do, that would be a different matter. It would also be a different planet.

There is a reason why the ICRC and other big-budget humanitarians like MSF exist and engender considerable support. The same point holds true for UN agencies, for example the World Food Program, UNICEF, and the UN Refugee Office (UNHCR). They are needed and cannot be easily duplicated. Local or ad hoc groups most of the time could not replace them – at least not for the foreseeable future, although the locals often do considerable good in their own way. This reality is underplayed by both Slim and Barnett. In Somalia in the early 1990s, when the ICRC became a focal point for dealing with mass starvation and malnutrition in that conflict situation, the ICRC had to basically re-create and acti-vate the Somalia Red Crescent in order to demonstrate a local partner in its important food relief program. There were certainly no other local humanitarian organizations who had the resources and expertise to do what needed to be done.

When Slim writes that "current calls to 'de-colonize' humanitarian aid make good moral and political sense if they lead to high-performing national networks that still encourage international norms, humanitar-ian solidarity and practical cooperation on transnational problems like war, climate, migration and health,"[9] he is avoiding a lot of reality about local humanitarian actors in today's world, although it may be politically incorrect to say so.[10]

Then there is the recurring and related issue of neutral, or more broadly NIIHA, status. Regardless of the capabilities of the Russian Red Cross, it is not going to be welcome in Ukraine. Regardless of how one views the independence of the Armenian Red Cross, it is not going to be welcome in Azerbaijan. Regardless of how many local citizens aid groups were active in Ukraine, they are not going to be given a role on the Russian side, especially on protection matters. Moreover, for some of the local Ukrainian aid efforts, some aid trickled down to relatives or friends in the military. And so on down the list of interstate conflicts. And in armed conflicts, which are fundamentally internal, the same gen-eral point holds. There is a need for humanitarian action that is per-ceived as neutral. This is why the ICRC got into field activities in the first place, especially after observing highly nationalistic National RC Societies in the Franco–Prussian War in 1870–1871. Dunant's vision of the preeminence given to National Societies had to be modified and this became broadly recognized. There is often a beneficial humanitarian role for neutral outsiders as compared to locals. Some experienced ICRC staff will even say privately that in some conflict situations an outside Western presence, even if white, is welcomed by the locals.

This need for a neutral intermediary is true for both assistance and especially protection in the narrow sense. The ICRC has built up that neutral image, with the mistakes common to all human endeavors, over more than 160 years. True, sometimes ICRC staff are killed or taken hostage, but the big picture is that the organization has a good record in being able to act in conflicts – and tries hard to keep it that way. New, ad hoc, local, and national humanitarians will not easily replicate that neutral image. Ukraine from February 2022 shows the special status of the ICRC based on its independent neutrality and experience in armed conflicts, both regarding prisoner affairs and establishment of humanitarian corridors for the extraction of civilians from imminent danger. This status, based on a record for effective action across cases and years, simply cannot be duplicated by "local" humanitarians.

What particularly strikes this author, noting that Slim had an inside view of the ICRC, is his lack of enthusiasm for large and bureaucratized humanitarians. This fits well with my analysis of the dangers inherent in a larger ICRC operating according to standard corporate management practices. Slim had already flagged the issue of bureaucratic humanitarians,[11] and he returns to that yellow flag in his new book. ICRC leaders would do well to take full note of that factor.

Photograph 18.2 In 2008 ICRC Director of Operations Pierre Krähenbühl introduces staff member Andreas Notter at a press conference. Notter had been taken hostage by an armed group in the Philippines, held for months, then freed by the action of others. Increasingly ICRC headquarters has had to calculate where it is safe for particular staff members, with differing personal characteristics, to operate. At the time of writing four ICRC staff members remained missing.

I suspect the ICRC already does so to some extent. I suspect it calculates where it is safe for a mobile staff person, say a Swede or Dane, to operate. I suspect it also wrestles with the following scenario: where outside/mobile staff cannot be safely placed, do the local ICRC staff members manifest the necessary NIIHA values, and financial trustworthiness and expertise, to run a humanitarian program then being discussed. All this is part of the new ICRC trying to operate in brutal conflicts – as in, say, East Africa dealing with Al Shabab, or in northeast Nigeria dealing with Boko Haram, or Yemen or South Sudan or Mozambique or Myanmar – to choose a relevant sample of situations.

It is doubtful that the ICRC at this point could return to the canary-in-the-mineshaft model of smallness and early warning to others. So the ICRC is probably stuck with its present size and management style – albeit with some reductions. To raise more money and do more good, the ICRC may wind up having sold its humanitarian soul to the gods of finance and visibility – meaning visibility within policymaking circles. So far the indicators are mixed, based on what we know about staff commitment to NIIHA values, but the game of humanitarian action is not over. The bigger, more bureaucratic ICRC is indeed new. An evaluation of size and commitment a generation from now will be interesting to read (for those still interested who are alive and well, with sound mind, which will not be me!).

As mentioned in the last chapter, but it bears repeating, in early 2023 with major budget cuts coming, an open letter circulated among staff criticizing how the leadership had handled planning. It picked up over 1,000 cosigners in the first twenty-four hours. There was concern about the perceived integrity of the organization among beneficiaries who had been promised this or that help. And of course there was concern about staff jobs. Some recently hired were likely to be let go – mostly in the field but also at headquarters.

Space does not allow full treatment of all of Slim's projections and recommendations about the future of global humanitarianism. My present work is, after all, not a book review. Slim is well regarded for his publications about the ethics of humanitarianism. His new book reflects that orientation in stressing the need to end a Western-based inequality in global humanitarian affairs. The other side of the coin of the push for localization is the argument that too much money goes to the Western-based establishment humanitarians such as the ICRC.[12] He sees the ICRC through that prism. And he has a point about expanding humanitarian roles along with expanding bureaucracies. But he, like Barnett, gives short shrift to what the ICRC brings to conflict situations in terms of experienced neutral roles, grounded in both law and diplomacy.

His orientation can be easily seen when he writes: "This superior white male gaze and its paternalist tendency has run deeply through the 160-year history of wartime humanitarianism catalyzed by Dunant. It still does."[13]

And, as quoted at the top of this chapter: "today's humanitarians have recognized a proliferation of new needs that would have been unimaginable to Dunant at Solferino, and which make humanitarian aid increasingly ambitious, complicated, expensive and utopian."[14]

And finally for present purposes: "New generation humanitarians everywhere must design an aid system that is more broadly and fairly based across the world, and that extends in networks well beyond the core system funded mainly by Western governments. In this process, Western humanitarians should re-purpose to focus much more on enabling local and national humanitarian institutions, as originally envisaged by Dunant."[15]

On some topics the ICRC is no doubt in agreement with his projections. Seville 2.0, already covered in detail in Chapter 6 on the RC Movement, shows increasing semantic attention to the role of National RC Societies. Both the ICRC and RC Federation are pledged, under Seville 2.0, to help National RC Societies develop. Moreover, the ICRC is already using cash transfers to some civilians affected by violence so they can make their own decisions about how to use that assistance. All that does not look like neocolonialism in humanitarian affairs.

Both irregular protracted conflicts and more traditional armed conflicts show the pressing need to focus on dangers to civilians, as Slim says – without of course forgetting about traditional protection of detained combatants. Future armed conflicts – at least among some states – are likely to feature actions in outer space, cyber space, and personal space, as he argues. The war in Ukraine in 2022, and other examples, already validates Slim's analysis in terms of an expanded battle space that required new thinking and clarification of humanitarian norms. The war was also fought in the media and with much use of advanced technology. Chapter 13 reviewed some ICRC efforts to adjust IHL to some new realities via customary international law, and particularly regarding cyber attacks and cyber war, as examples of ICRC attentiveness to change.

As for Slim's interpretations about how humanitarians should be preparing for a big war among major states, history may give us an evaluation on that projection in due course. The conventional war in Ukraine (as of late summer 2023) should give any rational state pause about resorting to war with an opponent of even roughly comparable capabilities, given the destructiveness of Russian strategy and tactics, and determined persistence on the Ukrainian side as supported by Western technology, even without escalation of various types. And if one should stumble into a nuclear war, certainly beyond a few tactical nukes, the ICRC and IHL will simply become irrelevant. It is not possible to observe traditional humanitarian distinctions and limitations in strategic nuclear war, complete with strategic cyber war, which is exactly why the ICRC, usually focused on the laws of war, is a peace organization on that one issue – opposing all nuclear wars.

II Final Comments

If for the moment we can assume that states and armed nonstate actors will continue to avoid Armageddon or something close to it, what are we to finally make of the ICRC as it has moved from five Genevans in 1863 – with no guaranteed budget and no staff support – to international organization status in 2022 with a budget of over US$2 billion employing a workforce of over 20,000 persons? How do we properly sum up its record across more than 160 years and in particular the years since the Cold War; with multiple wars both international and internal; with lots of riots, rebellions, and massacres; with two world wars; with a long Cold War; with the decolonization process leading to many more territorial states; and now with the complexities and challenges of the last thirty years after the demise of the classic East–West conflict?

I have a colleague who wrote a book entitled *Would the World Be Better without the UN?*[16] In similar vein I pose the question of whether the world would be better off without the ICRC. My answer is a categorical no. As the ICRC said in the midst of the 2022 international armed conflict in Ukraine: "A world without neutral and impartial humanitarian action is a bleaker, more dangerous place for victims of conflict, and for us all."[17] I believe the ICRC should be a candidate for the Nobel Peace Prize each and every year.

It is present in every violent hellhole of the world – from South Sudan to Yemen, from Syria to the DRC, from Ukraine to Ethiopia and Myanmar. In a wide-ranging exit interview, Peter Maurer said he was very proud that the ICRC had negotiated a presence in all the major wars and other major violence during his tenure.[18] (What it does with that access is fair game for analysis, as I have tried to show via such examples as Syria – and Ukraine in the Epilogue.) It is active on the ground and in diplomatic capitals, probing to maximize its humanitarian protection and assistance, often emerging literally from a basement (as in Mariupol, Ukraine) or a forced suspension of activity for reasons of insecurity (as in Yemen) to continue with trying to do as much good for victims/beneficiaries as the situation allows.

From about 1990 to 2020, it recorded more than seventy-five staff killed during field assignment. (The numbers are slightly soft due to several reasons, among them some lack of precision about the exact circumstances of death in some cases.) Six were murdered at point blank range in Chechnya. Several were intentionally shot in Afghanistan. Four are missing as of summer 2023. A former director-general remarked that he had never gone longer than four months without a staff member taken hostage. A former high official remarked about how searing it was to learn of the death or kidnapping of staff during his time in office. As of 2021, the leading situations showing attacks on various aid workers (comprised of shootings, assaults, kidnappings, or bombings), were, in order: South Sudan, Afghanistan, Syria, Ethiopia, and Mali.[19] The ICRC was active in all of them.

Overlapping with its field activities in about 100 nations was a constant effort to limit political violence via IHL and related norms, keeping a stiff upper lip, as the British would say, facing disappointment after disappointment in trying to get fighting parties to observe limits in the

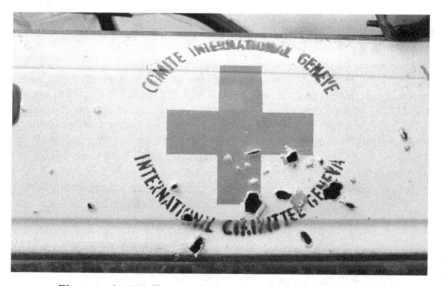

Photograph 18.3 Damage from rocket shrapnel, ICRC vehicle, Kabul, Afghanistan, 1994. Eash year the ICRC organizes a ceremony remembering those killed on missions. For a long time, the ICRC so recognized only expatriate staff – who were overwhelming European. Now it has a "one staff" policy, trying to recognize the equal importance of both resident and mobile staff, both the locals and the internationals.

name of at least a minimum regard for humane values. It is no wonder that Peter Maurer was ready for retirement after ten years of dealing with Putin and Assad, the Myanmar junta, armed militias in the Sahel and eastern DRC, and on and on. One can empathize when he went to Moscow in early 2022 and sought restraint from a Russian leadership that had been demonstrably brutal in places like Chechnya and Syria. The Putin regime had not just pursued something close to total war in several situations but had also killed Russian dissidents and locked up Russian critics. From the Stalinist Putin regime Maurer was expected to extract a commitment to humane policies.

Some readers might be surprised by the views above praising the ICRC, given earlier chapters and their close examination of different subjects. But I recall the old line about doing the analysis first, before one gets to praise or blame. There is no doubt that the ICRC has made mistakes. Some are major, like the inadequate response to the Holocaust. Some are almost major, like failing to properly contest Mussolini's atrocious policies in Abyssinia. Some linger, like a failure to fully control for Swiss nationalism in the light of what is required of cosmopolitan NIIHA values. Some are arguably of a minor and passing nature, like having the president on the WEF board of trustees or sometimes suspending sound judgment when trying to develop good relations with Beijing. (Some critics think these are major issues.) These topics and more have been covered in the preceding pages and will not be rehashed now. There is no organization – political, humanitarian, or otherwise – that has endured for over 160 years and has been free of mistakes great and small.

It is easy for some in a comfortable position on the sidelines to say that trying to limit the horrors of political violence actually encourages that violence by making it seem more humane at the margins. The view was decidedly otherwise by Nelson Mandela, who endured twenty-seven years of imprisonment and emerged with appreciation for the respite from despair that ICRC prison visits produced. The view is no doubt similar for the many women raped in the DRC or South Sudan or the Sahel and whom the ICRC transported to safe areas and arranged medical and psychological care. The view is without doubt similar for the many people forcibly displaced by political violence and whom the ICRC helped restore to stability and an income through its economic security programs. The view is definitely similar for those in Afghanistan and elsewhere who lost limbs to violence but were fitted by the ICRC with prosthetics and then given funding and training so as to be reintegrated into active society – and this over at least a thirty-year period.

It is this ethics of small and semi-small deeds, combined with bigger strategies of legal development and Movement calculation, always insufficient and inadequate, that would be absent in a world without the ICRC. MSF, valuable at it is, cannot completely fill the void, concentrating as it does mainly on medical policies. Various UN agencies, valuable as they are, cannot completely fill the void, lacking as they do the ICRC image of competent neutrality.[20] (The ICRC's overhead expenses for administration and fundraising were about 9 percent of budget. The UNHCR's was about 30 percent, with most of that expense going to fundraising. Charity Navigator, a rating agency, gave the UNHCR only a two-star rating out of a possible four.) One can go down the list of humanitarian agencies, or sometimes humanitarian agencies, and not find an adequate replacement for the unique ICRC. In 2022, the UNHCR said it had no experience in running humanitarian corridors for civilian convoys exiting a fighting space, as then being discussed for Ukrainian cities like Mariupol. The ICRC did, and after many hinderances was able to help thousands move away from deadly danger in that war – in cooperation with UN diplomacy to be sure.

Lest one be swept up into a hagiography of the organization that was characteristic of much earlier literature, it bears restating that many questions remain about the ICRC, now and in the future. Does it properly calculate the limits to its action, for example on the matter of the double nexus or links to development? Does it have the right calculus about relations with the other units of the Movement? Has it grown too big, too fast to the detriment of staff commitment and NIIHA values? Is the organization too much affected by different presidents who are brought in from the outside and manifest changing styles and personal fixations, even defects? (Coming from Bern, they almost always think their knowledge of diplomacy is superior to "amateurish" ICRC personnel, yet the latter have been negotiating with wily governmental and nongovernmental actors around the world.) Has the ICRC after the Sommaruga era been too reticent, too compliant with the preferences of fighting parties, too hesitant to push the envelope of humanitarian values by saying – even in measured terms – when a particular fighting party has failed to meet the terms of IHL? These and other questions comprise a continuing discussion worth having, given the importance of the ICRC to global humanitarianism today.

Mark Twain, when supposedly told that a newspaper had published his obituary, apparently commented wryly that accounts of his death were greatly exaggerated. Likewise, forecasts about the decline of the ICRC are certainly premature. The old ICRC – small, all Swiss, tightly focused, quick to act in the field – has indeed died. There is a new one extant – larger, multinational, more bureaucratic, with a sprawling applied mandate. The West has funded its ambitions at least until recently. Indeed, its major donors have agreed about its strategic objectives. But that does not mean that all ICRC extant policies should be continued. It seems time, especially with looming budget cuts once again, for those with full information to take stock after a period of rapid change, to cut some programs and not just trim some details here and there, and to make sure its current role is properly anchored in necessary activities in keeping with Dunantist values. A new president with maybe a reconfigured governing board would be a good time to construct from the inside the proper balance sheet about the contemporary ICRC.

Notes

1 Hugo Slim, *Solferino 2.0: Warfare, Civilians and Humanitarians in the Twenty First Century* (London: Hurst, 2022), p. 180.
2 Ibid.
3 Hugo Slim, "You Don't Have to Be Neutral to Be a Good Humanitarian," *The New Humanitarian*, August 27, 2020, www.thenewhumanitarian.org/opinion/2020/08/27/humanitarian-principles-neutrality (accessed November 12, 2022).
4 Scott Anderson, *The Man Who Tried to Save the World: The Dangerous Life and Mysterious Disappearance of an American Hero* (New York: Random House, 1999).
5 "The Humanitarian Club: Hierarchy, Networks, and Exclusion," chap. 5 in Michael N. Barnett, Jon C. W. Pevehouse, and Kal Raustiala, eds., *Global Governance in a World of Change* (Cambridge: Cambridge University Press, 2020), www.cambridge.org/core/books/global-governance-in-a-world-of-change/humanitarian-club/5B998C985F7281BD50874AF13AC9CA13 (accessed November 12, 2022). See also Michael Barnett and Peter Walker, "Regime Change for Humanitarian Aid," *Foreign Affairs*, July–August 2015, www.foreignaffairs.com/articles/world/2015-06-16/regime-change-humanitarian-aid (accessed December 17, 2020).
6 Robert Michels, *Political Parties: A Sociological Study of the Oligarchic Tendencies of Modern Democracy* (New York: The Free Press, 1962).
7 There is a related view that not just the international humanitarian enterprise but also the global human rights system is essentially a colonial project in which the powerful northwestern developed states tell the others what to do and how to do it. See, for example, Abdullah Ahmed An-Naim, *Decolonizing Human Rights* (Cambridge: Cambridge University Press, 2022). See especially his introductory chapter which is thoughtful but not the last word on the subject.
8 The interview contains several long passages on localization – too long and numerous to be reproduced here – but one can read them and decide whether they indicate clarity about alternatives. *The New Humanitarian*, September 2022, cited in the previous chapter. In a key passage Maurer said: "I think we are in a different stage of history. I'm very skeptical about grand bargains, less on bargains than on grand. And I'm very skeptical on overall frameworks showing the path forward." Here one sees the case-by-case diplomat, skeptical of doctrine, theory, or big-picture solutions. One muddles through, case by case, with attention to the specifics of each case.

9 Slim, *Solferino 2.0*, p. xxxix.

10 I am aware that in this section of my conclusion I run the risk of being seen as a reactionary or insensitive analyst – or perhaps politically incorrect – in some circles. Earlier Slim and David Rieff had some differing opinions about the proper role or scope of humanitarian assistance. At one point Slim referred to Rieff as a Luddite. So much for civilized debate among authors. Hugo Slim, "Is Humanitarianism Being Politicized: A Reply to David Rieff," HD, Centre for Humanitarian Dialogue, meeting at The Hague, The Netherlands, October 8, 2003, p. 3: "David and other 'back to basics' humanitarian Luddites might already regard these ideals as 'too developmental' or 'too political' or too much trying to be 'part of the solution.'" https://hdcentre.org/wp-content/uploads/2016/07/Is-Humanitarianism-Being-Politicised-October-2003.pdf (accessed December 9, 2022).

11 Hugo Slim, "Reflections of a Humanitarian Bureaucrat," *Humanitarian Law & Policy*, January 9, 2020, https://blogs.icrc.org/law-and-policy/2020/01/09/reflections-humanitarian-bureaucrat/ (accessed November 12, 2022).

12 Tariro Tandi and Immaculate Mugo, "Rethinking the Accountability of Funders," *Open Global Rights*, July 8, 2022, www.openglobalrights.org/rethinking-the-accountability-of-funders/ (accessed November 12, 2022).

13 Slim, *Solferino 2.0*, p. 161. See also Michael N. Barnett, ed., *Paternalism beyond Borders*, (Cambridge: Cambridge University Press, 2016).

14 Slim, *Solferino 2.0*, p. 180.

15 Ibid, pp. 213–214.

16 Thomas G. Weiss, *Would the World Be Better without the UN?* (Cambridge: Polity Press, 2018).

17 ICRC, "Ukraine: As Humanitarian Crisis Deepens, Parties Need to Agree on Concrete Measures; Misinformation Risks Lives," March 29, 2022, www.icrc.org/en/document/ukraine-humanitarian-crisis-deepens-parties-urgently-need-agree-concrete-measures (accessed November 12, 2022).

18 *The New Humanitarian*, September 2022.

19 Humanitarian Outcomes, as reported in "The World in Brief," *The Economist*, August 19, 2022, https://view.e.economist.com/?qs=12dc4c84c981e0737794204b4ce8b7ada5d26d74f783f80fea19a5a490a6b1e9390d2575010cf393c2e4ec51a0806d7b000ae7b0b0e559c960e80e2c2f8f19825ebcbc10dd1cfa86fcde6f9d7473bf81. For the more detailed original report, see Relief Web, "Aid Worker Security Report: Figures at a Glance 2022," posted July 30, 2022, originally published July 25, 2022, https://reliefweb.int/report/world/aid-worker-security-report-figures-glance-2022 (accessed November 12, 2022).

20 It is worth noting, as I do in the Epilogue, that the UN did not defer to the ICRC even in POW matters in the Ukraine war, establishing a monitoring mission that interviewed extant or released POWs on both sides. This occurred in the context of ICRC prolonged silence about many particulars on such topics as treatment of POWs and some other IHL issues.

Epilogue
The War in Ukraine – Challenges and Controversies

I want to point out that we did not find support from the International Committee of the Red Cross. We do not see that they are fully fighting to gain access to the camps, where Ukrainian prisoners of war and political prisoners are held. Neither are they helping to find deported Ukrainians. This self-withdrawal is the self-destruction of the Red Cross as an organization that was once respected.

Volodymir Zelensky, president of Ukraine, November 16, 2022

As this book project was being concluded, Russia invaded Ukraine and created the greatest international armed conflict in Europe since 1945 – dwarfing the atrocious but much smaller Balkan wars centered initially on Bosnia following the breakup of Yugoslavia in the 1990s. A full accounting of the ICRC in the war in Ukraine will obviously have to await the passage of time and more space, but one can give some preliminary and tentative observations. Mostly I limit analysis to the period between the start of the war and President Peter Maurer's departure from that office in fall, 2022.

The case of Ukraine reminds us again that while a narrow legal and judicial emphasis has it uses and importance, there is a policymaking process going on that involves choices among competing principles, values, and interests. No law implements itself. On the part of both belligerents and humanitarian third parties, choices are made about strategy and tactics. This process of policy choice is part of what can be termed "humanitarian politics," one central aspect of which is the struggle by third parties to elevate humanitarian values in the strategy and tactics of warring sides.[1] Actors such as the ICRC face a myriad of choices in deciding when and how to try to advance the values found in IHL.

The conclusion to this Epilogue will summarize humanitarian politics and the ICRC in the Ukrainian case by in arguing that: the ICRC tried very hard to play its traditional role in armed conflict, faced major challenges (as in most other wars), achieved some considerable good, made some controversial choices, and left a complex overall record that provides ample grist for the mill of future reflections. It was clear enough after about one year of that war that the Geneva headquarters struggled to be fully accepted by the two belligerents and struggled as well to develop a convincing communications policy about IHL.

I   Introduction

The ICRC was slow to get going immediately after the February 24, 2022 invasion and manifested major problems with its image on the Ukrainian side. Its problems on the Russian side were more substantive in that the attackers' strategy and tactics often did not fit well with the norms of IHL. In particular, Geneva's early silence on detention matters was troubling to many. This last subject brought up once again the old subject of discretion versus public statements – and how to interpret its doctrine on the subject. In general, that policy guideline said that the organization might go public about repeated violations of IHL if quiet diplomacy had proved disappointing *and* a public accounting was in the interest of victims. The ICRC almost never decides that going public on specifics is in the interest of victims, especially when a great or intermediate power is directly involved.[2]

An initial ICRC statement at the start of the war was brief and mainstream, emphasizing the norms of IHL that should be followed.[3] In fact, the two belligerents quietly accepted that they were involved in an international armed conflict to which IHL applied. This was different from Syria, to take one example, where President Assad from 2011 never accepted that he faced an armed conflict, insisting that his enemies were terrorists and that the situation remained below the level even of an internal armed conflict. Regarding Ukraine, in public Moscow rejected for many months the word "war" to describe its actions, preferring "special military operation." States were still playing semantical games with the word "war" at the G-20 meeting during fall 2022, although Putin finally used the word "war" in public in late December. But with the ICRC the two belligerents agreed early on that IHL for IAC (international armed conflict) applied in principle.

The situation meant that the ICRC could proceed directly to advocacy for – or general Protection under – the specifics of the 1949, 1977, and other law without spending time discussing the proper legal framework.[4] Agreement in the abstract, of course, certainly did not mean proper application of the law on particulars. Nevertheless, while early on President Putin of Russia apparently saw himself engaged in retaking land that was truly or rightfully Russian, and while he initially dismissed

Ukrainian identity and nationalism as artificial, being the product of outside mischief by "Nazis," which seemed to mean anyone who disagreed with his views, his officials did not object to the ICRC's reference to full IHL.

In February 2022 the ICRC was not especially well positioned for the outbreak of hostilities. It did not always have experienced and assertive staff on the ground in Ukraine. The ICRC was somewhat slow to get its field operations properly underway. Early violence saw many ICRC staff confined to quarters for safety reasons, although some activity occurred. The ICRC head of delegation in Ukraine was replaced, along with some other staff members. Several experienced staff persons were either recalled from retirement or transferred to Ukraine from other offices. Its program of emergency deployment was activated. It seems it was typical of large international humanitarian agencies to take some weeks to become operational in Ukraine.[5]

Top ICRC officials had little recent and direct experience with international armed conflict involving major powers of the type seen in the Ukraine war. Much ICRC activity was focused on "protracted conflicts" with levels of violence that rose and fell in "fragile societies" in non-Western areas. Organizational history, precedent, and "doctrine" about major wars were not at the top of concerns in Geneva. In the early months of the war the International Red Cross and Red Crescent Movement, including the ICRC, received about 10 percent of the donations made for humanitarian actors active in the war.[6] Several months into the fighting the ICRC had about 700 personnel on the ground in Ukraine, about 400 of them expats, carrying out many of the expected functions pertaining to IHL, despite complex challenges.

II   Civilian Protection

The ICRC and its partners, mainly about fifty National RC Societies from primarily Western nations, made cash payments to some displaced or especially needy persons; provided food and water, hygiene kits, blankets, and other material to some needy civilians; delivered a variety of medical supplies to various hospitals; and in general carried out the usual wartime relief activities. Many medical institutions had been damaged in the early fighting, as documented by the World Health Organization and other sources. A Red Cross publication in August 2022 indicated that 350 health-care facilities in Ukraine had been attacked.[7] Special attention was given to the evacuation from war zones of disabled, older, and especially needy persons – often in difficult conditions requiring complex negotiations. The total of ICRC and Movement efforts to help civilians was quite substantive, summarized early on by a public statement in late June,[8] then again in late August, as already cited.

Conditions were very difficult for any of the humanitarians active in Ukraine early in the war. Some aid personnel were killed from actors such as Caritas or the Hare Krishna movement. The scorched earth campaign adopted by Moscow, plus lack of reliable communication among invading units, made it highly difficult to carry out humanitarian activities amidst the dangerous uncertainty. No doubt this situation accounted for some of the early criticisms of the ICRC from the Ukrainian side.[9] The ICRC team in Ukraine was early on unable to do much partly because of the security situation, then was blocked from arranging exit corridors for endangered civilians despite its desire to do so.

Photograph E.1 The Russian full invasion of Ukraine in early 2022 presented the ICRC with a major international war for which it was not fully prepared. Its top officials had little hands-on experience with violence on this scale, but after a slow start it delivered much assistance to civilians in Ukraine under difficult conditions. Here in 2022 two staff members carry out damage assessment in an area that has been attacked and administer first aid to a local whose residence has been destroyed. Despite its efforts – included arranging corridors for the extraction of civilians from fighting areas, which required complicated diplomacy – the organization faced reputational challenges, especially on the Ukrainian side.

It can be said in general that Ukrainian nationalism, cohering and intensifying as the country faced unprovoked and brutal attack, and comprising a major asset in military operations, did not easily accommodate neutral organizations, some of which – including the ICRC – were sometimes seen as either lethargic or pro-Russia. Those seeing themselves as exercising legitimate self-defense against a brutal aggression do not always have charitable views toward neutrals, or even toward IHL itself, which applies to both defenders and invaders.

Despite criticism from the Ukrainian side, much ICRC help to civilians could be seen as offsetting some of the effects of Russian attacks through its de facto impact. This was so, for example, when the ICRC brought in water tankers and other basic supplies to the city of Kherson, as the Russian retreat was accompanied by continued shelling of the city's infrastructure from across the Dnieper River. At least in their public statements, high Ukrainian officials seemed to discount the value of that and similar ICRC assistance to civilians, disappointed as they were with ICRC diplomacy and failure to obtain broad access to Ukrainian POWs and other detainees held on the Russian side – explained further later.

The ICRC created in Geneva a special branch of the Central Tracing Agency, staffed with multilingual personnel, to try to track the fate of those detained or missing, receiving tens of thousands of inquiries.[10]

Civilian distress increased when Russia escalated attacks on power stations and electrical grids and other infrastructure vital to civilian society in the fall of 2022. Moscow admitted the attacks while claiming they were legally permissible as the power grids serviced military as well as civilian facilities. (The West itself has employed this kind of argument about dual use targets in 1999 when NATO bombed bridges and other targets in Belgrade as the West was contesting Serbian policies in Kosovo.) Escalating civilian hardship to weaken morale and support became part of Russia's evident military strategy – as in other wars in Syria and Chechnya. Civilians and their vital support systems suffered not just as collateral damage in traditional military campaigns but as intentionally targeted.

Consistent with its preferred practices, an ICRC statement noted that attacks on civilians and civilian infrastructure was a violation of IHL; but it did not explicitly call out Russian policies or get into the legal details – preferring to give an accounting of its extensive civilian assistance, generally impressive, as of the fall of 2022.[11]

Material support for war refugees in neighboring countries was mostly but not entirely provided by other units in the Movement, not primarily by the ICRC, which was an agreed division of labor in principle. As far as an outsider could tell, there was mostly adequate cooperation among the ICRC and the Ukrainian Red Cross and about fifty other National RC Societies. The ICRC interviewed refugees in Poland and elsewhere about what had been seen or experienced. This was important for the tracing of missing persons and for discreet representations to the fighting parties. This information was not shared with those seeking to build prosecutions for war crimes. As in Syria, millions of civilians were uprooted by the war both as refugees and internally displaced persons – in the Ukraine case amounting to about one-third of the national population. This problem increased with time and with the expansion of Russian attacks on infrastructure like electrical stations. There was a certain ebb and flow of civilians across borders, related to the ebb and flow of the war, such as in and out of Poland, which made precise and stable numbers difficult to establish.

The ICRC had various contacts with the Russian Red Cross (RRC), as did other Red Cross agencies. But once again the perennial question arose of how a National Red Cross Society might be faithful to NIIHA values (neutral, independent, and impartial principles in humanitarian action) when its government might expect it to be supportive of domestic or strategic politics.[12]

Ukraine and its Red Cross took exception to RRC activities that lent support to Russian families whose members were fighting in Ukraine, a program organized by the government, asking that the RRC be suspended from the Red Cross Movement.[13] But such RRC activity was what most National Societies did in wartime, boosting the morale of national fighting forces while remaining unarmed and avoiding direct participation in the fighting. Early on the Ukraine complaint about certain activities by the RRC was basically ignored by the ICRC and other Red Cross leaders in Geneva. Kyiv's demand raised complex and indeed embarrassing issues for the Movement and Red Cross fundamental principles. It was not a well-considered move by Kyiv but showed the depth of its nationalism and quest for support.

Other ICRC offices in some conflict situations were reduced slightly, with some staff transferred to Ukraine, but all offices continued to function more or less as usual in other conflicts. The ICRC made efforts to see that these other situations of violence were not forgotten. ICRC President Maurer, for example, called attention publicly to the situation in northeastern Syria.[14] These other conflicts were stressed when ICRC officials visited Washington, DC. It was true that the Western focus on Ukraine sucked much of the air – and money – out of the global humanitarian system. But the ICRC did what it could to contest this trend, even while making a major commitment to the European war. Its appeal for funds for Ukraine was *overfunded*.

Despite delay and many difficulties, the ICRC – acting in tandem with the United Nations – did help arrange humanitarian corridors for the safe evacuation of hundreds of civilians from some conflict areas.[15] It was no small achievement to arrange over several days the safe movement of sizable numbers of traumatized civilians through dangerous military checkpoints during active hostilities.[16] Regardless of figures about funding of aid, the ICRC brought to the humanitarian table in this war its reputation and expertise about various forms of Protection. By comparison, the UNHCR, the UN refugee office, indicated it has no experience in such matters as devising humanitarian corridors.

A particularly difficult problem was the fate of children taken from Ukrainian areas that legally fell under the Fourth GC from 1949 pertaining to occupied territory. This problem existed from 2014 and again from February 2022, regardless of whether Moscow claimed the Ukrainian areas as Russian. Under international law, territory captured in armed conflict does not confer ownership on the controlling party. While there

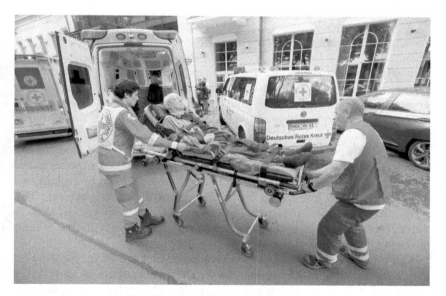

Photograph E.2 The ICRC in the war in Ukraine often worked with partners from the rest of the RC Movement and gave much attention in its assistance operations to the elderly and disabled. Here, ICRC staff work with personnel from the German Red Cross to evacuate a man away from the fighting in Mykolaiv to Moldova by way of Odesa in May 2022.

had been much attention to this subject in the Middle East, given Israel's taking of much new territory during and after the 1967 war, the subject did not receive comparable early public attention regarding Ukraine.

According to some media reports, many children had been taken from Ukraine and given new lives, and passports, as Russians.[17] This issue had not been addressed by any specific ICRC public statement in the first months of the war. Such a statement would directly contest Russian policy. The ICRC, in the face of various critiques from the Ukrainian side, did state that it would never be a party to forced relocation.[18] Ukrainian officials stressed this subject in at least two public statements in fall 2022, criticizing the ICRC for its alleged lack of dynamism on the subject.[19]

President Zelensky said of the ICRC at the G-20 meeting in fall 2022, as quoted at the start of this Epilogue:

> I want to point out that we did not find support from the International Committee of the Red Cross. We do not see that they are fully fighting to gain access to the camps, where Ukrainian prisoners of war and political prisoners are held. Neither are they helping to find deported Ukrainians. This self-withdrawal is the self-destruction of the Red Cross as an organization that was once respected.[20]

Relatedly, early in the war the ICRC mentioned the possibility of opening an office in Rostov, or Rostov-on-Don, in Russia in order to help with civilian issues on the Russian side – whether pertaining to adults or children. This was sometimes seen in Ukraine as facilitating objectionable Russian policies involving the fate of detained Ukrainians in areas controlled by Russian-backed separatists or deeper into Russian territory. It did not help matters that the town of Rostov was associated with past atrocities stemming from the Second World War. In the light of these complications the ICRC finally backtracked from its initial Rostov plans. It had been placed on the defensive and had to explain and justify its original intentions, before beating a diplomatic retreat. The ICRC denied that it was engaged in forced relocation of persons, already noted, but the damage had been done as a matter of perception – at least in some Ukrainian circles.

The International Criminal Court issued an arrest warrant for Russian President Putin and his top official on children's affairs in early 2023 precisely for the deportation and transfer of children from occupied territory, prohibited by the Fourth Geneva Convention of 1949. Given this fact, to some it was embarrassing that the ICRC had not spoken out about this violation of IHL. However much the ICRC may have discussed the issue with Russian officials, which was not clear, for Geneva the matter had remained in the realm of quiet diplomacy. It was also not clear why the ICC prosecutor had singled out the one issue of deportation of children, given that the UN had reported on a very long list of asserted war crimes at about the same time as the ICC arrest warrant.[21]

Early in spring of 2022 Mauer had gone to Kyiv and pressed his mainstream arguments.[22] On the one hand, his going to the scene of conflict, not without some personal risk, dramatized humanitarian concerns. On the other hand, many violations of IHL in this armed conflict originated not with Ukrainian officials but rather on the Russian side.[23] Maurer was not received by President Zelensky, whereas on a later trip to Moscow he was given the red carpet treatment.

It was reasonably clear that sometimes Ukrainian fighters fired from apartments and other civilian structures, as reported by various news magazines such as *The Economist*, although this occasional fact did not explain at all the broad extent of Russian attacks on civilians and civilian infrastructure. When Amnesty International issued a report about Ukrainian use of, or positioning military resources near, civilian structures to launch attacks,[24] the resulting Western media criticism of that human rights advocacy organization[25] showed that: (a) much of the West simply did not want to hear about Ukrainian controversial policies, and (b) the advocacy organization had not been careful in framing its report. Whether this Western backlash against Amnesty in London, when it criticized Ukrainian policies, had any effect on the ICRC HQ in Geneva when considering public statements is an interesting question.

Similar to Rwanda in 1994, regarding Russian attacks on cities including Mariupol the ICRC made clear what was happening to civilians through various statements, often on Twitter: "the human suffering is simply immense;" "the situation is really apocalyptic;" "the level of destruction is beyond all words and imagination;" "our team found devastation." In May from Warsaw, President Maurer said that civilian destruction in the war was "abhorrent and unacceptable."[26] There were, in fact, many ICRC public statements about IHL and the Ukraine war, but they were sporadic, not concentrated, and not part of a coherent and cohesive communications policy. One could learn, for example, that an ICRC warehouse in Mariupol, not then operative but well-marked by the Red Cross emblem, was attacked – presumably by Russian forces.

After his visit to Kyiv, Maurer also undertook personal diplomacy in Moscow where he had already met several times with some of the leading policymakers. He was clear in his philosophy of quiet diplomacy, as he said when receiving an award in Geneva earlier.[27] He was searching for the intersection of state interests and IHL norms, no doubt trying to get Russian decision-makers to recognize their self-interest in pursuing policies that spared the civilian population and their vital infrastructure, protected prisoners whether combatant or civilian, and in other ways respected IHL. This diplomacy: (a) was based on a realistic under-standing of how most governments operated, with much attention to self-interest; (b) at least officially believed that there was some common humanitarian ground among belligerents regardless of reputation for brutality; and (c) followed ICRC doctrine, based on lessons from the Holocaust, namely that the ICRC had to first try quiet but dynamic diplomacy even if the prospects for success were dim.

However, some ICRC former officials believed that in international armed conflicts such as Ukraine the organization should be insistent on state's legal obligations under IHL. They believed that the ICRC was overly affected by much experience in internal armed conflicts and "other violence" and used to negotiating its objectives rather than demanding compliance with IHL in international war, a law universally accepted. They faulted the contemporary ICRC for departing from some past ICRC practices in calling out violations of IHL in international war.

In his Moscow visit, whatever the substance of discussions, Maurer was filmed and photographed in friendly relations with Russian Foreign Minister Sergei Lavrov. These images did not play well in Ukraine and elsewhere and was acknowledged to this author as a faux pas by certain officials in the ICRC. That an experienced diplomat like Maurer would allow himself to be seen as less than business-like and almost jovial in a war setting was surprising. Such an optic may trace back to his disregard for images and reputation evident in other settings.[28]

On his way out the door at the end of his presidency in late September 2022, Maurer gave several unrestricted interviews, which he had mostly avoided up until then. In one of them he was asked about the images of his smiling relationship with the Russian foreign minister. Maurer, who could be very careful with his words, did not exactly deny having made a mistake, but once again he downplayed the subject of images while changing the subject. He said:

The same photo that exists with Sergey Lavrov exists probably with 100 other foreign ministers in the world. So there is a question of context, the question of whether this is the right choreography. But it was the right thing to go to Moscow. And it was the right thing to continue, on a day-to-day basis, to be in touch with the Russian authorities, with the Ukrainian authorities, with the local authorities in Ukraine, in order to carve out the space for our work. That's the baseline, and that's what is important. The rest is also a little bit of a distraction from what is essential.[29]

In subsequent days after his Moscow trip Maurer did indeed have many conversations with officials in Moscow, discussing with them various IHL matters. There was also a considerable dialogue between other ICRC and Russian officials. But some damage had been done via his ill-advised public presentations in Moscow. Continuing criticism of the ICRC on the Ukrainian side probably did not help the work of the Ukrainian Red Cross and its partners. The photo-ops and film no doubt played some role in the mounting criticism, even if there was other disinformation circulating on social media that sought to discredit the ICRC's role in Ukraine. Some of this disinformation about the ICRC became such that the organization spoke out against it.[30] Again, in the quiet bilateral contacts between the ICRC and especially Russian officials, we do not know the nature of ICRC diplomacy –for example, how vigorous and assertive it was in defense of IHL. Or, if not assertive, was low-key diplomacy appropriate given views held by key Russian officials?

III   POW Protection

In early October 2022 Ukraine's President Zelensky launched his first broadside of criticism against the ICRC for failing to protect Ukrainian POWs.[31] He repeated a slightly broader attack on the ICRC at the G-20 meeting that fall, already noted.[32] At this time the ICRC did not have full access to Russian POWs held by the *Ukrainian* side, as Russian officials accurately said. A UN report, based on interviews with POWs or former POWs from both sides, concluded that the Ukrainians too were violating their obligations under IHL regarding POWs.[33] This was confirmed by another UN report in March 2023, already cited. Several videos circulated in social media apparently showing Ukrainian forces mistreating or killing Russian military captives, already mentioned in a reference note. It was likely that Zelensky, in criticizing the ICRC, was trying to put more pressure on the Russians indirectly, by pushing the ICRC to push Moscow – and to distract from Ukrainian defects under IHL. Already, even before the two Zelensky broadsides of that fall, some criticism in Ukrainian news sources blamed the ICRC for, inter alia, not being dynamic in pressing Russian authorities to grant the organization full access to POWs as required by IHL.[34] From August 2022, Kyiv suspended the few ICRC visits then occurring to its POW facilities, in retaliation against Russian obstructions on that same issue.

However, according to reliable interviews, in the winter of 2022–2023 the Ukrainian Ministry of Justice commended the ICRC for its humanitarian efforts, including on POW affairs. It seems that on the Ukrainian side the ICRC ran workshops on the proper management of POW camps and discussed with Kyiv the topic of using civilian structures to attack the enemy,[35] as well as providing instruction about the proper process for collection of information pursuant to possible war crimes.

This record suggests either that there was a disconnect between the Office of the President, critical of the ICRC, and other parts of the Ukrainian administrative state, much more appreciative of the ICRC. Or it suggests that the Office of the President was playing a double game, fully understanding the role of the ICRC but using public criticism of Geneva to try to pressure Russia into better protection for Ukrainian detainees.

The ICRC responded to the first Zelensky public blast by, inter alia, issuing a press release in measured terms in which it again asked for access to all those detained under IHL rules on both sides.[36] It followed up by pointing out that it was ready to visit all POWs but needed the approval of the belligerents, which had the primary duty to respect IHL. It had said something similar once before when it was criticized for not having regular access to the Olenivka prison in eastern Ukraine under

Photograph E.3 Even before the full Russian invasion of Ukraine in February 2022, the ICRC had been one of the few humanitarian agencies active in the eastern part of the country from 2014, when Moscow took control of Crimea and intervened in various ways in the Donbas region. In the lower-level violence that ensued, the ICRC provided much assistance, especially concerning civilian water supplies and helping to keep schools operating. It also pursued its protection mandate. Here, a staff member deals with detention matters in Mariupol in the Donetsk region in 2019. (The man on the right is unidentified.)

Russian control where some fifty Ukrainian POWs or more had been killed in a suspicious explosion. (The ICRC, which knew of the Olenivka facility, had been there before the explosion but was not carrying out visits at the time of the blast, asked to go to the explosion site to bring medical and other assistance.[37] That request was ignored by Russia, at least in the first eighteen months of its invasion.) Unfortunately over time, there was the pattern that the ICRC only said something detailed about POWs in public when it was criticized for not being dynamic enough. This pattern was injurious to the ICRC's image, at least in some circles.

As reports were published in the Western media about bad conditions and treatment for prisoners held especially by Russia and its allies in eastern Ukraine, some based on eye-witness accounts, the ICRC was indeed in a difficult position.[38] Sometimes the fighting parties agreed to prisoner exchanges, from time to time mediated by Turkey or Saudi Arabia or the United Arab Emirates, or some other third party, and the prisoners formerly held by the Russian side would speak to the media about the ill treatment they had received.[39] Then there were multiple media reports about conditions under Russian control when those areas were taken over by Ukrainian forces. Moreover, there was that UN report in the fall, by a mission to Ukraine under the Office of the High Commissioner for Human Rights, based on interviews with current or former detainees from both sides, without governmental supervision.[40] This report indicated much mistreatment of POWs by both sides. A new video circulated on social media in the fall apparently showing the killing of Russian POWs by the Ukrainian side.

During most of 2022 the ICRC lacked regular access to all, or even most, POWs. A Russian diplomat said in mid-October that the Russian side held some 6,000 Ukrainian POWs.[41] The ICRC had said it had access to a few hundred. The Ukrainian side, while criticizing the ICRC, never fully addressed its own defective policies under the norms of IHL. Western media, being largely pro-Ukraine, did not press Kyiv on this subject.

In the early months of the war there had been a glimmer of progress on POW issues, but this promise proved mostly stillborn. When holdout Ukrainian fighters finally surrendered in Mariupol, ICRC representatives were present on the vehicles that transported the disarmed fighters to Russian detention. They also were able to register the names of many of the POWs, important for future developments (some of those who surrendered refused this opportunity). This episode showed that an ICRC presence was still seen as a guarantee of immediate personal security, by both sides, and that the ICRC was following the terms of the Third GC from 1949 and activating the work of the Central Tracing

Agency, as already noted, in trying to keep track of detained fighters and others such as the missing.[42] But again, for a time the ICRC was denied regular access to most POWs held in detention on both sides.

It remains unclear at the time of writing how dynamic and appropriate ICRC efforts were regarding attempted protection of detainees. (Attention to POWs should not preempt concern about interned civilians, also legally protected under IHL.) In the short term it does not matter if, in fifty years, when ICRC archives are opened, those records show much about the organization's discrete bilateral efforts. In the short term, the ICRC faced reputational challenges, not just from Ukrainians but from a broader circle of observers and analysts. The general impression created, at least in some circles, was humanitarian failure and organizational weakness. This view may have been misguided, or overstated, but it existed.

It was relevant that some statements by high-ranking Russian officials were vitriolic about Ukrainian fighters, suggesting, for example, that they deserved death by hanging. Such statements indicated a disregard for the basic principles behind IHL pertaining to prisoners – namely that once out of the fight by injury or capture they were entitled to a humanitarian quarantine.[43]

To recapitulate, while there was much attention in the Western media to Russian attacks on civilians and civilian infrastructure, there was some growing attention early on to detainee – especially POW – affairs. Some ICRC alumni could not understand the lack of public attention to detainee matters in early ICRC public communiqués. The view inside the organization was that protection matters were proceeding in the correct direction, if quite slowly and very incompletely, with much awareness of defects under IHL, but that the critics should have confidence in the ICRC's handling of this traditional area of ICRC expertise.

IV   ICRC Communication Policy

Given evident indiscriminate warfare in Russian targeting policies in Ukraine as well as widely reported evidence of many other probable war crimes involving torture and summary execution of those detained, some observers viewed ICRC early statements as overly cautious. This view was reinforced by the ICC arrest warrant for illegal deportations from occupied territory, on which the ICRC had remained quiet. Some well-informed former officials recalled what President Sommaruga had said about the Bosnia war in 1992. At a conference in London, Sommaruga had first noted that quiet efforts had been made to Protect persons in that brutal conflict but to little effect. And so in his view it was proper to move on to public appeals. The point to be noted here is that Sommaruga then became rather specific about who was doing what to whom. By naming specific locations of humanitarian problems, it was easy enough for his audience to understand the targets of his concern. Without exactly naming the offending parties, by mentioning locales and by also describing the fate of victims, there was not much ambiguity about the specifics of humanitarian abuses in his references to the Bosnian war.[44]

Especially in international armed conflict regulated by extensive law universally agreed to by states, the ICRC had something of a tradition – I would say fuzzy and inconsistent but still identifiable – of releasing much public information about what it did and what it was prevented from doing, even if ICRC officials avoided harsh commentary on some specifics like allegations of particular war crimes.

In Ukraine, if early high-level ICRC statements were bland, over time the ICRC record on public communications seemed not much different from the Bosnian case at least in terms of dangers to civilians and civilian infrastructure. This was documented above by noting Twitter messages and various other statements, such as by President Maurer in Warsaw in May. I have already cited two summary statements, mostly about civilian Protection, in late May and late August 2022 – the latter on behalf of the Movement and cosponsored by the IFRC – the union of the National RC Societies.

The ICRC did adhere to its doctrinal statements about public communications and how to respond to reports of violations of IHL. That is to say, the ICRC avoided public comments about alleged specific war crimes and the like, especially since some slight progress was being made on some humanitarian issues. Also, official summary statements on the war by the Geneva HQ required much internal consultation, and some leaders seemed to think HQ summary statements not only time consuming but also somewhat dated in an era of Twitter widely used by journalists and others.

However, an op-ed in a Swiss newspaper in September 2022, written by a former head of ICRC communications, seemed on target.[45] In the past in international war, the Geneva HQ had often provided an overview of humanitarian issues, indicating in general terms what the organization had and had not been allowed to do – as per the reference above to Sommaruga and Bosnia. Months into the war in Ukraine no such overview had been issued that included much information on detention matters or forced transfer if not internment of civilians. As argued in the op-ed, all parties to the four 1949 Geneva Conventions were legally obligated to "respect and ensure respect for" that treaty law (Common Article 1). It was difficult for third-party states to do that without an authoritative account of humanitarian issues from Geneva. Geneva's lack of accounting also gave up the possibility of some public pressure on the belligerents. Various Twitter feeds were arguably not an adequate substitute.

A similar argument by a former official of the Swiss Red Cross, who was also a former official of the IFRC, appeared slightly later in the Swiss press.[46] This op-ed likewise called for more public accounting by the ICRC, noting there were repeated violations of IHL in Ukraine that would justify such a public statement. It noted some previous ICRC public accounting in other international armed conflicts. In general, it was highly critical of the organization and its very broad discretion in the Ukraine war.

Some ICRC personnel and offices were quite unhappy with the ICRC communications record emanating from Geneva.

Particularly on POW matters, I would say that early ICRC complete discretion then led to a situation where events forced the ICRC to say more, but even then many outsiders wanted a more comprehensive overview. When a suspicious explosion killed Ukrainian POWs at Olenivka in late July, already mentioned, the Geneva HQ issued several statements, one of which was significant. It gave some specifics about what the ICRC knew and when it knew it. The statement made clear to any alert reader that Russia was in violation of its obligations under the Third Geneva Convention from 1949 dealing with POWs.[47]

Slightly later it seemed that the ICRC director-general, still under public pressure for failing to obtain systematic and full access to the Olenivka prison, began to inch toward a more general accounting of what the ICRC had and had not been able to achieve on detention matters.[48] He said the organization had access to some POWs on both sides but no access to most of them. He said that ICRC early discretion about events did not necessarily have to last forever, a point already said to be communicated to the belligerents in bilateral diplomacy. But an official and centralized communications strategy including POWs and interned civilians still was absent by late summer 2023.

In early 2023 the Associated Press, a respected news service, did a story on Ukrainian civilians detained by Russia.[49] There was no mention of the ICRC. This could stem from lack of awareness by Associated Press reporters. But it was hard to see how the ICRC could successfully aspire to be the "go to" private agency on IHL if an in-depth story on protection of wartime civilian internees by an establishment news agency did not reference the ICRC at all. Almost certainly, the ICRC's policy of almost total discretion on protection matters, or its release of some information only when criticized, and its lack of a centralized and well-considered communications policy contributed to the situation. Whatever the facts in play, as perhaps will be established by archival research in the future, at the time of events there was a broad perception of ICRC weakness and failure.

This author was impressed by a very strong and clear ICRC statement in December 2022 challenging the Taliban's new restrictions on women in Afghanistan.[50] The statement was not only morally and logically powerful, but it took a clear public stance against a government's announced policy – even though the situation at that time was not legally one of armed conflict. There was no similar strong statement about, particularly, POW affairs in the Ukraine war, much less about civilian prisoners and those transferred out of occupied territory. In the Ukrainian war, the ICRC seemed to shy away from strong and clear statements challenging the policies of one side or the other on matters of detention and forcible transfer. As a result, the ICRC was pushed into piecemeal statements by events – and constantly trying to catch up to the existence of broad criticism.

The image of the ICRC held in some circles was thus one of timidity about, and compliance with, many violations of IHL by the fighting parties. Outsiders do not know if ICRC quiet diplomacy was much more assertive and clearer than its public diplomacy. Geneva officials said they had been very clear in their bilateral diplomacy. Outsiders do not know how obstinate Russian officials were in bilateral discussions with the ICRC, and whether, for example, the moderates were few and weak compared to hardliners. Did the ICRC have good contacts in the Kremlin and military corridors of power, beyond Sergei Lavrov and the Foreign Ministry? Did Lavrov have influence in these other power centers? Most Western media sources remained biased in favor of Ukraine, as noted above, which had indeed been brutally attacked without military provocation, and did little reporting on Kyiv's violations of IHL.

Two further observations about public statements can be noted. First, Sommaruga had spoken out well after the start of the Bosnian war, whereas when Maurer went to Kyiv and then Moscow the fighting was still in early stages. Second, however, it can also be noted that Sommaruga's strong and relatively specific rhetoric about humanitarian issues in the Bosnian war had slight impact on that nasty conflict. Sommaruga's statements about Bosnia were similar to the ICRC's rather specific statements about Rwanda in 1994, already covered, and with equally disappointing results. Sommaruga, however, had protected ICRC integrity and reputation with his public diplomacy.

In his last meeting with a variety of officials at the start of the UN General Assembly in New York in early fall 2022, the author was told that Maurer met again with Lavrov. It was clear enough that matters were still unsatisfactory regarding ICRC access to detained combatants and civilians, not to mention extensive attacks on civilian targets. There were no pervasive security guarantees from the Russian Ministry of Defense that would allow traditional and legally mandated ICRC activities, especially pertaining to protection. There was an expansion, rather than reduction, of Russian attacks on civilian areas as the war continued. The Russians began using Iranian kamikaze drones to hit Ukrainian populated areas and power plants vital to the civilian population. Extensive areas of Ukraine were without electrical power and safe water and adequate heat.

It was evident that a number of critics believed the ICRC should have been more assertive in its public diplomacy, both about Russian attacks on civilian targets and Russian limits on detention visits. (As already noted, the Western media did not focus much on the Ukrainian record, while independent reporting from the Russian side was virtually impossible since one could be locked up for questioning the official version of affairs.)[51] How could the ICRC claim to be the guardian of IHL if it departed from at least some tradition and refused to publish a White Paper or overview of IHL issues in the war?

In the past, for example in the Iran–Iraq war of 1980–1988, when Iran blocked ICRC visits to Iraqi POWs, since Teheran was pressuring Shia Iraqis to renounce their government, even arranging for the roughing up of the ICRC delegate Jean Fallet, the ICRC publicly stated that its visits were being blocked.[52] Also in the past, for example at the 1981 International Red Cross Conference in Manilla, the ICRC had successfully pushed for a Conference resolution naming three armed conflicts where the ICRC had been blocked from carrying out its usual duties: the Ogaden region (involving Ethiopia and Somalia); the Western Sahara (involving Algeria and Morocco and their allies); and Afghanistan (then involving the Soviet Union as well as the central government and various armed nonstate actors).[53] And in the Middle East, for example in 1992, President Sommaruga issued a long statement about IHL over the past five years including the Israeli–Palestinian conflict, stating candidly inter alia that in the ICRC's view Israel's introduction of Jewish settlements in the West Bank violated the Fourth Geneva Convention of 1949 and was detrimental to events in that occupied territory. The fact that the Israeli government had a different view of the applicability of the Fourth Geneva Convention pertaining to occupied territory did not prevent the ICRC statement.[54]

Thus by the time of the Ukraine war, there was some precedent for speaking out, at least in the form of a general accounting or overview, about difficulties in achieving systematic prisoner visits and other traditional ICRC roles. (Not that ICRC leaders in 2022, busy with many pressing problems, had a good grasp of historical precedent. Some were little interested in ICRC history, feeling that almost everything was different in current times. Some ICRC officials were simply new to major international war and did not have a ready grasp of past organizational practice in that type of conflict.) Some ICRC leaders seemed to take a dim view of established ICRC doctrine, feeling that it was a limiting factor in a context that demanded change and flexible diplomacy.

Was it that the ICRC had grown more cautious in its use of public information in order to try to generate pressure on the belligerents to respect IHL? Or was it that ICRC leaders in Geneva were deferring to those dealing daily with particularly Russian officials and who felt that the limited humanitarian achievements were very fragile and subject to reversal? Or, still further, had ICRC officials just become too compliant with the wishes and sensitivities of public authorities most of the time and gotten into the habit of not rocking the boat?

Through fall 2022 there had indeed been some limited humanitarian progress: some extraction of civilians from danger, considerable civilian assistance, some visits to detainees, some return of mortal remains of deceased, some success in locating persons through the Central Tracing Agency, and ongoing dialogues at high level with both belligerents. All of these developments were subject to further limitations or termination.

Through the first nine months of the war, clearly the ICRC decided that mostly discretion on specific POW affairs (not to mention specifics on targeting civilians, detained civilians, and transferred children) was the best way to advance Protection matters at that time, and no outsider has the information necessary to evaluate that decision in real time. It seems that at the Geneva HQ there was much discussion especially about public statements and POW affairs, with exchanges of views at the highest levels among the professionals. Discretion, with a few careful exceptions, was a consciously chosen stance, rightly or wrongly.

Some at ICRC HQ thought that an early public overview or taking stock of IHL issues, going beyond evident civilian Protection and covering sensitive matters of detention and transfer, would not be win-win but lose-lose. Rather than alerting others and putting public pressure on the belligerents, such an accounting would arguably provoke a backlash from especially hardline Russian officials, but maybe also Ukrainian leaders, and damage ICRC continuing efforts. This posture left the ICRC open to much criticism, deserved or not, especially since quiet bilateral diplomacy had not produced major positive results early on – beyond the provision of much civilian assistance.

Was this state of affairs in 2022 going to be eventually the 1930s and 1940s all over again, with the ICRC accused of lack of dynamism and guilty of timidity or compliance in protection matters? Was it too deferential to the sensitivities of the belligerents, at the expense of both victims and its own reputation long term?

Or was it correct that given the realities it faced, discretion and a low-key approach over time was the best policy? After all, presumably ICRC policy was set in a collective process. Moreover, on other occasions ICRC leaders had shown awareness of the mistakes of the ICRC in the 1930s and 1940s in not being dynamic enough with European fascists in quiet bilateral diplomacy.[55]

In fall 2022 a Swiss German-language news magazine featured this exchange as part of a long interview with outgoing President Maurer (as translated for me into French):

WELTWOCHE: Est-il vrai que l'on a l'impression que vous êtes plutôt du genre réservé?

MAURER: Oui, c'est sans doute vrai. Si je vois ne serait-ce qu'une chance minime de faire un pas en avant via la confidentialité, je choisis cette voie.[56]

(QUESTION: Is it true that one has the impression that you're mostly in the category of a reserved person?

ANSWER: Yes, it is without doubt true. If I see only a minimal chance to make a forward step by confidential means, I choose that path.)

Hence Maurer was presumably a strong force for discretion on protection matters in the Ukraine war throughout his presidency. We simply do not know if Maurer's preferences carried the day rather automatically, or whether there was vigorous debate about how to proceed and what to say in public among the organization's key policymakers. Certainly there was some discussion at HQ in Geneva, but in general there was much deference to a strong-willed president.

In an interview given to a Swiss newspaper in September 2022,[57] President Maurer made a statement on the subject of POWs in the Ukraine war:

Nous avons des accès, et en même temps nous en manquons beaucoup. Nous avons pu rendre visite à quelques centaines de prisonniers de guerre des deux côtés, tout en constatant – si je prends comme valeur exacte les chiffres avancés par les ministres de la défense d'Ukraine et de Russie – un écart substantiel avec le fait que plusieurs milliers de personnes sont détenues de chaque côté. Cette différence nous préoccupe énormément et nous essayons vraiment de la combler avec les deux pays afin de pouvoir travailler de la manière que prévoit le droit international humanitaire. Ce que je trouve positif, c'est que ni la Russie, ni l'Ukraine n'ont remis en cause notre droit à visiter les prisonniers de guerre. Cet écart avec la pratique résulte donc plutôt d'une question de confiance envers le CICR comme intermédiaire neutre. Ce n'est pas une objection politique, contrairement à beaucoup d'autres endroits du monde où on vous dit non parce qu'on conteste le rôle du CICR. Ici il n'y a pas de contestation.

(We have access [to POWs], and at the same time we lack access to a lot of them. We were able to visit a few hundred prisoners of war on both sides, while noting – if I take as an exact value the figures put forward by the Defense Ministers of Ukraine and Russia – a substantial discrepancy with the fact that several thousand people are being held on each side. We are very concerned about this difference and we are really trying to bridge it with both countries so that we can work in the way that international humanitarian law provides. What I find positive is that neither Russia nor Ukraine has questioned our right to visit prisoners of war. This discrepancy with practice is therefore rather a question of confidence in the ICRC as a neutral intermediary. This is not a political objection, unlike many other places in the world where you are told no because the ICRC's role is being challenged. Here there is no dispute.)

This statement fit with much of what we knew about the state of affairs in the fall of 2022, namely that the two belligerents accepted in principle the applicability of IHL for IAC, but that there were tensions over the activities of the ICRC. It seems that the tensions, ironically enough, at least for a time, might have been greater on the Ukrainian side.

While Russian Foreign Minister Lavrov may have had some quibbles here and there regarding the ICRC, he seemed to have a friendly relationship with ICRC President Maurer. Moreover, the usual reason given for lack of adequate POW visits, at least from the Russian side, was difficulty in making practical arrangements for detention visits (as well as for humanitarian corridors for civilian extraction). A statement from a Russian diplomat in Geneva, for what it was worth, which can be debated, indicated appreciation for the role of the ICRC and did not mention anything about lack of neutrality.[58] One guesses that on the Russian side, the military, security, and high political figures simply did not want the ICRC impeding their various brutal policies. After all, as already noted, Kyiv had collected information on over 60,000 suspected war crimes by Russia. It was not that the ICRC lacked neutrality. It was that many Russian policies were in violation of IHL rules. It is highly suspicious that Moscow kept blocking ICRC unrestricted visits to Olenivka POW prison after the deadly explosion there, suggesting the Russians had something to hide.

Moreover, as the war continued, some Russians were conscripted and rushed into battle with a minimum of training. A *Washington Post* interview with two fighters from the Wagner Group, a mercenary organization, recently captured in eastern Ukraine, confirmed reports of little military training for these former common criminals in Russia who were released from prison and had their criminal records purged if they agreed to fight in Ukraine. (The interview also confirmed harsh conditions and brutal treatment within the Russian military forces, including Wagner mercenary units. If brutality among Russians was evident, could one expect broad humanitarian policies toward various Ukrainians?)[59]

One can safely assume that these Russian fighters pressed into rapid service got little or no training in the laws of war. Still further, the brutal Wagner group – as already noted a private security firm alleged to have committed atrocities in the Sahel, and some fighters under the command of the brutal Chechnyan leader Ramzan Kadyrov – were also fighting for Moscow in Ukraine. It is highly unlikely they paid much attention to IHL rules Protecting civilians or captured combatants.

On the Ukrainian side, from early on through the G-20 meeting in early November, there were repeated charges from different sources about the ICRC being pro-Russian and/or negligent regarding both civilian and POW matters. There was an evident dislike of the ICRC on the Ukrainian side. Some key leaders were clearly anti-ICRC. Early ICRC slowness to act, the nature of its original team in the country, the images of the ICRC president in friendly interactions with the Russian foreign minister, its public silence on any number of highly questionable Russian policies, its inability to gain timely access to the Olenivka prison where Ukrainian prisoners had been killed, all made for a negative ICRC image on the Ukrainian side.

In this context the ICRC may have feared that a public accounting of the fate of IHL norms including detention and transfer may have antagonized both sides, who had plenty to be embarrassed about. The embarrassment may actually have been greater on the Ukrainian side, not because the Russian side had the better humanitarian record – far from it. But it was the Ukrainians who had been publicly castigating the ICRC, while a public accounting might show much quiet and proper effort by the ICRC in support of IHL and many insufficient responses by Kyiv despite the howls of public protest against Geneva.

V   Tentative Conclusions

If various interlocutors could be believed, new ICRC President Mirjana Spoljaric from October 2022 was reviewing the situation, examining her options, and proceeding in a careful and low-key manner. It is now clear that, in addition to visiting both Kyiv and Moscow, she was contacting key allies of both Ukraine and Russia, looking for support of ICRC initiatives. Some of these other leaders might or might not focus on ICRC concerns and IHL, given that they all had other fish to fry regarding military and economic affairs. It is also possible that that the new president and other ICRC leaders might come to the same conclusion that was dominant in the Maurer era – namely that the time and conditions were not right for a public "White Paper" on the status of IHL issues in the Ukraine war that would include many specifics about detention and transfer as well as civilian distress.

There was a potential complication for the ICRC role in the Russian–Ukraine war, that being the policy of the Swiss government. In 2022 the Swiss departed from a strong version of neutrality concerning the war in Ukraine and followed their European trading partners in levying sanctions on the Putin government and his supporters who held various types of property in Switzerland. Bern had already done so to a lesser extent in 2014 when Moscow annexed Crimea and stirred up separatists in the Donbas region of Ukraine (in Luhansk and Donetsk). By then Bern had announced a campaign to win an elected seat on the UN Security Council, which was successful in June 2022, whatever role that quest at the UN might have played in the development of a tougher Swiss policy toward Russia. Debate in Bern about a tougher approach to Putin's policies continued well into 2023.

As of late summer 2023, there was no clear evidence that Swiss foreign policy, or Maurer's membership on the board of trustees of the World Economic Forum (WEF) from 2014 to 2022, had greatly affected relations between the ICRC and authorities in Moscow regarding Ukraine. It seemed that Maurer's access to Foreign Minister Lavrov and others was helpful up to a point. But hardliners in the Putin regime had the availability of manufactured grounds for dismissing ICRC overtures seeking a traditional role in the war in Ukraine – by claiming the ICRC was biased against Moscow as just an arm of the hostile Swiss government. If such persons existed in the Putin inner circle or within the Russian military, it would have been better for the ICRC not to have signed the 2013 and 2017 protocols to the 1993 headquarters agreement between Bern and Geneva extolling their very close relations.[60] Again, a more rigorous stance on NIIHA values would have been preferable, emphasizing ICRC independence from both the Swiss government and the WEF, these two actors having taken anti-Putin positions.

In sum, of the first year of the war in Ukraine regarding the ICRC, the organization was certainly trying to play its traditional roles regarding IHL in that conflict. It would be crucial for the long-term evaluation of the organization to eventually know the nature of its discreet diplomacy. Its prolonged silence on many specifics and its lack of an evident strategic communications policy created the image of compliance and unwillingness to energetically challenge some belligerent policies that violated IHL. By comparison, it looked bold in challenging the Taliban in Afghanistan regarding the status of women (and quietly worked out a way to continue many of its activities there), but less bold in the Ukraine war in defending IHL. But caution and much discretion might have been a wise orientation in order to avoid collapse of the limited humanitarian good achieved early on. The ICRC did give confidential briefings about its work to major donors and supportive states.

It was clear that the Geneva HQ had indeed discussed its options and had consciously decided that avoidance of most specific public criticism – direct or indirect – was the best way to advance humanitarian concerns, at least through the early months of the war. The organization had said much in bits and pieces about civilian destruction, but very little systematically and early on about detainee and transfer affairs.

Geneva's relations with both belligerents were delicate and tenuous, which probably contributed to its preference to avoid a public accounting of relevant IHL norms, or general White Paper on the subject, fearing a double backlash that would make humanitarian matters worse. Ukrainian nationalism was broad and deep, with a clear tendency to criticize the role of neutrals. Russian policy was broadly brutal, as had been the case in Chechnya and Syria, not to mention Mali through the actions of the Wagner group, with meager attention to IHL, whatever the Russian spokesperson might claim. Once again, the ICRC found itself in a complex setting in which charity toward enemies and cooperation with neutral humanitarians was at times close to the disappearing point.

A   Postscript

In late 2022, Ukraine allowed a resumption of ICRC visits to Russian POWs held by Kyiv. This occurred despite continuing complaints from Kyiv that the ICRC had been "inactive" on Ukrainian POWs held by Russia.[61] It was hoped in Geneva that this unblockage by Kyiv would produce further ICRC visits to Ukrainian POWs held by Russia. That hope was at least partially realized by the end of 2022. Yet many blockages still remained, and it was clear that IHL was not being implemented by the belligerents as it should have been.

A tentative judgment about IHL and detention of POWs was that ICRC quiet diplomacy had been at least partially vindicated on the matter of POW visits, given some slight expansion of ICRC visits at the end of 2022, and that probably ICRC contacts with important third parties had contributed to a change in Ukrainian policy. Kyiv shifted in deciding that the best way to protect Ukrainian POWs in Russian hands was not to block and castigate the ICRC as a pressure tactic but to improve its own record under the Third Geneva Convention according to the logic of reciprocity. Making appeals based on legal obligation and the precise wording of legal texts was relevant, but almost certainly not the most important factor in actual policy developments.

In the war in Ukraine as in other armed conflicts (and situations of other violence), there was a humanitarian politics in play with the ICRC almost always involved in specific developments on the ground. No legal system implements itself. There are always a variety of actors who take a variety of decisions both for and against IHL. At some point in the future there would be various final accounts of what humanitarian Protections were achieved in Ukraine for civilians and fighters *hors de combat*. There would also be fuller accounts of the ICRC record in relation to IHL in Ukraine. This essay presents an early step in that direction.

Notes

1 See further Forsythe, *Humanitarian Politics*.
2 Support for statements of fact, or interpretations of facts, not otherwise documented or explained at length can be found in the preceding chapters.
3 ICRC, "Statement from ICRC President Peter Mauer on the Armed Conflict in Ukraine," February 24, 2022, www.icrc.org/en/document/statement-icrc-president-peter-maurer-conflict-ukraine (accessed November 11, 2022).
4 Following ICRC usage, the author uses the concept of protection in two ways, as explained in preceding chapters.
5 Humanitarian Outcomes, "Enabling the Local Response: Emerging Humanitarian Priorities in Ukraine March–May 2022," June 2022, www.humanitarianoutcomes.org/sites/default/files/publications/ukraine_review_2022.pdf (accessed November 11, 2022).
6 Ibid.
7 ICRC and IFRC, *Six Months of Armed Conflict in Ukraine*, 22 August 2022, www.icrc.org/en/document/six-months-armed-conflict-ukraine-red-cross-red-crescent-movement-report (accessed December 30, 2022).
8 ICRC, "Ukraine: Humanitarian Situation Deteriorates as Major Cities Bear the Brunt of Heavy Fighting," June 22, 2022, www.icrc.org/en/document/ukraine-humanitarian-situation-deteriorates-major-cities-bear-brunt-heavy-fighting (accessed December 29, 2022).
9 Lily Hyde, "Evacuation Challenges and Bad Optics: Why Ukrainians Are Losing Faith in the ICRC," *The New Humanitarian*, May 2, 2022, www.thenewhumanitarian.org/news-feature/2022/05/03/the-icrc-and-the-pitfalls-of-neutrality-in-ukraine (accessed November 11, 2022).
10 Nick Cumming-Bruce, "Ukrainians Flood a Red Cross Hotline for Help Finding Missing Loved Ones," *New York Times*, August 23, 2022, www.nytimes.com/2022/08/23/world/europe/ukraine-missing-red-cross.html (accessed November 11, 2022); Frederic Koller, "Visit exclusive d'un

dispositive que le CICRC n'avait plus active depuis la Deuxieme Guerre mondiale," *Le Temps*, October 19, 2022, www.letemps.ch/monde/visite-exclusive-dun-dispositif-cicr-navait-plus-active-deuxieme-guerre-mondiale (accessed November 11, 2022).

11 ICRC, "Immense Damage to Civilian Infrastructure Will Cause Immense Suffering as Winter Looms," November 2, 2022, www.icrc.org/en/document/russia-ukraine-international-armed-conflict-immense-damage-essential-infrastructure (accessed December 21, 2022).

12 In preceding chapters there is a discussion of the links between the ICRC, the IFRC, the National Red Cross or Red Crescent Societies, and their recent agreement on cooperation, called Solferino 2.0.

13 Yahoo News, "Ukrainian Red Cross Demands Strict Measures against Russian Red Cross for Fundraising for Russia's Mobilised," October 24, 2022, www.yahoo.com/now/ukrainian-red-cross-demands-strict-224324161.html (accessed February 7, 2023).

14 For an analysis of how the global humanitarian system tilted in favor of Ukraine, at the expense of attention to humanitarian needs in other conflicts, see Corinne Redfern, "How the Focus on Ukraine Is Hurting Other Humanitarian Responses," *The New Humanitarian*, July 7, 2022, www.thenewhumanitarian.org/news-feature/2022/07/07/Ukraine-aid-Russia-invasion-funding-donors (accessed November 11, 2022).

15 ICRC, "Ukraine: As Humanitarian Crisis Deepens."

16 ICRC, "Ukraine: More Than 170 Civilians Evacuated from Azovstal and Mariupol Area in Third Safe Passage Operation," May 8, 2022, www.icrc.org/en/document/more-150-civilians-evacuated-azovstal-and-mariupol-area-third-safe-passage-operation (accessed November 11, 2022).

17 Sarah El Deeb, Anastasiia Shvets, and Elizaveta Tilna, "How Moscow Grabs Ukrainian Kids and Makes Them Russians," *Associated Press*, October 13, 2022, https://apnews.com/article/ukrainian-children-russia-7493cb22c90 86c6293c1ac7986d85ef6 (accessed November 24, 2022). Emma Bubola, "Using Adoptions, Russia Turns Ukrainian Children into Spoils of War," *New York Times*, October 22, 2022, www.nytimes.com/2022/10/22/world/europe/ukraine-children-russia-adoptions.html (accessed November 24, 2022). Nicholas Kristof, "Russian Traffics in Ukrainian Children," *New York Times*, November 23, 2022, www.nytimes.com/2022/11/23/opinion/russia-ukraine-children.html (accessed November 24, 2022).

18 ICRC, "Ukraine: As Humanitarian Crisis Deepens."

19 "Ukraine Seeks G20 Focus on Russian Deportations of Children," *Reuters*, November 9, 2022, https://newsinfo.inquirer.net/1691111/ukraine-seeks-g20-focus-on-russian-deportations-of-children (accessed November 16, 2022). "Zelensky at G20 Summit," *UKRINFORM*, November 16, 2022, www.ukrinform.net/rubric-ato/3614516-zelensky-at-g20-summit-if-russia-wants-to-end-this-war-let-it-prove-it-with-actions.html (accessed November 16, 2022).

20 UKRINFORM, "Zelensky at G20."

21 ICC press release, March 17, 2023: "Situation in Ukraine: ICC Judges Issue Arrest Warrants against Vladimir Vladimirovich Putin and Maria Alekseyevna

Lvova-Belova," www.icc-cpi.int/news/situation-ukraine-icc-judges-issue-arrest-warrants-against-vladimir-vladimirovich-putin-and (accessed March 20, 2023). And UN Human Rights Council, "Report of the Independent International Commission on Ukraine," March 15, 2023, www.ohchr.org/sites/default/files/documents/hrbodies/hrcouncil/coiukraine/A_HRC_52_62_AUV_EN.pdf (accessed March 20, 2023).

22 ICRC, "ICRC President: The Suffering in Mariupol Must Not Become the Future of Ukraine," March 17, 2022, www.icrc.org/en/document/icrc-president-suffering-mariupol-must-not-become-future-ukraine (accessed November 11, 2022).

23 One media report said that the Ukrainians had compiled a dossier by early 2023 containing reference to over 60,000 war crimes incidents by Russians. Liz Sly, "66,000 War Crimes Have Been Reported in Ukraine. It Vows to Prosecute Them All," *Washington Post*, January 23, 2023, www.washingtonpost.com/world/2023/01/29/war-crimes-ukraine-prosecution/ (accessed February 1, 2023). As for Ukrainian behavior, some videos circulated of Ukrainian fighters abusing Russian POWs, and some publicity was given to particular Russian POWs, a violation of IHL.

24 Amnesty International, "Ukraine: Ukrainian Fighting Tactics Endanger Civilians," August 4, 2022, www.amnesty.org/en/latest/news/2022/08/ukraine-ukrainian-fighting-tactics-endanger-civilians/ (accessed November 12, 2022).

25 See, for example, Max Boot, "What's Up with Amnesty International and Its Moral Myopia on Ukraine?," *Washington Post*, August 8, 2022, www.washingtonpost.com/opinions/2022/08/08/amnesty-international-ukraine-russia-war-crimes/ (accessed February 4, 2023).

26 ICRC, "Ukraine: Level of Death, Destruction, and Misery Abhorrent and Unacceptable," May 5, 2022, www.icrc.org/en/document/ukraine-level-death-destruction-misery-abhorrent-and-unacceptable (accessed December 29, 2022).

27 www.fondationpourgeneve.ch/program/programme-2022/ (accessed February 6, 2023); www.youtube.com/watch?v=8WdXnvp0yso, circa 7 minutes and 15 seconds into the verbal exchange recorded on the video (accessed February 6, 2023).

28 See further preceding chapters.

29 *The New Humanitarian*, "In Conversation with Peter Maurer: An Exit Interview with the ICRC President," September 26, 2022, www.thenewhumanitarian.org/interview/2022/09/26/Peter-Maurer-ICRC-interview-localisation-humanitarian-reforms-neutrality (accessed November 11, 2022).

30 Stéphane Bussard, "Une campagne de désinformation massive déstabilise le CICRC," *Le Temps*, March 28, 2022, www.letemps.ch/monde/une-campagne-desinformation-massive-destabilise-cicr (accessed Novembre 11, 2022).

31 Reuters, "Ukraine's Zelensky Says Red Cross Inactive on Prisoners of War," October 13, 2022, www.reuters.com/world/ukraines-zelenskiy-says-red-cross-inactive-prisoners-war-2022-10-13/ (accessed November 11, 2022); Oliver Slow, "Ukraine War: Kyiv Demands Red Cross Visit Notorious Prison," *BBC*, October 13, 2022, www.bbc.com/news/world-63251927?piano-modal (accessed November 11, 2022).

32 Reuters, "Ukraine's Zelensky."

33 UNHCHR, "Ukraine/Russia: Prisoners of War," November 15, 2022, www .ohchr.org/en/press-briefing-notes/2022/11/ukraine-russia-prisoners-war, (accessed November 19, 2022).

34 Olha Hlushchenko, "List of Dead in Olenivka Partially Confirmed," *Ukrainska Pravda*, August 3, 2022, https://news.yahoo.com/list-dead-olenivka-partially-confirmed-213159739.html (accessed November 11, 2022).

35 On the latter subject see Amnesty International, "Ukraine: Ukrainian Fighting Tactics Endanger Civilians."

36 ICRC, "Russia-Ukraine International Armed Conflict: ICRC Asks for Immediate and Unimpeded Access to Prisoners of War," October 14, 2022, www.icrc.org/en/document/ukraine-russia-icrc-asks-immediate-and-unimpeded-access-to-all-prisoners-of-war (accessed November 11, 2022).

37 ICRC, "Olevnika Prison Facility: Prisoners of War and ICRC's Role," August 3, 2022, www.icrc.org/en/document/olenivka-penal-facility-prisoners-war-and-icrcs-role.

38 Luke Harding, "'Absolute Evil': Inside the Russian Prison Camp Where Dozens of Ukrainians Burned to Death," *The Guardian*, August 6, 2022, www.theguardian.com/world/2022/aug/06/russian-prison-camp-ukrainians-deaths-donetsk (accessed November 11, 2022).

39 Dan Lamothe, "Americans Captured by Russia Detail Months of Beatings, Interrogation," *The Washington Post*, October 1, 2022, www.washingtonpost .com/national-security/2022/10/01/alex-drueke-andy-huynh-russian-prisoners/ (accessed November 11, 2022).

40 UNHCHR, "Ukraine/Russia: Prisoners of War."

41 Jamey Keaton, "Russian Official Says 'Practical' Issues Delay Visit to POWs," *Associated Press*, October 20, 2022, https://apnews.com/article/russia-ukraine-geneva-europe-prisoners-of-war-treatment-95fb7d015fb3034b54d9b311bdfe f45c (accessed August 10, 2023).

42 ICRC, "Ukraine: ICRC Registers Hundreds of Prisoners of War from Azovstal Plant," May 19, 2022, www.icrc.org/en/document/ukraine-icrc-registers-hundreds-prisoners-war-azovstal-plant (accessed November 11, 2022).

43 BBC, "Ukraine Condemns Russia's 'Humiliating Death' Tweet after Prison Attack," July 31, 2022, www.bbc.com/news/world-europe-62363225 (accessed November 12, 2022). Shaun Walker, "'I Hate Them,' Dmitry Medvedev's Journey from Liberal to Anti-Western Hawk," *The Guardian*, August 1, 2022, www.theguardian.com/world/2022/aug/01/dmitry-medvedev-journey-liberal-anti-west-hawk-russia (accessed November 12, 2022).

44 B. G. Ramcharan, ed., *The International Conference on Former Yugoslavia: Official Papers*, Vol. 1 (Leiden: Brill, 1997), pp. 121–123.

45 Alain Modoux, "Sous-informé, états ne peuvent pas faire respecter le droit international humanitaire," *Le Temps*, September 13, 2022, www.letemps .ch/opinions/sousinformes-etats-ne-peuvent-faire-respecter-droit-international-humanitaire (accessed November 12, 2022).

46 Pierre de Senarclens, "Ukraine: le silence du CICRC," *Le Temps*, November 24, 2022, www.letemps.ch/opinions/ukraine-silence-cicr (accessed February 5, 2023).

47 ICRC, "Olenivka Prison Facility."

48 Boris Mabillard, "Nous ne se pouvons faire que ce que les parties au conflit acceptent que l'on fasse," *Le Temps*, September 6, 2022, www.letemps.ch/monde/directeur-general-cicr-ne-pouvons-faire-parties-conflit-acceptent-lon-fasse (accessed November 12, 2022).

49 Hanna Arhirova and Dasha Litvinova, "Ukrainian Civilians Vanish and Languish in Russian-run Jails," *Associated Press*, January 17, 2003, https://apnews.com/article/russia-ukraine-government-donetsk-business-prisons-59837e2f8006bfd1dc3347522e87efc5 (accessed February 2, 2023).

50 ICRC, "Afghanistan: ICRC Deeply Concerned for Millions of Women and Girls," December 25, 2022, www.icrc.org/en/document/afghanistan-icrc-deeply-concerned-millions-women-and-girls (accessed December 29, 2022).

51 Jacques Pilet, "Le CICR sous le feu des critiques," *Bon Pour La Tete* May 20, 2022, https://bonpourlatete.com/actuel/le-cicr-sous-le-feu-des-critiques (accessed November 12, 2022).

52 ICRC, Annual Report 1980, https://library.icrc.org/library/docs/DOC/RA_1980_ENG.pdf (accessed November 13, 2022). Reference to ICRC release of protection details in the Iran-Iraq war is found at p. 51 and *passim*.

53 Resolutions of the XXIVth International Conference of the Red Cross, pp. 318–345, https://international-review.icrc.org/sites/default/files/S0020860400021549a.pdf (accessed November 12, 2022).

54 Cornelio Sommaruga, "Respect for International Humanitarian Law: ICRC Review of Five Years of Activity 1987–1991," *International Review of the Red Cross*, 286 (February 1992), pp. 74–93. https://international-review.icrc.org/sites/default/files/S0020860400082395a.pdf (accessed November 12, 2022).

55 In preceding chapters there is a discussion of ICRC relations with Italian Fascists and German Nazis.

56 Roger Koeppel, "La neutralité reste indispensable: Peter Maurer, président du CICR, parle de guerre et de paix," *Die Weltwoche*, October 6, 2022. Original in German. https://weltwoche.ch/story/der-ukraine-krieg-markiert-eine-trendwende/ (accessed November 14, 2022).

57 Aline Jaccottet, "Peter Maurer: 'Pour obtenir du soutien, le CICR doit le mériter'," *Le Temps*, September 13, 2022, www.letemps.ch/monde/peter-maurer-obtenir-soutien-cicr-meriter (accessed November 13, 2022).

58 Keaton, "Russian Official Says 'Practical' Issues Delay Visit."

59 Steve Hendrix and Serhil Koralchuk, "Bloodied Wagner Fighters Captured in Ukraine Recount Path from Prison to War," *Washington Post*, February 23, 2023, www.washingtonpost.com/world/2023/02/23/wagner-mercenaries-captives-war-ukraine/ (accessed February 23, 2023).

60 Explained in preceding chapters.

61 Alona Mazurenko, "President's Office Creates Human Rights Headquarters Amid International Red Cross Inaction," *Ukrainska Pravda*, November 9, 2022, www.pravda.com.ua/eng/news/2022/11/9/7375616/ Naturally the ICRC declined to participate in this "office" since it was a Ukrainian maneuver to publicly criticize Russian policies.

Annex

ICRC ORGANIZATIONAL CHART

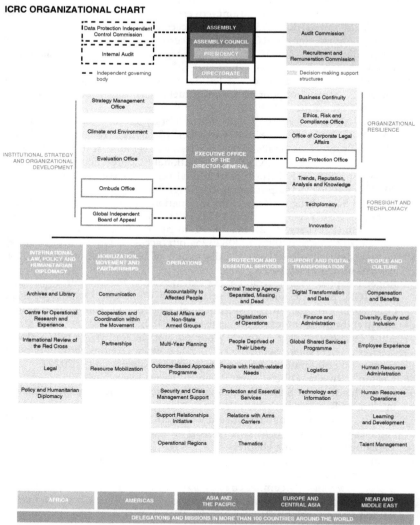

As at 31.12.2022

Source: ICRC Annual Report 2022.

Index

Page numbers in *italic* indicate figures

Printed in the USA
CPSIA information can be obtained
at www.ICGtesting.com
LVHW022242250124
769704LV00008BA/142